Prentice-Hall
General Science

FOR GRADES 6—9

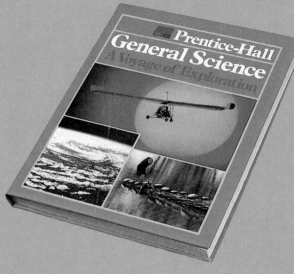

Plus...

Complete Teaching Package

for Success in Science

Flexible Content

PRENTICE-HALL GENERAL SCIENCE

A Voyage of Adventure
emphasis on
life science

A Voyage of Discovery
emphasis on
physical science

A Voyage of Exploration
emphasis on
earth science

The only general science program that provides total coverage for one-, two-,
and three-year courses

Three separate texts that can be used independently or in conjunction with one
another

Two units each of Life Science, Earth Science, and Physical Science topics in
each text

Carefully controlled reading level throughout each text

Introducing the Authors:

DEAN HURD

Physical Science Instructor
Carlsbad High School
Carlsbad, CA

SUSAN M. JOHNSON

Associate Professor of
  Biology
Ball State University
Muncie, Indiana

GEORGE F. MATTHIAS

Earth Science Instructor
Croton-Harmon
  High School
Croton-on-Hudson,
  New York

**CHARLES WILLIAM
McLAUGHLIN**

Chemistry Instructor
Central High School
St. Joseph, Missouri

EDWARD BENJAMIN SNYDER

Earth Science Instructor
Yorktown High School
Yorktown Heights,
  New York

JILL D. WRIGHT

Associate Professor of
  Secondary Education
Tennessee Technological
  University
Cookeville, Tennessee

Total Teaching Support

Annotated Teacher's Edition

Everything you need to know about teaching General Science successfully is provided in the Annotated Teacher's Edition. On-page answers provide easy access to key information

Laboratory Manual and Annotated Teacher's Edition

At least one laboratory investigation is keyed to every chapter to reinforce and extend facts and concepts. The Annotated Teacher's Edition provides answers, tips, and suggestions for conducting successful labs

Teacher's Resource Book

Each text has its own Teacher's Resource Book full of activities for every student ability level; daily lesson plans for each chapter that incorporate all the program components into one easy-to-use guide; skills worksheets; SAT-format unit and chapter tests; master forms; and computer-related information—everything you need to make your classes run smoothly (even your larger classes!)

General Science Courseware

As the leading software publisher, Prentice-Hall presents a wide variety of software designed to enhance and extend your General Science curriculum. Only Prentice-Hall courseware offers review, reteaching, glossaries, basic skills instruction, simulations, tests, and a complete management system

Organized to Enhance

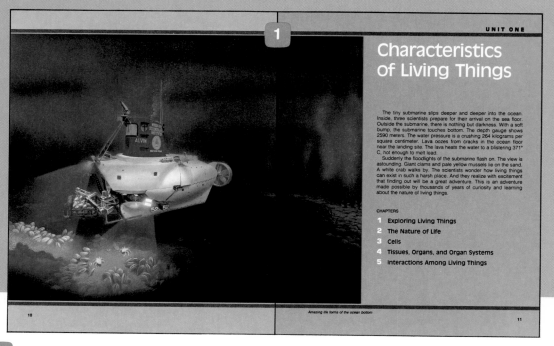

UNIT ONE

Characteristics of Living Things

The tiny submarine slips deeper and deeper into the ocean. Inside, three scientists prepare for their arrival on the sea floor. Outside the submarine, there is nothing but darkness. With a soft bump, the submarine touches bottom. The depth gauge shows 2590 meters. The water pressure is a crushing 264 kilograms per square centimeter. Lava oozes from cracks in the ocean floor near the landing site. The lava heats the water to a blistering 371° C, hot enough to melt lead.

Suddenly the floodlights of the submarine flash on. The view is astounding. Giant clams and pale yellow mussels lie on the sand. A white crab walks by. The scientists wonder how living things can exist in such a harsh place. And they realize with excitement that finding out will be a great adventure. This is an adventure made possible by thousands of years of curiosity and learning about the nature of living things.

CHAPTERS

1 Exploring Living Things
2 The Nature of Life
3 Cells
4 Tissues, Organs, and Organ Systems
5 Interactions Among Living Things

10   *Amazing life forms of the ocean bottom*   11

1 Bold attractive unit openers with vivid introductory paragraphs capture students' interest. List of chapters introduces upcoming topics

2 Attention-grabbing chapter openers bring science into the real world of students with up-to-date stories and anecdotes to maintain interest

3 Sections are listed and clearly stated objectives are keyed to section numbers to help students set and attain goals

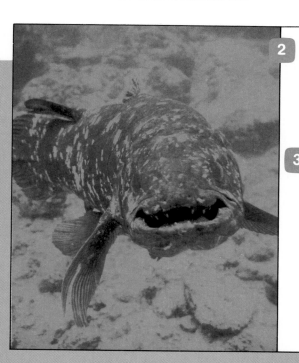

6 Classification

CHAPTER SECTIONS
6-1 History of Classification
6-2 Modern Classification Systems
6-3 Systems of Classification

CHAPTER OBJECTIVES
After completing this chapter, you will be able to:
6-1 Describe the work of Carolus Linnaeus.
6-1 Explain binomial nomenclature.
6-2 List the seven major classification groups.
6-3 Give some general characteristics of the plant, animal, protist, monera, and fungi kingdoms.

The people fishing from the boat could not believe their eyes. Lying in the boat's net was a fish none of them ever had seen before. It stretched more than 1.5 meters from the tip of its ugly nose to the end of its fan-shaped tail. Large steel-blue scales covered its body. A powerful lower jaw hung down from a frightening face. But most peculiar of all, its fins were attached to what appeared to be stubby legs!

The unusual fish, caught at the mouth of the Chalumna River in South Africa, was taken to a local museum. There M. Courtenay-Latimer, a South African museum curator, happened to see the fish. After searching through many books, she had found no description of the strange fish. However, she knew of someone who might be able to solve the riddle. That someone was Professor J. L. B. Smith, an African fish expert. So M. Courtenay-Latimer preserved and sent the fish to Professor Smith.

The scientist was shocked. He later wrote, "I would hardly have been more surprised if I met a dinosaur on the street." Professor Smith was looking at an animal thought to have become extinct more than 60 million years ago. Yet, in a flash, Professor Smith had been able to identify the fish as a coelacanth (SEE-luh-kanth). The discovery was exciting because coelacanths are thought to be closely related to fish that evolved into four-footed land animals.

What led Professor Smith to make his startling identification? A knowledge of biological classification, a special system that helps scientists to identify and name organisms.

Rare photograph of a coelacanth   131

Science Reading Skills

4 Numbered section heads outline each chapter and break up the text for increased comprehension of concepts

5 Flowing narrative style and "bite-size" paragraphs provide readability without diluting content

6 Large detailed illustrations animate the text and informative captions reinforce and extend it

7 New terms are boldfaced, phonetically respelled, and defined in context

8 Large charts graphically organize and present key concepts for better understanding

Figure 5-21

GEOLOGIC HISTORY OF THE EARTH

Enrichment and Reinforcement

9

SCIENCE GAZETTE

(Adventures in Science)

Jane Goodall
and the Chimps of Gombe Stream

Deep in the heart of the African jungle, Jane Goodall has been doing research among the wild animals. She is studying our closest living relative, the chimpanzee.

Goodall has always wanted to study the animals in Africa. When she was a young girl, she was inspired by Rudyard Kipling's jungle tales. Ever since reading Kipling's vivid descriptions of the jungle and its inhabitants, Goodall has known where she wanted to spend her time.

For more than 20 years, Goodall has lived at Gombe Stream, Tanzania's Game Preserve on Lake Tanganyika. She is both an ethologist, a person who studies animal behavior, and a primatologist, a person who studies primates. She hopes that her studies will help scientists better understand prehistoric and present-day humans.

In 1960, she stepped off a small boat and came face to face with the majestic mountains of Africa. Over the years, she has learned to live with blistering heat and drenching rain. She has learned how to travel in a country with deep valleys, high mountains, and steep gorges. She has adjusted to living among threatening animals such as cobras and leopards.

But for the first few months after her arrival, Goodall was in despair. Until she discovered wild pig and baboon trails, she had to fight her way through dense underbrush to do her research. Although she could hear the loud calls of the chimps and the rustling of the leaves as the chimps moved, she rarely saw them. They would always run when they heard her approaching. After eight months, Goodall had not come within 500 yards of the chimps. She was about to give up!

Suddenly her luck changed. A chimp she had named David Greybeard came shyly to her camp one day. He continued coming to the camp every day. After two weeks of observing her camp, David Greybeard actually took a banana from Goodall's hand. The other chimps, after seeing their leader's bold move, gradually allowed Goodall to get close to them too.

At about the same time, Goodall began to make some amazing discoveries. One of the most important is that chimps use objects as tools. Once again, David Greybeard was the star of the show. Goodall saw David Greybeard and a female chimp she had named Flo strip the leaves from thin branches. They then went over to a termite mound. For protection, termites seal the tops of their tunnels. Chimps look for these protective coverings and peel them off. Goodall watched as David and Flo dipped their branches into the tunnels and pulled them out covered with termites. The chimps then ate the termites off the sticks, just as you might take a piece of meat from a fork. Goodall also noticed that the chimps would go out of their way to select sticks and carry them to termite nests that were far away.

Chimps often chew leaves, which they then use as "sponges" to soak up drinking water from places such as hollows in logs.

This behavior seems to show that the chimps not only are able to use tools, but can think about their use ahead of time.

In time, Goodall was able to observe other chimp behavior. She saw another male, Evered, strip the leaves off a small branch and stuff them into his mouth. He chewed them for a short time and took them out of his mouth. He then dipped them, like a sponge, into a fallen log to get water. Goodall observed that the other chimps also used leaves to get water. So she collected some leaves and chewed them in order to understand what the chimps were doing. She found that chewing the leaves before dipping them helped to increase their absorbency.

When Goodall is not at Gombe Stream, she and her son live in Palo Alto, California, where she does laboratory research. However, she much prefers studying in the wild. Even in California, she keeps in touch with what is happening at Gombe by corresponding with her assistants there. She has lived among the wild chimps for more than twenty years. If asked why she chooses to live her life this way, Goodall replies that it is her "inborn love of the place and the beasts."

Jane Goodall (left) and companion observe the behavior of an adult and a young chimp.

302

---

9 The articles of the Science Gazette are designed to motivate students of all ability levels. They can be used to stimulate class discussions, as the basis for short essay assignments, to introduce or wrap up lessons on unit topics, and to build science reading skills

10 Career opportunities are introduced in every chapter for students with different career objectives

11 Margin activities, including laboratory, field, library, writing, vocabulary, and computational activities, promote interest and skill development

---

10

Career: *Special Effects Technician*

HELP WANTED: SPECIAL EFFECTS TECHNICIAN High school diploma required. Fine arts or carpentry training helpful. Best candidates will have completed courses in film technology and special effects. However, hard workers who display a willingness to learn will also be considered.

Deep in space, a small ship passes swiftly through the icy particles in the rings of Saturn. Suddenly a huge warship appears. It is too late to surrender. The warship takes aim and fires. In an instant, the small ship is shattered into a thousand pieces, each of which is left behind to become a permanent member of the rings of Saturn. Is this scene taking place in the distant future? Not really. You have simply entered the world of the **special effects technician**.

Special effects have often been called "movie magic." However, a special effects career is actually a blend of artistic creativity and scientific knowledge. In fact, the role of science in special effects is more important today than ever before. In order to shoot the short scene with the spaceships among the rings of Saturn, up to a hundred people are required. A spaceship may appear enormous on the screen, but it is probably only a few centimeters long. It is made by a special effects person who is an expert in miniatures. To do so requires skill in building models, of course, but the person must also understand the mathematics of building models to scale.

Computers, too, play a role in modern special effects. You may think a spaceship is flying through space, but chances are it is not moving at all. Instead, cameras programmed by computers circle around, above, and below the ship. The cameras do the moving, but your eye cannot tell the difference. The result is pure pleasure. It may take a team of computer programmers and camera technicians months to prepare for such a scene.

The world of special effects can make an interesting career combining a strong interest in science with a love of art. If you would like more information on a career in special effects, write to Universal Studios, Special Effects Department, 100 Universal City Plaza, Universal City, CA 91608.

Figure 2-6 ... ith solved ... of ... seismologists when she explained how P waves bend and change speeds as they move through the earth's outer and inner cores.

... about her discovery in 1936.
... ientists using more sensitive in-
... eloped an even clearer picture of

... ate of the size of the inner core
... ccurate. Scientists now calculate
... e inner core is about 1300 kilo-
... re about 2250 kilometers thick
... core. The outside boundary of
... about 2900 kilometers beneath
... Add these three numbers to-
... he approximate distance from
... the actual center of the earth—

... earthquake waves, scientists have
... about the earth's core. For ex-
... earned that the hot outer core is
probably a region of constantly churning liquid,

Activity

Mohorovicic's Discovery

The boundary between the crust and the mantle is called the Moho after Andrija Mohorovicic. Write a 300 word essay explaining how Mohorovicic discovered this boundary. Your essay should emphasize all of the following vocabulary words: crust, focus, mantle, Moho, P waves, S waves, and seismograph.

11

485

Mean Success for Every Student

LABORATORY ACTIVITY

A Moldy Question

Purpose
In this activity, you will investigate variables that may affect the growth of bread mold.

Materials (per group)
2 jars with lids
2 slices of bread
1 medicine dropper

Procedure
1. Put half a slice of bread into each of two jars. Moisten each half slice with ten drops of water. Cap the jar tightly. Keep one jar in sunlight and place the other in a dark closet.

2. Observe the jars every day for two weeks. Record your observations. Does light seem to influence mold growth?
3. Ask your teacher what you know about the effect of light on mold. Was your conclusion correct? What other conditions might influence mold growth?
4. Did you think of temperature and moisture? Light, temperature, and moisture are all possible variables. Design a second experiment to test the effect of light on mold growth. Change one of the other variables one variable at a time. Other groups will test the other two variables. You can pool your results and draw conclusions together.

Observations and Conclusions
1. In your second experiment, what variables were you testing? Did you have a control for your experiment? If so, describe it.
2. Study the class data for this experiment. What variables seem to affect mold growth?
3. Cathy set up the following experiment. She placed a piece of orange peel in each of two jars. She added 3 milliliters of water to jar 1 and placed it in the refrigerator. She added no water to jar 2 and placed it on the windowsill in the kitchen. At the end of the week, she noticed more mold growth in jar 2. Cathy concluded that light, warm temperature, and no moisture are ideal conditions for mold growth. Discuss the accuracy of Cathy's conclusion.

Medicine dropper
Water

CHAPTER SUMMARY

1-1 What Is Science?
▪ A scientific method is a process used by scientists to discover facts about nature.

▪ The basic steps of any scientific method are stating the problem, gathering information, forming a hypothesis, experimenting, recording and analyzing data, and stating a conclusion.

▪ The three main branches of science are physical science, earth science, and life science.

▪ Density is a measure of the amount of mass in a given volume of an object.

▪ Temperature is measured on the Celsius scale, which has 100 degrees between the freezing point and the boiling point of water.

1-3 Tools of a Scientist
▪ A spectroscope breaks up light into its particular colors.

▪ A laser produces a kind of concentrated light.

Figure 15-11 *Each subatomic particle in the nucleus is thought to be made up of a different combination of three quarks.*

SECTION REVIEW
1. What two particles are found in the nucleus?
2. Define atomic number; isotopes.
3. Where are the electrons in an atom found?

---

12 Every chapter includes a full-page Laboratory Activity that promotes interest through hands-on experience and guarantees success through easy-to-follow instructions

13 Concise summary is keyed to every section

14 Section Reviews offer immediate reinforcement of concepts

15 Multiformat chapter review allows you to evaluate students' grasp of facts, concepts, and applications. For easy access, answers are on the page in the Annotated Teacher's Edition

---

CHAPTER REVIEW

Multiple Choice
Choose the letter of the answer that best completes each statement.

1. The meter is the basic unit of
   a. volume.
   b. mass.
   c. length.
   d. density.
2. A kilometer is equal to
   a. 1000 meters.
   b. 100 meters.
   c. 10 meters.
   d. 39.4 inches.
3. The liter is the basic unit of
   a. mass.
   b. length.
   c. density.
   d. volume.
4. A liter contains
   a. 1000 milliliters.
   b. 100 kilometers.
   c. 100 centimeters.
   d. 1000 centimeters.
5. The kilogram is the basic unit of
   a. mass.
   b. length.
   c. density.
   d. volume.

6. A kilogram is equal to
   a. 100 grams.
   b. 10 grams.
   c. 1000 grams.
   d. 1000 liters.
7. Density is defined as the mass per unit
   a. length.
   b. volume.
   c. weight.
   d. degrees Celsius.
8. Pure water freezes at
   a. 100° C.
   b. 32° C.
   c. 10° C.
   d. 0° C.
9. To record visible energy, use a(n)
   a. X-ray telescope.
   b. reflecting telescope.
   c. radio telescope.
   d. infrared telescope.
10. Karl Jansky discovered
   a. X-rays.
   b. radio waves.
   c. infrared rays.
   d. ultraviolet rays.

Completions
Fill in the word or words that best complete each statement.

1. A process that scientists use to find facts about nature is called a(n) _____
2. A(n) _____ is a suggested solution for a problem.
3. The part of an experiment without the variable is called the _____
4. A(n) _____ is divided into 100 equal units called centimeters.
5. The _____ is the basic unit of volume in the metric system.
6. _____ is a measure of the amount of matter in an object.
7. Telescopes that use a series of lenses are called _____ telescopes.
8. A(n) _____ telescope detects heat energy coming from objects in space.
9. _____ from space cannot be detected because the atmosphere blocks them.
10. Karl Jansky discovered _____ waves from space.

True or False
Determine whether each statement is true or false. If it is true, write "true." If it is false, change the underlined word or words to make the statement true.

1. An experiment is performed to solve a problem or test a hypothesis.
2. A control is that part of an experiment without the variable.
3. A meter is divided into 100 equal units called millimeters.
4. One kilogram is equal to 100 grams.
5. If you went to the moon, your mass would decrease.
6. Density can be defined as mass per unit volume.
7. An optical telescope records X-rays from space.
8. The size of a telescope is given by the diameter of its lens or mirror.
9. Radio waves are scattered or blocked by the atmosphere.
10. Hunches can play an important part in making scientific discoveries.

Discussion Topics
Write a brief paragraph discussing each of the following.

1. Briefly discuss the basic steps of a scientific method.
2. Discuss how the Viking life-detecting experiment was carried out.
3. Explain how refracting and reflecting telescopes differ.
4. Describe what a radio telescope looks like and how it works.
5. Explain how radio waves were discovered.

EXPAND YOUR KNOWLEDGE

Couper, H., and T. Murtach. *Heavens Above! A Beginner's Guide to the Universe.* New York: Watts.
   Here is a beautifully illustrated and accurate book on many different topics in astronomy. The book opens with a log from an alien spaceship visiting our solar system for the first time.
Marten, M., and J. Chesterman. *The Radiant Universe: Electronic Images from Space.* New York: Macmillan.
   From millions of available photographs, the authors have selected the very best, which are beautifully reproduced here. These photographs include shots from the Apollo, Mariner, Viking, and Voyager missions and Landsat photographs of Earth.
McAleer, N. *The Cosmic Mind-Boggling Book.* New York: Warner.
   This book consists of short stories that together make up an accurate picture of what the universe is like. Many excellent NASA photographs are also included.

30

32

33

Prentice-Hall
General Science

COMPLETE • FLEXIBLE • EASY-TO-USE

For more information, please write to:

PRENTICE-HALL INC.
Educational Book Division
Englewood Cliffs, N.J. 07632

PRENTICE-HALL EDUCATIONAL BOOK DIVISION

Printed in U.S.A.

▄▆ Prentice-Hall
General Science
A Voyage of Adventure

Dean Hurd

Physical Science Instructor
Carlsbad High School
Carlsbad, California

Susan M. Johnson

Associate Professor of Biology
Ball State University
Muncie, Indiana

George F. Matthias

Earth Science Instructor
Croton-Harmon High School
Croton-on-Hudson, New York

Charles William McLaughlin

Chemistry Instructor
Central High School
St. Joseph, Missouri

Edward Benjamin Snyder

Earth Science Instructor
Yorktown High School
Yorktown Heights, New York

Jill D. Wright

Associate Professor
  of Secondary Education
Tennessee Technological University
Cookeville, Tennessee

Prentice-Hall, Inc., Englewood Cliffs, New Jersey 07632

ISBN 0-13-697475-9

10 9 8 7 6 5 4 3 2

Prentice-Hall of Australia, Pty. Ltd., Sydney
Prentice-Hall of Canada Inc., Toronto
Prentice-Hall Hispanoamericana, S.A., Mexico
Prentice-Hall of India Private Ltd., New Delhi
Prentice-Hall International, Inc., London
Prentice-Hall of Japan, Inc., Tokyo
Prentice-Hall of Southeast Asia Pte. Ltd., Singapore
Editora Prentice-Hall do Brasil Ltda., Rio de Janeiro
Whitehall Books Limited, Wellington, New Zealand

Contents

To the Teacher

RATIONALE OF THE PROGRAM

Science education is a vital force in helping your students to recognize the critical importance of scientific developments in today's world—and tomorrow's. The authors and editors of *Prentice-Hall General Science* have designed this textbook and its auxiliary materials to meet this educational goal. This program provides your students with the basic knowledge of science as related to themselves and their own range of experiences. And this program goes further. It makes it possible for young people to use their abilities to make intelligent decisions that relate to a broad perspective, to develop an appreciation of all branches of science. Historical achievements in the fields of science, career paths, and some ideas about the future will all contribute to the growth and development of your students.

BALANCED SCIENCE PROGRAM

The *Prentice-Hall General Science* program has been developed in accordance with basic principles of science education. The program offers a balance between textual material and investigative material, with enough flexibility to suit your individual teaching style and classroom needs.

Within the textual material, relevant recent facts are used to build science concepts. Illustrations, teaching captions, and in-text questions encourage students to participate, to draw on previously learned information, to make judgments, and to inquire, thus forming a basis for conceptual learning.

The factual and conceptual learning is highlighted and reinforced by the Marginal activities and Laboratory Investigations provided in the program. Through these investigations, students gain first-hand experience with learning skills and processes such as *observing, classifying, identifying, measuring, inferring, hypothesizing, interpreting, and predicting.*

READABILITY AND STUDENT COMPREHENSION AND INTEREST

The authors and editors of *Prentice-Hall General Science* have taken many steps to improve readability of this text in order to facilitate student comprehension and interest.

Prentice-Hall General Science is designed with an open, clean format with exciting and relevant visuals to enhance student interest. The text is written in a style that appeals to and accommodates the wide range of levels of comprehension found at the junior high or middle school level. The readability of the text has been carefully controlled so that most students at this level will be able to understand the science content and concepts presented.

Studies have shown that students often feel hindered and frustrated by scientific terms because these words are alien to them, are usually difficult to pronounce, and are hard to remember. To remedy this situation, *Prentice-Hall General Science* introduces scientific terms in boldface type. Definitions accompany the new terms, and, in most instances, phonetic pronunciation guides are also provided. In addition, photographs and illustrations, most of which are in full color, visually reinforce the text material, thereby acting as an aid to readability and comprehension. Most photographs and illustrations have been provided with an explanatory caption.

Other aids to readability and comprehension include single-concept paragraphs, frequent in-text questions, section checkup questions, chapter summaries, and end-of-chapter questions. These features help to make the text more readable by providing immediate learning evaluations and by continually eliciting student participation and response.

Yet another readability aid is the Science Gazette articles that appear at the end of every unit. These articles reinforce and extend the material presented in the chapters. Each article can be utilized as a science reader in order to improve a student's ability to read science materials.

Features of the Student Text

Prentice-Hall General Science has been set up to provide a flexible and varied approach to teaching science. The text has been divided into six units, sufficiently self-contained to be taught separately and in any order. Of the six units, two deal primarily with life science topics; two deal primarily with earth science topics; and two deal with physical science topics. Naturally, since science cannot be compartmentalized into discreet packets of information, there are areas in which one branch of science overlaps another. However, in order to retain the flexibility of the program and allow the teacher to begin with any unit he or she desires, any concept or definition introduced for the first time in a unit is considered unfamiliar and taught as if the topic is a new one. Thus, if density is discussed in the first unit and again in a subsequent unit, that term will be boldfaced and defined in both units.

UNIT OPENERS

Each unit begins with a two-page spread that includes a large, dramatic photograph. Accompanying the photograph is a short overview that both introduces the topics to be discussed in the unit and provides motivational text to capture student interest. A listing of the chapters in the unit is also included in the unit opening spread.

CHAPTER OPENERS

Each chapter begins with a two-page spread. Like the unit openers, large photographs are employed to ''grab'' student attention immediately. A short, concise caption informs the reader as to the nature of the photograph. The photograph can also be readily identified through the chapter opening text. This text, often written in an anecdotal style, serves to entice the student to read further. Intriguing questions and unusual data are employed to hold the student's attention and to thrust the student into the text with the desire to find out more about the topic.

Also included in the chapter opening spread is a list of the main sections in each chapter. This listing serves as an instructional outline for both student and teacher. Moreover, specific objectives are keyed directly to the main sections. Thus, the chapter opener serves the dual purpose of initiating the student's desire to learn more about the material and of alerting the student to the material in the chapter.

CHAPTER SECTIONS

As noted, each main chapter section is listed in the chapter opening. These sections are numbered consecutively on both the chapter opening page and in the text itself. This numbering of chapter sections provides an easy method of cross-referencing chapter objectives with their corresponding sections. Furthermore, numbering the main sections helps distinguish the main topics in the chapter from the subtopics. Subtopics in each main section are set apart and boldfaced.

Within each main section are numerous photographs and illustrations that help teach and reinforce the topics found in that section. Most visuals are large and in color to further hold student interest. Data charts are interspersed in the text as well, to provide further information.

At the end of every main section is a Section Review. These review questions, usually short answer questions, allow the teacher to quickly verify whether the important topics in that section have been grasped by the student.

MARGINAL ACTIVITIES

In most cases, each main numbered section of the text contains at least one marginal activity. These activities can be used in a variety of ways including homework, extra credit, or class projects. Each activity is keyed as to academic level—either average, remedial, or enriched—in the teacher's material that follows. This material contains a detailed discussion of each chapter. Such activities include library and field studies, hands-on activities, and activities that relate to other disciplines such as mathematics, social studies, vocabulary skills, reading skills, and dictionary skills.

CAREERS

Each chapter contains a career feature that introduces students to a possible career choice in science related to that particular chapter. The career feature begins with a simulated ''help wanted advertisement'' describing the academic training required for that career. Careers, it should be noted, range from those requiring a high school diploma to those requiring a doctorate. Each career feature consists of a full-color photograph depicting a person in this career at work, a description of the work done by people in this career, and an address to which interested students may write for further information. Career awareness and information encourages students to contemplate their own futures.

LABORATORY ACTIVITIES

Each chapter contains one full-page laboratory activity just prior to the chapter summary page. Such activities provide students with the opportunity to work in the laboratory and actively participate in investigating science problems. Most of the activities are designed to reinforce concepts presented in the text, but a few are designed to supplement the material in the text. Easy-to-obtain materials are used in such activities.

Each laboratory activity clearly outlines the Purpose of the activity, the Materials needed, and the Procedure to follow. The Procedure is set up in an easy to follow step-by-step system. A section entitled Observations and Conclusions allows the student to use the data collected in the activity and draw upon that data to determine a specific conclusion or to further establish a scientific concept.

END OF CHAPTER MATERIALS

Chapter Summary and Vocabulary

At the end of every chapter is a chapter summary section. The summary is divided into groupings based on the main numbered sections in the chapter. Under each grouping is a list of key sentences that describe the most important concepts presented in the chapter. The chapter summary might be considered a detailed outline of the chapter content.

Following the summary is a listing of the vocabulary words included in the chapter. The vocabulary words include all the boldfaced terms from the chapter.

Chapter Review

The chapter review includes a wide variety of questions in three distinct formats. Ten multiple choice questions begin the review. The questions are listed in the order in which the content is introduced in the chapter. Following the multiple choice section are ten completion questions. Again, these questions follow the content order established in the chapter. The same is true for the ten true and false questions. These questions are of the type that the student must not only identify an incorrect statement, but then must make it correct by substituting the correct word or phrase into the statement. Following these questions are several discussion topics. Discussion topics often call upon the student to relate the information presented in the chapter to everyday life.

Expand Your Knowledge

A listing of books that extends and reinforces the information in the chapter is included at the end of every chapter. A short discussion explains the nature of the book.

Gazette Preview

In the chapter review ending each unit, a short gazette preview is included. This preview alerts the student that the Science Gazette is about to begin.

SCIENCE GAZETTE

At the end of every unit, is a section entitled Science Gazette. Each Science Gazette is a Science Reader, which consists of three different types of articles. One type, called an Adventure in Science, profiles a particular scientist and the path the scientist took, or is taking, to make a significant discovery. The second type of article, called an Issue in Science, presents a nonbiased discussion of a contemporary scientific issue. The third type of article, called a Future in Science, presents a possible future scenario based on current scientific theory, experimentation, or data.

The articles of the Science Gazette have been carefully chosen and designed to maximize the motivation of students of all levels in their study of science. Each article is related to topics presented in the unit. The articles can be used to stimulate class discussions, as the basis for individual short essay homework assignments, to introduce or wrap-up lessons on related topics, and to develop science reading skills.

A discussion of the Science Gazette articles and the most appropriate time to introduce them are included in the chapter by chapter teacher's material in this book. Also, specific activities and handouts geared directly to the Science Gazette articles are included in the Teacher's Resource Book in the ''Science Reading Skills'' section.

APPENDICES

Appendix A introduces students to the *metric system* and provides a comparison of the units of the metric system with the equivalent units of the customary system. Appendix B instructs students on the use of laboratory balances. Appendix C introduces students to the proper use of the *microscope* and the method for making a *wet-mount slide.*

GLOSSARY

Scientific terms introduced in the text are listed in the Glossary in alphabetical order, followed by definitions and, where necessary, pronunciation guides.

INDEX

The Index provides students with an easy-to-use reference listing of subjects covered in the text.

Other Components of *Prentice-Hall General Science*

LABORATORY MANUAL—STUDENT EDITION

Each textbook has an accompanying laboratory manual. The manuals are 8½ inches by 11 inches, are five-hole punched, and are consumable. Each laboratory activity is keyed to a particular chapter in the student text. There is at least one lab per chapter. These laboratory investigations provide a traditional laboratory approach to the topics presented in the text and employ standard laboratory equipment.

Each investigation begins with background information for the student, a purpose (posed as a question), a comprehensive list of materials, a step-by-step procedure, and a question and answer section. Also, a section called Going Further allows industrious students to do further experiments.

LABORATORY MANUAL—ANNOTATED TEACHER'S EDITION

Each annotated teacher's edition provides answers to questions posed in the investigations, includes set-up instructions, and suggests possible

places to purchase special equipment, if any is required.

TEACHER'S RESOURCE BOOK

Each Teacher's Resource Book, or TRB, contains a wide variety of material for the teacher, most of which is clearly keyed to various academic levels. Materials in the TRB are presented on a chapter-by-chapter basis, that is correlated to the chapters in the student text and presented in the same sequence. Materials for each chapter include:

a. Pretest and posttest
b. Chapter lesson plan integrating all components of the PHGS program
c. At least 3 blackline master activities—each keyed to academic level
d. Transparency master
e. Vocabulary review puzzles
f. Laboratory investigation

In addition to the chapter-by-chapter materials, each TRB contains unit and final tests; computer-related materials; a student safety contract; and many other materials that can be copied and handed out for use in class for enrichment or for remediation.

Finally, activities designed to test science reading skills, which are correlated with the Science Gazette articles in the student text are included in each TRB.

GENERAL SCIENCE COURSEWARE

Prentice-Hall Computer Software Programs

provide a vast multiprogram project under the general title: General Science Courseware. Such courseware employs "state of the art" graphics in order to present on the computer screen events, concepts, and data that cannot be presented in the traditional classroom setting. The goal of Prentice-Hall Courseware is to allow the student—through a maximum of student participation and interaction—to master science material that cannot be easily grasped through the printed word, through laboratory experiences, or by using other traditional classroom materials and techniques.

Features of the Annotated Teacher's Edition

LIST OF ACTIVITIES AND CAREERS (page T-8)

A comprehensive listing of all activities and careers in this book is included. Furthermore, the page on which that activity or career may be found is also included.

LIST OF SUPPLIERS AND ADDRESSES OF LABORATORY MATERIALS (page T-10)

For teacher convenience, a list of names and addresses of suppliers of laboratory materials is included.

LIST OF AUDIOVISUAL SUPPLIERS AND ADDRESSES (page T-11)

Suggested audio-visual materials for each chapter are provided in the Teaching Aids for Units and Chapters section of the *Annotated Teacher's Edition*. For easy ordering of A-V materials, a list of suppliers and their addresses is provided in the *Annotated Teacher's Edition*.

LIST OF COMPUTER SOFTWARE SUPPLIERS AND ADDRESSES (page T-11)

For teacher convenience, a list of names and addresses of suppliers of computer software is included.

COMPREHENSIVE LIST OF LABORATORY MATERIALS (pages T-11-T-14)

This list supplies the teacher with the type and

amount of materials and equipment needed to complete the laboratory activities presented in the text. Only easy-to-obtain materials are needed to complete the activities. Also included is the chapter number of the Laboratory Activity in which each item will be used.

SAFETY GUIDELINES (page T-14)

For your convenience, a list of Do's and Don't's for science classroom safety has been provided. It is suggested that this list be read or reproduced for your class. A list of field trip safety tips is also included.

TEACHING AIDS FOR UNITS AND CHAPTERS (pages T-17-T-72)

This portion of the *Annotated Teacher's Edition* takes you through each unit, chapter, and chapter section, detailing concepts developed in the student text and providing suggested learning goals for your students; additional information for chapters and chapter sections, suggested activities, student answers, related films and filmstrips, and reference books for the teacher and interested students. Initially, the teaching outline considers each unit in detail in a *Unit Overview* that discusses the major concepts developed in the unit. Following the Unit Overview, the main points in each chapter are discussed in a *Chapter Overview*. Each chapter section is then detailed in the Teaching Strategy section. Any marginal activity found in that chapter section is then discussed and keyed to academic level (average, remedial, or enriched). Following the teaching strategy sections, the end of chapter laboratory activity is discussed. The amount of time and preparation is provided for the teacher, as well as any alternate materials if applicable. All questions posed in the laboratory activity are answered as well. Finally, a section entitled Going Further is included. This section provides the teacher with an activity or activities designed to supplement the concepts presented in the laboratory activity.

At the end of every chapter discussion are the possible answers to the Discussion Topics in the student's text. All other answers posed in the student's text, however, are answered in red on the page the question appears in your Annotated Teacher's Edition.

The bibliography that appears in the Teaching Aids section includes books appropriate for teacher reference as well as student use. A list of audio-visual materials that might be used during a particular chapter is also included. Finally, in chapters that end a unit, a discussion of the Science Gazette articles that follow each unit is included.

ANNOTATED PAGES OF THE STUDENT TEXT

You will find the following types of annotations printed throughout the text:

Answers to In-text Questions: Throughout the reading, questions are posed to the students. These questions are marked in red in the Annotated Teacher's Edition.

Answers to Section Review Questions: Following each chapter section there are Section Review questions. Answers to these questions appear in red.

Below each unit title and chapter title is an annotation indicating the pages of the teaching outline that contain information on teaching aids for that section.

Answers to end of chapter questions: All multiple choice, completion, and true and false questions found in the chapter review are answered in red in the Annotated Teacher's Edition on the page on which the questions appear.

List of Activities and Careers

MARGINAL ACTIVITIES (cont.)

CAREERS

List of Suppliers

LABORATORY MATERIALS AND ADDRESSES

Carolina Biological Supply Company
Burlington, NC 27215

DAMON/Educational Division
115 Fourth Avenue
Needham, MA 02194

Edmund Scientific Company
103 Gloucester Pike
Barrington, NJ 08007

Fisher Scientific Company
Educational Materials Division
4901 W. LeMoyne Ave.
Chicago, IL 60651

Hubbard Scientific Company
P.O. Box 104
Northbrook, IL 60062

La Pine Scientific Company
6001 Knox Avenue
Chicago, IL 60018

Prentice-Hall, Inc.
Educational Book Division
PO Box 900
Englewood Cliffs, NJ 07632

Sargeant-Welch Scientific Company
7300 North Linder Avenue
Skokie, IL 60076

Science Kit, Inc.
777 East Park Drive
Tonawanda, NY 14150

Scientific Glass Apparatus Company
737 Broad Street
Bloomfield, NJ 07003

Turtox
5000 W. 128 Place
Alsip, IL 60658

A-V SUPPLIERS AND ADDRESSES

BFA

BFA Educational Media
CBS Educational Publishing
A Division of CBS, Inc.
2211 Michigan Avenue
Santa Monica, CA 90404

Cor

Coronet Films
65 East South Water Street
Chicago, IL 60601

CRM/McGraw-Hill

Contemporary/McGraw-Hill Films
1221 Avenue of the Americas
New York, NY 10020

EBE

Encyclopedia Britannica
Educational Corporation
425 N. Michigan Avenue
Chicago, IL 60611

Eye Gate

Eye Gate Media
146-01 Archer Avenue
Jamaica, NY 11435

NGS

National Geographic Society
Educational Services
Dept 79
Washington, DC 20036

PH Media

Prentice-Hall Media
150 White Plains Road
Tarrytown, NY 10591

Walt Disney

Walt Disney Educational Media Company
500 South Buena Vista Street
Burbank, CA 91521

COMPUTER SOFTWARE SUPPLIERS

Carolina Biological Supply Company
2700 York Road
Burlington, NC 27215

Datatech Software Systems
19312 East Eldorado Drive
Aurora, CA 80013

Educational Dimensions Group
P.O. Box 126
Stamford, CT 06904

Focus Media, Inc.
839 Stewart Avenue
Garden City, NY 11530

Prentice-Hall, Inc.
Educational Book Division
Englewood Cliffs, NJ 07632

Comprehensive List of Laboratory Materials

Item	Quantities per group	Chapter
Alum	50 g	18, 19
Animal shelter building materials	1	5
Antacid, or seltzer, tablet	1	20
Ants	12	10
Balance, triple-beam	1	14, 17, 19
Ball bearings	4	22
Barium nitrate solution, 0.5M	4 mL	15

Beakers		
100 mL	4	20
250 mL	3	14, 19, 21, 22
500 mL	1	8, 17
Borax	25 g	18
Bread	2 slices	1
Broom	1	13
Bunsen burner	1	15, 21, 23
Calcium nitrate solution, 0.5M	4 mL	15
Can, metal, with secure seal	1	23
Clay	small piece	22
Cookbooks	3	4
Copper sulfate	25 g	18
Cotton wadding	10 cm	10
Cover slips	4	3, 7
Dental floss	50 cm	18
Dictionary, or encyclopedia	1	4
Dissecting needle	1	11
Ferric nitrate, $Fe(NO_3)_3$	2.4 g	14
Flask, or peanut butter jar with screw top	1	14
Food coloring blue, green, red, yellow	1 bottle of each	16
Funnel, glass	1	21
Glucose	5.4 g	17
Graduated cylinders		
50 mL	1	15
100 mL	1	19, 20
250 mL	1	15, 17
Hanger, wire coat	1	7
Hydrochloric acid, 6M	50 mL	15
Ice, crushed	150 mL	17
Jars with lids	2	1
Lab coat	1 per student	15
Lithium nitrate solution, 0.5M	4 mL	15
Magnifying glass	1	8, 10, 11, 18
Mammal photographs	2 to 3 sets (14 classes)	12
Marshmallows, large	25	16
Medicine droppers	4	1, 7
Menu, school lunch	1	2
Metric ruler	1	11, 13, 19, 22
Microscope	1	3, 7
Mushroom caps	1	8

Newspaper, small piece	1	3
Nylon stocking	1	7
Objects of various masses	1 set of 3	13
Oven mitten	1	23
Owl pellet	1	11
Pan, shallow	1	10
Paper		
construction, black (20 cm × 28 cm)	1 sheet	10
construction, white (20 cm × 28 cm)	14 sheets	12
white (20 cm × 28 cm)	13 sheets	2, 5, 6, 8, 11, 20
Paper towel	1	9
Pencils		
glass-marking	1	9, 17, 18, 19, 20
graphite	2	2, 6, 11, 20, 22
Petri dishes	5	9, 18
Photograph, magazine	1	3
Pin	1	10
Plastic bottles		
200 mL	1	10
2 L	1	10
Plastic container	1	19
Plastic wrap, 10 cm square	1	10
Potassium nitrate solution, 0.5M	4 mL	15
Potassium thiocyanate, KSCN	1 g	14
Reference books		
on mammals	1	12
on nutrition	1	2
on wildlife	1	5
Rock salt	few crystals	14
Rubber band	1	7
Rubber gloves	1 pair per student	15
Safety goggles	1 pair per student	15, 21, 23
Salt		
coarse	100 mL	17
table	25 g	18
Salt water, 3 different concentrations	200 mL of each	22
Sand	1 small bag	19
Scissors	1	10
Seeds, corn	4	9
Shoe boxes	3	13
Slides, microscope	4	3, 7
Sodium chloride	1.8 g	17
Sodium nitrate solution, 0.5M	4 mL	15
Soil, sandy	1 small bag	10

Stick, wooden	1	7
Stirring rod	1	18, 19
Straw, plastic drinking	1	22
String, 50 cm	1	7
Strontium nitrate solution, 0.5M	4 mL	15
Sucrose (table sugar)	35.2 g	17, 18
Tape		
adhesive, water-resistant	1 small roll	7, 10
masking	1 small roll	9
·transparent	1 small roll	12
Test tubes		
large with stoppers	8	14, 17
medium with stoppers	7	7, 15
small	1	14
Test tube brush	1	15
Test tube clamp	1	15
Test tube holder	1	15
Test tube rack	1	15, 17
Thermometer, −10° to 100° C	1	17
Toothpicks	1 small box	16
Tripod	1	21, 23
Varnish, or hair spray	1 small can	8
Water		
distilled	1 L	15
tap	3.015 L	14, 15, 17, 18, 20, 21, 22, 23
Wire gauze	1	21, 23
Wire loop with wooden handle	1	15

Safety Guidelines

SCIENCE CLASSROOM SAFETY DO'S AND DON'T'S

It is suggested that you read this section to your class, or distribute copies. Also, see the safety handout in your Teacher's Resource Book.

The scientific laboratory is a place of adventure and discovery. Some of the most important events in scientific history have happened in laboratories. The antibiotic powers of penicillin were discovered in a laboratory. The plastics used today for clothing and other products were first made in a laboratory. The list is almost endless. Although work in a laboratory can be fun and exciting, it can also be dangerous if rules of safety are not followed. Here are some rules for you to follow:

Do

1. Wear protective goggles when working with chemicals, burners, or any substance that might get into your eyes. Many materials in a lab can cause injury to the eyes and even blindness.

2. Learn what to do in case of specific accidents such as getting acid in your eyes or on your skin. (Rinse acids on your body with lots of water.)
3. Before starting any Laboratory Investigation or other experiment, make a list of the things that could go wrong that might hurt you. Then make a list of what you should do if the accident happens.
4. Make sure you have a fire extinguisher nearby to put out a fire.
5. Work with a friend, when you can, under the supervision of a science teacher or adult who understands lab safety rules.
6. Work in a well-ventilated area.
7. Learn how to use first aid to quickly treat burns, cuts, and bruises. Seek help if you are injured.
8. Read directions for an experiment carefully two or more times. Follow the directions exactly as they are written.

Don't

1. Mix chemicals ''for the fun of it.'' You might produce an explosive reaction that could seriously injure you.
2. Taste, touch, or smell any chemical that you don't know for a fact is harmless. Many chemicals are poisonous.
3. Heat any chemical that you are not instructed to heat. A chemical that is harmless when cool can be dangerous when heated.
4. Heat a liquid in a closed container. The expanding gases produced may blow the container apart, injuring you.
5. Perform an experiment in which you must connect wires to house current. You could electrocute yourself. (Use dry cells instead.)
6. Tilt a test tube toward yourself or anyone else (or hold it upright) when you are heating its contents. (Always tilt the tube away from yourself and others.)
7. Perform any experiment for which you do not have written instructions (in a text or from your teacher).

FIELD TRIP SAFETY

This text offers a variety of field investigations, or field trips, that can be used to extend your students' studies and interests in science. Although the program outlined in this book can be successfully carried out within the confines of a classroom, the suggested field investigations have been included to provide an opportunity for your students to have first-hand evidence and experiences outside of the classroom. Though numerous field investigations have been suggested in the student text and in the *Annotated Teacher's Edition,* the number of field investigations can be limited by combining expected outcomes of several field investigations into one. For example, one field investigation at the zoo may suggest to students that they observe animals and their habitats. Another field investigation may suggest to students that they observe animal behavior or interactions. Data for these two investigations can be collected during one trip and then used when needed.

The success of a field trip or investigation depends on careful preparation, both by you and your students. The following suggestions are made to help you organize and conduct a field trip or investigation successfully.

1. **Site Selection:** The text suggests possible field trip sites, but it is up to you to select an appropriate field trip site for your students, depending upon your locale. To aid you in making the necessary arrangements, we suggest that you make a school file of available sites in your area. The file should contain specific instructions concerning who to contact at the site, directions or a map to the site, fees (if any), the hours the site is open to the public, and availability of meal facilities and restrooms.

   It is suggested that you make a visit to the site prior to the field trip to inspect the facilities. While you are there, locate and inventory work-study areas. Make a list of specific equipment your students will need and note the site restrictions and danger spots. Also note facilities for the handicapped if any of your students have physical limitations.

2. **Planning the Trip:** Be sure that the field trip is justified in view of the school's educational program and your individual lesson objectives. Request written permission for the trip from school personnel and keep this written permission on file. After being granted permission, send a written statement of your destination, departure and arrival times, mode

of transportation, and necessary expenditures to each student's parent or guardian.

Meanwhile, provide time in class for advance research on the site. Correlate the projected field trip with your lessons and text material. Tell your students the why, where, and when of the field trip. Be sure to inform them of any special equipment or clothing they will need—special shoes, shorts, hand lenses, notebooks, and so on.

3. **The Actual Field Trip:** Make a head count of your students at each boarding and departure and periodically during the trip. Each adult should be provided with a list of the students he or she is to supervise and should remain with that group throughout the entire trip. While you're on the way to the site, discuss the investigation with your students. Have them note and list things they observe on the way—wooded areas, rock formations, signs of pollution, and so on. When you arrive at the site, keep the group together unless you have planned otherwise.

Make certain the students understand the purpose of the field trip. Have them make sketches, drawings, plans, or maps or take notes. Do not allow students to remove anything from its natural setting unless carefully selected items are taken for observation and returned to their natural habitats.

Most importantly, be enthusiastic but don't rush. Don't try to crowd too much into one field trip. Keep in contact with the individuals in the group and be alert for the "teachable moment."

4. **Follow-up Activities:** A good field trip provides a base experience for other class activities. While you are returning to the school, have students exchange ideas and discuss their experiences and observations at the site. Encourage students to ask questions and propose future activities related to the field trip. Schedule individual or group reports and have the students evaluate the trip.

Later, you may want to have your students prepare exhibits or displays using their sketches, maps, photographs, or other materials from the trip. Have them use the library to investigate questions arising from the trip. A number of library investigations can usually be proposed after a successful field trip. Remember, the learning value of a field trip depends largely on you and the type of follow-up activities you provide or encourage.

UNIT ONE
Characteristics of Living Things

pp. 10–119

OVERVIEW

This unit deals with the general characteristics of life forms. As the unit introduction suggests, life forms can vary in remarkable ways and can become adapted to seemingly hostile environments. You might begin your teaching of the unit by asking students to list as many kinds of living things as they can and then asking them to describe similarities among them. The actual biological similarities may well elude them, because these similarities have to do with the basic processes of life and with cells and internal structures that are not ordinarily visible.

Chapter 1 serves as an introduction to the study of living things. In a more general sense, it introduces students to the methods of science. Chapter 2 deals with the nature of life—the processes, needs, and basic chemistry of living things. Chapter 3 describes the structure and functions of the basic unit of life, the cell. Chapter 4 treats the higher levels of anatomical organization—tissues, organs, and organ systems. Chapter 5 deals with the basic interactions between living things.

CHAPTER

1 Exploring Living Things

pp. 12–33

OVERVIEW

W. P. Coombs's analysis of dinosaur tracks, described in the chapter introduction, illustrates scientific reasoning at its best, bringing out both its logical and its creative aspects. This entire chapter deals essentially with the nature of science—that is, science considered not as a collection of facts but as a process. Throughout your teaching—not only of this chapter but of the course as a whole—you should stress to students that by learning the methods of science, they too can act as scientists, and that simply memorizing sets of facts discovered in the past is not sufficient for the study or practice of science.

This chapter serves as an introduction to life science, as well as to scientific method, which is illustrated in a biological context. After studying the steps biologists tend to follow in their investigations, students then go on to learn about measurement in science, the equipment used in biology, and the fortuitous aspects of important scientific breakthroughs in the past.

SECTION

1-1 What Is Science?

pp. 14–20

Teaching Strategy

The title and content of this section may at first seem somewhat at odds to some students: The title hints at a static definition of science, whereas the content deals with scientific method. There is no contradiction, however, as you should point out to students, because science is a process that is describable in terms of the steps scientists actually follow in doing their work. There is no single sequence of steps that is rigidly followed; however, there is an underlying logic to the overall process of scientific method, which allows the scientist to work from a foundation of previous knowledge toward new hypotheses that can be verified or falsified through careful experimentation.

As you teach students about the sequence of steps used to solve the particular biological problem (the ability of rattlesnakes to find their wounded prey) described in this section, ask them to consider why those steps were followed. Ask students how they might have gone about solving this and other scientific problems, and try to get them to recognize that scientific method involves application of processes that make sense in the context of the particular problems being investigated. They may discover that problem-solving methods they have used themselves in real-life situations are not very far removed from many of the methods used by scientists.

Similarity and Diversity in Living Things

This activity allows students to apply information-gathering and observation skills in a familiar context, that of their own neighborhood. It also asks them to compare and contrast living things and thus to make the sorts of discriminations necessary in biology.

ACTIVITY

Theories and Laws
p. 16 (Enriched)

This activity will help students understand the difference between a theory and a law. Refer students to page 37 (theory of spontaneous generation) and pages 335–336 (Boyle's and Charles's Laws).

ACTIVITY

Early Scientists
p. 18 (Average)

This activity helps students to develop library research skills, which are also important in science. Encourage them to bring out in their reports the aspects of scientific method used by the scientists whose contributions they are researching.

SECTION

1·2 Scientific Measurements
pp. 20–24

Teaching Strategy

In this section, some of the most basic quantities measured by scientists—length, volume, mass, weight, density, and temperature—are discussed. You should be especially careful to point out the distinction between mass and weight and to continue to distinguish clearly between them throughout the course, since students tend to confuse the two quantities.

The metric system, which is used to express measurements in science, is also explained. The rationality of this system, which is based on units of ten, can easily be made apparent to students. Thus, their changeover from thinking in terms of English measurement, with its unwieldy units and cumbersome conversions, to "thinking metric" should not be too difficult, especially if you completely avoid using English units once the metric units have become familiar.

ACTIVITY

Practicing Metric Measurements
p. 22 (Average)

In this activity, students apply their knowledge of metric units of length to the measurement of familiar objects, whose dimensions they may be used to thinking of in terms of English units. They should also be able to find a number of products (in particular, food items) whose masses and volumes are expressed, on their containers, in metric as well as English units.

ACTIVITY

Comparing Temperatures
p. 24 (Remedial–Average)

This activity serves to reinforce mathematical word-problem skills involving large numbers. By dividing $20,000,000°$ C by $3700°$ C, students should arrive at the correct answer, which is approximately 5405.

SECTION

1·3 Tools of a Scientist
pp. 24–28

Teaching Strategy

The tools described in this section are some of those used by life scientists. Of these, your school probably has available only the light microscope (and perhaps the computer). Familiarize your students with the structure and operation of the light microscope, which they can make use of in various laboratory activities. Have them do more library research on the other, more specialized devices, or arrange for a class trip to a large biological laboratory that uses such devices.

You may wish to refer to the units of measurement discussed earlier and explain the use of "tools" in the making of such measurements—such as the balance, the graduated cylinder, and the Celsius thermometer, all of which your students will need to use in their science studies.

SECTION

1-4 Science and Discovery pp. 28–29

Teaching Strategy

The role of luck, hunches, and other "non-logical" aspects of scientific discovery is discussed in this section. Point out once again that scientific method as actually followed by successful scientists does not consist of a set of rigid steps but always involves adaptation to and creative use of unexpected aspects of the situation being investigated. You may wish to have students do library research on other important discoveries in life science, such as the discovery of penicillin. Many of these discoveries involved unexpected turns of events, and all required creativity and flexibility, as well as patience, precision, and thoroughness on the part of the scientists involved.

ACTIVITY

A Lucky Find p. 29 (Remedial–Average)

This activity helps build vocabulary and essay-writing skills. It also helps reinforce students' understanding of the fortuitous discovery of Bonamo and Grierson described in this section. Have students read their essays to the class.

LABORATORY ACTIVITY

A Moldy Question p. 30

This activity will require a few minutes out of each of about five class periods over a two-week period. It can be begun once Section 1-1 has been completed.

Answers to questions in Procedure: 2. Light has little influence on mold growth. 3. Other conditions include temperature, moisture, and the presence of preservatives.

Observations and Conclusions: 1. The variable chosen will vary. The control will be a similar jar and piece of bread that does not contain the variable (moisture, for example) but is otherwise identical to the other, experimental setup. 2. Moisture and high (but not too high) temperatures have a positive effect on mold growth.

3. The experiment was not well designed because Cathy varied more than one condition at the same time and therefore could not tell which variable was responsible for the difference in mold growth. The experiment should thus be redesigned, and it should also be repeated several times.

Going Further: Have students repeat their experiments, using different types and brands of bread, including breads that do not contain preservatives.

Discussion Topics p. 33

1. The steps include stating the problem, gathering information on the problem, forming a hypothesis, testing the hypothesis by experimenting, recording and analyzing the data, and stating a conclusion.
2. Mass is a measure of the amount of matter and is constant for an object. Weight is a measure of the force of gravity acting on an object and can change.
3. A compound light microscope uses light to observe objects, whereas an electron microscope uses particles called electrons.
4. Lasers can be used as "light scalpels" to cut and seal off blood vessels, and they can be used to destroy clumps of cancer cells. Computers can help in diagnosis, prescription, and information gathering.
5. Discoveries are sometimes made because of chance or luck rather than through strict adherence to scientific method, as is illustrated in the discovery of extremely ancient fossils by Bonamo and Grierson.

BIBLIOGRAPHY

Clark, M. E. *Contemporary Biology: Concepts and Implications.* Philadelphia, Pa.: W. B. Saunders.

Dixon, B. *What Is Science For?* Westhampton, N.Y.: Collins.

Samuel, E. *Order in Life.* Englewood Cliffs, N.J.: Prentice-Hall.

Smith, R., and W. M. Reid. *Guide to the Literature of the Life Sciences.* Minneapolis, Minn.: Burgess.

The Microscope: Light Field Illumination, film loop, PH Media.

The Scientific Method, film, Encyclopaedia Britannica.

What Is Science?, film, Coronet.

CHAPTER

2. The Nature of Life   pp. 34–55

OVERVIEW

This chapter describes the general characteristics of living things. It does not deal with the anatomical aspects of living things or with the basic unit of life, the cell, which is treated in Chapter 3.

After a discussion of the properties of organisms in the first section of the chapter, the needs of living things are detailed. As the chapter introduction, with its description of Miller's experiments, suggests, an understanding of these properties and characteristics must be based on analysis of the chemistry of living things, which is covered in the final section of this chapter. You may wish to point out to students that the composition of the gases used by Miller was similar to that of the atmosphere of the young Earth. Our atmosphere no longer contains appreciable amounts of hydrogen sulfide, methane, ammonia, and hydrogen; however, the atmosphere of the planet Jupiter does, and there is speculation whether life forms might develop there.

SECTION

2-1 Characteristics of Living Things   pp. 36–43

Teaching Strategy

Point out to students that although it is difficult to state a definition of the word ''life,'' it is possible to distinguish life from nonlife by recognizing the characteristics of all living things. One of these characteristics is biogenesis, or the property of coming only from other living things. Redi, Spallanzani, and Pasteur proved the principle of biogenesis when they disproved the theory of spontaneous generation. Other properties of living things include movement, metabolism (with its

many processes), growth and development, response, and reproduction. Students may be able to list, in their own words, most of these characteristics. When you teach them about stimulus and response, you may also ask them for examples drawn from their own experience.

ACTIVITY

Disproving Spontaneous Generation   p. 37 (Average)

Encourage students to examine the findings of the three scientists in terms of the logic of their scientific thought and methods. This is relatively simple to do in the cases of Spallanzani and Pasteur, who turned out to be correct in their rejection of the theory of spontaneous generation. However, even Needham, who incorrectly held to this theory, formulated hypotheses, conducted experiments, and came to conclusions in a logical, scientific manner, although there were problems with certain aspects of his experimental setups and, of course, in his failure to recognize that life forms could have entered the system from outside.

ACTIVITY

Observing Stimulus-Response Reactions   p. 43 (Average)

This activity serves to demonstrate the presence of stimulus-response mechanisms in human beings. Although students may feel that the reflexes observed in steps 1 and 4 involve learned behavior to some extent, the dilation-contraction reflex of the pupils observed in steps 2 and 3 is clearly automatic and cannot be controlled by the subject.

SECTION

2-2 Needs of Living Things   pp. 44–48

Teaching Strategy

You may wish to ask students to name various things they need from their environment in order to survive. You will probably find that most will be able to list food, water, and energy (light or heat, as well as other forms). Encourage them to relate these needs to the characteristics of life they learned about earlier—in particular, metabolism, whose processes require the input of matter and energy from the environment.

Point out that although all organisms have in common the various needs described, their particular requirements may differ considerably. Consideration of different kinds of organisms that live under very different environmental conditions should help to make this point.

ACTIVITY

Body Water   p. 45 (Remedial–Average)

This activity not only illustrates that a great deal of the body's mass is water but also reinforces mathematical skills. Particular answers will vary, depending on the masses of the students. In each case, the student should multiply 0.65 by his or her mass, in kilograms. The water content of a 50.0-kg student, for example, is about 32.5 kg.

ACTIVITY

Temperature Range   p. 47 (Average)

This exercise illustrates the wide range of temperature extremes on the earth and also reinforces subtraction skills. Since a negative number is involved, the exercise may be difficult for some students. If so, you may suggest that these students "count" from the lower to the higher temperature. The answer is 147° C.

ACTIVITY

Swamp Story   p. 48 (Remedial–Average)

This activity tests students' understanding of basic concepts covered in this chapter, as well as reinforcing vocabulary skills and encouraging students to express their ideas creatively. Have students read their stories to the class.

SECTION

2-3 Chemistry of Living Things   pp. 48–51

Teaching Strategy

The point of this section is to introduce only the most basic chemical concepts to provide an overview of some of the major classes of substances found in living things. These substances include carbohydrates, fats and oils, and proteins. Do not attempt to introduce more chemistry than is absolutely necessary; the goal is simply to provide students with enough knowledge to be able to continue with their general study of living things and to take up the study of the cell. If you have already covered Units Three and Four, which deal with physical science, however, you may wish to go into more detail, using terms such as "atoms" and "molecules."

ACTIVITY

A Healthful Diet   p. 51 (Average)

By doing this activity, students not only learn a bit more about the chemistry of foods and of the human body but also develop a heightened awareness of the importance of a balanced diet. Students may wish to make daily charts of their intake of foods from the various groups, over a period of a week or two, and perhaps use the experience to improve the quality and balance of the food they ingest.

LABORATORY ACTIVITY

You Are What You Eat   p. 52

This activity, which will require one class period, should be done when the final section of the chapter has been completed.

Observations and Conclusions: 1. Answers will vary.

Going Further: You may wish to have students research federal guidelines for school lunch programs. They may attempt to determine restrictions on certain foods and requirements for balanced menus.

Discussion Topics   p. 55

1. The characteristics of living things include the necessity of their coming from other living things, movement, metabolism (which involves ingestion, digestion, respiration, and excretion), growth and development, the possession of a typical life span, response, and reproduction.

2. The sun is the primary source of energy. Plants use the sun's energy to make food. Some animals eat the plants, which have stored the energy, and other animals may eat these animals. In this way, the sun's energy is passed on from one living thing to another.

BIBLIOGRAPHY

Keeton, W. T. *Biological Science*. New York: Norton.

Stare, F. J., and M. McWilliams. *Living Nutrition*. New York: Wiley.

Tuckerman, M. M., and S. J. Turco. *Human Nutrition*. Philadelphia, Pa.: Lea and Febiger.

Ward, B. *Food and Digestion*. New York: Watts.

A-V MATERIALS

Breathing and Respiration, filmstrip, BFA Educational Media.

Excretion, filmstrip, McGraw-Hill.

Reproductive System, filmstrip, McGraw-Hill.

The Human Body: Nutrition and Metabolism, filmstrip, Coronet.

CHAPTER

3 Cells   pp. 56–78

OVERVIEW

This chapter deals with the cell, the basic unit of life. As the chapter introduction indicates, cells have existed for billions of years and have developed the most amazing adaptations and the most complex interrelations within multicellular organisms. The first section of the chapter deals with the basic structure and functions of the living and nonliving parts of the cell and with the differences between plant and animal cells. The second section describes the processes of diffusion, osmosis, and reproduction (including mitosis and meiosis).

SECTION

3-1 Cell Structure and Function   pp. 58–67

Teaching Strategy

This section introduces students to the structure of cells by taking them on an imaginary journey through a cell. Follow this same approach in your teaching, since it will help hold students' attention. The imaginary-journey approach can be as exciting when applied to the cell as it is when applied to space.

In this section, the cell wall, cell membrane, nucleus, endoplasmic reticulum, ribosomes, mitochondria, vacuoles, lysosomes, and chloroplasts are covered. As you teach students about these structures, have them use the microscope to observe each one. Prepared slides are available from biological supply houses. Be sure that students have a clear grasp of the interrelated functions of the various cellular structures. Also, take the time to make them aware of the differences in structure and function between plant and animal cells; their knowledge on this subject will be helpful when you later teach them about plants and animals considered as entire organisms.

ACTIVITY

The Nature of Protoplasm   p. 60 (Average–Enriched)

Many thousands of chemical substances are present in protoplasm. Most students should be able to make charts that display the names and relative proportions of the most common of these substances. More advanced students, or students with a grasp of or an interest in the basic principles of chemistry, may be able to go further in their research and analysis. If you have already covered Units Three and Four, you may wish to have students organize their information in terms of the atoms and molecules involved and to use the concepts of "mixture" and "solution" in their presentations.

ACTIVITY

Word Clues   p. 65 (Remedial–Average)

This activity helps to build language skills. Once the meanings of the prefixes have been grasped, you may wish to ask students to find other words that contain them.

SECTION

3-2 Cell Activities   pp. 67–73

Teaching Strategy

This section moves from consideration of the structure and function of individual parts of the cell to an examination of some of the activities and processes characteristic of the cell as a whole. In explaining cell metabolism, refer students to the more detailed description of metabolic processes presented in the preceding chapter. In explaining cell reproduction, do not attempt to explain the specifics of sexual or asexual reproduction in organisms considered as a whole; concentrate, rather, on the cellular level. You may wish, however, to go into greater detail on cell division, pointing out the stages involved in this process and having students use prepared slides to observe these stages.

ACTIVITY

The Big Egg   p. 70 (Average)

The expansion of the hard-boiled egg that occurs as a result of osmosis should be apparent. Students may wish to attempt to observe the reverse osmotic process by placing a hard-boiled egg in a concentrated saltwater solution.

ACTIVITY

How Many Cells? p. 71 (Remedial–Average)

This activity reinforces mathematical skills and demonstrates the rapidity of cell division. After 90 minutes, there will have been 9 divisions, so the total number of cells will be 2^9, or 512. You may wish to have students attempt to calculate the number present (ideally) after 24 hours. The number, 2^{144}, is astronomically high.

LABORATORY ACTIVITY

Things Look Different
Under a Microscope   p. 74

This activity, which will require one class period, can be done at any time during the course of the chapter.

Answers to questions in Procedure: 4. The letter seems to move in a direction opposite to that in which it is actually moved. 5. The entire letter is no longer visible, and the ink no longer appears to be solid but takes on a dotted appearance.

Observations and Conclusions: 1. The letter chosen will be enlarged and will appear reversed and upside down.

Going Further: Have students use the microscope to observe other small objects, such as cork cells, onionskin cells, or crystals of sugar and salt.

Discussion Topics   p. 77

1. Students may argue that the chloroplasts would best be implanted in cells of the digestive system (to provide food) or in skin cells, which would be exposed to light.
2. Mitosis, in which exact duplicates of cells are formed, cannot introduce new characteristics into offspring. Meiosis (which involves chromosomal halving), together with fertilization (the combination of chromosomes from the two parents that occurs later), typically gives an offspring characteristics that are different from those of either parent.

BIBLIOGRAPHY

Dowben, R. *Cell Biology*. New York: Harper & Row.

Stein, H., and D. L. Nanney. *The Biology of Cells*. New York: Wiley.

Swanson, C. P. *The Cell*. Englewood Cliffs, N.J.: Prentice-Hall.

A-V MATERIALS

Cells: A First Film, film, BFA Educational Media.

Cell Biology: Life Functions, film, Coronet.

Learning About Cells, film, Encyclopaedia Britannica.

The Living Cell: An Introduction, film, Encyclopaedia Britannica.

CHAPTER

4   Tissues, Organs,
and Organ Systems   pp. 78–92

OVERVIEW

The preceding chapters dealt with the nature of life and with the basic unit of life, the cell. This chapter deals with the higher levels of organization in multicellular organisms: the tissues, organs, and organ systems. There must be close coordination between structures within a given level—for example, between cells within a tissue or between organs within an organ system. Such coordination is essential to the performance of complex activities—for example, the hunting activity of the cheetah described in the chapter introduction.

You may wish to begin by having students list three or four activities they perform daily. Later, they can research the tissues, organs, and organ systems that are involved in each activity.

SECTION

4-1 Division of Labor pp. 80–81

Teaching Strategy

This short section describes in a general way the division of labor, or allotment of functions, characteristic of healthy multicellular organisms. Such organisms (especially in the higher phyla) tend to have clearly differentiated body parts. Students may be asked to list the major visible structures of a familiar organism and describe the functions carried out by each structure.

The division of labor that is characteristic of separate body parts is also an attribute of the smaller structures that make up these parts. Refer students to the preceding chapter to ensure that they are familiar with the general characteristics of all cells before going on to teach them about the specializations of different kinds of cells.

ACTIVITY

Division of Labor p. 81 (Average)

This activity introduces students to the concept of biological coordination by means of an analogy to the cooperation within a community of human beings. You may wish to point out later that such groups of like organisms, or populations, are often referred to as a sixth level of biological organization beyond the five discussed.

SECTION

4-2 Organization of Living Things pp. 81–87

Teaching Strategy

This section describes the cells, tissues, organs, and organ systems that represent the levels of or-

ganization within an organism. As you teach students about various kinds of cells and tissues, make use of prepared microscope slides to make clear the special features of each. You may wish to have students do library research on various organs or organ systems of human beings or other organisms and report to the class on the anatomy and physiology of these structures.

ACTIVITY

An Amazing Feat p. 87 (Remedial-Average)

This activity illustrates the extraordinary ability of a particular organism to coordinate its bodily structures in order to fly. To do this activity, students are required to review a basic mathematical skill. They must multiply 80 beats/second by 60 seconds/minute by 5 minutes to come up with the correct answer: 24,000 beats.

LABORATORY ACTIVITY

Have You Tasted These? p. 88

This activity, which will require one class period, should be done when the chapter has been nearly completed.

Answers to Questions in Procedure: 2. Tripe: muscular lining of stomachs of ruminants; sweetbreads: pancreas or thymus of calf; chitterlings: intestine of pig; escargot: snail; sushi: muscle of fish; jerky: dried muscle of cattle; suet: fat of sheep or cattle; marrow: tissue that fills cavities of bones of cattle; pâté de foie gras: liver of goose; caviar: fish eggs.

Observations and Conclusions: 1. Tripe: tissue; sweetbreads: organ; chitterlings: organ; escargot: organism; sushi: tissue; jerky: tissue; suet: tissue; marrow: tissue; pâté de foie gras: organ; caviar: cells. 2. Answers will vary.

Going Further: Suggest to students that they or other members of their families shop for some of these or other unusual foods, and prepare and sample them.

Discussion Topics p. 91

1. A simple organism is typically unicellular; a

complex one contains many cells that function together according to the various levels of organization.

2. The pyramid will have five levels, with ''cells'' at the bottom.
3. Answers will vary, and may include body temperature, digestive processes, and emotional-physical changes, such as those resulting from fear.
4. Answers will vary. On hearing a wakeup alarm, sense organs receive information that they convey via the nervous system. On rising, muscles are moved due to nervous stimuli. Eating and digesting breakfast requires the use of muscles and of the organs of ingestion and digestion.

BIBLIOGRAPHY

Elson, L. M. *It's Your Body.* New York: McGraw-Hill.

Harrison, R. J., and W. Montagna. *Man.* Englewood Cliffs, N.J.: Prentice-Hall.

Nourse, A. E., et al. *The Body.* New York: Time, Inc.

A-V MATERIALS

Man: The Incredible Machine, film, National Geographic Society.

The Heart and Circulatory System, film, Encyclopaedia Britannica.

The Human Nervous System, 8 filmstrips, PH Media.

CHAPTER

5 Interactions Among
Living Things   pp. 92–128

OVERVIEW

Having learned about the relationship of parts within an organism, students are now ready to study the relationships between organisms. This chapter deals with such interactions, as well as with the nonliving environment within which they occur. The relationships within ecosystems are, in general, extremely complex, as the chapter introduction suggests, and can change dramatically as conditions change. However, the basic principles involving the groupings of organisms and the food, energy, and symbiotic relationships within ecosystems are fairly simple to comprehend. These principles will be taken up in the several sections of this chapter.

SECTION

5-1 Living Things and Their
Environment   pp. 94–100

Teaching Strategy

This section introduces some of the basic terminology of the study of ecology. Carefully review the definitions of ''environment,'' ''ecosystem,'' ''community,'' and ''population''; these terms are often confused by students. Use examples to clarify the meanings of these terms and to explain the concepts of ''habitat'' and ''niche,'' the latter of which is often incorrectly understood as a spatial rather than a role-related concept. Point out that populations have different niches because they have different food needs, hunting habits, and ways of protecting themselves. You may wish to have students make a list of animals native to their area and to ask them to describe the habitats and niches of these animals.

ACTIVITY

Identifying Interactions   p. 97 (Average)

Encourage students to make on-site observations of the ecosystem they choose, and remind them that, as in all field trips, they should not go alone and they should inform an adult of their whereabouts. Explain that their observations should be analyzed and presented in terms of the ecological concepts covered in this chapter. Ask them to share their results with the class. Display their drawings and diagrams and use them to illustrate some of the points you will make in your teaching of the rest of the chapter.

SECTION

5-2 Food and Energy
in the Environment   pp. 100–107

Teaching Strategy

In this section, students are introduced to the distinction between producer (autotrophic) and consumer (heterotrophic) organisms. Food chain and food web diagrams are also introduced as aids to understanding the food relationships between organisms. Take special care to provide examples of energy level diagrams, since this concept is especially difficult for students. You may wish to invite an environmentalist to address the class on food and energy relationships and other ecological topics.

ACTIVITY

Drawing a Food Web   p. 105 (Average)

This exercise gives students practice in analyzing feeding relationships. They might draw arrows that point from grass to mice and deer, from deer to mountain lions, from mountain lions to vultures, and from all these organisms to bacteria, which serve as decomposers.

ACTIVITY

Your Place in a Food Chain   p. 107 (Average–Enriched)

Students should be able to derive a food chain for each of the major components of each meal. Certain of the foods may contain a large number of ingredients, whose separate food chains may be difficult to determine. Students should be encouraged to do library research on the organisms from which the various ingredients and foods were described and to report their findings to the class.

SECTION

5-3 Relationships in an Ecosystem   pp. 107–115

Teaching Strategy

The basic competitive and symbiotic relationships between organisms are discussed in this section. There are many interesting examples of commensalism, mutualism, and parasitism that you might use to illustrate these categories of symbiosis. For example, a small bird called the Egyptian plover "plays dentist" to a crocodile in a mutualistic relationship, the plover feeding on bloodsucking leeches found inside the crocodile's mouth. Ask students to do library research to

come up with other examples and to relate their findings to what they have already learned about food chains.

Also ask students to do reports on disturbances to ecosystems. These reports should include examples of damage caused by human activity. You may wish to set up class discussions or debates on industrial development versus environmental protection.

ACTIVITY

Shady Survival   p. 109 (Remedial–Average)

This activity reinforces mathematical skills. Students must multiply 65 percent (or 0.65) by 140 and then multiply 35 percent (or .035) by 140. The answer is 91 sugar maples and 49 red maples.

ACTIVITY

Changes in Populations   p. 115 (Average)

By doing this library activity, students will learn about factors that limit population size. Have students explain the concept of population cycle, using this and other examples, taken both from their experience and from further library research.

LABORATORY ACTIVITY

They Call It Home   p. 116

This activity, which can be done at any point in the chapter, will require about two class periods, or an equivalent amount of at-home time.

Observations and Conclusions: 1. Answers will vary. 2. Animals build shelters for protection, as food-storage sites, as breeding sites, and for other reasons that depend upon the particular animal. 3. The animal might attempt to use other materials. However, some animals will not use substitute materials.

Going Further: Have students design and build a diorama to contain the shelter and to depict the animal's natural habitat.

Discussion Topics   p. 119

1. The tickbird eats the ticks. This is an example of mutualism, since both organisms benefit.

2. Answers will vary. Students might suggest including protected park lands in the city and minimizing air and water pollution.

BIBLIOGRAPHY

Boughey, A. S. *Ecology and Population.* New York: Macmillan.

McNaughton, S., and L. L. Wolf. *General Ecology.* New York: Holt, Rinehart and Winston.

Street, P. *Animal Partners and Parasites.* New York: Taplinger.

A-V MATERIALS

Ants: Backyard Science, film, BFA Educational Media.

Interrelationships of Living Things, filmstrips, Eyegate.

Nature's Half Acre, film, Walt Disney.

Science Gazette   pp. 120–127

The Gazette Adventure, "Archie Carr and the Mystery of the Vanishing Sea Turtles," may be read after Chapter 5, the last chapter in the unit. The article broadens the discussion of living things and the environments in which they live. Students may be surprised to learn that even such temporary dwelling places as clumps of floating seaweed harbor ecological communities. You may have students research other unusual ecological communities and write short papers on communities that interest them. Another option is to have each student draw his or her favorite community, showing the organisms in the community and perhaps indicating feeding relationships among the organisms.

The Gazette Issue, "Pests or Pesticides: Which Will It Be?," will show students how a knowledge of ecology can literally save lives. Once again, this article would be best appreciated after students have read Chapter 5, particularly the last subsection, entitled "Balance in the Ecosystem." Students will see how ecology is applied to common agricultural problems. You may want to have students try to come up with ways in which an awareness of the ecology could solve problems in your area. List the problems on the chalkboard in one column and the ecological solutions in another. You may want to expand the discussion to include the state in which you live.

Following Chapters 3 and 4, have students read the Gazette Future, "The Computer That Lives!" While the chapters provide very basic information about cells, tissues, organs, and organ systems, the gazette article presents an extraordinary, futuristic glimpse into what would be a medical breakthrough—a living computer implanted in a person's brain. In the article, the computer replaces damaged nerves in the brain to allow the patient, Ronda, to see again. Students should be able to understand how the computer works, in what sense it is "alive," and how the parts of the body interact with the computer to make it effective. Encourage students' creativity as you elicit from them other uses for living computers.

Classification of Living Things

OVERVIEW

The material in this unit deals with the classification of a great diversity of living things. To give students an appreciation for this diversity, you might direct their attention to the unit-opening photo and to other general nature photos that they have brought in to class. Ask them to pick out and identify as many of the living things as they can in such photographs. You might also ask them to describe the characteristics of these living things so completely that other people would be able to guess the names of the things without looking at the picture. Students might be asked to play this description guessing game in class.

Chapter 6 deals with the general problem of taxonomic classification. Chapters 7 to 12 deal with the characteristics of various groups of living things: viruses, bacteria, protists, nonvascular plants and plantlike organisms, vascular plants, invertebrate animals, nonmammalian vertebrate animals, and mammals. You might point out to students that taxonomists do not all agree on which classification system is the best. For example, some favor a three-kingdom system (protists, plants, animals), whereas others favor a five-kingdom system (protists, monerans, fungi, plants, animals). No one system can be considered the correct one. However, all classification systems have one thing in common: They result from an attempt to group living things on the basis of their similarities and differences.

CHAPTER

6 Classification

pp. 130–145

OVERVIEW

The chapter-opening text describes the discovery of a lobe-finned fish called the coelacanth that had been thought to be extinct. This discovery is an exciting example of the application of taxonomic principles. In this chapter, students will study the history of biological classification and nomenclature and will learn how various kinds of living things are classified and named today. In the process, they will learn the general charac-

teristics of living things. As you teach this material, point out the importance of careful observation, description, and comparison—important aspects of scientific method—in the taxonomic process.

SECTION

6-1 History of Classification pp. 132–135

Teaching Strategy

Present the problem of classification as one that has always existed for human beings, who are curious about the characteristics and uses of all the things in their environment. Explain how the science of taxonomy progressed. Ask students what general characteristics they would use in classification and how they might have improved on the early work done in this field.

ACTIVITY

What's in a Name?

p. 134 (Average)

Students should enjoy searching for the clues in the chapter introduction that will tell them why the scientific name for the coelacanth is *Latimeria chalumnae*. After being caught at the mouth of the Chalumna River, the fish was seen by M. Courtenay-Latimer. She was responsible for having the fish identified. Hence the coelacanth is named for her and for the river in which it was caught.

SECTION

6-2 Modern Classification System

pp. 135–138

Teaching Strategy

Point out the advantage of a standard biological nomenclature for living things. Explain the seven-level classification (from kingdom to species) in present use. The mnemonic device described on page 137 should help students remember the names and order of the levels. Carefully review the various examples of classification that are given on page 139.

ACTIVITY

The Secret Code   p. 137 (Remedial)

Students can have some fun with this idea of making up sentences in which the first letter of each word stands for a classification grouping. Going from the largest to the smallest grouping, the letters are *k, p, c, o, f, g, s.* Students can also reverse the order and go from the smallest to the largest grouping with the letters *s, g, f, o, c, p, k.*

ACTIVITY

Early Taxonomists   p. 138 (Average)

Try to develop in students an appreciation for early attempts at systematic classification. Point out the historical progression of the ideas involved. Encourage students to see the taxonomic work of each scientist in the context of an entire life-work—especially for Aristotle, who made great contributions in a number of different areas.

SECTION

6-3 Systems of Classification   pp. 140–141

Teaching Strategy

Begin by asking students what two basic groups they would use to classify all living things. The answers "plant" and "animal" will almost surely come to mind. Point out several of the basic differences between plants and animals, some of which may surprise students, who may have thought of all animals as capable of motion and all plants as stationary. Go on to explain the protist kingdom, which is used to classify certain unicellular organisms; the moneran kingdom, which includes bacteria and blue-green algae; and the fungi kingdom, whose molds and mushrooms should be familiar to students.

ACTIVITY

Natural History Museum   p. 141 (Enriched)

Individual students who plan to do this activity should prepare for it by doing more research on the differences among organisms in the various kingdoms. Have the students report to the class on their museum trip and on their findings.

LABORATORY ACTIVITY

Whose Shoe Is That?   p. 142

This activity should be done after Section 6–2 has been completed. It will require one class period.

Observations and Conclusions: 1. If a proper and complete classification system has been devised, any given shoe out of the group of six should be uniquely identifiable.

Going Further: 1. Devise a classification system for a set of ten different fruits, flowers, or vegetables. 2. Devise a classification system for students to use in grouping their classmates. Explain that only objective characteristics such as eye color, height, and hair color are to be used and that terms such as "pretty" or "underweight" are not to be used.

Discussion Topics   p. 145

1. Linnaeus used similarities in form and structure in his classification system.
2. Modern scientists use large and microscopic structures, chemical makeup, and behavior to classify and name organisms.
3. An autotroph, such as an oak tree, uses chlorophyll to make its own food from simpler substances. A heterotroph, such as a dog, does not contain chlorophyll and cannot make its own food.

BIBLIOGRAPHY

Clark, M. E. *Contemporary Biology: Concepts and Implications.* Philadelphia: W. B. Saunders.

Dixon, B. *What Is Science For?* Ontario, Canada: Collins.

Samuel, E. *Order in Life.* Englewood Cliffs, N.J.: Prentice-Hall.

A-V MATERIALS

Carolus Linnaeus, film, Encyclopaedia Britannica.

Classifying Plants and Animals, film, Coronet.

7 Viruses, Bacteria, and Protists pp. 146–167

OVERVIEW

Because of their extremely small size, viruses, bacteria, and protists may seem mysteriously abstract to students. However, this mystery angle can be used to present important material. For example, the chapter introduction, on Legionnaires' Disease, is presented as a scientific mystery. Much can be made of diseases and their invisible causes. In this way, the enormous effects of such organisms on other living things, including human beings, can be taught in an interesting manner.

SECTION

7-1 Viruses pp. 148–152

Teaching Strategy

Continue the "mystery-story" approach as you teach students about the discovery of viruses. The story of this discovery can be used to reinforce student learning of scientific method.

Because they are not cells and carry out few of the functions of organisms, viruses are often considered chemical rather than biological entities. Since even scientists disagree on this subject, you may ask students what *they* think, requiring first that they list the functions they believe necessary to living things.

You may wish to invite a doctor or public-health agent to visit your class. This person can discuss with students how viral diseases are spread, diagnosed, treated, and prevented.

SECTION

7-2 Bacteria pp. 152–158

Teaching Strategy

A lesson on bacteria is a good opportunity review—or introduce—the topic of cell structure. However, you should point out that bacteria, unlike most other kinds of cells, lack a nucleus; that is, they are prokaryotes. Although bacteria are unicellular and prokaryotic, some of them have amazing adaptations. You may wish to mention one type of bacterium that can distinguish north from south by means of tiny internal sacs that contain magnetite. Prepared slides of cocci, bacilli, and spirilla, easily obtained from biological supply houses, can demonstrate this.

After discussing the life functions of bacteria, be sure to spend some time pointing out the helpfulness to human beings of certain types of bacteria; many students believe that all bacteria are harmful.

ACTIVITY

Benefiting from Bacteria p. 154 (Enriched)

Student essays on useful bacteria could mention how bacteria are used to make such common foods as cheese and vinegar. Bacteria are used to make antibiotics to treat a wide variety of illnesses. Many chemicals are made by bacterial action. By causing decay, bacteria rid the earth of the bodies of dead organisms and enrich the soil. Essays could focus on any one process or on a number of processes.

ACTIVITY

Botulism p. 157 (Average)

Student research on this topic is well worth the time spent. It is important to know that improperly preserved foods can become dangerously contaminated with the bacterium responsible for botulism. Have students report their findings to the class and share them with their parents.

SECTION

7-3 Protozoans pp. 158–163

Teaching Strategy

In this section, members of four protozoan phyla are discussed: amoebas (phylum Sarcodina), paramecia (phylum Ciliophora), *Euglena* (phylum Mastigophora), and *Plasmodium* (phylum Sporozoa), the protozoan that causes malaria. This discussion of protozoans provides many opportunities for discussing the life functions and structures of eukaryotes, or cells that contain a nucleus.

ACTIVITY

A Protozoan Population   p. 158 (Average)

Students must first convert 30 meters into centimeters by multiplying by 100. Then students should divide 3000 by 1.5 to determine the answer. There would be 2000 *Pelomyxa palustrius* protozoans in the pond.

ACTIVITY

Harmful Microorganisms   p. 160 (Average)

This activity allows students to learn more about a number of different disease-causing viruses, bacteria, and protists. You might ask students to research other diseases of which they have heard and to present their findings to the class.

ACTIVITY

Protozoan Models   p. 163 (Enriched)

This activity allows students who are accomplished in model making to prepare protozoan models. Check the models carefully and use them as classroom displays.

LABORATORY ACTIVITY

Collecting Protists   pp. 164

This activity should be done after the entire chapter has been read. It will require one classroom period of actual laboratory work, as well as several hours of field and library work.

CAUTION: Make sure that students do not go to ponds by themselves when they collect protists.

Observations and Conclusions: Using a reference book, students should be able to collect, identify, and draw at least some of the following protists (among others): *Acanthocyst, Amoeba, Ichthyophthirius, Lacrymaria, Paramecium, Stentor, Stylonychia, Tetrahymena, Tokophyra, Urostyla, Volvox, Vorticella, Zoothamnium.*

Going Further: Have students collect samples of protists from other bodies of water such as streams and, if possible, bodies of salt water. Have them use reference works to identify the protists.

Discussion Topics   p. 167

1. Iwanowski and Beijerinck attempted to discover bacteria that they believed were the cause of the tobacco mosaic disease. But even plant juices from which bacteria had been filtered out were able to spread the disease. Beijerinck concluded correctly that the juices contained viruses, which are much smaller than bacteria.
2. Viruses are not cells. Unlike cells, they cannot reproduce on their own, although they do contain hereditary material. Viruses cannot perform the other life functions of cells either.
3. Viruses reproduce in living cells by attaching themselves to the cell and injecting their hereditary material. The cell then makes more viruses, which burst from the cell.
4. Autotrophic bacteria contain chlorophyll and can make their own food. Heterotrophic bacteria cannot make their own food.
5. Some bacteria can spoil food and cause diseases of people, animals, and food crops.
6. The roots of alfalfa contain lumps that hold nitrogen-fixing bacteria that replace the nitrogen compounds in soil. Without such compounds, many other crops would be unable to grow.

BIBLIOGRAPHY

Andrewes, C., H. G. Perreira, and Wildy. *Viruses of Vertebrates.* 4th ed. New York: Macmillan.

Dixon, *Magnificent Microbes.* New York: Atheneum.

Hook, E. W., ed. *Current Concepts of Infectious Diseases.* New York: Wiley.

A-V MATERIALS

Paramecium, Parts 2 and 3, film loop, PH Media.

Protists: Threshold of Life, film, National Geographic Society.

The Flagellates, Parts 1 and 2, film loops, PH Media.

The Protist Kingdom, film, BFA Educational Media.

8 Nonvascular Plants and Plantlike Organisms   pp. 168–191

OVERVIEW

This chapter deals with plants and plantlike organisms that lack specialized conducting, or vascular, tissues and that lack true roots, stems, leaves, and flowers. With so few characteristics in common with higher plants, these organisms may not seem to students to be plants at all. In fact, in the five-kingdom classification system, blue-green algae are monerans and fungi are classified in the fungi kingdom.

As you teach, point out some of the structural features—such as the presence of cell walls—that nonvascular plants and plantlike organisms have in common. Then discuss their more obvious differences. In Chapter 9, you should compare and contrast vascular plants with the nonvascular ones treated in this chapter. Throughout, you should attempt to impart to students an appreciation for the importance of plants and other photosynthetic organisms, since without the oxygen they produce, hardly any forms of life—certainly no human life—could exist.

SECTION

8-1 Algae   pp. 170–178

Teaching Strategy

Point out the wide variety of different algae found in different environments and mention that algae have a number of practical uses—for example, in toothpaste and highway lane paint. The various algae discussed are, by and large, distinguished according to color (blue-green, green, brown, golden, and so on), which should make it easier for students to remember them. In teaching students about blue-green algae, refer to the interesting account of stromatolites in the chapter introduction.

ACTIVITY

Algae Life Cycles   p. 172 (Average)

The information gathered by students should be of use and interest to other students. Display

their labeled diagrams of the rather complicated life cycles involved, and refer to them as you describe the various types of algae.

ACTIVITY

Algae Classification   p. 174 (Remedial)

The five kinds of algae in the plant kingdom and their phyla are golden algae, Chrysophyta; brown algae, Phaeophyta; red algae, Rhodophyta; fire algae, Pyrrophyta; and green algae, Chlorophyta. See the chapter sections for the characteristics of each phylum.

ACTIVITY

Collecting Algae   p. 176 (Average)

Students may succeed in collecting samples of a number of different species of algae. The drawings of the various samples seen through a microscope should be displayed, and students should be encouraged to conduct library research to attempt to identify the algae.

SECTION

8-2 Fungi   pp. 178–184

Teaching Strategy

Fungi are interesting and, to many students, rather peculiar. Thus it may be easy for students to remember that fungi form their own kingdom. The fungi are heterotrophs; that is, they are unable to make their own food. The various fungi to be discussed in this section—mushrooms, yeasts, and molds—are similar in their lack of chlorophyll but differ in many respects, such as methods of reproduction. Some fungi, such as yeast, can reproduce by budding, whereas others, such as mushrooms, typically reproduce by producing spores. You might want to give students an appreciation for the prolific nature of spore production in some mushrooms by mentioning that the spores produced by a single puffball mushroom, if placed in groups of 20 in individual square meters, would cover an area the size of the state of Pennsylvania.

ACTIVITY

Cheeses   p. 183 (Average)

This interesting activity gives students the opportunity of learning about the use of certain molds in cheeses. Ask students to give reports on how the various cheeses are made. You might even consider bringing in samples of cheeses, such as bléu, Roquefort, Brie, and Camembert, and allowing students to observe and taste the samples.

SECTION

8-3 Lichens and Slime Molds   pp. 184–186

Teaching students about lichens, combinations of algae and fungi, will allow you to introduce the important concept of symbiosis, which will figure in other chapters of this book. You might ask students to collect samples of lichens and to observe them with a microscope and draw what they see. Mention that some useful substances, such as the acid-base indicator litmus, are derived from lichens.

Slime molds are quite astonishing organisms, taking on an almost animallike quality during the plasmodium phase of their life cycle. Ask interested students to conduct library research on this life cycle and to share their findings.

ACTIVITY

Observing a Slime Mold   p. 186 (Enriched)

Slime molds may be rather difficult to find, so this investigation should probably be carried out only by patient and observant students. Such students may even be able to bring in living samples of slime molds. They should also collect the moist bark or wood to which the molds are clinging, and they should keep the samples moist.

SECTION

8-4 Mosses and Liverworts pp. 186–187

Teaching Strategy

Mosses and liverworts are members of a division of plants called Bryophyta. Ask students to use a hand lens to observe some mosses. Point out

that although bryophytes are green plants that may superficially resemble larger plants, the apparent "leaves," "stems," and "roots" or bryophytes are different from the true leaves, stems, and roots of larger plants, which contain vascular tissue. The life cycle of mosses, with their characteristic alternation of generations, is interesting, and you may ask students to do library research on this topic.

You should also point out to students that certain plants that are popularly called mosses—such as Spanish moss and reindeer moss—are not true mosses. Spanish moss is actually related to the pineapple, and reindeer moss is a lichen.

LABORATORY ACTIVITY

Making Spore Prints   pp. 188

This activity, which requires two class periods several days apart, should be done after Section 8-2 has been completed.

Observations and Conclusions: 1. A spore print consisting of lines radiating outward like spokes should be visible. 2. The magnifying glass should reveal the small, dotlike spores that make up the print. 3. The fruiting body of the mushroom produces spores on the surfaces of small reproductive structures called basidia. These structures are located on the gills that radiate outward on the underside of the cap. The spores germinate under the proper conditions of moisture and light, producing new mushrooms.

Going Further: Have students repeat the activity, using mushrooms of different kinds that you provide. However, this time have them use a small knife or laboratory spatula to scrape the spores together, instead of spraying the prints. Students should record the colors that are revealed and use reference books to identify the kinds of mushrooms involved, on the basis of the appearance of the cap and the color of the scrapings.

Discussion Topics   p. 191

1. Algae have certain characteristics in common with plants, such as cell walls. Algae, like large green plants, contain chlorophyll and are autotrophs. Fungi do not have chlorophyll.
2. Certain green algae are used in some sewage and water purification systems because they

remove poisonous materials from water. They may be used in the future as oxygen sources in closed environments, such as spaceships.

3. Fungi cannot make their own food because they do not contain chlorophyll.

4. The mushroom contains a fruiting body, or cap. On the underside of the cap are gills, which contain spores. The cap is at the top of a stalk that has a ring near the top. The mushroom absorbs food from the soil through threadlike hyphae.

5. Fermentation is an energy-releasing process in which sugars and starches are changed into alcohol and carbon dioxide. Yeast is used in baking because the carbon dioxide it releases through fermentation produces tiny bubbles that cause the dough to rise.

6. Symbiosis is a relationship in which two different kinds of organisms live together. Lichens illustrate symbiosis.

BIBLIOGRAPHY

Bold, C., and C. L. Hundell. *The Plant Kingdom.* Englewood Cliffs, N.J.: Prentice-Hall.

Brodie, J. *Fungi: Delight of Curiosity.* Toronto: University of Toronto Press.

Burns, *The Plant Kingdom.* New York: Macmillan.

A-V MATERIALS

Algae, Fungi, and Lichens, filmstrip, Eyegate.

Kingdom of Plants, filmstrip, National Geographic Society.

CHAPTER

9 Vascular Plants pp. 192–215

OVERVIEW

The plants discussed in this chapter have specialized vascular tissue, or tubes that transport material throughout the plant. They are classified in the division *Tracheophyta.* Vascular plants vary greatly in structure and appearance. However, most of them have in common true roots, stems, and leaves and are autotrophic.

Attempt to awaken students' interest by discussing the importance of plants as oxygen producers, in textile and construction-material production, and in the formation of fossil fuels.

Point out that certain vascular plants are among the longest-lived and largest organisms on the earth. The vascular system of such plants gives them support for growth and a considerable advantage over most nonvascular plants, which tend to be quite small and short-lived. Use the chapter introduction to sensitize students to the need for more education about plants and about conservation in general.

SECTION

9-1 Ferns pp. 194–196

Teaching Strategy

This section deals with ferns, which are members of the subdivision Pteropsida. Ferns, like most vascular plants, have true roots, stems, and leaves. However, you should defer a complete discussion of these structures, as well as of xylem and phloem (the vascular conducting tubes), until the following section, where they are treated in greater depth. The alternation-of-generations characteristic of fern reproduction will give you the opportunity to discuss both asexual and sexual reproduction.

ACTIVITY

Observing Ferns p. 196 (Average)

The two reproductive stages of ferns are dramatically different in appearance. This activity should allow students the opportunity of observing the large frond-leafed sporophyte generation in nature. They will also be able to grow the tiny prothallus gametophyte generation in the classroom and to observe the resultant formation of new sporophytes that develop by means of sexual reproduction. Have students display their drawings, both of the actual ferns and of the fern life cycle as pictured in reference books.

SECTION

9-2 Seed Plants pp. 196–204

Teaching Strategy

During the teaching of this and the following sections, you may wish to have students plant fast-germinating seeds, such as beans, in order to observe firsthand the structures and growth processes characteristic of seed plants. This section deals with the structure of roots, stems, and leaves and with the process of photosynthesis. The subject of reproduction is taken up in the two sections that follow.

You may wish to relate to students some interesting facts about plant structures. For example, the total length of the root system of a single rye plant is more than 609,000 meters. To awaken their interest in leaves, you may ask them to make a leaf collection. If they do this in the fall, you might point out that the pigments responsible for the brilliant colors of autumn leaves are always present in the leaves but are masked by green chlorophyll, which breaks down as temperatures decrease.

ACTIVITY

Transport Tubes   p. 198 (Average)

In this activity, students will be able to observe the transport of water and dye up the stem of plant segments to the leaves. The xylem tissues, which carry the liquid, can be made out as dots in the cross sections and, in particular, as rings of dots in the woody twigs.

ACTIVITY

Annual Rings   p. 200 (Average)

The growth rings of most severed tree trunks should be quite easily visible. You might caution students that the number of rings is not an exact indicator of the age of a tree, because in some years more than one growth layer can be added.

ACTIVITY

Xylem Transport   p. 201 (Average)

Students must convert centimeters to meters in order to divide. So 5 centimeters/sec becomes .05 meters/sec. Students should then divide 200 meters by .05 meters/sec. The answer is 4000 seconds, or 66.6 minutes, or 1.1 hours. This is how long it takes the water to reach the top of the tree.

ACTIVITY

Insect-Eating Plants   p. 202 (Remedial)

Plants such as the Venus' flytrap are fascinating to students and are interesting to research. If possible, order some insect-eating plants and allow students to observe them in the classroom.

SECTION

9-3   Gymnosperms   pp. 204–206

Teaching Strategy

The gymnosperms are true seed-bearing plants. Unlike angiosperms, which are treated in the next section, the four orders of gymnosperms do not produce flowers or fruits. You might ask students to collect and bring in pollen and seed cones and to use reference works to identify the conifers that produced them.

SECTION

9-4   Angiosperms   pp. 206–211

Teaching Strategy

This section deals primarily with the reproductive structures and processes of angiosperms, or flowering and fruit-producing plants. The processes of pollination, fertilization, and seed production and dispersal are discussed. You may wish to have students bring in sample flowering plants for in-class observation. Students may even attempt to grow new plants from the seeds produced by certain of these plants, such as petunias. You might also ask individual students to do reports on different kinds of flowers, both monocots and dicots. Students may be interested to know that flowers range in size from less than 1 centimeter to up to 1 meter across (the flower of the *Rafflesia* plant, for example).

ACTIVITY

Plant Responses   p. 211 (Average)

The tropisms mentioned are responses to light (phototropism), gravity (geotropism), water (hydrotropism), touch (thigmotropism), and chemical substances (chemotropism). The information gathered can be used to plan classroom demonstrations of these tropisms.

LABORATORY ACTIVITY

Geotropism

p. 212

This activity should be done after the chapter has been completed. It will require half of one class period plus about 10 minutes out of each of the next four or five class periods. If students have not done the activity on tropisms, they may need to do a bit of library research to achieve a full understanding of what they observe in this activity.

Observations and Conclusions: 1. The roots of all the seeds grew in the direction of the earth. The stems grew in the opposite direction. 2. Gravity pulls downward in the same direction for all the seeds. The seeds thus all respond in the same direction. (Chemicals in the plant called auxins become concentrated on the lower side of the stem, which produces more cell elongation on this side, causing the stem to turn upward. Auxins in the roots inhibit growth on their lower side, while the upper side continues to grow, resulting in downward growth for the roots.)

Going Further: Have students use corn seeds to study phototropism—the growth response to light. They should allow the corn seeds to germinate along the edges of a glass beaker, with a bright light overhead. They should then repeat the experiment, with the light source below.

Discussion Topics

p. 215

1. In the asexual stage, spores are produced on the undersides of fronds. The spores fall and produce the tiny, heart-shaped prothallus of the sexual stage. The prothallus produces male and female cells, which unite and produce a new asexual-stage fern.
2. Roots anchor plants in the ground, absorb water and minerals from the soil, and sometimes store food. Stems support the plants, hold up leaves to the light, and transport water, minerals, and food.
3. Herbaceous stems are green and soft and tend to be found in annual plants. Woody stems are rigid, have large amounts of xylem, and tend to be found in perennial plants.
4. Carbon dioxide enters through the stomata, water enters through the roots and stems, and oxygen is released through the stomata.

5. Gymnosperms produce uncovered seeds and produce no flowers or fruits. Angiosperms produce flowers and fruits, which contain the seeds.
6. In self-pollination, pollen is transferred from a stamen to a pistil of the same flower or of another flower on the same plant. In cross-pollination, the transfer occurs between stamens and pistils in flowers on different plants.

BIBLIOGRAPHY

Devlin, R. *Plant Physiology.* New York: D. Van Nostrand.

Galston, A. W., et al. *Life of the Green Plant.* Englewood Cliffs, N.J.: Prentice-Hall.

Fahn, A. *Plant Anatomy.* 2nd ed. Elmsford, N.Y.: Pergamon Press.

A-V MATERIALS

Flowering Plants, filmstrip with cassette, Eyegate.

Flowers: Structure and Function, film, Coronet.

Green Plants and Sunlight, film, Encyclopaedia Britannica.

The Photosynthesis and Respiration Cycle, film, Churchill.

CHAPTER

10 Animals: Invertebrates

pp. 216–251

OVERVIEW

This chapter and the two that follow deal with the animal kingdom. The present chapter, on invertebrates, includes animals that range from the sponge to the clam to the ant and may come from any phylum but Chordata. These animals, classified as they are in many different phyla, differ from one another in a great many respects. They also differ greatly from the vertebrate organisms most students think of when the word "animal" is mentioned. As you deal with the animals covered in this chapter, review the general characteristics of animals that all these organisms have in common: They are heterotrophic, multicellular, and have cells that lack cell walls but do have a nucleus. Point out that even invertebrates have amazing physical and social adaptations, such as those of the bees discussed in the chapter introduction.

SECTION

10-1 Characteristics of Invertebrates pp. 218–219

Teaching Strategy

Have students observe invertebrates, such as insects and earthworms, firsthand, and make lists of their similarities and differences. Also, have them contrast the properties of invertebrates with those of the vertebrates with which they are familiar. Point out that all invertebrates lack a backbone and that such organisms actually make up more than 90 percent of animal species.

SECTION

10-2 Sponges pp. 219–221

Teaching Strategy

Point out that sponges, which are members of the phylum Porifera, are generally considered to be the simplest animals and that the cells in a given sponge can act quite independently of one another. However, a sponge is an organism and not merely a collection of cells, as is demonstrated by the amazing fact, pointed out in this chapter, that a sponge broken into clumps of cells can regroup itself into its original shape. You may wish to add that sponges can reproduce both asexually (by budding and by regeneration) and sexually (by producing gametes, which unite to form zygotes, which in turn develop into free-swimming larvae).

ACTIVITY

Sponge Growth p. 220 (Average)

Students must convert kilograms into grams, which results in 3000 grams. Students must then divide 3000 grams by 28 grams to get 107. So a sponge must filter 107 tons of water to reach a mass of 3 kilograms.

SECTION

10-3 Coelenterates pp. 221–225

Teaching Strategy

This section deals with members of the three classes of the phylum Coelenterata: Hydrozoa (which includes hydras), Scyphozoa (which includes jellyfish), and Anthozoa (which includes sea anemones and corals). You may wish to set up an experiment in which students can observe response and food getting in hydras. Obtain hydras and brine shrimp from a biological supply house and have students study the interaction between the two, using a depression slide and a microscope or hand lens.

SECTION

10-4 Worms pp. 225–229

Teaching Strategy

Three different phyla of organisms are collectively known as worms: flatworms (phylum Platyhelminthes), roundworms (phylum Nematoda), and segmented worms (phylum Annelida). Point out that although all the worms are invertebrates, have elongated, legless bodies, and have three layers of body cells, they differ greatly in other respects. Earthworms, for example, are more highly developed in many of their organ systems than flatworms. You may wish to have students observe the behavior of the flatworm *Planaria,* which is readily available from biological supply houses. Planarian feeding can be studied, as well as the amazing ability of slit or divided planarians to regenerate.

ACTIVITY

Flukes p. 227 (Average)

Many parasitic worms, such as the liver flukes, have complicated and interesting life cycles. You might expand this activity by having students research other parasitic worms, such as the tapeworm, trichina, and ascarid.

ACTIVITY

Symmetry p. 228 (Enriched)

The concept of symmetry—in its general geometrical aspects, as well as its specifically biological ones—is difficult for many students to grasp. Students who investigate radial and bilateral symmetry may wish to make up charts containing drawings of characteristic organisms, including a few familiar vertebrates, such as human beings, as well as invertebrates.

SECTION

10-5 Mollusks pp. 229–233

The phylum Mollusca includes clams, mussels, scallops, and oysters (class Pelecypoda), snails, slugs, and conchs (class Gastropoda), and octopuses, squids, and chambered nautiluses (class Cephalopoda), the latter group being the most highly developed and the only one that has a closed circulatory system. If you live near the coast, you may wish to suggest shell gathering and identification as an activity. If you do, be sure to caution students not to go near the water by themselves.

The introductory paragraphs in this section, about giant squids, should prove interesting to students. You may wish to add the information that such creatures can measure 19 meters from tip of head to end of tentacles. Their only known natural enemy is the sperm whale.

ACTIVITY

Shell Collecting p. 230 (Remedial)

Students will enjoy this activity; many of them may have been collecting shells for years on their own. Most students will be curious about the names of shells they are already familiar with from seeing them on the beach. They will also be proud to display their finds in the classroom. Be sure to remind students always to do their shell collecting in pairs or groups and to exercise caution when they are looking for shells near the water's edge.

SECTION

10-6 Spiny-Skinned Animals pp. 234–236

Teaching Strategy

The spiny-skinned invertebrates discussed in this section are classified in the phylum Echinodermata. Starfish, sea urchins, and sand dollars are familiar examples of echinoderms. Such creatures typically exhibit radial symmetry and possess a distinctive water-vascular internal canal system. The starfish is an interesting organism to most students, both because of its beautiful shape and because of its amazing ability to open the shells of clams to obtain food. You may wish to point out that the sunflower starfish, a 20-armed organism, can measure up to 80 centimeters across (40 centimeters from center to end of arm).

SECTION

10-7 Arthropods pp. 236–241

Teaching Strategy

Of all animal phyla, the phylum Arthropoda contains by far the largest number of species and of individual members. Arthropods live in practically all environments. They include the only invertebrates that are able to fly.

This section deals only with crustaceans, centipedes and millipedes, and arachnids. Insects, the largest class of arthropods, are taken up in the following section. Point out the general characteristics of arthropods—such as jointed legs and exoskeleton—and detail the differences among characteristic members of the classes discussed in this section. You may wish to invite experts on the various arthropods to speak to the class and show specimens. You may also wish to take students on a guided nature walk and ask them to do library research on the arthropods they observe.

SECTION

10-8 Insects pp. 241–247

Teaching Strategy

This section can only scratch the surface on the subject of insects, whose class (Insecta) is the largest in biology. General anatomical, developmental, and behavioral characteristics of insects are stressed, rather than differences among the many orders of insects. You may wish to assign to various students the activity of doing library research on these orders and of reporting their results to the class. As is suggested below, advanced students may wish to raise silkworms and butterflies and observe their metamorphic changes. Some students may wish to do library research on the social behavior of insects, such as bees. When you teach the subsection ("Insect

Behavior'') that deals with this subject, refer to the chapter introduction.

ACTIVITY

Role Playing   p. 243 (Remedial)

This section on insects will give students plenty of options from which to choose their favorite insect. Encourage students to observe the insect of their choice before beginning their essays. But also allow students to use their imagination in writing a day in the life of their insect. The essays can be both factual and fanciful.

LABORATORY ACTIVITY

Observing an Ant Farm   p. 248

This activity will require roughly one class period plus several minutes from each of about five other periods over the course of about one month. Because of the long span of time involved, the activity may be done at the beginning of the chapter, although it most closely relates to the final section, on insects.

Preparation Suggestions and Cautions: You may wish to cut the tops from the 2-L plastic bottles yourself. If you have students do it, be sure to caution them to be very careful with scissors. Check each ant farm yourself to be sure it is well sealed, so that ants cannot escape.

Observations and Conclusions: 1. Sketches should show various chambers used for food storage and for egg and larva tending (if a queen ant is present), and they should also show a network of tunnels. 2. If different classes of ants are present, different activities should be visible (for example, food gathering and larva tending by female workers, egg laying by queens, and perhaps mating between queens and short-lived winged males). The division of labor and cooperation among ants in a colony demonstrate why ants are called social insects.

Going Further: Have advanced students raise silkworms or butterflies and observe their metamorphic changes. You may obtain kits from a biological supply house.

Discussion Topics   p. 251

1. Some insects, such as flies, eat plants that human beings use for food. Others, such as moths, eat fabrics commonly used for clothing. Still others, such as termites, eat the wood used in constructing houses.

2. The sea anemone protects the clownfish against predators by means of stinging cells; the clownfish, in turn, attracts other fish, which are then trapped by the anemone. The earthworm releases a kind of ''sweat'' that helps it glide away from predators more quickly and that also warns other earthworms of danger. The squid releases a dye into the water to hide itself and confuse predators; it then uses its water-propulsion system to move quickly away. Various insects exhibit a wide variety of defensive behaviors and features, including stingers, camouflage, and markings that frighten predators.

3. In metamorphosis, insects pass through four stages: egg, larva (which is hatched from an egg), pupa (which is wrapped in a covering secreted by the larva), and adult (which emerges from the pupa).

4. Invertebrates get food by the following methods: filtering water (sponges, bivalve mollusks), stinging prey and bringing it into the central body cavity (hydra), breaking down their own body organs, which later regenerate (planarian), absorbing food from hosts in which they live parasitically (tapeworm, hookworm), eating dead plant and animal matter in soil through which they burrow (earthworm), forcing open shells by means of tube feet (starfish), catching prey in silk webs (spider), sucking blood through specialized mouthparts (mosquito), and collecting nectar and making honey (bee).

BIBLIOGRAPHY

Blaney, W. M. *How Insects Live.* New York: E. P. Dutton.

Buchsbaum, R. *Animals Without Backbones.* Chicago: University of Chicago Press.

Swan, L. A., and C. S. Papp. *The Common Insects of North America.* New York: Harper & Row.

Wells, M. *Lower Animals.* New York: McGraw-Hill.

Whiteley, D. *The Oxford Book of Invertebrates.* New York: Oxford University Press.

A-V MATERIALS

Animals Without Backbones, filmstrip, Encyclopaedia Britannica.

Crustaceans, film, Encyclopaedia Britannica.

Insects, film, Encyclopaedia Britannica.

Planaria, film loop, PH Media.

CHAPTER

11 Animals: Vertebrates   pp. 252–279

OVERVIEW

This chapter deals with four major groups of vertebrates (which, like all vertebrates, are members of the phylum Chordata): fish (superclass Pisces), amphibians (class Amphibia), reptiles (class Reptilia), and birds (class Aves). The remaining major group of vertebrates, the mammals (class Mammalia), will be treated in the following chapter. All vertebrates have in common an internal skeleton and a spinal column made up of vertebrae that encloses a nerve cord. In other respects, they may differ markedly.

SECTION

11-1 Fish   pp. 254–260

Teaching Strategy

Use the chapter introduction on the anglerfish as a bridge to interest students in the behavior and adaptations of fish. This section describes the characteristics of three classes of fish: the jawless fish (class Agnatha, which includes lampreys), the cartilaginous fish (class Chondrichthyes, which includes rays and sharks), and bony fish (class Osteichthyes, which includes flounder, trout, perch, and many other well-known fish). Point out the general characteristics of all fish and review them as you proceed, so that students recognize both the similarities and the differences among members of the different classes of fish. A classroom aquarium or a visit to a large public aquarium will be helpful in developing student interest.

ACTIVITY

Vertebrate Body Systems p. 255 (Enriched)

This activity should probably be assigned only to advanced students, because it requires a good understanding of organ systems and an interest in comparative anatomy. The charts, if well executed, should be of considerable use to you later as you compare the systems of mammals with those of other vertebrates.

ACTIVITY

Comparing Sizes   p. 257 (Average)

Students will have a greater appreciation for the massiveness of great white sharks if they compare their own size to that of a shark. Perhaps the best way for students to compare sizes is for them to draw a shark to scale on a piece of graph paper. They can then draw a young person, who is about 1.4 meters tall and weighs about 41 kilograms, over the outline of the shark. This will clearly illustrate how much bigger than a person a shark is.

ACTIVITY

Salmon   p. 259 (Average)

The reproductive cycle of salmon, which includes a dramatic swim upstream, should be of interest to most students. The activity can be extended to include reports on the life cycles of other kinds of fish.

SECTION

11-2 Amphibians   pp. 260–264

Teaching Strategy

Members of two orders of amphibians are covered in this section: frogs and toads (order Salienta), and salamanders and newts (order Caudata). In pointing out the general characteristics of amphibians, you may wish to mention that not all amphibians have legs: The so-called caecilians (in order Apoda) are wormlike in appearance. All amphibians do have moist skin and gills that are present in larvae and that are replaced by lungs in adults. They also spend some time on land and some in water, and they lay their eggs in water. Chronologically, they were probably among the first vertebrates to emerge from the water.

You may wish to plan a laboratory activity on frog dissection. If possible, supplement this with an activity on which live frogs and tadpoles are observed.

SECTION

11-3 Reptiles pp. 264–271

Teaching Strategy

A trip to a natural history museum or at least a presentation on dinosaurs, reptiles of the Mesozoic Era (sometimes known as the Age of Reptiles), should awaken in students a lively interest in the subject of reptiles. Section 11-3 deals with members of three orders of reptiles: snakes and lizards (order Squamata), turtles and tortoises (order Chelonia), and alligators and crocodiles (order Crocodilia). Internal fertilization and the laying of leathery eggs on land are important characteristics of reptiles. Another is their cold-bloodedness, which you should explain and later contrast with the warmbloodedness of birds and mammals. Incidentally, there is speculation at present that some dinosaurs may have been warmblooded.

ACTIVITY

A Symbiotic Relationship p. 270 (Remedial)

Students can easily find out about the relationship between the Egyptian plover and the Nile crocodile. The plover picks leeches and bits of food off the crocodile's teeth. The crocodile gets its teeth cleaned, and the plover gets a free meal. You may encourage students to bring in nature magazines in which this and other symbiotic relationships are pictured.

SECTION

11-4 Birds pp. 271–275

Teaching Strategy

Members of the class Aves are in some ways the most highly evolved of the nonmammalian vertebrates. They are warmblooded and have a four-chambered heart, and most of them are capable of flight as well as motion on land. They are also the only organisms that have feathers. The adaptations of various kinds of birds for flight, feeding, breeding, and migration are extremely interesting, and the material presented on this subject can be supplemented with reports, including illustrations, done by students. Other activities can include making bird feeders for home or schoolyard and observing the birds that are attracted.

ACTIVITY

Finding the Way Home p. 274 (Average)

To determine the answer, students must divide 10,000 by the number of days in two months, or 62. This will give them the answer of 161.3 kilometers a day as the distance traveled by the homing pigeon.

ACTIVITY

Bird Watching p. 275 (Average)

This activity requires only a little patience, an observant eye, and an interest in birds. Students can use small field guides to identify birds and larger reference works to learn about their fascinating behaviors and adaptations. Artistic students may make and display color sketches of the birds they observe. Students interested in photography may take and exhibit snapshots.

LABORATORY ACTIVITY

Classifying Vertebrate Bones in Owl Pellets p. 276

This activity actually serves as a bridge between this chapter and the one that follows, since it has to do with both the feeding habits of a bird and the skeletal structure of the vertebrates (mostly mammals) on which it feeds. The activity, therefore, should be done when the chapter has essentially been completed. It will require about two class periods, including identification time.

Preparation Suggestions: Owl pellets can be ordered from biological supply houses.

Observations and Conclusions: 1. Answers will vary, depending on the kinds of skulls present. 2. The long bones generally are used to support the animal and are used in moving. The bones of the skull are used to protect the brain. Some of the bones, such as the teeth and jawbones, are used in feeding. The ribs protect the internal thoracic organs. The vertebrae protect the spinal cord.

Going Further: 1. This laboratory activity can be used to teach students about food webs. Inform them that an owl regurgitates, on the average, two pellets per day. Thus students can easily calculate the average number of animals eaten by an owl per year. They can also assume that each of the animals eaten required about 4.5 kilograms of grain per year. Have students do library research on food webs and report to the class the general information and its specific applications to the owl-rodent-grain food web, including a chart or drawing. 2. Have students use reference books to study the complete skeletal structure of the various animals whose bones they observed in this activity. Have them make labeled sketches and display the sketches in the classroom.

Discussion Topics   p. 279

1. Jawless fish lack scales, fins, and jaws and have skeletons made of cartilage; some, such as the lamprey, suck out the body fluids of other fish. Cartilaginous fish have jaws and skeletons made of cartilage. Bony fish have skeletons made of hard bone.
2. Answers will vary, depending on student opinions.
3. Reptiles, unlike amphibians, have dry, scaly skins that are resistant to drying out. Their eggs are protected by a leathery shell, so that they do not dry out and need not be laid in water.
4. Some birds navigate long distances by observing the sun and other stars. Others follow coastlines or mountain ranges. Still others may have magnetic centers in their brains that are used as a sort of compass.

BIBLIOGRAPHY

Curry, J. *Animal Skeletons.* New York: Crane, Russak.

Dorst, J. *The Life of Birds.* New York: Columbia University Press.

Walker, E. P. *Mammals of the World.* 3rd ed. Baltimore, Md.: Johns Hopkins University Press.

Young, J. Z. *The Life of Vertebrates.* 2nd ed. New York: Clarendon Press.

A-V MATERIALS

Fish of Arkansas, film, Arkansas Dept. of Parks and Tourism.

In the Company of Birds, film, Information Service of India.

Marine Life Preview, film, Marineland of Florida.

Reptiles, film, Encyclopaedia Britannica.

CHAPTER

12 Mammals   pp. 280–301

OVERVIEW

The class Mammalia includes the most complex organisms in nature. This chapter treats the three major groupings of mammals, which vary widely in appearance, characteristics, habitat, and behavior: the egg-laying mammals (order Monotremata), the pouched mammals (order Marsupialia), and the placental mammals (which comprise a number of orders).

Students have more knowledge of mammals than they do of any other kinds of organisms, and this greater experience usually means heightened interest on their part. You may wish to begin by asking the class to name as many mammals as they can. You can keep the list on a chalkboard and refer to the various entries as you cover the corresponding orders of mammals.

SECTION

12-1 Characteristics of Mammals   pp. 282–283

Teaching Strategy

Point out that the strange platypus students read about in the chapter introduction is just as surely a mammal as are the more familiar dogs, cats, horses, and cattle of their experience. All types of mammals have certain characteristics in common: they have highly developed brains, possess fur or hair during at least a part of their lives, feed their young with milk, are warm-blooded, have a four-chambered heart, and use internal fertilization. Review these characteristics periodically as you cover the other sections of this chapter.

ACTIVITY

Pet Mammals   p. 283 (Remedial)

This activity provides an excellent means of motivating students to learn more about mammals and to extend their powers of observation by studying the nonhuman living things with which they are most familiar. Students will enjoy reporting on the behavior of their pets, and by doing library research they can compare this behavior with that of the same types of animals as found in nature, in the undomesticated state. You may wish to augment this activity with observation of in-classroom pets, such as gerbils, hamsters, and guinea pigs. The students can care for the animals, keep records of the amounts of food and water they consume, observe their behavior and development, and so on.

SECTION

12-2   Egg-Laying Mammals   pp. 284–285

Teaching Strategy

The animals in the order Monotremata are unusual not only in appearance but in the fact that they are the only mammals that lay eggs. Point out that fertilization itself, however, takes place internally, as is the case for all mammals. You may wish to ask students to bring in magazine photographs of these and other mammals, and you may wish to show films of the mammals, with special attention to mammals, such as the monotremes, that students will probably never have the opportunity of observing in nature.

ACTIVITY

What's the Difference?   p. 285 (Average)

Students can glean information about anteaters from the chapter itself. Encourage them to find the characteristics of anteaters in the chapter and then write a paragraph in their own words. This assignment is a good test of reading comprehension. Students can also do further research in the library on the different types of anteaters.

SECTION

12-3   Pouched Mammals   pp. 285–287

Teaching Strategy

The members of the order Marsupialia, which include koalas and kangaroos, are interesting to observe, so, if possible, you may wish to plan a class field trip to a zoo to observe these and other mammals. In terms of reproduction, the marsupials are intermediate between the more primitive monotremes and the more advanced placental mammals: They give birth to young (rather than laying eggs), but these young are quite undeveloped and must live for some time in pouches on the mother's body, rather than completing early development within her body, as placental mammals do.

SECTION

12-4   Placental Mammals   pp. 287–297

Teaching Strategy

You may wish to direct students to diagrams of placental-uterine structure in pregnant placental mammals to help clarify the anatomical and physiological characteristics involved in the gestation of such mammals. The placental mammals discussed in this section are the insect eaters, such as moles and shrews (order Insectivora); the flying mammals, or bats (order Chiroptera); the flesh-eating mammals, such as dogs and cats (order Carnivora) and walruses and seals (order Pinnipedia); the "toothless" mammals, such as anteaters, sloths, and armadillos (order Edentata); the trunk-nosed mammals, or elephants (order Proboscidea); the hoofed mammals, such as pigs and cows (order Artiodactyla) and horses and tapirs (order Perissodactyla); the gnawing mammals, or rodents, such as squirrels and mice (order Rodentia); the "rodentlike" mammals, such as rabbits (order Lagomorpha); the water-dwelling mammals, such as whales and porpoises (order Cetacea) and manatees (order Sirenia); and the primates, such as monkeys, apes, and human beings (order Primates). Compare and contrast these different groups of mammals. You may wish to assign different groups to different students for further library research or special projects.

ACTIVITY

The Fastest Runner   p. 290 (Average)

First, students must calculate how many seconds are in an hour by using the following equation:

$$1 \text{ hr } \times \frac{60 \text{ min}}{\text{hr}} \times \frac{60 \text{ sec}}{\text{min}} = 3600 \text{ sec.}$$

Then they must divide 100 kilometers by 3600 seconds to get the answer of .28 kilometers/sec.

ACTIVITY

Useful Mammals p. 292 (Remedial–Average)

This is a good activity for slower students as well as average students to work on, because it not only is interesting and relevant to human beings but also provides an opportunity for reviewing the particular characteristics that led to the specific uses of the animals. You can also extend it to bring in the issues of ecological relationships and conservation. Interesting class discussion and debate can be generated as a result of gathering information on this subject.

ACTIVITY

Migration of Mammals   p. 294 (Average)

Migration studies at this grade level are usually limited to studies of birds; however, the migration patterns of certain mammals are also interesting. The maps drawn by students can be referred to as you teach about the flying, hoofed, and water-dwelling mammals involved.

ACTIVITY

Museum Visit   p. 296 (Average)

If you live near a natural history museum, a student field trip should be considered a must. Prior outlining and planning on the part of the students will make for a more rewarding experience, since the number of relevant exhibits in such a museum may be very large. You may wish to assign particular preparations and on-site note-taking responsibilities to different students, perhaps limiting each to one or two orders of mammals. You might plan an entire period of oral reports by the various students who participated.

LABORATORY ACTIVITY

Classifying and Comparing Mammals   p. 298

This activity will require the equivalent of roughly two class periods. However, students may do much of the work at home or in the library. The activity should be scheduled to coincide with the coverage of the final sections of the chapter.

Preparation Suggestions: The 14 major orders of mammals are Monotremata, Marsupialia, Insectivora, Chiroptera, Carnivora, Edentata, Proboscidea, Perissodactyla, Rodentia, Lagomorpha, Sirenia, Cetacea, Pinnipedia, and Primates. Be sure to choose mammals that belong to each of these orders. Label each picture, using a number or letter code, for future identification.

Observations and Conclusions: 1. Monotremes are egg-laying mammals. Marsupials give birth to rather undeveloped young that complete their early development in a pouch on the mother's body. 2. Mammals other than marsupials complete their early development inside the mother's body rather than in a pouch outside it. 3. Answers will vary. Students may place Sirenia, Cetacea, and Pinnipedia together in one group, for example, and Insectivora, Rodentia, and Lagomorpha in another. 4. Mammals have hair, produce milk, have a highly developed brain, are warmblooded, and have a four-chambered heart.

Going Further: You may wish to choose an order, such as Carnivora, that contains many mammals that are familiar to students and to ask the students to research the families that make up the order. Then give them pictures of mammals from the various families and ask them to identify the family of each.

Discussion Topics   p. 301

1. Egg-laying mammals lay eggs that do not hatch inside the mother's body. Pouched mammals

do not lay eggs but give birth to only partially developed young, which complete their early development inside a pouch on the mother's body. The young of placental mammals complete their early development totally within the mother.

2. Pouched animals include koalas, kangaroos, and opossums. Their young are born live, not hatched from eggs, and they are only partially developed, completing their development in a pouch on the mother's body.

3. Carnivores tend to have well-developed incisors and canines for biting, tearing, and shredding and for defense. They tend to have muscular legs, which help them pursue prey, and to have sharp claws to hold the prey.

4. Groups (and examples) of mammals include insect-eating mammals (shrew), flying mammals (bat), flesh-eating mammals (lion), "toothless" mammals (anteater), trunk-nosed mammals (elephant), hoofed mammals (horse), gnawing mammals (rat), rodentlike mammals (rabbit), water-dwelling mammals (whale), and primates (monkey).

BIBLIOGRAPHY

Carrington, R., and the editors of Time-Life Books. *The Mammals.* Alexandria, Va.: Time-Life Books.

Sanderson, I. I. *Living Mammals of the World.* New York: Doubleday.

A-V MATERIALS

Animals with Backbones, filmstrip, Eyegate.

Mammals, film, National Geographic Society.

Mammals and Their Characteristics, film, Coronet.

Science Gazette   pp. 302–309

The Gazette Adventure for this unit, "Jane Goodall and the Chimps of Gombe Stream," could be used in conjunction with Chapter 12, particularly Section 12-4, "Placental Mammals." In the last subsection, on primates, there is a reference to scientists who have observed chimpanzees using tools. This is a good opportunity to discuss backing up a statement with hard evidence. Jane Goodall has observed just what is described in the subsection—chimps using twigs to remove insects from logs. Students should be led to see that observing chimps in the wild is both an adventure and an important scientific step toward understanding human behavior.

The Issue, "Conservationists to the Rescue?" can be used to broaden the discussion of mammals stimulated by the material presented in Chapter 12. Students' opinions could be elicited on what characteristics of various mammals might make them easy targets for extinction. After finishing Chapter 12, students may be particularly sensitive to the idea of certain kinds of mammals being allowed to disappear. You may want to play "devil's advocate" to draw students out on why and how they think different endangered species of animals could be saved.

With the Future, "The Corn Is as High as a Satellite's Eye," the discussion of plants begun in Chapter 9 could be expanded. In Section 9-2, "Seed Plants," reference is made to planting a vegetable garden. You may want to take this opportunity to introduce the idea of alternative growing methods that may become necessary in the future. The Gazette article also reminds students of the difficulties involved in growing crops the traditional way. Students may have their own ideas on how and where plants of the future may be grown. Encourage creative thinking with a positive approach to any discussion on this topic.

Matter

OVERVIEW

This unit deals with the properties of matter. It describes how these properties are measured and how they are used to classify matter. Mass and volume, the general properties of matter, are covered in Chapter 13, which also introduces students to the concept of density. Chapter 14 explains physical and chemical changes and describes the basic phases of matter: solid, liquid, and gas.

CHAPTER

13 General Properties of Matter   pp. 312–327

OVERVIEW

The general nature of matter and the properties that all matter has in common—mass and volume—are described in this chapter. The concepts of weight and density are also introduced. You may wish to begin by asking students what they think these terms mean, explaining that the precise scientific definitions may be quite different from popular notions about these concepts—in particular, that of weight. Explain that understanding how to use these terms scientifically and how to measure weight and density enables scientists to solve many problems and unravel many mysteries, such as that of the *Mary Rose,* described in the chapter introduction.

SECTION

13-1   Matter   pp. 314–315

Teaching Strategy

Precisely because matter is so pervasive, students sometimes have difficulty in dealing with it in its general, abstract sense. Have them actually choose one of the objects they see around them and attempt to describe its properties. Ask them to use categories, such as color and length, to describe the object, and then explain that such categories are useful in describing all kinds of objects, all of which are matter.

SECTION

13-2   Mass   pp. 315–316

Teaching Strategy

Mass is the most important general property of matter. In fact, mass and matter are so closely related that each is used in defining the other. Thus, mass is a measure of the amount of matter in a thing, and anything that has mass is matter. Stress the constancy of mass of any object (you will later explain that weight contrasts with mass in this respect). In this section, mass is explained in terms of inertia, or the ability to resist changes in motion. Mass can also be defined in terms of gravitation, but explicit use of the term "gravitational mass" should probably be avoided at this point, since it may cause confusion when you introduce the concept of weight.

If students have not already read Chapter 1, carefully go over the nature of measurement in science. Explain the metric system and the units of mass. Have students actually determine the mass of some objects by using a triple-beam balance.

ACTIVITY

Demonstrating Inertia   p. 316 (Average)

Students will be able to observe that an object, such as a coin, at rest tends to remain at rest. Rapid removal of the card will not cause the coin to move horizontally to any significant extent, so the coin will fall almost straight down into the glass below it.

SECTION

13-3   Weight   pp. 317–318

Teaching Strategy

Gravity and weight are both widely misunderstood concepts. Explain that gravity is not simply a property of the earth but an attraction that operates between all objects in the universe. All things that have mass are attracted by gravitational force. However, the amount of gravitational force that happens to be acting on an object at any given moment is not a good measure of the amount of matter in the object. This is because the attraction depends upon the attracting body's mass and distance, which may vary, not simply on the mass of the object, which is constant. Point out that scientists use the term ''weight'' to express this attraction and that weight can vary depending on conditions. You may wish to add that weight is measured in newtons, force units that are completely different from units of mass, such as the gram.

ACTIVITY

Weight Changes   p. 318 (Average)

By doing this activity, students can come to recognize that weight is not constant but depends upon gravitational attraction. They will also learn that using units other than metric units—even fictitious units such as the ''jupe''—does not affect the ratio of gravitational attractions exerted on an object by different attracting bodies, such as the planets Earth and Jupiter and the moon. On Earth, the weight would be 100 jupes; on the moon, it would be 16.7 jupes.

SECTION

13-4   Volume   p. 319

Teaching Strategy

This brief section teaches students about another general property of matter—its ability to take up space, or exhibit volume. Explain the metric units of volume and show students how to use the graduated cylinder to measure volume.

ACTIVITY

Volume of a Solid   p. 319 (Average)

By doing this activity, students will learn to subtract initial from final volume to determine the volume of an immersed solid. Ask students whether this method will work for all solids.

SECTION

13-5   Density   pp. 320–323

Teaching Strategy

In teaching about mass-to-volume ratios, have students do actual density determinations for various pure liquids and solids. Explain that the density of each kind of material is a characteristics property of that material and can be used to identify it. Have them practice doing calculations using the density formula, both in its usual form and rearranged.

ACTIVITY

Describing Properties   p. 320 (Average)

This activity permits students to improve their powers of observation, classification, and description. You may wish to set the activity up as a contest, using teams of students to guess the identities of the samples from the descriptions given by the other students.

ACTIVITY

Archimedes and
the Crown   p. 322 (Average)

By doing this library activity, students will learn about Archimedes' principle that an object immersed in a fluid undergoes an apparent weight loss (is buoyed up by an amount) that is equal to the weight of the fluid that it displaces. You may also wish to have students research Archimedes' achievements in the fields of geometry, mechanics, optics, and astronomy.

LABORATORY ACTIVITY

Inertia   p. 324

This activity, which will require one class period, should be done when Section 13-1 has been completed.

Observations and Conclusions: 1. An object's mass causes it to resist changes in motion, or exhibit inertia. 2–3. The boxes that contained more mass had greater inertia and were not set in as rapid a motion as were the lighter boxes. 4. Use one object as a standard. Perform inertia (motion-resistance) tests on it and on other objects and assign mass values on this basis.

Going Further: Have students drop unequal (and nonbuoyant) masses through air to observe whether mass affects rate of fall. It turns out not to, as Galileo discovered. This actually indicates that the ratio of inertia to gravitational mass is equal for all objects.

Discussion Topics   p. 327

1. Students may suggest determining the mass of air and showing that air has volume.
2. Weight could be reduced simply by changing position relative to the center of the earth, but such a change would not improve the fit of clothing. The statement should be changed to read: "I have to lose mass."
3. Aluminum's density is low, making it relatively light and therefore useful for airplane construction. Cast iron's relatively high density makes it more useful for heavy-machine construction.
4. Students may suggest doing various tests to determine its properties. These tests might include determining hardness and density.

BIBLIOGRAPHY

Goodstein, D. L. *States of Matter.* Englewood Cliffs, N.J.: Prentice-Hall.

Levere, T. H. *Affinity and Matter: Elements of Chemical Philosophy.* New York: Oxford University Press.

Solomon, J. *Structure of Matter.* New York: Halsted Press.

A-V MATERIALS

Investigations in Science: Properties of Matter, 3 filmstrips, BFA Educational Media.

Matter and Energy, film, Coronet.

Matter and Energy: Properties of Matter, filmstrip, Singer Educational Division.

CHAPTER

14 Physical and Chemical Changes   pp. 328–349

OVERVIEW

In the preceding chapter, students learned about general properties of matter. In this chapter, they will study those properties that distinguish different kinds and forms of matter. They will learn about the physical states, or phases, of matter and about changes of phases. The energies associated with such changes can be used to explain paradoxes such as the one described in the chapter introduction: freezing water can be used to save an orange crop. Students will also study chemical properties and chemical changes.

SECTION

14-1 Physical Properties and Changes   pp. 330–331

Teaching Strategy

Explain a physical change as one that affects the form, shape, or other relatively superficial properties of a sample of matter but not the kind of matter. Have students prepare lists of physical changes; the lists will be of use later in contrasting physical changes with chemical changes.

If you use a dissolving process to demonstrate physical changes, avoid utilizing ionic substances such as sodium chloride, which undergo dissociation of ions (which can be considered a chemical change) when dissolved. Instead, use molecular substances, such as sucrose, whose molecules are not changed by the dissolving process.

SECTION

14-2 The Phases of Matter   pp. 331–337

Teaching Strategy

Explain to students that matter can exist in different states, or phases. Describe and give examples of matter in the solid, liquid, and gas phases, pointing out that solids have definite shape and volume, that liquids have definite volume and indefinite shape, and that gases have indefinite shape and volume. Explain the differences in terms of the arrangements of and distances between particles. Avoid introducing the terms ''atom'' and ''molecule,'' however.

If possible, demonstrate the gas laws, at least in a qualitative fashion, using air-filled balloons. If you have access to a vacuum pump and bell jar, you can also place a filled balloon in the jar, evacuate surrounding air, and show that the balloon's volume increases as the opposing pressure, which normally prevents the balloon from expanding, is decreased. Ask students to try to explain this phenomenon.

ACTIVITY

Boyle's Law   p. 335 (Average)

Students must apply Boyle's Law to carry out these simple calculations, which serve to reinforce mathematical skills. The volumes vary inversely with pressure. The answers follow: final pressure = $\frac{1}{3}$ of original pressure; final pressure = 2 times original pressure; final pressure = $\frac{1}{2}$ of original pressure.

ACTIVITY

Temperature and Pressure of a Gas   p. 336 (Average–Enriched)

Students will observe that the temperature and pressure of the tires rise. Although they may guess that Charles's Law can be used to explain this phenomenon, it turns out that this gas law is usable only if pressure remains constant and volume is permitted to vary. However, the volume of the tires is constant. A gas law called Gay-Lussac's Law must be used. It states that, given constant volume, the temperature and pressure of a gas vary directly.

SECTION

14-3 Phase Changes   pp. 337–342

Teaching Strategy

Explain solid-liquid and liquid-gas phase changes in terms of the placement of particles in the phases. Bring in the concept of energy to account for the ability of matter to go from phase to phase. Demonstrate the phase changes, using

a thermometer to show that temperature is constant during the changes. You may wish to ask students where they think the heat energy that is added to melting solids or boiling liquids is going, since it is not showing up as a temperature increase. The answer is that it is being stored as potential energy.

If you have access to a vacuum pump, you can demonstrate the dependence of boiling point on atmospheric pressure. Place a beaker of warm (but not already boiling) water in a bell jar and evacuate the air. The water will begin to boil.

ACTIVITY

Comparing Melting Points   p. 338 (Remedial)

This activity reinforces mathematical skills. Students must divide 3700° C by 801° C. The answer is approximately 4.6.

ACTIVITY

Holding Particles Together   p. 341 (Average)

By doing this library activity, students will learn about cohesive forces that act between particles and about energy stored during phase changes. Have them report their findings to the class.

ACTIVITY

An Almost-Ruined Day   p. 342 (Average)

This activity gives students the opportunity to express themselves creatively and to reinforce their understanding of the scientific terms used to describe phases and phase changes. Encourage them to read their stories to their classmates.

SECTION

14-4 Chemical Properties and Changes   pp. 342–345

Teaching Strategy

Contrast chemical changes with physical changes, explaining that during chemical changes, particles change and recombine. Point out that, regardless of whether a change is chemical or physical, the mass of the object does not change. Have students do the end-of-chapter laboratory activity, which illustrates the law of conservation of mass.

Demonstrate some simple nonreversible chemical reactions, pointing out that these changes, unlike phase changes, cannot be "undone" simply by putting the process "in reverse." Again, avoid introducing the concepts of the atom and the molecule. These concepts are treated in Unit Four.

LABORATORY ACTIVITY

Conservation of Mass   p. 346

This activity, which should be done when Section 14-4 has been begun, will require one class period.

Observations and Conclusions: 1. The total mass did not change. 2. The total mass did not change.

Going Further: Have your students demonstrate that mass does not change during a phase change. Have them find the mass of a beaker containing ice cubes, and then have them find the mass of the system again after the ice cubes have melted.

Discussion Topics   p. 349

1. Denver is at higher altitude. Atmospheric pressure is lower in Denver than it is in New York, so the boiling point is also lower. Therefore, the boiling water is not as hot, and more cooking time is required.
2. The moving air promotes more rapid evaporation of perspiration, which cools the body.

BIBLIOGRAPHY

Azaroff, L. V. *Introduction to Solids.* Huntington, N.Y.: Krieger.

Booth, V. H., and M. Bloom. *Elements of Physical Science: The Nature of Matter and Energy.* New York: Macmillan.

Toulmin, S., and J. Goodfield. *The Architecture of Matter.* Chicago: University of Chicago Press.

A-V MATERIALS

Matter and Energy: Physical and Chemical Changes, filmstrip, Singer Educational Division.

Matter, Matter Everywhere—Mixing, Dissolving, film, Coronet.

Matter, Matter Everywhere—Solid, Liquid, Gas, film, Coronet.

The Nature of Matter, film or videocassette, CRM/McGraw-Hill.

Science Gazette   pp. 350–357

The Gazette Adventure on W. Lincoln Hawkins, "He Solved the Puzzle of the Aging Wires," shows students how knowledge of the properties of matter is put to use. This Gazette article can be read in conjunction with either chapter in the unit but perhaps would be better understood after students have completed both chapters. The properties of lead are contrasted with the properties of polyethylenes, and students can speculate on how Hawkins narrowed down the list of chemicals until he found those that had the properties he needed to make plastic almost indestructible. Students can also discuss Hawkins' work in terms of chemical changes. To apply his knowledge of the properties of matter, Hawkins had to know how to use and control chemical reactions. Students should see clearly how interrelated all these aspects of matter are.

The Gazette Issue "Energy from a Volcano?" will be most meaningful to students after they have read Sections 14-2 and 14-3 on the phases of matter. Reading this article in conjunction with Chapter 14, students should be able to explain how a volcano's energy could be tapped. When students read the subsection called "The Behavior of Gases," they will understand why the steam from natural hot springs is powerful enough to heat buildings in Iceland, Italy, New Zealand, and the United States (California). Have students discuss volcanoes and geothermal energy as they relate to Boyle's and Charles's laws.

The Gazette Future about a house of tomorrow, " 'Wired' to the Sun," ties together the properties of matter, discussed in Chapter 13, and the phases of matter, discussed in Chapter 14. Both aspects of matter are integral to the concept of a house that makes its own electricity. In such a house, photovoltaic cells are filled with crystals of the elements silicon and germanium. Sunlight falling on the cells is converted directly into electricity. Students may be interested in exploring the properties of silicon and germanium, which will elucidate further how solar panels work. Properties of matter are also important relative to the building materials used in the house. Students should be made aware of this. Phases of matter come under consideration in the storage of solar energy in the house's hot-water heater. Interested students may research just how this process works and report on it to the rest of the class.

Structure of Matter

OVERVIEW

In this unit, students learn about the particles that make up matter and about the basic chemical classification of substances. Chapter 15 treats atoms and molecules, which are tiny building blocks of substances. Chapter 16 covers elements and compounds, the two categories of pure substances, or materials that contain only one kind of molecule. Elements contain only one kind of atom in their molecules, whereas compounds contain more than one kind of atom. Chapter 17 deals with the categories of physical combinations of substances: heterogeneous and homogeneous mixtures and solutions, which are especially "well-mixed" homogeneous mixtures.

If you have not already covered Unit Three, you should explain to students the nature and general properties of matter and the metric units used to measure matter. This explanation will give students the foundation they need to study the structure of matter.

CHAPTER

15 Atom and Molecules   pp. 360–375

OVERVIEW

By reading this chapter, students learn about changing concepts of the structure of matter from Greek times to the present. They are introduced to the idea of the atom as the basic building block of matter and to the discoveries that led to our modern theory of atomic structure and subatomic particles. Finally, they learn about the concept of the molecule, which will be taken up again in the following chapter.

SECTION

15-1 An Atomic Model of Matter   pp. 362–365

Teaching Strategy

In this section, students learn about the historical development of the atomic theory from the time of Democritus to that of Rutherford. Have students do more research on the work of some of the atomic theorists and also on philosophers, such as Aristotle, who held to a nonatomic theory of the basic "elements" fire, air, water, and earth.

You may wish to point out that Thomson discovered the electron by using a cathode-ray tube. Such tubes are used today in televisions, in which a beam of electrons is directed in such a way as to cause a bright image to appear on a screen.

Point up the logic of the theories of Thomson and Rutherford, who, although they were wrong in certain important respects, contributed to our knowledge of the structure of the atom. Show how their experiments helped suggest and support their theories. Encourage students to make physical representations of the atomic models of these two scientists.

ACTIVITY

A Mental Model   p. 363 (Average)

This activity will help students develop the ability to form hypotheses on the basis of indirect observation. The difficulty involved in doing this will help bring out the difficulties faced by atomic scientists, who cannot directly observe atoms.

SECTION

15-2 Structure of the Atom   pp. 365–370

Teaching Strategy

Although there are more than 200 kinds of subatomic particles, students need learn about only three of them—the proton, the neutron, and the electron. You may wish to encourage interested students to do library research on some of the other particles, however, and to report their findings to the class.

Have students practice the simple calculation necessary to figure out the number of neutrons in an atom, given its atomic number and its total number of neutrons and protons. You may wish to inform students that this total number is called the mass number and is used to distinguish between isotopes. Have interested students do library research on some of these isotopes (such as C-14) and their uses.

Even the basic concepts of quantum mechanics are difficult for most students, so take sufficient time to make clear the energy-level structure of electrons in the atom. You should know that although electrons are described here as exhibiting a whirling motion about the nucleus, they actually cannot be said to have a path. Only probabilistic statements can be made about their positions and motions.

ACTIVITY

An Atomic Model   p. 366 (Average)

By doing this library activity, students will learn about the contributions of four major twentieth-century scientists to our understanding of the atom. Have students report their findings to the class.

ACTIVITY

Electron Arrangement   p. 369 (Average)

Students will practice assigning electrons to energy levels and reinforce their understanding of atomic structure in this activity. The answers follow: sodium: 2 (electrons in first level), 8 (electrons in second level), 1 (electron in third level); nitrogen: 2, 5; chlorine: 2, 8, 7; lithium: 2, 1; neon: 2, 8; argon: 2, 8, 8.

SECTION

15-3   The Molecule   pp. 370–371

Teaching Strategy

The point of this brief section is simply to explain that atoms can bond together to form molecules and that a molecule is the smallest particle of a substance that has all the properties of that substance. You should know that molecules, as separate entities that make up a substance, need not actually have more than one atom each; the molecules of noble gases, such as helium, are monatomic.

Do not attempt to go into detail on bonding. You may wish to introduce students to the basic use of molecular-model kits, however.

LABORATORY ACTIVITY

Flame Tests   p. 372

This activity, which will require one class period, should be done when Section 15-2 has been completed. It not only introduces students to a useful test for identifying substances but also helps to clarify the concepts of electron energy levels. Have students be very careful when handling the hydrochloric acid and when using the Bunsen burner.

Observations and Conclusions: 1. Flame tests are often used to confirm the identity of an unknown metal since compounds of Group I and II metals impart characteristic colors to a Bunsen burner flame.

Going Further: You may wish to give students an "unknown"—a salt containing one of the elements investigated in the laboratory activity—and ask them to do a flame test to identify the element.

Discussion Topics   p. 375

1. Number of electrons = Z; number of protons = Z; number of neutrons = A–Z.
2. One isotope is less massive than the other. The more massive one produces a solid whose density is greater than that of ordinary liquid water and therefore sinks.
3. There are 27 possibilities, including those in which a single molecule contains two different isotopes of hydrogen.

BIBLIOGRAPHY

Condon, E. V., and H. Odabasi. *Atomic Structure.* New York: Cambridge University Press.

Conn, G. K. *Atoms and Their Structure.* New York: Cambridge University Press.

Koester, L., and A. Steyerl. *Neutron Physics.* New York: Springer-Verlag.

Electrons and Protons in Chemical Change, 2 filmstrips, PH Media.

Matter and Molecules: Into the Atom, filmstrip, Singer Educational Division.

Measuring Electron Charge and Mass, 2 filmstrips, PH Media.

The Nucleus: Composition, Stability, and Decay, filmstrip, PH Media.

CHAPTER

16 Elements and Compounds pp. 376–389

OVERVIEW

This brief chapter provides an account of the classification of pure substances, or substances that contain only one kind of molecule. The two basic groups of pure substances—elements and compounds—are taken up, and students are introduced to the use of chemical symbols, formulas, and equations. As the chapter introduction, about Sherlock Holmes and criminology, suggests, a knowledge of chemical classification is necessary for solving many of the world's mysteries. Use this mystery-solving approach in your teaching.

SECTION

16-1 Elements pp. 378–381

Teaching Strategy

Point out that elements are pure substances that contain only one kind of atom. Explain the use of one- and two-letter symbols to represent the elements. Have students do research on the sources and uses of some of the elements.

Atomic structure is not taken up in this book. However, if you wish, you may have advanced students do library research on atoms.

ACTIVITY

Getting to Know the Elements p. 378 (Average)

Have students choose solid elements, such as iron, copper, carbon, aluminum, and zinc, that are not dangerous. Students should indicate on their charts the symbols and sources of the elements, as well as their uses (in construction, coins, and so on).

SECTION

16-2 Compounds pp. 382–385

Teaching Strategy

Explain that compounds, which have more than one kind of atom in each molecule, are pure substances because all the molecules in any given compound are the same. When you cover Chapter 17, you will wish to remind students of this fact to contrast compounds with mixtures, which are not pure substances.

Explain the use of letter symbols and subscripts in chemical formulas. Have students practice writing and interpreting such formulas and identifying the kinds of elements present.

Explain how chemical equations are written and how they are balanced through the use of coefficients. You may wish to point out that equations must be balanced because they must reflect the law of conservation of mass, which states that matter can be neither created nor destroyed.

Do not attempt to give an account of ionic or covalent bonding or of the categories of chemical reactions; these topics will be taken up in another book. You may wish, however, to demonstrate some chemical reactions, such as the electrolytic decomposition of water into its elements, which are produced in a 2:1 ratio by volume.

ACTIVITY

Naming and Counting Atoms p. 385 (Remedial–Average)

This activity helps to reinforce undestanding of chemical formulas and the subscripts they contain. $NaHCO_3$ contains 1 sodium atom, 1 hydrogen, 1 carbon, and 3 oxygen; $C_{12}H_{22}O_{11}$ contains 12 carbon, 22 hydrogen, and 11 oxygen.

LABORATORY ACTIVITY

Marshmallow Molecules p. 386

This activity requires one class period plus two overnight drying periods. It should be done when Section 16-2 has been begun.

Answers to Questions in Procedure: B2. The balanced equation is $1N_2 + 3H_2 \rightarrow 2NH_3$. B3. The balanced equation is $2Cu_2O + C \rightarrow 4Cu + CO_2$

Observations and Conclusions: 1. One N_2 and three H_2 are needed. 2. Four Cu atoms are produced. 3. Three O_2 molecules are produced.

Going Further: Have students construct other molecules and balance the corresponding chemical reactions. Some examples follow: $C + 2H_2 \rightarrow CH_4$ (methane); $2K + Cl_2 \rightarrow 2KCl$; $H_2 + N_2 + 3O_2 \rightarrow 2HNO_3$ (nitric acid).

Discussion Topics   p. 389

1. The symbols and formulas are the same throughout the world. This permits scientists to communicate without misunderstanding or the need to translate symbols of one system to other systems.
2. The changing of subscripts would change the identity of substances. The equation is supposed to represent the formation of water (H_2O), not hydrogen peroxide (H_2O_2). The balanced equation makes use of coefficients: $2H_2 + O_2 \rightarrow 2H_2O$.

BIBLIOGRAPHY

Ahrens, L. H., ed. *The Origin and Distribution of the Elements.* Elmsford, N.Y.: Pergamon.

Donohue, J. *Structure of the Elements.* New York: Wiley.

Schroeder, H. A. *Elements in Living Systems.* New York: Plenum.

A-V MATERIALS

A Look at Chemical Changes, film, CRM/McGraw-Hill.

Matter and Molecules: The Matter of Elements, filmstrip, Singer Educational Division.

CHAPTER

17 Mixtures and Solutions   pp. 390–403

OVERVIEW

The last chapter deals with pure substances, or substances whose molecules are all the same. This chapter deals with mixtures, or physical combinations of substances, in which more than one kind of molecule is present. Such mixtures make up almost all the materials around us; pure substances are quite rare in nature. As students learn by reading the chapter introduction, even objects as familiar and seemingly simple as a hamburger may contain thousands of components.

Students are introduced to the properties of mixtures. They then learn about the basic classes of mixtures—heterogeneous and homogeneous—and about solutions, a subclass of homogeneous mixtures.

SECTION

17-1 Properties of Mixtures pp. 392–394

Teaching Strategy

Explain to students that the components of mixtures are physically, rather than chemically, combined. Point out that the substances in a mixture keep their identities and most of their properties and can be separated from each other. You may wish to demonstrate this point by using several methods to separate some simple mixtures such as iron fillings and sulfur (which are separable by means of a magnet), sand and water (separable by filtration), or sugar and water (separable by evaporation). Explain that even gaseous mixtures may be separated into their components—for example, by condensation and then distillation, as is done with air, whose components boil off at different temperatures.

ACTIVITY

A Mixture Collection   p. 393 (Average)

It should be easy for students to find examples of mixtures and display them. Have them do library research to identify the chemical components of some of the mixtures they have chosen.

SECTION

17-2 Types of Mixtures   pp. 395–396

Teaching Strategy

Display examples of heterogeneous and homogeneous mixtures, and prepare one or two of each kind in class. Point out that such mixtures differ in the degree to which their components are "well-mixed," heterogeneous mixtures containing different kinds of particles that are large enough to be seen. Explain the differences between suspensions and colloids. When you teach students about solutions (in the following section), contrast solutions and colloids, showing that a beam of light produces a visible "track" in the latter, whose particles are large enough to scatter the light, but not in the former.

17-3 Solutions   pp. 397–399

Teaching Strategy

Explain the properties of solutions and introduce the terms "solute" and "solvent." Technically speaking, the solute is the component whose phase, if isolated, would be different from that of the solution in which it is dissolved. For example, in a sugar-water solution, sugar is the solute because it is a solid dissolved in a solution that is liquid; water is the solvent because, like the sugar-water solution, it is liquid. However, it is appropriate for students to think of the solute as the material that is dissolved and to think of the solvent as the material that does the dissolving. Have students prepare solutions and study the properties of solutions and effects such as freezing-point depression and boiling-point elevation (see "Laboratory Activity: Examination of Freezing-Point Depression").

Introduce the concept of solubility, explaining that solubility can be expressed in various ways, but avoid attempting to introduce molarity and molality, which presuppose an understanding of the concept of the mole (a set of 6.02×10^{23} molecules). You may wish to demonstrate the formation of precipitates, or low-solubility salts, that result when certain ions are brought together in too high a concentration. Some of these precipitates are of colors different from those of the substances used to make them. For example, colorless solutions of lead nitrate $(Pb(NO_3)_2)$ and potassium iodide (KI) combine to produce a brilliant yellow precipitate of lead iodide (PbI_2).

You may wish to explain to students that no substance is, strictly speaking, insoluble, since all substances dissolve at least to a slight degree.

However, solubility may be so low as to be negligible.

ACTIVITY

Water Dissolves Most Substances   p. 398 (Average)

Students can do this simple activity at home. They will learn that some household substances, such as sugar and salt, are very soluble in water, whereas others, such as flour and cooking oil, have low solubility.

ACTIVITY

Expressing Solubility   p. 399 (Average)

This library activity gives students the opportunity to learn the meanings of certain terms used in discussing solutions. You may wish to have them actually prepare examples of dilute and concentrated solutions, or of saturated or supersaturated solutions, to illustrate these concepts.

LABORATORY ACTIVITY

Examination of Freezing-Point Depression   p. 400

This activity, which will require two class periods, should be done when Section 17-3 has been begun.

Observations and Conclusions: 1. It lowers the freezing point. 2. It doubles or nearly doubles the amount of freezing-point depression (about $1.86°$ C for solutions 2 and 4; about $3.72°$ C for 3 and 5; about $3.72°$ C for solution 6; and about $7.44°$ C for solution 7). 3. The kind of substance does not seem to have much effect. (This is true for nonionic substances. The depression is about $1.86°$ C for a 1-molal, or $1\ m$, solution. Solutions 2 and 4 were both $1\ m$. However, solution 6 was of the same concentration—as you may wish to inform your students—and its freezing-point depression was about twice as great. This is because each NaCl unit dissociated into 2 ions, so a $1\text{-}m$ solution produced a $2\text{-}m$ solution of ions.)

Going Further: You may wish to have students measure the effect on the freezing point of water when ethyl alcohol is added. Ask them why they think such substances are used in antifreeze. As an alternative, you may wish to have them study boiling-point elevation in saltwater solutions.

Discussion Topics   p. 403

1. Heterogeneous mixtures contain large clumps of particles that will not fit through the small openings of most filters. The particles in solutions are very well mixed or are mixed on the molecular level, and are small enough to pass through.
2. Answers will vary.
3. The sugar would dissolve rapidly and completely in the hot tea. Dissolving would occur much more slowly in the cold tea.

BIBLIOGRAPHY

Stone, A. H., and D. Ingmanson. *Crystals from the Sea: A Look at Salt.* Englewood Cliffs, N.J.: Prentice-Hall.

Stone, A. H. *The Chemistry of a Lemon.* Englewood Cliffs, N.J.: Prentice-Hall.

Zubrowski, B. *Messing Around with Baking Chemistry: A Children's Museum Activity Book.* Boston: Little, Brown.

A-V MATERIALS

Matter and Molecules: Clue-Compounds and Changes, filmstrip, Singer Educational Division.
Naming Chemical Substances, Parts 1 and 2, filmstrip, PH Media.

Science Gazette   pp. 404–411

With the Gazette Adventure, "Peter Armbruster and the Search for an Unknown Element," students will see that atomic research has come a long way since Rutherford's day. The contrast between his research and the type of experiments going on today would be most dramatic if the Gazette article were read in conjunction with Chapter 15. Students may find it difficult to appreciate the significance of Armbruster's achievement, but if you trace the development of atomic research from 1897 to the present, students will have more of a feeling for how scientists strive to unlock the mysteries of the unknown.

After completing Chapter 15, have students read the Gazette Issue, "Wasting Time: The Nuclear Clock Ticks Down." Students may not yet be aware of the relationship between atoms and nuclear power. Having students do some research on nuclear power plants will show them the importance of atomic experiments. Be sure students come away with the knowledge that nuclear energy comes from the splitting of the nuclei of atoms of uranium or plutonium (nuclear fission). The problem of nuclear waste can be contrasted, in debate, with the advantages of nuclear energy. Students should have no trouble finding articles on this subject in the news and should be encouraged to bring them into class for continuing discussion.

To complete the broadening of the scope of Chapter 15, have students read the Gazette Future, "The Right Stuff—Plastics," at this time. By now, after having read the Gazette Adventure and Issue, students should no longer have any doubts about the importance of atoms and molecules and the necessity for atomic research. In this article, they see yet another application of scientific knowledge about atoms and molecules—the creation of superstrong, light plastics. Have interested students research monomers and polymers and report their findings to the class. Elicit from students a list of objects made of plastic. The list should fill the chalkboard. Have students speculate about future uses of plastics in keeping with the theme of the Gazette Future.

Composition of the Earth

OVERVIEW

This unit deals with the substances that make up the earth—their properties, formation, combination, and changes. The unit introduction presents the problem of investigating the planet's composition as a sort of journey to the center of the earth. Have your students read this interesting introduction and, as you cover the unit, try to work into your teaching the metaphor of an ongoing journey into a mysterious and fascinating realm.

Chapter 18 deals with minerals that make up the earth, explaining basic chemical concepts in the process. Chapter 19 describes the rocks that result from the physical combination of the chemical substances that make up minerals. Chapter 20 describes the composition of soil and its formation from weathered rock and organic material.

CHAPTER

18 Minerals

pp. 414–431

OVERVIEW

This chapter discusses the nature and composition of minerals. The basic physical and chemical characteristics of minerals, as well as the practical methods by which they are identified, are discussed.

The chapter also describes the uses of minerals. Many of these applications, such as the removal of metals from ores, have a history that extends back for millennia. The use of certain hard and beautiful minerals as gemstones is also discussed. The chapter introduction, with its account of the mystery surrounding the Orloff diamond, should awaken student interest in this subject.

SECTION

18-1 What Is a Mineral?

pp. 416–424

Teaching Strategy

This discussion of the nature of minerals makes use of only the most basic chemical principles. The

definition of "element" is given, though the concept of "atom" is not introduced. More advanced students may wish to learn more about atoms and elements and about the compounds that they make up. If you have not already covered the unit on the structure of matter (Chapters 15–17), you may wish to direct these students to relevant passages of that unit.

The process of identifying minerals is described in this section. The tests for hardness, streak, heft, color, luster, and cleavage and fracture are detailed in the context of an interesting particular situation—the attempt of a prospector to discover and identify gold and to differentiate it from other substances that resemble it.

As you teach students about these tests, you should demonstrate the tests with actual minerals. Have students conduct some of the tests themselves. Mineral samples, as well as slides, can be obtained from science supply houses. You might also plan a visit to a natural history or geology museum to examine collections. Point out that the oldest minerals discovered so far on the earth are some zircon crystals from Australia that are 4.2 billion years old. Point out also that new minerals are sometimes discovered; for instance, armalcolite, tranquillityite, and pyroxferroite were discovered in moon rocks collected on the Apollo mission.

ACTIVITY

Rock-Forming Minerals

p. 419 (Average)

Students will be interested in applying their newfound knowledge of rocks and minerals to find and identify various samples gathered in their own areas. Allow them to display their collections in the classroom and to describe the identification methods they used.

ACTIVITY

A Gem of a Gem!

p. 420 (Average)

To find the mass of the largest gem, students must multiply 520,000 by 200 by setting up the following equation: 520,000 carats × 200 milli-grams/carat = 104 kilograms.

SECTION

18-2 Uses of Minerals   pp. 424–427

Teaching Strategy

This section deals with only two general uses of minerals: the use of metals extracted from ores and the use of gems. It would be helpful, there-fore, to call students' attention to the table on page 424, which describes a number of other mineral uses.

You may wish to direct interested students to reference works that describe the actual chemical processes involved in ore extraction. These and other students may also be interested in research-ing the use of a bacterium that is used to remove metals such as copper from ores. The bacterium digests the ores. Other students may wish to learn more about gems and gem cutting. You may wish to invite a gemologist or jeweler to the class to talk about precious and semiprecious stones, to demonstrate stone-cutting principles, and to discuss units, such as the carat, that are used to measure the mass of stones. One carat is equal to 200 milligrams.

ACTIVITY

Rubies, Sapphires, and Emeralds   p. 426 (Average)

Interested students may wish to share with the class the results of their library research, which may include maps that show the regions in which gems are found. They may also wish to combine this research with visits to jewelry stores and in-terviews with jewelers.

LABORATORY ACTIVITY

Forming Mineral Crystals   p. 428

This activity fits in best immediately after Sec-tion 18-1. It will require two class periods about two days apart.

Observations and Conclusions: 1. Regularly shaped crystals grew on the dental floss and around the edge of the flat-bottomed dish.

2. Sugar: slanted rectangles, white crystals; alum: octahedrons, hexagons, or slanted rectangles and colorless crystals; borax: slanted rectangles, color-less crystals; copper sulfate: slanted rectangles, green or blue crystals. 3. Answers and charts will vary.

Going Further: Have students attempt to grow larger crystals of alum by growing small seed crystals in the bottom of a dish and then suspend-ing these crystals from dental floss in a saturated alum solution in a flask. This saturated solution should then be permitted to evaporate slowly for about one week.

Discussion Topics   p. 431

1. Minerals, unlike nonminerals, are natural substances formed in the earth and composed of one or more elements. Minerals are not products of living things.
2. Some physical properties used to identify minerals are hardness, the ability to scratch or be scratched by other materials; streak, the color of a mineral in powder form; heft, the apparent weight or heaviness; color; and luster, the way the mineral reflects light.
3. Types (and examples) of nonmetallic lusters are glassy (quartz), pearly (mica), greasy (serpentine), brilliant (diamond), and silky (malachite).
4. Some minerals and their uses follow: alum—in cosmetics, dyes, water purification; bauxite—as a source of aluminum; calcite—in medicine, toothpaste, building materials; corundum—in emery boards, and for grinding and polishing; feldspar—in pottery, china, glass; graphite—in pencils, as a lubricant; halite—as table salt; hematite—as a source of iron; jade—in making vases; malachite—in jewelry and table tops; quartz—in radios, radar, televi-sions; sulfur—in matches, medicine, rubber, gunpowder.
5. Impurities, or small traces of various minerals, give red and blue color, respectively, to aluminum oxide in rubies and sapphires and give green color to beryl in emeralds.

BIBLIOGRAPHY

Desautels, P. E. *Rock and Minerals.* New York: Grosset and Dunlap.

Dietrich, R. V., and B. J. Skinner. *Rocks and Rock Minerals.* New York: Wiley.

Frye, K. *Modern Mineralogy.* Englewood Cliffs, N.J.: Prentice-Hall.

Mason, A. *The World of Rocks and Minerals.* New York: Larousse.

A-V MATERIALS

Minerals (Problem of Conservation series), film, Encyclopaedia Britannica.

Rocks and Their Minerals, 20 slides, Singer Educational Division.

Rocks and Minerals, film, BFA Educational Media.

CHAPTER

19 Rocks   pp. 432–449

OVERVIEW

This chapter deals with the three basic types of rock: igneous, sedimentary, and metamorphic. The formation and characteristics of these types are presented, with examples. The changes of rock from type to type are treated in the final section of the chapter, on the rock cycle. Remind students that rocks are physical aggregates of minerals, each of which is made up of a chemical substance. The rocks can occur in beautiful or striking formations, such as the so-called Giant's Causeway, which is discussed in the chapter introduction.

SECTION

19-1 Rocks of Liquid and Fire: Igneous Rocks   pp. 434–437

Teaching Strategy

Obtain slides of various igneous rocks from a scientific supply house and allow students to examine them to appreciate their structure and texture. Do the same for rocks of the other types that will be covered in the following sections.

The formation of igneous rocks from magma is discussed in this section. The appearance of magma, as lava, at the earth's surface may be seen by students in dramatic photos or films of erupting volcanoes. The igneous rock (including basalt, obsidian, and pumice) formed in this way at the earth's surface is described in the subsection "Extrusive Rocks," whereas the igneous rock (such as granite) formed inside the earth is described in the subsection "Intrusive Rocks."

You may wish to point out to students that certain large islands, such as Hawaii, Japan, the Philippines, and Iceland, were formed volcanically from basalt. Point out these islands on a map, and select students to do library research on the topography and natural history of these islands. Some students may even wish to research island formation, as well as other igneous formations, in terms of subsurface earth activity and tectonic plate theory.

SECTION

19-2 Rocks in Layers: Sedimentary Rocks   pp. 437–440

Teaching Strategy

The layered rocks called sedimentary rocks are discussed in this section. Such rocks are categorized according to the origin of the sediments and the process of rock formation. Fragmental rocks are made up of rock particles mixed with and cemented together by sand or clay. Organic rocks are formed from the remains of once-living plants and animals. Chemical rocks are typically formed by evaporation.

Conglomerate rocks, which are a variety of fragmental rock, can be enormous in size. The largest single exposed rock discovered on the earth is a conglomerate. Called Mount Augustus, it is located in western Australia. Mount Augustus is 8 kilometers long and about 3 kilometers across. By the way, the term "puddingstone," which, as the text states, was once used to refer to conglomerate rocks, came from "Yorkshire pudding," the name of a lumpy-looking English pudding.

ACTIVITY

Coral Conversions   p. 440 (Average)

To determine how many meters long the Coral Reef is, students must use the following equation:

$$2000 \text{ kilometers} \times 1000 \text{ meters}/1 \text{ kilometer}$$
$$= 2{,}000{,}000 \text{ meters.}$$

To change meters to centimeters, students must multiply 2,000,000 by 100 to get an answer of 200,000,000 centimeters. To compare this distance to the distance across the United States, students should use the following equation:

$$\frac{2000 \text{ km}}{4517 \text{ km}} \frac{\text{(Coral Reef)}}{\text{(U.S.)}} = .44$$

So the Coral Reef is almost half as long as the United States.

SECTION

19-3 Rocks That Change: Metamorphic Rocks   pp. 441–443

Teaching Strategy

Metamorphic rocks are formed when other kinds of rock undergo changes of form or structure called metamorphism. The metamorphic rocks marble, slate, and quartzite are discussed in this section.

Encourage students to collect rocks of all three basic types and to bring the rocks to class. They should collect the specimens from different sites and note the sites. If they use a hammer to break off specimens, warn them to wear safety goggles to protect their eyes against flying fragments. Tell them to conduct their searches with one or more partners. You can direct the students to reference books or field guides that will help them to identify the rocks they have collected. The samples may be labeled and displayed in the classroom.

ACTIVITY

Rock Quarries   p. 441 (Average)

The general information gathered on quarrying can be augmented with information on specific quarries in your local area. Students may wish to write to or visit the quarries, and they may even receive samples of the stones quarried there, together with detailed information on the removal, processing, and eventual uses of the stones. Students may also wish to interview and observe the work of people who use these materials, such as masons and sculptors.

ACTIVITY

A Rock Walk   p. 443 (Remedial)

Students need not actually take a walk through a rocky area to write their essays. In fact, a real walk might not allow them to ''see'' all three kinds of rock mentioned, while an imaginary walk certainly would. Encourage students' creativity by having them set the scene for their sightings by describing terrain and other physical characteristics of the rocky landscape.

SECTION

19-4 The Rock Cycle   pp. 444–445

Teaching Strategy

The changes that characterize the so-called rock cycle include not only the metamorphism discussed in the preceding section but also the melting into magma of various rocks and the re-formation of igneous rocks. Because of the complexity of the changes that may figure in the rock cycle, you should make use of flow diagrams, photos, and actual specimens to make the discussion more understandable to students. You may wish to plan a trip to a natural history museum that has a large rock collection and exhibits on rock changes, or you may wish to invite a geologist to your class to discuss the rock cycle.

ACTIVITY

Changes in Rocks   p. 445 (Average)

Observing gravestones may reveal weathering and erosive processes in various kinds of stone, including igneous (granite) and metamorphic (marble) rocks. Caution students to seek prior permission of custodians of the cemeteries that they visit.

LABORATORY ACTIVITY

Making a Sedimentary Rock   p. 446

This activity will require one class period plus about 10 minutes of a second period about one to three days later. It should be done when Section 19-2 is completed.

Observations and Conclusions: 1. The color of the rock formed should not be much different from that of the original sand. The rock will probably resemble many kinds of sandstones in its general characteristics. 2. Small grains are cemented together, as in real sandstone. 3. It will be more brittle, tending to crumble between the fingers, and the cementing alum will dissolve in water, releasing the grains of sand. Its density will probably be lower than that of most sandstones.

Going Further: The steps described in this activity can be repeated after a piece of "sandstone" has been formed. New layers can thus be deposited on the same stone, and students can be asked to look for evidence of this stratification in the larger stone that is eventually produced.

Discussion Topics   p. 449

1. Obsidian is glassy-looking and does not contain crystals, whereas granite is crystalline and grainy. Obsidian is extrusive and is formed by rapid cooling, whereas granite is intrusive and is formed by slow cooling, which gives large crystals a chance to form.
2. Sedimentary rocks form when layers of material are laid down over a period of time and are often cemented together. Such rocks are often formed in water and can contain the remains of once-living things that were deposited on the floor of the body of water.
3. Fragmental rocks, such as sandstone, are made up of rock fragments mixed with sand or clay and cemented together. Organic rocks, such as limestone, are built up from the remains of living things. Chemical rocks, such as rock salt, are formed by evaporation of water.
4. The granite may be worn down. The fragments may be reduced to powdery sediments made up mainly of quartz sand grains, which may mix with water and minerals such as aluminum to form clay, which may in turn become part of the soil. The powdery sediments may alternatively be deposited in water and be cemented together to form sedimentary rocks, such as sandstone. After such rocks are deeply buried, high pressure and temperature may change the stone into metamorphic quartzite, which may be eroded, at the earth's surface, or may be melted to magma inside the earth, only to cool and form granite once again.

BIBLIOGRAPHY

Blatt, H., G. V. Middleton, and R. C. Murray. *Origin of Sedimentary Rock.* Englewood Cliffs, N.J.: Prentice-Hall.

Fay, G. *Rockhound's Manual.* New York: Barnes & Noble.

Shakley, M. L. *Rocks and Man.* New York: St. Martin's.

A-V MATERIAL

Earth Science: The Rock Cycle, filmstrip, Singer Educational Division.

Investigating Rocks, 9 filmstrips, Encyclopedia Britannica.

Minerals and Rocks, film, Encyclopedia Britannica.

CHAPTER

20 Soils   pp. 450–467

OVERVIEW

This chapter deals with the layers and the organic and inorganic components of soil. The process of soil formation through weathering is also discussed. This process, which involves the breakdown of rocks, was treated in less depth in the preceding chapter, which focused on changes and interconversions of the rocks themselves.

The soils in different regions of the earth differ from one another owing to environmental and biological factors that affect the leaching of minerals and the formation of humus. These different types of soils are discussed in Sections 20-2 to 20-6. They include tropical rain forest soil, temperate forest soils, prairie grassland soil, desert soil, and tundra soil. The various soil regions often differ dramatically in the life forms that are present, as is illustrated in the chapter introduction, which deals in an interesting way with the temperate-forest–prairie-grassland boundary in the United States.

SECTION

20-1   Soil   pp. 452–455

Teaching Strategy

This section of the chapter deals with the topsoil, subsoil, and parent rock layers and with the organic (humus) and inorganic (weathered rock) components of soil. The field investigation on soil layers is an important one, and you may wish to use it as the focus of your teaching, referring frequently to students' own findings. In any case, sample soil cores or appropriate diagrams are invaluable in conveying the idea of soil structure to students.

ACTIVITY

Studying Soil Layers   p. 452 (Average)

The depth of the various soil layers in the samples dug out by students will depend on various general and local factors. You may wish to have students make drawings of their findings and display them in the classroom. In certain regions, very little topsoil will be present. In such cases, you may wish to have students relate their findings to the environmental conditions. Library research into the topic of erosion, along with class discussion, would be well worth the time spent, because erosion, which poses a serious threat in many regions of the world, is an important topic.

ACTIVITY

Rain Forest Death Rate   p. 454 (Average)

For students to calculate how many hectares of rain forest would have to be destroyed each day to make the Academy's yearly estimate correct, they would have to divide 20 million by the 365 days in a year. The answer is that about 100,000 hectares or 247,000 acres a day are destroyed if 20 million hectares are destroyed each year. (Note that 1 hectare equals 2.47 acres.)

SECTION

20-2   Tropical Rain Forest Soil   pp. 455–457

Teaching Strategy

Students are unlikely to have had any direct experience with conditions in tropical rain forests, since none exist in the continental United States. Tropical rain forest soil is found in Hawaii, however. You must convey to students that, despite the lushness of vegetation and animal life in tropical regions, the soil is quite poor in minerals. The large plant forms are able to exist because of the year-round rapid decay of dead plant parts and animals, which provides food for the plants. In this section and in the sections that follow, the key to student understanding of the soils in the regions discussed lies in explaining the degrees to which leaching and humus formation occur. Therefore, make sure that these two processes are thoroughly understood before continuing.

SECTION

20-3   Temperate Forest Soils   pp. 457–459

Teaching Strategy

The temperate forest region covers large areas of the United States, particularly in the eastern third of the country. The loss of minerals by leaching into subsoil is significant in such regions, which accounts in part for the fact that smaller plants often are not present in large numbers, especially in northern regions, where mineral-poor evergreen needles cover the forest floor and cool temperatures make for a slow rate of humus formation.

You may wish to ask students to bring in photographs of the various forms of plant and animal life found in temperate forest regions and to do library research on them. You may also wish to invite experts on climate zones and on soil structure and conservation to address the class.

Leaching   p. 459 (Remedial)

Have students go through Chapter 20 to write their essays on the effects of leaching on the various soil types. Students may want to write an overview based on the information given in the chapter, or they may be encouraged to concentrate on the leaching problems in one type of soil. In the latter case, students will have to supplement the text material with library research.

SECTION

20-4   Prairie Grassland Soil   pp. 460–461

Teaching Strategy

The region of prairie grassland extends throughout most of the midwestern United States as far west as the Rocky Mountains. The thick, rich layer of topsoil characteristic of this region resulted from the blowing of soil into the region from the west and from the thick humus layer built up by the decay of grasses. The leaching of minerals out of the topsoil is minimized by the generally sunny weather and high winds, which promote rapid evaporation. Here again, knowledge of the rates of humus-formation and leaching are necessary to an understanding of the soil and of the life forms its supports.

ACTIVITY

The Use of Fertilizers   p. 460 (Average–Enriched)

This activity can be carried out at varying levels of sophistication, depending on the background, ability level, and interest of the student. More advanced students may wish to concentrate on the chemical nature and aspects of fertilizers, and they may wish to learn more about the chemical composition of these substances and of the components of soil. Other students may limit themselves to a more qualitative and descriptive approach to fertilizer use. The issues surrounding such use are rather controversial, and may be dealt with in class discussion or debates.

SECTION

20-5   Desert Soil   pp. 461–462

Teaching Strategy

Point out to students that nearly an eighth of the world's land surface has desert soil. Such soil is mineral-rich because there is little rainfall to promote leaching. However, it contains little humus because of the relatively low density of plant life and the low rate of decay. The biological adaptations to desert conditions are fascinating and can provide interesting library research topics. Cacti are particularly interesting, with their widespread, shallow root systems, their ability to conserve water by closing their pores during the day, and their sharp spines, which discourage animals from attempting to eat or draw water out of them.

SECTION

20-6   Tundra Soil   pp. 462–463

Teaching Strategy

The permafrost that characterizes tundra soil can extend for considerable depths below the surface in regions near the earth's poles. The lack of different soil layers due to the constant mixing that results from freezing and thawing is a distinguishing characteristic of tundra soil. Students may wish to do library research on the methods used to grow food and raise animals in the hostile tundra region. Encourage them also to draw maps of the continents, using different colors to indicate all the various regions and soil types they have studied.

LABORATORY ACTIVITY

Determining Rates of Weathering   p. 464

This activity will require about half of a class period. It should be done when Section 20-1 has been completed.

Observations and Conclusions: 1. The broken tablet reacted more quickly than the unbroken one. 2. In general, the greater the surface area, the higher the reaction rate. 3. The graph, which plots weathering rate (*y*-axis) versus particle size (*x*-axis), should show a curve that extends from upper left to lower right in the first quadrant, indicating that rate tends to decrease as particle size increases.

Going Further: Have students investigate the rate of other reactions as a function of surface area. You might try reactions involving dissolving, or perhaps combustion—illustrating, for example, the rapid rate of burning of steel wool, which has a high exposed surface area. Warn students to be careful when working with a flame. They should wear safety goggles, use tongs, and have a pan of water nearby.

Discussion Topics   p. 467

1. With soil, the earth is able to support an amazingly wide variety of living things that are adapted to particular environmental and soil conditions. If there were no soil, very few kinds of land organisms could exist.

2. Leaching washes many minerals out of tropical rain forest soil because of the heavy rainfall. There is less leaching in temperate forest zones because there is no heavy year-round rainfall. There is still less leaching in prairie grassland soil because sunlight and high winds foster rapid evaporation of water. Desert soils undergo very little leaching of minerals because rainfall is so light. In tundra areas, water is often permanently frozen under the surface, although there is frequent mixing of soil owing to freezing and thawing.

3. She was probably referring to the fact that some aspects of soil formation can take place very quickly (for example, the sudden breaking of a rock under the right conditions), whereas others (such as the formation of a thick, humus-rich layer of topsoil) may take a very long time.

4. The Antarctic has very little precipitation, which explains why it is considered to be a desert despite its coldness.

BIBLIOGRAPHY

Bloom, A. L. *The Surface of the Earth.* Englewood Cliffs, N.J.: Prentice-Hall.

Carroll, D. *Rock Weathering.* New York: Plenum.

Ollier, C. D. *Weathering.* New York: Longman.

Watkins, J. S., M. L. Bottino, and M. Morisawa. *Our Geological Environment.* Philadelphia: W. B. Saunders.

A-V MATERIALS

Erosion, film, BFA Educational Media.

Geologic Weathering, 20 slides, Singer Educational Division.

Soil: Its Meaning for Man, filmstrip, PH Media.

Science Gazette   pp. 468–475

The Gazette Adventure on Maria Reiche and her work in the Nazca Desert in Peru can be read in conjunction with Section 20-5, "Desert Soil." The Adventure will help students to visualize the nature of desert soil and climate. It reinforces the description of desert terrain provided in Chapter 20. The way in which the Peruvian Indians created the Nazca Lines and the lines' longevity should intrigue students. You may want to remind students that if the lines had been drawn in another part of the world or in different soil, they would not exist today. Also, Reiche's determination to solve the mystery of the lines, under the very trying climactic conditions of the desert, might be a good subject for a thought-provoking discussion.

The Gazette Issue, "Diving for Natural Treasures: A Risky Business?," will add to students' knowledge of minerals, a subject dealt with in Chapter 18. While reading Sections 18-1 and 18-2, you may want to have students learn about the minerals on the ocean floor. Beginning with some of those listed in the Issue—manganese, tungsten, vanadium, cobalt, and so on—you may want students to research the uses of certain less common minerals or to try to find pictures of them or how they are used. Students can also be urged to explore the ecological remifications of mining, both on land and under the waves. A topic for debate could be the necessity of mining versus the effects of mining operations on miners and on the ecology.

To continue the subject of mining begun in connection with Chapter 18, the Gazette Future may be read at this time. It provides a fanciful look at an imaginary mining operation of the future. Students may contrast real-life mining operations with those pictured in the Gazette. The practicality and logistics of mining asteroids should spark students' imaginations and make for an interesting discussion.

Structure of the Earth

OVERVIEW

As the unit introduction implies, the different regions of the earth and its atmosphere are inter-related and affect one another. Thus, for example, a mountain can result from volcanic activity that originates deep inside the earth. This activity not only changes surface features of the planet but also—because of dust and gases it releases—affects the atmosphere.

Chapter 21 deals with the internal structure of the earth, including the core, mantle, and crust. Chapter 22 describes the earth's surface features. Chapter 23 discusses the structure and composition of the earth's atmosphere.

CHAPTER

21   Internal Structure of the Earth   pp. 478–499

OVERVIEW

This chapter not only describes the internal features of our planet but also explains how information on these features was obtained. Thus, it follows the chronology of scientific discovery and illustrates the application of scientific method. Studies of earthquakes and interpretations of the findings of these studies are discussed. The information on the structure of the core, mantle, and crust that resulted from the studies is presented, and the chapter concludes with a discussion of the theory of plate tectonics.

SECTION

21·1   The Earth's Core and Earthquake Waves   pp. 480–486

Teaching Strategy

Present the seismologic studies that are described in terms of the unfolding of evidence in a scientific mystery. Make sure that before you reveal the conclusions scientists came to with regard to the earth's structure, you have made clear the basic facts about seismology. A visit to a geo-logic institute, observatory, or museum would be of great help in this area. You might also invite a seismologist to address your students, show them some seismographs, and tell them about seismo-logic activity in their area. You might use a Slinky® or similar coil toy to demonstrate the difference between longitudinal P waves and transverse S waves.

Review scientific method with students and have them analyze the indirect discovery of the core in terms of observation, hypothesis, conclusion, and so on.

ACTIVITY

How Many Earths?   p. 485 (Average)

This activity involves a computation, by division, that helps not only to reinforce mathematical skills but also to reveal the enormity of astronomical distances, even when compared with very large geologic distances. The answer to the question is about 11,628 earths. In order to arrive at the right answer, students must divide 150 million km by 12,900 km, the diameter—not the radius—of the earth.

SECTION

21·2   Exploring the Earth's Mantle   pp. 486–492

Teaching Strategy

Mohorovicic's discovery of the Moho, or boundary between the crust and mantle, is another example of scientific method. Have interested students do further research on this discovery and report their findings to the class (see "Activity: Mohorovicic's Discovery").

The discussion of rift valley flow that ends this section will be resumed in the following section. To bridge the two sections, you might ask students what they think ultimately happens to all the material that rises from the rifts and ask them to consider whether this process could continue indefinitely without some counteracting process that returns material to the mantle.

ACTIVITY

Visiting the Earth's Core   p. 487 (Average)

Jules Verne's novel *A Journey to the Center of the Earth* makes delightful reading. Students will enjoy contrasting Verne's imaginative account with their own newly gained knowledge of the earth's structure.

ACTIVITY

Drilling into the Earth   p. 488 (Average)

By doing this activity, students will learn about the successes and failures of attempts at drilling into the earth's mantle to discover more about its structure and composition. Have them make a report to the class of their findings, which should include the information that drillings have shown that rocks near the Mid-Ocean Ridge are younger than those farther away.

SECTION

21-3   The Earth's Crust and Floating Continents   pp. 492–495

Teaching Strategy

The discussion of the earth's crust and of the trenches through which older crust moves back down into the mantle serves to round out students' understanding of the processes that create and move the continents. Have students do library research on plate tectonics and prepare maps showing plates and plate movement in the earth as a whole or in our region of it.

ACTIVITY

Making a Model of the Earth's Interior   p. 493 (Remedial–Average–Enriched)

This activity should serve to make the earth's internal structure more concrete, especially for students who have difficulty visualizing structures that are not directly observable. Students of average or above-average ability can do further research on the composition of the various layers and include corresponding labels in their models.

ACTIVITY

Mohorovicic's Discovery   p. 495 (Average)

This activity not only helps provide students with more information on the mantle-crust boundary but also serves to reinforce vocabulary and composition skills. You might devise vocabulary or essay activities on other topics, such as plate tectonics, as well.

LABORATORY ACTIVITY

Building an Active Geyser   p. 496

This activity, which requires about 30 minutes, should be done soon after the point has been made that the earth's interior contains a great deal of heat. The activity may be done by you as a demonstration, if you prefer.

Observations and Conclusions: 1. Water should spurt periodically from the funnel stem. 2. Heated rock below the surface of the earth provides the heat energy. 3. Increased heat energy would cause more frequent or more vigorous eruption, assuming an unlimited water supply. 4. A reduction in the amount of either heat or water could cause the stoppage. 5. The heat source and water supply must be fairly constant.

Going Further: You may wish to have students do library research on the underground structure of actual geysers and compare it with the experimental setup. You might also ask them to construct a model of the structure of geysers.

Discussion Topics   p. 499

1. Heat from the earth's core sets up churning motions in the solid-liquid rocks of the mantle. As in a pot of soup on a stove, the hottest material, nearest the source of heat, rises to the top, where it cools and sinks back down, only to be reheated.
2. Continents may sink when, for example, large sheets of ice are deposited on them. They may rise when such ice melts away, just as a cargo ship may sink or rise in the water as the ship becomes heavier or lighter by addition or removal of cargo.

BIBLIOGRAPHY

Jacobs, J. A. *The Earth's Core.* New York: Academic Press.

Sawkins, F. J., et al. *The Evolving Earth.* New York: Macmillan.

Sparks, J., and A. Bourne. *Planet Earth: Earth's Atmosphere and Crust.* New York: Doubleday.

A-V MATERIALS

Earth in Change—The Earth's Crust, film, Encyclopaedia Britannica.

Strata—The Earth's Changing Crust, film, BFA Educational Media.

The Earth's Crust, filmstrip, Singer Educational Division.

CHAPTER

22   Surface Features of the Earth   pp. 500–521

OVERVIEW

The preceding chapter describes the interior of the earth. Chapter 22 describes the earth's surface. Of course, the processes covered in Chapter 21, such as plate movement and the upwelling of magma from the interior, account for many of the external features of the planet, as the introduction to this chapter suggests.

The landmasses of the earth, with their specific physical features, are discussed. Then the fresh and salt water of the earth is described, and the water cycle is introduced as a way of explaining not only the movement of liquid water but also the water transfer that occurs between the atmosphere and the earth's surface.

SECTION

22-1   The Earth's Surface: Landmasses   pp. 502–511

Teaching Strategy

In this section, the various physical features and landscapes of the earth, such as mountains, plateaus, and plains, are discussed. As you teach students about these features and about the seven major continents that contain them, remember to tie the information to the geological processes that created them. Also, make use of globes and maps to help locate landmasses, mountain ranges, and so on. Topographical maps are very useful for this purpose; you can order some that are specific to your own region and then ask students to use clay or plaster of Paris to make three-dimensional scale models of the region. Students may also wish to display photographs of interesting physical features they have observed in their travels. They can then do library research on the formation and physical details of these features.

ACTIVITY

Earth's Mountains   p. 506 (Remedial–Average)

This activity reinforces mathematical problem-solving skills. Students must multiply the total land area by ⅕. The answer is 29,660,000 square kilometers. You can extend this activity by having students calculate the area occupied by other physical features, such as plains and plateaus, or by making such calculations for their own geographical region.

ACTIVITY

Sizes of Continents   p. 508 (Average)

Students gain specific information on the areas of the earth's major landmasses by doing this exercise. They also learn about a simple geometrical technique used to estimate area. Be sure that the grid size of the graph paper they use is appropriate. If the squares are too large, the estimate will not be accurate; if they are too small, it will take too long to count them. You may wish to have students calculate the mathematical ratios for the continental areas. All students should obtain the same values, regardless of what grid size they have chosen.

ACTIVITY

Surface Features p. 510 (Remedial–Average)

This activity not only reinforces learning of the physical features of landmasses but also builds vocabulary and essay-writing skills. The essays will probably vary considerably in content and style. Encourage students to share their work with the class.

22-2 The Earth's Surface: Water pp. 511–517

Teaching Strategy

As you teach students about running, standing, and frozen water, refer to globes and maps, as you did in the last section. Encourage students to research the bodies of water in their area and to get information on the water table and on the history of local drought or flooding problems.

The point of this section is not simply to describe features of the earth's water but also to explain the passage of water from form to form. The concept of the water cycle is used to do this. If, in their studies of physical science, students have already gained some knowledge of the phases and phase changes of matter, you can refer them to what they have learned about evaporation and condensation on the molecular level and about the energies involved in these processes, which on a global scale are prodigious. Each year, for example, more than 313,000 cubic kilometers of water is "pumped out" of the ocean by the water cycle; enormous amounts of energy are absorbed from sunlight during this evaporation process and are released during the condensation that occurs later.

ACTIVITY

Community Water Supply p. 512 (Average)

Students learn about the ground- or surface-water sources of their drinking water by doing this activity. Prepare them for their field trip by having them do some prior library research on water in their region. If it is not possible to arrange a field trip to the water-treatment plant, you may be able to invite a representative of such a plant to your school to address the class.

ACTIVITY

Reservoirs p. 517 (Average)

This activity can be combined with the preceding one if the principal source of fresh water is your area's reservoirs. If you have covered electric-energy generation in your teaching, you may encourage students to do further research on the use of reservoirs in such power generation.

LABORATORY ACTIVITY

Examining Differences Between Fresh and Salt Water p. 518

This activity, which will require one class period, should be done soon after Section 22–2 has been begun. Preparation suggestion: Use a saturated solution of sodium chloride and water for the most dense solution. Then dilute this solution to half and quarter strength to make the other two solutions.

Observations and Conclusions: 1. The fresh water was least dense, the solution with the most dissolved salt was most dense. 2. It would be more deeply submerged. 3. It would float higher. 4. It would float higher in salt water than in fresh water. 5. The density becomes lower.

Going Further: Have students repeat the activity using liquids other than water. Ethyl alcohol and various oils may be used for this purpose.

Discussion Topics p. 521

1. Mountain landscapes contain individual features that rise at least 610 meters above the surrounding land. Plateaus are raised flat regions. Plains are lower flat regions and can occur along coasts or inland.
2. Mountains can form by slow folding and wrinkling of the earth's crust, by the breaking of the crust into blocks, and by lava and ashes that rise through cracks in the crust.
3. The Colorado Plateau began rising as the Rocky Mountains were forming. It was originally a single broad structure but was carved into many steep-walled plateaus by the Colorado River and its branches.
4. Coastal and inland plains are both flat and low-lying and tend to have rich soil. The soil of

coastal plains comes from soil-carrying rivers and from shallow oceans, and it tends to build up the plains. The soil of inland plains comes from rivers, and the plains themselves are formed by the wearing down of mountains and hills.

5. Their rich soil deposited by rivers, their plentiful rainfall, and the lack of flooding problems account for their high quality as farming land.

6. Water evaporates from the oceans and freshwater sources. As it cools, it condenses back to liquid and falls as precipitation. The cycle then begins again.

BIBLIOGRAPHY

Bradshaw, M. J., et al. *The Earth's Changing Surface*. New York: Halsted Press.

Hart, J. F. *The Look of the Land*. Englewood Cliffs, N.J.: Prentice-Hall.

Ross, D.A. *Introduction to Oceanography*. Englewood Cliffs, N.J.: Prentice-Hall.

Suckling, E. E. *The Seas*. New York: McGraw-Hill.

A-V MATERIALS

Landforms on the Earth's Crust, 20 slides, Singer Educational Division.

Ocean Currents, 2 filmstrips, PH Media.

The Earth: Mountains, filmstrip, Singer Educational Division.

The Earth: Oceans, filmstrip, Singer Educational Division.

CHAPTER

23 Structure of the Atmosphere pp. 522–541

OVERVIEW

As the chapter introduction suggests, the earth's atmosphere is not undifferentiated but has a definite structure. This chapter deals with the height and properties of the four principal regions, or layers, of the atmosphere. The regular variations of temperature and gas density that characterize the atmosphere as a whole are also treated. The chapter's final section deals with the earth's magnetosphere, a magnetic field that extends beyond the atmosphere.

SECTION

23-1 The Layers of the Atmosphere pp. 524–535

Teaching Strategy

The story of Glaisher and Coxwell's balloon exploration of the atmosphere makes an exciting introduction to this section. Their discovery of the decrease of density and temperature in the lower atmosphere as altitude increases was an important one, revealing that the properties of the atmosphere are not constant throughout its range.

Point out to students that the division of the atmosphere into its four principal layers is based on the direction of temperature variation with altitude. In the troposphere, or lowest level, the temperature decreases with increasing altitude. In the stratosphere, or second level, it increases. In the mesosphere, the third and coldest level, it decreases. In the thermosphere, the fourth and warmest level, it increases. However, as is pointed out in this section of the chapter, temperature range is not the only distinguishing feature of the various layers. Pressure, composition, and degree of turbulence also differ. You may wish to have students do more research on these specific features of the atmospheric layers, such as the ozone region, the jet stream, and the ionosphere, with its auroras.

Some students may wish to make scale drawings of the atmosphere, indicating its structure and features. If they include the earth in their drawings, they will readily observe that the atmosphere—or at least those layers that contain significant amounts of gas—is not like a huge balloon in which our planet floats but is more like a thin skin that fits tightly around it. The importance of minimizing pollution of the atmosphere becomes all the more clear to students when they realize just how little atmosphere there is, relatively speaking.

ACTIVITY

Air Pressure p. 526 (Average)

You may wish to do this activity yourself as a demonstration. If you have students do it, caution them to be very careful when using matches and to have a pan of water and a fire extinguisher at hand.

The hard-boiled egg will be drawn into the bottle. The reason is that the pressure inside the bottle decreases as a result of the combustion, and the outside pressure, now no longer balanced by pressure within, can push the egg inside.

ACTIVITY

Hurricanes and Tornadoes   p. 528 (Average)

Students should report to the class their overall findings on these storms. Some of them may wish to include maps showing hurricane or tornado occurrences by state or region. Other students may wish to research the history of certain particularly destructive storms, especially those that may have affected their own area in the past.

ACTIVITY

Distances Between Collisions of Air Particles   p. 532 (Remedial–Average)

This activity reinforces mathematical word-problem-solving skills. Students must multiply 12,000 meters by 550 and then divide the product by 1000 to convert it to kilometers. The answer is 6600 kilometers. You may wish to point out that the particles are much closer together than this but because of their extreme smallness, they travel a long distance before "finding" one another.

ACTIVITY

Listening to the Radio   p. 535 (Average)

Students will typically find that they can receive signals from more and farther stations at night. The increased altitude of the ionosphere at night enables radio waves to travel farther before being reflected, increasing the total efficient distance they tend to travel.

SECTION

23-2   The Magnetosphere   pp. 535–537

Teaching Strategy

The principal focus of this section is not the earth itself or the cause of its magnetism but rather the planet's surrounding magnetic field. Thus, in introducing the concept of the magnetosphere, you should simply point out that the earth acts like a large magnet and avoid discussing in too much depth the structure and composition of its iron-and-nickel core. You may wish to mention, however, that the planet's magnetic poles have reversed 171 times in the last 76 million years.

The concept of auroras and the ionosphere, discussion of which ended the preceding section, can be picked up again at this point. Charged particles coming from the sun interact with charged particles already trapped in the magnetosphere. Light energy is given off, resulting in the shimmering effects of auroras. Some of your students may wish to do research on solar flares and on the Van Allen radiation belts that surround the earth.

LABORATORY ACTIVITY

Using Atmospheric Pressure to Crush a Can   p. 538

This activity, which requires about 30 minutes, should be done shortly after Section 23-1 has been begun. Be sure that students are very careful in working with the Bunsen burner and heated can. Caution students to wear safety goggles during these parts of the experiment.

Observations and Conclusions: 1. The can was crushed inward. The water vapor inside condensed to liquid, resulting in reduced gas pressure inside. The unbalanced outside air pressure pushed in the can. 2. The can may be heated again, vaporizing the water. It can then be reopened when its sides have been pushed out to their normal position. (If students actually attempt to do this, they must be very careful not to overheat the can or to have their faces or hands near the jet of escaping steam.)

Going Further: Given that average atmospheric pressure amounts to about 1 kg/cm², students can calculate the total atmospheric "pressure" (figured here in equivalents of mass rather than force) pushing against the entire surface of the can. They should measure the can and calculate its surface area, in cm², and then multiply by 1 kg/cm². The result will be surprisingly large.

Discussion Topics   p. 541

1. At this elevated altitude, the air is less dense. It therefore offers less resistance to the passage of objects through it. Beamon was able to jump farther because of this lowered air resistance.
2. An airplane flying eastward may use the jet stream, which flows from west to east, as a tail wind to help speed the plane in its motion. An airplane flying westward cannot make use of the jet stream and thus tends to move more slowly.

BIBLIOGRAPHY

Goody, R., and J. C. Walker. *Atmospheres.* Englewood Cliffs, N.J.: Prentice-Hall.

Riehl, H. *Introduction to the Atmosphere.* New York: McGraw-Hill.

A-V MATERIALS

Meteorology: The Atmosphere, filmstrip, Eyegate.

The Air Around Us, filmstrip, CRM/McGraw-Hill.

The Atmosphere and Its Effect, filmstrip, Eyegate.

The Atmosphere in Motion, film, Encyclopaedia Britannica.

Science Gazette   pp. 542–549

The Gazette Adventure, entitled "William Haxby Maps the Invisible Ocean Floor," could be read after Chapter 21. It would be particularly effective if read in conjunction with the last subsection of Section 21-2, which discusses how the ocean floor is built up, or with Section 21-3, which discusses how the continents and ocean floor ride on plates. The Gazette article could be used to expand the discussion of floating continents as it brings in the phrases "continental drift" and "plate tectonics." Students will see how knowledge of the earth's crust, including the ocean floor, may be applied to earthquake prediction. You may want to have students draw their own imaginative maps of a section of ocean floor as they "see" it.

"Should People Build Lakes?," the Gazette Issue, could be used in conjunction with Section 22-2 to reinforce students' understanding of surface water's effects on climate and vegetation on land. This article has interesting implications in relation to the water cycle that you may have some students explore. Have students consider the effects of artificial lakes on the environment. For debate purposes, select some students to defend artificial lakes and others to condemn them. Students will be called upon to present cogent arguments to support their positions. You may also want to appoint a committee of students to check on the health of a local lake, whether natural or artificial, and report their findings to the class.

The Gazette Future, "The Longest Winter," would make an intriguing addition to Chapter 23. Have students identify the layer of the atmosphere that "acts as a window for sunlight but as a blanket for heat." You may have students research the effects of pollution on the ozone layer in the stratosphere or have them discuss the effects of nuclear war on the atmosphere and the possible ramifications such effects might have for survivors of a nuclear strike. You may want to have students write papers on this subject, stressing the scientific rather than the political aspects of nuclear war. Students should have no trouble researching this topic, for it is much in the news.

■■ Prentice-Hall
General Science
A Voyage of Adventure

Prentice-Hall
General Science
A Voyage of Adventure

Dean Hurd
Physical Science Instructor
Carlsbad High School
Carlsbad, California

Susan M. Johnson
Associate Professor of Biology
Ball State University
Muncie, Indiana

George F. Matthias
Earth Science Instructor
Croton-Harmon High School
Croton-on-Hudson, New York

Charles William McLaughlin
Chemistry Instructor
Central High School
St. Joseph, Missouri

Edward Benjamin Snyder
Earth Science Instructor
Yorktown High School
Yorktown Heights, New York

Jill D. Wright
Associate Professor
   of Secondary Education
Tennessee Technological University
Cookeville, Tennessee

Prentice-Hall, Inc., Englewood Cliffs, New Jersey 07632

Prentice-Hall General Science Program

Student Text and Annotated Teacher's Edition

Laboratory Manual and Annotated Teacher's Edition

Teacher's Resource Book

General Science Courseware

Other Programs in this series

Prentice-Hall General Science © 1986
A Voyage of Discovery

Prentice-Hall General Science © 1986
A Voyage of Exploration

General Science Reviewers

John K. Bennett
Science Specialist
State Department of Tennessee
Cookeville, Tennessee

Sue Teachey Bowden
Department of Science Education
East Carolina University
Greenville, North Carolina

Edith H. Gladden
Curriculum Specialist
Division of Science Education
Philadelphia, Pennsylvania

Gordon Neal Hopp
Carmel Junior High School
Carmel, Indiana

Stanley Mulak
Science Supervisor
Springfield School District
Springfield, Massachusetts

Richard Myers
Science Instructor
Cleveland High School
Portland, Oregon

Reading Consultant

Patricia N. Schwab
Chairman, Department of Education
Guilford College
Greensboro, North Carolina

ISBN 0-13-697418-X

10 9 8 7 6 5 4 3 2

Prentice-Hall of Australia, Pty. Ltd., Sydney
Prentice-Hall Canada Inc., Toronto
Prentice-Hall Hispanoamericana, S.A., Mexico
Prentice-Hall of India Private Ltd., New Delhi
Prentice-Hall International, Inc., London
Prentice-Hall of Japan, Inc., Tokyo
Prentice-Hall of Southeast Asia Pte. Ltd., Singapore
Editora Prentice Hall do Brasil Ltda., Rio de Janeiro
Whitehall Books Limited, Wellington, New Zealand

Photograph credits begin on page 572

Cover Photographs

The top cover photograph shows a honeybee in flight as it approaches a flowering plant. (Stephen Dalton, *Animals Animals*) The photograph on the left is of a group of rocks on the shore of Lake Superior. (Robert P. Carr, *Bruce Coleman*) The photograph on the right shows a steaming hot spring in Yellowstone National Park. (Steven Fuller, *Earth Scenes*)

Back Cover Photographs

Top center, Bryon Crader/*Tom Stack & Associates;* Top right, O.S. Pettingill, Jr./*Photo Researchers;* Bottom left, Center for Astrophysics; Bottom center; Breck P. Kent/*Earth Scenes;* Bottom right, Nicholas Devore/*dpi*

Contents

Digestive system

Cells

5

UNIT THREE Matter 310-357

UNIT FOUR Structure of Matter 358-411

Characteristics of Living Things

For an overview of this unit, see pages T-17 to T-27. You may want to check the Laboratory Activity following each chapter, as well as the activities and investigations for this unit in your Teacher's Resource Book and Annotated Teacher's Edition, Laboratory Book, so that materials can be ordered, gathered, or prepared in advance.

The tiny submarine slips deeper and deeper into the ocean. Inside, three scientists prepare for their arrival on the sea floor. Outside the submarine, there is nothing but darkness. With a soft bump, the submarine touches bottom. The depth gauge shows 2590 meters. The water pressure is a crushing 264 kilograms per square centimeter. Lava oozes from cracks in the ocean floor. The lava heats the water to a blistering 371° C, hot enough to melt lead.

Suddenly the floodlights of the submarine flash on. The view is astounding. Giant clams and pale yellow mussels lie on the sand. A white crab walks by. The scientists wonder how living things can exist in such a harsh place. And they realize with excitement that finding out will be a great adventure. This is an adventure made possible by thousands of years of curiosity and learning about the nature of living things.

CHAPTERS

1 Exploring Living Things

2 The Nature of Life

3 Cells

4 Tissues, Organs, and Organ Systems

5 Interactions Among Living Things

Amazing life forms of the ocean bottom

1 Exploring Living Things

For a chapter overview, teaching strategies, answers to all activities, a list of A-V materials, and a chapter bibliography, see pages T-17 to T-20.
Consult your Teacher's Resource Book and Annotated Teacher's Edition, Laboratory Book for additional activities and teaching aids.

CHAPTER SECTIONS

CHAPTER OBJECTIVES

After completing this chapter, you will be able to:

1-1 Describe the various steps of a scientific method.

1-2 Make and understand metric measurements.

1-3 Explain the difference between a light microscope and an electron microscope.

1-3 Describe several tools used by biologists.

1-4 Discuss the recent discovery of some land animals that lived more than 380 million years ago.

A howling wind shook the walls of the wooden temporary building at Rocky Hill, Connecticut. Torrents of rain swept over the building's roof. With a groan, the building suddenly fell apart.

Unknown to the scientists at Rocky Hill, where the Connecticut State Dinosaur Park is located, the collapse of the building was soon to lead to an unexpected discovery. For later, when the earth was moved to make room for the new building, strange scratches were found on the exposed rock. An expert on dinosaurs, Dr. W. P. Coombs, Jr., of Western New England College in Massachusetts, was contacted.

Dr. Coombs took one look at the mysterious scratches and immediately knew what they were—dinosaur footprints. But there was more to the story. The scratches appeared in groups of three. Dr. Coombs concluded the scratches were made by an animal having three toes with sharp claws. They were clearly the marks of a meat-eating dinosaur.

Carefully, the scientist measured the distance between the footprints—130 centimeters. Dr. Coombs reasoned that only a very large animal, perhaps the 7-meter-long *Megalosaurus*, could take such long strides. There was something very peculiar about the footprints, however. Only the tips of the dinosaur's toes seemed to have touched the rock. But *Megalosaurus* did not run on its toes, at least not on land.

Dr. Coombs could draw only one conclusion. The prints were made under water, which kept most of the animal's weight off the rock. Dr. Coombs had discovered the first evidence of swimming, meat-eating dinosaurs. A simple accident, a sharp eye, and some smart detective work had led to a scientific discovery.

Megalosaurus—the first swimming, meat-eating dinosaur

1-1   What Is Science?

The universe around you and inside of you is really a collection of countless mysteries. It is the job of scientists to solve those mysteries. And, like any good detective, a scientist uses special methods to find truths about nature.

These truths are called facts. An example of a fact is that the earth is populated with millions of different kinds of living things. But science is more than a list of facts. Jules Henri Poincaré, a famous nineteenth-century French scientist, put it this way: "Science is built up with facts, as a house is with stones. But a collection of facts is no more a science than a heap of stones is a house."

So scientists go further than simply discovering facts. Scientists try to use facts to solve larger mysteries of nature. In this sense, you might think of facts as clues to scientific mysteries. An example of one of these larger mysteries is how the relatively few and simple organisms of three billion years ago gave rise to the many complex organisms that inhabit the earth today.

Figure 1-1 *It is a fact that this red diamondback rattlesnake injects poison into its prey. It is a hypothesis that the rattler locates its injured victim by following the smell of its own venom.*

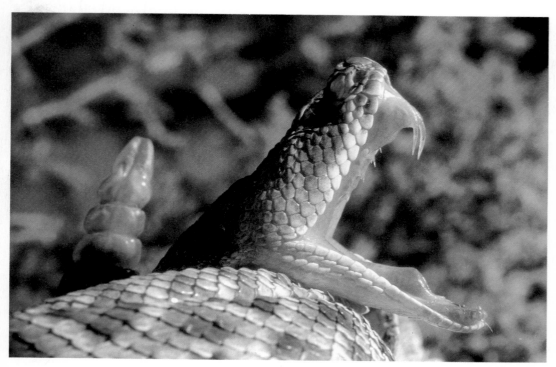

Scientific Methods

To uncover scientific facts and solve scientific mysteries, scientists can use any one of a number of **scientific methods.** There are various basic steps in these methods. But these steps need not be followed in any particular order, although some orders make more sense than others. Sometimes the order in which a scientist tries to solve a mystery depends on the nature of the mystery. The basic parts of any scientific method are the following:

1. Stating the problem
2. Gathering information
3. Suggesting an answer for the problem
4. Performing an experiment to see whether the suggested answer makes sense
5. Recording and analyzing the results of experiments or other observations
6. Stating conclusions

The following example shows how a scientific method was used to solve an actual problem. As you will see, the basic steps of a scientific method often overlap.

Stating the Problem

Most people know enough to walk the other way if they should run into a rattlesnake. However, if you could safely observe a rattler, you would discover a rather curious kind of behavior.

With fangs flashing and body arching, the deadly rattler strikes. The snake's fangs quickly inject poisonous venom into its victim. Then, in a surprise move, the rattler allows the wounded animal to run away! But the rattlesnake will not miss its intended meal. After waiting for its poison to take effect, the rattler follows the trail of the injured animal.

Although the rattler cannot see well, somehow it manages to find its victim on the dense, dark, forest floor. Clearly, something leads the snake to its prey. What invisible trail does the snake follow in tracking down its bitten prey? This is a *problem* that scientists recently tried to solve.

Figure 1-2 *The rattler does not have an especially keen sense of sight. Its pit organs detect the body heat given off by this field mouse.*

Gathering Information on the Problem

The first step in solving a scientific problem is to find out or review everything important related to it. For example, the scientists trying to solve the rattlesnake mystery knew that a rattlesnake's eyes are only sensitive to visible light. However, they also knew that a pair of organs located under the animal's eyes detects invisible light in the form of heat. These heat-sensing pits pick up signals from warmblooded animals. The signals help the snake to locate its intended prey. But the heat-sensing pits cannot help the snake find a wounded victim that has run many meters away. Some other process must be responsible for that.

The scientists knew that a rattler's tongue "smells" certain odors in the air. The rattler's tongue picks up these odors on an outward flick. The odors enter the snake's mouth on an inward flick. The scientists also knew that the sight or smell of an unbitten animal did not trigger the rattler's tracking action. Using all this information, the scientists were able to suggest a solution to the problem.

Forming a Hypothesis

A suggested solution is called a **hypothesis** (high-PAH-thuh-sis). A hypothesis is almost always formed after the information related to the problem is carefully studied. But sometimes a hypothesis is the

Activity

Theories and Laws

Scientists sometimes use observations and experiments to develop a theory. A theory is a broad scientific explanation for things that happen in nature. If the theory is tested and confirmed, it may become a law.

Using books and reference materials in the library, find out about a theory in life science that became a law.

result of creative thinking that often involves bold, original guesses about the problem. In this regard, forming a hypothesis is like good detective work, which involves not only logic, but hunches, intuition, and the taking of chances.

To the problem, "What invisible trail does a rattler follow in tracking down its prey?" the scientists suggested a hypothesis. The scientists suggested that *after the snake wounds its victim, the snake follows the smell of its own venom to locate the animal.*

Experimenting

The scientists next had to test their hypothesis by performing certain activities and recording the results. These activities are called *experiments.* Whenever scientists test a hypothesis using an experiment, they must make sure that the results of the experiment clearly support or do not support the hypothesis. That is, they must make sure that one, and only one, factor affects the results of the experiment. The factor being tested in an experiment is called the variable. In any experiment, only one variable is tested at a time. Otherwise it would not be clear which variable had caused the results of the experiment.

Emphasize to your students that conclusions are made only after an experiment has been performed many times.

Figure 1-3 *Sinking its fangs into its victim, the rattler injects the mouse with deadly poison.*

In the rattlesnake experiments, the scientists tested whether the snake's venom formed an invisible trail that the snake followed. The venom was the variable, or single factor, that the scientists wanted to test. The scientists performed the experiment to test this variable.

First, the scientists dragged a dead mouse that had been struck and poisoned by a rattlesnake along a curving path on the bottom of the snake's empty cage. When the snake was placed in its cage, its tongue flicked rapidly, its head moved slowly from side to side, and it followed the exact trail the scientists had laid out. The results seemed clear, but the scientists had one more experiment to perform.

To be sure it was the scent of the venom and no other odor that the snake followed, the scientists ran a **control** experiment. A control experiment is run in exactly the same way as the experiment with the variable, but the variable is left out. So the scientists dragged an unbitten dead mouse along a path in the cage. The experiment was exactly the same, except this mouse had not been poisoned. This time the snake seemed disinterested. Its tongue flicked very slowly and it did not follow the path.

Recording and Analyzing Data

The rattlesnake experiments were repeated many times, and the scientists carefully recorded the **data** from the experiments. Data include observations such as measurements.

Stating a Conclusion

After analyzing the recorded data, the scientists *concluded* that the scent of venom was the only factor that could cause a rattlesnake to follow its bitten victim. Rattlesnake venom is made up of many different substances. Exactly which ones are responsible for the snake's behavior are as yet unknown. As is often the case in science, a solution to one mystery brings to light another mystery. Using scientific methods similar to those described here, scientists hope to follow a path that leads to the solution to this new mystery.

Activity

Early Scientists

The science of biology owes a great deal to the work of many early scientists. Using books and reference materials in the library, look up the following names.

Anton van Leeuwenhoek

Robert Hooke

Leonardo da Vinci

Gerty Radnitz Cori

Write a brief report about the scientists, including information about the contribution of each.

Branches of Science

Science is divided into many branches according to subject matter. Each branch is made up of a small or large topic in science. There are three main branches of science.

Life science   Life science deals with living things and their parts and actions. Smaller branches of life science include **zoology,** the study of animals, and **botany,** the study of plants.

Earth science   Earth science is the study of the earth and its rocks, oceans, volcanoes, earthquakes, atmosphere, and other features. Usually, the earth sciences also include **astronomy.** Astronomers explore nature beyond the earth. They study such objects as stars, planets, and moons.

Physical science   Physical science is the study of matter and energy. For example, some physical scientists explore what substances are made of and how they change and combine. This branch of physical science is called **chemistry.** Other physical scientists study forms of energy such as heat and light. This is the science of **physics.**

Figure 1-4   *Life science includes the study of animals such as these penguins who nest in Antarctica.*

Figure 1-5   *The earth-orbiting Space Shuttle Challenger (left) helps gather important information about the nature of the earth and the universe beyond. The laws of motion, a part of the science of physics, explain how Olympic cyclists speed along their circular track (right).*

SECTION REVIEW

1. What is a hypothesis?
2. Why does an experiment have only one variable?
3. What are the three main branches of science?
   1. A suggested solution to a problem
   2. To make it clear which factor caused the results of the experiment
   3. Life science, earth science, physical science

1-2 Scientific Measurements

As part of the process of experimenting and gathering information, scientists must make accurate measurements. The scientists may need to know the size of a cell or the temperature of a bird's body. They must also be able to share their information with other scientists. To do this, scientists must speak the same measurement "language." The common language of measurement in science used all over the world is the **metric system.**

The metric system is a decimal system, or a system based on ten. That is, each unit in the metric system is ten times larger or ten times smaller than the next unit. Metric calculations are easy to do because they involve multiplying or dividing by ten. Some frequently used metric units and their abbreviations are listed in Figure 1-6.

Figure 1-6 *The metric system is easy to use because it is based on units of ten.*

COMMONLY USED METRIC UNITS

Length

Length is the distance from one point to another.

A meter is slightly longer than a yard.

1 meter (m) = 100 centimeters (cm)

1 meter = 1000 millimeters (mm)

1 meter = 1,000,000 micrometers (μm)

1 meter = 1,000,000,000 nanometers (nm)

1 meter = 10,000,000,000 angstroms (Å)

1000 meters = 1 kilometer (km)

Mass

Mass is the amount of matter in an object.

A gram has a mass equal to about one paper clip.

1 kilogram (kg) = 1000 grams (g)

1 gram = 1000 milligrams (mg)

1000 kilograms = 1 metric ton (t)

Volume

Volume is the amount of space an object takes up.

A liter is slightly larger than a quart.

1 liter (L) = 1000 milliliters (mL) or 1000 cubic centimeters (cm^3)

Temperature

Temperature is the measure of hotness or coldness in degrees Celsius (°C).

0°C = freezing point of water

100°C = boiling point of water

Length

The **meter** is the basic unit of length in the metric system. One meter is equal to 39.4 inches. Sometimes scientists must measure distances much longer than a meter, such as the distance a bird may fly across a continent. To do this, scientists use a unit called a kilometer. The prefix *kilo-* means 1000. So a kilometer is 1000 meters, or about the length of five city blocks.

A hummingbird, on the other hand, is too small to be measured in meters or kilometers. So scientists use the centimeter. The prefix *centi-* means that 100 of these units make a meter. Thus there are 100 centimeters in a meter. The hummingbird is only about 5 centimeters long. For objects even smaller, another division of the meter is used. The millimeter is one thousandth of a meter. The prefix *milli-* means 1/1000. One meter equals 1000 millimeters. In

Figure 1-7 *Scientists use many tools to study their world. A metric ruler (top, left) measures length. A graduated cylinder (top, right) helps measure the volume of liquids. A triple-beam balance (bottom, left) may be used to measure mass. And a Celsius thermometer is used to measure temperature.*

bright light, the diameter of the pupil of your eye is about 1 millimeter. Even this unit is too large to use when describing the sizes of the smallest germs, such as the bacteria that cause sore throats. These germs are measured in micrometers, or millionths of a meter, and nanometers, or billionths of a meter.

Volume

The amount of space an object takes up is called its volume. The **liter** is the basic unit of volume in the metric system. The liter is slightly larger than the quart. Here again scientists use divisions of the liter to measure smaller volumes. The milliliter, or cubic centimeter, is $\frac{1}{1000}$ of a liter. There are 1000 milliliters, or cubic centimeters, in a liter. The volumes of both liquids and gases are measured in liters and milliliters. For example, a scientist may remove a few milliliters of blood from an animal in order to study the types of substances the blood contains.

Mass and Weight

The **kilogram** is the basic unit of mass in the metric system. **Mass** is a measure of the amount of matter in an object. Your experience tells you that there is more matter in a tree trunk than in a leaf. Therefore, a tree trunk has more mass than a leaf.

One kilogram is slightly more than two pounds. For smaller units of mass, the gram is used. Remember that the prefix *kilo-* means 1000. There are 1000 grams in a kilogram. One milligram measures an even smaller mass, $\frac{1}{1000}$ of a gram. How many milligrams are there in one kilogram? 1,000,000

Mass is not the same as **weight.** Weight is a measure of the force of attraction between objects due to **gravity.** All objects exert a force of gravity on other objects. The strength of the force depends on the mass of the objects and the distance between them. You may not be aware of it, but the gravity of your body pulls the earth toward you. At the same time, the gravity of the earth pulls you toward its center. The mass of the earth is, however, much greater than your mass. As a result, the force of gravity you exert is very small compared to that of the earth. You remain on the surface of the earth because of

Figure 1-8 *Astronaut Bruce McCandless, weightless in space, uses his jet-powered backpack and foot restraint to maneuver around the Space Shuttle Challenger.*

the force of the earth's gravity. And it is the size of this force that is measured by your weight. As the distance between objects decreases, the force of gravity between them increases. Therefore, you would weigh a little more at sea level than on the top of a mountain. At sea level, you are closer to the center of the earth.

It may be apparent to you now that mass is a constant and weight is not. Because weight can change, it is not a constant. For example, a person who weighs a certain amount on Earth would weigh much less on the moon. Can you explain this? The force of gravity of the moon is about one sixth that of the earth. Therefore, a person's weight on the moon would be one sixth that on the earth. The mass of the person, however, does not change. It is the same on the moon or the earth because the amount of matter in the person does not change.

DENSITY   The measurement of how much mass is contained in a given volume of an object is called its **density.** Density can be defined as the mass per unit volume of a substance. The following formula shows the relationship between density, mass, and volume.

$$\text{density} = \frac{\text{mass}}{\text{volume}}$$

Activity

Comparing Temperatures

The internal temperature of the sun is almost 20,000,000° C. The core of the earth is about 3700° C. How many times hotter is the sun than the earth?

Density is an important concept because it allows scientists to identify and compare substances. Each substance has its own characteristic density. For example, the density of water is 1g/cm³ while that of butterfat is 0.91g/cm³. Based on this data, will butterfat sink or float in water? Float

Temperature

Scientists measure temperature according to the **Celsius** scale, in degrees Celsius. The fixed points on the scale are the freezing point of water at sea level, 0° C, and the boiling point of water, 100° C. The range between these points is 100 degrees, and each degree is ¹/₁₀₀ of the difference between the freezing point and boiling point of water. Normal human body temperature is 37° C, while some birds maintain a body temperature of 41° C.

SECTION REVIEW

1. What are the basic units of length, volume, and mass in the metric system? 1. Meter, liter, kilogram
2. What is the difference between mass and weight?
3. What is density and why is it an important scientific measurement?

2. Mass, a measure of the amount of matter, is constant. Weight, a measure of the force of gravitational attraction, can vary.
3. Mass per unit volume; to identify and compare substances

1-3   Tools of a Scientist

Scientists use a wide variety of tools to explore the world around them. Tools may be as simple as paper and pencil or as complex as computer video systems. The scientist chooses the tools most useful for solving a specific problem.

Microscopes

Have you ever looked through a magnifying glass to examine a leaf or the body of an insect more closely? If so, you used a simple **microscope.** A microscope is an instrument that produces an enlarged image of an object. A magnifying glass is a simple

Figure 1-9 *On this unmagnified fruitfly (top), notice the two large, red structures, which are the eyes. Then look at the head of the fruitfly, which is magnified 60 times (center). The two rounded structures on each side of the head are the eyes. A scanning electron microscope produced this detailed, three-dimensional image of the eye of the fruitfly (bottom).*

microscope because it has only one **lens.** A lens is a curved piece of glass that bends light rays as they pass through it. In certain lenses, this bending increases the size of an object's image.

THE COMPOUND LIGHT MICROSCOPE Optical, or light, microscopes that have more than one lens are called **compound light microscopes.** These microscopes use light to make an object look up to 2000 times larger than it really is. Compound light microscopes can be used to examine the cells in your body.

ELECTRON MICROSCOPES An **electron microscope** does not use light to magnify the image of an object. Instead, it uses a beam of tiny particles called electrons. Pictures produced by this beam are focused on a television screen or photographic film. Electron microscopes can magnify objects hundreds of thousands of times. One type, the scanning electron microscope, or SEM, produces a three-dimensional

Career: *Electron Microscopist*

HELP WANTED: ELECTRON MICROSCOPIST Bachelor's degree in histotechnology preferred. Training in the operation of the electron microscope and the interpretation of electron micrographs required.

Until the invention of the electron microscope in the 1930s, scientists examined the inner structures of living things by viewing slices of plant and animal tissues through light microscopes. Light microscopes magnify only large cell structures, not tiny structures. The tiny cell structures can be seen only when viewed through an electron microscope. Users of electron microscopes need special training and extensive practice before they become **electron microscopists.** Once their skill is developed, they can use the electron microscope to bring objects as small as bacteria, viruses, or even atoms into focus.

Electron micrographs are photographs of specimens seen through the electron micro-

scope. By studying these photographs, research scientists learn more about the normal activities of cells. Human tissue micrographs help doctors diagnose patients.

Electron microscopists work in hospitals, universities, and research laboratories. If you wish to know more about a career in electron microscopy, write to the National Society for Histotechnology, P.O. Box 36, Lanham, MD 20706.

image. Biologists use electron microscopes to study such things as viruses and parts of cells.

Lasers

A simple microscope uses light and lenses to magnify an image. The laser uses light in an entirely different way than a microscope does. A laser produces a narrow, intense beam of light. Lasers have many biological uses. A laser beam can be a surgeon's "light scalpel," cutting and sealing off blood vessels. Lasers can also be used to destroy clumps of cancer cells.

Computers

Computers are electronic devices that collect, analyze, display, and store data. They have a wide range of uses in the biological sciences. In medicine, for example, computers help doctors diagnose diseases and prescribe treatments. Computers also help researchers gather information about the structure and function of cells and the activities of all living things.

Seeing Through Barriers

In order for scientists to learn more about living things, they must be able to view the inside of organisms *from the outside*. Certain tools make this investigation possible.

X-RAYS   Invisible radiations known as X-rays have been used by scientists for almost one hundred years. X-rays easily pass through barriers such as skin and muscle but tend to be blocked by more dense materials such as bone. The result is a picture of the interior of an object. X-rays are most useful for taking pictures of bones inside an organism.

CAT   A relatively new technique, Computerized Axial Tomography scanning, or CAT scan, provides a two-dimensional picture of an object. A beam of radiation may take as many as 720 separate exposures of the object. A computer then constructs a picture by combining and analyzing each exposure. CAT scans are used to produce pictures of the head and other body parts.

Figure 1-10   *Lasers produce a narrow, concentrated beam of light that can be used in medicine to cut through, destroy, or repair damaged tissue.*

Figure 1-11   *Top view of computer-generated image of a DNA molecule.*

Figure 1-12 *This image of a person's head (left) was produced by CAT scanning. NMR images (right) help scientists study the internal structure of body parts.*

NMR Another tool for seeing and studying the inside of objects is Nuclear Magnetic Resonance, or NMR. This tool uses magnetism and radio waves to produce images. With no apparent harmful effects on living tissue, NMR promises to be a valuable tool for studying the structure of body cells and how they function.

SECTION REVIEW

1. Explain the difference between the compound light microscope and the electron microscope.
2. Name three other tools of the scientist and briefly explain their uses.

1. One uses light to magnify the object, the other uses beams of electrons.
2. Lasers: to repair or destroy damaged tissue; computers: to collect, analyze, display, and store data; X-rays, CAT, NMR scans: to observe internal structures

1-4 Science and Discovery

Scientific discoveries are not always made by following a scientific method. Sometimes a discovery is made because of luck, a hunch, or because a scientist has found a new way of looking at a problem.

Recently, two American biologists Dr. Patricia Bonamo and Dr. James Grierson discovered a special group of fossils. While looking for extinct plant specimens in rocks from northern New York, these scientists found something different and unexpected. Instead of plant fossils, the scientists discovered fossils of some of the first land animals.

Fossilized centipedes, shells and claws of spiderlike creatures, and a single mite were discovered.

There was much that was amazing about this discovery. The centipede, only about 2.54 centimeters long, had its many pairs of legs well preserved. The sense organs of several of the spiderlike creatures were easily recognizable.

Scientists described the fossils as looking as though "they might have died yesterday." But these organisms had not died "yesterday," and that was the most amazing discovery of all. Tests showed that the animals had died about 380 million years ago! Until this discovery, the earliest totally land-living animals ever discovered had been 300 million years old. Drs. Bonamo and Grierson had turned back the birthday of such animals by 80 million years.

"When we first saw the animals in our samples, we thought they might have fallen in by accident, from the light fixtures or cracks in the wall. But one spiderlike animal had its legs still embedded in the rock." This statement by Drs. Bonamo and Grierson shows how their fossil discovery was an exciting piece of good luck. But it is also an example of scientists recognizing something special when they see it.

SECTION REVIEW

1. What does this fossil discovery indicate about the appearance of land-living animals?
2. In what way was this fossil discovery a combination of accident and scientific method?

1. They date back at least 380 million years.
2. Accident: scientists were looking for plant fossils; scientific method: scientists recognized what was present and made hypotheses, observations, conclusions

Activity

A Lucky Find

Write five sentences that help describe the discovery made by Drs. Bonamo and Grierson. In each sentence, use one of the following words.

botany
data
hypothesis
metric system
scientific method

LABORATORY ACTIVITY

For further instructions, see page T-19.

A Moldy Question

Purpose

In this activity, you will investigate variables that may affect the growth of bread mold.

Materials *(per group)*
2 jars with lids
2 slices of bread
1 medicine dropper

Procedure

1. Put half a slice of bread into each of two jars. Moisten each half slice with ten drops of water. Cap the jars tightly. Keep one jar in sunlight and place the other in a dark closet.

Medicine dropper

Water

Jar 1
(in sunlight)

Bread

Jar 2
(in darkness)

2. Observe the jars every few days for about two weeks. Record your observations. Does light seem to influence mold growth?

3. Ask your teacher what scientists know about the effect of light on mold growth. Was your conclusion correct? Think again. What other conditions might have affected mold growth?

4. Did you think of temperature? How about moisture? Light, temperature, and moisture are all possible variables in this activity. Design a second experiment to retest the effect of light on mold growth—or to test one of the other variables. Test only one variable at a time. Other groups of students will test the other two variables. Then you can pool your results and draw your conclusions together.

Observations and Conclusions

1. In your second experiment, what variable were you testing? Did you have a control for your experiment? If so, describe it.

2. Study the class data for this experiment. What variables seem to affect mold growth?

3. Cathy set up the following experiment: She placed a piece of orange peel in each of two jars. She added 3 milliliters of water to jar 1 and placed it in the refrigerator. She added no water to jar 2 and placed it on a windowsill in the kitchen. At the end of a week, she noticed more mold growth in jar 2. Cathy concluded that light, a warm temperature, and no moisture are ideal conditions for mold growth. Discuss the accuracy of Cathy's conclusion.

CHAPTER SUMMARY

1-1 What Is Science?

■ A scientific method is a process scientists use to discover facts and truths about nature.

■ The basic steps of any scientific method are stating the problem, gathering information, forming a hypothesis, experimenting, recording and analyzing data, and stating a conclusion.

■ An experiment should have only one variable, or factor being tested, and a control, or the same experiment without the variable.

■ The three main branches of science are life science, earth science, and physical science.

1-2 Scientific Measurements

■ The metric system is the system of measurement used in science.

■ The meter is the basic unit of length in the metric system.

■ The liter is the basic unit of volume in the metric system.

■ The kilogram is the basic unit of mass in the metric system.

■ Mass is a measure of the amount of matter in an object. Weight is a measure of the attraction between objects due to gravity.

■ Density is the measurement of the amount of mass that is contained in a given volume of an object.

■ The Celsius temperature scale has 100 degrees between the freezing and boiling points of water.

1-3 Tools of a Scientist

■ The compound light microscope and the electron microscope magnify small objects and produce enlarged images of them.

■ Lasers and computers have important applications in biology.

■ X-rays, CAT, and NMR can provide pictures of internal body structures.

1-4 Science and Discovery

■ Sometimes luck or a hunch, combined with observation and thought, can lead to a scientific discovery.

VOCABULARY   *Define the following terms.*

astronomy p.19
botany p.19
Celsius p.24
chemistry p.19
compound light microscope p.26
control p.18
data p.18
density p.23
electron microscope p.26
gravity p.22

hypothesis p.16
kilogram p.22
lens p.26
liter p.22
mass p.22
meter p.21
metric system p.20
microscope p.24
physics p.19
scientific method p.15

variable p.17
weight p.22
zoology p.19

CHAPTER REVIEW

Multiple Choice

Choose the letter of the answer that best completes each statement.

1. The branch of physical science that deals with the composition of substances, their changes and combinations is
   a. astronomy.
   b. chemistry.
   c. physics.
   d. botany.

2. The basic unit of length is the
   a. liter.
   b. gram.
   c. meter.
   d. kilogram.

3. One kilometer is equal to
   a. 1000 meters.
   b. 1/1000 meter.
   c. 100 meters.
   d. 10 meters.

4. One centimeter is equal to
   a. 100 meters.
   b. 1/100 meter.
   c. 10 meters.
   d. 1000 meters.

5. The liter is the basic unit of
   a. volume.
   b. mass.
   c. weight.
   d. density.

6. The basic unit of mass is the
   a. liter.
   b. gram.
   c. kilogram.
   d. meter.

7. The amount of mass contained in a given volume of an object is called
   a. gravity.
   b. temperature.
   c. area.
   d. density.

8. The freezing point of water is
   a. 32° C.
   b. 0° C.
   c. 100° C.
   d. 212° C.

9. A device doctors can use to perform surgery is the
   a. X-ray.
   b. CAT scan.
   c. NMR.
   d. laser.

10. Fossils of animals and plants provide evidence about
   a. rock formations.
   b. oceans.
   c. the history of life on the earth.
   d. Scotland.

Completions

Fill in the word or words that best complete each statement.

1. A suggested solution to a problem usually based on information related to the problem is called a(n) _____hypothesis_____.

2. The factor being tested in an experiment is the _____variable_____.

3. The branch of earth science that includes the study of stars, planets, and moons is _____astronomy_____.

4. The _____metric_____ system is the system of measurement used in science.

5. The prefix _____milli-_____ means 1/1000.

6. One meter is equal to _____100_____ centimeters.

7. _____Mass_____ is a measure of the amount of matter in an object.

8. Water boils at _____100_____ ° C.

9. A(n) _____microscope_____ is an instrument that magnifies an object and produces an enlarged image of it.

10. A narrow beam of intense light is produced by a(n) _____laser_____.

True or False

Determine whether each statement is true or false. If it is true, write "true."
If it is false, change the underlined word or words to make the statement true.

1. The process used by scientists to discover facts and truths about nature is called a <u>scientific method</u>. T

2. Recorded observations that often involve measurements are called <u>conclusions</u>. F (data)

3. The <u>control</u> experiment is the experiment without the variable. T

4. <u>Botany</u> is the study of animals. F (Zoology)

5. The prefix <u>kilo-</u> means 1000. T

6. The basic unit of volume is the <u>meter</u>. F (liter)

7. The force of attraction between objects is called <u>gravity</u>. T

8. Your <u>weight</u> on the moon would be the same <u>as</u> it is on the earth. F (mass)

9. A <u>mirror</u> is a curved piece of glass that bends light rays as they pass through it. *

10. A <u>magnifying glass</u> is an example of a simple microscope. T

* F (lens)

Discussion Topics Answers appear on page T-19.

Write a brief paragraph discussing each of the following.

1. Describe briefly the basic steps of a scientific method.

2. Explain the difference between mass and weight.

3. Discuss the difference between a compound light microscope and an electron microscope.

4. Describe how lasers and computers are being used in biology.

5. Discuss the role of chance or luck in making a scientific discovery.

EXPAND YOUR KNOWLEDGE

Land, B. *The New Explorers: Women in Antarctica.* New York: Dodd, Mead.
> The experiences of over 15 women scientists doing research in Antarctica in areas ranging from biochemistry to volcanology are highlighted.

National Geographic Society. *Hidden Worlds.* Washington, D.C.: National Geographic Society.
> Using striking photographs, this book spurs the reader's imagination by illustrating how modern imaging techniques reveal the otherwise invisible world around us.

Smith, N. F. *How Fast Do Your Oysters Grow? Investigate and Discover Through Science Projects.* New York: Messner.
> An introduction to investigation, discovery, and scientific method through excellent explanations and illustrations.

2 The Nature of Life

For a chapter overview, teaching strategies, answers to all activities, a list of A-V materials, and a chapter bibliography, see pages T-20 to T-22.

Consult your Teacher's Resource Book and Annotated Teacher's Edition, Laboratory Book for additional activities and teaching aids.

CHAPTER OBJECTIVES

After completing this chapter, you will be able to:

2-1 Discuss the basic characteristics of all living things.

2-1 Describe metabolism and the activities involved in metabolism.

2-2 Discuss the basic needs of all living things.

2-3 Distinguish between elements and compounds.

2-3 Describe the organic compounds that are the building blocks of life.

Slowly, the scientist fills the clear glass flask. First he pours in three colorless gases. The odor is awful—a combination of rotten eggs and swamp gas that stings the scientist's nose and brings tears to his eyes. Now the scientist adds two more gases. Nothing seems to happen. The flask looks empty. But the gases it contains may be changed into something very special, if everything goes right!

The mixture needs a spark to produce the necessary change. The scientist sends a surge of electricity through the flask again and again. Suddenly, a sticky brown coating begins to form on the walls of the flask. The mixture of gases inside is changing—turning into substances that scientists believe may help them solve a key mystery of life.

Magic? It may seem to be, and at times the scientist may seem to be a magician. But this exciting experiment was actually performed, and its results are being used by scientists today as they attempt to study the "stuff of life."

In 1952, the American scientist Stanley Miller mixed together three foul-smelling gases: hydrogen sulfide, methane, and ammonia. To this mixture he added hydrogen, a colorless, odorless gas, and gaseous water. Then he passed an electric current through the colorless mixture. Soon a brown tarlike substance streaked the sides of the container. Dr. Miller analyzed the tarlike substance and found that it contained several of the same substances that make up all living things. From nonliving chemicals, Stanley Miller had made some of the building blocks of life.

Primitive Earth, on which life evolved

Figure 2-1 *A great variety of animals and plants inhabit the earth. The llama (top, left)* may not be as familiar to you as the lovely crocus *(bottom, left).* The baobab tree (top, right) *and the aardvark (bottom, right)* may also be unfamiliar. Yet all are made up of the same basic elements.

2-1 Characteristics of Living Things

Whether you live in the city or in the country, even the shortest walk will show you that there is an enormous variety of living things on the earth. In fact, scientists estimate that there are more than five million different types of plants and animals, ranging from one-celled bacteria to huge blue whales. Yet all living things are composed almost entirely of the same basic elements: carbon, hydrogen, nitrogen, and oxygen. These elements make up the gases Miller placed in his glass flask. These four elements along with iron, calcium, phosphorus, and sulfur all link together in chains, rings, and loops to form the stuff of life.

Well-known chemical rules govern the way these elements combine and interact. But less well understood is what gives this collection of chemicals a very special property—the property of life.

Life from Life

People did not always understand that living matter is so special. Until the 1600s, many people believed in the theory of **spontaneous generation.** According to this theory, life could spring from non-living matter. For example, people believed that mice came from straw and frogs and turtles developed from rotting wood and mud at the bottom of a pond.

In 1668, an Italian doctor named Francesco Redi disproved this theory. In those days, maggots, a wormlike stage in the life cycle of a fly, often appeared on decaying meat. People believed that the rotten meat had actually turned into maggots, and that flies formed from dead animals. In a series of experiments, Redi proved that the maggots hatched from eggs laid by flies. Today there is no doubt that living things can arise *only* from other living things.

Now let's look at some of the characteristics that make living things special. These characteristics distinguish even the smallest organism from a lifeless streak of brown tar on a laboratory flask.

Activity

Disproving Spontaneous Generation

Redi's conclusions were not well accepted. The controversy over the theory of spontaneous generation continued for many years. Each of the men listed below was involved in either proving or disproving the theory. Using books and reference materials in the library, find out what contribution each man made to a better understanding of living things.

John Needham

Lazzaro Spallanzani

Louis Pasteur

Figure 2-2 *Redi's experiment helped disprove spontaneous generation. No maggots were found on the meat in jars covered with netting or tightly sealed. Maggots appeared on the meat only when flies were able to enter the jars and lay eggs.*

Open jars   Tightly sealed jars   Jars covered with cloth netting

Figure 2-3 *The arctic tern* (left) *survives by commuting between the Arctic and the Antarctic. The larval crab* (right) *gets around by hitching a ride on a jellyfish.*

Movement

The arctic tern is a small, gull-like bird that at first glance may not appear to be a record breaker. See Figure 2-3. Yet for seven months of every year, the arctic tern is in flight, covering a distance of nearly 32,000 kilometers. The tern begins its journey near the Arctic, travels south to its winter quarters in the Antarctic, and then flies back north again. Its yearly trip gives the tern the "long-distance record" for birds in flight. An ability to move through the environment is an important characteristic of many living things.

Animals must be able to move in order to find food and shelter. In times of danger, swift movement can be the difference between safety and death. Of course, animals move in a great many ways. Fins enable fish such as salmon to swim hundreds of kilometers in search of a place to mate. The kangaroo uses its entire body as a giant pogo stick to bounce along the Australian plains looking for scarce patches of grass upon which to graze.

Most plants do not move in the same way animals do. Only parts of the plants move. The stems of the common houseplant *Pothos* bend toward the sunlight coming through windows. Its leaves turn to catch the sun's rays.

Metabolism

Building up and breaking down is a good way to describe the chemical activities that are essential to life. During some of these activities, simple substances combine to form complex substances. These substances are needed for growth, to store energy, and to repair or to replace living materials. During other activities, complex substances are broken down, releasing energy and usable food substances. Together, these chemical activities in an organism are called **metabolism** (muh-TA-buh-li-zuhm). Metabolism, then, is another characteristic of living things.

Metabolism includes many chemical reactions that go on in the body of a living thing. However, metabolism usually begins with eating.

INGESTION All living things must either take in food or produce their own food. For most animals, **ingestion,** or eating, is as simple as putting food into their mouths. But some organisms, such as worms that live inside animals, absorb food directly through their skin.

Green plants do not have to ingest food because they make it. Using their roots, green plants absorb water and minerals from the soil. Tiny openings in the underside of their leaves allow carbon dioxide to enter. The green plants use the water and carbon dioxide, along with energy from the sun, to make food.

DIGESTION Getting food into the body is the first step in metabolism, but there is a lot more to metabolism than just eating. The food must be digested in order to be used. **Digestion** is the process by which food is broken down into simpler substances. Later, some of these simpler substances are reassembled into more complex materials for use in the growth and repair of the living thing. Other simple substances store energy that the organism will use for its many activities.

RESPIRATION Organisms combine oxygen with the products of digestion to produce energy. The energy is used to do all the work of the organism. The process by which living things take in oxygen and use it to produce energy is called **respiration.**

Figure 2-4 *Until baby thrushes are old enough to fly, they must rely on their mother for food.*

Figure 2-5 *A cougar (left) could not run very fast without the energy produced during respiration. Dolphins (right) also need oxygen for respiration, so they continually surface for breaths of air.*

Land animals like yourself have lungs that remove oxygen from the air. Most sea animals have gills that absorb oxygen dissolved in water. Some sea animals, however, come to the surface to breathe with their lungs. Whales, porpoises, and dolphins are examples of air-breathing sea animals. Some of these animals can remain under water for as long as 120 minutes!

Plants, too, need oxygen to stay alive. Most plants absorb oxygen through tiny pores in their leaves. Plants use oxygen for respiration, as do almost all living things. For respiration is the main process that provides energy necessary to living things. You get this energy by combining the foods you eat with the oxygen you breathe. The amount of energy a food can supply is measured in units called Calories.

EXCRETION Not all the products of digestion and respiration can be used by the organism. Some products are waste materials that must be released. The process of getting rid of waste materials is called **excretion.** If waste products are not removed, they will eventually poison the organism.

Growth and Development

Standing under a giant oak tree, you might marvel at the fact that it grew from a tiny acorn. Within that acorn, metabolic activity produced a supply of energy from stored food. The acorn used this energy to begin to grow into a tree. Without the energy of metabolism, no living thing can grow. And growth is one of the characteristics of living things.

Figure 2-6 *A tiger swallowtail caterpillar* (left) *will grow and develop into an adult butterfly* (right).

But growing things do more than just increase in size. They also develop and become more complex. Sometimes this development results in dramatic changes. A tadpole, for example, swims for weeks in a summer pond. However, one day that tadpole becomes the frog that sits near the water's edge. And surely the caterpillar creeping through a garden gives little hint of the beautiful butterfly it will soon become. Certainly development must be added to your list of the characteristics of living things.

Different organisms grow at different rates. A person will grow from a newborn baby to an adult in about 18 years. But puppies become adult dogs in only a few years. And a lima bean seed becomes a bean plant in just a few weeks. Some living things, such as certain insects, can change from an egg to an adult within a few days.

Life Span

One of the important characteristics of living things is **life span,** or the maximum length of time a particular organism can be expected to live. Life span varies greatly from one type of organism to another. For example, an elephant lives for about 60 or 70 years. A bristlecone pine tree may live to be 5500 years old!

In certain organisms, growth and development take up most of the life span. The mayfly, for example, spends two years in lakes or ponds growing and

Figure 2-7

MAXIMUM LIFE SPANS	
Organism	**Life Span**
Adult mayfly	1 day
Marigold	8 months
Mouse	1–2 years
Dog	13 years
Horse	20–30 years
Alligator	56 years
Asiatic elephant	78 years
Blue whale	100 years
Human	117 years
Tortoise	152 years
Bristlecone pine	5500 years

Figure 2-8 *The adult mayfly* (left) *lives for only about one day. The bristlecone pine* (right) *has a life span of about 5500 years.*

Figure 2-9 *Even if they must swim thousands of kilometers, most salmon return to the same stream in which they were hatched to lay their eggs.*

developing into an adult. However, the adult lives for only about one day. It finds a mate and starts a new family of mayflies. Then it dies.

Response

When the alarm clock rings in the morning, you wake up. The smell of eggs and toast makes your mouth water as you hurry to breakfast. On your way to school, you stop at a red light. In just a matter of several hours, you have reacted to signals in your surroundings that determine much of your behavior.

Scientists call each of the signals to which an organism reacts a **stimulus.** A stimulus is any change in the environment, or surroundings, of an organism that produces a **response.** A response is some action or movement of the organism.

Some stimuli come from outside the organism's body. For example, smells and noises are stimuli to which you respond. So is tickling. Light and water are stimuli to which plants respond. Other stimuli come from inside an organism's body. A lack of oxygen in your body is a stimulus that often causes you to yawn.

Some plants have special responses that protect them. For example, when a gypsy moth caterpillar chews on the leaf of an oak tree, the tree responds by producing bad-tasting chemicals in its other leaves. The chemicals discourage all but the hungriest caterpillars from eating these leaves. Can you think of responses that help you protect yourself?

Blinking, flinching, running, coughing, or sneezing

Reproduction

You probably know that dinosaurs that lived 230 million years ago are now extinct. Yet crocodiles, which appeared before dinosaurs, are still living today. An organism becomes extinct when it no longer produces other organisms of the same kind. In other words, all living things of a given kind would become extinct if they did not reproduce.

The process by which living things give rise to the same type of living thing is **reproduction.** Crocodiles, for example, do not produce dinosaurs. Crocodiles only produce more crocodiles. You are a human, and not a water buffalo, a duck, or a tomato plant, because your parents are human. An easy way to remember this is *like produces like.*

There are two different types of reproduction: **sexual reproduction** and **asexual reproduction.** Sexual reproduction usually requires two parents. Most higher forms of plants and animals reproduce sexually.

Some living things reproduce from only one parent. This is asexual reproduction. This type of reproduction can be as simple as an organism dividing into two parts. Bacteria reproduce this way. Yeast form growths called buds, which break off and then form new yeast plants. Geraniums and African violets can grow new plants from part of a stem, root, or leaf of the parent plant. All of these examples demonstrate asexual reproduction.

Sexual and asexual reproduction have an important function in common. In each case, the offspring receive a set of very special chemical "blueprints," or plans. These blueprints determine the characteristics of that type of living thing and are passed from one generation to the next.

Figure 2-10 *Strawberries reproduce asexually when their stems produce bundles of roots, each of which forms a new plant.*

Activity

Observing Stimulus-Response Reactions

Listed below are a few stimuli that produce responses known as reflexes. Observe your reaction, or that of your classmates or family members, to each stimulus.

1. Hold your hands close to a friend's face. Quickly clap your hands. Watch your friend's eyes as you do this. What happens?

2. Cover one of your eyes for a minute. Then remove your hand and at once look in a mirror. Describe the changes in your eye.

3. While looking in a mirror, shine a flashlight into your eyes. What happens to the size of your pupils?

4. Cut a slice of lemon. Bring it close to your mouth or, if you choose, put it in your mouth. What is your reaction?

SECTION REVIEW

1. What is the theory of spontaneous generation, and what did Redi's experiments reveal about the theory? 1. That life could spring from nonlife; that it was false

2. What is metabolism? What are some processes that are part of metabolism?

3. What are the six basic characteristics of living things?

2. Chemical building-up and breaking-down activities in an organism; ingestion, digestion, respiration, excretion

3. Movement, metabolism, growth and development, life span, response, reproduction

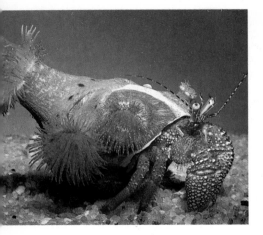

Figure 2-11 *This empty shell is home to a hermit crab, as well as to the sea anemones growing on the shell.*

2-2 Needs of Living Things

Living things do not live in a vacuum. They interact with one another and with their environment. Of course, these interactions are as varied as are the living things themselves. Birds, for example, use dead twigs to build nests, but they eat live worms and insects. Crayfish build their homes in the sand or mud of streams and swamps. They absorb a chemical called lime from these waters to build a hard body covering. Crayfish rely, however, on living snails and tadpoles for their food. And some people rely on crayfishes for a tasty meal!

It seems clear, then, that living things depend on both the living and nonliving parts of their environment. In order for a living organism to survive, the environment must supply all of the organism's many needs.

Energy

All living things need energy. The energy can be used in different ways. A lion uses energy to chase and capture its prey. The electric eel defends itself by shocking its attackers with electric energy.

What is the source of this energy so necessary to living things? The primary source of energy for most living things is the sun. Plants use the sun's light energy to make food. Some animals feed on plants and in that way obtain the energy stored in the plants. Other animals may then eat the plant eaters. In this way, the energy from the sun is passed on from one living thing to another.

Figure 2-12 *These glowworm larvae (left) use energy to produce light. The original source of energy for all living things, worms as well as grasses, is the sun (right).*

Figure 2-13 *Many animals and plants have unusual ways of obtaining food. The woodpecker finch (left)* uses a twig to get at insects in the bark of trees. The *Venus' flytrap snares a grasshopper with special leaves (right).*

Food and Water

Have you ever heard the saying "You are what you eat"? Certainly this saying does not mean you will become a carrot or a hamburger if you eat these foods. But it does tell you that what you eat is very important. Food is a need of living things.

FOOD The kind of food organisms eat varies considerably. You would probably not want to eat eucalyptus leaves, yet that is the only food a koala eats. A diet of wood may not seem tempting, but for the termite it is a source of energy and necessary chemical substances. And surely a green plant's diet of simple sugar would not suit your taste.

Although all plants and animals must obtain food to live, some do it in very unusual ways. For example, the Venus' flytrap has special leaves that attract insects. When an insect lands on these leaves, they immediately close and trap the insect. Then the plant slowly digests the insect.

WATER Although you would probably not enjoy it, you could live a week or more without food. But you would die in a few days without water. It may surprise you to learn that 65 percent or more of your body is water. Other living things are also made up mainly of water.

Aside from making up much of your body, water serves many other purposes. Most substances dissolve in water. In this way, important chemicals can be transported easily throughout an organism. The blood of animals and the sap of trees, for example, are mainly water.

Activity

Body Water

About 65% of your body mass is water. Using your mass in kilograms, determine how much water you contain.

Most chemical reactions in living things cannot take place without water. Metabolism would come to a grinding halt without water. And it is water that carries away many of the metabolic waste products produced by living things. For green plants, water is also a raw material needed to make food.

Air

You already know that oxygen is necessary for the process of respiration. Most living things get oxygen directly from the air or from air that has dissolved in water. When you breathe out, you release the waste gas called carbon dioxide. However, this gas is not wasted. The green plants around you use carbon dioxide in the air to make food.

Living Space

Do you enjoy hearing the chirping of birds on a lovely spring morning? Surprisingly, the birds are not simply singing. Rather, they are staking out their territory and warning intruders to stay away.

Often there is only a limited amount of food, water, and energy in an environment. As a result, only a limited number of the same kind of living thing can survive there. That is why many animals defend a certain area that they consider to be their living

Most of the earth's atmosphere is made up of the gas nitrogen. But few living things can use this gas. However, certain microscopic organisms living in the nodules of plant roots can convert nitrogen in the air into nitrogen compounds that help plants grow.

Figure 2-14 *Here two bighorn sheep are engaged in battle.*

space. The male sunfish, for example, defends its territory in ponds by flashing its colorful fins at other sunfish and darting toward any sunfish that comes too close. You might think of this behavior as a kind of **competition** for living space.

Competition is the struggle among living things to get the proper amount of food, water, and energy. Animals are not the only competitors. Plants compete for sunlight and water. Smaller, weaker plants often die in the shadow of larger plants.

Proper Temperature

During the summer, temperatures as high as 58°C have been recorded on the earth. Winter temperatures can dip as low as −89°C. Most organisms cannot survive at such temperature extremes because many metabolic activities cannot occur at these temperatures. Without metabolism, an organism dies.

Actually, most organisms would quickly die at far less severe temperature extremes if it were not for **homeostasis** (ho-mee-o-STAY-sis). Homeostasis is the ability of an organism to keep conditions inside its body the same even though conditions in its external environment change. Maintaining a constant body temperature, no matter what the temperature of the surroundings, is part of homeostasis. Birds and certain other animals, such as dogs and horses, produce enough heat to keep themselves warm at low temperatures. Trapped air in the feathers of birds keeps

Activity

Temperature Range

Calculate the range in temperature between this highest recorded temperature, 58°C, and this lowest, −89°C.

Figure 2-15 *Coldblooded turtles* (left) *must absorb the sun's heat to keep warm. Flowers such as these coltsfoots* (right) *can grow in extremely cold conditions.*

You may wish to summarize this section by having students use their knowledge of the five basic needs of living things to determine whether they could live on Mars.

Activity

Swamp Story

Using at least five of the following vocabulary words, write a 200-word story about animal life in a swamp.

coldblooded
competition
homeostasis
life span
metabolism
stimulus
response
warmblooded

them cool when temperatures get too high. Panting and sweating do the same for dogs and horses. Animals that maintain a constant body temperature are called warmblooded animals. Warmblooded animals can be active during both day and night, in hot weather and in cold.

Animals such as reptiles and fish have body temperatures that can change somewhat with changes in the temperature of the environment. These animals are called coldblooded animals. To keep warm, a coldblooded reptile, such as a crocodile, must spend part of each day lying in the sun. At night, when the air temperature drops, so does the crocodile's body temperature. The crocodile becomes lazy and inactive. Coldblooded animals do not move around much at relatively high or low temperatures.

SECTION REVIEW

1. Name five basic needs of living things.
2. What is the relationship between the sun and the energy needed by all living things?
3. What is the difference between warmblooded organisms and coldblooded organisms? 1. Energy, food, water, air, living space, proper temperature 2. The sun is the primary source of this energy.
3. Warmblooded: maintain constant body temperature; coldblooded: body temperature varies with temperature of environment

2-3   Chemistry of Living Things

What do a diamond, foil wrap, and a light bulb filament have in common? These objects look very different and certainly have very different uses, but all are examples of **elements.** An element is a pure substance that cannot be broken down into any simpler substances by ordinary means. A diamond is the element carbon. Foil wrap is the element aluminum. And the light bulb filament is the element tungsten. Carbon, oxygen, hydrogen, nitrogen, copper, gold, and sulfur are elements.

When two or more elements are chemically joined together, **compounds** are formed. Water is a compound made up of the elements hydrogen and oxygen. Table salt, which you probably use to flavor your food, is a compound made up of sodium and chlorine. Sand and glass are compounds composed of the elements silicon and oxygen. There are thousands of different compounds all around you. In fact, you are made up of many compounds. Scientists classify compounds in two groups.

Inorganic Compounds

Compounds that may or may not contain the element carbon are called **inorganic compounds.** Most inorganic compounds do not contain carbon. However, carbon dioxide is an exception. Table salt, ammonia, rust, and water are examples of inorganic compounds.

Organic Compounds

Many compounds contain carbon, which is usually combined with other elements such as hydrogen and oxygen. These compounds are called **organic compounds.** There are more than three million different organic compounds. Some of these compounds are the basic building blocks of life. They include families of compounds such as carbohydrates, fats and oils, proteins, enzymes, and nucleic acids.

CARBOHYDRATES The main source of energy for living things is **carbohydrates.** Carbohydrates are made up of the elements carbon, hydrogen, and oxygen. Sugar and starch are two important carbohydrates. Fruit and candy contain sugar. Potatoes, rice, noodles, and bread are sources of starch. What are some foods that you eat that contain sugar and starch? Answers will include various kinds of fruits and candies, as well as potatoes and breads.

All carbohydrates are broken down inside the body into a simple sugar called **glucose.** The body then uses glucose to produce the energy needed for life activities. If an organism has more sugar than it needs for its energy requirements, it will store the sugar for later use. The sugar is stored as starch. Starch is a stored form of energy.

FATS AND OILS Energy-rich organic compounds made up of carbon, hydrogen, and oxygen are **fats** and **oils.** Fats are solid at room temperature; oils are liquid at room temperature.

Figure 2-16 *The active element sodium* (top) *combines chemically with poisonous chlorine gas* (center) *to form crystals of ordinary table salt* (bottom).

Figure 2-17 *The foods on this picnic table provide the organic compounds that are the basic building blocks of life.*

Fats can provide twice as much energy as carbohydrates. Foods high in fat, such as butter, cheese, milk, nuts, and some meats, should be included in your diet, but not to excess. Fats are stored by the body as body fat. And although this stored fat helps keep you warm, protects your internal organs from injury, and gives you energy, it can make you overweight.

PROTEINS Like carbohydrates and fats, **proteins** are organic compounds made up of carbon, hydrogen, and oxygen. But proteins also contain the element nitrogen and sometimes the elements sulfur and phosphorus. Some important sources of proteins are eggs, meat, fish, beans, nuts, and poultry.

The building blocks of proteins are **amino acids.** There are about 20 different types of amino acids. But because amino acids combine in many ways, they form thousands of different proteins.

Career: *Enzymologist*

HELP WANTED: ENZYMOLOGIST Requires Ph.D. in biochemistry and experience in this field. Needed for research project. Will investigate the action of various poisons on enzymes found in living things.

Two young children enter the hospital emergency room sweating and complaining of headaches and nausea. They have eaten the pits of some purple berries they found growing in a field. Although the berries themselves were harmless, the pits contained poisonous chemicals called cyanides. Scientists know that in the body cyanides quickly combine with an important respiratory enzyme. When this enzyme is bonded with cyanide, the enzyme can no longer perform its normal, vital job. As a result, cells cannot use oxygen in the process of metabolism.

Scientists who do research into the action of enzymes are called **enzymologists.** They isolate, analyze, and identify enzymes. They determine the enzyme's effects on body functions. The human body contains more than one thousand different enzymes. Enzymologists know much about these enzymes.

Enzymes are now being used in the manufacture of detergents, bread, cheese, and coffee. Physicians use enzymes for cleaning wounds, dissolving blood clots, and treating certain diseases. Enzymologists are learning how enzymes can be helpful in cleaning up the environment.

Enzymologists can use their knowledge and skill in industry, in public and private research institutes, and in colleges and universities. To learn more about this career, write to the American Society of Biological Chemists, 9650 Rockville Pike, Bethesda, MD 20014.

Proteins perform many jobs for an organism. They are necessary for the growth and repair of body structures. Proteins are used to build body hair and muscle. Proteins provide energy. Some proteins, such as those in blood, carry oxygen throughout the body. Other proteins fight germs that invade the body. Still other proteins make chemical substances that start, stop, and regulate many important body activities.

ENZYMES A special type of protein that regulates chemical activities within the body is called an **enzyme.** Enzymes act as **catalysts.** A catalyst is a substance that speeds up or slows down chemical reactions, but is not itself changed by the reaction. Without enzymes, the chemical reactions of metabolism could not take place.

NUCLEIC ACIDS Do you remember the "blueprints" of life discussed earlier? These blueprints are organic chemicals called **nucleic acids.** Nucleic acids are very large compounds that store information that helps the body make the proteins it needs. The nucleic acids control the way the amino acids are put together so that the correct protein is formed. This process is similar to the way a carpenter uses a blueprint to build a house. Now you understand why nucleic acids are called the blueprints of life.

One nucleic acid is **DNA,** deoxyribonucleic acid. DNA stores the information needed to build a protein. DNA also carries "messages" about an organism that are passed from parent to offspring. Another nucleic acid, **RNA,** ribonucleic acid, "reads" the DNA messages and guides the protein-making process. Together, these two nucleic acids contain the information and carry out the steps that make each organism what it is.

SECTION REVIEW

1. What is the basic difference between inorganic and organic compounds? 1. All organic compounds contain carbon; most inorganic compounds do not.
2. Of what importance are carbohydrates, fats and oils, and proteins to living things?
3. What are two nucleic acids? What is the function of each of these nucleic acids? 2. Carbohydrates provide energy. Fats and oils also produce energy and provide warmth and protection. Proteins are used for growth and repair, to provide energy, and to regulate body activities. 3. DNA stores information needed to build proteins and carries "messages" that are passed from parent to offspring. RNA "reads" DNA messages and guides protein making.

Activity

A Healthful Diet

A balanced diet is designed to give you all the foods necessary for good health. Foods from each of the basic food groups should be included in a balanced diet.

Using books and reference materials in the library, find out what the basic food groups are and what foods are included in each group. Based on this information, prepare a sample diet for yourself. Compare this diet with the foods you actually eat. Determine how healthful your present diet is.

LABORATORY ACTIVITY

For further instructions, see page T-21.

You Are What You Eat

Purpose

In this activity, you will study your school's lunch menus for one week.

Materials *(per group)*

School lunch menus for the current week
Pencil
Paper
Reference book or textbook on foods
and nutrition

Procedure

1. Obtain a copy of your school's lunch menus for one week.
2. Make a table listing the four basic food groups: meat group, vegetable-fruit group, milk group, bread-cereal group. For each day of the week, place the items from the menu in the appropriate food group.

Meat Group	Vegetable-Fruit Group	Milk Group	Bread-Cereal Group
Hamburger			Roll

Carbohydrates	Fats	Proteins
Roll		Hamburger

3. Make a second table listing the three major nutrients: carbohydrates, fats, and proteins. List those foods containing large amounts of these nutrients under the proper heading.
4. On a third table, identify those foods that are plants or plant products and those that are animals or animal products.

Plants or Plant Products	Animals or Animal Products
Roll	Hamburger

Observations and Conclusions

1. Study the data you have collected and organized. What conclusions can you draw regarding your school's lunch program? Do the foods seem to represent a balanced diet? Do foods in certain categories appear much more often than foods in some other categories? What changes, if any, would you make in the menus?

CHAPTER SUMMARY

2-1 Characteristics of Living Things

■ The elements most abundant in living things are carbon, hydrogen, nitrogen, and oxygen.

■ Metabolism is the sum of all chemical activities essential to life. Ingestion, digestion, respiration, and excretion are metabolic activities that occur in all organisms.

■ Life span is the maximum length of time a particular organism can be expected to live.

■ A living thing reacts to a stimulus, which is a change in the environment, by producing a response.

■ Reproduction is the process by which organisms produce offspring.

2-2 Needs of Living Things

■ Living things need energy for metabolism. The primary source of energy for all living things is the sun.

■ All living things need food and water.

■ Oxygen in the air or dissolved in water is used by all organisms during respiration. Carbon dioxide is used by plants to make food.

■ Competition is a struggle for food, water, and energy. *Living space*

■ Homeostasis is the ability of an organism to keep conditions constant inside its body when the outside environment changes.

■ Warmblooded animals maintain a constant body temperature. Coldblooded animals have body temperatures that change with changes in the external temperature.

2-3 Chemistry of Living Things

■ Elements are pure substances that cannot be broken down by ordinary chemical means. Compounds are formed when two or more elements are chemically joined.

■ Most inorganic compounds do not contain the element carbon. Organic compounds do contain carbon. The organic compounds important to living things are carbohydrates, fats and oils, proteins, enzymes, and nucleic acids.

■ DNA and RNA are two important nucleic acids. They carry the information for and control the building of proteins that make each organism what it is.

VOCABULARY   *Define the following terms.*

amino acid p.50
asexual reproduction p.43
carbohydrate p.49
catalyst p.51
coldblooded p.48
competition p.47
compound p.48
digestion p.39
DNA p.51
element p.48
enzyme p.51

excretion p.40
fat p.49
glucose p.49
homeostasis p.47
ingestion p.39
inorganic compound p.49
life span p.41
metabolism p.39
nucleic acid p.51
oil p.49
organic compound p.49

protein p.50
reproduction p.43
respiration p.39
response p.42
RNA p.51
sexual reproduction p.43
spontaneous generation p.37
stimulus p.42
warmblooded p.48

CHAPTER REVIEW

Multiple Choice

Choose the letter of the answer that best completes each statement.

1. The theory that life could spring from non-living matter is called
   a. spontaneous respiration.
   b. spontaneous generation.
   c. asexual reproduction.
   d. homeostasis.

2. The building up and breaking down of chemical substances necessary for life is called
   a. reproduction.
   b. excretion.
   c. competition.
   d. metabolism.

3. The process of combining oxygen with the products of digestion to produce energy is called
   a. reproduction.
   b. ingestion.
   c. excretion.
   d. respiration.

4. Which of these organisms cannot produce offspring by asexual reproduction?
   a. yeast
   b. bacterium
   c. human being
   d. geranium plant

5. The gas in air used by plants to make food is
   a. oxygen.
   b. nitrogen.
   c. carbon dioxide.
   d. hydrogen.

6. The struggle among living things to obtain the resources needed to live is called
   a. competition.
   b. homeostasis.
   c. metabolism.
   d. spontaneous generation.

7. Which of these is a warmblooded animal?
   a. fish
   b. bird
   c. reptile
   d. crocodile

8. Which of these is an example of a substance made entirely of a single element?
   a. diamond
   b. table salt
   c. water
   d. glass

9. Carbohydrate is to glucose as
   a. fat is to oil.
   b. protein is to amino acid.
   c. DNA is to RNA.
   d. hydrogen is to oxygen.

10. The complex compound that carries the information needed to make protein from amino acids is
    a. carbohydrate.
    b. homeostasis.
    c. glucose.
    d. DNA.

Completions

Fill in the word or words that best complete each statement.

1. _____Metabolism_____ is the sum of all the chemical activities essential to life.

2. The process by which food is broken down into simpler substances is _____digestion_____.

3. The process by which living things produce offspring is called _____reproduction_____.

4. A response is the reaction of an organism to a(n) _____stimulus_____.

5. All organisms directly or indirectly receive energy from the _____sun_____.

6. The substance that makes up most living things and is necessary for metabolic reactions is _____water_____.

7. The ability of an organism to maintain a constant internal environment when external conditions change is called _____homeostasis_____.

8. A pure substance that cannot be broken down into simpler substances by ordinary chemical means is called a(n) _____element_____.

9. Most inorganic compounds do not contain the element _____carbon_____.

10. Because it can influence the rate of chemical reactions without itself changing, an enzyme is an example of a(n) _____catalyst_____.

True or False

*Determine whether each statement is true or false. If it is true, write "true."
If it is false, change the underlined word or words to make the statement true.*

1. Most forms of life are composed almost entirely of <u>carbon</u>, hydrogen, nitrogen, and oxygen. T

2. The theory of <u>spontaneous combustion</u> states that life can spring from nonliving matter. F (spontaneous generation)

3. The process by which an organism puts food into its body is <u>digestion</u>. F (ingestion)

4. Green plants use <u>carbon dioxide</u> and <u>water</u> to make food. T

5. The process of getting rid of waste material is called <u>reproduction</u>. F (excretion)

6. The maximum length of time a particular organism can be expected to live is called its <u>life span</u>. T

7. Animals that maintain a constant body temperature are <u>coldblooded</u> animals. *

8. Ammonia, carbon dioxide, and water are examples of <u>inorganic compounds</u>. T

9. Stored <u>fat</u> helps keep you warm and protects your internal organs from injury. T

10. <u>DNA and RNA</u> guide the protein-making process in living things. T

* F (warmblooded)

Discussion Topics   Answers appear on page T-21.

Write a brief paragraph discussing each of the following.

1. List and describe five characteristics of living things.

2. All plants and animals get energy from the sun. Explain how this can be.

EXPAND YOUR KNOWLEDGE

Adler, I. *How Life Began.* New York: John Day.
    This book explains how the organic compounds of living organisms may have developed from inorganic compounds and how simple chemicals become complex proteins.
Silver, D. *Life on Earth.* New York: Random House.
    This paperback, part of the *Library of Knowledge,* is a good general introduction to biology, as it clearly explains the various life functions.

Cells

For a chapter overview, teaching strategies, answers to all activities, a list of A-V materials, and a chapter bibliography, see pages T-22 to T-23.

Consult your Teacher's Resource Book and Annotated Teacher's Edition, Laboratory Book for additional activities and teaching aids.

CHAPTER OBJECTIVES

After completing this chapter, you will be able to:

3-1 Describe the structure and function of the living and non-living parts of a cell.

3-1 Distinguish between a plant cell and an animal cell.

3-2 Compare the processes of diffusion and osmosis.

3-2 Explain the importance of reproduction to a living organism.

3-2 Describe the processes of mitosis and meiosis.

When it first appeared on earth about 3.5 billion years ago, it was a tiny structure made up of tinier parts alive with activity. As the years passed, it changed a bit here and a bit there. New parts developed through unknown processes. And it became able to do increasingly different and fascinating jobs—it could build complex chemicals, it could release bursts of energy, and eventually it could even move by itself.

Millions of years later it would join not only with others of its kind, but with others not quite like it. Together they would form the most amazing inhabitants of the universe—living things with many harmonious parts, such as plants that grow from the soil and animals that race over it.

Today these tiny structures still exist. They are a bridge to the distant past. They are the building blocks of all living things. They are cells! Cells are fascinating and, in many ways, very mysterious objects. Scientists continue to probe the secrets of cells like explorers journeying through parts of an uncharted world.

Root tip cells magnified 125 times

3-1 Cell Structure and Function

You are about to take an imaginary journey. It will be quite an unusual trip because you will be traveling inside a living organism, visiting its tiny cells.

All living things are made up of one or more **cells,** which are the basic units of structure and function. Most cells are too small to be seen without the aid of a microscope. In fact, most cells are smaller than the period at the end of this sentence. Yet within these tiny cells are even smaller structures that carry out the activities of the cell. You may recall from Chapter 2 that these activities include storing and releasing energy, building and repairing cell parts, getting rid of waste materials, responding to the environment, and increasing in number.

There are many types of cells. For example, human cells include muscle cells, bone cells, and nerve cells. In plants, there are leaf cells, stem cells, and root cells. However, whether in an animal or a plant, most cells share certain similar characteristics. So hop aboard your imaginary ship and prepare to enter a

Figure 3-1 *A typical animal cell*

Nucleolus — Vacuole

Nucleus —

Cell membrane

Cell wall

Nuclear membrane —

Endoplasmic reticulum —

Ribosome —

Cytoplasm

Mitochondrion —

Chloroplasts

Figure 3-2 *A typical plant cell*

typical plant cell. You will begin by sailing up through the trunk of an oak tree. Your destination is that box-shaped structure directly ahead. See Figure 3-2.

Cell Wall

Entering the cell of an oak tree is a bit difficult. First you must pass through the **cell wall.** Strong and stiff, the cell wall is made of cellulose, a nonliving material. Cellulose is a long chain of sugar molecules that the cell manufactures. Although the cell wall is hard, it does allow water, oxygen, carbon dioxide, and certain dissolved materials to pass through it. So sail on through.

The rigid cell wall is found only in plant cells. This structure helps give protection and support so the oak tree can grow tall. Think for a moment of grasses and flowers that support themselves upright. No doubt you can appreciate the important role the cell wall plays for the individual cell and for the entire plant.

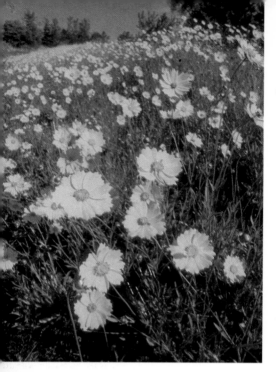

Figure 3-3 *The cell wall gives support and protection to plant cells, enabling grasses, flowering plants, and trees to grow upright.*

The outer covering of a plant cell, the cell wall, is not elastic and flexible as is the cell membrane. Thus, the cell does not change shape easily under pressure.

The cell membrane is made up of protein molecules scattered within and throughout a double layer of fat molecules. As these molecules move, they aid in the transport of materials through the membrane.

Activity

The Nature of Protoplasm

Protoplasm, the living material of the cell, is made up of many different elements and compounds. Using books and reference materials in the library, find out what substances make up protoplasm, how much of the protoplasm each substance represents, and some characteristics of each substance. Prepare your research in the form of a chart.

Cell Membrane

Once past the cell wall, you prepare to enter the living material of the cell. Biologists call all the living material in *both* plant and animal cells **protoplasm.** Protoplasm is not a single structure or substance. It is a term used to describe all the living materials in a cell.

The first structure of protoplasm you encounter is a thin, flexible envelope called the **cell membrane.** In a plant cell, the cell membrane is just inside the cell wall. In an animal cell, the cell membrane forms the outer covering of the cell. Look again at Figures 3-1 and 3-2.

The cell membrane has several important jobs. You can discover one of its jobs on your own. Push down on your skin with your thumb. Your skin does not break, does it? Now lift your thumb. The skin bounces back to its original position. Your skin can do this because the cell membrane around each skin cell is elastic and flexible. It allows the cell to change shape under pressure. The flexible cell membrane also keeps the protoplasm of the cell separated from the environment outside the cell.

As your ship nears the edge of the cell membrane, you notice that there are tiny openings in the membrane. You steer toward an opening. Suddenly, your ship narrowly misses being struck by a chunk of floating material passing out of the cell. You have discovered another job of the cell membrane. This membrane helps control the movement of materials into and out of the cell.

Everything that the cell needs, from food to oxygen, enters the cell through this membrane. And harmful waste products exit through the cell membrane. In this way, the cell stays in smooth-running order, keeping conditions inside the cell the same even though conditions outside the cell may change. This ability of a cell to maintain a stable internal environment is called homeostasis. Now sail on to an important structure inside the living cell.

Nucleus

A large oval structure comes into view just ahead of you. This structure is the control center of the cell—the **nucleus** (NOO-klee-uhs), which acts as the

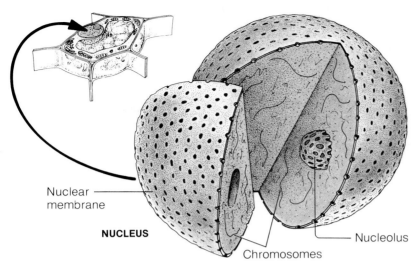

Nuclear membrane

NUCLEUS

Chromosomes

Nucleolus

Figure 3-4 *This nucleus of a typical cell* (left) *shows the nuclear membrane, chromosomes, and nucleolus. In this photograph of the nucleus* (right), *the arrows point to tiny pores in the nuclear membrane.*

"brain" of the cell. See Figure 3-4. The nucleus regulates all cell activities.

NUCLEAR MEMBRANE The thin membrane that separates the nucleus from the protoplasm of the cell is called the **nuclear membrane.** This membrane is similar to the cell membrane in that it allows materials to pass into and out of the nucleus. Small openings, or pores, are spaced regularly around the nuclear membrane. Each pore acts as a passageway into and out of the nucleus. Set your sights for that pore ahead and carefully glide into the nucleus.

CHROMOSOMES Those thick, rodlike objects floating in the nucleus are called **chromosomes.** Steer very carefully to avoid colliding with and damaging the delicate chromosomes. For the chromosomes direct the activities of the cell and pass on the traits of the cell to new cells.

The large, complex molecules that make up the chromosomes are compounds called nucleic acids. You may recall from Chapter 2 that nucleic acids store the information that helps a cell make the proteins it needs. And proteins are necessary for life. Some proteins, for example, are used to form structural parts of the cell such as the cell membrane. Other proteins make up different enzymes and hormones used inside and outside the cell. Enzymes and hormones regulate cell activities.

The two nucleic acids that make up the chromosomes are DNA and RNA. You can think of these nucleic acids as the "blueprints" of life. Working together, DNA and RNA store the information and carry out the steps in the protein-making process—a process necessary to life. The DNA remains in the nucleus. But the RNA, carrying its protein-building instructions, leaves the nucleus through a nuclear pore. So hitch a ride on the RNA leaving the nucleus and continue your exploration of the cell.

NUCLEOLUS As you prepare to leave the nucleus, you see a small, dense object float past. It is the **nucleolus** (noo-KLEE-uh-luhs), or "little nucleus." You are looking at a cell structure whose function remains something of a mystery. Biologists know that

Career: *Medical Artist*

HELP WANTED: MEDICAL ARTIST
Advanced degree in medical illustration required. College background in biology or zoology desirable. Needed to prepare accurate and creative drawings for medical textbooks.

Have you ever looked at a health book or a magazine about health that did not have diagrams? Probably not, because many concepts and objects related to health cannot be easily understood by reading only words. For example, cell structures and functions, body parts, and organism development can best be "described" through the use of drawings. Making such drawings is the job of a special group of artists.

Artists who create visual materials dealing with health and medicine are **medical artists.** Sometimes their work involves viewing a specimen through various kinds of microscopes in order to draw it. Or a medical artist may dissect and study the parts of animals and plants. Some medical artists work closely with surgeons or other kinds of doctors in order to pre-

pare accurate drawings of medical conditions.

Most medical artists are employed by publishers, medical, veterinary, or dental schools, or by hospitals with programs in teaching and research. To receive more information about this field, write to the Association of Medical Illustrators, Route 5, Box 311F, Midlothian, VA 23113.

the nucleolus is made up of RNA and protein. And they believe this tiny structure may play an important role in making proteins for the cell.

Endoplasmic Reticulum

Outside the nucleus, floating in a clear, thick fluid, your ship needs no propulsion. For here the jellylike material called **cytoplasm** is constantly moving. Cytoplasm is the term for all the protoplasm, or living material of the cell, *outside* the nucleus.

Steering will be a bit difficult here because many particles and tubelike structures are scattered throughout the cytoplasm. You cannot help noticing a maze of tubular passageways that leads out from the nuclear membrane. These clear tubes form the **endoplasmic reticulum** (en-doh-PLAZ-mik ri-TIK-yuh-luhm). See Figure 3-5.

The endoplasmic reticulum is involved in the manufacture and transport of proteins. You can see that it is well suited for its job. Its network of passageways spreads throughout the cell. Proteins made in one part of the cell can pass through the endoplasmic reticulum to other parts of the cell. Other materials can be transported to the outside of the cell through this system.

Figure 3-5 *The endoplasmic reticulum* (left) *manufactures and transports proteins. In this photograph of the endoplasmic reticulum* (right), *the dark dots lining the tubelike passageways are ribosomes.*

ENDOPLASMIC
RETICULUM

Ribosomes

Ribosomes

Look closely at the inner surface of one of the endoplasmic passageways. Attached to the surface are grainlike bodies called **ribosomes,** which are made up mainly of the nucleic acid RNA. Ribosomes are the protein-making sites of the cell. The RNA in the ribosomes, along with the RNA sent out from the nucleus, directs the production of proteins. Ribosomes are well positioned as they not only help make proteins, they "drop" them directly into the endoplasmic reticulum. From there the proteins go to any part of the cell that needs them.

Not all ribosomes are attached to the endoplasmic reticulum. Some float freely in the cytoplasm. Watch out! There go a few passing by. The cell you are in has many ribosomes. What might this tell you about its protein-making activity? It makes a great deal of protein.

Mitochondria

As you pass by the ribosomes, you see other structures looming ahead. These structures are **mitochondria** (migh-toh-ĸon-dree-uh; singular: mitochondrion), which are the main source of energy for the cell. Somewhat larger than the ribosomes, these rod-shaped structures are often referred to as the "powerhouses" of the cell. See Figure 3-6.

Figure 3-6 *The mitochondrion is the "powerhouse" of the cell.*

MITOCHONDRION

Inside the mitochondria, simple food substances such as sugars are broken down. Large amounts of energy are released during the breakdown of sugars. The mitochondria gather this energy and store it in special energy-rich molecules. These molecules are convenient energy packages that the cell uses to do all its work. The more active a cell is, the more mitochondria it has. Some cells, such as a human liver cell, contain more than 1000 mitochondria. Would you expect your muscle cells or your bone cells to have more mitochondria? Muscle cells

Because mitochondria have a small amount of their own DNA, some scientists believe that they were once tiny organisms that invaded living cells millions of years ago. The DNA molecules in the mitochondria were passed from one generation of cells to the next as simple organisms evolved into complex ones. Now all living cells contain mitochondria. No longer invaders, mitochondria are an essential part of living cells.

Vacuoles

That large, round, water-filled sac you see floating in the cytoplasm of this plant cell is called a **vacuole** (VA-kyoo-ohl). Both plant and animal cells have vacuoles. However, plant cells often have one very large vacuole while animal cells have a few small vacuoles.

Vacuoles act like storage tanks. Food, enzymes, and other materials needed by the cell are stored inside the vacuole sacs. Vacuoles also can store waste products. In plant cells, vacuoles are the main water-storage areas. When water vacuoles in plant cells are full, they swell and make the cell plump. This plumpness keeps a plant firm. During its lifetime, a plant cell may increase to 500 times its original size because of an increase in the amount of water in its expanding vacuoles.

Lysosomes

If you carefully swing your ship around the lake-like vacuole, you may be lucky enough to see a **lysosome.** Lucky because lysosomes are common in animal cells but not often observed in plant cells.

Explain to your students that mitochondria make proteins for their own growth and reproduction. This is a good example of parts of cells working independently as well as for the good of the entire cell.

Activity

Word Clues

The definition of a word can often be determined by knowing the meaning of its prefix. Choose five of the following words, look up the prefix for each, and tell how it relates to the definition.

chloroplast
protoplasm
mitochondria
vacuole
chromosome
lysosome
cytoplasm

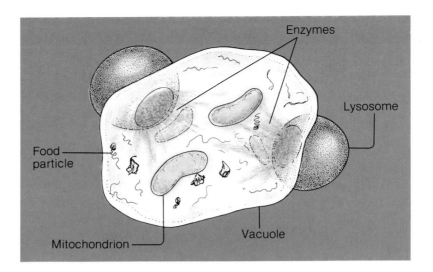

Figure 3-7 *Enzymes from a lysosome digest the contents of a vacuole.*

Lysosomes are small, round structures involved with the digestive activities of the cell. See Figure 3-7. Lysosomes contain enzymes that break down large food molecules into smaller ones. Then these smaller food molecules are passed on to the mitochondria, where they are "burned" to provide energy.

Although lysosomes digest substances in the cytoplasm, you need not worry about your ship's safety! The membrane surrounding a lysosome keeps the enzymes from escaping and digesting the entire cell. However, lysosomes do digest whole cells when the cells are injured or dead. In an interesting process in the growth of a tadpole into a frog, lysosomes in the tadpole's tail cells digest the tail. Then this protoplasmic material is reused to make new body parts for the frog.

Chloroplasts

Your journey is just about over, and you will soon be leaving the cell. But first look around you. Floating in the cytoplasm are large, irregularly shaped structures that are easily sighted. They are green! These structures are **chloroplasts,** and they contain a green pigment called chlorophyll. Chlorophyll captures the energy of sunlight and uses it to make food for the plant cell.

Chloroplasts are found *only* in plant cells. However, the sea slug, an animal, often eats plants that

CHLOROPLAST

Figure 3-8 *Chloroplasts* (left), *the food-making sites, are found only in the cells of green plants* (right).

contain chloroplasts. After the sea slug digests the plant, some of the chloroplasts get into the cells of its digestive system. There the chloroplasts continue to make food just as they do in a plant. The process goes on for a week or so and provides the sea slug's cells with food for energy.

SECTION REVIEW

1. What does protoplasm mean? 1. All the living material in a cell
2. What two nucleic acids are found in the nucleus? 2. DNA, RNA
3. Name the structures in the cytoplasm needed for the manufacture and transport of proteins. 3. Ribosomes, endoplasmic reticulum
4. Describe three differences between plant cells and animal cells. 4. Plant cells have cell wall, chloroplasts, few lysosomes, and one large vacuole rather than several small ones.

3-2   Cell Activities

Each structure within a cell performs a vital activity. And the cell as a whole carries out the chemical processes necessary to life. This tiny unit, basic to all forms of life, is like a miniature factory that produces many kinds of chemicals. Like any factory, a cell must have energy to do work. Working day and night, a cell traps, converts, stores, and uses energy. Obtaining and using energy is one of the most important activities of a living cell.

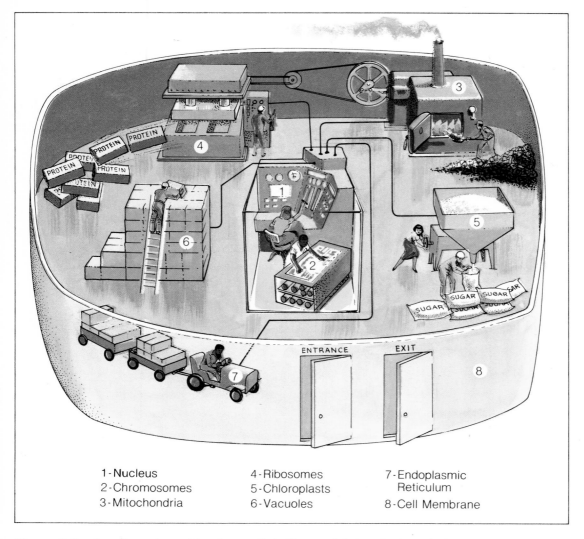

1 - Nucleus   4 - Ribosomes   7 - Endoplasmic
2 - Chromosomes   5 - Chloroplasts   Reticulum
3 - Mitochondria   6 - Vacuoles   8 - Cell Membrane

Figure 3-9 *A cell, such as this plant cell, is like a miniature factory that carries out all the activities necessary to life.*

Metabolism

Even while you sleep, you need energy to keep you alive. But where does this energy come from? Cells provide it. Although cells do not *make* energy, they do *change* energy from one form to another. Cells obtain energy from their environment and convert it into a usable form.

This conversion process is very complex. And it involves many chemical reactions. Some reactions break down molecules. Other reactions build new molecules. The sum of all the building-up and breaking-down activities that occur in a living cell is called **metabolism.**

Think for a moment of all the things cells do: grow, repair structures, absorb food, manufacture proteins, get rid of wastes, and reproduce. The energy for these activities is locked up in the molecules in food. As a result of metabolism, the stored energy in food is set free so it can be used to do work.

Diffusion

Remember how you sailed through the cell membrane to enter the cell? Well, the substances that get into and out of the cell do the same thing. Food molecules, oxygen, water, and other materials enter and leave the cell through openings in the cell membrane by a process called **diffusion.**

Why does diffusion occur? Molecules of all substances are in constant motion, continuously colliding with one another. This motion causes the molecules to spread out. The molecules move from an area where there are more of them to an area where there are fewer of them. See Figure 3-10.

If there are many food molecules outside the cell, for example, some diffuse through the membrane into the cell. At the same time, waste materials built up in the cell pass out of the cell by diffusion.

You can observe the process of diffusion for yourself. Drop some ink into a glass of water and watch what happens. The drop of ink spreads throughout the water, getting lighter in color as the ink molecules move through the liquid.

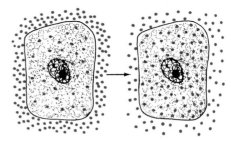

Higher concentration of substance outside the cell

Equal amounts of substance on both sides of cell membrane

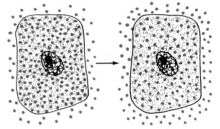

Higher concentration of substance inside the cell

Equal amounts of substance on both sides of cell membrane

Figure 3-10 *Diffusion is the movement of molecules of a substance into a cell (top) or out of a cell (bottom). Substances move from places where they are more* <u>*concentrated*</u> *to places where they are less concentrated.*

Figure 3-11 *The cell membrane is selective, permitting oxygen and food molecules to enter and waste materials to leave.*

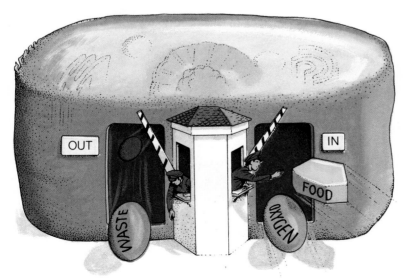

In a plant cell, as water fills the large vacuole, the cytoplasm and nucleus get pushed against the cell wall, creating turgor pressure. A loss of turgor pressure is called plasmolysis and causes leaves and stems to wilt.

Figure 3-12 *Normal red blood cells* (left) *will shrink* (center) *if too much water leaves the cells. If too much water enters the cells, they will swell* (right).

If substances can move into and out of the cell through the membrane, what keeps the protoplasm from oozing out? What keeps harmful materials from moving in? The cell membrane safeguards the contents of the cell because it is selective. That is, it permits only certain substances, mainly oxygen and food molecules, to diffuse into the cell. Only waste products such as carbon dioxide are allowed to diffuse out of the cell.

Osmosis

Water is the most important substance that passes through the cell membrane. In fact, about 80 percent of protoplasm is water. Water passes through the cell membrane by a special type of diffusion called **osmosis.** During osmosis, water molecules move from a place of greater concentration to a place of lesser concentration. This movement keeps the cell from drying out.

Suppose you put a cell in a glass of salt water. The concentration of water outside the cell is lower than the concentration of water inside the cell. So water leaves the cell, and the cell starts to shrink. If too much water leaves the cell, the cell dries up and dies.

Now, if the cell was put in a glass of fresh water instead of salt water, just the opposite occurs. Water enters the cell, and the cell swells. This happens because the concentration of water is lower inside the cell than outside the cell. As you might imagine, if too much water enters the cell, the cell bursts.

Figure 3-13 *In these normal plant leaf cells* (left), *the movement of too much water from the cell vacuoles causes the cell contents to shrink away from the cell wall* (right).

Reproduction

How many cells do you think you are made of? The number of cells in an organism depends on its size, and so no specific number can be given. But you may be surprised to learn that as an adult, you will consist of about 50 thousand billion cells! All of these cells come from just one original cell.

GROWTH AND DEVELOPMENT Body cells must undergo reproduction in order for the total number of cells to increase and for the organism to grow. These cells reproduce by dividing into two new cells. Each new cell, called a daughter cell, is identical to the other and to the parent cell. How does this process occur?

If a parent cell—a skin cell, leaf cell, or bone cell, for example—is to produce two identical daughter cells, then the exact contents of its nucleus must go into the nucleus of each new cell. In other words, the "blueprints" of life in the parent cell must be passed on to each daughter cell. Now, if the parent cell simply splits in half, each daughter cell would get only half the contents of the nucleus—only half the "blueprints." It would no longer be the same kind of cell—a skin cell, leaf cell, or bone cell.

Fortunately, this is not what happens. For just before a cell divides, all the material in the nucleus is duplicated, or copied. The duplication and division of the nucleus and of the chromosomes is called **mitosis** (migh-TOH-sis).

Activity

How Many Cells?

Suppose a cell splits in half every 10 minutes. How many cells will there be after 1½ hours?

Figure 3-14 *During mitosis, each chromosome is duplicated before the nucleus divides. In this drawing, the magician represents a nucleus. And the balloons represent chromosomes.*

You may wish to tell your students that a normal human body cell has 46 chromosomes.

Figure 3-15 *In one stage of mitosis, the chromosomes in the nucleus are duplicated (left). In another stage, one of each pair of chromosomes moves to the opposite ends of the nucleus (center). Finally, the nucleus splits and two new cells with identical chromosomes are formed (right).*

Mitosis is a very complex process that occurs in several stages. During mitosis, each chromosome in the nucleus makes a copy of itself. See Figure 3-14. When the nuclear membrane disappears, one set of chromosomes moves to one end of the parent cell, and the other set of chromosomes moves to the opposite end. A new nuclear membrane forms around each set of chromosomes. The parent cell then divides into two. Each daughter cell contains an exact copy of the chromosomes of the parent cell. The complete "blueprint" of life is passed from one cell to another. The two new skin cells are exactly like the parent skin cell and so are able to do the same job. And the two new nerve cells are identical in form and function to their parent nerve cell.

Mitosis, then, is the process by which the cells of an organism reproduce to form exact copies of one another. Through mitosis, both plants and animals grow larger, repair damaged parts, and replace dead

Courtesy Carolina Biological Supply Company

cells. For example, the root tip of a plant contains many cells undergoing mitosis. The formation of new cells makes the root longer and allows it to push through the ground toward water.

PRODUCTION OF OFFSPRING   Mitosis is a method to reproduce cells inside an organism. However, there is another kind of reproduction in which a new organism comes from two parents. This is called sexual reproduction. Sexual reproduction involves the joining of two special types of cells—the male sex cell and the female sex cell—in a process known as fertilization. The offspring of fertilization contains a *combination* of the chromosomes of the male sex cell and the female sex cell.

Sex cells reproduce by a special type of cell division called **meiosis** (migh-OH-sis). Meiosis is a form of cell division that *halves* the number of chromosomes in a male or female sex cell as it forms. When the sex cells later join, the offspring gets half its chromosomes from the male and the other half from the female. The offspring's cells now have the same number of chromosomes as the cells of the parents.

Figure 3-16 *Sexual reproduction produces offspring that have a combination of the characteristics of the parents.*

SECTION REVIEW

1. What is metabolism?
2. Describe the process of osmosis.
3. What process causes an organism to grow?

1. Sum of building-up and breaking-down activities in a cell
2. Water passes from a place of greater concentration to a place of lesser concentration
3. Mitosis

LABORATORY ACTIVITY

For further instructions, see page T-23.

Things Look Different Under a Microscope

Purpose

In this activity, you will examine newspaper and magazine paper under a microscope.

Materials *(per group)*

Microscope
Microscope slide
Cover slip
Small pieces of newspaper print
Small pieces of colorful magazine
    photographs

Procedure

1. Obtain a small piece of newspaper print and place it on a clean microscope slide. Cover the slide with a cover slip.
2. Place the slide on the stage of the microscope. The newspaper should be facing up and be in the normal reading position. **CAUTION:** *Always use a cover slip to protect the objective lens from coming into contact with the material being observed.*
3. With the low-power objective in place, follow your teacher's directions for focusing on a letter.
4. While focusing on a letter, move the slide to the left. Which way does the letter seem to move? Now move the slide to the right. Which way does the letter seem to move this time?
5. While looking through the eyepiece, adjust the slide so that a letter is in the center of your field of view. Now, looking at the stage and objectives from the side, revolve the nosepiece until the high-power objective clicks into place. Using *only* the fine adjustment knob, bring the letter into focus. Describe what you see. Now follow the same

MICROSCOPE PARTS AND THEIR FUNCTIONS

1. **Arm**   Supports the body tube
2. **Eyepiece**   Contains the magnifying lens you look through
3. **Body tube**   Maintains the proper distance between the eyepiece and objective lenses
4. **Nosepiece**   Holds high- and low-power objective lenses and can be rotated to change magnification
5. **Objective lenses**   Low-power lens usually magnifies 10 times; high-power lens usually magnifies 40 times
6. **Stage clips**   Hold the slide in place
7. **Stage**   Supports the slide
8. **Diaphragm**   Regulates the amount of light let into the body tube
9. **Mirror**   Reflects the light upward through the diaphragm, the specimen, and the lenses
10. **Base**   Supports the microscope
11. **Coarse-adjustment knob**   Moves the body tube up and down for focusing
12. **Fine-adjustment knob**   Moves the body tube slightly to sharpen the image

steps using magazine paper.

Observations and Conclusions

1. What letter did you choose? How does this letter appear when viewed through the microscope? Focus on another letter. How does it appear? What conclusion can you draw about the way objects appear when viewed under the microscope?

CHAPTER SUMMARY

3-1 Cell Structure and Function

■ The cell wall, found only in plant cells, is made of nonliving cellulose and gives protection and support to the cell.

■ Protoplasm is all the living material of a cell.

■ The cell membrane is a thin, flexible membrane that regulates the movement of materials into and out of the cell.

■ The control center of the cell is the nucleus. It is surrounded by the nuclear membrane.

■ Chromosomes found in the nucleus are made of nucleic acids, which are the "blueprints" of life.

■ Cytoplasm is all the protoplasm outside the nucleus.

■ The endoplasmic reticulum, a network of tubelike passageways, is the site of the manufacture and transport of proteins.

■ Ribosomes, often attached to the endoplasmic reticulum, are the protein-making sites.

■ Mitochondria are the "powerhouses" of the cell.

■ Vacuoles store food, water, enzymes, and waste products.

■ Lysosomes play a role in the digestive activities of the cell.

■ Chloroplasts, found only in green plant cells, capture the energy of the sun and use it to make food for the cell.

3-2 Cell Activities

■ The sum of all the activities that occur in a living cell is called metabolism.

■ Food, oxygen, water, and other materials enter and leave the cell by a process called diffusion.

■ Water passes through the cell membrane by a type of diffusion called osmosis.

■ Mitosis is the duplication and division of the nucleus and of the chromosomes during cell division, which results in daughter cells identical to the parent cell.

■ During the formation of the male and female sex cells, meiosis takes place and the chromosome number is halved.

VOCABULARY   *Define the following terms.*

cell p.58	**endoplasmic reticulum** p.63	**nucleolus** p.62
cell membrane p.60	**lysosome** p.65	**nucleus** p.60
cell wall p.59	**meiosis** p.73	**osmosis** p.70
chloroplast p.66	**metabolism** p.68	**protoplasm** p.60
chromosome p.61	**mitochondria** p.64	**ribosome** p.64
cytoplasm p.63	**mitosis** p.71	**vacuole** p.65
diffusion p.69	**nuclear membrane** p.61	

CHAPTER REVIEW

Multiple Choice

Choose the letter of the answer that best completes each statement.

1. The cell wall is made of a nonliving material called
   a. protoplasm.
   b. nucleic acid.
   c. cellulose.
   d. chromosomes.
2. The cell membrane
   a. provides protection for the cell.
   b. keeps the cell's inner contents together.
   c. regulates the movement of materials into and out of the cell.
   d. does all of these.
3. The "brain" of the cell is its
   a. nucleus.
   b. mitochondria.
   c. ribosomes.
   d. cytoplasm.
4. The rodlike structures that direct the activities of the cell and pass on traits to new cells are the
   a. chloroplasts.
   b. chromosomes.
   c. ribosomes.
   d. lysosomes.
5. The network of passageways that transports proteins throughout the cell is known as the
   a. nuclear membrane.
   b. endoplasmic reticulum.
   c. mitochondria.
   d. vacuole.
6. Food, water, and wastes are stored in
   a. lysosomes.
   b. chromosomes.
   c. ribosomes.
   d. vacuoles.
7. Food-making structures found in cells of green plants are called
   a. chloroplasts.
   b. chromosomes.
   c. chromoplasts.
   d. mitochondria.
8. Water usually moves through a cell membrane from an area of
   a. lesser concentration to greater concentration.
   b. equal concentration to equal concentration.
   c. greater concentration to lesser concentration.
   d. none of these.
9. The total number of cells in an organism increases as a result of
   a. respiration.
   b. reproduction.
   c. homeostasis.
   d. diffusion.
10. Each daughter cell gets an exact copy of the chromosomes of the parent cell by
    a. mitosis.
    b. diffusion.
    c. homeostasis.
    d. osmosis.

Completions

Fill in the word or words that best complete each statement.

1. All the living material in a cell is called ____protoplasm____.

2. The ability of a cell to maintain a stable internal environment even if external conditions change is called ____homeostasis____.

3. Two important nucleic acids are ____DNA____ and ____RNA____.

4. Simple food substances are broken down and the energy they release is stored in structures called ____mitochondria____.

5. A plant remains firm because inside its cells are sacs called _____vacuoles_____ that fill up with water.

6. Structures common to animal cells that are involved in the digestive activities of the cell are called _____lysosomes_____.

7. The passage of food, oxygen, water, and other materials in and out of a cell is called _____diffusion_____.

8. When only water enters or leaves a cell, the process is called _____osmosis_____.

9. As a result of mitosis, the daughter cells have chromosomes that are _____the same as_____ those of the parent cell and each other.

10. During _____meiosis_____, the chromosome number in the male sex cell and in the female sex cell is halved.

True or False

Determine whether each statement is true or false. If it is true, write "true."
If it is false, change the underlined word or words to make the statement true.

1. The outer covering of the <u>animal</u> cell is the cell wall. F (plant)

2. The <u>cytoplasm</u> controls all activities. F (nucleus)

3. Chromosomes are made of <u>nucleic acids</u>. T

4. All the living material outside the nucleus is called <u>protoplasm</u>. F (cytoplasm)

5. <u>Ribosomes</u> are the protein-making sites of the cell. T

6. The green pigment found in special structures of a plant cell is called <u>chromatin</u>.*
* F (chlorophyll)

7. The sum of all the activities that occur in a living cell is called <u>metabolism</u>. T

8. If a cell is placed in a glass of salt water, water will <u>enter</u> the cell. F (leave)

9. The duplication and division of the nucleus and of the chromosomes is called <u>mitosis</u>. T

10. The chromosome number in the male sex cell and in the female sex cell is halved during <u>fertilization</u>. F (meiosis)

Discussion Topics Answers appear on page T-23.

Write a brief paragraph discussing each of the following.

1. If it were possible to implant chloroplasts in human cells, which cells would be the best sites? Explain your answer.

2. Compare the processes of mitosis and meiosis in terms of introducing new characteristics into the offspring.

EXPAND YOUR KNOWLEDGE

Cobb, V. *Cells: The Basic Structure of Life.* New York: Watts.
What are cells made of? What is a diseased cell? How do cells reproduce? Find out the answers in this fascinating book.

Silverstein, A., and V. B. Silverstein. *Cells: Building Blocks of Life.* Englewood Cliffs, N.J.: Prentice-Hall.
Here is the amazing story of how a cell is formed, what it is made of, and how it works with other cells to make up multicellular organisms.

4 Tissues, Organs, and Organ Systems

For a chapter overview, teaching strategies, answers to all activities, a list of A-V materials, and a chapter bibliography, see pages T-23 to T-25.

Consult your Teacher's Resource Book and Annotated Teacher's Edition, Laboratory Book for additional activities and teaching aids.

CHAPTER OBJECTIVES

After completing this chapter, you will be able to:

4-1 Explain what is meant by division of labor in living things.

4-2 Describe the five levels of organization of living things.

4-2 Explain how the levels of organization of living things are dependent upon one another.

Poised high upon the edge of a jagged rock, the cheetah seems almost motionless. Yet every muscle is tensed and ready to spring into action.

Its nostrils quiver as the familiar scent of an antelope reaches its nose. The sleek animal's back arches, its ears prick up to catch even the faintest sound in the bushes below, and its tongue slowly and smoothly licks its lips.

In anticipation, the cheetah's heart pounds faster and its breathing quickens. A low, menacing sound escapes from its throat. Its paws curl more tightly around the rock as its limbs flex and tighten, flex and tighten. Its flanks ripple with excitement, and juices pour into its mouth as it prepares to descend upon its prey.

The unsuspecting antelope calmly grazes on the plain just below. A young antelope lies near, secure in the protection of its parent. Above them, the cheetah silently readies itself for attack. Every part of the animal—from the smallest cell to its entire body—is working together to ensure that the cheetah will eat well this night.

Cheetah in search of prey

Figure 4-1 *Multicellular organisms, such as this beetle and the green plant upon which it feeds, carry on a wide variety of complex activities.*

Figure 4-2 *Different parts of this bat's body work in harmony with each other as the bat prepares to attack. If the tree frog's body parts work well together, the frog may escape.*

4-1 A Division of Labor

Bacteria lead very simple lives. They do not walk, run, or listen to music. They do not see, smell, talk, or shake hands. They just grow, divide, and then grow some more. A cheetah, on the other hand, leads a life that is not that simple. Its life includes activities like roaming the plains, climbing trees, hunting for food, and playing with other cheetahs.

The whole body of a bacterium is made up of one cell. On its own, that single cell must do all the jobs that keep a bacterium alive. This accounts, in part, for the simple lives bacteria live. A cheetah, however, is multicellular—it is made of a great many cells. And these numerous cells are organized into the different parts of the cheetah's body, enabling the animal to carry out more complex activities than a single-celled bacterium can.

Some of the cheetah's body parts, such as muscle cells, are relatively small and simple. Other parts, like strands of muscle fibers, are larger and more complex. Still other parts, the cheetah's heart and circulatory system, for example, are even larger and more complex. However, all the different parts, whether small or large, interact with each other, perform their special functions, and keep the cheetah alive.

Within the body of the cheetah, as within most living things, there is a **division of labor.** Division of labor means that the work of keeping the organism alive is divided among the different parts of its body. Each part has a specific job to do. And as the part does its special job, it works in harmony with all the other parts to keep the organism healthy and active.

The concept of division of labor is used here to refer to the idea of specialization or differentiation of cells.

SECTION REVIEW

1. What is the basic difference between a bacterium and an organism such as the cheetah?
2. What is meant by the term "division of labor" in living things?

1. Bacterium—one-celled, leads simple life; cheetah—multicellular, leads complex life
2. Work of keeping the organism alive is divided among different parts of its body.

4-2 Organization of Living Things

The arrangement of specialized parts within a living thing is sometimes referred to as levels of organization. There are five basic levels of organization, arranged from the smallest, least complex structure to the largest, most complex structure.

The five levels of organization that will be discussed here are: cells, tissues, organs, systems, organism.

Level One: Cells

In Chapter 3, you learned that all living things are made up of **cells.** Cells are the building blocks of life; they are microscopic units of structure and function of all organisms. Some living things are made of only one cell. A bacterium is a one-celled organism, as is an amoeba. For these organisms, the single cell exists as a free-living organism. It does all the jobs that keep the organism alive.

In multicellular organisms, different cells perform specialized tasks. Muscle cells, for example, help the cheetah move through its environment, climb rocks, and spring to attack. Nerve cells receive and send messages throughout the cheetah's body. Every kind of cell, however, depends on other cells for its survival and for the survival of the entire organism. Those muscle cells move only when set into action by nerve cells. And both muscle cells and nerve cells rely on blood cells for oxygen.

Explain to your students that there are levels of organization below the cell: cell parts, molecules, atoms.

Figure 4-3 *Cells come in different shapes and sizes, as you can see from these nerve* (left), *muscle* (center), *and blood cells* (right).

Level Two: Tissues

In a multicellular organism, cells usually do not work alone. Cells that are similar in structure and function are joined together to form **tissues.** Tissues are the second level of organization.

Like the single cell of the bacterium, each tissue cell must carry on all the activities needed to keep that cell alive. But at the same time, tissues perform one or more specialized functions in an organism's body. In other words, tissues work for themselves as well as for the good of the entire living thing.

For example, bone cells in the cheetah form bone tissue, a strong, solid tissue that gives shape and support to the bodies of animals. Blood cells are part of blood tissue, a liquid tissue responsible for carrying food, oxygen, and wastes throughout the cheetah's body. Some muscle tissue helps move the cheetah's legs, neck, and other body parts. Another kind of muscle tissue enables its heart to pump blood. A third type of muscle tissue lines its stomach and helps the cheetah digest its meal.

Plants have tissues too. The leaves and stems of a plant are covered by a type of tissue called epidermis, which protects the plant and prevents it from losing water. Tissue known as xylem (ZIGH-luhm) conducts water and dissolved minerals up through

Figure 4-4 *The sundew plant has special hairlike tissues that produce a sticky fluid that traps insects.*

the stems to the leaves. And another special tissue called phloem (FLOH-em) brings food made in the leaves back down to the stems and roots.

Level Three: Organs

The cheetah is a clever hunter. Stalking about on its padded feet, it uses its keen senses of smell, sight, and hearing to locate its prey. Then, as its lungs fill with oxygen, it moves with incredible speed and strikes down its victim with a blow of its front paws.

The cheetah's eyes, ears, nose, and lungs are several of the **organs** that help the animal find food and stay alive. Organs are groups of different tissues working together. The cheetah's heart, for example, is an organ composed of nerve tissue, muscle tissue, and blood tissue. Each tissue does its special job. Nerve tissue signals the muscle tissue to contract. Muscle tissue contracts and causes the heart to pump the blood tissue. Blood tissue carries oxygen and wastes to and from every cell in the cheetah's heart— and eventually to cells throughout the entire body.

Figure 4-5 *Various organs in the cheetah's body work together so that the animal can run as fast as 115 kilometers per hour.*

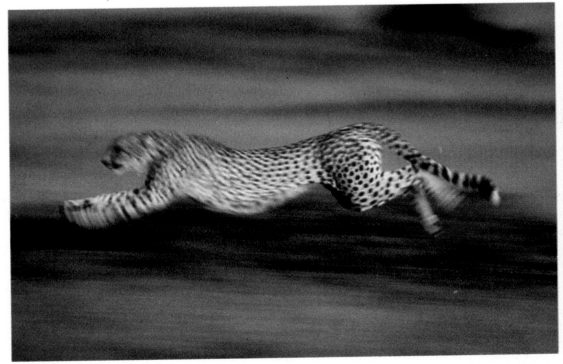

Lungs, heart, spleen, pancreas, gall bladder, bladder, liver, etc.

Figure 4-6

ORGAN SYSTEMS

System	Function
Skeletal	Protects and supports the body
Muscular	Supports the body and enables it to move
Skin	Protects the body
Digestive	Receives, transports, breaks down, and absorbs food throughout the body
Circulatory	Transports oxygen, wastes, and digested food throughout the body
Respiratory	Permits the exchange of gases in the body
Excretory	Removes liquid and solid wastes from the body
Endocrine	Regulates various body functions
Nervous	Conducts messages throughout the body to aid in coordination of body functions
Reproductive	Produces male and female sex cells

You are probably familiar with the names of many of the organs that make up your body. Your brain, stomach, kidneys, and skin are some examples. Can you name some others?

Plants have organs too. Roots, stems, and leaves are common plant organs. Like animal organs, plant organs are made up of groups of tissues performing the same function. For example, various tissues in the leaf help this organ make food for the plant.

Level Four: Systems

Like cells and tissues, organs seldom work alone. They "cooperate" with each other to form specific **systems.** A system, then, is a group of organs that work together to perform certain functions.

The cheetah is able to spot its prey because its sense organs—its eyes, ears, and nose—do their job. They receive messages in the form of sights, sounds, and smells. The cheetah's brain processes this information. And its spinal cord and nerves send out impulses to all parts of its body so that the animal is able to prepare to attack. Each of these organs, doing its individual job as well as working together with other organs, forms part of the cheetah's nervous system.

A living thing cannot survive unless all its systems are "go." For example, its digestive system must receive, carry, break down, and absorb food. Its excretory system must remove certain waste materials from its body. And its endocrine system must make chemical substances called hormones. Hormones speed up or slow down the activities of many organs. They also play a part in the growth and development of the organism.

The organs that make up a system vary in number and complexity from one kind of living thing to another. For example, a very simple animal called the hydra has a nervous system that is a simple net of nerves spread throughout the organism. More complex animals, such as the earthworm, have a more highly organized system of nerves and a primitive brain. The most highly developed animals, people, for example, have nervous systems consisting of a complex brain, a spinal cord, and nerves.

You may wish to discuss how breathing systems vary in complexity from one organism to another. Amoeba take in oxygen directly through cell membranes. Earthworms breathe through their moist skin. Fish have gills. Land animals have the most complex systems consisting of trachea and lungs.

Figure 4-7 *The skin of the camel (left), part of its excretory system, helps it get rid of waste materials and excess heat. The circulatory system of the eucalyptus tree (right) brings water and other substances to the very top of the tree.*

Career: *Histologic Technician*

HELP WANTED: HISTOLOGIC TECHNICIAN Position involves preparation of tissue for microscopic study and detection of cell features that suggest disease or damage. Completion of a formal training program or an associate degree program in histotechnology required.

New drugs and chemical food additives are constantly being manufactured and introduced into the marketplace. Before these substances can be used, however, they must be carefully tested to ensure that they are safe for human use. The United States Food and Drug Administration requires these tests. Controlled amounts of a new drug or additive are given to research animals over a period of time. Scientists then study the tissues of the animals, looking for possible damage or disease.

People who prepare animal or plant tissue for microscopic study are called **histologic technicians** or histotechnologists. They prepare tissue by first treating it with special chemicals that prevent decomposition of the tissue. They then remove water from the tissue so that they can place it in liquid wax. The wax quickly hardens and gives support to the tissue

so that the tissue can be sliced into extremely thin sections with a very sharp knife. The sections are placed on microscope slides and are stained with various dyes that help to distinguish tissue structures. A specially trained technician or a doctor examines the slide.

Opportunities for histologic technicians exist in various fields of medicine, in marine biology, and in certain areas of industrial and university research. For further information, write to the National Society for Histotechnology, 5900 Princess Garden Parkway, Suite 805, Lanham, MD 20706.

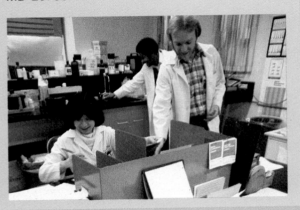

Level Five: Organisms

Throughout this chapter, you have been reading the word "organism." Perhaps you have already determined what an **organism** is. An organism is an entire living thing that carries out *all* the basic life functions. You, like the cheetah, are an organism. A buttercup is an organism, as are a cactus, a caribou, and a whale. Even a one-celled bacterium is an organism. The organism is the highest level of organization of living things.

A complex organism is a combination of organ systems. Each system performs its particular function, but all the systems work together to keep the organism alive. Without the smooth operation of any one of its systems, a living thing could not survive.

The behavior of the cheetah you read about earlier is the result of many systems performing their specific functions and interacting with other systems. For example, when the cheetah's nervous system senses the antelope's presence, it signals the muscular system. The cheetah's spine arches, its tail goes

Figure 4-8 *Levels of organization in an organism*

Figure 4-9 *Survival often depends on the cooperation of body parts—from simple cells to complex systems.*

straight back, and its hind legs extend forward. In this position, the cheetah is able to accelerate to speeds of 75 to 115 kilometers per hour. The nervous system also alerts organs of the endocrine system, which increase their production of hormones. As a result, the cheetah's heart rate increases and more oxygen than usual is delivered to the muscle cells. As you can see, no one process or one system is independent of the others.

Cells, tissues, organs, systems, organisms. By now one thing should be clear to you: Each level of organization interacts with every other level. And the smooth functioning of a complex organism is the result of all its various parts working together.

The antelope, of course, is also an organism. The parts of its body must work together as well. In fact, once the antelope spots the cheetah lying in wait, its body parts work fast and furiously to spare it an untimely death at the paws of the cheetah. Often the cheetah wins this deadly battle, but this time the antelope and its young escape into the bush—just as the cheetah is about to jump and pounce. Tonight, at least, the cheetah will go hungry.

Activity

An Amazing Feat

Bone and muscle work together to perform amazing feats. A hummingbird can stay in one place in midair by beating its wings 80 times per second. How many beats is this in 5 minutes?

SECTION REVIEW

1. What is meant by levels of organization of a living thing? 1. Arrangement of specialized parts within a living thing

2. List and define the five levels of organization of living things. 2. Cells: units of structure and function; tissues: groups of cells working together; organs: groups of tissues working together; systems: groups of organs working together; organism: entire living thing that carries out all basic life functions

LABORATORY ACTIVITY

For further instructions, see page T-24

Have You Tasted These?

Purpose

In this activity, you will be introduced to some unusual foods that are derived from cells, tissues, and organs of various animals.

Materials *(per group)*

Dictionary or encyclopedia
Cookbooks

Procedure

1. Examine the following list of foods:

tripe	jerky
sweetbreads	suet
chitterlings	marrow
escargot	pâté de foie gras
sushi	caviar

   How many of these foods can you identify?
   How many of them have you eaten?

2. Using a dictionary, encyclopedia, or cookbook, look up the foods that no one in the class was able to identify. Name the animal that is the source of each of these foods. From what part of the animal is each of these foods derived?

Observations and Conclusions

1. Classify each of these foods using the levels of organization you learned in this chapter as categories: cells, tissues, organs, organ systems, organisms.
2. List other animal organs that are used as foods. How many of these have you tasted? How were these foods prepared?

CHAPTER SUMMARY

4-1 A Division of Labor

■ In a one-celled organism, the single cell performs all the activities necessary to keep the organism alive.

■ In multicellular organisms, different parts of the body have specific jobs to do. This division of labor keeps the organism alive.

4-2 Organization of Living Things

■ The least complex level of organization of living things is the cell. The cell is the basic unit of structure and function of all organisms.

■ Cells that are similar in structure and function are joined together to form tissues.

■ Groups of different tissues work together as organs.

■ A group of different organs working together to perform certain functions is known as a system.

■ An organism is an entire living thing that carries out all the life functions. Complex organisms are made up of systems. The organism is the highest level of organization of living things.

VOCABULARY   *Define the following terms.*

cell p.81
division of labor p.81
organ p.83

organism p.86
system p.84
tissue p.82

CHAPTER REVIEW

Multiple Choice

Choose the letter of the answer that best completes each statement.

1. In a bacterium, the single cell carries on
   a. digestion only.
   b. respiration and digestion only.
   c. all life functions.
   d. excretion only.

2. The concept of various body parts each doing a specific job is called
   a. division of labor.
   b. reduction division.
   c. differentiation.
   d. specialization.

3. The basic units of structure and function of all organisms are the
   a. bones.
   b. systems.
   c. cells.
   d. tissues.

4. Multicellular organisms have
   a. one cell.
   b. many cells.
   c. solar cells.
   d. no cells.

5. Cells that are similar in structure and function are joined together to form
   a. organs.
   b. systems.
   c. tissues.
   d. organisms.
6. Xylem, phloem, and epidermis are examples of plant
   a. organs.
   b. tissues.
   c. cells.
   d. systems.
7. Roots, stems, and leaves are examples of plant
   a. organs.
   b. cells.
   c. tissues.
   d. bones.
8. The highest level of organization in living things is the
   a. cell.
   b. organ.
   c. organism.
   d. system.
9. From the most complex to the least complex, the levels of organization of most living things are
   a. organism, systems, organs, tissues, cells.
   b. systems, cells, tissues, organs, organism.
   c. organism, systems, organs, cells, tissues.
   d. cells, tissues, organs, systems, organism.
10. In order for any multicellular organism to stay alive,
   a. each level of organization must perform its specific job.
   b. all levels of organization must interact with one another.
   c. neither of these.
   d. both of these.

Completions

Fill in the word or words that best complete each statement.

1. The least complex level of organization in a living thing is the basic unit of structure called the _____cell_____.

2. Messages are received and transmitted throughout a complex organism's body by _____nerve_____ cells.

3. The type of tissue that helps an organism move is _____muscle_____ tissue.

4. Xylem and phloem are examples of plant _____tissue_____.

5. The type of tissue that carries oxygen and wastes to and from cells of the heart is _____blood_____ tissue.

6. Eyes, kidneys, and skin are examples of animal _____organs_____.

7. Roots, stems, and leaves are common plant _____organs_____.

8. Systems are made up of different _____organs_____ that work together to perform a certain activity.

9. Chemical substances called _____hormones_____ are produced by the endocrine system and regulate the activities of many organs of the body.

10. A(n) _____organism_____ is an entire living thing made up of systems that carries out all the basic life functions.

True or False

Determine whether each statement is true or false. If it is true, write "true." If it is false, change the underlined word or words to make the statement true.

1. A bacterium is a <u>multicellular</u> organism. *
2. Within complex organisms, there is a <u>division of labor</u> among the different parts of the body. T
3. There are <u>seven</u> basic levels of organization in living things. F (five)
4. The unit of structure and function of living things is the <u>nucleus</u>. F (cell)
5. Groups of cells similar in structure and activity are called <u>tissues</u>. T
6. Organs are made up of groups of different <u>systems</u>, each performing its particular job. F (tissues)

7. The heart, lungs, and eyes are examples of animal <u>organs</u>. T
8. Leaves are important plant <u>tissues</u>. F (organs)
9. An organism is composed of many <u>tissues</u>, each carrying out a specific life function. F (systems)
10. An organism <u>can</u> survive without the smooth operation of any one of its basic systems. F (cannot)

* F (one-celled)

Discussion Topics   Answers appear on pages T-24–T-25.

Write a brief paragraph discussing each of the following.

1. Explain the difference between a simple organism and a complex organism.
2. Using the idea of a pyramid, make a drawing that illustrates the five basic levels of organization in living things.
3. Describe some changes in the internal activities and external conditions of an organism that the nervous system might monitor and respond to.
4. Using the sequence of activities that takes place from the time you wake up in the morning to the time you leave for school, describe how the systems of your body might work with each other.

EXPAND YOUR KNOWLEDGE

Flanagan, G. L. *Window into an Egg*. New York: William R. Scott.
  This book probes the day-by-day development of a chicken. Many excellent photographs help make this material exciting and clear.
Kelly, P. M. *The Mighty Human Cell*. New York: John Day.
  This book tells the remarkable story of human cells—what they look like, how they live, how they grow and reproduce. Learn the very important functions that cells perform to help people stay alive.
Milne, L., and M. Milne. *The How and Why of Growing*. New York: Atheneum.
  How and why do living things grow? This book explains the process of growth in animals, plants, and bacteria.
Silverstein, A., and V. B. Silverstein. *The Reproductive System: How Living Creatures Multiply*. Englewood Cliffs, N.J.: Prentice-Hall.
  The authors discuss topics such as mating habits and parental care.

5 Interactions Among Living Things

For a chapter overview, teaching strategies, answers to all activities, a list of A-V materials, and a chapter bibliography, see pages T-25 to T-27.

Consult your Teacher's Resource Book and Annotated Teacher's Edition, Laboratory Book for additional activities and teaching aids.

CHAPTER SECTIONS

CHAPTER OBJECTIVES

After completing this chapter, you will be able to:

5-1 Relate the concepts of an ecosystem, a community, a population, a habitat, and a niche to one another.

5-2 Explain the food and energy relationships that exist between producers and consumers in an ecosystem.

5-2 Describe a food chain, food web, and energy pyramid.

5-3 Explain why competition among organisms occurs in every ecosystem.

5-3 Compare the symbiotic relationships of commensalism, mutualism, and parasitism.

For more than 30 years, Great Gull Island in Long Island Sound, New York, has been an exciting outdoor laboratory for ornithologists, or people who study birds. The ornithologists have been studying two graceful sea birds—the common tern and the roseate tern.

Gradually, a dangerous inhabitant of the island began to take control and threaten the lives of the terns. This enemy was grass! Scientists know that terns need bare, sandy beaches on which to build nests and raise their young. By 1981, the beaches of Great Gull Island were covered with grass. Human efforts to remove it were useless. Were the terns doomed?

A hundred years ago, Great Gull Island had a large population of field mice called voles. These voles fed on the roots and stems of the island's grasses. But by 1981 voles had long been gone from the island. Could voles now be brought back to the island in an effort to save the terns?

Scientists captured 36 voles and set them loose on the island. Over the next three years, the tern population soared. So did the vole population at first. Then it suddenly shrank. The little voles had eaten up much of their food supply. Will the vole population bounce back? Will a natural balance of living things return to Great Gull Island? Scientists hope so, but only time will tell.

Vole on Great Gull Island

5-1 Living Things and Their Environment

Deep within the cool, dark waters of the earth's oceans lives an unusual variety of animals and other living things. Some animals glow like streetlights in the dark, attracting their prey with their light. Other animals swim very slowly, using huge eyes to find their way in a nighttime world. The only other living things that can survive in these waters are the fungi. Fungi do not need light to live.

On land, in a lush tropical rain forest, tall trees with clinging vines form a giant umbrella. This umbrella blocks the sun and casts a permanent shadow on the forest floor. In the treetops, brightly colored

Figure 5-1 *An environment includes all the living and nonliving things that interact with one another.*

Environment

Animals

Plants

Nonliving

parrots munch on seeds while monkeys chatter to one another. Snakes and lizards climb up and down the tree trunks in search of food. And long-nosed anteaters calmly make their way on the ground.

The deep sea and a rain forest are only two of many different **environments** found on the earth. An environment includes all the living and nonliving things with which an organism may interact. Other environments include deserts, grasslands, polar regions, and cities. You can think of each kind of environment as being like a giant spider web. However, the threads of this web are not spun from silk. The threads of an environmental web are the plants, animals, soil, water, temperature, and light found there.

Consider for a moment what happens when an insect gets caught in a spider's web. As one thread of the web is disturbed, the shaking motion is transferred to all the threads that are part of the web. So a spider resting some distance from the trapped insect suddenly receives a signal that dinner is nearby!

In an environmental web, all the living and nonliving things make up different threads. Some threads are delicate. Others are hardy. But all have one thing in common: Like a real spider web, changes in one thread may be transmitted to and have an effect on other threads in the environment.

In order to understand the changes that can occur in an environment, and how they can affect the environment, you must study the science called **ecology.** Ecology is the study of the relationships and interactions of living things with one another and with their environment. Scientists who study these interactions are called ecologists.

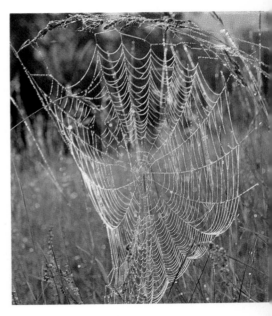

Figure 5-2 *Like the threads of a spider web, the various parts of an environment are interconnected. Changes in one part of the environment can affect other parts.*

Ecosystems

Living things inhabit many different environments. From the poles to the equator, life can be found underground, in air, in water, and on land. A group of organisms in an area that interact with each other, together with their nonliving environment, is often called an **ecosystem.** An ecosystem can be as tiny as a drop of pond water or a square meter of a garden. Or it can be as large as an ocean or an entire forest.

Figure 5-3 *These copepods are among the animals that live in pond water.*

If, for example, you look at a drop of pond water through a microscope, you will see a world of living things. Tiny plants, such as diatoms and green algae, float through the water in this microscopic ecosystem. Rotifers and copepods, very small animals, chase after these plants and eat them.

In the forest ecosystem, other microscopic organisms can be found. Some live in the soil and feed off dead animals and plants. Much larger living organisms such as foxes roam through the forest looking for food, while birds fly above. The foxes eat earthworms, birds, fruits, and small animals such as mice. Fox families live in burrows, which are holes dug into the ground. The trees of the forest supply shelter for birds, which eat insects and earthworms. From this example you can see that the various threads or factors in an ecosystem are interdependent. In other words, the plants, animals, and nonliving parts of the ecosystem all interact with one another.

Figure 5-4 *The deciduous forest is the ecosystem for many plants and animals that interact with one another.*

Communities

An ecosystem is composed of both living and nonliving things. The living part of any ecosystem—all the different organisms that live together in that area—is called a **community.** Fish, insects, frogs, and plants are members of a pond community. The insects, birds, small animals, and trees make up a community in a forest ecosystem. Are these living things interdependent? If you have ever observed pond life, you may know the answer to this question. Frogs eat insects, and fish eat tadpoles. Insects eat plants, as do some of the fish.

In a desert ecosystem's community, insects and birds feed on plants. Other animals, such as lizards, feed on insects and bird eggs. And larger animals eat lizards. Can you see a pattern to these communities? The plants are a source of food to plant-eating animals. And the rest of the organisms feed on the plant eaters and on other animals. So although not all the animals in these communities eat plants, they could not exist without them! Perhaps you are asking yourself what plants eat. Most plants make their own food, as you will soon learn in the next section.

Activity

Identifying Interactions

Ecosystems are all around you. Choose one particular ecosystem—for example, an aquarium, swamp, lake, park, or city block—and study the interactions that occur among the living and nonliving parts of the ecosystem. Include drawings and diagrams in your observations.

You may wish to expand the concept of communities by telling your students that although communities are orderly, changes do occur within them. Use the changes in a forest during autumn as an example: leaves change color, die, and fall off the trees; birds may leave in search of better living conditions.

Populations

You probably live in a community. And you know from your experience that your community is made up of many different kinds of living things: people, dogs, cats, birds, fish, roses, and daisies.

Figure 5-5 *A community is made up of many different populations. On these plains in Kenya, Africa, two populations—zebras and impalas—graze.*

Each kind of living thing makes up a **population** in the community. A population is a group of the *same* type of organism living together in the same area. For example, all the trout living in a lake are a population of trout. All the mesquite bushes surviving in the desert make up another population.

Different ecosystems support different populations of plants and animals. You might expect to see squirrels in a park near your home. The park is the squirrel's natural environment. But, certainly, you would be quite surprised to see a group of zebras grazing there! For the natural environment of zebras is the African plain.

In any ecosystem, the most successful organisms are those that are best adapted to their environment. Perhaps the finest example of an animal population that is well adapted to its environment is the tortoise of the Galapagos Islands. Located in the Pacific Ocean off the western coast of South America, the Galapagos Islands are the home of two different kinds of tortoises. On some of the islands, the tortoises have short necks and shells that hang over the backs of their necks. These shells act like stiff collars and prevent the tortoises from raising their heads. On other islands of the Galapagos, the tortoises have long necks and the part of the shells above their necks is high. These tortoises can raise their heads.

The tortoises with the short necks and low shells live on islands where food is close to the ground. So these tortoises do not have to raise their heads to find food. The tortoises with long necks and high shells live on islands where the only vegetation these animals can eat is high off the ground. So the tortoises must raise their heads high in order to reach food. In other words, each kind of tortoise is adapted to its own environment in ways that help it obtain food.

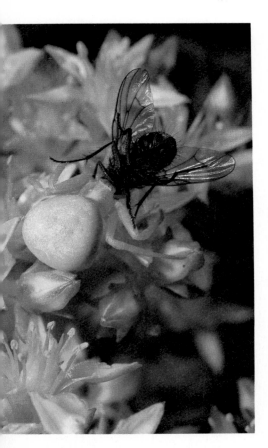

Figure 5-6 *The yellow crab spider is well adapted to its environment. Looking much like a yellow mustard flower, it easily attracts insects and then traps them.*

Habitats and Niches

Where would you look for deer in a forest? Would you look for them in the same places you would look for birds or snakes? Probably not. You would expect to find deer among the trees and bushes of the forest; the birds in the branches of the trees; and the snakes in the soil.

Figure 5-7 *The habitat of these condors is the high, barren peaks of the Andes Mountains of South America.*

The forest contains a community of living things. And each member of that community has a certain place where it lives. The place in which an organism lives is called its **habitat.** A burrow, a tree, or a cave is a habitat. A habitat provides food and shelter for an organism. Plants have habitats too. The beautiful orchid, for example, grows from the branches of tall trees in the rain forest. The branches of these trees are the orchid's habitat.

In addition to a habitat, each organism in a community plays a particular role. The organism has a **niche,** or "occupation." A niche is everything the organism does and everything the organism needs within its habitat. And an organism's niche can affect the lives of other organisms.

Beavers, for example, build dams across streams, creating small lakes. The waters of the stream no longer rush along, wearing down the stream banks. Plants can now grow alongside the lake. Fish, such as trout, can make their home in the calm waters of the lake, and songbirds can nest along the quiet banks. Meanwhile, the beaver lives in an underwater home that it makes from sticks and mud. So the beaver's niche not only makes a home for the beaver, it also makes a habitat in which other animals and plants can thrive.

Organisms in an ecosystem can share the same habitat without any problems, but they *cannot* occupy the same niche. This fact seems obvious since sharing the niche would mean competing for the same

Habitats sometimes overlap. If the organisms do not eat the same food, however, there is usually no problem. For example, the squirrel inhabits the inside of a hollow tree trunk and gets its food from among the leaves on the ground. These leaves may be the habitat of a land snail. But since the snail is not looking for the same food as the squirrel, the overlapping of habitats causes little interaction between the two animals.

Figure 5-8 *The dam that this beaver is building will become its underwater home, as well as a habitat for other animals and plants.*

food and space. Here is an example of how similar organisms in a habitat occupy different niches.

Three types of birds are found on the Galapagos Islands. The three types of birds are the blue-footed booby, the red-footed booby, and the white booby. These three birds all feed on the same kind of fish in the nearby waters. However, the blue-footed booby feeds close to shore, while the red-footed booby flies further out to sea to catch its food. And the white booby dives for its meals in the water in between. Can you think of another example of organisms sharing habitats but not niches?

Foxes and wolves in a forest, trout and bass in a lake, etc.

SECTION REVIEW

1. What is ecology?
   1. Study of relationships and interactions of living things with one another and with their environment

2. What is the difference between a community and a population?
   2. Community includes all organisms in an ecosystem; population includes only organisms of same type

3. What is an organism's habitat? Its niche?
   3. Habitat: place in which organism lives; niche: everything organism does and needs in its habitat

5-2 Food and Energy in the Environment

All living things need energy in order to live. They use energy to carry on all the basic life functions. For most living organisms, the immediate source of energy is the food they eat. But this food can be traced all the way back to green plants, which use the sun's energy. Thus, all the energy used by plants and animals comes directly or indirectly from the sun.

Green Plants: Food Factories

Green plants have one very important advantage over other living things. They can make their own food, while most other living things cannot. Plants make food by the process of **photosynthesis.** During photosynthesis the green parts of plants, especially the leaves, capture the energy of sunlight and use it to make glucose, a type of sugar. The glucose is formed when the plants chemically combine water and carbon dioxide. The reason green plants can carry on photosynthesis is that they contain the green pigment chlorophyll. It is the chlorophyll that captures the energy of sunlight. In addition to glucose, oxygen is also produced during photosynthesis. In fact, photosynthesis is an important source of oxygen on the earth. If it were not for green plants, animals would quickly use up all the oxygen available to them.

Because green plants use the energy of the sun directly to make their own food, they are called **autotrophs** (AWT-uh-trohfs), or "self-feeders." Plants use glucose to provide energy for carrying out life functions. But plants also combine the glucose with other chemicals to make starches, fats, and proteins. As you can see, photosynthesis is a very important process to green plants. But photosynthesis is also very important to animals. Can you guess why this process is so important?

By photosynthesis, plants provide oxygen and food for animals.

Interactions Among Organisms

In every ecosystem, organisms can be divided into groups based on how they obtain their food. Do not forget, however, that the organisms in an ecosystem are interdependent.

PRODUCERS Green plants make their own food and are thus the food **producers** of the ecosystem. Animals cannot make their own food. They must eat either plants or other animals that eat plants.

Figure 5-9 *The leaves of green plants are food factories that make glucose during photosynthesis.*

Figure 5-10 *Indian pipe plants lack chlorophyll and cannot make their own food. But a certain fungus that lives on nearby green plants forms a bridge to the Indian pipe plants. The fungus takes in glucose from the green plants. And the Indian pipes take the glucose from the fungus.*

CONSUMERS   An organism that feeds directly or indirectly on producers is called a **consumer.** Consumers are also called **heterotrophs** (HET-uhr-uh-trohfs), or "other-feeders."

There are many kinds of consumers. Some organisms such as mice, insects, and rabbits are plant eaters. Snakes, frogs, and wolves are flesh eaters. They consume animals that are plant eaters or animals that feed on plant eaters.

In the northern parts of Norway, Sweden, and Finland, a plant called the reindeer moss carries on photosynthesis. Reindeer feed on the reindeer moss. And people who live in this area eat the reindeer. Can you identify the producers and consumers?

A special type of animal consumer feeds on the bodies of dead animals. These organisms are called **scavengers.** Jackals and vultures are examples of scavengers. So are crayfish and snails, who "clean up" lake waters by eating dead organisms.

DECOMPOSERS   After plants and animals die, organisms called **decomposers** use the dead organic matter as a food source. Unlike scavengers, decom-

Figure 5-11 *Organisms are classified as producers, consumers, or decomposers, depending on how they get their food. Producers are autotrophs. Consumers and decomposers are heterotrophs.*

Producer   Consumer   Consumer

Decomposer

posers break down dead plants and animals into simpler substances. In the process, they return important materials to the soil and water. You may be familiar with the term "decay," which is often used to describe this process. Bacteria and mushrooms are examples of decomposers.

Figure 5-12 *The small stickleback fish, which feeds on water fleas, is about to become food for the larger pike fish (left). Spotted hyenas are often scavengers (right).*

Career: *Game Warden*

HELP WANTED: GAME WARDEN College degree in zoology, ecology, or wildlife management desired. Must be familiar with animal behavior and habitats within this state.

The crack of the rifle broke the peaceful quiet of the forest, turning the game warden's attention from the nest full of screeching young robins to more serious matters. This was not the hunting season so there was no reason for anyone to use a gun in the forest. The warden walked carefully to the spot from where the sound seemed to come, calling out "hello" so as not to be mistaken for a target.

This is a scene from the duties of the **game warden.** Each state has rules and regulations protecting its wildlife. The game warden's job is to enforce these rules. They may warn offenders, fine them, arrest them, and confiscate guns, equipment, and any illegally killed animals if necessary.

Game wardens have other duties, too. They keep accurate records of the wildlife in their areas. They are responsible for planning con-

trolled hunts. Wardens issue hunting permits and conduct safety programs to educate hunters. During emergency situations, they may take part in rescue operations.

If you are interested in this career, write to the National Park Service, U.S. Department of the Interior, 18th & C Streets, NW, Washington, DC 20240.

Figure 5-13 *In this Antarctic food chain, microscopic plants known as diatoms (top)* are the food of *zooplankton (top, center),* tiny water animals. The zooplankton are then eaten by krill (bottom, center), shrimplike animals. Krill feed many creatures, including popeyed squid (bottom). *The right whale (bottom, right)* feeds on both krill and squid.

Decomposers are essential to the ecosystem for two reasons. They rid the environment of dead plant and animal matter. But even more important, decomposers return substances such as nitrogen, carbon, phosphorus, sulfur, and magnesium to the environment. These substances then are used by other plants to make food, and the cycle begins again. If the nutrients were not returned to the environment, organisms within that ecosystem could not survive for long.

Food Chains and Food Webs

Within an ecosystem, there are food and energy links between the different plants and animals living there. A **food chain** illustrates how groups of organisms within an ecosystem get their food and energy.

Green plants are autotrophs, or producers. So they are the first link in a food chain. Animals that eat the green plants are the second link. And animals that eat animals that eat plants are the third link.

Here are two examples of food chains. On land, a grasshopper eats a plant. A bird then eats the grasshopper. Finally, a snake eats the bird. In a freshwater pond, microscopic green plants are eaten by water fleas. In turn, the water fleas become the food of minnows, or small fish. Larger fish such as perch and bass feed on the minnows. If no animal eats the perch or bass, it will eventually die and become a source of food for a scavenger like the crayfish. As the perch or bass decays, important substances are returned to the lake water. The microscopic green plants use these substances to make their food. The

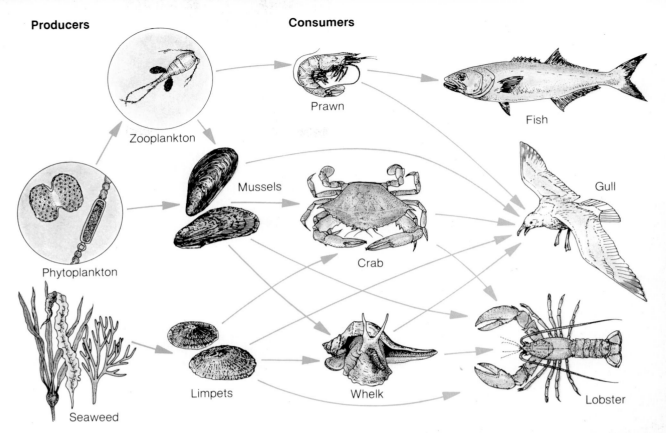

Producers

Zooplankton

Phytoplankton

Seaweed

Consumers

Prawn

Fish

Mussels

Crab

Gull

Limpets

Whelk

Lobster

Figure 5-14 *This ocean food web is a complex overlapping of many individual food chains.*

food chain goes on and on. This food chain could have been extended beyond the perch or bass. Can you think of who the next consumer might be? Bear or person

Food chains are good descriptions of how food energy is passed from one organism to another. But interactions among organisms often are more complex because most animals eat more than one type of food.

For example, in a saltwater environment, sea snails eat various types of seaweed. But seaweed is also eaten by other small fish. And these small fish may become food for larger fish, birds, and octopuses. There are several different food chains involved here, and they overlap to form a **food web.** A food web includes all the food chains in an ecosystem that are connected together. See Figure 5-14.

Feeding and Energy Levels

A feeding level is the location of a plant or an animal along a food chain. Because green plants produce their own food, they form the first feeding level. Consumers that eat plants form the second

Activity

Drawing a Food Web

Using the following plants and animals, draw the food web as you think it might exist: grass, mice, deer, mountain lions, vultures, bacteria.

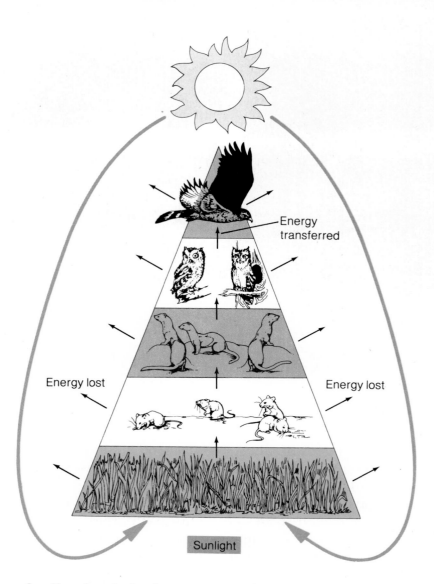

Figure 5-15 *In this food chain, grasses and other plants make their own food by photosynthesis. Mice feed on the grasses and are consumed by weasels. In turn, owls feed on weasels. Owls also become a source of food for the hawks. At each point along the food chain, some energy is lost.*

feeding level. And consumers that eat animals that eat plants form a third feeding level.

At each feeding level, however, much of the energy in food is lost. Each organism at a particular feeding level uses up some of the energy locked in food to carry out its life activities. In addition, a great deal of energy is lost in the form of heat as it is transferred from one feeding level to another. What does this mean for living things at higher energy levels? There is less energy available to organisms at each higher level. The loss of energy as it moves through a food chain can be pictured as an energy pyramid. See Figure 5-15. The energy pyramid represents the decreasing amount of energy available at each feeding level.

Since the autotrophs, or producers such as green plants, support all other living organisms on the earth, they form the base of the energy pyramid. This first level is very broad. Each level above the first level is made up of consumers. And each successive level of consumers in the pyramid is narrower than the one beneath it. As energy moves through the pyramid, from the first feeding level up through all the other levels, much of it is lost.

SECTION REVIEW

1. What is photosynthesis? 1. Process by which green plants make food
2. What is the difference between autotrophs and heterotrophs? 2. Autotrophs make their own food; heterotrophs do not.
3. What is a food chain? A food web?
3. Food chain shows food and energy links between organisms in an ecosystem. Food web includes all the overlapping food chains in an ecosystem.

Activity

Your Place in a Food Chain

Every time you eat, you are assuming a particular place in a food chain. You can determine your place in a food chain through the following activity.

Make a list of all the foods you ate for breakfast, lunch, and dinner. For each food, determine the food chain, using a pyramid to represent your findings. Be sure to answer the following questions.

1. Who are the producers?
2. Who are the consumers?
3. At what level are you a consumer?

5-3 Relationships in an Ecosystem

Whether an ecosystem is a huge patch of ocean bottom or just a dark corner of a forest floor, all the living and nonliving things in it must interact successfully in order for the ecosystem to survive. From

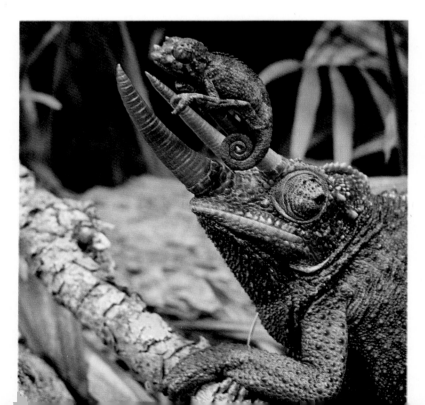

Figure 5-16 *Living things, such as this adult and young chameleon, must interact with other living and nonliving things in the ecosystem. If conditions are right and organisms can find food, water, and shelter, they will reproduce and increase their populations.*

Figure 5-17 *The snowshoe hare shares its habitat with moose. During the cold winter, the hare must successfully compete with the moose for food, or else the hare will die.*

Competition need not always occur when different species of animals or plants live near each other. Three different types of warblers all live in the same forest and have similar diets. However, each type of warbler feeds at a different height in the trees, thus avoiding competition for food.

their environment, all the living organisms must be able to obtain food, water, and shelter. Given the right conditions, the plant and animal populations can reproduce themselves and increase their number. However, if certain living and nonliving factors in the environment interfere with the growth of the population, the size of the population will be limited.

Competition

Ecosystems often cannot satisfy the needs of all the living things in a particular habitat. When there is only a limited amount of food, water, shelter, or even light in an environment, **competition** occurs. Competition is a type of relationship in which organisms struggle with one another and their environment in order to obtain the materials they need to live.

Most of the relationships among living things in an ecosystem are based on competition. The moose and the snowshoe hare, for example, share the same habitat and compete for the same food. Birch trees are the most important food source for these two animals. However, the small hares can hardly compete with the large, hungry moose. So the hares may face a shortage of food, and possibly death, during the cold winter.

Competition often has a positive effect on an ecosystem. Through natural competition, different populations of animals usually are prevented from growing so large that they disrupt the ecosystem. But sometimes outside forces can unbalance natural competition. For example, people interfered with such a natural plan when they introduced rabbits to Australia in 1788. The rabbits had few natural enemies, so the rabbit population grew very quickly. By the middle of the 1800s, these harmless-looking animals were stripping the grasslands bare of vegetation. Cattle herds that also grazed on this vegetation were threatened with starvation. Finally, a disease-causing virus was given to many of the rabbits by scientists. These rabbits died, and so the cattle were saved from starvation.

Plants, too, compete with one another for light, carbon dioxide, minerals, and water. In the forest, plants usually compete for light. Tall trees soak up plenty of sunlight. Smaller trees that also need sunlight may not survive in the shade of these big trees. However, shade can be an advantage to some trees. The red maple tree is hardier than the sugar maple tree, and it usually outnumbers the sugar maple tree in a forest. But the sugar maple tree can grow in the shade, and the red maple tree cannot. So if a young red maple tree and a young sugar maple tree are competing for space and food in the shade of a forest, the sugar maple tree will be more likely to survive.

Symbiotic Relationships

Instead of competing with one another, some plants and animals survive by "living together" and helping one another. Such a partnership is called **symbiosis** (sim-bee-OH-sis). Symbiosis is a relationship in which one organism lives on, near, or even inside another organism. A symbiotic relationship may benefit either one partner or both partners in the relationship. Some symbiotic relationships may sound rather strange to you. But no matter how odd they may seem, all symbiotic relationships have one thing in common. They provide the means by which one or both of the organisms can survive.

COMMENSALISM High in the branches of a tree, a large, fierce hawk called the osprey builds a big platform-shaped nest for its eggs. Smaller birds such as sparrows and wrens set up their homes beneath the osprey's nest. Because the osprey eats mostly fish,

Activity

Shady Survival

Suppose 140 trees are growing in a shaded area of a forest. Of those trees, 65 percent are sugar maples and 35 percent are red maples. How many trees of each kind are there?

Figure 5-18 *In an example of commensalism, small birds such as this sparrow* (left) *make their homes beneath the nests of large, fish-eating osprey* (right). *The presence of the fierce osprey provides protection for the little birds.*

these smaller birds are in no danger from the osprey. In fact, the little birds obtain protection from their enemies by living close to the fierce hawk.

Beautiful tropical orchids survive in dense jungles by growing high above the shade. There among the branches of trees, the flowers get a great deal of sunlight. The roots of these flowers are exposed, so they can take water right out of the air. The tree does not benefit from this relationship. It simply plays the role of "good neighbor."

Both of these symbiotic relationships are examples of **commensalism.** In commensalism, one organism in the partnership benefits. The other organism is neither helped nor harmed.

In another example of commensalism, whales make good neighbors for tiny, crusty-looking animals called barnacles. If you could swim alongside a whale, you would see these barnacles attached to the whale's sides. There the barnacles get a free ride through vast areas of the ocean, which greatly increases their chances of finding food. The whale, unharmed by the barnacles, simply ignores its tiny passengers!

MUTUALISM Some relationships are necessary for the survival of both organisms. This type of symbiosis is called **mutualism** and is helpful to both organisms. Food and protection are two common reasons organisms share such a partnership.

Figure 5-19 *This furry ratel (left) works with the honey guide bird (right) so that both can find their favorite foods—honey and beeswax.*

In certain areas of Africa, a small bird known as the honey guide bird lives in a mutualistic relationship with a furry little animal called a ratel. The honey guide bird loves to eat beeswax, but it is too small to break into a bee's nest easily. The ratel likes honey, but it cannot always find a supply on its own. So the two animals work together. The honey guide locates a bee's nest and chirps loudly for the ratel. The ratel moves toward the sound. This chirping and following continues until the ratel reaches the bee's nest. With its sharp claws, the ratel rips the nest open and enjoys a fine feast. The honey guide bird then gets its chance to finish the beeswax.

Strange, undersea creatures called tubeworms create an unusual team with bacteria. At the bottom of the Pacific Ocean in an area near the Galapagos Islands, cracks in the ocean floor leak hot water. This water contains a foul-smelling substance called hydrogen sulfide. Nearby, tubeworms that are three meters long grow together in small bunches. The tubeworms, which lack intestines for digesting food, attach themselves to the ocean bottom, looking very much like rubbery flagpoles bending in the breeze. Each worm has a red, blood-filled organ sticking out of the top of its white tube. These red organs filter the hydrogen sulfide out of the water. Inside the tubeworms, bacteria use the hydrogen sulfide to carry on chemical reactions that release energy. The bacteria use this energy to make food for themselves. The tubeworms also can use the food made by the bacteria. They do not need to digest it, so the absence of intestines is not a problem. This strange relationship between tubeworms and bacteria allows these two organisms to survive deep in the inky darkness of the ocean bottom.

In some cases of mutualism, an animal will help feed another in return for protection. Large fish-eating birds called herons and ibises make their nests in the trees of the Florida swamps. At the base of these trees live poisonous snakes, who gather there to catch pieces of fish the birds may drop. At the same time these snakes are getting a free meal, they are providing protection for the herons and ibises. For the poisonous snakes keep away raccoons and other animals that would feast on the birds' eggs and baby chicks.

Figure 5-20 *Poisonous snakes live at the base of the tree in which this white ibis makes its nest. They keep raccoons and other animals away from the ibis's eggs and baby chicks.*

Two other examples of mutualism are the shark and remora and the termite and its intestinal protozoa.

Figure 5-21 *The relationship between these water buffaloes and tickbirds is an example of mutualism. The tickbirds feed on tiny insects they pluck from the buffaloes's hides, and the buffaloes get a good cleaning.*

Figure 5-22 *The vinelike dodder plant is a parasite. It benefits by getting all its food from its host plant, which is harmed by the relationship.*

As you can see, mutualism can occur in just about any ecosystem. All that is necessary is the need for two organisms to cooperate with each other in order that they both may survive.

PARASITISM So far you have seen that in a relationship between two organisms, both may benefit or just one may benefit. In the relationship called **parasitism,** however, one partner not only does *not* benefit but is actually harmed by the other organism. The organism that benefits is the parasite. The organism that the parasite lives off and harms is called the host. A parasite has special adaptations that help it to take advantage of its host.

The sea lamprey, a very primitive fish that lacks jaws, is a blood-sucking parasite. This strange-looking fish resembles a swimming tube that has fins on its back. The lamprey's round mouth acts as a suction cup by which the lamprey attaches itself to other fish. Even as the victim tries to shake the lamprey loose, the parasite's toothed tongue carves a hole in the fish and sucks out its blood. Small fish often die from loss of blood. However, a successful parasite does not usually kill its victim. Can you explain why? If it did, it would lose its food source.

Plants, as well as animals, can be parasites. The dodder plant lives by obtaining all of its food from host plants, such as clover and alfalfa. Wrapping its pale stem around the host plant, the dodder pushes its "suckers" onto its host. Then it releases itself completely from the soil and stays attached to the host plant for support and food.

Balance in the Ecosystem

An ecosystem is a finely balanced environment in which living things successfully interact in order to survive. Disturbance in this balance in one part of the ecosystem can cause problems in another part of the ecosystem. Such disturbances can be the result of nature or of human interference.

A natural disaster regularly strikes the giant panda, which lives in the bamboo forests of China and Tibet. The bamboo plants, which make up most of the panda's diet, produce seeds about once every 100 years. Then the bamboo plants die. It takes the new bamboo plants several years to grow large enough for the pandas to eat them. During this time, the pandas face a serious shortage of food. Many of them die. *

Ecologists do not always have to study the death of living things in order to understand the importance of interdependence among organisms in an ecosystem. Sometimes such interdependence can be studied by observing the rebirth of an ecological system.

In May of 1980, Mount St. Helens, a volcano in the state of Washington, exploded. Thousands of trees, shrubs, flowers, and animals were destroyed by the eruption. Volcanic ash covered the soil as far away as 14 kilometers from the volcano. What had once been a beautiful, green forest soon looked like

Figure 5-23 *In May of 1980, the lush, green forests of Mount St. Helens (top, left) were destroyed by a volcanic eruption. Volcanic ash covered the soil (top, right). But within a month, life began to appear amid the fallen trees and ash (center). A year later, flowers began to bloom and birds and insects returned to the area (bottom). An ecosystem had been reborn.*

* Although this phenomenon is not completely understood, the century bamboo plants that grow in these forests all produce seeds and die at the same time, creating the serious shortage of food for the pandas.

the barren surface of the moon. Within a month, however, life began to return to the area. Roots of the red-flowered fireweed bush and other plants that had survived pushed growing stems up through the ash. These plants attracted insects such as aphids, which feed on the juices of the fireweed. In turn, birds came into the area to feed on insects. Spiders crawled on the ash-covered surface. When these animals died, their bodies fertilized the ash, returning important nutrients to the soil. Hoofed animals such as elk wandered through the area, breaking up the ash cover and leaving holes through which more seeds could sprout.

Once plant and animal life started again, relationships among organisms were reestablished. What was once a bleak, lifeless landscape is now an area filled with colorful flowers, green shrubs, and growing trees. Scientists are carefully studying this area for clues to the secret of how living things can turn a barren land into a lively ecosystem inhabited by interdependent organisms.

People can often be the cause of the destruction of an ecological system. Mono Lake, in eastern California, is a beautiful saltwater lake fed by streams of melting snow from the Sierra Nevada Mountains. Two small islands within Mono Lake attract thou-

Figure 5-24 *The ecosystem of Mono Lake (left), once disturbed by human interference, is now returning to its delicate balance (right).*

sands of birds, especially sea gulls. More than 80 species of birds nest on these islands and feed on the lake's shrimp, flies, and algae. That is, until 1981. During the summer of that year, many baby sea gulls were found dead. How strange this seemed to be for an ecosystem that had long provided food, water, and shelter for the sea gull population. As people investigated the situation, they discovered that the ecosystem had been disturbed by actions taken far away from the lake many years before.

About 40 years ago, the city of Los Angeles began to use water from the major streams that feed into Mono Lake. Less and less water emptied into Mono Lake, and the lake began to dry up. Thousands of acres of dust formed where there was once water.

As the amount of water in the lake decreased, the concentration of salt dissolved in the water increased. The shrimp that sea gulls fed on could not survive in water so salty. As the shrimp died, less food was available for the sea gulls. Baby sea gulls starved to death.

To make matters worse, as the water level in Mono Lake dropped, a land bridge that connected the shore to the nesting islands formed. Coyotes crossed this bridge, killed many sea gulls, and invaded the gulls' nests.

Many people want to save Mono Lake. They realize that human actions have damaged the lake and disturbed an ecosystem. Without a water conservation plan, Mono Lake will continue to dry up. And the delicate balance between living and nonliving things in this ecosystem will be seriously altered.

Mono Lake illustrates how important it is to understand how an ecosystem operates and how it can be damaged by human activity. With this sort of knowledge, people can save the environment, and perhaps even improve it!

Activity

Changes in Populations

Isle Royale is a long, narrow island in Lake Superior, 25 kilometers from the shore of Canada. In the early 1900s, a few moose reached the island and within 20 years increased their population to more than 2000.

During the next 40 years, the moose population underwent several changes. Using books and other materials in the library, find out what changes occurred on Isle Royale and what caused the changes. Include answers to the following questions in your report.

1. What are limiting factors and in what ways do they affect a population?

2. How do birth and death rates affect a population?

3. What is the definition of a population cycle?

SECTION REVIEW

1. What is symbiosis? 1. Relationship in which organisms live together for the benefit of either or both of the partners

2. Compare the relationships of commensalism, mutualism, and parasitism.

3. What are the two main causes of disturbances in the balance within an ecosystem?

2. Commensalism: one organism benefits, the other is unaffected; mutualism: both organisms benefit; parasitism: parasite benefits, host is harmed.

3. Natural changes and human interference

LABORATORY ACTIVITY

They Call It Home

For further instructions, see page T-26.

Purpose

In this activity, you will learn about some animals that build elaborate and interesting shelters.

Materials *(per group)*

Wildlife encyclopedia or other reference
  books
Paper
Colored pencils or crayons
Materials for shelter building

Procedure

1. Animals must use available materials to create their homes. Some animals dig burrows; some live in hollow trees. Other animals build very elaborate and unusual shelters. Choose one of the following animals and find out what kind of shelter it builds:
   beaver
   trapdoor spider
   termite
   cliff swallow
   titmouse
   prairie dog
   fighting fish
   mud dauber wasp
2. Learn all you can about how the animal constructs its home. Draw a picture of the animal's shelter and make a list of materials used to create it.
3. Working alone, or in a group, build a model of your animal's shelter. Whenever possible, use the same kind of materials that the animal would use.

Observations and Conclusions

1. How long did it take you to construct the shelter? How long do you think it would take the animal to make the same shelter?
2. Why do animals build shelters? List as many reasons as you can.
3. What do you think would happen if some of the materials that an animal usually used to build its shelter were not available?

CHAPTER SUMMARY

5-1 Living Things and Their Environment

- Ecology is the study of the relationships and interactions of living things with one another and with their environment.

- An ecosystem is a group of organisms in an area that interact with each other, together with their nonliving environment.

- The living part of an ecosystem is called the community.

- A population is a group of the same type of organism living together in the same area.

- Different ecosystems support different living things.

- The place in a community in which an organism lives is its habitat. Its niche is its role in the community. Habitats can overlap, but organisms cannot share the same niche.

5-2 Food and Energy in the Environment

- Green plants are autotrophs because they make their own food by photosynthesis.

- Green plants are the producers in an ecosystem; heterotrophs are the consumers.

- Scavengers feed on dead animals.

- Decomposers are organisms that break down dead plants and animals into simpler substances during the decay process. As a result, important substances are returned to the soil and water.

- A food chain illustrates how groups of organisms within an ecosystem get their food and energy.

- Food chains often overlap or connect to form food webs.

- Each plant or animal in a food chain has a particular location called a feeding level.

- At each successive level in a food chain, energy is lost. The loss of energy as it moves through a food chain can be pictured as an energy pyramid.

5-3 Relationships in an Ecosystem

- Competition among organisms for food, water, and shelter exists in all ecosystems.

- Symbiosis is a relationship in which two organisms live together for the benefit of either one or both of the partners.

- In commensalism, one organism in the partnership benefits.

- A relationship in which both partners benefit is called mutualism.

- In parasitism, one organism benefits but only by harming the other organism.

- An ecosystem is a finely balanced environment in which living things successfully interact in order to survive.

- Disturbances in an ecosystem can be caused by nature or by human interference.

Vocabulary   *Define the following terms.*

autotroph p.101
commensalism p.110
community p.97
competition p.108
consumer p.102
decomposer p.102

ecology p.95
ecosystem p.95
environment p.95
food chain p.104
food web p.105
habitat p.99

heterotroph p.102
mutualism p.110
niche p.99
parasitism p.112
photosynthesis p.101
population p.98

producer p.101
scavenger p.102
symbiosis p.109

CHAPTER REVIEW

Multiple Choice

Choose the letter of the answer that best completes each statement.

1. The study of the relationships of living things and their environment is called
   a. commensalism.
   b. parasitism.
   c. ecology.
   d. botany.

2. A forest is an example of a(n)
   a. ecosystem.
   b. population.
   c. food chain.
   d. niche.

3. A group of the same type of organism living together in the same area is a(n)
   a. ecosystem.
   b. habitat.
   c. niche.
   d. population.

4. An organism's "occupation," or role, in an ecosystem is called its
   a. niche.
   b. habitat.
   c. community.
   d. level.

5. Green plants make their own food by
   a. mutualism.
   b. adaptation.
   c. population.
   d. photosynthesis.

6. In order to make food, green plants need
   a. water, carbon dioxide, and sunlight.
   b. oxygen, carbon dioxide, and sunlight.
   c. glucose, oxygen, and carbon dioxide.
   d. glucose, nitrogen, and phosphorus.

7. A whale is an example of a(n)
   a. producer.
   b. autotroph.
   c. consumer.
   d. scavenger.

8. How plants and animals in an ecosystem get their food can be described by a(n)
   a. energy web.
   b. food chain.
   c. population pyramid.
   d. symbiotic relationship.

9. Two organisms living together for the benefit of both is an example of
   a. commensalism.
   b. parasitism.
   c. decay.
   d. mutualism.

10. The delicate balance of an ecosystem can be disturbed by
    a. nature.
    b. human interference.
    c. both of these.
    d. neither of these.

Completions

Fill in the word or words that best complete each statement.

1. A group of organisms and their nonliving environment is a(n) ____ecosystem____.

2. The place in a community in which an organism lives is called its ____habitat____.

3. The process by which a green plant makes its own food is called ____photosynthesis____.

4. Organisms that feed on the bodies of dead animals are called ____scavengers____.

5. Organisms known as ____decomposers____ break down dead plants and animals.

6. When food chains overlap or are connected together, a(n) ____food web____ is formed.

7. Energy loss through a food chain can be pictured as a(n) ____energy pyramid____.

8. There is always ____competition____ among organisms for food, water, light, and shelter.

9. In _____mutualism_____ each animal benefits from the partnership.

10. An organism that lives off and harms its host is called a(n) _____parasite_____.

True or False

Determine whether each statement is true or false. If it is true, write "true."
If it is false, change the underlined word or words to make the statement
true.

1. The study of the relationships of living things to one another and to their environment is called etymology. F (ecology)

2. The living part of an ecosystem is called a community. T

3. A tree, a cave, or a pile of leaves is an example of an organism's habitat. T

4. Green plants can make food because they contain carotene. F (chlorophyll)

5. An organism that cannot make its own food is called a(n) autotroph. F (heterotroph)

6. Decomposers help return important substances to the environment. T

7. The first link in a food chain are the consumers such as green plants. F (producers).

8. Within a food chain, there is more energy available at each higher feeding level.*

9. Most relationships among living things in an ecosystem are based on competition. T

10. Synthetic relationships provide the means by which one or both organisms can benefit by living together. F (Symbiotic)

* F (less)

Discussion Topics Answers appear on page T-26.

Write a brief paragraph discussing each of the following.

1. The African tickbird lives on the back of the rhinoceros, where it picks bloodsucking ticks off the back of this huge animal. What type of symbiosis is this? Explain.

2. Pretend you are in charge of building a city. Explain what design features you would use in order to make the city part of the existing ecosystem.

EXPAND YOUR KNOWLEDGE

Mabey, R. *Oak & Company.* New York: Greenwillow.
    The life cycle of an oak is used to show the fabric of a community.

Coming Up·····SCIENCE GAZETTE·······

Starting on the next page you will find three special articles. The first tells an exciting story about a scientist. The second tells about a battle of ideas. And the last looks into the future. Each of the articles has been written so you will enjoy reading it. As you read, you may want to jot down thoughts that come to mind. You might then write a report telling what you thought about the articles. Or you might just want to read the articles for the fun of it.

Adventures in Science

The articles of this *Science Gazette* have been carefully chosen and designed to inspire and motivate students of all levels in their study of science. Each article is related to one or more topics presented in the unit. See the "Science Reading Skills" section in your Teachers' Resource Book for specific activities and handouts. Also, for further instructions, see page T-27 in this book.

Archie Carr and the Mystery of the Vanishing Sea Turtles

The great sea turtle mystery: Now you see them, now you don't. And now you see them again. Year after year, millions of newly hatched sea turtles leave their nests on sandy beaches and disappear into the sea. Then, larger and one year older, they begin to pop up hundreds of kilometers from their original homes. Where have the turtles been? What have they eaten? How do these little creatures survive in the vast, stormy oceans?

For many years, these questions puzzled Dr. Archie Carr, who is now a research scientist at the University of Florida in Gainesville. Carr says that ever since he was a young boy, he had wanted to be a scientist and study animals. Turtles have always been of special interest to him. In the late 1940s and early 1950s, Carr visited museums in the United States, Europe, South America, and Africa in order to study their turtle collections. During these trips, he noticed something odd. The museums had specimens of newly hatched sea turtles, called hatchlings. And the museums also had sea turtles that were about a year old and were as large as dinner plates. But the museum did not have sea turtles that were older than hatchlings but younger than one year old. Apparently, no sea turtles of that age had ever been found!

The Lost Sea Turtles

Archie Carr decided to find out where these "lost" sea turtles were. Working like a detective, he started gathering clues to the mystery. He walked along beaches where mother sea turtles laid their eggs. He talked to people who lived near the beaches and to people who fished in the waters offshore. But Carr couldn't find anyone who had seen baby sea turtles after they had hatched. The babies seemed to be hiding from everyone for the first year of their lives.

Carr knew that newly hatched sea turtles leave their nests on the sandy beaches of Florida, Panama, and Costa Rica and head straight for the sea. He also knew that the

Dr. Archie Carr conducts his sea turtle research while at sea.

floating animals and plants called plankton. So even if there were no sargassum rafts, hatchlings could survive by floating along with the currents and eating the plankton.

Sea turtle hatchlings spend the first year of their lives clinging to seaweed floating on the surface of the water.

ocean currents far offshore push together clumps of seaweed. The seaweed, called sargassum, floats on the surface of the water. The sargassum collects to form large "rafts" that drift along with the currents. These rafts are more than just large clumps of seaweed. They are ecological communities that house various life forms.

The Plot Thickens

By 1967, Carr had developed a hypothesis about what happens to hatchling sea turtles. According to Carr, hatchlings swim out to sea and climb onto the sargassum rafts. The rafts give them shelter and food. At the same time, the drifting rafts carry the hatchlings hundreds or even thousands of kilometers from their home beaches. After about a year, the turtles find their way back to shore—a new shore, far from home.

There was one problem with this explanation, however. Not all the waters off the beaches where sea turtles hatch have sargassum rafts. Did that mean Carr's explanation was wrong? Not at all. Carr knew that even where the currents did not form sargassum rafts, they did push together tiny

Put to the Test

Archie Carr's hypothesis was interesting, but was it correct? He and other scientists began to look for young sea turtles in sargassum that was floating in the sea off beaches where the sea turtles hatched. One day the scientists were examining a tangle of sargassum. Suddenly, something moved. A tiny head poked out of the seaweed. It belonged to a sea turtle! Soon a hungry bird plucked the turtle off the raft. Birds knew where to find the young turtles, even if people didn't.

Carr now knows that the hatchlings become part of the ecological community of the sargassum raft. They eat small shrimp, snails, crabs, and jellyfish that also inhabit this community. In turn, the sea turtles are food for other animals. Pelicans, sea gulls, and other hungry birds swoop down and snatch some of the turtles off the rafts. Despite this and storms at sea that tear the rafts apart, enough sea turtles survive to reproduce and begin the sea turtle adventure again.

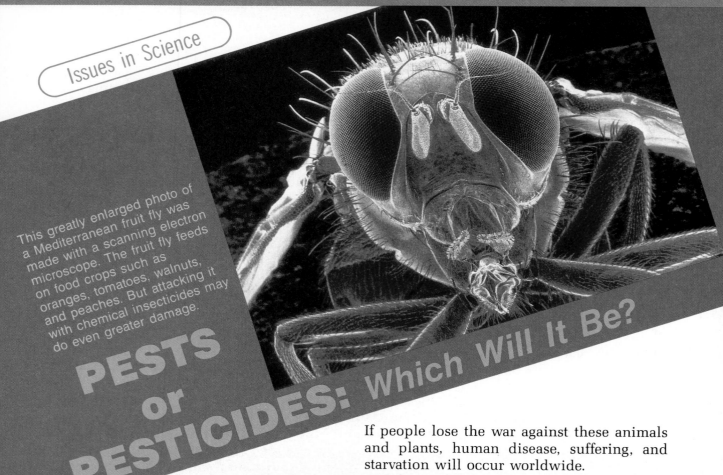

Issues in Science

This greatly enlarged photo of a Mediterranean fruit fly was made with a scanning electron microscope. The fruit fly feeds on food crops such as oranges, tomatoes, walnuts, and peaches. But attacking it with chemical insecticides may do even greater damage.

PESTS or PESTICIDES: Which Will It Be?

There is a war being fought right now that has been going on for thousands of years. It is a fight for survival against armies that far outnumber the earth's entire human population. It is the war people wage against insects, rats, mice, weeds, and fungi.

Some insects, rats, and mice carry deadly diseases such as malaria and typhoid fever. Throughout history, diseases carried by pests have killed hundreds of millions of people. These animals also threaten food supplies around the world.

Other threats to world food supplies are weeds and fungi. Weeds compete with crops for water and nutrients. Some fungi cause plant diseases that result in huge crop losses.

If people lose the war against these animals and plants, human disease, suffering, and starvation will occur worldwide.

Today people have many weapons to use in the fight against insects, rodents, and unwanted plants. During the past few decades, scientists have made or discovered many chemicals that kill pests. These chemicals, which are called pesticides, have helped increase food production by killing the pests that destroy crops and eat stored food. Pesticides have also saved many human lives by killing disease-carrying pests.

Unfortunately, people have not always used pesticides wisely. Farmers and others who use pesticides have accidentally killed useful animals and plants. Also, incorrect use of certain pesticides has made it harder to kill some pests. That is because many pests are now able to withstand assaults of deadly chemicals. In other words, the pests have become resistant to the pesticides.

In addition, pesticides are sometimes washed into rivers and streams, where they kill fish and other animals. Winds can spread pesticides over hundreds or thousands of miles. This pollutes areas far from where the chemical was used to kill pests. Pesticides have injured and killed people in all parts of the world.

So now we face a difficult problem. How can we save crops and kill disease-carrying insects without harming the environment?

The Other Side of Pesticides

There are now about 35,000 different pesticides on the market. Each year in the United States alone, about one-half billion kilograms of these chemicals are used by farmers, homeowners, and industry.

Specific pesticides called herbicides and fungicides have helped farmers to reduce crop losses due to weeds and fungi. Yet during the past 30 years, the amount of crops destroyed by insects has nearly doubled. This is true despite the fact that farmers have been using more powerful insecticides in greater quantities than ever before!

Incorrect use of pesticides may account for the alarming comeback of malaria in countries where it had been practically wiped out. More than 200 million people in Asia, Africa, and Latin America suffer from this disease, which is spread from person to person by mosquitoes. Perhaps because of overspraying of crops, mosquitoes are becoming resistant to insecticides that used to control them.

This begins when a few resistant insects survive after being sprayed with insecticide. These survivors then produce more mosquitoes that are resistant to the insecticide. In a short time, most of the population of insects in the sprayed area is resistant.

Insecticides can also kill the natural enemies of insect pests. For example, insecticides have killed ladybugs in some apple orchards. Now there are no more ladybugs in these orchards to keep apple-eating insects, such as mites, under control.

Because of the harmful effects of pesticides, some people believe that these chemicals are

One way to combat insect pests is to spray them from the air with chemical insecticides. But this method, called crop dusting, also affects living things other than pests.

too dangerous to use. But those in favor of using pesticides disagree. They say that pesticides would not be so dangerous if people knew how to use them properly.

For example, pesticides should not be sprayed in fields when the wind is blowing. When the wind is blowing, much of the pesticide is blown away. The pesticide then travels to pollute the air people breathe, the water they drink, and the rivers and lakes in which fish swim. People should also be taught to use only as much pesticide as they need for a particular job. This would reduce the over-spraying that can lead to resistant pests.

New Weapons

One way to lessen our dependence on pesticides is to understand how crops and insects interact with their environments. The study of how living things interact with their environments is called ecology. Ecology provides clues to how to control pests by changing the environment of either the pest or its victim.

Farmers use pesticides against such destructive insects as the tobacco hornworm. The hornworm attacks many kinds of crops, including these tomato plants. However, pesticides can also harm helpful insects, animals, and even people.

For example, a plant called barberry often carries a fungus that causes a disease called black stem rust. When barberry grows near wheat, the rust spreads from the barberry to the wheat. Some farmers have protected their wheat from black stem rust by destroying nearby barberry plants rather than by spraying fungicide.

Other diseases can be controlled by crop rotation. Periodically planting crops other than cabbage in a cabbage field is an example. This method prevents disease-causing organisms that attack only cabbage from building up in the soil.

Also, scientists might discover new chemicals that are harmful only to pests. For example, scientists at the University of Georgia discovered that the oil in orange peels kills fire ants, wasps, and fleas but is harmless to other animals.

Not all new types of pest control are so down-to-earth, however. By studying how the crop-eating desert locust interacts with its environment, scientists have been able to use satellites to fight this pest.

The desert locust is a flying insect related to the grasshopper. From time to time, millions of these locusts gather and sweep across Africa and India, eating every crop and blade of grass in their path. No weapons have been able to stop these insects once they take flight. But in recent years, satellites orbiting the earth have been taking pictures of areas in Africa and India where locusts might breed. Scientists can identify possible breeding areas by the amount of moisture they contain. If satellite photos show that an area is moist enough for locust eggs to survive there, scientists warn the people that may be threatened. The people can then concentrate their pesticide spraying in these areas.

The better we understand how living things interact with their environments, the more clues we will find for controlling pests without using large amounts of chemicals.

Ronda and her family lived in a space settlement on Pluto. One day, a strong radiation storm swept across the Purple Mountains of their planet. There had been many such storms on the planet in the year, 2101. The module in which Ronda and her family lived had been directly in the path of the storm. Somehow, radioactive dust penetrated the sealed glass that served as windows in the module. As a result, Ronda was blind. Radiation had destroyed the nerves that carried the electrical signals from Ronda's eyes to her brain. Her brain could no longer interpret what her eyes were "seeing."

Months after the storm, Ronda sat nervously in a plush armchair in the waiting room of Venus General Hospital. Today was the day the bandages would be removed from her eyes. Ronda was terrified that the operation to restore her sight might have been a failure. She did not want to rely on a seeing-eye robot for the rest of her life.

As the doctors removed the bandages, Ronda thought about the computer that had been implanted in her brain. No larger than a grain of rice, the computer was programmed to record all the images Ronda's eyes picked up and then translate them into messages her brain could understand. The computer was designed to work exactly like the eye nerves that had been destroyed.

The bandages fell from Ronda's eyes. She could see! The living computer inside her head had restored her sight.

Today scientists believe that living computers will be a reality in the not-so-distant

THE COMPUTER THAT LIVES!

Vacuum tubes like these made the first computers possible.

The computers of the 1950s used transistors instead of vacuum tubes.

Today, thousands of transistors are packed onto a silicon chip.

future. Living computers, like the one in Ronda's brain, require no outside power source and never need to be replaced. To understand how living computers may be possible, let's look briefly at how computers have evolved since the 1800s.

The first computers, made up of clunky gears and wheels, were turned by hand. They had only the simplest ability to answer questions based on the information stored inside them. By 1950, computers were run by electricity and operated with switches instead of gears. Information was stored when thousands of switches turned on and off in certain ways. While a lot of information could be fed into electrical memory banks, the computers of the 1950s were still very crude. In fact, the typical 1950s computer took up an entire room and could do less than many video-arcade games of the 1980s.

Time Marches On

The computers of the 1980s contain thousands of switches and can be placed on a tabletop. The reason for the compactness of these computers is the silicon chip. Engineers can put hundreds of switches on a tiny piece of the chemical silicon. These tiny pieces of silicon, known as chips, are manufactured using laser beams and microscopes. It is these chips that record the information when, for example, you tell a computer your name.

But even with the silicon chip, modern computers cannot really think creatively or reason. And a computer has less sense than an ordinary garden snail. Experts feel that in order for computers to "graduate" to higher-level tasks, a whole new way must be developed of storing information in them. The key to developing a new system of information storage may lie in molecules of certain chemicals.

Why molecules? Scientists know that when some molecules are brought together, interesting changes take place. For example, electricity can jump from one molecule to another almost as if tiny switches were being shut on and off between them. Can we learn how to work these tiny switches? If so, then perhaps a whole new type of computer could be built!

This new computer might be able to hold more information in a single drop of liquid than today's computer could store in an entire roomful of chips. As you can imagine, the molecules in this computer of the future would have to be pretty special. And they would have to be produced in a new way.

Leave It to Bacteria

One of the most popular current ideas concerning how these molecules could be produced is: Let bacteria do it for us! Bacteria

A complex network of protein molecules, such as the one in this drawing, may be the electrical switches in computers of the future.

Current flow

Protein

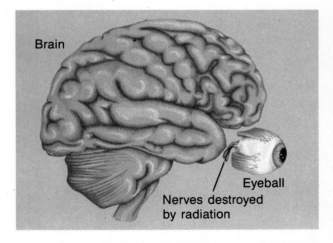

Remember that bacteria need food to make molecules. Suppose that the computer in Ronda's brain was fed by her own blood, like all the other cells in her body. If this were the case, Ronda's computer would live as long as Ronda herself.

It may be many years before the living computer becomes a reality. Scientists must learn more about such things as how molecules react together, and how they can be programmed. But many scientists await the day when they can look at a computer and say, "It's alive."

When nerves connecting the eye to the brain are destroyed, no electrical signals can be carried. A person cannot see. By implanting a computer the size of a grain of rice, the person's sight is restored. The computer is designed to work exactly like the eye nerves.

Brain

Eyeball

Nerves destroyed by radiation

Brain

Ronda's new computer in place of nerves

are all around us. They constantly break down very complicated chemicals into molecules. Bacteria are at work in our bodies, in our food, and in our environment every minute of every day. Some scientists feel that bacteria could be "taught" to make special molecules. These molecules, when mixed together, could produce the flow of electricity needed to make a computer.

Of course, bacteria cannot be taught in the same sense that people can. Bacteria are not able to "learn." However, scientists can now *control* bacteria in many unusual ways. There are new techniques available that allow scientists to combine two different types of bacteria to produce a third, totally different type. In the future, bacteria may produce chemicals that have never been seen before.

In terms of a living computer, imagine that some bacteria have been taught to make special molecules. These bacteria could be grown in a special container and fed a particular substance to produce certain molecules. If the molecules could be told, or programmed, to do the right things, you would have a computer. And the computer would actually be alive because the bacteria live, grow, and produce molecules inside their container.

Think about the living computer implanted in Ronda's brain that allowed her to see again.

Deer in pond ecosystem

Classification of Living Things

For an overview of this unit, see pages T-28 to T-45. You may want to check the Laboratory Activity following each chapter, as well as the activities and investigations for this unit in your Teacher's Resource Book and Annotated Teacher's Edition, Laboratory Book, so that materials can be ordered, gathered, or prepared in advance.

On a small pond in northern Minnesota, tiny water-striding insects glide along the slate-blue surface, paying little attention to the deer standing near the pond. Beneath the water, a hungry pop-eyed minnow follows the rapid movement of the insects. The pleasant odors of pond grasses drift to the twitching nostrils of a cottontail rabbit standing beside the edge of the pond. Suddenly, without warning, the croak of a bullfrog breaks the calm silence.

Not far away, a camper with binoculars observes this tiny slice of nature. "There must be some kind of order to this," she thinks to herself. The woman tries to remember the ways in which living things are grouped. Then she smiles as she remembers a strange sentence: "Kings play cards on fat green stools." This sentence is a kind of code that reveals the way living things are grouped. See page 137 for the secret of the code.

CHAPTERS

6 Classification

For a chapter overview, teaching strategies, answers to all activities, a list of A-V materials, and a chapter bibliography, see pages T-28 to T-29.

Consult your Teacher's Resource Book and Annotated Teacher's Edition, Laboratory Book for additional activities and teaching aids.

CHAPTER OBJECTIVES

After completing this chapter, you will be able to:

6-1 Describe the work of Carolus Linnaeus.

6-1 Explain binomial nomenclature.

6-2 List the seven major classification groups.

6-3 Give some general characteristics of the plant, animal, protist, monera, and fungi kingdoms.

The people fishing from the boat could not believe their eyes. Lying in the boat's net was a fish none of them ever had seen before. It stretched more than 1.5 meters from the tip of its ugly nose to the end of its fan-shaped tail. Large steel-blue scales covered its body. A powerful lower jaw hung down from a frightening face. But most peculiar of all, its fins were attached to what appeared to be stubby legs!

The unusual fish, caught at the mouth of the Chalumna River in South Africa, was taken to a local museum. There M. Courtenay-Latimer, a South African museum curator, happened to see the fish. After searching through many books, she had found no description of the strange fish. However, she knew of someone who might be able to solve the riddle. That someone was Professor J. L. B. Smith, an African fish expert. So M. Courtenay-Latimer preserved and sent the fish to Professor Smith.

The scientist was shocked. He later wrote, "I would hardly have been more surprised if I met a dinosaur on the street." Professor Smith was looking at an animal thought to have become extinct more than 60 million years ago. Yet, in a flash, Professor Smith had been able to identify the fish as a coelacanth (SEE-luh-kanth). The discovery was exciting because coelacanths are thought to be closely related to fish that evolved into four-footed land animals.

What led Professor Smith to make his startling identification? A knowledge of biological classification, a special system that helps scientists to identify and name organisms.

Rare photograph of a coelacanth
This photograph was taken in the Indian Ocean near the Comoro Islands.

Figure 6-1 *Thousands of years ago, people drew this painting on a cave wall in Spain. What message does the painting communicate?*

The painting shows the types of animals the people hunted.

6-1 History of Classification

Thousands of years ago, people began to recognize that there were different groups of living things in the world. Some animals had claws and sharp teeth and roamed the land. Others had feathers and beaks and flew in the air. Still others had scales and fins and swam in the water.

People also made observations about plants. Not only did plants vary in shape, size, and color, but some were good to eat while others were poisonous. In a similar sense, some animals, such as those with sharp teeth, were very dangerous, while others, such as those with feathers, were relatively harmless.

Without knowing exactly what they were doing, these people developed simple systems of *classification*. Classification is the grouping of living things according to similar characteristics. Knowledge of these characteristics helped people to survive their environment. For example, they quickly learned to fear the sharp-toothed animals and to hunt the feathered ones.

Perhaps these people painted pictures on the walls of caves to communicate this knowledge. See Figure 6-1. Today, similar but much more complex information is found in the drawings, photographs, and words in scientific books. This information is organized into the science of classification, which is called **taxonomy** (tak-SAH-nuh-mee). The scientists who work in this field are called taxonomists. The purpose of taxonomy is to group all the plants and animals on earth in an orderly system. This system helps to provide a better understanding of the relationships among living things. Meaningful names are given to newly discovered animals and plants based on taxonomy. Sometimes taxonomy even helps solve biological riddles of the past.

Early Classification Systems

In the fourth century B.C., the Greek philosopher Aristotle first proposed a system to classify life. He placed the animals into three groups. One group included all animals that flew, another group included those that swam, and a third group included those that walked.

Aristotle classified animals according to the way they moved. Although this system was useful, it caused problems. According to Aristotle, both a bird

Figure 6-2 *From these photographs, you might think that both of these animals are classified as bears. The grizzly bear (*left*) does belong to the bear family, but the panda (*right*) is actually a close relative to the raccoon.*

and a bat would fall into the same flying group. Yet in some basic respects, birds and bats are very different. Birds, for example, are covered with feathers. Bats, on the other hand, are covered with hair.

Although the system devised by Aristotle would not satisfy today's taxonomists, it was the first attempt to develop a scientific and orderly system of classification. Aristotle's classification system was used for almost 2000 years.

In the seventeenth century, John Ray, an English biologist, set an enormous goal for himself. He decided to collect, name, and classify all the plants and animals in England. But unlike Aristotle, Ray based his system of classification on the internal anatomy of plants and animals. He examined how they behaved and what they looked like as well. Ray was the first person to scientifically use the term **species** (SPEE-sheez). A species is a group of organisms that are able to interbreed, or produce young.

John Ray achieved his goal. Moreover his work aided in the development of more complete and accurate classification systems.

The Work of Carolus Linnaeus

The eighteenth-century Swedish scientist Carolus Linnaeus spent the major part of his life developing a new system of classification. The system placed all living things into plant and animal groups according to similarities in form or structure.

Linnaeus also developed a simple system for naming organisms. Before Linnaeus developed his naming system, plants and animals had been identified by a series of Latin words. These words described the physical features of the organism. Sometimes five or six Latin words were used to describe a single organism!

Linnaeus devised a simpler naming system of **binomial nomenclature** (bigh-NOH-mee-uhl NOH-muhn-klay-cher). In this system, each plant and animal are given two names, a **genus** (plural: genera) name and a species name. For example, you could think of the genus name as your family name. The species name could be thought of as your first name. Like your family, a genus may consist of several closely related organisms or only one species.

1. What is taxonomy? 1. Science of classification
2. How did the classification systems of Aristotle and Ray differ?
3. What is meant by binomial nomenclature?

2. Unlike Aristotle, Ray based his system of classification on the internal anatomy of plants and animals.

3. System of giving each plant and animal two names: a genus and a species name

6-2 Modern Classification Systems

Today, 200 years after Linnaeus completed his work, scientists consider many additional factors when classifying organisms. Of course, scientists still examine large internal and external structures, but they also examine microscopic structures. Scientists even analyze the chemical makeup of an organism.

Although such a classification system may at first seem complicated, it is really quite simple. The modern system of classification does two jobs. First, it groups organisms according to their _basic_ characteristics. Second, it gives a _unique name_ to an organism that scientists all over the world can use and understand. For example, in North and South America

Figure 6-3 _Scientists often use skeletons of animals to help in classification. Notice how the similarity of forelimb structures of these animals helps to classify them as being part of the same group, in this case, mammals._

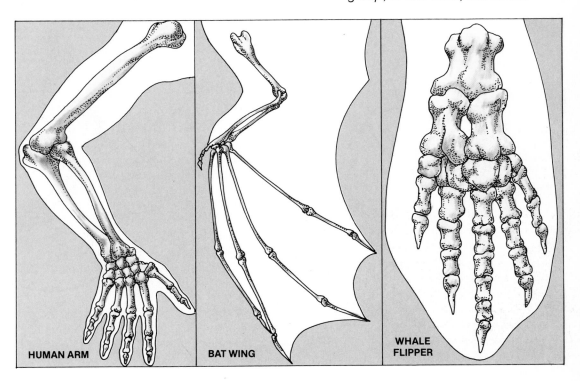

HUMAN ARM

BAT WING

WHALE FLIPPER

one large cat is called a <u>mountain lion</u> by some people, a <u>cougar</u> by others, and a <u>puma</u> by still others. If these people were to talk to one another about the animal, they might think they were talking about three different animals. But scientists throughout the world use only one name for this large cat, *Felis concolor*. This name easily identifies the cat to all scientists, no matter where they live or what language they speak.

Classification Groupings

In scientific classification, there are seven major groups. The <u>largest group</u> is called a **kingdom.** All animals, for example, belong to the animal kingdom, and all plants belong to the plant kingdom. The second largest group is called a **phylum** (FY-luhm;

In the plant kingdom, the word "division" is used more than the word "phylum."

Career: *Zoo Keeper*

HELP WANTED: ZOO KEEPER High school diploma required. Minimum one year experience as an apprentice zoo keeper needed. Must like animals and be tolerant of both animal and human behavior. Apply in person.

Today is a big day at the zoo. The arrival of a male and female giraffe is expected from Africa. For months, everyone has prepared for the new exhibit. Gardeners planted fruit trees bearing the giraffe's favorite food. In addition, zoo architects designed and built a new home, while tour guides learned the habits of the newcomers. Everyone wants to make sure the giraffes will be safe and comfortable. If all goes well, the pair will breed and produce young giraffes.

At first, the giraffes will be kept away from other animals. Once tests show they are strong and healthy, the **zoo keeper** will help move them to their new home. The zoo keeper will also be responsible for giving food and water to the giraffes. Other responsibilities of the zoo keeper include keeping the animals' area clean and observing and recording their behavior.

The zoo keeper usually is the first to notice any medical problems as well as to treat minor injuries or ailments. However, serious problems must be reported to the senior zoo keeper.

Of the many people working at the zoo, zoo keepers come into the most direct contact with the animals. In fact, zoo keepers sometimes bathe and groom the animals. Occasionally, zoo keepers answer visitors' questions about the inhabitants of the zoo. For further career information, write to the American Association of Zoo Keepers National Headquarters, 635 Gage Boulevard, Topeka, KS 66606.

Figure 6-4 *The variety of living things in a rain forest, such as this one in Uganda, Africa, is greater than in any other place on the surface of the earth. Here gorillas share their territory with countless different plants and animals.*

plural: phyla). Each phylum is made up of **classes.** Within each class are **orders.** In turn, each order is divided into **families** that consist of many related genera. Each genus usually is divided into one or more species.

The words for an organism's genus and species make up its scientific name. The genus name is capitalized, but the species name begins with a small letter. For example, the genus and species name for a wolf is *Canis lupus*. These two names identify the organism. Although most of these names are in Latin, some are in Greek. Scientists estimate that there are at least three million and perhaps as many as ten million different species alive today. Many of them have yet to be identified and named.

Classifying an Organism

Figure 6-5 shows the classification groupings of several organisms. Each grouping indicates something about the organism's characteristics. For example, the lion belongs to the order Carnivora.

The Secret Code

How can you remember the correct classification sequence from the largest to the smallest group? You can do this by remembering the sentence "*Kings play cards on fat green stools.*" The first letter of each word is the same as the first letter of each classification group from the largest to the smallest. For example, *k* stands for kingdom, *p* stands for phylum, and so on.

CLASSIFICATION OF FIVE DIFFERENT ORGANISMS

	Lion	Onion	Paramecium	Yogurt-making Bacterium	Edible Mushroom
Kingdom	Animalia	Plantae	Protista	Monera	Fungi
Phylum	Chordata	Angiospermophyta	Ciliophora	Eubacteriacea	Basidiomycetes
Class	Mammalia	Monocotyledonae	Ciliatea	Schizomycetes	Homobasidiomycetes
Order	Carnivora	Liliales	Hymenostomatida	Eubacteriales	Agaricales
Family	Felidae	Liliaceae	Paramecidae	Lactobacillaceae	Agaricaceae
Genus	*Panthera*	*Allium*	*Paramecium*	*Lactobacillus*	*Agaricus*
Species	*leo*	*cepa*	*caudatum*	*bulgarius*	*campestris*

Figure 6-5

ACTIVITY

Early Taxonomists

Using reference materials in the library, look up the following taxonomists:

Aristotle
John Ray
Carolus Linnaeus
Ernst Haeckel

Write a brief report about each. Include answers to the following questions in your report: When and where did each person live? What was the major contribution of each person to the science of taxonomy?

"Carnivora" is the Latin word for flesh eater. Many other familiar organisms also belong to this order such as dogs, raccoons, and bears. Look at Figure 6-5 again and notice that the lion is in the family Felidae. This family contains not only the lion but other cats, including ordinary house cats.

This knowledge allows you to have a very good idea of how a lion acts and looks even if you have never seen one in person. You can do this because lions and house cats are in the same family. But lions and house cats are not in the same genus and species, which indicates they are somewhat different. For example, taxonomists include the lion in the genus *Panthera* along with other large cats. All cats in the genus *Panthera* roar; they do not purr. Other cats, including house cats, are in the genus *Felis*. They, of course, purr and do not roar. Finally, the species name for the lion is *leo*. In this case, the lion, *Panthera leo,* is the animal that you see jumping through hoops in the circus or lounging lazily in a cage at your local zoo. *Felis domesticus* is the scientific name for your playful pet cat.

SECTION REVIEW

1. What are the seven major classification groups?
2. What is the scientific name for an onion?

1. Kingdom, phylum, class, order, family, genus, species
2. *Allium cepa*

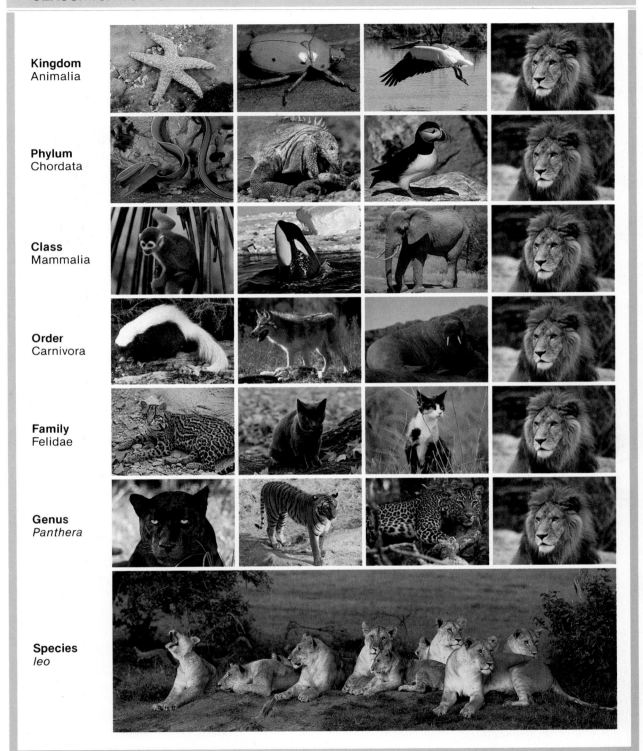

Kingdom
Animalia

Phylum
Chordata

Class
Mammalia

Order
Carnivora

Family
Felidae

Genus
Panthera

Species
leo

Figure 6-6 *Examine each row from top to bottom. What pattern do you discover?* The similarities among organisms increases as the animals are classified from kingdom to species.

6-3 Systems of Classification

In Figure 6-5, you may have noticed that some organisms were not in the plant or animal kingdoms. The paramecium, for example, is usually placed in a kingdom called Protista. Scientists invented this kingdom to include organisms that did not seem to fit into either the plant or animal kingdoms. Later, two more kingdoms called Monera (muh-NIHR-uh) and Fungi (FUHN-jigh) were added to many modern classification systems. So, today, most scientists use a five kingdom system of classification. The members of these five kingdoms are: plants, animals, protists, monerans, and fungi.

PLANTS   Most plants are **multicellular,** or many-celled, organisms that contain specialized tissues and organs. A few plants are **unicellular,** or one-celled. Some algae are examples of unicellular plants. In general, plants are **autotrophs** (AWT-uh-trohfs). Autotrophs are organisms that can make their own food from simple substances. Most plants contain chlorophyll, a green pigment necessary for making food.

Figure 6-7   *The ability to move from place to place is one way scientists distinguish the wasp, a member of the animal kingdom, from the berry bush, a member of the plant kingdom.*

Figure 6–8 *The unicellular paramecium is a member of the Protista kingdom. This paramecium is magnified 200 times.*

ANIMALS   Only multicellular organisms are in the animal kingdom. These organisms have tissues and most have organs and organ systems. Unlike plants, animals do not contain chlorophyll and are not able to make their own food. They depend upon autotrophs. These organisms are called **heterotrophs** (HET-uh-roh-trohfs).

PROTISTS   The Protista kingdom includes most unicellular organisms. Microscopic protozoans such as paramecia are found in this kingdom.

MONERANS   All of the earth's bacteria are found in the Monera kingdom. One kind of algae, the blue-green algae, are also in the Monera kingdom. Like protists, monerans are unicellular. However, the cells of monerans do not contain a well-defined nucleus. The nucleus is the control center of a cell.

FUNGI   As you might expect, the world's wide variety of fungi make up the Fungi kingdom. The kinds of fungi you are probably most familiar with are mushrooms and molds. Fungi share many characteristics with plants. However, fungi do not contain the green pigment chlorophyll. So, unlike plants, fungi cannot make their own food.

SECTION REVIEW

1. In what kingdom are most protozoans found?
2. Define multicellular and unicellular.

   1. Protist
   2. Multicellular means many-celled. Unicellular means one-celled.

141

LABORATORY ACTIVITY

For further instructions, see page T-29.

Whose Shoe Is That?

Purpose

In this activity, you will develop a classification system for shoes.

Materials *(per group of 6)*
Students' shoes
Pencil and paper

Procedure

1. At your teacher's direction, remove your right shoe and place it on a work table.
2. As a group, think of a characteristic that will divide all six shoes into two kingdoms. For example, you may first divide the shoes by the characteristic of color into the brown shoe kingdom and the nonbrown-shoe kingdom.
3. Place the shoes into two separate piles based on the characteristic your group has selected.
4. Next, working only with those shoes in one kingdom, divide that kingdom into two groups based on a new characteristic. The brown shoe kingdom, for example, may be divided into a shoelace group and a non-shoelace group.
5. Further divide these groups into subgroups. For example, the shoes in the shoelace group may be again separated into shoes with rubber soles and shoes without rubber soles.
6. Continue to divide the shoes by choosing new characteristics until you have only one shoe left in each group. Identify the person who owns this shoe.
7. Now repeat this process working with the nonbrown shoes.

Observations and Conclusions

1. Test your shoe classification system for accuracy by doing the following: Have a member of your group hold up a shoe. Starting with the kingdom, classify it according to the system you have just developed. The system should lead you to the correct person's name.

CHAPTER SUMMARY

6-1 History of Classification

▬ The science of classification is called taxonomy.

▬ Aristotle was the first person to develop a classification system for living things. His system was used for almost 2000 years.

▬ In the seventeenth century, John Ray, an English biologist, introduced a classification system that became the foundation of modern systems.

▬ In the eighteenth century, Carolus Linnaeus, a Swedish scientist, devised a system for naming organisms called binomial nomenclature. Linnaeus also developed a classification system based on the structural similarities of organisms.

6-2 Modern Classification Systems

▬ Today, scientists classify organisms according to structural, chemical, and other similarities.

▬ Organisms are classified into seven groups. In order of decreasing size, these groups are kingdom, phylum, class, order, family, genus, and species.

6-3 Systems of Classification

▬ A five-kingdom system of classification consists of plants, animals, protists, monerans, and fungi.

▬ Autotrophs can make their own food.

▬ Heterotrophs are organisms that cannot make their own food.

VOCABULARY   *Define the following terms.*

autotroph p.140

binomial nomenclature p.134

class p.137

family p.137

genus p.134

heterotroph p.141

kingdom p.136

multicellular p.140

order p.137

phylum p.136

species p.134

taxonomy p.133

unicellular p.140

CHAPTER REVIEW

Multiple Choice

Choose the letter of the answer that best completes each statement.

1. The first person to propose a classification system was
   a. Ray.
   b. Linnaeus.
   c. Aristotle.
   d. Haeckel.

2. A group of organisms that are able to interbreed is a
   a. species.
   b. family.
   c. genus.
   d. kingdom.

3. What language is used most often to name organisms in modern classification systems?
   a. French
   b. Latin
   c. English
   d. German

4. The largest classification group is the
   a. species.
   b. order.
   c. phylum.
   d. kingdom.

5. A classification group that is smaller than an order is
   a. kingdom.
   b. phylum.
   c. family.
   d. class.

6. A classification group that is larger than an order is
   a. genus.
   b. species.
   c. family.
   d. class.

7. A genus can be divided into a(n)
   a. phylum.
   b. order.
   c. species.
   d. family.

8. The term "Protista" refers to a
   a. class.
   b. kingdom.
   c. genus.
   d. species.

9. Which organism is a heterotroph?
   a. frog
   b. maple tree
   c. seaweed
   d. spinach

10. The animal kingdom is made up of only
    a. autotrophs.
    b. unicellular organisms.
    c. multicellular organisms.
    d. families.

Completions

Fill in the word or words that best complete each statement.

1. The science of classification is known as _____taxonomy_____.

2. In classification, the two-word naming system is known as _____binominal nomenclature_____.

3. The first word in a scientific name is the _____genus_____.

4. In classification, the largest group is called a(n) _____kingdom_____.

5. The smallest classification group is a(n) _____species_____.

6. The second largest group is a(n) _____phylum_____.

7. The Latin word for flesh eater is _____carnivora_____.

8. A paramecium is a member of the _____protist_____ kingdom.

9. An organism that can make its own food is called a(n) _____autotroph_____.

10. An organism that can not make its own food is called a(n) _____heterotroph_____.

True or False

Determine whether each statement is true or false. If it is true, write true. If it is false, change the underlined word or words to make the statement true.

1. Aristotle introduced the term "species." F (Ray)
2. In Linnaeus's classification system, the smallest group was the genus. F (species)
3. The correct classification order from largest to smallest groups is kingdom, phylum, class, order, family, species, genus. *
4. The scientific name for a lion is *Panthera leo*. T
5. The scientific name for a wolf is *Canis lupus*. T

6. Multicellular organisms are composed of only one cell. F (unicellular)
7. In a five-kingdom classification system, bacteria are classified as plants. F (monerans)
8. Green plants are heterotrophs. F (autotrophs)
9. Animal cells contain chlorophyll. F (Plant)
10. Heterotrophs are organisms that cannot make their own food. T

*F (...genus, species)

Discussion Topics Answers appear on page T-29.

Write a brief paragraph discussing each of the following.

1. What type of characteristics did Linnaeus use to develop his classification system?
2. What are some characteristics scientists use to classify and name organisms?

3. How do an autotroph and a heterotroph differ? Give an example of each.

EXPAND YOUR KNOWLEDGE

Perkins, M. *My Wild Kingdom: An Autobiography*. New York: Dutton.
    This book is an interesting story about the life of Marlin Perkins, the director of three zoological gardens and the narrator of the popular television program "Wild Kingdom." Perkins clearly states his ideas on the conservation of natural habitats.
Simon, S. *Strange Creatures*. New York: Four Winds/Scholastic.
    This book contains a collection of 21 of the most unusual kinds of animals on the earth. There is a full-page drawing for each creature and a story about the animal's habits.
Venino, S. *Amazing Animal Groups*. Washington, D.C.: National Geographic Society.
    This book describes the activities of some fish, birds, insects, and mammals. The author includes excellent color photographs of these activities.

7 Viruses, Bacteria, and Protists

For a chapter overview, teaching strategies, answers to all activities, a list of A-V materials, and a chapter bibliography, see pages T-30 to T-31.

Consult your Teacher's Resource Book and Annotated Teacher's Edition, Laboratory Book for additional activities and teaching aids.

CHAPTER SECTIONS

CHAPTER OBJECTIVES

After completing this chapter, you will be able to:

7-1 Describe the structure of viruses.

7-1 Explain viral reproduction.

7-2 List and describe the three basic shapes of bacteria.

7-2 Describe the structure of a bacterial cell.

7-2 Explain the difference between bacteria that are autotrophs and those that are heterotrophs.

7-3 Name the parts of the amoeba, the paramecium, and *Euglena* and give the functions of each part.

7-3 Describe the life functions of the amoeba, the paramecium, and *Euglena.*

7-3 Describe a sporozoan.

In July of 1976, the city of Philadelphia was full of people wearing navy blue military caps. These people were members of the American Legion, a veterans' organization that was holding its yearly convention in what is known as "the city of brotherly love." However, before the month was out, Philadelphia might well have been called "the city of brotherly fear." For shortly after the close of the convention, a serious disease struck many of the legionnaires.

What caused the frightening illness, which was given the name "Legionnaires' Disease"? One possible cause was a microorganism, a living thing too small to be seen without the aid of instruments such as microscopes. But what particular microorganism? There were millions.

Dr. Joseph McDade of the Center for Disease Control at Atlanta, Georgia, was one of the medical detectives trying to solve the mystery of Legionnaires' Disease. If a microorganism was responsible for Legionnaires' Disease, McDade would find it. Early in 1977 he discovered the microorganism responsible.

The microorganism McDade identified was a new bacterium, a kind of germ. Fortunately, the new bacterium could be treated with an old kind of medicine called erythromycin, which adds another twist to this strange story. Erythromycin is made by bacteria. So the illness caused by one kind of bacteria was cured by a substance produced by another kind of bacteria.

Erythromycin crystals

7-1 Viruses

In 1892, a terrible disease swept through certain areas of Russia. Victims of the disease were not people or even animals. They were plants—tobacco plants. Because tobacco was a very important crop, many people were interested in discovering the cause and, perhaps, a cure for the disease. One of these people was a 28-year-old Russian botanist, or plant expert, named Dimitri Iwanowski.

By the late 1800s, scientists had discovered that many diseases of human beings, animals, and plants were caused by unicellular microorganisms called **bacteria** (singular: bacterium). These discoveries were made possible by hard work and the invention of powerful light microscopes. These microscopes made visible microorganisms never seen before. Based on these discoveries Iwanowski assumed the tobacco disease was also caused by bacteria. So he set out to devise an experiment to identify them.

Iwanowski's procedure was simple. He would gather some infected tobacco leaves, crush the leaves, and collect the juice. Then he would pass the juices through a filter whose holes were so small that bacteria could not slip through. Finally, Iwanowski would place the pure juices on healthy tobacco plants. He

Figure 7-1 *Tobacco mosaic disease causes healthy tobacco plant leaves* (left) *to become spotted* (right).

reasoned the plants would remain healthy and this would be proof that bacteria were the cause of the disease.

All this reasoning made very good sense. And Iwanowski performed his experiment perfectly. The only problem was that the healthy plants caught the disease. Iwanowski thought his experiment was a failure. He thought his filters were not well made and that cracks in them must have let through the disease-causing bacteria. However, Iwanowski was wrong. He had made a great discovery without recognizing it. The recognition came six years later from Delft, Holland, about 1600 kilometers to the east.

Viruses—Smaller than Bacteria

In 1898, the Dutch microbiologist Martinus Beijerinck, was also working on the devastating disease of tobacco plants. A microbiologist is a scientist who studies **microbiology,** or the science of microorganisms. Using the best microscopes, Beijerinck searched for bacteria in the diseased, spotted leaves of tobacco plants. He also searched in their filtered juices and in the material trapped by filters that should have contained bacteria. Like Iwanowski's, Beijerinck's experiments seemed to end in failure. He could find no bacteria. Nevertheless, the filtered juices from diseased plants continued to cause healthy plants to become infected.

These repeated observations led Beijerinck to draw a momentous conclusion that had escaped Iwanowski. The filtered juices from diseased plants caused infection, but the juices did not contain bacteria. Therefore, they contained something else that caused infection, a germ much smaller than bacteria. This germ was too small to be visible even under the lenses of the most powerful light microscope. Beijerinck named this germ a **virus,** which comes from the Latin word for poison.

Almost 40 years passed before Wendell Stanley, an American scientist, isolated the virus that caused the disease in tobacco leaves. He called it the tobacco mosaic virus. The word "mosaic" refers to the pattern of spots found on the leaves of diseased plants. See Figure 7-1.

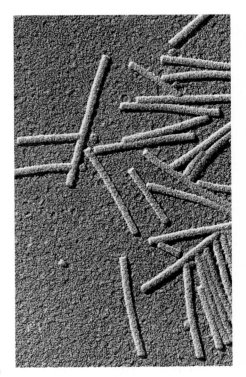

Figure 7-2 *These rod-shaped objects are tobacco mosaic viruses.*

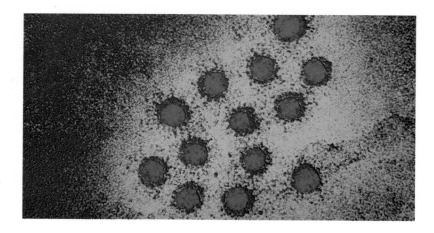

Figure 7-3 *These red spheres, magnified 70,000 times, are viruses that cause a type of liver disease called hepatitis A.*

Since the discovery of the tobacco mosaic virus, scientists have found that there are many different kinds of viruses. By studying many of these viruses, scientists have learned a great deal about the function and structure of viruses.

What Is a Virus?

Living things come in many shapes and sizes. However, all living things seem to have one thing in common. They all contain cells. Some organisms consist of only a single cell. Other organisms, such as yourself, are made up of many cells. Unlike these organisms, viruses are not cells and do not contain cells. Viruses are tiny particles that contain hereditary material.

Because viruses are not cells, they cannot perform the life functions of living cells. They cannot, for example, take in food or get rid of wastes. In fact, about the only similarity that viruses share with cells is that viruses are able to reproduce. However, viruses cannot reproduce on their own. They need the help of other living cells. For this reason, many scientists consider viruses an unusual form of life. Other scientists strongly disagree and do not classify viruses as living things. Thus, it might help if you think of viruses as being on the threshold of life.

Structure of Viruses

A virus has two basic parts, a core of hereditary material and an outer coat of protein. The hereditary material in the virus's core may be either **DNA,** *deoxyribonucleic acid,* or **RNA,** *ribonucleic acid.* DNA and RNA are substances that control the production of new viruses.

Surrounding the DNA or RNA in the virus is a protein coat. The coat is much like the shell of a turtle. Like the turtle's shell, the protein coat encloses and offers some <u>protection</u> to the virus. In fact, the protein coat is so protective that some viruses survive after being dried and frozen for many years.

With the invention of the electron microscope in the 1930s, scientists were able to see and to study the shapes and sizes of certain viruses. Some viruses, such as those that cause the common cold, have 20 surfaces. Each of these surfaces is in the shape of a triangle that has equal sides. Other viruses look like small threads, while still others resemble small spheres. Some even resemble small spaceships. See Figure 7-5.

Reproduction of Viruses

In order to understand how a virus reproduces, causing disease, you can examine the activities of one kind of virus called a **bacteriophage** (bak-TEE-ree-uh-fayj). A bacteriophage is a virus that infects bacterial cells. The word "bacteriophage" means "bacteria eater."

Figure 7-4 *Viruses vary in size from about 10 to 250 nanometers, or nm. A nanometer is equal to one millionth of a millimeter. Compare the sizes of the viruses on the right to the large bacterium on the left.*

Figure 7-5 *This drawing shows the structure of a bacteriophage, which attacks bacterial cells. The photograph is of the same virus magnified 190,000 times.*

KEY

 Bacteriophage

Protein coat

Bacterial hereditary material

Viral hereditary material

Figure 7-6 *Viruses reproduce in cells. A virus attaches to the cell and injects its heredity material. The cell then makes more viruses, which burst from the cell.*

In Figure 7-6, you can see how a bacteriophage attaches its tail to the outside of a bacterial cell. The virus quickly injects its hereditary material directly into the living cell. The protein coat is left behind and discarded by the virus. Once inside the cell, the virus's hereditary material takes control of all of the bacterial cell's activities. As a result, the bacterial cell is no longer in control. The cell begins to produce new viruses rather than its own chemicals.

Soon the bacterial cell fills up with new viruses, perhaps as many as several hundred. Eventually, the bacterial cell bursts open. The new viruses are released and infect nearby bacterial cells. This process continues until all living bacterial cells have been infected by the virus.

The viruses that attack plants, animals, and people may vary in size and shape. However, all viruses act in much the same way as bacteriophages.

SECTION REVIEW

1. What was the first virus to be isolated?
2. Name the two parts of a virus.
3. What is a bacteriophage?

1. Tobacco mosaic virus
2. Core of hereditary material (DNA or RNA) and an outer coat of protein
3. Virus that infects bacterial cells

7-2 Bacteria

Unlike viruses, bacteria clearly are living organisms. At one time, scientists placed bacteria in the plant kingdom because, like plants, bacteria have **cell walls.** The cell wall is the outermost boundary of plant and bacterial cells. The cell wall helps the cells of these organisms to keep their shape. Today, most classification systems consider bacteria as monerans. You may recall from Chapter 6 that monerans are members of the Monera kingdom. Like all other monerans, bacteria are unicellular.

Bacteria are considered the simplest organisms. However, bacteria are more complex than they may appear. Each cell performs the same basic functions that more complex organisms, including you, perform.

Figure 7-7 *Bacteria are grouped and named according to their three basic shapes. Spherical bacteria are called cocci* (left), *rodlike bacteria are called bacilli* (center), *and spiral-shaped bacteria are called spirilla* (right).

Scientists now recognize a fourth group of bacteria called the spirochetes, which have a corkscrew shape.

Bacteria are among the most numerous organisms on earth. Scientists estimate there are about 2.5 billion bacteria in a gram of garden soil. And the total number of bacteria living in your mouth is greater than the number of people who have ever lived.

Scientists classify bacteria into three basic groups according to shape. Bacteria that resemble spheres are called **cocci** (KAHK-sigh; singular: coccus). Those bacteria that look like rods are called **bacilli** (buh-SIL-igh; singular: bacillus). Still others resemble spirals. These bacteria are called **spirilla** (spigh-RIL-uh; singular: spirillum). See Figure 7-7.

Structure of Bacteria

All bacteria have a **cell membrane** on the inside of the cell wall. The cell membrane controls which substances enter and leave the bacterial cell. Unlike most other cells, the hereditary material of bacteria is not confined in a **nucleus** (NOO-klee-uhs; plural: nuclei). The nucleus is a spherical structure within a cell that directs all the activities of the cell. Instead, the hereditary material is spread throughout the **cytoplasm** in the cell. The cytoplasm is the jellylike material found inside the cell membrane.

Figure 7-8 *This drawing shows the typical structure of a bacterium.*

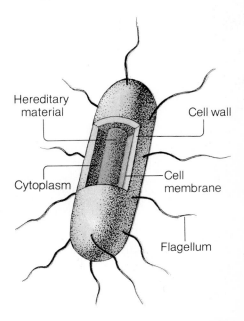

Hereditary material

Cell wall

Cytoplasm

Cell membrane

Flagellum

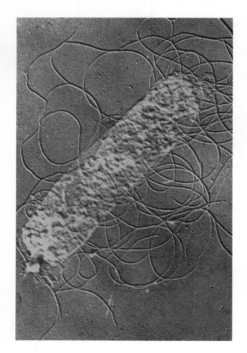

Figure 7-9 *The bacterium,* Proteus vulgaris, *uses its many whiplike flagella to move through water.*

Many bacteria are not able to move on their own. However, they can be carried from one place to another by air and water currents, clothing, and other objects. Other bacteria have special structures that help them move in watery surroundings. One type of structure is a **flagellum** (fla-JEL-um; plural: flagella). A flagellum is a long, thin, whiplike structure that propels the bacterial cell. Some bacteria may have many flagella.

Life Functions of Bacteria

Bacteria are in water, air, and the upper layers of soil. In fact, bacteria live almost everywhere, even in places where other living things cannot survive. For example, some bacteria were discovered living in volcanic vents at the bottom of the Pacific Ocean south of Baja, California. Temperatures here are as high as 250° C. Unlike most living things, some bacteria can thrive without oxygen. However, all bacteria need water or they eventually die.

Most bacteria are heterotrophs. These bacteria feed on other living things or on dead things. Bacteria that feed on living organisms are called **parasites** (PA-ruh-sights). These bacteria cause infections in

Figure 7-10 *Bacteria that live in Morning Glory Pool, a very hot spring in Yellowstone National Park, make up the blue-green growth.*

Figure 7-11 *Saprophytic bacteria of decay break down material in a dead tree and return important substances to the soil.*

people, animals, and plants. Bacteria that feed on dead things are called **saprophytes** (SA-pruh-fights). Why are saprophytes among the most important organisms found on earth?

Some bacteria are autotrophs. Like green plants, some of these food-making bacteria use the energy of sunlight to produce food. Other bacteria use the energy in substances such as sulfur and iron to make food.

Conditions may become unfavorable for bacteria. If the food, water, or air supply of bacteria becomes used up, some bacteria form microscopic **endospores.** An endospore is shaped like a ball or oval and is surrounded by a thick protective membrane. The protective membrane enables the endospores to survive long periods of boiling and disinfectant chemicals. When food, air, and water again become available, the endospores develop into active bacteria.

Most bacteria reproduce by **binary fission.** In binary fission a cell divides into two cells. Under the best conditions, most bacteria reproduce quickly. Some types can double in number every 20 minutes. At this rate, after about 24 hours the offspring of a single bacterium would have a mass greater than 2 million kilograms, or as much as 2000 small cars. In a few more days, their mass would be greater than that of the earth. Obviously, this does not happen.

Figure 7-12 *These bacteria are splitting in two, a process of reproduction called binary fission. Which of the three basic groups of bacteria are reproducing here?* Cocci.

* They break down the dead remains of plants and animals into substances that can be used by other organisms.

In the real world, the rate of reproduction slows down because the bacteria soon use up their food, water, and space. They also produce wastes that eventually poison them.

Helpful Bacteria

Most types of bacteria are not harmful and do not cause disease. For example, many food products, especially dairy products, are produced with the help of bacteria. Bacteria are needed to make cheeses, butter, yogurt, and sour cream. Some species of bacteria are used in the process of tanning leather.

Some helpful bacteria are used to fight other, harmful bacteria. These helpful bacteria, for example, can help produce **antibiotics.** Antibiotics destroy or weaken disease-causing bacteria. Scientists also have found a way to turn certain types of bacteria into "chemical factories." The DNA within these bacteria is changed. The bacteria then produce large

Career: *Bacteriologist*

HELP WANTED: BACTERIOLOGIST
College degree required; master's or Ph.D. desirable. Strong background in science necessary. Applicant should be creative and innovative. Position involves testing and research. Past experience as lab helper/technician an asset.

The specially equipped plane landed at the Atlanta airport. Within minutes, white-coated technicians rushed the test tube the plane was carrying to the Center for Disease Control. There, under strict laboratory conditions, the contents of the test tube were analyzed.

Through the powerful lens of the microscope, a tiny rod-shaped object became visible. Was it a living organism? The answer soon became obvious. Twenty minutes later a second rod-shaped object became visible under the lens of the microscope. The organism had reproduced.

Now a more important question had to be answered. Could this rod-shaped bacteria cause disease in human beings? Was it related to a type of bacteria that had caused diseases such as diphtheria, typhoid fever, and plague in the past? A **bacteriologist** would determine the type of bacteria it was and whether or not it was dangerous. In San Francisco, a sick patient and her doctor waited eagerly for the results.

Many bacteriologists specialize in identifying unknown microorganisms from the 2000 or so known types of bacteria. Others try to devise methods to combat harmful bacteria. Still others study how disease-causing bacteria may be spread in our environment. For further information on this career, write to the American Society of Microbiology, 1913 I Street N.W., Washington, DC 20006.

amounts of important substances such as insulin. Insulin helps to control the rate at which the human body breaks down sugar. People who do not produce enough of their own insulin can use the insulin produced by the bacteria.

Certain bacteria, called nitrogen-fixing bacteria, can make nitrogen compounds from nitrogen gas in the atmosphere. Nitrogen-fixing bacteria turn nitrogen gas, which plants cannot use for food, into nitrogen compounds that plants can use for food. These nitrogen-fixing bacteria often appear as lumps on the roots of plants such as alfalfa. See Figure 7-13. Nitrogen-fixing bacteria also help replace the nitrogen compounds in the soil. Without such nitrogen-fixing bacteria, most nitrogen compounds in the soil would be quickly used up and plants could no longer grow.

Harmful Bacteria

Although most bacteria are harmless, and some are helpful, a few can cause trouble. The trouble comes in a number of forms—food spoilage, diseases of people, diseases of farm animals and pets, and diseases of food crops. Fortunately, there are a number of defenses against attacks by harmful bacteria.

FOOD SPOILAGE Spoilage can be prevented or slowed down by heating, drying, salting, or smoking foods. Each one of these processes prevents or slows down the growth of bacteria. Milk, for example, is heated to 71° C for 15 seconds before it is placed in containers and shipped to the grocery or supermarket. This process, called pasteurization, destroys most of the bacteria that would cause the milk to spoil quickly. Heating and then canning foods such as vegetables, fruits, meat, and fish are also used to prevent bacterial growth. But if the foods are not sufficiently heated before canning, bacteria can grow inside the can and produce poisons called **toxins.**

HUMAN DISEASES These diseases caused by bacteria include strep throat, certain kinds of pneumonia, diphtheria, tuberculosis, and whooping cough. Some of these diseases can be prevented by an immunization shot. Others can be treated with antibiotics.

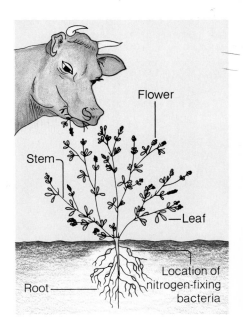

Figure 7-13 *Nitrogen-fixing bacteria on the roots of alfalfa plants convert nitrogen gas in the air to nitrogen compounds that enter the soil. These compounds are needed by plants for growth.*

Activity

Botulism

Perhaps the most powerful poison known is produced by the bacterium *Clostridium botulinum.* This bacterium needs no oxygen and can thrive in improperly sealed canned goods. People who become infected with this bacterium are said to have botulism, or food poisoning. Botulism is a serious, often fatal, disease. Using reference materials in the library, find out how to prevent botulism when canning foods. How can you detect if a canned food may be infected with botulism? How is the disease treated if a person becomes infected?

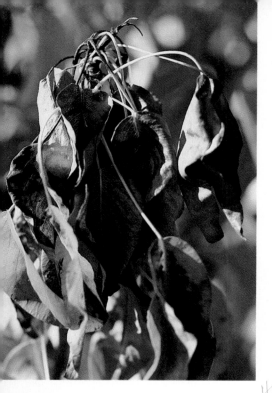

ANIMAL DISEASES   Bacteria cause diseases in animals. These diseases include anthrax, which attacks sheep, horses, cattle, and other large farm animals, and fowl cholera, which attacks chickens. Vaccinations can prevent both diseases.

PLANT DISEASES   These diseases caused by bacteria include fire blight of apples and pears and soft rot of vegetables. There are many ways of treating plant diseases, including the use of antibiotics and various chemicals.

SECTION REVIEW

1. What are the three basic shapes of bacteria?
2. What are two ways in which bacteria are helpful? Harmful?

1. Spheres-cocci; rods-bacilli; spirilla-spirals
2. Helpful bacteria - aid in production of dairy products and antibiotics and used in the tanning of leather. Harmful bacteria - can cause food spoilage and diseases of people, farm animals, pets, and food crops.

Figure 7-14   *Leaves on this pear tree have been attacked by a bacterial disease called fire blight.*

Figure 7-15   *The radolarian, a protozoan, is surrounded by a hard silicon shell.*

7-3 Protozoans

Two billion years ago, the earth was a strange and barren place. No animals roamed the land, swam in the sea, or flew in the air. No trees, shrubs, or grasses grew from the soil. From the air, the earth looked gray, brown, and blue. But even though it looked lifeless, an unseen new form of life was taking hold in its blue waters. This form of life, the **protozoans,** represented a giant step in the parade of living things that would follow. Protozoans are unicellular animal-like organisms. The protozoans still inhabit the world's seas, lakes, rivers, and ponds.

Protozoans differ in many ways from the bacteria that first inhabited the earth. For one thing, protozoans do not have cell walls. They do contain a distinct cell nucleus, which contains hereditary material. Protozoans are, in fact, the first animal-like organisms to evolve on the earth. For this reason, they were given their name, which comes from the Greek words for "first animal." However, protozoans are not true animals and are classified in the Protista kingdom.

Amoebas

Amoebas (uh-MEE-buhz) make up one of the simplest groups of protozoans. Although some amoebas are visible to the unaided eye, most are microscopic. Under the microscope, an amoeba looks like a blob of jelly.

The amoeba moves slowly in a watery environment by extending its cell membrane and cytoplasm. This extension is called a **pseudopod** (soo-duh-pahd), or "false foot." When the pseudopod is fully extended, it pulls the amoeba along with it.

Activity

A Protozoan Population

The largest existing protozoan is *Pelomyxa palustrius.* It may grow to a length of up to 1.5 centimeters. If all the *Pelomyxa palustrius* in a 30-meter-long pond were placed end-to-end and equaled the pond's length, how many would be present in the pond?

Figure 7-16 *This drawing shows the structure of a typical amoeba. The photograph of the amoeba was magnified 160 times.*

Activity

Harmful Microorganisms

Using reference materials in the library, prepare a report on the following diseases.

measles

smallpox

amoebic dysentery

poliomyelitis

pneumonia

tetanus

In your report, include information about how these diseases are transmitted to human beings. Also include what types of treatment are used to prevent or cure the diseases.

The amoeba also uses pseudopods to obtain food. As the amoeba nears a small piece of food, such as a smaller protozoan, the amoeba extends its pseudopod around the food. Soon the food particle is engulfed, or surrounded, by the pseudopod. A spherical **food vacuole** (VAK-yoo-ohl) in the pseudopod forms around the engulfed food particle. The food vacuole releases special digestive chemicals, called enzymes, in order to break down the captured food. The digested food can then be taken in and used by the amoeba. The waste products left behind in the food vacuole are eliminated through the cell membrane.

To supply itself with energy, the amoeba requires oxygen as well as food. Oxygen passes from the watery environment into the amoeba through the cell membrane. At the same time, waste products, such as carbon dioxide, pass out of the amoeba through the cell membrane. Excess water in the amoeba is pumped out through the cell membrane by a **contractile vacuole.**

Like bacteria, amoebas reproduce by binary fission. A parent cell divides into two new identical cells. Each of these new cells has the same amount and kind of hereditary material as the parent cell.

Amoebas respond simply to changes in their environments. They are sensitive to bright light and move to areas of dim light. Amoebas are also sensitive to certain chemicals, moving away from some and toward others.

Ciliates

The protist kingdom also includes the ciliates (SIHL-ee-ayts). These protozoans have **cilia** (SIHL-ee-uh; singular: cilium). Cilia are small hairlike projections on the outside of the cells. Sweeping through the water like tiny oars, the cilia enable these organisms to move, and help them to obtain food. In addition, the cilia function as sensors through which these organisms receive information about their environment.

One of the most familiar ciliates is the paramecium (pa-ruh-MEE-shi-uhm; plural: paramecia). A hard membrane covers the outer surface of the paramecium. This membrane gives the paramecium its

Figure 7-17 *The drawing shows the wavelike motion of a cilium.*

A paramecium also has trichocysts, which are small poisonous dartlike threads. Trichocysts are found on the paramecium's outer surface and are often used to trap food and to protect the paramecium.

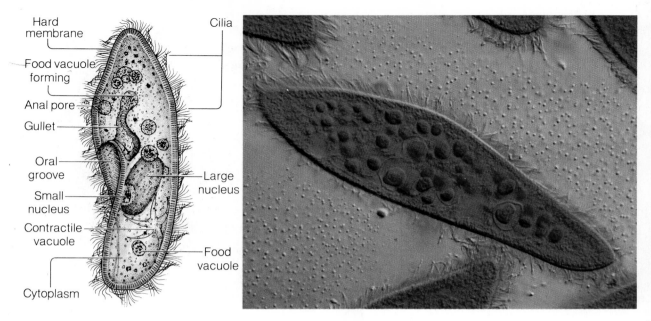

Figure 7-18 *This drawing shows the structure of a typical paramecium. The photograph of the paramecium was magnified 140 times.*

slipper shape. The cilia of the paramecium move food particles in the water into its **oral groove.** The oral groove is an indentation in the paramecium. <u>Food goes from the oral groove into the **gullet.**</u> The gullet is a funnel-shaped structure that ends at the food vacuole. The food vacuole distributes food particles as it moves through the organism. Undigested material is eliminated through the **anal pore.**

Located in the cytoplasm of paramecia are a small nucleus and a large nucleus. The small nucleus controls reproduction. The large nucleus controls all other life functions.

Reproduction in paramecia occurs in two ways. Like an amoeba, paramecia reproduce by binary fission. A paramecium may also share its hereditary material with another paramecium through a process called **conjugation** (kahn-joo-GAY-shuhn). During conjugation, two paramecia join together. Soon the larger nuclei disappear and the smaller nuclei divides in two. One of the smaller nuclei from each pair passes into a special tube joining both paramecia. After exchanging the hereditary material, the two paramecia move away from each other. A new small nucleus and a new large nucleus form in each of the two paramecia. Conjugation is beneficial because it allows paramecia to share hereditary characteristics that may help the paramecia become better able to survive a changing environment.

Flagellates

The flagellates include protozoans that have flagella. Most of the flagellates, such as *Euglena*, are unicellular. However, some flagellates, such as *Volvox*, form colonies, or clusters of cells.

There are two groups of flagellates. One group contains the green substance chlorophyll. These flagellates are autotrophs. *Volvox* is an example of this type of flagellate.

The second group of flagellates do not contain chlorophyll. They are heterotrophs. Most of these flagellates are parasites. Some of them cause disease such as African sleeping sickness. This group of disease-causing flagellates is transmitted to people and animals by the tsetse fly.

Figure 7-19 Volvox *are flagellates that form colonies.* Volvox *are autotrophs because they contain the green substance chlorophyll, which enables them to make their own food.*

Figure 7-20 *This drawing shows the structure of the autotrophic flagellate called* Euglena. *The photograph is of a typical* Euglena.

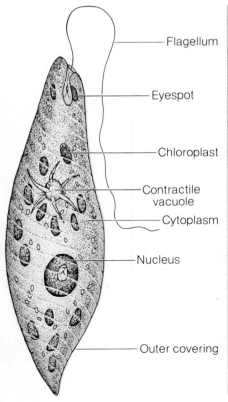

- Flagellum
- Eyespot
- Chloroplast
- Contractile vacuole
- Cytoplasm
- Nucleus
- Outer covering

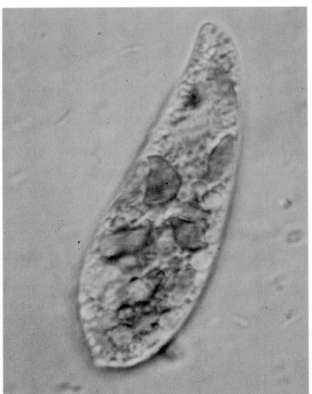

A flagellate that is both an autotroph and a heterotroph is *Euglena*. *Euglena* is an oval-shaped organism with one pointed end and one rounded end. The rounded end contains the flagellum. Also located in this area in the cytoplasm is the **eyespot.** The eyespot is a reddish structure that is sensitive to light. *Euglena* tends to move toward areas where there is enough light. *Euglena* use light energy to make their own food.

Like the amoeba and paramecium, *Euglena* reproduces by binary fission. However, unlike most protozoans, *Euglena* splits in two lengthwise. This type of division produces two cells that are mirror images of each other.

Sporozoans

Sporozoans are protozoans that cannot move from place to place. These organisms are parasites whose foods are the cells and body fluids of animals.

Many of these sporozoans have complicated life cycles. During their life cycles, sporozoans form spores. Each spore contains hereditary material and a small amount of cytoplasm. Eventually, the sporozoans release these spores. Each spore can develop into a mature sporozoan.

Perhaps the most familiar type of sporozoan is the organism that causes the disease malaria. This sporozoan is carried by the *Anopheles* mosquito. When an infected mosquito bites a human being, the mosquito injects its saliva, and the spores enter the person's body. The infected person soon begins to experience chills and fever, which are two symptoms of malaria.

SECTION REVIEW

1. What is a pseudopod?
2. What are cilia?
3. How do amoebas, paramecia, and *Euglena* reproduce?
4. What is the function of the eyespot in *Euglena*?
5. How do sporozoans differ from other protozoans?

1. Extension of an amoeba's cell membrane and cytoplasm, its "false foot"
2. Hairlike projections
3. All reproduce by binary fission; paramecia also reproduce by conjugation
4. Enables *Euglena* to move toward light
5. Sporozoans cannot move from place to place; have complicated life cycles

Activity

Protozoan Models

You can examine the structure of some protozoans by building models out of modeling clay or wheat paste. Using these materials and the illustrations in the text and other reference materials, construct a cross-section model of an amoeba, a ciliate, a flagellate, and a sporozoan. Mount each model on a piece of stiff cardboard. After the clay or wheat paste hardens, use different colors of paint to show the structures of each protozoan. Label all of the structures. What are some similarities among these organisms? Some differences?

LABORATORY ACTIVITY

For further instructions, see page T-31.

Collecting Protists

Purpose

In this activity, you will collect and identify microorganisms that live in pond water.

Materials *(per group)*
Wire coat hanger
Wooden stick
Water-resistant adhesive tape
String
Nylon stocking
3 test tubes and stoppers
3 medicine droppers
Rubber band
Microscope
Microscope slides and cover slips

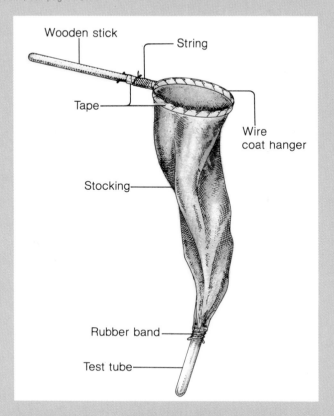

Procedure

1. Construct a dip net as shown in the drawing. First, bend a wire coat hanger into a circular loop with a short, straight handle.
2. Attach the wire handle to a wooden stick by tying the handle and stick with string and winding tape around them.
3. Next, use tape to attach the open end of a nylon stocking to the circular loop of wire.
4. In the toe end of the stocking, make a hole just large enough to allow a test tube to pass through. The open end of the test tube should be just inside the net. Attach the test tube to the stocking with a rubber band.
5. Go to a nearby pond with your teacher. **CAUTION:** *Do not go alone, and be sure to inform an adult where you are going.* As you walk along the pond's edge, slowly pull the dip net along the surface of the water. This will cause protists and water to collect in the test tube. Remove the test tube, together with its contents, and cover it with a stopper.

6. Using the other two test tubes, collect two more samples in the same way, one from 5 centimeters below the surface and one from about 30 centimeters below the surface. Label the samples.
7. Return to the classroom. Using a dropper, place a few drops of water from the test tube on a slide. Place a cover slip over the drop. Examine the slide under a microscope. Follow the same procedure with the other two test tubes.

Observations and Conclusions

1. Use reference books in the library to identify the microorganisms you observed and to learn more about them.
2. Make more careful drawings of the organisms you have identified, labeling their parts. Display your drawings in the classroom.

CHAPTER SUMMARY

7-1 Viruses

- Viruses cannot carry out any life processes unless within a living cell.

- Viruses are tiny particles that contain a center of either DNA or RNA surrounded by a protein coat.

- Reproduction of viruses occurs only when the virus invades a living cell.

- Bacteriophages are viruses that infect bacterial cells.

- When a virus's hereditary material enters a living cell, the virus takes control of the cell. The cell begins to produce new viruses, which are released from the cell.

7-2 Bacteria

- Bacteria are simple unicellular monerans.

- Bacteria have three basic shapes: cocci, bacilli, or spirilla.

- Bacterial cells have a cell wall and a cell membrane surrounding the cytoplasm. The hereditary material of a bacterial cell is spread throughout the cytoplasm.

- Some bacteria have flagella, or whiplike structures, that enable them to move.

- Some bacteria called autotrophs use energy from the sun or chemicals to make food.

- Bacteria that must obtain their food from other organisms are called heterotrophs.

- Bacteria usually reproduce by binary fission, or splitting in two.

7-3 Protozoans

- Protozoans are animal-like microorganisms. Their hereditary material is confined in a nucleus.

- Amoebas move and obtain food by the movement of their pseudopods. Amoebas reproduce by binary fission.

- Ciliates, such as paramecia, have hairlike cilia used for obtaining food and for movement.

- Paramecia reproduce by binary fission and conjugation.

- Flagellates use whiplike flagella to move. There are two groups of flagellates. The members of one group contain chlorophyll and can make their own food. The second group of flagellates do not contain chlorophyll and cannot make their own food.

- Sporozoans cannot move from place to place. Sporozoans are parasites and have complex life cycles.

VOCABULARY   *Define the following terms.*

anal pore p.161	**cilium** p.160	**flagellum** p.154	**pseudopod** p.159
antibiotic p.156	**coccus** p.153	**food vacuole** p.160	**RNA** p.151
bacillus p.153	**conjugation** p.161	**gullet** p.161	**saprophyte** p.155
bacteriophage p.151	**contractile vacuole** p.160	**microbiology** p.149	**spirillum** p.153
bacterium p.148	**cytoplasm** p.153	**nucleus** p.153	**toxin** p.157
binary fission p.155	**DNA** p.150	**oral groove** p.161	**virus** p.149
cell membrane p.153	**endospore** p.155	**parasite** p.154	
cell wall p.152	**eyespot** p.163	**protozoan** p.159	

CHAPTER REVIEW

Multiple Choice

Choose the letter of the answer that best completes each statement.

1. Viruses are
   a. shaped like spheres.
   b. shaped like tadpoles.
   c. shaped like cylinders.
   d. any of these shapes.
2. What is used to observe viruses?
   a. the unaided eye
   b. an electron microscope
   c. a light microscope
   d. all of these
3. The scientist who gave viruses their name was
   a. Martinus Beijerinck.
   b. Wendell Stanley.
   c. Dimitri Iwanowski.
   d. Anton van Leeuwenhoek.
4. The type of hereditary material in a virus may be
   a. DNA.
   b. RNA.
   c. either DNA or RNA.
   d. neither DNA nor RNA.
5. An organism that feeds on dead matter is called a(n)
   a. autotroph.
   b. saprophyte.
   c. parasite.
   d. flagellum.

6. An amoeba moves by means of
   a. flagella.
   b. cilia.
   c. pseudopods.
   d. conjugation.
7. Which organism reproduces by binary fission and conjugation?
   a. amoeba
   b. paramecium
   c. sporozoan
   d. *Euglena*
8. *Euglena* is an example of a(n)
   a. flagellate.
   b. ciliate.
   c. sporozoan.
   d. amoeba.
9. Which group of protozoans cannot move by themselves?
   a. amoebas
   b. ciliates
   c. flagellates
   d. sporozoans
10. The most familiar type of sporozoan causes
    a. pneumonia.
    b. tuberculosis.
    c. malaria.
    d. African sleeping sickness.

Completions

Fill in the word or words that best complete each statement.

1. A virus that infects a bacterial cell is called a(n) ___bacteriophage___.

2. The bacteria that look like rods are called ___bacilli___.

3. Bacteria usually reproduce by ___binary fission___.

4. Bacteria that make nitrogen compounds from nitrogen gas are called ___nitrogen-fixing bacteria___.

5. Some bacteria produce poisons called ___toxins___.

6. Paramecia move by means of ___cilia___.

7. The spherical structure in a cell that releases enzymes to digest food is the ___food vacuole___.

8. In paramecia, food particles are swept by cilia into an indented structure called a(n) _____oral groove_____.

9. A flagellate that is both an autotroph and a heterotroph is the _____Euglena_____.

10. The structure in *Euglena* that responds to changes in light is the _____eyespot_____.

True or False

Determine whether each statement is true or false. If it is true, write "true." If it is false, change the underlined word or words to make the statement true.

1. A virus is made up of hereditary material surrounded by a <u>protein coat</u>. T

2. The outermost boundary of a bacterial cell is the <u>cell membrane</u>. F (cell wall)

3. <u>Cilia</u> are long, thin, whiplike structures that are used to propel some microorganisms. *

4. <u>Saprophytes</u> are organisms that feed on living organisms. F (Parasites)

5. <u>Endospores</u> allow bacteria to survive unfavorable conditions. T

* F (Flagella)

6. <u>Protozoan</u> means false foot. F (Pseudopod)

7. In a paramecium, the <u>oral groove</u> is the funnel-shaped structure that ends in a food vacuole. F (gullet)

8. The <u>contractile vacuole</u> pumps excess water out of an amoeba. T

9. In a paramecium, undigested material is eliminated through an opening called the <u>anal pore</u>. T

10. *<u>Euglena</u>* is an example of a flagellate. T

Discussion Topics   Answers appear on page T-31.

Write a brief paragraph discussing each of the following.

1. What contributions did Dimitri Iwanowski and Martinus Beijerinck make to the study of viruses?

2. Explain the differences between viruses and cells.

3. How do viruses reproduce?

4. What is the difference between bacteria that are autotrophs and those that are heterotrophs?

5. Explain why some bacteria are harmful.

6. Explain why a farmer may choose to plant a field of alfalfa every few years.

EXPAND YOUR KNOWLEDGE

Asimov, I. *How Did We Find Out About Germs?* New York: Walker.
> The author discusses how scientists discovered that bacteria can cause disease.

Curtis, H. *The Marvelous Animals: An Introduction to the Protozoa.* New York: Natural History Press.
> This book explores the world of protozoa. What living things are in a drop of pond water? Are they plants? Are they animals? You decide.

Nourse, A. E. *Viruses.* New York: Watts.
> The author discusses Jenner's and Pasteur's discovery of vaccination. Also included in this book is a short history of viruses that ends with the present use of vaccines and the reason for the difficulty in producing a universal flu vaccine.

⑧ Nonvascular Plants and Plantlike Organisms

For a chapter overview, teaching strategies, answers to all activities, a list of A-V materials, and a chapter bibliography, see pages T-32 to T-34.

Consult your Teacher's Resource Book and Annotated Teacher's Edition, Laboratory Book for additional activities and teaching aids.

CHAPTER OBJECTIVES

After completing this chapter, you will be able to:

8-1 Give the characteristics of algae and list some examples.

8-2 Give the characteristics of fungi and list some examples.

8-3 Describe lichens and slime molds.

8-4 Describe the characteristics of mosses and liverworts.

The sun blazes in a cloudless sky. Far to the east, a tall pillar of orange smoke billows from an erupting volcano. The air, almost empty of oxygen, blows swiftly over the ocean, whipping up waves that crash against a huge sand bar. But there is no one here to witness or record these happenings. No people sail on this ocean or wade in the protected tidal pool, which is dotted with countless peculiar pillows of rock. No fish swim below the ocean's surface, nor do any birds fly above it. This is the world of 2.5 billion years ago. Here, there are no signs of life—except for those strange rocky pillows. One day in the future scientists will recognize these softly rounded rocks as the first structures built by living things.

Scientists call these softly rounded rocks stromatolites, which comes from Greek words that roughly mean "mattress of stone." But what living thing could build these 2.5-billion-year-old stony mattresses? The answer is blue-green algae. Undisturbed in protected pools of very salty water, the blue-green algae grew even larger and larger. As they did so, they produced a rocky mineral called lime. The lime piled up—year after year, century after century—and built a seascape of gray-brown cushions. And in certain parts of the world, such as in Shark Bay on the northwest coast of Australia, the process still goes on.

Stromatolites in Shark Bay, Australia

8-1 Algae

In a northern California forest, a giant redwood tree over 200 years old stands through a violent rainstorm. Deep in the soil the tree's roots soak up water. Soon thin tubes in the tree's trunk will carry the water nearly 60 meters to the top of the tree. Without these tubes, the redwood could not bring water to its millions of living cells.

If you were walking through this forest, you would probably marvel at the height of the redwood tree. However, unless you looked closely, you might not notice a smaller plant growing on the bark near the bottom of the tree. Unlike the redwood, this plant cannot grow to majestic heights. It is one of the earth's **nonvascular** (nahn-VA-skyuh-ler) **plants.** These plants do not have transportation tubes to carry water and food throughout the plant.

The plant living on the bark of the redwood tree is a type of **alga** (AL-guh; plural: algae—AL-gee). Algae are the largest group of nonvascular plants. Because algae have no way of transporting water and food over long distances, they must live near a source of water and food.

Figure 8-1 *The green patches floating on the surface of this lake are colonies of threadlike algae.*

Nonvascular plants such as the algae are often called simple plants. Simple plants lack true stems, leaves, and roots. However, do not let the term "simple" fool you. Nonvascular plants have managed to survive for hundreds of millions of years while other forms of life have come into being and then died off. In fact, through their long history nonvascular plants have become well adapted to many different environments on the earth.

Where Algae Live

No doubt you enjoy a visit to the zoo. Walking past one of the cages, you might notice a greenish stump hanging from a large branch. You look more closely and you see that the stump is breathing. The stump is alive! Looking at the small plaque on the cage, you discover that the "stump" is an animal called the three-toed sloth. Interestingly, the hair of this and many other three-toed sloths is the home for certain green algae. Because the sloth is such a slow-moving animal, it is unable to escape if there is danger. The algae's green color helps the sloth to blend in with its surroundings until the danger has passed. In return, the sloth gives the algae a place to live.

Most algae, of course, do not live on sloths. Algae live in many different places. The majority of algae live in watery environments such as oceans, ponds, and lakes. See Figure 8-2. Other algae grow in the soil, on the sides of houses, and at the base of trees. Certain species of algae thrive in the near-boiling water of hot springs such as those in Yellowstone National Park. Other algae grow in snow as well as in the icy waters of such places as the Antarctic continent, home of the South Pole.

Structure of Algae

Some species of algae are unicellular, or one-celled, and can only be seen with a microscope. Quite often unicellular algae group together to form colonies. These colonies may even attach themselves to one another and form chains of algae.

Beaches often become littered with seaweed after a heavy storm. Seaweed is one type of multicellular

In your discussion on algae, you may wish to mention plankton, which are the tiny organisms that float or drift near the surface of the water. Those that carry on photosynthesis, such as the algae, are called phytoplankton. Those that do not carry on photosynthesis consist mainly of protozoans called zooplankton.

Figure 8-2 *Several kinds of seaweeds, which are types of algae, washed up on a New England beach.*

algae. Multicellular algae can grow quite large. The giant kelp, for example, may stretch over 30 meters.

Whether unicellular or multicellular, all algae are autotrophs, or organisms that can make their own food. All algae contain **chlorophyll,** a green substance found in green plant cells. Chlorophyll is used in the process of **photosynthesis** (foh-tuh-SIN-thuh-sis). In photosynthesis, plants use the energy in sunlight to make their own food. Plants make food by combining carbon dioxide from the air with water and minerals from the soil. During the process of photosynthesis, oxygen is released from the plant.

Early in the earth's history there was very little oxygen in the atmosphere. In time, algae and other simple green plants, along with certain bacteria, released vast amounts of oxygen into the air. Eventually there was enough oxygen in the air to allow other forms of life to develop. If it were not for these simple green plants, no animals or people would now exist on the earth. And, as a matter of fact, if green plants were to suddenly vanish from the earth, oxygen in the air would soon become so rare that most living things would vanish.

Algae have several similarities and differences. Most algae reproduce by binary fission. Others have very complicated life cycles. Regardless of these differences, scientists have placed the algae into six groups. The groups are arranged according to the color of the algae.

Blue-Green Algae

In 1883, on the island of Krakatoa in Indonesia, a great volcano exploded. The sound of the explosion was heard by people thousands of kilometers away. In an instant, all living things on the island were destroyed, leaving behind only bare rock. Yet a few years later, one form of life had begun to grow on the barren island. This living thing was a blue-green alga.

Soon a layer of blue-green algae carpeted much of the island. The layer of algae eventually became so thick that plants were able to grow on top of it. Today, as they did before the volcanic eruption, many kinds of plants live and flourish on the island of Krakatoa.

ACTIVITY

Algae Life Cycles

Using reference materials in the library, find out more about the life cycles of the different groups of algae. Summarize your findings by drawing labeled diagrams of each type of life cycle.

172

Blue-green algae are considered to be the simplest of all algae. In fact, unlike all other algae, blue-green algae are not considered plants. They are placed in the Monera kingdom, along with bacteria. All blue-green algae need to live is sunlight, nitrogen and carbon dioxide gas from the air, and a few minerals in their water supply. It is likely that they were the first organisms to grow on land.

Blue-green algae are special for other reasons. Some blue-green algae can remove nitrogen gas from the air and combine the nitrogen with other substances to make nitrogen compounds. In this way, blue-green algae help provide the nitrogen compounds that plants need to live. Normally, farmers must use fertilizers to replace nitrogen compounds used by green plants. However, in places like Asia where blue-green algae live in the water, farmers can plant rice year after year without the need of fertilizers. The blue-green algae fertilize the rice paddies naturally.

Not all blue-green algae are blue-green in color. In some algae, the blue-green substance is masked by another substance. For example, one species of blue-green algae is actually red. It lives in the Red Sea, which accounts for the sea's name.

Figure 8-3 *Algae are found in many environments on the earth. These blue-green algae* (left) *are in a hot spring in Yellowstone National Park. Some blue-green algae* (right) *grow below the frozen surface of Lake Hoare in Antarctica.*

Figure 8-4 *The green alga* (left), *magnified 50 times, forms "water nets" on ponds.* Spirogyra (right) *is a green alga that forms filaments and is found in pools of fresh water.*

Green Algae

The year is 2001. Deep in space, a silvery ship is on its second year in a four-year journey to study the planets. On board, the two astronauts are about to finish dinner. Although they brought along enough food to last the entire journey, they could not carry enough oxygen to last several years. Are the astronauts doomed to suffocate in space? Of course not.

In a tiny room near the back of the ship lies a tub of water filled with green algae. The green algae use the carbon dioxide wastes exhaled by the astronauts to make food during photosynthesis. In return, the algae release their own waste, oxygen, for the astronauts to breathe. If you looked closely at the tub, you could see bubbles containing oxygen floating toward the surface. In this way, the astronauts and the green algae support each other's lives.

This scene is one that will not be played out for some time. However, scientists today are hard at work developing methods of growing green algae in closed environments. These methods will allow the algae to produce the oxygen future travelers will use in their explorations of space.

Right now you can find green algae only at home on the earth. Most green algae live in the water, but some plants may grow on the branches, stems, and leaves of trees. A few types of green algae may anchor themselves to rocks and pieces of wood.

Golden Algae

Every morning and evening you probably brush your teeth. Chances are that the last thing you would consider brushing with is algae. Yet a part of many toothpastes is made of golden algae. Do not let their name fool you, however. Golden algae all contain the green substance chlorophyll. Their golden color comes from a mixture of orange, yellow, and brown substances in their cells.

The most common, and certainly the most attractive, golden algae are the diatoms (DIGH-uh-tuhms). If you looked at diatoms through a microscope, they would resemble tiny glass boxes. See Figure 8-5. The appearance of diatoms is due to a glassy material in their cell walls. When diatoms die, their tough glass-like walls remain. In time, the walls collect in layers and form deposits of diatomaceous (digh-uh-tuh-MAY-shuhs) earth. Diatomaceous earth is a coarse, powdery material. For this reason, it is often added to toothpastes to help polish teeth. Moreover, be-

Figure 8-5 *Diatoms have cell walls made of silica, a glasslike substance. The diatoms (left) show their many different shapes. The single diatom (right) is magnified 3000 times.*

Collecting Algae

Some algae may be found on the bark on the side of a tree. These algae appear as masses of green material. Locate such a tree and carefully remove some of this green material. Be sure that you remove some bark along with the algae. Place the algae in a dish containing a small amount of water. Cover the dish to keep the bark moist.

After a few days, scrape off some of the green material and place it on a glass slide containing a drop of water. Cover the water and green material with a cover slip. Examine the slide under the low and high powers of the microscope. How does this alga compare with the photographs in Figure 8-4? Draw and label this alga under low and high power.

Figure 8-6 *The brown alga,* Sargassum, *provides a home for the Sargassum filefish and the Sargassum crab. The tiny grape-shaped structures are air bladders, which help to keep the alga afloat.*

cause diatomaceous earth reflects light, it is also added to the paint used to indicate separate traffic lanes on highways.

Brown Algae

For centuries, sailors whispered tales of a huge sea within a sea in the Atlantic Ocean southeast of Bermuda. This sea, the Sargasso Sea, the sailors said was filled with endless tangles of brown seaweed. The name of the sea comes from the brown *Sargassum* algae that grow in great amounts in this part of the Atlantic Ocean. Legend had it that ships trapped in this thick growth of seaweed would remain here forever, forming a fleet of dead ships guarded by skeletons. Today, some people believe that the sailors traveling with Christopher Columbus mutinied not out of fear of falling off the side of the earth, but out of fear of being trapped in the Sargasso Sea.

The legends about the Sargasso Sea are merely a product of people's strong imagination. However, the brown algae that float there are very real. The *Sargassum* lie, on or near the ocean's surface. There they are able to receive enough sunlight to perform photosynthesis. They stay near the surface because they have **air bladders.** Air bladders are tiny grape-shaped structures. These air bladders act like inflatable life preservers.

Brown algae, such as *Sargassum,* are the largest and most complex of the algae. Most brown algae live in salt water and are called seaweeds or kelps. Some brown algae float freely while others remain attached to the sea floor.

Red Algae

Red algae, named for a red substance found in their cells, make up another large group of algae. Some red algae produce a jellylike material called agar (AH-guhr). Agar is a substance on which scientists grow bacteria.

Red algae can grow to be several meters long, but they never reach the size of brown algae such as *Sargassum.* Red algae usually grow attached to rocks on the ocean floor. Their red color allows them to absorb a part of sunlight that can penetrate deep into the ocean. For this reason, some species of red algae grow as far as 200 meters below the ocean's surface.

Fire Algae

In the winter and spring of 1974, the waters near the west coast of Florida suddenly turned brown and red. Soon thousands of dead fish washed up on shore. One young boy became very ill after eating clams taken from the area. This was not the first time a "red tide" had struck a Florida beach, or, for that matter, other beaches in the United States. Red tides have swept onto beaches in such places as New England and Los Angeles.

The red tide is not a tide at all. It is a large group of unicellular fire algae. Fire algae range in color from yellow-green to orange-brown. Some of these fire algae produce poisons. These poisons can injure or kill living things.

If you observed fire algae through a microscope, you would notice something interesting. Fire algae have cell walls that look like plates of armor. In addition, fire algae have two flagella that help propel them forward. So the algae might look like tiny submarines spinning through the water like tops.

Figure 8-7 *Unlike brown algae which float free, red algae usually are attached to rocks on the ocean floor. Red algae also are smaller and more delicate than brown algae.*

Figure 8-8 *Notice that the cell wall of this fire alga, magnified 5000 times, looks like armor plates. This particular fire alga can cause "red tides."*

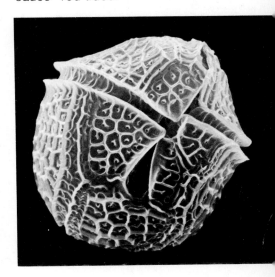

Some fire algae have a characteristic that has amazed sailors since they first set sail on the world's oceans. These sailors often saw a strange glow at night in the water behind their ships. What the sailors did not know was that the glow was produced by fire algae. This glow is called **bioluminescence** (bigh-oh-loo-muh-NE-suhns), which means "having living light." The glow is similar to that produced by fireflies, or "lightning bugs."

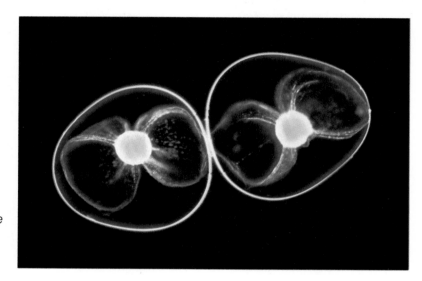

Figure 8-9 *These two fire algae cells produce a cold light, or a glow, called bioluminescence.*

SECTION REVIEW

1. What are nonvascular plants?
2. List the different groups of algae.
3. What is bioluminescence?

1. Plants that do not have transportation tubes
2. Blue-green, green, golden, brown, red, and fire
3. Glow produced by some fire algae

8-2 Fungi

In 1927, scientists discovered a deadly elm tree disease in England. The disease, called Dutch elm disease, caused the leaves of the trees to wither. Eventually, the trees died. You would think that elm trees in the United States, separated from England by the Atlantic Ocean, would be safe. However, despite repeated warnings, wood of the English elm trees was shipped to this country to make furniture. By 1930, Dutch elm disease had struck trees in Ohio.

Figure 8-10 *The elm tree* (left) *has been attacked by a fungus that causes Dutch elm disease. This disease is carried by the bark beetle whose wormlike larva* (right) *burrow through the bark of the tree.*

Today, Dutch elm disease has spread to almost every state in the country. The disease is carried from tree to tree by insects called bark beetles. However, as scientists learned, Dutch elm disease actually is caused by a type of **fungus,** (FUHNG-guhs; plural: fungi) carried by the beetles.

Like algae, fungi are nonvascular. But unlike algae, fungi have no chlorophyll and, therefore, cannot perform photosynthesis. Because fungi must obtain their food from living or once-living organisms, they are heterotrophs.

Fungi that live and grow on other living things are called parasites. The fungus that kills elm trees is an example of a parasite. Other parasitic fungi grow on and destroy crop plants, which people depend upon for food. Fungi can also attack people directly, as anyone who has ever suffered from the itching of athlete's foot can tell you. Animals, too, can be victims of fungi. Some fungi, for example, infect fishes, including those that are raised in home aquariums.

Other species of fungi get their food from once-living organisms. These fungi are called saprophytes. They, along with many types of bacteria, are the earth's "clean-up crew." These fungi decompose, or

Figure 8-11 *The four shelflike structures growing on this tree are shelf fungi. These fungi are parasites and get their food from the living tree.*

Figure 8-12 *Fungi have many shapes and can be very colorful. The bird's nest (top left), morel (top right), scarlet cup (bottom left), and death cup (bottom right) are different kinds of fungi.*

break down, dead plant and animal matter. These broken-down products become the foods of other living things. Without saprophytes, dead plants and animals would soon litter and pollute the earth.

Structure of Fungi

Fungi have several types of structures. Most members of the Fungi kingdom have threadlike structures called **hyphae** (HIGH-fee; singular: hypha). These hyphae produce special chemicals called enzymes. The enzymes digest or break down the cells of living or dead organisms. The broken-down cells and their chemicals are used by fungi as food. Fungi absorb food through the walls of the hyphae.

Most fungi reproduce by means of spores. These spores are contained in special **fruiting bodies.**

Fruiting bodies are structures that form from the closely packed hyphae. When the spores are released and land in moist areas, such as on the forest floor, they grow into new fungi.

Mushrooms

Have you ever ordered a pizza with all the trimmings? If so, you probably ate one type of fungi called the mushroom. All you may know about the mushrooms on pizza is that they taste good. But the pizza maker has to know a lot more because certain mushrooms are poisonous, and poisonous mushrooms on a pizza certainly would not improve sales.

Fortunately, the mushrooms on pizzas and stocked on grocery shelves come from special farms and are safe to eat. However, mushrooms that grow in the wild often are not safe to eat. One of the most poisonous wild mushrooms is the death cup. This well-named mushroom produces a poison that acts much like the venom of a rattlesnake. Since most people cannot tell the difference between poisonous and nonpoisonous mushrooms, wild mushrooms should never be picked or eaten.

The umbrella-shaped part of the mushroom you probably are most familiar with is the mushroom's **cap.** It is actually the mushroom's fruiting body, which contains spores. See Figure 8-13. The cap can be any color, depending on the species of mushroom. The cap is at the top of a **stalk,** a stemlike

Spores

Fruiting body

Cap

Gills
Spores
Ring

Stalk

Hyphae

Figure 8-13 *As a mushroom develops, the fruiting body emerges from under the ground and releases spores. These spores then develop into new mushrooms.*

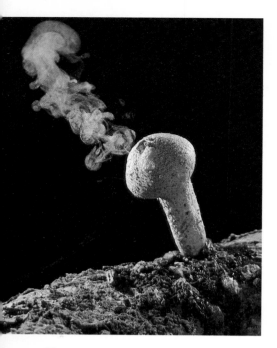

Figure 8-14 *When a water droplet hits this puff ball fungus, the fungus responds by releasing a cloud of spores.*

Figure 8-15 *Yeasts reproduce by budding, as shown in this photograph. The cells that result can form new yeast colonies.*

structure that has a ring near its top. If you were to turn the mushroom upside down, you would see its **gills.** The gills are the mushroom's spore factories.

Not all mushrooms resemble the types that you see in the grocery store. The puffball, for example, looks like a giant softball and can grow up to 60 centimeters in diameter. When a raindrop hits the puffball, a tiny puff of "smoke" is given off. The puff of smoke contains thousands of spores. See Figure 8-14.

Yeasts

Most people cannot help but stop and take a deep breath when they pass a bakery. There is something about the aroma of fresh bread that excites our senses. The next time you pass a bakery you might whisper a soft thank-you to another type of fungi, the yeasts.

Yeasts, like other fungi, have no chlorophyll. They obtain their energy through a process called **fermentation.** During fermentation, sugars and starches are changed into alcohol and carbon dioxide gas. At the same time, energy is released.

Bakers add yeast to bread dough. As the dough bakes, the yeast produces carbon dioxide. This causes the bread to rise. The carbon dioxide also produces millions of tiny bubbles in the bread, which you can see as holes in a slice of bread.

Although yeasts are unicellular, they can clump together to form chains of cells. Yeasts reproduce by forming spores or by **budding.** See Figure 8-15. During budding, a portion of the yeast cell pushes out of the cell wall and forms a tiny bud. In time, the bud forms a new yeast.

Molds

Centuries ago people treated infections in a rather curious way. They often placed decaying breads, cheeses, and fruits such as oranges on the infection. Although the people did not have a scientific reason to do this, every once in a while the infection was cured. What these people did not and could not know was that the cure was due to a type of fungus, called mold, which grows on certain foods.

In 1928, the Scottish scientist, Sir Alexander Fleming found out why this treatment worked. Fleming discovered that a substance produced by the mold *Penicillium* could kill certain bacteria that caused infections. Fleming named the substance penicillin. Since that time penicillin, an antibiotic, has saved millions of lives.

You have probably seen the common mold that grows on bread. This mold looks like tiny fluffs of cotton. Actually, these fluffs are groups of long hyphae that grow over the surface of bread. Shorter hyphae grow down into the bread and resemble tiny roots. The shorter hyphae release the enzymes that break down chemicals in the bread. The broken-down chemicals are foods for the mold and are absorbed by the hyphae. See Figure 8-16.

Perhaps you have noticed tiny black spheres on bread mold. These spheres are spore cases, which produce spores. The spores are carried from one place to another through the air. When the spores land on food, they begin to develop into a new mold.

Figure 8-16 *Bread mold reproduces by producing spores. They are released from structures called spore cases. Long hyphae anchor the mold to bread. Short hyphae absorb food from bread.*

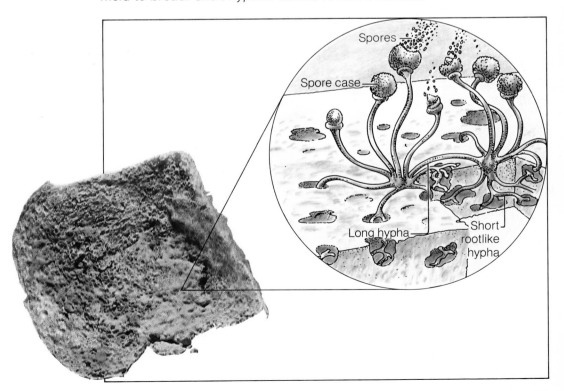

**HELP WANTED: MUSHROOM GROW-
ER** Must know basics of mushroom
growing and have an interest in botany.
High school diploma needed. Business
and marketing courses desirable.

People have been using mushrooms to flavor food for thousands of years. Usually the
mushrooms were found growing wild in fields.
It was not until the late 1800s that mushrooms
were grown on a large scale in the United
States for sale in the marketplace.

Mushroom growers must grow their crop
indoors, where conditions can be controlled.
The growers keep careful watch over the special devices that control temperature, humidity,
and ventilation. In addition, mushroom growers
must know how to identify and treat diseases
of mushrooms.

Growers work in all stages of mushroom
production. Because mushrooms live on dead
or decayed matter, growers prepare mixtures
of corn and hay. This mixture is placed in a
shallow bed and then steam heated to destroy
harmful insects, worms, and fungi. Then the
hyphae, or cottony masses of material from
which the mushrooms will develop is planted in
the mixture of corn and hay and covered with
a layer of soil.

Two to three months later, the mushrooms
are picked just before the gills appear under
the caps. The mushrooms are sent to large
canning companies or supermarkets the same
day they are picked. Some mushroom growers
sell directly to consumers. If becoming a mushroom grower appeals to you, you can write to
the American Mushroom Institute, P.O. Box
373, Kennett Square, PA 19348.

SECTION REVIEW

1. How are fungi different from algae?
2. What are hyphae?
3. How do yeast cells reproduce?
4. What is penicillin?

1. Fungi are heterotrophs
2. Threadlike structures in fungi that produce enzymes
3. By budding
4. An antibiotic produced by a mold

8-3 Lichens and Slime Molds

Suppose someone asked you what kind of organism can live in the hot, dry desert as well as the
cold, wet Arctic. What if the person added that this
organism can also survive on bare rocks, wooden

poles, the sides of trees, and even the tops of mountains? You might reply that no one organism can survive in so many different environments. In a way, your response would be right. For although **lichens** (LIGH-kuhnz) can actually live in all of these environments, they are not one organism but two. A lichen is made up of a fungus and an alga that live together. Combined, these two organisms can live in many places that neither could survive in alone.

The fungus part of the lichen provides the alga with water and minerals that the fungus absorbs from whatever the lichen is growing on. The alga part of the lichen uses the minerals and water to make food for the fungus and itself. This type of relationship, in which two different organisms live together, is called **symbiosis** (sim-bigh-OH-sis).

Lichens are called pioneer plants because they are often the first plants to appear in rocky, barren areas. Lichens release acids that break down rock and cause it to crack. Dust and dead lichens fill the cracks, which eventually become fertile places for other organisms to grow. In time, the rocky area may become a lush, green forest.

Figure 8-17 *This green structure with the red top is a lichen. A lichen is made up of an alga and a fungus that live together.*

Figure 8-18 *The lavender, bloblike organism growing on this dead leaf is a slime mold.*

While walking through a forest, you may have seen a bloblike organism growing in moist areas, on dead leaves, rotting logs, and other types of decaying material. This organism is called a **slime mold.** It gets its name from the two stages that it goes through during its life cycle.

In one of the slime mold's stages, it resembles a jellylike mass of protoplasm, engulfing and digesting food like a giant amoeba. In the other stage, the slime mold develops fruiting bodies like its cousin the mushroom. The fruiting bodies produce spores. The spores develop into new slime molds.

SECTION REVIEW

1. What is a lichen?
2. Define symbiosis.
3. Where are slime molds found?

1. A fungus and an alga that live together
2. Relationship in which two different organisms live together
3. In moist areas, and on dead leaves and rotting logs

8-4 Mosses and Liverworts

In a barren cold part of northern Europe, above the Arctic Circle, is the country of Lapland. Its rocky landscape has a few small trees and beds of lichens and **mosses.** The people who live in this icy place are

Figure 8-19 *The rounded structures at the top of these haircap mosses are capsules. Spores are produced within these capsules.*

called Lapps. For them, everything in their environment is important, including the mosses. Because the mosses are soft and keep in warmth, the Lapps use them to line their baby cradles.

Classified as nonvascular plants, mosses live not only in Lapland but almost everywhere in the world. They are found near or on the ground, close to sources of water. Mosses absorb water through root-like structures called **rhizoids** (RIGH-zoids). Because mosses contain chlorophyll, they make their own food through photosynthesis. They live in damp and cool places such as the shaded surfaces of trees and rocks.

Although **liverworts** share characteristics with mosses, they are different plants. Liverworts live in similar places and possess rhizoids. However, liverworts are usually smaller and look different from mosses. Each liverwort looks like a tiny green leaf, although it is not a real leaf. Some liverworts look like miniature livers, which explains how these simple plants got their name. Certain liverworts have a special way of reproducing. New plants grow from pieces broken off older plants. See Figure 8-20.

Figure 8-20 *The small, flat, green plants growing on the rock are liverworts.*

SECTION REVIEW

1. What is the function of a rhizoid?
2. How are liverworts like mosses? Unlike mosses?

1. Absorption of water
2. They both live in similar places and have rhizoids. However, liverworts, are smaller and look different from mosses.

LABORATORY ACTIVITY

For further instructions, see page T-33.

Making Spore Prints

Purpose

In this activity, you will make a spore print of a mushroom.

Materials *(per group)*

1 fresh mushroom cap
Sheet of white paper
Large beaker
Magnifying glass
Clear varnish or hair spray

Procedure

1. Examine a mushroom cap and make a sketch of the gills on the underside of the cap.
2. Place the mushroom cap, gill side down, on a sheet of white paper. Cover the cap with a large beaker, open end down. Do not disturb the mushroom and beaker.
3. After several days, carefully remove the beaker and lift off the mushroom cap. You should now find a spore print on the paper.
4. Spray the paper with clear varnish or hair spray in order to make a permanent spore print.
5. Using a magnifying glass, examine the print.

Observations and Conclusions

1. What did you observe on the paper when you removed the cap? Name the structures that you are observing.
2. What did use of the magnifying glass reveal?
3. Explain your print in terms of the reproduction of mushrooms.

CHAPTER SUMMARY

8-1 Algae

■ Algae are nonvascular organisms that lack true stems, roots, and leaves.

■ Algae contain chlorophyll, a green substance needed for photosynthesis.

■ Algae are placed into six groups according to their color. They are grouped as blue-green, green, golden, brown, red, and fire algae. All but the blue-green are plants.

8-2 Fungi

■ Fungi are nonvascular organisms that lack true stems, roots, and leaves.

■ Unlike algae, fungi do not contain chlorophyll.

■ Fungi are heterotrophs. Some fungi are parasites, organisms that feed on other living things. Others are saprophytes, organisms that feed on once-living organisms.

8-3 Lichens and Slime Molds

■ Lichens are made up of two organisms, a fungus and an alga, that live together. This type of relationship is called symbiosis.

■ Slime molds are found in moist areas on once-living leaves, rotting logs, and other types of decaying material.

8-4 Mosses and Liverworts

■ Mosses are nonvascular plants that have rootlike structures called rhizoids. Rhizoids help to absorb water from the soil.

■ Liverworts are smaller than mosses. Some liverworts reproduce when pieces of the plant break off older plants.

VOCABULARY   *Define the following terms.*

air bladder p.176
alga p.170
bioluminescence p.178
budding p.182
cap p.181

chlorophyll p.172
fermentation p.182
fruiting body p.180
fungus p.179
gill p.182

hypha p.180
lichen p.185
liverwort p.187
moss p.186
nonvascular plant p.170

photosynthesis p.172
rhizoid p.187
slime mold p.186
stalk p.181
symbiosis p.185

CHAPTER REVIEW

Multiple Choice

Choose the letter of the answer that best completes each statement.

1. The green substance in plants needed for photosynthesis is
   a. diatomaceous earth.
   b. hypha.
   c. chlorophyll.
   d. rhizoid.

2. Algae whose gritty, glasslike skeletons form a substance used in toothpaste are
   a. blue-green algae.
   b. green algae.
   c. golden algae.
   d. red algae.

189

3. Structures that enable brown algae to float near the surface of the water are
   a. rhizoids.
   b. hyphae.
   c. fruiting bodies.
   d. air bladders.

4. What structures do fire algae use for movement?
   a. rhizoids
   b. cilia
   c. flagella
   d. pseudopodia

5. Most fungi have threadlike structures called
   a. caps.
   b. hyphae.
   c. fruiting bodies.
   d. stalks.

6. Yeasts change sugars into alcohol and carbon dioxide during
   a. budding.
   b. fermentation.
   c. symbiosis.
   d. conjugation.

7. An important product produced by the *Penicillium* mold is
   a. chocolate milk.
   b. toothpaste.
   c. fertilizer.
   d. an antibiotic.

8. The black, rounded structures in bread mold produce
   a. rhizoids.
   b. spores.
   c. fruiting bodies.
   d. hyphae.

9. Mosses have rootlike structures that are called
   a. hyphae.
   b. stalks.
   c. caps.
   d. rhizoids.

10. A plant that is very similar to a moss is a(n)
   a. mushroom.
   b. alga.
   c. liverwort.
   d. fungus.

Completions

Fill in the word or words that best complete each statement.

1. All plants that lack true roots, stems, and leaves are ____nonvascular____.

2. The process by which green plants make their own food is ____photosynthesis____.

3. An example of a golden alga is a(n) ____diatom____.

4. In most fungi, spores are contained in special ____fruiting bodies____.

5. The umbrella-shaped part of a mushroom is the ____cap____.

6. In a mushroom, the cap is found at the top of a(n) ____stalk____.

7. A puffball is an example of a(n) ____mushroom____.

8. Yeasts reproduce by forming spores or by ____budding____.

9. A relationship in which two different organisms live together is ____symbiosis____.

10. A moss absorbs water from its environment with its rootlike ____rhizoids____.

True or False

Determine whether each statement is true or false. If it is true, write "true."
If it is false, change the underlined word or words to make the statement
true.

1. Most algae live in a <u>watery</u> environment. T
2. Algae contain <u>chlorophyll</u>. T
3. Blue-green algae are considered to be the <u>most complex</u> of all algae. F (Brown)
4. Diatoms are examples of <u>red</u> algae. F (golden)
5. *Sargassum* is an example of a brown alga. T
6. Some <u>brown</u> algae are capable of bioluminescence. F (golden)
7. Dutch elm disease is caused by a <u>fungus</u>. T
8. Fungi are <u>autotrophs</u>. F (heterotrophs)
9. Yeasts are unicellular <u>algae</u>. F (fungi)
10. A <u>slime mold</u> is made up of an alga and a fungus. F (lichen)

Discussion Topics Answers appear on page T-33.

Write a brief paragraph discussing each of the following.

1. Why are most algae and no fungi classified as plants?
2. What are some uses of green algae?
3. Why are fungi called heterotrophs?
4. Describe the structure of the mushroom.
5. What is fermentation? Why are yeast cells used in baking bread?
6. Define symbiosis and give an example.

EXPAND YOUR KNOWLEDGE

Johnson, S. A. *Mushrooms*. Minneapolis, Minn.: Lerner.
  This book explains how mushrooms and other fungi obtain their food, grow, and reproduce. It includes many colorful photographs.
Shuttleworth, F. S., and H. S. Zim. *Non-Flowering Plants*. New York: Golden Press.
  Most of this book is devoted to algae and fungi. Many colorful drawings are included to help identify these plants.

Vascular Plants

For a chapter overview, teaching strategies, answers to all activities, a list of A-V materials, and a chapter bibliography, see pages T-34 to T-36.

Consult your Teacher's Resource Book and Annotated Teacher's Edition, Laboratory Book for additional activities and teaching aids.

CHAPTER SECTIONS

CHAPTER OBJECTIVES

After completing this chapter, you will be able to:

9-1 Describe the characteristics of ferns.

9-2 Give the functions of roots, stems, and leaves in seed plants.

9-2 Describe photosynthesis and transpiration.

9-3 Describe the characteristics of gymnosperms.

9-4 Describe the characteristics of angiosperms.

9-4 List the parts of the flower and describe their function in pollination and fertilization.

9-4 Discuss the processes of seed dispersal and seed germination.

Life at the top of Mount Washington in New Hampshire is not easy. Winds often whip through the air at more than 160 kilometers an hour. Winter temperatures can dive to −40°C. Yet even in this harsh environment, living things can survive. As a matter of fact, one of the rarest plants in the world lives here. The tiny plant, less than 5 centimeters tall, is called the Robbins cinquefoil (SINK-foil). This plant is able to survive the wind and cold because it grows under patches of snow and ice. The snow and ice act as a blanket that protects the plant from low temperatures and from blowing away.

Today, there are fewer than 4000 Robbins cinquefoil plants in the world. However, it is not the cold environment that threatens them, but rather people. Hikers enjoying the pleasures of Mount Washington often walk near the plant. As they do, they kick away some of the soil around the plant. Without the soil, new seeds cannot grow, which endangers the future of the plant.

Can the Robbins cinquefoil be saved? The federal government has gone to great lengths to protect the plants. But, in the end, it will be up to people to save the Robbins cinquefoil. Through education and understanding, people will know next time to step around a tiny plant growing at the top of a tall mountain.

Robbins cinquefoil on Mount Washington

9-1 Ferns

Imagine walking through a rain forest, such as Washington State's Olympic National Park. As you enter, you immediately feel the cool dampness of the air. Tall trees, such as firs, spruces, and cedars, are everywhere. Mosses drape the branches and trunks of trees and hold moisture like a sponge.

As you continue your walk, you notice feathery green leaves above some moss plants. Many of these leaves belong to ferns. Unlike mosses, which are nonvascular plants, ferns are **vascular plants.** Vascular plants contain transporting tubes that carry material throughout the plant. Remember that mosses must live close to the ground. Mosses have no transporting tubes to carry water and nutrients to their parts.

Ferns are one of the oldest plants on the earth. They appeared more than 300 million years ago and soon became the most abundant type of plant. These ferns were as large as trees. Today, some ferns the size of trees are still found in tropical rain forests.

Most ferns disappeared as the earth's climate changed. All that remained of some ferns was dead

Figure 9-1 *The photograph on the left shows tree ferns as they appear today in a rain forest in Costa Rica. The photograph on the right shows a model of a fern forest during the Carboniferous period.*

plant material. This material later formed great coal deposits. Most living or once-living material contains carbon. Because coal is made up mostly of carbon, the geological period in which ferns were abundant is called the Carboniferous Period.

Structure of Ferns

As vascular plants, ferns have true leaves, stems, and roots. In fact, a fern's **fronds,** or leaves, are the part of the plant you usually notice. See Figure 9-2. For the most part, developing fern leaves are curled at the top and resemble the top of a violin. Because of their appearance, these developing leaves are called fiddleheads. As they mature, the fiddleheads uncurl until they reach their full size.

Following the leaves down toward the ground, you find the **rhizome** (RIGH-zohm), or stem of the fern. In some ferns, the rhizome looks like a large fuzzy, brown caterpillar with leaves. The rhizomes of many ferns grow along the surface of the soil. In other types of ferns, the rhizomes grow beneath the ground. Roots grow from the rhizomes and anchor the ferns to the ground. The roots also absorb water and minerals for the plant.

Transporting tubes travel throughout the fern's leaves, stems, and roots. These tubes carry materials throughout the plant. These special tubes allow the fern to grow taller than nonvascular plants.

Reproduction of Ferns

As the fern grows, it goes through two stages in its life cycle. If you were to look at both stages of the same plant, you would think that each was a different plant.

The fern uses a different type of reproduction in each stage. In the first stage of a fern's life cycle, small brown structures appear on the underside of the fronds. These structures are spore cases and contain spores. See Figure 9-3. Once the spore cases ripen, they open and release spores. Spores are carried through the air and eventually fall to the ground. If growth conditions are favorable, the spores begin to grow into new fern plants. The development of new organisms from spores is an

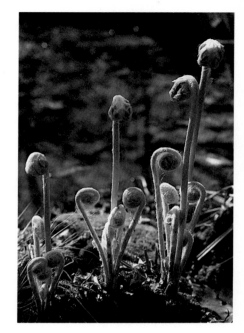

Figure 9-2 *The curled structures at the tops of these ferns are called fiddleheads because they resemble the tops of violins. Fiddleheads are the developing fronds, or leaves, of ferns.*

Figure 9-3 *The tiny brown spots on the underside of this fern frond are spore cases. Spore cases contain spores.*

Observing Ferns

Visit an area, such as a park or nature center, in your neighborhood where ferns grow. Such areas usually have lots of shade and moisture. Examine a fern plant. Observe the brown spots on the underside of the fronds. These spots are the spore cases and contain the spores.

Carefully remove a frond and place it in a small plastic bag. Plant the frond on top of a pot of moist soil. Be sure that the spore cases are facing down. Make sure that the soil is always moist.

In about four weeks, you will notice new ferns growing. What type of reproduction has occurred? Using reference material, draw the life cycle of a fern.

Figure 9-4 *The sticklike structure growing out of the avocado fruit is a developing plant. This plant grew from the seed within the avocado.*

example of **asexual reproduction.** Asexual reproduction is the formation of an organism from a single parent.

The next stage of a fern's life cycle begins as the spores grow into structures that do not resemble their parents. These structures look like tiny heart-shaped green plants. The plants develop special tissues that produce male and female sex cells. The male sex cell is called the sperm and the female sex cell is called the egg. Both are located on the plant. The sperm unites with the eggs by swimming across the plant through dew and rainwater.

The united sperm and egg grow into a new fern plant. This plant is similar in appearance to the plant with fronds that produced spores. The new fern plant was produced by **sexual reproduction.** In sexual reproduction, an organism develops from the uniting of two different sex cells.

Although the fern's life cycle seems complicated, it is successful. Ferns have survived, with little change, for millions of years.

SECTION REVIEW

1. How are vascular plants different from nonvascular plants?
2. What is a frond? A rhizome?
3. What is the difference between asexual and sexual reproduction?

1. Vascular plants contain transporting tubes, while nonvascular plants do not. 2. A frond is a fern's leaf, while a rhizome is the fern's stem. 3. In asexual reproduction, an organism develops from a single parent. In sexual reproduction, an organism develops from the uniting of two different sex cells.

9-2   Seed Plants

If you wanted to plant a vegetable garden, you would begin by loosening the soil. Also you would have to make sure that your garden had a source of water. Only then would you plant your **seeds.** A seed contains a young plant, stored food, and a seed coat. With proper care, the seeds in your garden would begin to grow and, after a few months, produce adult plants loaded with vegetables.

Like ferns, seed plants have roots, stems, leaves, and go through the same two reproduction stages during their life cycles. Seed plants are divided into

Figure 9-5 *This zucchini squash plant is an example of an angiosperm. Angiosperms produce seeds covered by a protective wall and flowers.*

two groups based on the structure of their seeds. In **gymnosperms** (JIM-nuh-sperms), the seeds *are not* covered by a protective wall. In **angiosperms** (AN-jee-oh-sperms), the seeds *are* covered by a protective wall.

Seed plants are among the most numerous plants on the earth. Also, they are the plants with which most people are familiar. The trees in the forest, the vegetables in a garden, and the cotton plant are all examples of seed plants. What other seed plants can you name?

Roots

Anyone who lives near trees no doubt has seen what a violent storm can do to them. The tremendous force of the storm's wind can pull a tree right out of the ground. A large hole marks the spot where the tree once was anchored to the ground. If you were to look carefully at the exposed base of the tree, you would notice small and large structures that resemble tentacles. These structures are the tree's roots, which anchor the plant in the ground. Roots also absorb water and minerals from the soil. In addition, the roots of some plants, such as those of the

Figure 9-6 *Although all roots absorb materials from the soil and anchor a plant to the soil, they do not all look the same. Notice the differences in the roots of the banyan trees (left), grasses (top right) and carrots (bottom right).*

Activity

Transport Tubes

Obtain a medium-sized jar and fill it one-quarter full of water. Add a few drops of red vegetable coloring to the water and stir thoroughly. Place a celery stalk with leaves and a twig from a tree or shrub in the jar.

After 24 hours, remove the celery and twig from the water and examine each. With a knife, cut off and discard the portion of the celery stalk and twig that were under the surface of the colored water. **CAUTION:** *Be very careful when using a knife.* Now carefully cut a small section across the bottom of both remaining sections. How do the two sections differ? What is the name of the tubes that transported the colored water up to the top of the plant?

carrot, store food for the plant. The roots of some plants, such as those of turnips, go straight down. Other plants, such as the grasses, have slender roots that spread out in many directions. See Figure 9-6.

Tiny <u>root hairs</u> cover the surface of many roots. Root hairs are microscopic extensions of single cells. The root hairs greatly increase the surface area of the root. They allow the plant to take in water and minerals from the soil. The minerals pass through the root hairs into tissue called **xylem** (ZIGH-luhm). The xylem tissue forms tubes that carry water and minerals from the roots up through the plant. The roots also contain another kind of tissue called **phloem** (FLOH-uhm). Phloem tissue forms tubes that carry food substances down from the plant's leaves.

Stems

Have you ever seen a group of maple trees with buckets attached to their trunks and wondered what was going on? Remember that the stem, or trunk, of the tree contains xylem and phloem tissue. Within these tissues, there flows a liquid called sap. The sap in the xylem tissue contains water and minerals, while the phloem tissue's sap contains sugary plant food. Usually, the sugary sap moves downward. At certain times of the year in some trees, such as the sugar maple, the sap moves both up and down. The sap is collected from sugar maple trees and used to produce the maple syrup that you pour over your breakfast pancakes!

Stems also contain a tissue called **cambium** (KAM-bee-uhm). Cambium is the growth tissue of the stem. New xylem and phloem cells are produced in the cambium, causing the wood in the stem to become

Figure 9-7 *Maple syrup comes from the sap of certain types of maple trees. This tree is being tapped for its sugary sap.*

Figure 9-8 *In a stem, the xylem transports water and other materials from the roots up to the leaves. The phloem conducts sap from the leaves down to the roots. Cambium is the growth tissue of the plant and produces new xylem and phloem cells.*

Figure 9-9 *The age of a tree can be determined by counting the number of rings in its stem. Each ring represents one year's growth.*

ACTIVITY

Annual Rings

Find a sawed-off tree stump or a fallen tree. Count the number of annual rings to determine the age of the tree. Notice the widths of different rings. A wide ring is produced during a year of heavy rainfall, while a narrow ring is produced during a year of little rain. Closely examine one ring. Within each ring, you should be able to see a wide growth area and a narrow growth area. Which of these areas do you think took place in the spring? In the summer? Explain why.

thicker. Each year, as a new layer of xylem cells grows, it wraps itself around the layer before it. Because each layer is one year's growth of xylem cells, these layers are called **annual rings.** Scientists estimate the age of a tree by counting its annual rings.

Plant stems vary in size, shape, and function. The trunk, branches, and twigs of a tree are all stems. Some plants, such as the cabbage, have stems so short that you probably would not recognize them.

Stems provide the means for the transportation of water, minerals, and food. Another function of the stems is to support the other parts of the plant. In addition, the stems hold the leaves up in the air so that they can receive sunlight and make their own food.

Although most stems grow vertically and above the ground, some grow like roots. In some plants, such as the iris and lily of the valley, the stems grow horizontally and under the ground. Like those of ferns, these stems are called rhizomes. Other underground stems called tubers store food. The potato, for example, is a tuber. The "eyes" of the potato are buds. Each bud is capable of developing into a new potato plant. Certain spring plants, such as onions and tulips, produce a short, thick stem called a bulb.

Figure 9-10 *A potato is actually a special kind of stem called a tuber that grows under the ground. The fingerlike structures growing on the potato are actually new potato plants.*

Figure 9-11 *Stems are either herbaceous or woody. The soft, green herbaceous stems on the left are of a daisylike plant. On the right are the rigid woody stems of trees.*

Bulbs have thick leaves that contain food for the plant. When planted, the bulbs develop into new plants.

Stems may be placed into two groups based on their hardness. A **herbaceous** (her-BAY-shuhs) **stem** is green and soft. Sunflowers, eggplants, peas, beans, and tomatoes are examples of plants with herbaceous stems. Most plants that have herbaceous stems are annuals. An annual is a plant that completes its life cycle within one growing season. A plant's life cycle begins when the plant starts to grow from a seed and ends when the plant produces its own seeds. Wheat, rye, and tobacco plants are examples of annuals.

Unlike herbaceous stems, **woody stems** are rigid. These stems have large amounts of woody xylem tissue. Plants that have woody stems are called perennials (puh-REN-ee-uhls). A perennial is a plant that lives for more than two growing seasons. Included in the group of perennial plants are trees and woody shrubs. Plants that live for two growing seasons are called biennials (bigh-EN-ee-uhls). Biennials

201

Figure 9-12 *Leaves come in a wide variety of types and shapes. The tulip tree leaf* (left) *is a simple leaf, while the poison ivy leaf* (right) *is a compound leaf.*

may be either herbaceous or woody. Many garden vegetable plants, such as beets, celery, carrots, and cabbage, are biennials.

Leaves

Have you ever heard of the drug digitalis (di-ji-ᴛᴀʟ-is)? It is given to people who have certain types of heart problems. This drug is not made in a laboratory. It is made from the dried leaves of a garden flower called the foxglove. The leaves are found growing along the stem of the plant.

Plant leaves vary greatly in shape and size. For example, leaves of the foxglove are long and oval-shaped. Pines, firs, and balsams have needle-shaped leaves. Other plants have flat, wide leaves. Most leaves have a stalk and a blade. The stalk connects the leaf to the stem, while the blade is the thin, flat part of the leaf. Most of the cells in which food making takes place are in the blade.

In addition, there are two types of leaves. Some leaves have only one blade and are called simple leaves. The silver maple leaf and apple leaf are examples of simple leaves. Leaves such as the black locust and buckeye have two or more blades. These are examples of compound leaves.

Whatever their shape, leaves are very important structures. Within the leaves, the sun's energy is trapped and used to produce food. This process is called **photosynthesis.** It is the largest and most important manufacturing process in the world.

Activity

Insect-Eating Plants

The leaves of some plants contain special chemicals or mechanical traps that catch insects. These plants are called insectivorous plants.

Visit the library and look up information about insectivorous plants. How does each plant capture its prey? Do these plants also perform photosynthesis? Record your findings in a written report.

In photosynthesis, the sun's light energy is captured by <u>chlorophyll</u>, the green substance in plants. The sun's energy is used to combine water from the soil and carbon dioxide from the air. The food made by this combination is a sugar called <u>glucose</u>. Glucose is used by the plant for growth and to repair its parts. Glucose can be stored in special areas in the roots and stems. Photosynthesis also yields a waste product—oxygen! Of what value is this product of photosynthesis? Oxygen is needed by most living things to produce energy.

Photosynthesis is a complicated process, although an equation can be used to sum up what occurs. An equation is the scientist's shorthand for describing a reaction. This is the equation for photosynthesis.

$$\text{carbon dioxide} + \text{water} \xrightarrow[\text{chlorophyll}]{\text{sunlight}} \text{glucose} + \text{oxygen}$$

$$6CO_2 + 6H_2O \xrightarrow[\text{chlorophyll}]{\text{sunlight}} C_6H_{12}O_6 + 6O_2$$

In photosynthesis, carbon dioxide enters the leaves through **stomata** (STOH-muh-tuh; singular: stoma). Stomata are openings in the surface of the leaf. Although most plants have stomata on the lower surface of their leaves, some plants have stomata on the top surface of their leaves. Stomata also permit oxygen to pass out of the leaf into the air.

Figure 9-13 *This section of a leaf shows the tissues and structures found in various parts of the leaf.*

Figure 9-14 *Plants release excess moisture, which can be seen on the inside of the jar. The process by which plants release excess water through the leaves is called transpiration.*

Figure 9-15 *These palmlike trees are cycads, which grow in tropical areas. The cones at the top of the trees are the reproductive structures.*

The stomata also regulate water loss through the leaves of a plant. This regulating process is called **transpiration.** You might be surprised at the amount of water that a plant can give off. Scientists estimate that a single corn plant can give off more than 200 liters of water during a single growing season. This water is enough to fill a very large bathtub. Of course, this amount is not all the water a plant takes in during its growing season. Although the corn plant takes in much more water, the plant uses much of it to make glucose.

If you closely examined a leaf section, you would be able to see how a living food factory works. The outer protective layer of the leaf is called the **epidermis** (E-puh-DER-mis). The epidermis contains many stomata. Each stoma is surrounded by two sausage-shaped structures called **guard cells.** Guard cells regulate the opening and closing of the stomata. When the guard cells swell, the stoma opens and carbon dioxide enters the leaf. When the guard cells relax, the stoma closes. Most stomata are open during the day and closed at night.

Some leaves have a waxy <u>cuticle</u> (KYOO-ti-kuhl) that covers the epidermis. The cuticle prevents the loss of too much water from the leaf. Within the leaf are two thin layers of food-making cells, which contain chlorophyll. In addition, the leaf has small veins that contain xylem and phloem tissue.

SECTION REVIEW

1. What are the functions of the roots?
2. What is xylem tissue? Phloem tissue?
3. What are the functions of the stem?
4. Define annual, biennial, and perennial.
5. What is the equation for photosynthesis?

1. Anchor the plant in the soil, absorb water and minerals from the soil, and store food for the plant
2. Xylem tissue forms tubes that carry materials up through the plant. Phloem tissue forms tubes that carry materials down through the plant.

9-3 Gymnosperms

The word "gymnosperm" comes from two Greek words meaning uncovered and seed. The three main groups of gymnosperms are the <u>cycads</u> (SIGH-cads), gingkoes (GING-kohs), and <u>conifers</u> (KOH-nuh-fers).

3. Transport materials up and down plant, support plant parts, and hold leaves up
4. An annual lives only one season; a biennial lives two seasons; and a perennial lives for more than two. 5. See page 203.

The cycads are tropical trees that look like small palm trees or ferns. Cycads have leaves that look like a feathery crown. In the center of the leaves is a large cone. The trees have either male or female cones. Inside the male cones are **pollen.** Inside the female cones are **ovules** (OH-vyools). Pollen contain male sex cells called sperm. Ovules contain female sex cells called eggs. The pollen is carried to the female cones by wind. After a male and female cell join, a seed forms. As the seeds mature, part of the cone dries up and releases the seeds, which fall to the ground. Soon these seeds develop into new cycad plants.

The second group of gymnosperms, gingkoes, contains only one species, which is commonly called the maidenhair tree. Gingkoes come from China and now grow on many streets in the United States. The gingko can grow as tall as 30 meters and has fan-shaped leaves. As with the cycads, male and female cones are found on separate gingko plants. After the female and male sex cells join, yellowish seeds form. These seeds on the female gingko are about the size of a cherry and have an awful odor. In fact, the odor is so bad that only male gingko trees are planted on city streets.

The largest group of gymnosperms is the conifers. The word "conifer" means cone-bearing. Like the gingkoes and cycads, they have cones that produce pollen or ovules. Conifers are woody plants that live in the temperate areas of the world.

Figure 9-16 _Gingko, or maidenhair, trees are often planted along city streets._

Figure 9-17 _The conifers, or cone-bearing plants, grow in forests in many cool areas of the world._

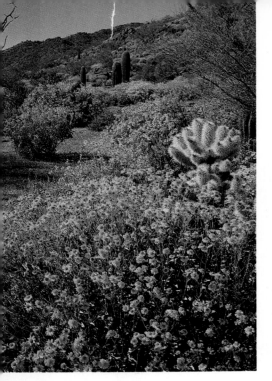

Figure 9-18 *These wild desert plants produce colorful structures called flowers, a characteristic of angiosperms. Flowers contain the male and female structures of the plant.*

Most conifers, such as pines, cedars, firs, spruces, and hemlocks are called evergreens. Evergreens are trees that appear to keep their needles or leaves year round. Actually, evergreens lose leaves while adding new ones. The needles or leaves may remain on an evergreen tree for 2 to 12 years.

SECTION REVIEW

1. What are the three main groups of gymnosperms?
2. What are evergreens?

1. Cycads, gingkoes, and conifers
2. Trees that appear to keep their needles or leaves year round

9-4 Angiosperms

Angiosperms make up the largest group of plants in the world. They are the plants that make the earth's landscape come alive with color—angiosperms produce **flowers!** However, flowers provide more than beautiful colors and pleasant smells. Flowers are structures containing the reproductive organs of angiosperms.

Angiosperms differ in size and living environment. Plant sizes range from the tiny duckweed, a water plant less than 1 millimeter long, to a giant redwood tree 100 meters tall. Some angiosperms, such as the orchids, live in rain forests where the air

Figure 9-19 *The seeds of a gymnosperm are not covered by a fleshy fruit, while those of an angiosperm are.*

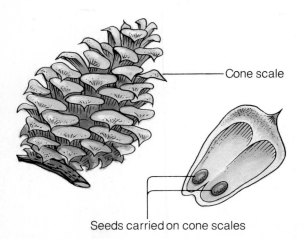

GYMNOSPERM

Cone scale

Seeds carried on cone scales

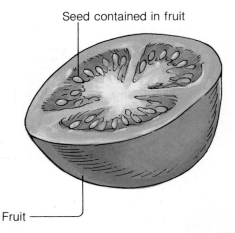

ANGIOSPERM

Seed contained in fruit

Fruit

and ground are moist constantly. Others, such as the cacti, live in deserts where rain may fall only once a year.

Like gymnosperms, angiosperms form seeds and have leaves, stems, and roots. However, these two groups of plants differ from each other in several ways. The most obvious difference is that only angiosperms produce flowers.

Flowers

When a flower is still a bud, it is enclosed by leaf-like structures called **sepals** (SEE-puhls). Sepals protect the flower. The sepals open and reveal the flower's **petals.** The colors and shapes of the petals attract insects, which play a vital role in the reproduction of flowering plants. See Figure 9-20.

Around the male and female reproductive organs of the flower are the petals. The **stamens** (STAY-muhns) are the male organs of the flower. In most flowers, each stamen has two parts. The filament is stalklike and supports the anther. The anther produces the pollen, which contains the sperm.

In the center of the flower are the **pistils.** The pistils are the female organs of the flower. Most flowers have two or more pistils. Some flowers, such as the sweet pea and clover, have only one pistil. The pistils of most flowers have three parts. At the base of the flower is the hollow ovary (OH-vuh-ree). The ovary contains egg cells. A slender tube, called the

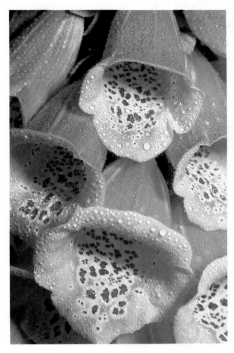

Figure 9-20 *The patterns inside the petals of this foxglove plant act as a "landing strip" for insects. These patterns help to guide insects to the male and female reproductive structures within the flower.*

Figure 9-21 *In the photograph, some of the petals have been removed to show the structures inside a flower. The drawing of the flower indicates the names of these structures.*

Petals

Pistil: Female
Stigma
Style
Ovary

Stamen: Boy
Anther
Filament

Sepals

207

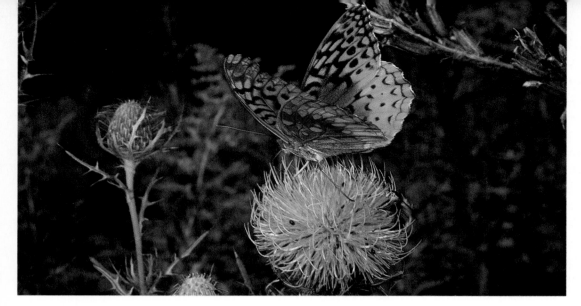

Figure 9-22 *Insects, such as this butterfly, help to transfer pollen from one flower to another.*

style, connects the ovary to a sticky structure at the top of the pistil. This structure is called the stigma (STIG-muh).

In flowers, reproduction occurs in two stages. First, the pollen must be transferred to the stigma. This stage is called **pollination.** In *self*-pollination, pollen is transferred to the stigma of the same flower, or to the pistil of another flower on the same plant.

When pollen is transferred from the flower of one plant to the stigma of another plant, *cross*-pollination occurs. In this kind of pollination, pollen grains are carried from flower to flower by wind, insects, and birds. Usually, cross-pollinated plants have large sweet-smelling flowers. These features help to attract insects and birds.

Because the stigma surfaces of all flowers are sticky, the pollen grains cling to it. Once pollen reaches the stigma, a tube pushes its way down the style to an ovule in the ovary. The sperm from the pollen grain then travels down the tube to the ovule. When the sperm unites with an egg, **fertilization** occurs. Fertilization is the second stage in flower reproduction.

The fertilized egg becomes a seed and the ovary develops into a **fruit.** A fruit is the ripened ovary that encloses and protects the seed. Apples and cherries are examples of fruits.

If it were not for the activities of insects such as bees, moths, and butterflies, many flowering plants would not be able to reproduce. In some cases, only one species of insect can cross-pollinate a single species of plant. For example, in a species of Central American yucca plant, the stamens of the flowers can be reached only by a curved object. That object is the long noselike tube of a particular small moth.

The moth lands on a flower and gathers pollen from the stamen. After rolling the pollen into a ball, the moth flies off to another yucca flower. There the moth crawls deep into the flower, punches a hole in the flower's ovary, and lays its eggs inside the ovary. Then, for some reason not known to scientists, the moth creeps up to the top of the flower's stigma and pushes down the ball of pollen. This action pollinates the yucca. Without this special relationship, both the moth and the yucca would quickly vanish from the earth.

Career: *Nursery Manager*

HELP WANTED: NURSERY MANAGER Requires two- or four-year degree in horticulture. Business background in marketing and management desirable. Nursery or greenhouse experience helpful. Apply in person.

Nearly every community has a garden center that provides its customers with the plants and supplies they need for their homes and gardens. If you pass by a garden center in April, you see pots of tulips and daffodils on display. In July, petunias and other colorful flowers catch your eye. Piles of pumpkins appear in October, and rows of pine trees emerge in December. However, all these plants are not grown at the garden center. They are ordered and delivered by a nursery.

Nurseries are run under the direction of **nursery managers.** The managers supervise the growing of plants and flowers from seeds, seedlings, or cuttings until they are large enough to sell. Nursery managers make sure nursery workers properly fertilize, weed, transplant, and apply pesticides to the plants. In addition, nursery managers make sure that proper inventory records are kept and that the orders placed by garden centers are filled quickly.

Nursery managers also make many business decisions, such as choosing new equipment, deciding how much money to spend on the growing of various plants, and determining the kinds of plants to sell. Nursery managers also are involved in planning chemical use, in deciding which new plant varieties should be planted, and in directing the building of storage areas. If you enjoy owning a business that involves working with plants, write to the American Society for Horticultural Science, 701 North Saint Asaph Street, Alexandria, VA 22314.

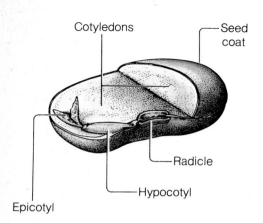

Figure 9-23 *This bean seed is an example of a dicot, which contains two cotyledons. Within the seed is an embryo plant, which is made up of the epicotyl, radicle, and hypocotyl.*

Figure 9-24 *The stage in a plant's development when a seed begins to grow is called germination. Notice how the roots and stem grow.*

Seeds

A seed is a tiny package that can develop into a new plant—if conditions are right. Surrounding the seed is a coating that develops from the ovule's wall. Like your winter coat, the seed coat protects what is inside it. Within the seed is a tiny embryo plant and the endosperm. The endosperm is a tissue that contains food the plant will need until it can make its own food.

If you were to remove the seed coat of a bean seed carefully, the seed would divide into two halves. These halves are called **cotyledons** (kaht-uh-LEE-duhnz). A cotyledon is the embryo plant's leaflike structure that stores food. Angiosperms have one or two cotyledons. Those angiosperms that have one cotyledon are called monocotyledons, or monocots. Grasses, orchids, and irises are examples of monocots. Angiosperms with two cotyledons, such as cacti, roses, and peas, are called dicotyledons, or dicots.

Most seeds remain dormant, or inactive, for a short time after being scattered. If there is enough moisture and oxygen, and the temperature is just right, most seeds go through a process called **germination** (jer-muh-NA-shuhn). Germination is the early growth stage of an embryo plant. Some people call this stage "sprouting."

When germination begins, part of the embryo below the cotyledon starts to grow down into the soil. This part of the embryo is called the hypocotyl (high-puh-COT-uhl) and will become the plant's stem. The upper part of the embryo is called the epicotyl (ep-uh-COT-uhl). The epicotyl becomes the leaves, while a part called the radicle gives rise to roots. See Figure 9-24.

Seed Dispersal

After seeds ripen, they usually are scattered far from where they were made. The scattering of seeds is called seed dispersal (di-SPER-suhl). Seeds are dispersed in many ways. Have you ever picked a dandelion puff and blown away all its tiny fluffy seeds? If you have, you have helped to scatter the seeds. Usually, the wind scatters dandelion seeds.

Figure 9-25 *Seeds are dispersed, or scattered, in many ways. Seeds of the milkweed* (left) *and red maple* (center) *are dispersed by the wind. The seeds of the burdock are carried by people's clothes or animal fur.*

Maple and elm seeds also travel on the wind with the help of their winglike structures. In addition, human beings and animals play a part in seed dispersal. For example, burdock seeds have spines that stick to people's clothing or animal fur. People or animals may pick up the seeds on a walk through a field or forest. At some other place, the seeds may fall off and eventually start a new plant.

The seeds of most water plants are scattered by floating in oceans, rivers, and streams. The coconut, which is the seed of the coconut palm, floats in water. This seed is carried from one piece of land to another by ocean currents.

Other seeds are scattered by a kind of natural explosion, which sends the seeds flying into the air. This is how the dwarf mistletoe disperses its seeds. The popping open of a dwarf mistletoe's seed case can shoot its seeds up to a distance of 15 meters.

SECTION REVIEW

1. What is a flower?
2. What is pollination? Fertilization?
3. What conditions are necessary for seed germination?

1. Flowers are structures that contain the reproductive organs of angiosperms.
2. Pollination is the transfer of pollen from one flower to another. Fertilization is the joining of the sperm and ovule (egg).   3. Moisture, oxygen, and proper temperature

LABORATORY ACTIVITY

For further instructions, see page T-36.

Geotropism

Purpose

In this activity, you will observe how gravity affects the growth of a seed.

Materials *(per group)*

4 corn seeds soaked in water for
   24 hours
Paper towels
Petri dish
Masking tape
Wax pencil

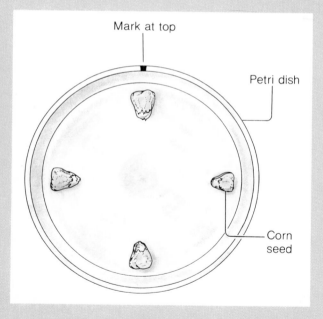

Mark at top

Petri dish

Corn seed

Procedure

1. Arrange four soaked corn seeds in a petri dish. The pointed ends of the seeds should all point toward the center of the dish. One of the seeds should be at the 12 o'clock position of the circle, and the other seeds at 3, 6, and 9 o'clock.
2. Place a circle of paper towel over the seeds. Then pack the dish with enough pieces of paper towel so that the seeds will be held firmly in place when the other half of the petri dish is put on.
3. Moisten the paper towels with water. Cover the petri dish and seal the two halves together with a strip of masking tape.
4. Mark one point of the sealed edge of the dish with the wax pencil, near one of the seeds. Stand the dish up so that this point is on top.
5. Put the dish, on its edge, in a completely dark place with the mark at the top.
6. Observe the seeds each day for about one week. Make a sketch of them each day. Be sure to return the dish and seeds to their original position when you have finished.

Observations and Conclusions

1. What happened to the corn seeds? In which direction did the roots and the stems grow?
2. Explain your observations in terms of geotropism, or the effect of gravity on plant growth.

CHAPTER SUMMARY

9-1 Ferns

- Vascular plants contain tubes that carry material throughout the plant.

- Ferns have true leaves, stems, and roots.

- In asexual reproduction, new fern plants develop from spores.

- In sexual reproduction, fern plants develop from the uniting of a sperm and an egg cell.

9-2 Seed Plants

- A seed contains an embryo plant, stored food, and a seed coat.

- Seed plants are divided into two groups: gymnosperms and angiosperms.

- Roots are structures that anchor plants and absorb water and minerals.

- In the roots, minerals and water travel up the plant through the xylem. Food substances travel down the plant through the phloem.

- Stems support plant parts.

- Herbaceous stems are soft and green, while woody stems are rigid.

- During photosynthesis, the sun's energy is used to combine carbon dioxide from the air and water from the soil to produce glucose and oxygen.

- In transpiration, the stomata regulate the amount of water lost through the plant leaves.

- The leaf has an epidermis, two layers of food-making cells, and veins containing the xylem and phloem.

9-3 Gymnosperms

- Gymnosperms produce uncovered seeds.

- Cycads, gingkoes, and conifers are the three main groups of gymnosperms.

9-4 Angiosperms

- Angiosperms, or flowering plants, produce seeds with a protective covering.

- Flowers contain the male and female reproductive organs. The stamens produce sperm-containing pollen. The pistils contain the egg-producing ovary.

- Fertilization occurs when the sperm unites with the egg in the ovary. The ovary then develops into a fruit that encloses the seed.

- Seeds have one or two cotyledons. A cotyledon is the embryo plant's food storehouse.

VOCABULARY   *Define the following terms.*

angiosperm p.197
annual ring p.200
asexual reproduction p.196
cambium p.199
cotyledon p.210
epidermis p.204
fertilization p.208
flower p.206

frond p.195
fruit p.208
germination p.210
guard cell p.204
gymnosperm p.197
herbaceous stem p.201
ovule p.205
petal p.207

phloem p.198
photosynthesis p.202
pistil p.207
pollen p.205
pollination p.206
rhizome p.195
seed p.196
sepal p.207

sexual reproduction p.196
stamen p.207
stoma p.203
transpiration p.204
vascular plant p.194
woody stem p.201
xylem p.198

CHAPTER REVIEW

Multiple Choice

Choose the letter of the answer that best completes each statement.

1. The stem of a fern is called a
   a. frond.
   b. rhizome.
   c. fiddlehead.
   d. biennial.
2. Ferns produce spores during
   a. germination.
   b. fertilization.
   c. sexual reproduction.
   d. asexual reproduction.
3. Plant tissue that carries water and minerals up through the plant is called
   a. stoma.
   b. cambium.
   c. phloem.
   d. xylem.
4. Which of these structures is *not* a stem?
   a. bulb
   b. rhizome
   c. frond
   d. tuber
5. During photosynthesis, oxygen leaves the leaf through the
   a. stomata.
   b. rhizoids.
   c. guard cells.
   d. rhizomes.
6. Gymnosperms
   a. produce flowers.
   b. have seeds with no protective wall.
   c. have seeds with a protective wall.
   d. are found only in deserts.
7. Which structure produces pollen?
   a. pistil
   b. anther
   c. ovary
   d. style
8. The union of the sperm and the egg is called
   a. germination.
   b. transpiration.
   c. pollination.
   d. fertilization.
9. Seeds can be scattered by
   a. wind.
   b. water.
   c. people.
   d. all of these.
10. How many cotyledons does a monocot contain?
    a. one
    b. two
    c. three
    d. four

Completions

Fill in the word or words that best complete each statement.

1. A group of vascular plants that were abundant during the Carboniferous Period were the _____ferns_____.

2. Small brown structures on the underside of fern fronds produce _____spores_____.

3. The fern structures that absorb water and minerals from the soil are called _____roots_____.

4. In the stem, new xylem and phloem cells are produced by the _____cambium_____.

5. Leaves that have two or more blades are called _____compound_____ leaves.

6. The outer, protective cell layer of a leaf is the _____epidermis_____.

7. Conifers belong to a group of seed plants called _____gymnosperms_____.

8. During pollination, pollen grains cling to the sticky surface at the top of the pistil called the _____stigma_____.

9. When conditions are just right, a seed may go through a process of growth called _____germination_____.

10. The seeds of the coconut palm are dispersed by _____water_____.

True or False

Determine whether each statement is true or false. If it is true, write "true."
If it is false, change the underlined word or words to make the statement true.

1. In <u>sexual</u> reproduction, an organism develops from the union of an egg and a sperm. T

2. Seed plants absorb water and minerals through microscopic extensions of single cells called <u>guard cells</u>. F (root hairs)

3. One year's <u>growth of xylem cells</u> produces a layer called an <u>epidermis</u>. *

4. A <u>biennial</u> is a plant that lives for more than two growing seasons. F (perennial)

* F (annual ring)

5. The food made by a plant during <u>germination</u> is called glucose. F (photosynthesis)

6. The cuticle prevents the loss of too much <u>oxygen</u> from the leaf. F (water)

7. <u>Conifers</u> produce flowers. F (cones)

8. Angiosperms produce <u>cones</u>. F (flowers)

9. When a sperm unites with an egg in a flower's ovary, <u>pollination</u> occurs. F (fertilization)

10. A fruit is the ripened ovary that encloses and protects the seed. T

Discussion Topics Answers appear on page T-36.

Write a brief paragraph discussing each of the following.

1. Describe the two stages in the reproductive cycle of a fern.

2. Compare the functions of roots and stems.

3. Distinguish between herbaceous and woody stems.

4. The process of photosynthesis takes place in the leaves of a plant. Explain how the carbon dioxide and water needed for photosynthesis get into the leaves. Explain how the oxygen formed during photosynthesis is released.

5. Distinguish between gymnosperms and angiosperms.

6. Discuss the difference between self-pollination and cross-pollination.

EXPAND YOUR KNOWLEDGE

Barnard, P. *Don't Tickle the Elephant Tree: Sensitive Plants*. New York: Messner.
  This book relates the strange ways in which some plants behave. The author compares plant seeds to computers because both contain a lot of information.

Bauman, R. P. *Plants as Pets*. New York: Dodd, Mead.
  The author shows how plants make marvelous pets, which require only a minimum of care and attention. The book reviews plant selection, grooming, health, breeding, and even playing with your pet plant.

10 Animals: Invertebrates

For a chapter overview, teaching strategies, answers to all activities, a list of A-V materials, and a chapter bibliography, see pages T-36 to T-40.

Consult your Teacher's Resource Book and Annotated Teacher's Edition, Laboratory Book for additional activities and teaching aids.

CHAPTER OBJECTIVES

After completing this chapter, you will be able to:

10-1 Explain the difference between vertebrates and invertebrates.

10-2 Describe how sponges obtain food.

10-3 Describe the living conditions and food-getting methods of corals, sea anemones, and jellyfish.

10-4 Explain the difference between flatworms, roundworms, and segmented worms.

10-5 Name several characteristics of mollusks.

10-6 Describe the living habits of spiny-skinned invertebrates.

10-7 Name four major groups of arthropods and list their characteristics.

10-8 Describe the anatomy of insects and list their characteristics.

A hard-working person is often described as being "busy as a bee." But, you may wonder, just how busy is a bee? Kirk Visscher, a scientist, wondered the same thing. Visscher is an *entomologist* (en-tuh-MAHL-uh-jist), a person who studies insects.

Visscher observed bees living in a glass-enclosed colony. He knew that one group of bees had the job of cleaning up the hive. What he did not know was whether these clean-up bees also were responsible for removing dead bees from the hive. He soon realized that most bees in the colony did not pay much attention to dead bees. However, some bees would carry the dead bees away. These bees would fly hundreds of meters in the air before dropping off their dead companions. What proportion of the colony's bees did this job? To find out, Visscher painted dots on these bees and eventually counted them. He found that only about 2 percent of the bees in the colony had this very special task—beehive undertaking!

Did the undertakers act as clean-ups as well? To answer this question, Visscher placed tiny wooden models of dead bees in the colony. Only the clean-up bees removed the models. So it became clear that the task of undertaking belongs to only a certain group of bees.

Honeybee flying over a flower

10-1 Characteristics of Invertebrates

Animals! Just hearing the word brings a different image to almost everyone. Some people think of the fierce great cats in Africa. To others, the word brings to mind the friendly porpoise, certainly among the most intelligent of all animals. Of course, for a great many people the word "animal" reminds them of that cuddly puppy they had, or have, or have always wanted to get. All of these animals, no matter how different they may seem, have one thing in common. They are **vertebrates** (VER-tuh-brits). Vertebrates are animals with a backbone.

Figure 10-1 *There are many kinds of invertebrates, or animals without backbones. The skeleton butterfly* (top left), *hercules beetle* (top right), *giant clam* (bottom left), *and flame lobster* (bottom right) *are examples of invertebrates.*

On the other hand, almost nobody thinks of the earthworm crawling through the soil when the word "animals" is mentioned. Or the mosquito about to raise a bump on another victim. Or the jellyfish with its stinging cells always ready to poison a passing fish. And yet, these organisms are among a group of animals called **invertebrates** that make up more than 90 percent of all animal species. Invertebrates are animals without a backbone. They are found in just about every corner of the world.

All animals, including the invertebrates, are multicellular. Most have cells that perform specialized functions. Some cells, for example, are involved with the digestion of food. Other cells help circulate the digested food particles throughout the body. In many animals, these specialized cells are grouped together into tissues. Skin cells, for example, form skin tissue. Tissues that work together can be further organized into organs. For example, the lungs are organs made up of different tissues that work together to help you breathe. Finally, organs that work together often are grouped as organ systems. The mouth, stomach, and intestines all work together as part of the digestive system.

SECTION REVIEW

1. What are animals with backbones called?
2. What are animals without backbones called?

1. Vertebrates
2. Invertebrates

10-2 Sponges

Today, the sponge you use to wash the dishes or take a bath is probably made of synthetic material. In the past, however, people used natural, or real, sponges from the sea. A natural sponge is the dried remains of an animal that lives in the ocean, or as in a few cases, in fresh water. You might think a sponge, whether synthetic or natural, looks nothing like any animal you ever saw. In a way you would be right, for sponges seem to be totally unrelated to all other forms of animal life. For many years, in fact, sponges were classified as "plant-animals."

Figure 10-2 *Although there are different types of sponges, they all share the characteristic that their bodies contain many pores.*

ACTIVITY

Sponge Growth

A sponge must filter almost a ton of water through its body to grow in mass only 28 grams. To reach a mass of 3 kilograms, how many tons of water must a sponge filter?

Sponges lead a very simple life. They grow attached to one spot on the ocean floor, usually in shallow water. A sponge stays in that one spot its entire life unless a strong wave or current washes it somewhere else. The body of a sponge has a great many **pores,** or holes. Moving ocean water carries food and oxygen through the pores into the sponge. The sponge's cells remove <u>food</u> and <u>oxygen</u> from the water and, at the same time, <u>release waste products</u> into the water. Because the pores of a sponge are small, most sponges live in clear water that is free of floating matter that could clog the pores.

Sponge cells are unusual in that they function on their own without any coordination between one another. In fact, some people think of sponges as a colony of cells living together. However, despite their independent functioning, sponge cells have a mysterious attraction to one another. This attraction can be demonstrated easily by passing a sponge through a fine filter so that it is broken into clumps of cells.

Within hours, these cells reform into the shape of the original sponge. No other animal species shares this amazing ability of sponge cells to reorganize themselves.

SECTION REVIEW

1. How do sponges obtain food?
2. How do sponges remove waste products?
3. Why do most sponges live in clear waters that are free of floating matter?

1. Sponge cells remove food from the water that has entered through pores.
2. Sponge cells release waste products into water.
3. To keep their pores free of material

10-3 Coelenterates

In the shallow waters off the coast of Puerto Rico, a group of scientists drill into the sea floor. To an ordinary person, the scientists might appear to be hunting for oil and gas, or perhaps valuable minerals. However, these scientists are drilling through layers of coral in order to read a very special "diary"—a diary of the earth's past. The scientists have discovered that corals are extremely sensitive to environmental changes, including changes in temperature and the chemicals in sea water. These changes are recorded in the daily growth rings of coral. By studying the layers of coral that were laid down year after year for more than 500 million years, scientists hope to uncover evidence of past events. For example, many scientists believe the length of the earth's day has increased by several hours or more in the last few hundred million years. Scientists hope to find evidence for this increase in the coral growth rings.

Corals are among a group of animals called the coelenterates (si-LEN-tuh-rayts). Also included among the coelenterates are the jellyfish, the hydra, and the sea anemone (uh-NEM-uh-nee). All coelenterates contain a central cavity with only one opening. You can think of coelenterates as being cup-shaped animals with an open mouth. Tentacles with stinging cells called **nematocysts** (NEM-uh-toh-sists) surround the mouth of most coelenterates. Coelenterates use nematocysts to stun or kill other animals. It is no

Figure 10-3 Venus' flower baskets are sponges having glassy skeletons. These sponges have been on the earth at least 500 million years.

Figure 10-4 Meters below the surface of the ocean, these scientists use a coring machine to remove a sample of coral. Like trees, coral forms annual layers as it grows.

221

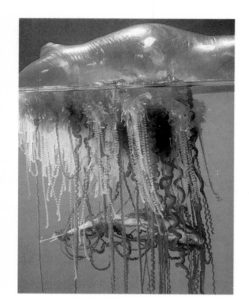

Figure 10-5 *Jellyfish, like this Portuguese man-of-war, use their tentacles to capture prey. Nematocysts, or stinging cells, on the tentacles then paralyze the prey.*

surprise, then, that the stinging cells are near the mouth. For after capturing an animal with their tentacles, coelenterates pull it into their mouth and then into their central body cavity. Once the food is digested, coelenterates then release waste products back out, through their mouth.

Unlike the sponges, coelenterates contain groups of cells that perform special functions. That is, coelenterates have specialized tissues. Some coelenterates like the jellyfish move about in the water using muscle tissues. Others, like the corals, remain in one place.

Corals

In the warm waters off the coast of eastern Australia lies one of the largest structures ever built by living things—the 2000-kilometer-long Great Barrier Reef. However, the reef was not built by people. Instead, it was built by tiny corals.

Corals, like all coelenterates, are soft-bodied organisms. However, corals use minerals in the water to build a hard protective covering of limestone. When the coral dies, the hard outer covering is left behind. Year after year, for many millions of years, generations of corals live and die, each adding a layer of limestone. In time, a coral reef such as the Great Barrier Reef forms. The outer layer of the reef, then, contains living corals. But underneath this

Figure 10-6 *When these brightly colored corals die, their skeletons remain. Over the years, the skeletons pile up, creating a coral reef.*

Figure 10-7 *Surrounding the mouth of this delicate-looking coral are tentacles, which are used to trap food.*

"living stone" are the remains of corals that may have lived when dinosaurs walked the earth.

Corals live together in <u>colonies</u> that can grow into a wide variety of shapes and colors. Some corals look like antlers, others like fans swaying in the water, while still others look like underwater brains.

At first glance, a coral appears to be little more than a mouth surrounded by stinging tentacles. See Figure 10-7. However, there is more to a coral than meets the eye. <u>Algae</u> live inside the coral's body. The algae help make food for the coral. And, since algae need sunlight to make food, corals must live in shallow waters where sunlight can reach them. This relationship between a coral animal and an alga plant is among the most unusual in nature.

Sea Anemones

Can you spot the clownfish swimming through the brightly colored plant in Figure 10-8? You might be surprised to discover that the "plant" is actually an animal—a type of coelenterate called a sea anemone. Sea anemones look like underwater <u>flowers</u>. However, the "petals" are really tentacles, and their brilliant coloring helps attract passing fish. When a fish passes over the anemone's stinging cells, the cells poison the fish. The tentacles then pull the fish into the anemone's mouth, and the stunned prey soon is digested.

The clownfish, however, is not harmed by the anemone. It swims safely through the anemone's

Figure 10-8 *The lavender-tipped "petals" in this photograph are actually the tentacles of a sea anemone. Notice the black and white clown fish swimming among the tentacles.*

Figure 10-9 *Jellyfish move with a jetlike motion by contracting their muscle cells. The long trailing tentacles are used to capture food.*

tentacles. In this way, the clownfish is protected from other fish that might try to attack it. At the same time, the clownfish serves as a kind of living bait for the anemone. Other fish see the clownfish, come closer, and are quickly trapped by the anemone. So the sea anemone and the clownfish live in harmony.

Jellyfish

If you ever swam in the ocean and saw a jellylike cup floating in the water, you probably knew enough to swim away. Most people quickly recognize this coelenterate, the jellyfish. While the jellyfish may look harmless, it can deliver a painful poison through its stinging cells. In fact, even when they are broken up into small pieces, the stinging cells remain active and can sting a passing swimmer who accidentally bumps into them. Of course, jellyfish do not have stinging cells merely to bother passing swimmers. Like the other coelenterates, jellyfish use the stinging cells to capture prey.

1. What are nematocysts?
2. Which of the coelenterates discussed have muscle tissue that can help move them about?
3. What type of coelenterate formed the Great Barrier Reef?

1. Stinging cells
2. Jellyfish
3. Corals

10-4 Worms

Have you ever wondered where natural pearls come from? If so, you might be surprised to find out that another group of invertebrates—the worms—is involved in the formation of many natural pearls. Natural pearls are formed inside of oysters. When a particular type of worm gets into an oyster, the worm acts as an irritant. The oyster's response to the irritant is to produce a hard material that surrounds the worm. That material is a pearl. Most natural Oriental pearls are formed in this manner.

Most people think of a worm as a slimy, squiggly creature. And, in fact, many are. However, there are other kinds of worms that look nothing like the worms used to bait fishing hooks. See Figure 10-10.

Figure 10-10 *Not all worms are slimy and squiggly. The plume worms (left) resemble feathered flowers, while the sea mouse (right) looks like a furry animal.*

Figure 10-11 *The planarians (top) and the tapeworm (bottom) are examples of flatworms.*

Flatworms

You have probably never seen a worm that looks like the one in Figure 10-11. This worm, a planarian, is a kind of flatworm. Flatworms, as you might expect, have flat bodies. Most planarians live in ponds and streams, often on the bottom of plants or on underwater rocks. Planarians feed on any dead plant or animal matter. However, when there is little food available, some planarians do a rather unusual thing. They break down their own organs and body parts for food. Later, the missing parts <u>regrow</u> when food is available again. In fact, if a planarian is cut into pieces, each piece eventually grows into a new planarian!

Not all flatworms are found on dead matter. Some are parasites and grow on or in living things. Tapeworms, for example, look like long flat ribbons and live in the bodies of many animals, including human beings.

The head of a tapeworm has special hooks that it uses to attach itself to the tissues of the **host,** or animal in which it lives. The tapeworm then takes food and water from its host. In return, the tapeworm gives back nothing.

Tapeworms can grow quite large inside the host. One of the largest tapeworms can live in human beings and grow to be 18 meters long. However, size is not always a good indicator of danger. The most dangerous tapeworm known to humans is only about 8 millimeters long and enters the body through microscopic eggs in food.

Roundworms

You probably have been told time and time again never to eat pork unless it is well cooked. Did you know that the reason has to do with the *Trichina* (trick-EE-nuh) worm? This worm lives in the muscle tissue of pigs. If a piece of pork is cooked improperly, the worm may survive and enter a human's body. In the body, the worm lives in the muscle tissue. The disease it causes, called <u>trichinosis</u> (tri-kuh-NOH-sis), can be very painful and is difficult to cure.

<u>*Trichina*</u> is a kind of roundworm. All roundworms resemble strands of <u>spaghetti</u> with pointed ends.

Roundworms live on land or in water. Many round-worms are animal parasites, although some live on plant tissue. One roundworm, the hookworm, infects more than 600 million people in the world each year. The worms enter the body by burrowing through the skin. Eventually, they end up in the in-testines where they live on the blood of the host.

Roundworms, like other worms, have both a head end and a tail end. In fact, worms were the first or-ganisms to develop with distinct head and tail ends. Connecting the two ends is a tube called the diges-tive tube. Food enters the tube in the head end and waste products leave through the tail end. Although this system may not seem very unusual, it is far more advanced than that of the coelenterates, which use a mouth for both taking in food and releasing wastes.

Segmented Worms

The worm you probably are most familiar with is the common earthworm. The earthworm is a type of segmented worm. As you might expect, its body is divided up into numerous segments, usually at least 100. Earthworms, of course, live in the soil. But other segmented worms may live in salty oceans or the fresh waters of lakes and streams. Segmented worms also include sandworms and leeches.

If you ever felt an earthworm, you know it has a slimy outer layer. This layer, made up of slippery mucus, helps the earthworm glide through the soil.

Activity

Flukes

Flukes are parasitic flat-worms that have interesting life cycles. Visit the library and look up the life cycle of the liver fluke. On a sheet of white paper, make a diagram of its life cycle. Use arrows to show its life path through the various hosts. How many hosts are there in one life cycle?

Figure 10-12 *This drawing shows that segmented earthworms have a well-developed digestive system.*

Mouth — Esophagus — Crop — Gizzard — Intestine — Bristles — Anus

The body shapes of invertebrates show either radial symmetry, bilateral symmetry, or asymmetry. Visit the reference section of your library. Using a dictionary, look up the meaning of the word "symmetry." Then use a science dictionary or science encyclopedia to define "radial" and "bilateral" symmetry, as well as "asymmetry."

Make a list of the invertebrates discussed in this chapter. On your list, indicate what type of symmetry is shown by each one.

Figure 10-13 *Individual earthworms contain both male and female structures. When two earthworms join together, sperm cells are exchanged and eggs are fertilized.*

Small bristles on the segments of earthworms also help it to pull itself along the ground.

Earthworms are good friends to have in the garden. As they pass through the soil, the earthworms feed on dead plant and animal matter. Earthworms create tiny passages as they move. Air enters these passages and improves the quality of the soil. Also, waste products released by earthworms help fertilize the soil.

Earthworms have a well-developed digestive system. After the earthworm eats the food, it passes through several structures before reaching the worm's **crop.** The crop is a saclike organ that stores food. From the crop, the food travels into the worm's muscular **gizzard.** The gizzard grinds up food and then passes it into the worm's intestine. Here, nutrients are removed and enter the worm's circulatory system.

The earthworm has a closed circulatory system. All of its body fluids are contained within small tubes. The fluids are pumped throughout the earthworm's body by a series of special vessels that act like a tiny "heart."

In the respiratory system of the earthworm, oxygen enters through the skin. The earthworm produces carbon dioxide gas, which leaves through the animal's skin. However, the skin must remain moist in order for gases to pass through. If an earthworm remains out in the heat of the sun, the skin dries out and the animal suffocates.

The earthworm's reproductive system has both male and female structures. In one part of the earthworm, sperm cells are produced. In another part, egg cells are made. However, despite the fact earthworms contain both types of reproductive cells, reproduction occurs through sexual reproduction. Earthworms mate at night when two worms join together and exchange sperm cells. The sperm of each worm unites with the eggs of the other worm. This process is called **fertilization.** Soon after, the worms move apart. Each worm then lays a number of fertilized eggs in a slimy shell or cocoon. Eventually, the young worms break out of the shell and crawl away.

Although earthworms have a simple nervous system, they are very sensitive to their environment. Earthworms seem to be able to both sense danger and warn other earthworms as well. They do so by releasing a kind of sweat that helps them glide away much faster and warns other worms in the area at the same time.

SECTION REVIEW

1. A planarian is an example of what type of worm?
2. Name two kinds of parasitic roundworms.
3. What organ in an earthworm breaks up food?

1. Flatworm
2. *Trichina* and hookworm
3. Gizzard

10-5 Mollusks

In 1873, two men and a young boy were fishing off the coast of Newfoundland in Canada when they spotted a dark object in the water. One of the men poked the object to see what it was. Suddenly, two large green eyes looked up at the men. Before they could move, the strange creature attacked their boat. A huge tentacle wrapped itself around the boat and began to pull it under. The two men were terrified, but the boy thought quickly and chopped through the tentacle with an axe. The water immediately turned jet black as the creature dove beneath the waves. Later, a part of the tentacle left in the boat was fed to hungry dogs on shore. Without knowing it, the boaters had destroyed one of the few parts of a giant squid ever recovered.

Although this story actually happened, most legends about giant squids are false. Giant squids do

Figure 10-14 *Giant squids can grow up to 17 meters in length. In this historical print, one of the few actual cases of a giant squid attacking people is shown.*

Figure 10-15 *Many types of mollusks are covered with a hard shell. Notice the different colors and patterns of these mollusk shells.*

ACTIVITY

Shell Collecting

Visit a seashore area. **CAUTION:** *When near water, always use the buddy system.* Search different areas of the beach and shoreline to find as many different types of shells as possible. Collect them in plastic bags to bring back to school.

At school, use field guides to identify the shells of your collection. Using an index card, prepare a file card for each. Record the genus and species name, the habits, and the habitat of each mollusk shell collected. On each shell, paint a number that matches the number on the index card. Display the collection in your classroom.

not normally attack boats. They usually live in deep ocean waters far from people. In fact, until 1980, when an entire giant squid body was found washed onto a Massachusetts shore, few scientists had ever seen or been able to study the legendary giant squid. Today the remains of this squid are on view in the Smithsonian Museum in Washington, D.C.

Giant squids are included among a group of invertebrates called mollusks (MAHL-uhsks). If you enjoy seafood, you are probably more familiar with other mollusks such as clams, oysters, octopuses, and normal-sized squids. You would not find giant squids on any menu, by the way, even if they could be easily found. They are rumored to taste like ammonia!

The word "mollusk" comes from the Latin word meaning soft. As you might expect, mollusks have a soft, fleshy body. However, many species of mollusks are covered with a hard shell. See Figure 10-15.

The bodies of most kinds of mollusks having outer shells are similar. Most mollusks have a thick muscular foot. The foot of some mollusks opens and closes their shells. In other species, the foot is used for movement. Some mollusks even use their foot to bury themselves in the sand or mud.

The head region of a mollusk generally contains the mouth and sense organs such as the eyes. The rest of the body contains various organs involved in reproduction, circulation, digestion, and other important processes. Covering much of the body is a soft **mantle.** The mantle is the part of a mollusk that produces the material that makes up the hard shell.

As the animal grows, the mantle enlarges the shell, providing more room for its occupant.

Mollusks are grouped according to certain characteristics. These characteristics include the presence of a shell, the type of shell, and the type of foot.

One-Shelled Mollusks

Many kinds of mollusks have only one shell and are called univalves. "Uni-" is the prefix that means one and "valve" is the word scientists use to mean shell. There are many kinds of univalves, which live in oceans, fresh waters, or on land. However, univalves that live on land still must have a moist environment to survive.

Univalves have an interesting feature in their mouth called the **radula.** The radula resembles a file used by carpenters to file wood. The radula files off bits of plant matter into small pieces that can be swallowed by the univalve. Some species of univalves can inject a poison through the radula that even can be a danger to people.

The land univalve you probably are most familiar with is the common garden snail. These snails move slowly along a trail of mucus that they produce. Because they release this slippery mucus, they are able to travel easily over rough surfaces because their body does not actually touch the ground. As you can see in Figure 10-16, univalves such as the snail have two eyes located on the end of two stalks sticking out of their head.

Figure 10-16 *This giant African land snail can grow to a length of about 20 centimeters. The tiny bumps on the end of each stalk are the snail's eyes.*

Figure 10-17 *Although this sea slug does not have a hard outer shell, it is a mollusk. Its shell, however, is internal.*

It may seem strange to you, but there is one kind of univalve that does not have any visible shell. It is the slug. See Figure 10-17. Many <u>slugs</u>, called sea slugs, live in ocean waters. However, some slugs live on land. Most people are familiar with the simple slugs they often find in moist areas.

Two-Shelled Mollusks

If you have been to the beach, you may have seen clam and mussel shells littering the shore. <u>Clams</u> and mussels are members of a group of mollusks called bivalves, or two-shelled mollusks. Bivalves move

Figure 10-18 *The chambered nautilus' shell (left) consists of many sections. The bay scallop (right) is a bivalve, or two-shelled mollusk. The blue dots are its eyes.*

through the water by clapping their two shells together, which forces water out between the shells. The force of the moving water propels the bivalve.

Bivalves do not have radula. Instead, they feed on small organisms in the water. Bivalves are often called filter feeders since they spend most of their time straining the water for food.

Head-Footed Mollusks

The most highly developed mollusks are the head-footed mollusks. These mollusks include the octopus, the squid, and the nautilus. Most head-footed mollusks do not have an outer shell, but do have some part of a shell within their body. An exception is the chambered nautilus. The nautilus shell consists of many chambers, or rooms. These chambers are small when the animal is young but increase in size as the animal grows. The nautilus constructs a new chamber as it grows. It lives in the outer chamber.

All of these mollusks have tentacles that are used to capture food and for movement. However, these mollusks differ in the number and type of tentacles they possess. The octopus, of course, has eight tentacles. Squids have ten tentacles, although two of them differ in shape from the other eight. These two tentacles are shaped like paddles.

Octopuses, squids, and nautiluses use a water propulsion system for movement. They force water out of a tube in one direction, which pushes them along in the opposite direction. Using this "jet" system, these animals can move away rapidly from danger. Squids and octopuses can also produce a purple dye. When they squirt this dye into the water, it hides the animal and confuses predators. The squid or octopus can then make good its escape. In the example earlier in the chapter, the water turned dark when the young boy chopped off the giant squid's tentacle for this reason.

Figure 10-19 *Most head-footed mollusks, such as the octopus* (top) *and the squid* (bottom), *do not have outer shells.*

SECTION REVIEW

1. What is the main function of the mantle?
2. How does the radula help univalves eat?
3. Name two mollusks often referred to as filter feeders.

1. Produces the material that makes up the hard shell
2. Files off bits of plants into small pieces
3. Clam and mussel

Figure 10-20 *The spiny structures in this photograph are the arms of the crown-of-thorns sea star, a spiny-skinned animal. This animal feeds on the soft bodies of living corals.*

10-6 Spiny-Skinned Animals

Earlier you read about the Great Barrier Reef and how it took millions of years to build. Today, the living corals on the surface of the reef are in danger of being destroyed. If they are, the reef will grow no larger. What is damaging the corals? A kind of starfish called the crown-of-thorns sea star is responsible for the damage. See Figure 10-20. The crown-of-thorns eats the soft body parts of the living coral and leaves an empty shell behind.

The crown-of-thorns is a member of a group of animals commonly called the spiny-skinned animals. As you might expect, these animals have a rough, spiny skin.

Starfish

Starfish are *not* fish. But most *are* shaped like stars. They have five or more arms that extend from a central body. On the bottom of these arms are thousands of tube feet that resemble tiny suction cups. These tube feet not only help the animal to move about, but do much more. For example, when a starfish passes over a clam, one of its favorite foods, the tiny tube feet grasp the clam's shell. The

Figure 10-21 *This starfish is using its suctionlike tube feet to open a clam's shell.*

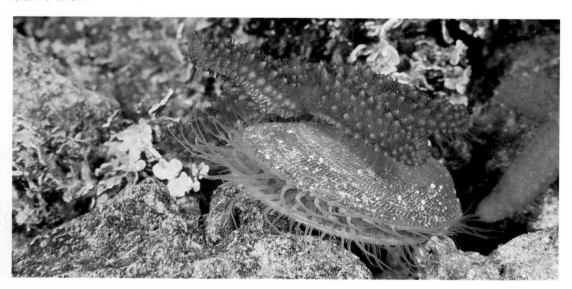

tube feet exert a tremendous force on the clam's shell, and eventually the shell opens. Then the starfish can eat a leisurely meal.

People who harvest clams from the ocean bottom have long been at war with starfish that destroy their clam beds. In the past, when starfish were captured near clam beds, they were cut into pieces and thrown back into the water. However, starfish have an amazing ability to regenerate, or grow back, missing body parts. So by cutting them up, all people did was make sure there would always be more and more starfish than before—exactly the opposite of what was wanted.

Other Spiny-Skinned Animals

Other spiny-skinned animals vary widely in appearance. Some, like the sea cucumber, resemble a vegetable. These animals usually are found lying on the bottom of the sea. Sea cucumbers lack arms. They slowly move along the sea's bottom with tube feet or by wiggling back and forth.

Sea lilies have many arms that look like the flower petals. These animals grow on stalks attached to the sea bottom. Most sea lilies remain in one spot for their entire lives.

Sea urchins and sand dollars are round and lack arms. They may be flat like the sand dollar, or dome-shaped like the sea urchin. Some species have long poisonous spines used for protection.

Figure 10-22 *Like starfish, the sea urchin* (left) *and the sand dollar* (right) *are also spiny-skinned animals.*

1. What spiny-skinned animal is causing severe damage to the Great Barrier Reef?
2. What does it mean to regenerate?
3. Name three spiny-skinned animals other than the starfish.

1. Crown-of-thorns sea star
2. To grow back missing body parts
3. Sea cucumber, sea lily, sea urchin, and sand dollar

10-7 Arthropods

The arthropods (AR-thruh-podz) are the most successful invertebrates on the earth. There are more species of arthropods than all the other animal species combined. Arthropods live in air, on land, and in water. Wherever you happen to live, you can be sure arthropods live there too. In fact, arthropods are our main competitors for food and, if left alone and unchecked, they would eventually take over the world.

The name "arthropod" means jointed legs, which are one of the main characteristics of these animals. Another characteristic of arthropods is a rigid outer covering called an **exoskeleton.** In some ways, an exoskeleton is similar to the suits of armor once worn by knights as protection in battle. One drawback of an exoskeleton is that it does not grow as the animal grows. So the arthropod's protective suit must be

Figure 10-23 *The rigid outer covering of this horseshoe crab is called an exoskeleton. An exoskeleton is characteristic of all arthropods.*

Figure 10-24 *Like all arthropods, these spider crabs have jointed legs and exoskeletons.*

Figure 10-25 *A hermit crab peers out from its borrowed shell atop a fire coral.*

shed and replaced from time to time. While the exoskeleton is being replaced, the arthropod is more vulnerable to attack from other animals.

Arthropods include a variety of animal groups. Among the many types of arthropods are crustaceans, centipedes and millipedes, arachnids, and insects.

Crustaceans

Do you see the two eyes peering out of the shell in Figure 10-25? These eyes belong to a hermit crab, a crab that uses discarded shells for its home. Crabs, along with lobsters, crayfish, and shrimp, are arthropods that are included among the crustaceans (kruh-STAY-shuhnz). All of these animals live in a watery environment. Crustaceans obtain their oxygen from the water through special structures called **gills.** Even the few land-dwelling crustaceans have gills and must live in damp areas to get oxygen.

The bodies of crustaceans are divided into segments. A pair of limbs or other body parts, such as claws, are attached to each segment. These limbs have many different functions, depending on the organism. The claws of some crabs, for example, are strong enough to enable them to open their favorite food, coconuts. Crabs use their claws to cut through the tough outer husk of a coconut to reach the tender flesh inside. Other limbs are adapted for walking. The female lobster even attaches clusters of eggs to the limbs beneath her tail. She carries the eggs in this way.

Crustaceans are able to regrow certain parts of their body. A crab for example, can grow new claws. The stone crab lives in the waters off the coast of Florida. Its claws are considered to be particularly good eating. When a stone crab is caught, one of its claws is broken off and the crab is returned to the water. In about a year's time, the broken claw has regrown. If the crab is unlucky enough to be caught again, that claw may once again be removed.

Centipedes and Millipedes

Figure 10-26 *Centipedes are carnivores. Here a centipede uses its claws to inject poison into its prey, a toad.*

Both centipedes and millipedes have been described as worms with legs. In fact, you probably think the main difference between centipedes and millipedes is the number of legs. Actually, both types of arthropods have many legs, and you cannot easily tell them apart by counting. Centipedes have one pair of legs in a segment, while millipedes have two pairs of legs in a segment. However, if you were a tiny earthworm crawling through the soil you would certainly know the difference between the two. Millipedes live on plants and simply would pass you by. Centipedes, however, are carnivorous and are active hunters. The centipede would use its well-developed claws to inject a poison into your body. So, for the earthworm, the difference between the two can mean the difference between life and death.

Arachnids

In Greek mythology, there is a legend of a young woman named Arachne who challenged the gods to a weaving contest. When the mortal Arachne won, the angered gods tore up her tapestry. Arachne hanged herself in sorrow. The gods, the legend goes, then changed her into a spider. Her tapestry became a spider's web. Today, spiders, along with scorpions, ticks, and mites, are all included in a group of arthropods called arachnids (uh-RACK-nidz). As you can guess, arachnids are named for the young Arachne.

The bodies of arachnids are divided into two main sections: a head-chest section and an abdominal section. Although arachnids vary in size and shape, they all have eight legs. So, if you ever find a small

Figure 10-27 *While under water, the diving spider breathes air it stores in bubbles.*

"bug," one way you can tell if it is an arachnid is to count its legs.

Arachnids live in many environments. Most spiders, for example, live on land. However, one spider lives underwater inside a bubble of air it brings from the surface. Scorpions, for the most part, are found in dry desert areas. Ticks and mites, however, live on organisms. They may live on a plant and stay in one place, or they may live on an animal and go wherever the animal goes.

Spiders catch their prey in different ways. Many spiders make webs of fine, yet very strong, strands of silk. Special glands in the abdomens of spiders secrete this silk. Spiders' webs are often constructed in

Figure 10-28 *Like many spiders, this spider traps its prey in a web.*

Figure 10-29 *The fishing spider (left) and the jumping spider (right) do not spin webs to catch their prey. These spiders hunt their prey.*

Figure 10-30 *The scorpion, an arachnid, is found in dry environments. Located at the tip of its tail is a stinger, which the scorpion uses to stab and poison its prey.*

complicated and beautiful patterns. You may be surprised to learn that the spider actually spins two different kinds of silk. Some strands of the silk are sticky. These strands catch and hold prey until the spider is able to kill it. Other strands are not sticky. These are the strands the spider uses when it walks around its web. Many spiders weave a new web every day. At night the spiders eat the strands of that day's web, recycling this material the following day when a new web is produced.

Some spiders hide and spring out to surprise their prey. The trapdoor spider lives in a hole in the ground covered by a door made of silk and hidden by dirt and pieces of plants. When an unsuspecting insect passes close to the trapdoor, the spider rushes out to catch it.

Once a spider catches its dinner, it uses a pair of fangs to inject venom, or poison, into its prey. Sometimes the venom kills the prey immediately. Other times it paralyzes the prey so that the spider can save living creatures trapped in its web for another day when it needs more food.

Scorpions are active mostly at night. They capture and hold their prey with their large front claws while they inject venom through the stinger in their tail. During the day, scorpions hide under logs, stones, or in holes in the ground. Campers have to be careful when they put their boots on in the morning because a scorpion may have mistaken a boot lying on the ground for a suitable place to hide to escape the heat of the day.

Ticks and mites live off the body fluids of animals and plants. Many ticks suck blood from larger animals. When they do this they may spread disease. Rocky Mountain spotted fever is spread to people through the bites of ticks. Some ticks and mites live on insects. Other mites live by sucking juices from plant stems and leaves. They may also spread disease.

SECTION REVIEW

1. What is an exoskeleton?
2. Through what structure do crustaceans take in oxygen from the water?
3. List three different arachnids.

1. Rigid outer covering
2. Gills
3. Spider, scorpion, tick, mite

10-8 Insects

By now you may have noticed that there is one group of arthropods, or animals with jointed legs, that has not been discussed. This group, of course, is the insects. However, it would be hard to overlook insects for too long since there are more kinds of insects than all other animal species combined. In fact, it has been estimated that there may be as many as

Figure 10-31 *Insects, like the may beetle* (left) *and the banded woollybear* (right), *vary greatly in appearance.*

300 million insects for every single person alive on the earth!

Along with birds and bats, certain insects are the only animals that can fly. Insects vary greatly in appearance. If you examine different insect species, for example, you would find that the mouth parts vary greatly. A mosquito's mouth resembles a tiny needle. It can push its needlelike mouth through an animal's skin and remove some of the animal's body fluids. Other insects have mouths that are adapted to eating parts of plants. If you have ever watched a caterpillar eating a leaf, you know how efficient these insects' mouths are.

Many insects compete directly with humans. Insects eat the plants we use for food. Others eat the clothes we wear. If you live in a house made of wood, you may be surprised to find that some species of insects, such as termites, may even be eating your house.

Insect Anatomy

A grasshopper is a typical insect in many ways. See Figure 10-32. Insects differ from arachnids whose bodies are divided into two sections. A grasshopper's body is divided into three main sections: a head, a thorax or chest section, and an abdominal

Figure 10-32 *The grasshopper is an insect. Like all insects, it has three pairs of legs. The pair of large hind legs help the grasshopper jump.*

section. Insects have three pairs of legs. In the grass-hopper, the three pairs of legs are not identical. One pair of legs is much larger than the other two pairs. This pair of legs enables the grasshopper to jump away as you approach.

If someone were to ask you what animal has five eyes, you might laugh. But if you took a look at the head of a grasshopper, you would find five eyes peering at you. The grasshopper has three simple eyes on the front of its head. These eyes only can detect light and dark. However, on the sides of its head are two compound eyes. Compound eyes contain many lenses. See Figure 10-33. These compound eyes can detect some colors, but they are best at detecting movement. This ability is important to an animal that is hunted daily by other animals for food.

Most insects have wings. The grasshopper has two pairs of wings, and it can fly quite well for short distances. Some kinds of grasshoppers can fly great distances in search of food. Insect flight varies from the gentle fluttering flight of a butterfly to the speedy flight of the hawkmoth, an insect that can fly as fast as 50 kilometers per hour.

Insects have an open circulatory system. Their blood usually is not contained within a system of blood vessels, as it is in humans. The blood moves around the inside of the insect's body, bathing the internal organs. An insect's blood carries food. But the blood does not carry oxygen. Insects do not have a well-developed system for moving oxygen into the body and waste gases out. Instead, they have a system of tubes that pass through the exoskeleton and into the insect's body. Gases move into and out of the insect's body through these tubes.

Insect Growth and Development

Insects spend a great deal of time eating, and they grow rapidly. Like other arthropods, insects must shed their exoskeleton as they grow. As insects develop, they pass through several stages. Some species of insects change their appearance completely as they pass through the different stages. This change in appearance due to development is known as **metamorphosis** (met-uh-MAWR-fuh-sis).

Figure 10-33 *Insects, such as this fly, have compound eyes. Within these eyes are many lenses, which enable the insect to detect the slightest movement of an object.*

ACTIVITY

Role Playing

Pick your favorite insect and imagine that you are that insect for one day. Write a 500-word essay describing all the events and encounters that occur on that day.

Figure 10-34 *During <u>metamorphosis</u>, an insect goes through a series of changes. The monarch butterfly begins life as an egg (top left),* then *becomes a larva, also known as a caterpillar (bottom left), and finally wraps itself up into a cocoon (right), where it becomes a pupa.*

Figure 10-35 *In the last stage of metamorphosis, the monarch has wings and other parts of a typical adult insect. These monarch butterflies are wintering in a tree in southern California.*

During metamorphosis, an insect passes through four distinct stages. The first stage is the egg. When the egg hatches, a **larva** emerges. A caterpillar, for example, is the larva of an insect that will one day become a butterfly or a moth. The larva spends almost all of its time eating and can eat all the leaves of a plant in a short time.

Eventually, the caterpillar begins the next phase, the **pupa** (PYOO-puh) phase. In this phase, the caterpillar secretes a covering made of silk or another material. It wraps itself in this cocoon and appears to be sleeping. But inside the cocoon remarkable changes take place. The pupa changes into an adult insect with a completely different appearance. It is often difficult to believe that a beautiful butterfly was once a creeping caterpillar.

Insect Behavior

Most insects lead solitary lives. They live alone. In this way, they do not compete directly with other members of their species for available food. They come together only to mate and to produce fertilized eggs. Insects attract mates in different ways. One way involves the giving off of a special scent, which you might think of as a kind of perfume. These scents are called **pheromones** (FER-uh-mohnz), extremely powerful chemicals that cannot be smelled by a human. However, even a small amount of a pheromone can be noticed by a potential mate over great distances. Some pheromones produced by female insects can attract a male located more than 11 kilometers away.

Other insects, known as social insects, cannot survive alone. These insects form colonies or hives. Ants, termites, some wasp species, and bees are social insects. They survive as a society of individual insects that perform different jobs. Many of these colonies are highly organized.

A beehive is a marvel of organization. Worker bees, actually infertile females, perform all of the work needed to ensure the survival of the hive. For example, worker bees supply the hive with food. They make the honey and the combs to store it. They feed the queen bee, whose only function is to lay huge numbers of eggs. Worker bees keep the

Figure 10-36 *Insect behavior often helps other organisms. This moth flies from flower to flower. As it does, it helps pollinate the flowers.*

Figure 10-37 *This large mound of soil was built by termites. Termites, like bees, are social insects and work and live together in a colony.*

queen bee clean as well as do the housekeeping for the hive. They also protect the hive. Male bees, whose only function is to fertilize the queen, are unable to feed themselves and so also are dependent upon the workers.

Defense Mechanisms

Insects have many defense methods to ensure their survival. Wasps and bees have stingers that they use to defend them against their enemies. Other insects are masters of camouflage. These insects survive because their bodies are not easily seen by their enemies. Some insects, for example, resemble sticks and twigs. Other insects resemble leaves or the

---

Career: *Beekeeper*

HELP WANTED: BEEKEEPER No special education required. Courses in beekeeping, agriculture, and business helpful. Will train to harvest honey from honeycombs and clean, repair, and inspect beehives.

The worker bee hovered over the flower while sucking nectar with its long tongue into its stomach. In the bee's stomach, special chemicals mixed with the nectar. When its stomach was full, it returned to its hive. At the hive it brought the nectar mixture back up through its mouth and placed it in a compartment or cell in the hive. As water evaporated from the mixture, the nectar changed to honey. Other bees placed a wax cap on the honey-filled cell. Honey stored in this way provides food for all the bees during the winter.

People who maintain hives of bees from which they collect honey and beeswax are called **beekeepers.** They sell the honey to bakeries for use in cookies and crackers or package it to sell in markets by the jar. The beeswax is sold for use in making candles, lipsticks, and polishes.

Beekeepers construct wooden boxes with removable frames as hives for the bees. The bees build honeycombs of wax on the frames, which contain many cells to receive the nectar mixtures. Bees are free to come and go so they can bring nectar from flowers back to the hive.

Anyone interested in beekeeping might begin by keeping a hive or two in a backyard or on a roof. Beginner colonies can usually be bought or rented from local beekeepers. For more information on a career working with fascinating insects, write to the New Jersey Beekeepers Association, 157 Five Point Road, Colts Neck, NJ 07722.

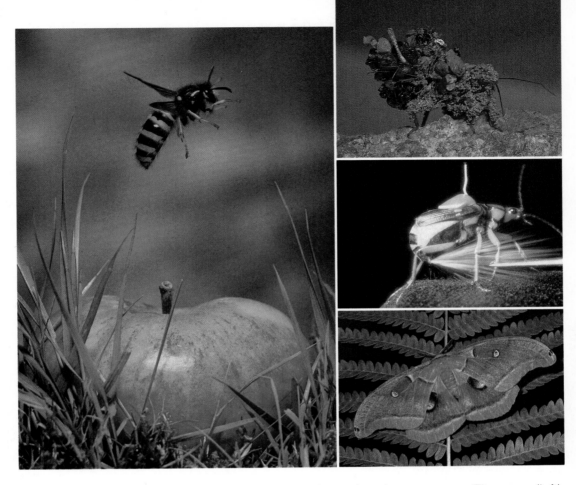

Figure 10-38 *Insects defend themselves in many ways. The wasp* (left) *uses its stinger, the assassin bug* (top right) *is camouflaged, the bombardier beetle* (center right) *sprays a foul-smelling chemical, and the eye spot coloring on this moth* (bottom right) *startles its predators.*

thorns of plants. Some insects have the ability to spray <u>foul-smelling</u> chemicals at an enemy. Other insects have <u>markings</u> that frighten birds and other animals that might eat them. In Figure 10-38, you can see two large "eyespots" on the wings of the moth. These spots startle predatory animals and may confuse a predator long enough for the insect to escape.

SECTION REVIEW

1. What are the three main sections of an insect's body?
2. What are the four stages of metamorphosis?
3. List three kinds of social insects.

1. Head, thorax, abdomen
2. Egg, larva, pupa, adult
3. Ants, termites, some wasp species, bees

LABORATORY ACTIVITY

For further instructions, see page T-39

Observing an Ant Farm

Purpose

In this activity, you will observe the behavior of a common invertebrate, the ant.

Materials *(per group)*

2-L plastic soft-drink bottle
200-mL plastic soft-drink bottle
Black construction paper
10-cm length of cotton wadding
Small bits of meat and bread (or other foods ants eat)
12 ants (from your teacher)

Scissors	Magnifying glass
Sandy soil	Shallow pan
Adhesive tape	Pin
Plastic wrap	

Black construction-paper sleeve

Plastic wrap with pinholes

Tape

Small bottle containing water

Large plastic bottle

Food

Cotton wadding

Pan containing water   Moist sandy soil

Procedure

1. Use the scissors *carefully* to cut about 10 cm from the top of a 2-L plastic bottle.
2. Fill a 200-mL plastic bottle with water, and place this bottle inside the 2-L bottle.
3. Use moistened sandy soil to fill the space that remains between the two bottles. The soil should come to about 5 cm of the top of the inside bottle.
4. Place the length of cotton wadding in the mouth of the inside bottle so that half of it is under the surface of the water and half hangs over the bottle, just above the soil.
5. Make a cover for the larger bottle by cutting a sleeve of construction paper about 10 cm wide. Tape the paper securely to the bottle.
6. Place a dozen ants, obtained from your teacher, on the surface of the soil. Also place the meat and bread bits on the soil.
7. Cover the opening of the paper sleeve with clear plastic wrap. Tape the wrap in place and use a pin to make about 10 small holes in the wrap.
8. Place the entire ant farm in a shallow pan of water.
9. Using the magnifying glass, observe the ant farm two or three times a week for about a month. If all the food has been taken by the ants, place more food on the surface. Remove any excess or moldy food. Add water to the inner bottle as the level drops. Replace the paper cover securely each time, using more tape.

Observations and Conclusions

1. Make sketches of the tunnels and chambers constructed by the ants.
2. Were there differences in behavior among the ants in the colony? What activities were carried out by the different ants? Why are ants said to be social insects?

CHAPTER SUMMARY

10-1 Invertebrates

▰ Vertebrates have backbones, while invertebrates have no backbones.

▰ All animals are multicellular, and most have specialized cells.

10-2 Sponges

▰ The cells of sponges remove food and oxygen from ocean water as the water flows through pores. The out-flowing water carries away waste products.

10-3 Coelenterates

▰ Coelenterates have a cup-shaped body with one opening. Examples include corals, sea anemones, and jellyfish.

▰ Most coelenterates have stinging cells called nematocysts on their tentacles. Coelenterates sting and capture their prey, which is digested in the central body cavity. Waste products are released through the mouth.

10-4 Worms

▰ Flatworms have flat bodies and live in ponds and streams. Flatworms can regrow missing or cut-off parts. Examples of flatworms are planarians and tapeworms.

▰ Roundworms resemble strands of spaghetti. Food passes from the mouth end to tail end through a digestive tube. Trichinosis is a disease caused by eating pork containing roundworms.

▰ Segmented worms, such as earthworms, have segmented bodies and live in soil, salt water, or fresh water.

▰ Earthworms have a digestive system with a crop and gizzard, a closed circulatory system, a moist skin for gas exchange, a sexual reproductive system, and a simple nervous system.

10-5 Mollusks

▰ Mollusks have soft bodies covered by a shell-producing mantle. Their muscular foot opens and closes the shell and permits movement. Snails, clams, and squids are examples of mollusks.

10-6 Spiny-Skinned Animals

▰ Starfish have tiny tube feet for movement and can regenerate missing parts.

▰ The spiny-skinned animals also include sea cucumbers, sea lilies, sea urchins, and sand dollars.

10-7 Arthropods

▰ Arthropods have jointed legs and an exoskeleton. The group includes crustaceans, centipedes and millipedes, arachnids, and insects.

10-8 Insects

▰ Insects have bodies divided into three parts, have three pairs of legs and an open circulatory system.

VOCABULARY *Define the following terms.*

crop p.228	gizzard p.228	mantle p.230	pore p.220
exoskeleton p.236	host p.226	metamorphosis p.243	pupa p.245
fertilization p.229	invertebrate p.219	nematocyst p.221	radula p.231
gill p.237	larva p.245	pheromone p.245	vertebrate p.218

[handwritten annotations: heart, mouth, Bristles, intestine, esophagus, anus]

249

CHAPTER REVIEW

Multiple Choice

Choose the letter of the answer that best completes each statement.

1. Tissues that work together are organized into
   a. cells.
   b. organs.
   c. organ systems.
   d. tissue systems.

2. Which of these invertebrate groups is responsible for building the Great Barrier Reef?
   a. sponges
   b. corals
   c. sea anemones
   d. jellyfish

3. Scientists hope to learn more about the earth's past by studying the daily growth rings of
   a. sponges.
   b. corals.
   c. segmented worms.
   d. mollusks.

4. Tapeworms are examples of parasitic
   a. flatworms.
   b. roundworms.
   c. segmented worms.
   d. earthworms.

5. Which of these is *not* a function of a mollusk's thick muscular foot?
   a. movement
   b. production of a hard outer shell
   c. digging
   d. opening and closing the shell

6. Which of these animals can regenerate lost body parts?
   a. crabs
   b. planarians
   c. starfish
   d. all of these

7. In which group of invertebrates do the animals have jointed legs and exoskeletons?
   a. coelenterates
   b. worms
   c. mollusks
   d. arthropods

8. Spiders belong to a group of invertebrates called
   a. coelenterates.
   b. crustaceans.
   c. arthropods.
   d. insects.

9. In which stage of metamorphosis is a caterpillar?
   a. egg
   b. larva
   c. pupa
   d. adult

10. The only function of the queen bee is to
   a. lay large numbers of eggs.
   b. do the beehive housekeeping.
   c. protect the hive.
   d. make the honey to store in combs.

Completions

Fill in the word or words that best complete each statement.

1. Animals without backbones are called ____invertebrates____.

2. The stinging cells found around the mouth of most coelenterates are called ____nematocysts____.

3. The painful disease caused by eating raw pork containing certain roundworms is called ____trichinosis____.

4. The ____hookworm____ is a roundworm which infects over 600 million people each year by burrowing through their skin.

5. Giant squids belong to a group of invertebrates called _____mollusks_____.
6. The structure that files off bits of plant matter in most mollusks is called _____radula_____.
7. The crown-of-thorns sea star is an example of a(n) _____spiny-skinned animal_____.
8. The rigid outer covering of an arthropod is called a(n) _____exoskeleton_____.
9. The changing appearance of insects as they pass through different stages is called _____metamorphosis_____.
10. The special scents produced by insects to attract mates are called _____pheromones_____.

True or False

Determine whether each statement is true or false. If it is true, write "true."
If it is false, change the underlined word or words to make the statement
true.

1. All animals are multicellular. T
2. The clownfish is protected from other fish by living in harmony with the stinging jellyfish. F (sea anemone)
3. Certain worms get into oysters causing the oysters to produce pearls. T
4. In an earthworm, the crop is the muscular organ that grinds up food. F (gizzard)
5. The soft radula covering the body of a mollusk produces the material making up the mollusk's hard shell. F (mantle)
6. Sea cucumbers, and sea lilies are examples of spiny-skinned animals. T
7. In crustaceans, the special structures that remove oxygen from water are called pores. F (gills)
8. Spiders are examples of crustaceans.*
9. Oxygen and waste gases pass out of the exoskeleton of an insect's body through gills. F (tubes)
10. In order to grow, insects must shed their mantles. F (exoskeletons)

* F (arachnids)

Discussion Topics   Answers appear on page T-39.

Write a brief paragraph discussing each of the following.

1. Discuss the ways in which insects compete with human beings. Give two examples.
2. Describe the protective method each of the following uses against predators: sea anemone, earthworm, squid, insect.
3. Explain the process of metamorphosis.
4. List the different methods invertebrates use to get food. For each method, give examples of those invertebrates that use it.

EXPAND YOUR KNOWLEDGE

Dallinger, J. *Grasshoppers*. Minneapolis, Minn.: Lerner.
    The book describes the types of habitats, eating habits, and reproductive activities of grasshoppers. Excellent photographs of the growth cycles, from nymph to adult, are included.
Johnson, S. A. *Snails*. Minneapolis, Minn.: Lerner.
    The author describes how land snails glide through the forest, grow up, and reproduce.

11 Animals: Vertebrates

For a chapter overview, teaching strategies, answers to all activities, a list of A-V materials, and a chapter bibliography, see pages T-40 to T-42.

Consult your Teacher's Resource Book and Annotated Teacher's Edition, Laboratory Book for additional activities and teaching aids.

CHAPTER SECTIONS

CHAPTER OBJECTIVES

After completing this chapter, you will be able to:

11-1 Describe the characteristics of vertebrates.

11-2 Explain the differences between toads and frogs.

11-3 Describe the adaptations that allow reptiles to live their entire lives on land.

11-4 List the four main categories of birds and their adaptations for flight.

A small fish swims past a rock. As it does, it notices a worm wriggling and moves closer to investigate. However, the fish is in for a deadly surprise. No, the worm is not at the end of a fishing line that leads to the surface. But it *is* being used as bait. In fact, the worm is attached to the rock, which is quietly watching the small fish. For the "rock" is not made of minerals; it is actually a fish called an anglerfish. And the "worm" is really an organ attached to the fish's head. In order to catch a meal, the anglerfish must wait patiently, as still as a rock.

The worm lures the fish closer. When the prey is near, the anglerfish takes a big gulp. The small fish ends up in the anglerfish's huge mouth.

To trap its prey, the anglerfish must remain very still and show unlimited patience. However, it can move quickly when it strikes. In fact, the strike of the anglerfish, one of the fastest in the animal kingdom, has been timed at less than 4/1000 of a second!

Anglerfish luring its prey

11-1 Fish

Around 500 million years ago, a tiny animal first appeared in the earth's oceans. This strange animal had no jaws. It did have fins, but they were not like the fins of modern fish. However, there was something very special about this animal—something that would group it with the many kinds of fish that were to come in later years. This early fish was the first animal with a backbone—the first vertebrate.

The main characteristic of all vertebrates, including fish, is a backbone, although you will read about some fish whose backbone is not made of bone at all! The bones that make up a vertebrate's backbone are called **vertebrae** (singular: vertebra). See Figure 11-1. The backbone is part of the vertebrate's internal skeleton, although, again, not all skeletons are made of bone. The skeleton provides support and helps give the body of a vertebrate its shape. One important advantage of an internal skeleton is that it increases in size as the animal grows. It does not have to be shed, as does the exoskeleton of an insect.

An important function of the backbone of a vertebrate is to protect the nerves of the spinal cord, which runs down through the center of the backbone. These spinal cord nerves connect the vertebrate's well-developed brain to nerves that carry information to and from every part of the body.

Figure 11-1 *Like all vertebrates, fish have a series of bones called vertebrae that make up their backbone.*

Figure 11-2 *Some fish, like these in the Coral Sea, travel in schools.*

Fish are the vertebrates that are best adapted to a life under water. Their smooth body, usually covered with scales, is streamlined, allowing them to glide through the water. Most fish have fins. Some fins keep a fish upright so that it does not roll over on its side. Other fins help the fish steer and stop. The side-to-side movement of the large tail fin propels the fish through the water. Rapid movement of its tail fin, for example, allows the pike to travel up to 12 times its body length in less than one second.

Like some invertebrates, fish take oxygen from the water through gills. As a fish swims, water passes through its gills. Oxygen passes from the water into blood vessels in the gills. Carbon dioxide wastes also pass out of the fish through the gills. Fish have well-developed digestive, circulatory, and nervous systems, as do the other vertebrates you will read about.

Fish live in all of the earth's waters, in both fresh and salt water. As you might expect, however, the same fish usually cannot live in both fresh and salt water. Also, while some fish, like the cod, may live in the cold waters of the Arctic, others, like the ferocious piranha, live in warm, tropical waters. If you take a tropical piranha and place it in arctic waters, it will soon die. Why? Fish are coldblooded. They have no internal control over their body temperature. So changes in their environment can affect their body temperature. If the change is severe, as from tropical to arctic waters, most fish will not survive. However,

Activity

Vertebrate Body Systems

Vertebrates have well-developed body systems. However, these systems are not the same in all vertebrates. The heart structure of fish, for example, differs from that of birds. Choose one of the systems listed below. Use posterboard and colored pencils to draw and label how a particular system changes from fish to amphibians to reptiles and finally through birds. See if you can include how the system changes in mammals, a kind of vertebrate you will read about in the next chapter. Select one of the following systems:

  nervous system
  digestive system
  circulatory system
  reproductive system
  excretory system

Figure 11-3 *(left) Fish are found in all the water environments on the earth. Some, like this ferocious piranha, are found only in warm, tropical waters.*

Figure 11-4 *(right) The lamprey, a jawless fish, attaches to other fish with its suction-cup mouth. Once attached, the lamprey uses its teeth to drill a hole into the other fish.*

since the water temperature in an area remains relatively constant compared to the temperature on land, fish have little trouble maintaining a constant body temperature as long as they remain in their native waters. This results in a saving of energy, for fish do not have to use food energy to keep warm.

Fish are divided into three groups. These groups are the jawless fish, the cartilaginous (kahr-tuh-LA-juh-nuhs) fish, and the bony fish.

Jawless Fish

Jawless fish are the most primitive of all fish. They are so primitive, in fact, that they lack scales and fins as well as jaws. In Figure 11-4, you can see the most common jawless fish—the lamprey. The lamprey looks like a snake with a suction-cup mouth at one end. Even though the fish has no jaws, this suction-cup mouth is very efficient. Using its mouth, the lamprey attaches itself to the soft belly of some other fish such as a trout. Then, with its teeth and rough tongue, the lamprey drills a hole into the fish and sucks out its blood and other body fluids. At one time, lampreys in the Great Lakes killed so many other fish that special poisons were used to kill lamprey young.

There is something else that makes jawless fish unusual. To find out what it is, take your ear between your fingers and move it back and forth a few times. Nothing breaks, does it? The reason is that you ear contains a flexible material called **cartilage.** In fact, before you were born your entire skeleton was made of cartilage. In time, the cartilage was replaced by bone, except in some places like your ear and the tip of your nose. The entire skeleton of a jawless fish is made of cartilage. The skeleton is never replaced by bone tissue. As you might expect, such a fish is very flexible and can be bent so that its head touches its tail without causing any damage to the fish.

Cartilaginous Fish

A monstrous figure moves slowly toward a group of skin divers. However, the divers are too intent on their swimming to notice the 18-meter-long fish as it approaches. Then, suddenly, just as it reaches them one of the divers turns and sees the creature. It is a shark! The diver signals her companions. But they do not swim away in fear, even though they are confronted by the largest shark on earth—the whale

Figure 11-5 *In spite of their enormous size, whale sharks are harmless to people. Whale sharks only eat microscopic plants and animals.*

Figure 11-6 *The great white shark* (left) *and the horn shark* (right) *are examples of cartilaginous fish.*

Figure 11-7 *Rays, such as this blue-spotted lagoon ray, swim by beating their huge fins much the same way as a bird flaps its wings when flying.*

shark. Instead, they grab the shark's top fin and playfully hitch a short ride. The divers know that the whale shark has little interest in people. It eats only microscopic plants and animals.

Sharks are included in a group of fish called the cartilaginous fish. Like those of jawless fish, sharks' skeletons are made of cartilage. But unlike the jawless fish, sharks definitely have jaws. See Figure 11-6. In fact, sharks are probably the most successful predators on earth. And they have been so for hundreds of millions of years. When you think of sharks, you probably think of the great white shark, which has a reputation for eating people. Great white sharks, along with a few other types, have been known to attack people occasionally. But for the most part sharks let people alone and prefer to be let alone as well.

Also included among the cartilaginous fish are skates and rays. These fish have two large, broad fins that stick out from their sides. They beat these fins to move through the water, much as a bird beats its wings to fly through air. Rays and skates often lie on the ocean bottom, where they use their "wings" to cover their bodies with sand and hide. When an unsuspecting fish or invertebrate comes near, the hidden skate or ray is ready to attack. Some rays have a poisonous spine at the end of their long, thin tail. However, they use this for defense, not to catch prey. Other rays are able to produce small charges of electricity to stun and capture prey.

Bony Fish

Anyone who has eaten a flounder or a trout knows why such fish are called bony fish. Their skeleton is composed of hard bones, many of which are quite small and sharp. That is one reason that many restaurants serve fish with the bones removed. Some of the bony fish, including the tuna and herring you may eat, travel in groups called schools. Because of this schooling behavior, these fish can be caught in large numbers at one time by fishing boats.

One important characteristic of bony fish is their **swim bladder.** The swim bladder is a sac that the fish can empty or fill with air. The swim bladder acts in much the same way as a life preserver that keeps people afloat. However, by letting air in and out of the bladder, a fish can float at any level in the water. That is why a fish can sleep under water and not sink, even though it is not moving its fins.

There are many different kinds of bony fish. Some have made remarkable adaptations to life in the water. The electric eel, for example, can generate considerable amounts of electricity. This eel, found in South American streams, uses the electricity it produces to stun its prey. The remora, a saltwater fish, uses a sucker to attach itself to a shark or other marine animal. It feeds on bits of food the shark leaves behind. Some fish, such as the flounder, are

Activity

Salmon

Many fish have interesting reproductive behaviors. But none is more unusual than that of the salmon. Using reference books from the library, study the reproductive cycle of the salmon. Find out where salmon spawn and how they get to their spawning grounds. Write a report on the topic, including what happens to salmon after they spawn.

Figure 11-8 *Fish are adapted in many different ways to a life under water. The stonefish (left) not only blends in with its surroundings, it also gives off a deadly poison through its spines. The deep sea fish (right) has large eyes, a huge mouth, fanglike teeth, and light-emitting organs that flash on and off.*

masters of camouflage. They are able to change color to match their surroundings. By changing to the same color as the ocean bottom, the flounder "hides" from predators.

Some fish that live in the dark ocean depths have developed light-producing organs that can flash on and off to attract prey. Other deep-sea fish have huge eyes to help them see in dim light.

You might think that all fish share one thing in common—a need to stay in water at all times. However, the mudskipper and the walking catfish have adaptations that allow them to come out of the water and spend some time on land. And the lungfish can bury itself in mud in order to survive a dry season during which the water of the stream or pond in which it lives evaporates.

Figure 11-9 *The mudskipper is a "fish out of water." It can crawl along the mud of tropical swamps and breathe air as well as water.*

SECTION REVIEW

1. What are vertebrae?
2. What material makes up the skeleton of lampreys and sharks?
3. What structure allows bony fish to float at any depth in the water, even when asleep?

1. Bones that make up a vertebrate's backbone
2. Cartilage
3. Swim bladder

11-2 Amphibians

In the forests of Colombia, South America, lives the Choco Indian tribe. Today, as they have done for centuries, these Indians hunt deer, monkeys, and even jaguar with poisoned arrows. To do so, the Indians must first capture a supply of a certain frog that lives in the area. They then collect a milky fluid from the frog's back. The tips of their arrows are dipped into this fluid, a poison so powerful that a few drops can kill several thousand mice. The common name for this frog is no surprise—it is called the arrow-poison frog.

The arrow-poison frog is included among a group of coldblooded animals called the amphibians. The word "amphibian" means "double life." Most amphibians do live a double life in the sense that part of it is spent in water and part is spent on land.

Figure 11-10 *This brilliantly colored frog is called an arrow-poison frog. The poisonous fluid in its skin can kill small animals.*

All amphibians, for example, are born from eggs laid in water. And even those which spend their entire lives on land must return to the water to reproduce. Why? The eggs of amphibians lack a hard outer shell and would dry out if they were not deposited in the water.

There is yet another reason amphibians cannot stray too far from water—or at least from a moist area. Amphibians breathe through their skin, but the skin must remain damp for them to take in oxygen in this way.

Frogs and Toads

Have you ever wondered where frogs and toads go in the winter when the temperature drops? Frogs and toads, like all amphibians, are unable to move to warmer climates. But they can survive. Frogs often bury themselves beneath the muddy floor of a lake during the winter. Toads dig through dry ground below the frost line. Then these amphibians go into a winter sleep called **hibernation.** During hibernation, all body activities slow down so that the animal can live on food stored in its body. The small amount of oxygen needed during hibernation passes through the amphibian's skin as it sleeps. Once warmer weather comes, the frog or toad awakes. If you live in the country, you can usually tell when this

Figure 11-11 *Amphibians such as the tree frog* (left) *and toad* (right) *lead a "double life." They spend part of their lives in water and part of them on land.*

happens. The night is suddenly filled with the familiar peeps, squeaks, chirps, and grunts that male frogs and toads use to attract their mates.

Frogs and toads appear similar in shape. But if you touch them, you can tell one difference immediately. Frogs have a smooth, moist skin. Toads are drier and are usually covered with small wartlike bumps. In many toads, the bumps behind the eyes contain a poisonous liquid, which the toad releases when attacked. The attacking animal quickly becomes sick and may even die.

Neither frogs nor toads have tails as adults. However, strange as it may seem, they do have tails when they hatch from eggs in the water. In this stage of their lives they are called tadpoles or polliwogs. A tadpole has gills to breathe under water and feeds on plants. Eventually the tadpole begins to undergo remarkable changes. Its tail begins to disappear. Two pairs of legs take shape. At the same time, its gills begin to close. Inside the tadpole's body, lungs are forming. Soon the tadpole will be an adult toad or frog, ready for its life on land.

If there is one thing most people know about adult toads and frogs, it is that they are excellent jumpers. The main reason for this is that the hind legs of a frog or toad are much larger than the front legs. It is these powerful hind legs that allow the animals to jump so well and helps them escape from

Figure 11-12 *All amphibians lay their eggs* (left) *in a watery environment. Each egg then hatches into a larval form called a tadpole* (right).

Figure 11-13 *The sticky tongue in a frog's mouth is well adapted for catching insects, such as this fly.*

enemies. The largest frog, the goliath frog of West Africa, can jump more than 3 meters with little effort! A frog's large hind legs are also useful in water, where they serve as paddles to propel the animal.

Unlike tadpoles, adult frogs and toads are carnivorous. They catch their prey with a most unusual tongue. The sticky tongue of a frog or toad is attached to the front of its mouth. To trap an insect or other prey, the frog or toad quickly flicks its tongue out of its mouth and catches the insect as it flies by.

Salamanders and Newts

An important ingredient of a witches' brew or magic potion was the eye of a newt. Well, there are no magic potions, but there really are newts. Newts, along with salamanders, are amphibians with tails. Like frogs and toads, these animals have two pairs of legs. However, their legs are not developed like those of a frog. Newts and salamanders cannot jump at all.

Since they are amphibians, salamanders and newts must live in moist areas. Some live in the water all their lives. Others may spend most of their life under a single tree stump. Like frogs and toads, salamanders and newts must lay their eggs in water.

Figure 11-14 *Like all amphibians, this spotted salamander must live in a moist area. Notice the mass of eggs below the salamander.*

263

1. What does the term "amphibian" mean? How does it apply to amphibians?
2. How do frogs survive the cold winter months?
3. When do frogs and toads have tails and gills? When do they have legs and lungs?

1. Double life; part of life spent in water, part spent on land
2. They go into hibernation.
3. Tails and gills as tadpoles; Legs and lungs as adults

11-3 Reptiles

On the barren, windswept shoreline of the Galapagos Islands in the Pacific Ocean, a group of iguanas (i-GWAH-nuhz) cling to the rocks. Wave after wave pounds against the rocks, but the iguanas do not let go. Then, without warning, the iguanas plunge into the cold sea in search of food. The iguanas did not suddenly become hungry. Instead, they basked on the rocks of the Galapagos until the sun warmed their bodies. Only then could these coldblooded animals enter the chilly waters. And once they become cold again in the water, they will have to return to the warm rocks and reheat their bodies.

The iguana, a kind of lizard, belongs to a large group of coldblooded animals called reptiles. Other reptiles include snakes, turtles, and alligators. Although many of these reptiles live in or near water,

Figure 11-15 *Sunning themselves on the shore of this Galapagos island, located off the west coast of South America, are marine iguanas. Marine iguanas are a type of reptile. A crab with red-tipped legs keeps them company.*

Figure 11-16 *Some reptiles, such as this gecko, must shed their skin as they grow.*

as do amphibians, they do not have to go through a water-dwelling stage in their lives. Reptiles have a dry and scaly skin that is resistant to drying out. So reptiles do not have to live in a moist environment. In fact, many reptiles are found in hot, dry deserts all over the world. However, some of these reptiles pay a price for their scaly covering. In order to grow larger, snakes and lizards must shed their skins. To do so, they actually crawl out of their old covering, leaving behind an empty, thin shell of skin.

The eggs of reptiles have a leathery protective shell. This shell prevents the contents of the egg from drying out. So reptiles do not have to return to the water to lay their eggs. Since the eggs are enclosed within a shell, reptiles have developed a system of internal fertilization. The eggs are fertilized within the female's body before the shell forms around the egg.

Snakes and Lizards

Most people are naturally fearful of snakes. They mistakenly think that all snakes are dangerous. But most snakes are not poisonous and will not harm people. In fact, most snakes are helpful. They eat small animals like mice and rats. However, a good rule to follow is: When in doubt, leave a snake alone!

Those snakes which *are* poisonous have developed special glands that produce their **venom,** or poison. Snakes inject their venom into their prey

Figure 11-17 *The king cobra* (left) *is the largest poisonous snake in the world. The emerald tree boa* (right) *squeezes its victim's chest so that it cannot breathe and suffocates.*

through special teeth called fangs. Four kinds of poisonous snakes are found in the United States: rattlesnakes, copperheads, water moccasins, and coral snakes. Other poisonous snakes, like the king cobra, the largest poisonous snake in the world, are found on other continents.

Snakes have developed several remarkable ways of finding prey. Many snakes are able to detect the body heat produced by their prey. They have special pits on the sides of their head that are extremely sensitive to heat. Their tongue is also used as a sense organ. When a snake flicks its tongue in and out of its mouth, it is actually tasting the air, trying to detect those molecules in the air that tell the snake that

Figure 11-18 *The Komodo dragons in this photograph are eating a goat. The largest lizards, Komodo dragons can grow to a length of 3 meters and weigh 113 kilograms.*

food is nearby. Snakes are deaf and have poor eyesight. But their other senses make up for these limitations.

A snake moves by wriggling its muscular body. The scales on its belly help the animal grip the ground and push itself forward. Many snakes, including the water moccasin, are quite at home in the water and can swim along at the surface or submerged.

Lizards differ from snakes in several ways. The most obvious difference is that lizards have legs. Lizards also have ears and can detect sounds. Most lizards are small and eat insects. However, one lizard, the Komodo dragon of Indonesia in Southeast Asia, is very large and looks like a prehistoric dinosaur. The Komodo dragon can swallow small pigs and chickens whole.

Lizards have developed various ways to trap prey. For example, the Gila (HEE-luh) monster, a lizard that lives in the American Southwest, poisons its prey. The Gila monster bites the prey, holds on tight, and rolls over on its side. Meanwhile, poison released from the lizard's lower jaw flows into the wound, aided only by the force of gravity. How does this differ from the way a snake poisons its prey?

Some lizards have developed special ways to protect themselves from becoming another animal's dinner. The chameleon is one of several kinds of lizard that can change color to match their surroundings. In this way, the chameleon hides from predators. Another lizard has an even stranger way of escaping.

* Snakes inject their venom through fangs.

Figure 11-19 (left) Gila monsters live in North American deserts and are one of two types of lizards that have a poisonous bite.

Figure 11-20 (right) Some lizards, such as the anole, have the ability to blend in with their surroundings. Can you find the anole in the photograph?

If caught by its tail, it will quickly shed the tail. The tail remains behind, wriggling on the ground. This action confuses the predator, and the lizard scampers to safety. Later, the lizard's body regenerates the missing tail.

Turtles and Tortoises

Turtles and tortoises are two reptiles that look alike but have adapted to different environments. Turtles spend most of their time in the water. Their legs are shaped like paddles and are used for swimming. Turtles can swim quite well; however, on land they move slowly. Tortoises spend most of their time on land. They have solid, stumpy legs used for walking. Tortoises also have claws on their feet that are used for digging.

Turtles and tortoises carry around with them shells made of plates. Although the shells offer the

---

Career: *Fish Farmer*

HELP WANTED: FISH FARMER High school diploma desired. Courses in fish behavior, fish physiology, fish diseases, and business helpful. Job involves outdoor work.

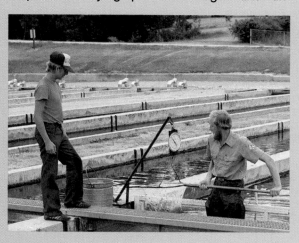

In Mark Twain's *Huckleberry Finn,* Huck recalls fixing breakfast for his friend and himself. "I fetched meal and bacon and coffee and coffeepot and frying pan and sugar and tin cups. . . . I catched a good big catfish, too, and Jim cleaned him with his knife and fried him." In early America, when you sat down to a tasty fish dinner, it meant that somebody had had good luck fishing that day. Now, however, chances are that the fish you ate recently was raised and bred on a fish farm. **Fish farmers** throughout America raise catfish, salmon, trout, bass, and other types of fish to be sold at a profit to restaurants and markets.

At a fish farm, farmers begin by stripping eggs from female fish. They place them in moist pans, where they fertilize them with sperm cells from male fish. The fertilized eggs are then kept warm to ensure growth. When the fish hatch and grow to be as long as a person's finger, they are called fingerlings and are moved to rearing ponds until fully grown.

If fish farming interests you and you live in an area that will support some type of fish farming, you can learn more by writing to the Marine Resources Research Institute, South Carolina Wildlife and Marine Resources Department, P.O. Box 12559, Charleston, SC 29412.

Figure 11-21 *The Ridley turtle* (left) *and giant tortoise* (right) *are examples of reptiles with shells. Turtles spend most of their time in water, while tortoises spend most of their time on land.*

animals some protection, they are heavy and slow the animals down. The backbones of these animals are fused to their top shell. Turtles and tortoises have no teeth. They have a beak similar in structure to the beak of a bird. Many of these animals eat plants as well as well as animals.

Turtles and tortoises can live for a very long time. The Galapagos tortoise, for example, may live for as long as 200 years. When sailors first discovered these animals, they captured them and brought them back to their ships. The animals were kept alive and used as a source of fresh meat on long ocean voyages.

A sea turtle called the green turtle is among the most outstanding navigators in the animal kingdom. Soon after the turtle eggs hatch, perhaps on a beach in Brazil, the young turtles head for the ocean. There they wander for many years over thousands of square kilometers. Eventually, the turtles mature and mate. Now they are ready to lay their own eggs. Where do these turtles go? Back to the same beach where they were born!

That beach may be hundreds of kilometers away, across an ocean surface that has no road signs or other markings. Yet the turtles find their way home. How? No one knows. And here is another fascinating mystery. No matter how far they spread out

Figure 11-22 *These American alligators are examples of reptiles that have hard outer skin and spend most of their time in water.*

through the ocean, turtles born on a particular beach find one another in the ocean and return together to that beach. One scientist observed a huge group of green turtles in a line that stretched for more than 100 kilometers. Each turtle was almost exactly 200 meters ahead of the next!

Alligators and Crocodiles

To most people, alligators and crocodiles are very similar in appearance. Actually there are some differences. The snout of an alligator is broader than the snout of a crocodile, which is narrower and more pointed. When a crocodile's mouth is closed, some of its bottom teeth are visible. When an alligator closes its mouth, none of its teeth are visible. Most people, of course, do not feel the need to examine the mouth of either of these animals closely enough to tell them apart!

Alligators and crocodiles spend most of the time submerged in water with only their eyes and nostrils showing above the surface. Both kinds of animals eat meat. Their diet consists mainly of fish and other animals that venture too close to their large mouths.

Alligators and crocodiles have unusual reproductive behavior. The female alligator builds a nest of rotting plants in which to lay her eggs. The rotting plants give off heat as they decompose. This heat keeps the eggs warm and helps them to develop. The alligators inside the eggs make low chirping sounds when they are about to hatch. The sounds

ACTIVITY

A Symbiotic Relationship

Look for information and write a short paragraph on the relationship between the Egyptian plover and the Nile crocodile.

are heard by the mother, who has remained nearby guarding her eggs. When she hears the hatchlings, she uncovers the eggs. The tiny alligators, looking like small copies of their parents, come out into the light of day. The female continues to care for the young for some time after they hatch. The male alligator also helps care for the young. This behavior is unlike the behavior of most reptiles, which usually leave their eggs after they are laid. Their young must care for themselves as soon as they hatch.

SECTION REVIEW

1. What is an important difference between the egg of an amphibian and the egg of a reptile?
2. Describe an important difference between the legs of a turtle and the legs of a tortoise.

1. The eggs of reptiles are leathery.
2. The turtle's legs are shaped like paddles while the tortoise's legs are solid and stumpy.

11-4 Birds

For many people, birds are the most fascinating and colorful animals on earth. Birds, along with bats and insects, are the only animals with the power of flight, although not all species of birds do fly.

The earliest known bird lived more than 150 million years ago, during a time when reptiles like the dinosaurs ruled the earth. In fact, this early bird had many of the characteristics of reptiles. For example, it had a long bony tail and sharp teeth. Modern birds have neither of these. However, there is no doubt that this early flying creature was a bird. For fossil evidence shows it had feathers, a characteristic that only birds have. If you look at a modern bird, you will notice another characteristic in common with reptiles. Birds have scales on their legs.

Birds are warmblooded. They have the ability to maintain a constant body temperature, despite the temperature of their environment. In Figure 11-23, you can see a group of penguins huddled together against the cold antarctic winds. Penguins trap their own body heat under an insulating coat of feathers. Birds like these penguins are able to withstand very cold temperatures. However, maintaining a high

Figure 11-23 *Birds have feathers and are warmblooded. These penguins can withstand the cold of Antarctica because they are insulated by a coat of feathers.*

body temperature requires birds to consume a great deal of food for energy. For the penguins, that means eating a lot of fish.

Types of Birds

Birds can be divided into four main groups: perching birds, water birds, birds of prey, and flightless birds. The perching birds are perhaps the most familiar. These birds have feet that are adapted for perching. Their feet can easily grasp a branch. Cardinals, robins, and sparrows are perching birds. The beaks of some of these birds may be long and thin like the beak of the hummingbird. This beak enables hummingbirds to reach deep into flowers for nectar. Other perching birds have beaks that are adapted for cracking seeds or catching insects. The macaw, a kind of parrot, has a beak that is strong enough to crack open tough Brazil nuts. The woodpecker has a beak that can open the bark of trees where insects, the food of woodpeckers, live.

Water birds have feet that are adapted for swimming. Ducks and geese are water birds with feet that resemble paddles. These birds glide across the surface of the water looking for food. All water birds can fly as well as swim.

Birds of prey are superb fliers and also have keen eyesight. Soaring high in the air, they can spot prey on the ground or in the water far beneath them. Birds of prey eat small animals including fish, reptiles, and other birds. Some, such as a certain eagle, even eat small monkeys.

Birds of prey are able to fly very fast. The peregrine falcon has been clocked at more than 125 kilometers per hour while diving at its prey. Birds of prey have sharp claws called **talons** on their toes. Talons enable the bird to grasp and hold its prey. Some eagles have talons that are longer than the fangs of a lion. Birds of prey also have strong, curved beaks that are used to tear their prey into pieces small enough to be swallowed.

The flightless birds include the ostrich of Africa, the largest bird alive today; the rhea of South America; and the emu and cassowary of Australia. Also included in this group are penguins, flightless birds that are able to "fly" through the water. All of these

Figure 11-24 *Perching birds, such as this macaw, live on land and spend their lives in trees or other high places when they are not flying. Macaws are members of the parrot family.*

Figure 11-25 *The paddlelike feet of the wood duck* (top left) *enables it to swim in water. The bald eagle* (bottom left) *has keen eyesight, sharp bill, and talons, or curved claws, for grasping prey. A road runner* (right) *can run as fast as 24 kilometers per hour.*

birds have small wings relative to the size of their bodies. All flightless birds except penguins have strong leg muscles that enable the birds to run quickly. These birds also use their strong legs for defense, kicking viciously at any enemy foolish enough to challenge them.

Adaptations for Flight

Birds have light, hollow bones—certainly an advantage to any flying animal. Birds are also covered with feathers. They usually have large feathers on their wings. These feathers provide lift, much as an airplane's wings lift it off the ground.

The feathers on the wings and most of the bird's body feathers are called **contour feathers.** These feathers are the largest and most familiar feathers. They give birds their streamlined shape. Other feathers, called **down feathers,** are short and fuzzy and act as insulation. Most birds have down feathers on their breasts. Down feathers are also found covering young birds after they hatch, but before contour feathers have grown in.

Breeding Habits and Development

Many birds have complicated behaviors. Bird songs are used to establish a territory, an area where the bird lives. The song chases other birds of the same species away. Establishing a territory is important because it ensures that few birds will compete for food and living space in the same area.

The bright feathers of some male birds are used to attract females. However, brightly colored feathers also make the bird more obvious to predators. So many birds sport bright colors only during the breeding season.

Some birds attract a mate by constructing a large and colorful nesting site. Male bowerbirds use bits of colorful material to call attention to themselves and thereby attract a mate. The male penguin, on the other hand, does not construct a colorful structure. Instead, he presents his intended mate with a pebble. The pebble indicates that he is ready to breed and care for a youngster.

Most birds build nests. These nests can be little more than a space hollowed out in the ground, or they can be quite elaborate like the nest of the weaverbird, which is actually more like a crowded apartment house in a big city. All of these structures are designed to protect the eggs and the young birds as they develop.

ACTIVITY

Finding the Way Home

The longest flight by a homing pigeon took two months and covered almost 10,000 kilometers. Assuming each month had 31 days, calculate the distance per day traveled by the homing pigeon.

Figure 11-26 *Birds are the most famous nest-builders. Weaver birds use their feet and bills to weave their enclosed nests of grass. These nests hang from tree branches.*

Unlike a reptile's egg, a bird's egg is encased within a hard, strong shell. The shell protects the developing bird and contains food for the bird. The shell, while seemingly quite solid, allows oxygen to pass into the egg and carbon dioxide to pass out.

Most birds incubate their eggs by sitting on them. This behavior keeps the eggs warm as the young develop. However, the penguin keeps its single egg warm by balancing it on the top of its feet and pressing down on the egg with its abdomen. The egg never rests on the cold ground.

Among birds, sometimes only one parent will incubate the eggs. In other species, both parents take turns incubating the eggs. After the eggs hatch, the young birds are quite helpless. They cannot fly to look for food. Their parents must bring them food and water until they are old enough to fly and take care of themselves.

Migration

Many birds **migrate,** or move to a new environment, during the course of a year. Some birds migrate over tremendous distances. For example, the American golden plover flies more than 25,000 kilometers when it migrates. Birds migrate for many reasons, but perhaps the most important reason is to follow seasonal food supplies.

Some birds fly south in the winter in search of food. The whooping crane, for example, flies south from its nesting area in Canada to winter on the Texas shore. Birds have developed extremely accurate mechanisms for migrating. Scientists have learned that some birds navigate, or find their way, by observing the sun and other stars. Other birds follow coastlines or other natural formations such as mountain ranges. Still other birds are believed to have magnetic centers in their brain. These centers act like a compass to help the bird find its way.

SECTION REVIEW

1. How do bird legs resemble lizard legs?
2. What are the four main categories of birds?
3. List three possible ways birds may navigate across great distances.

1. Birds' legs have scales.
2. Perching birds, water birds, birds of prey, and flightless birds
3. Observing the sun and other stars; following coastlines; or having magnetic centers in their brain

LABORATORY ACTIVITY

For further instructions, see page T-41.

Classifying Vertebrate Bones in Owl Pellets

Purpose

In this activity, you will identify undigested bones of small vertebrates present in a pellet coughed up by an owl.

Materials (*per group*)

Owl pellet
Metal dissecting needle or small spatula
Magnifying glass
Small metric ruler
Pencil and paper

Procedure

1. Observe the outside of an owl pellet and record your observations.
2. Gently break the pellet into two pieces.
3. Using a metal dissecting needle or small spatula, separate any bones and fur from the pellet. Also remove all fur from any skulls found in the pellet.
4. Group similar bones together in a pile. For example, put all skull bones in one group. Observe the skulls. Record the length, number, shape, and color of their teeth.
5. Now try to fit together bones from the different piles to form complete skeletons.

Observations and Conclusions

1. On the basis of your observations of the skulls, use the chart to identify the kinds of animals eaten by the owl.
2. What are the functions of the different bones you found?

Shrew	Upper jaw has at least 18 teeth. Skull length is 23 mm or less. Teeth are brown.	
House Mouse	Upper jaw has 2 biting teeth. Upper jaw extends past lower jaw. Skull length is 22 mm or less.	
Meadow Vole	Upper jaw has 2 biting teeth. Upper jaw does not extend past lower jaw. Molar teeth are flat.	
Mole	Upper jaw has at least 18 teeth. Skull length is 23 mm or more.	
Rat	Upper jaw has 2 biting teeth. Upper jaw extends past lower jaw. Skull length is 22 mm or more.	

CHAPTER SUMMARY

11-1 Fish

■ All vertebrates, including fish, have a backbone made up of bones called vertebrae. The backbone is part of their internal skeleton.

■ Jawless fish, such as the lamprey, are the most primitive fish.

■ Like that of jawless fish, the skeleton of cartilaginous fish is made of flexible cartilage, rather than hard bone. Examples of cartilaginous fish are sharks, skates, and rays.

■ Bony fish have a swim bladder that allows them to float at different levels in the water, even when asleep.

11-2 Amphibians

■ The term "amphibian" means "double life." Amphibians spend part of their lives on land and part in water.

■ The eggs of amphibians do not have hard shells. They must be laid in water or they will dry out.

■ Frog and toad eggs hatch into tadpoles. Tadpoles have gills and a tail.

■ As adults, frogs and toads develop lungs and legs. The powerful hind legs of these animals allow them to leap great distances.

■ Like frogs and toads, salamanders and newts have two pairs of legs.

■ Salamanders and newts are examples of amphibians with tails.

11-3 Reptiles

■ The eggs of reptiles have leathery shells and will not dry out when laid on land.

■ Most snakes are nonpoisonous. However, those snakes which are poisonous inject their venom through special teeth called fangs.

■ Snakes and lizards are covered with a scaly skin. They must shed their skins to grow larger.

■ Turtles are adapted for a life in the water. Tortoises are adapted for a life on land.

■ Alligators have a broader snout than do crocodiles.

11-4 Birds

■ Birds, along with bats and insects, are the only animals that can fly.

■ The four main groups of birds are perching birds, water birds, birds of prey, and flightless birds.

■ The beaks of many birds are adapted for the kinds of foods they eat.

■ Contour feathers give birds their streamlined appearance. Down feathers act as insulation.

■ Birds have many ways to attract a mate, including songs, brightly colored feathers, and unusual nests.

■ Many birds migrate long distances in search of food and warm climates.

warm blooded

VOCABULARY   Define the following terms.

cartilage p.257
contour feather p.273
down feather p.273
hibernation p.261
migrate p.275
swim bladder p.259
talon p.272
venom p.265
vertebra p.254

CHAPTER REVIEW

Multiple Choice

Choose the letter of the answer that best completes each statement.

1. All vertebrates have
   a. an exoskeleton.
   b. an internal skeleton.
   c. scales.
   d. a bony skeleton.
2. The fins of fish help them
   a. steer.
   b. swim upright.
   c. move through the water.
   d. all of these.
3. Cartilaginous fish do *not* include
   a. cod.
   b. sharks.
   c. rays.
   d. skates.
4. Tadpoles are the early stage of
   a. reptiles.
   b. frogs.
   c. newts.
   d. salamanders.
5. Amphibians with tails include
   a. frogs.
   b. toads.
   c. newts.
   d. lizards.
6. During a frog's life, it breathes through its
   a. skin.
   b. gills.
   c. lungs.
   d. all of these.
7. A snake *not* native to the U.S. is the
   a. coral snake.
   b. cobra.
   c. copperhead.
   d. rattlesnake.
8. One kind of poisonous reptile is the
   a. turtle.
   b. chameleon.
   c. Gila monster.
   d. crocodile.
9. Modern birds and reptiles have
   a. feathers.
   b. teeth.
   c. bony tail.
   d. scales on legs.
10. Which are warmblooded?
    a. fish
    b. birds
    c. reptiles
    d. amphibians

Completions

Fill in the word or words that best complete each statement.

1. The bones that make up a vertebrate's backbone are called _____vertebrae_____.
2. The backbone helps protect the nerves of the _____spinal cord_____.
3. The _____swim bladder_____ of bony fish allows them to float at different levels in the water.
4. The term _____amphibian_____ means "double life."
5. During the cold winter, frogs can go into a winter sleep called _____hibernation_____.
6. The peeps and grunts of male frogs are used to attract _____females_____.
7. The poison injected by certain snakes is called _____venom_____.
8. The sparrow is a kind of _____perching_____ bird.
9. _____Down_____ feathers act as insulation for birds.
10. Many birds _____migrate_____ to warmer climates in the winter.

278

True or False

Determine whether each statement is true or false. If it is true, write "true." If it is false, change the underlined word or words to make the statement true.

1. Jawless fish have a hard, bony skeleton. *
2. Most fish can live in both fresh and salt water. F (cannot)
3. The lamprey is a kind of bony fish. F (jawless)
4. Amphibians must live in a dry environment. F (moist)
5. The front legs of a toad are very powerful and help the toad jump. F (hind)
6. The tongue of a frog is attached to the front of its mouth. T

                                        * F (Bony)

7. Reptiles have developed a system of external fertilization. F (internal)
8. Tortoises are well adapted to a life in the water. F (on land)
9. Penguins are a kind of flightless bird. T
10. Contour feathers provide insulation for birds. F (Down)

Discussion Topics Answers appear on page T-42.

Write a brief paragraph discussing each of the following.

1. Name and describe the three types of fish.
2. Because the skins of alligators make excellent leather, these animals have been hunted almost to the point of extinction. Do you think such animals should be protected from hunters? Or do people have a right to hunt all animals, even if they are endangered?
3. Why are reptiles able to live in dry environments when amphibians are not?
4. What are the different mechanisms birds may use to navigate long distances?

EXPAND YOUR KNOWLEDGE

Rowland-Entwistle, T. *Illustrated Facts and Records Book of Animals.* New York: Arco.
> This is a well-organized and well-illustrated book covering both invertebrates and vertebrates. The author gives interesting records and facts concerning many of the animals.

Sadoway, M. *Owls: Hunters of the Night.* Minneapolis, Minn.: Lerner.
> This is a most informative book about 18 species of owls that live in the United States and Canada. Each type of owl is illustrated with a photograph.

Todd, F. S. *The Sea World Book of Penguins.* New York: Harcourt Brace Jovanovich.
> In this book, the author often relates his personal experience with penguins. This helps to make the reader feel that the information is accurate.

12 Mammals

For a chapter overview, teaching strategies, answers to all activities, a list of A-V materials, and a chapter bibliography, see pages T-42 to T-45.

Consult your Teacher's Resource Book and Annotated Teacher's Edition, Laboratory Book for additional activities and teaching aids.

CHAPTER SECTIONS

CHAPTER OBJECTIVES

After completing this chapter, you will be able to:

12-1 List the five main characteristics of mammals.

12-2 Describe the characteristics of egg-laying mammals.

12-3 Describe the characteristics of pouched mammals

12-4 Describe the characteristics of placental mammals.

12-4 Name ten groups of placental mammals and give an example of each.

Imagine yourself living in London at the end of the eighteenth century. In the newspaper, the headline "Explorers Discover Strange Creature in Australia" catches your eye. As you read on, you find out that when the first dried skins of the creature arrived at London's Natural History Museum, they were thought to be fakes. The creature had thick fur, webbed feet, and a beak like a duck's. No one had ever seen such a strange animal!

Years later, when English scientists examined the complete body of this creature, they discovered it was not a fake. The creature was real, no matter how strange it looked. But what was it? It had a bill like a bird's, feet like a frog's, and fur like a beaver's. Moreover, it laid eggs and fed its young milk. As hard as it might be for you to believe, scientists decided that the mysterious creature belonged to a certain group of animals called mammals, which includes lions, dogs, and people!

When it came time to decide what to call this weird animal, scientists searched for a name that would describe its strange features. First, the animal was called a platypus (PLAT-uh-puhs), which means "flat-footed." Soon after, scientists discovered that this name had already been given to a flat-footed beetle. Scientists made the name more descriptive and called it duck-billed platypus.

Duckbilled platypus

12-1 Characteristics of Mammals

A few hundred meters off the coast of California, a small group of animals playfully swim around one another. These whiskered animals are called sea otters. Sea otters spend most of their lives swimming in the ocean. While lying on its back, a sea otter can pound a closed shell against a rock balanced on its chest. The sea otter uses the rock to crack open the shell so that it can eat what is inside.

The sea otter seems rather intelligent. To prevent itself from being swept away by waves, the sea otter wraps itself in strands of giant seaweed growing offshore. The otter uses the seaweed much as an ocean liner uses giant ropes to hold itself close to a pier.

Sea otters belong to a group of vertebrates called mammals. There are about 4000 kinds of mammals on the earth. In addition to sea otters, duckbilled platypuses, lions, dogs, and people, this group also includes such animals as whales, bats, and elephants. Since scientists group together animals that have common characteristics, you might wonder what such different-looking animals could have in common.

All mammals have characteristics that set them apart from all other living things. As the tool-using sea otter showed, mammals are the most intelligent animals on the earth. The great intelligence of mammals springs from a brain that is better developed

Figure 12-1 *The sea otter spends most of its time lying on its back in the cold waters of the North Pacific Ocean. The otter uses the rock balanced on its chest to crack open clams.*

Figure 12-2 *As with most mammals, a thick coat of hair covers the body and provides warmth for llamas.*

than that of any other group of animals. Human beings, for example, have the most well-developed brain of all mammals and are the most intelligent of living things.

Mammals also have physical characteristics that set them apart. At one time during their lives, all mammals possess fur or hair. The fur or hair, if it is thick enough, acts like insulation and enables some mammals to survive in very cold parts of the world. Mammals also can survive in harsh climates because, like birds, mammals are warmblooded. The body temperature of mammals remains almost unchanged no matter what the temperature of their surroundings.

Unlike any other animal, female mammals feed their young with milk produced in **mammary glands.** In fact, the name of this group, "mammal," comes from the name for these glands. In addition, most mammals give their young more care and protection than do other animals.

Despite the characteristics that all mammals have in common, their young develop in different ways. This difference can be used to place mammals into three basic groups: egg-laying mammals, pouched mammals, and placental mammals.

SECTION REVIEW

1. List the five main characteristics of mammals.
2. What substance is produced by mammary glands?

Activity

Pet Mammals

If you have a pet cat, dog, mouse, gerbil, guinea pig, horse, or pig, then your pet belongs to the class Mammalia. Make observations of your pet mammal, for a few days. On a sheet of paper, make a list of your pet's behaviors. Next to each item, record what the behavior means to you. Do you think other animals of the same species behave the same way? How could you go about finding out if they do?

12-2　Egg-Laying Mammals

One of the strangest-looking animals lives in Australia and is called the spiny anteater. It has long claws, a tubelike nose, a covering of fur, and short, stiff spines like those of a porcupine. See Figure 12-3. But what makes the spiny anteater even more strange is that, although it is a mammal, it lays eggs! The spiny anteater and the duckbilled platypus are the only mammals that lay eggs.

Just after the female anteater lays her eggs, she places them into a pouch on her abdomen. The eggs hatch in seven to ten days. The young spiny anteaters feed on milk produced by their mother's mammary glands. Milk production, you may recall, is a characteristic of mammals.

The female platypus lays her one to three eggs in a burrow that she digs in the side of a stream bank. She stays with the eggs to keep them warm until they hatch. After the eggs hatch, the young platypuses feed on milk produced by their mother.

The unusual body parts of the spiny anteater help it gather its food, which consists of ants and termites. For example, its nose holds a sticky, wormlike

Figure 12-3　*This porcupinelike animal is actually a spiny anteater. Unlike all other kinds of mammals, the spiny anteater and the duckbilled platypus do not give birth to live young. Instead, they lay eggs that have a leathery shell.*

tongue that flips out to catch insects. When in danger, the spiny anteater uses its short powerful legs and curved claws to dig a hole in the ground and cover itself until only its spines are showing. These 6-centimeter-long spines scare almost any enemy!

Just as the spiny anteaters have special structures to search for and eat insects on land, the duckbilled platypus has special structures for hunting small animals under water. The platypus is a very good swimmer that has webbed paws and waterproof fur. When underwater, the platypus keeps its eyes closed and uses its soft bill to feel around for snails, mussels, worms, and sometimes small fishes.

ACTIVITY

What's the Difference?

Write a brief paragraph on the differences between the anteater and the spiny anteater.

SECTION REVIEW

1. Name the two egg-laying mammals.
2. Where do these two mammals live?

1. Spiny anteater and duckbilled platypus
2. Australia

12-3 Pouched Mammals

Mammals that have pouches are called **marsupials** (mahr-soo-pi-uhls). To most people, the word "marsupial" is associated with a kangaroo. But kangaroos are not the only marsupials. Some marsupials resem-

Figure 12-4 *The bandicoot (left) and wombat (right) are examples of marsupials, or pouched mammals. These mammals live in Australia or nearby islands.*

ble weasels and teddy bears. There are also marsupials that look like rats and mice.

One of the cuddliest and cutest of marsupials is the <u>koala</u> (koh-AH-luh). See Figure 12-5. The koala's ears are big and round and are covered by thick fur. Unlike most marsupials, the opening of the koala's pouch faces its hind legs rather than its head. Eucalyptus leaves are about the only type of food that koalas eat. Oils from these leaves are an ingredient in cough drops. So it is no wonder that koalas actually smell like cough drops! Because koalas eat only plant material, they are called **herbivores** (HER-bi-vorz).

Kangaroos

"At best it resembles a jumping mouse but it is much larger." These words were spoken in 1770 by the famous English explorer James Cook. He was describing an animal never before seen by Europeans. He later gave the name "kangaroo" to this strange animal.

Kangaroos live in the forests and grasslands of Australia. They have short front legs but long, muscular hind legs and tails. The tail helps the kangaroo to keep its balance and to push itself forward.

When a kangaroo is born, it is only 2 centimeters long and cannot hear or see. Although the kangaroo is only partially developed at birth, its front legs enable it to crawl as much as 30 centimeters to its mother's pouch. How the newborn kangaroo finds its way is a mystery. It would be like a person being blindfolded and earplugged and placed in the center of a strange room the size of half a football field. The person would then be asked to find a single doorway on the first try. After the young kangaroo crawls into the pouch, it stays there for about nine months, feeding on its mother's milk.

Opossums

Have you ever heard the phrase "playing possum" and wondered what it meant? When in danger, opossums lie perfectly still, pretending to be dead. In some unknown way, this behavior helps to protect the opossum from its predators.

Figure 12-5 *The young of some marsupials, such as the koala, hitch rides on their mother's back.*

Figure 12-6 *The most familiar marsupial is the kangaroo. A baby kangaroo, called a joey, rests in its mother's pouch.*

Figure 12-7 *The only marsupial that is native to North America is the opossum. Young opossums cling to their mother as she moves from place to place.*

The opossum is the only marsupial found in North America. It lives in trees, often hanging onto branches with its long tail. Opossums eat fruits, insects, and other small animals.

Female opossums may give birth to as many as 24 opossums at one time. Opossums are partially developed at birth and crawl along their mother's abdomen to her pouch. The newborn opossums are so tiny that all 24 of them could fit into a single teaspoon!

SECTION REVIEW

1. What is a marsupial? Give two examples.
2. What is a predator?
3. Name the only North American marsupial.

1. A pouched mammal; koala, kangaroo, opossum
2. Organisms that feed off other organisms
3. Opossum

12-4 Placental Mammals

Unlike egg-laying and pouched mammals, the young of placental (pluh-SEN-tuhl) mammals develop totally within the female. The females in this group of mammals have **placentas** (pluh-SEN-tuhs). The placenta is a structure through which the developing young receive food and oxygen while in the mother. The placenta also removes wastes from the developing young. After the young are born, female placental mammals supply their young with milk from mammary glands.

There are more than 20 groups of placental mammals. They are grouped according to how they

Figure 12-8 *Mammals that give birth to well-developed young are called placental mammals. Grizzly bears are examples of placental mammals.*

eat, how they move about, or where they live. Of these groups, ten are discussed in the sections that follow.

Insect-Eating Mammals

What has a nose with 22 tentacles and spends half its time in water? If you have given up, the answer is the star-nosed mole. The star-nosed mole gets its name from the ring of 22 tentacles on the end of its nose. See Figure 12-9. No other mammal has this structure. Each tentacle has very sensitive feelers, which enable the mole to find insects to eat and to feel its way around. Even though these moles have eyes, they are too tiny to see anything. The star-nosed mole spends part of its day burrowing beneath the ground and the other part of the day in the water. Star-nosed moles are found in northeastern United States and eastern Canada.

In addition to moles, hedgehogs and shrews are also insect-eating mammals. Because they are covered with spines, hedgehogs look like walking cactuses. When threatened by predators, hedgehogs roll up into a ball with only their spines showing. This action makes the hedgehog's enemy a little less enthusiastic about disturbing the tiny animal.

One type of shrew is the smallest mammal in the world. This animal, called the pygmy shrew, weighs

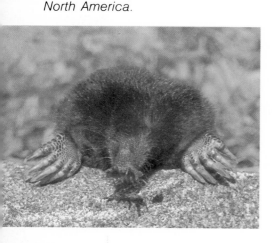

Figure 12-9 *The star-nosed mole has 22 tentacles, or feelers, at the end of its nose. This tiny insect-eating mammal lives in moist or muddy soil in parts of eastern North America.*

only 1.5 to 2 grams—as an adult! Because shrews are so active, they must eat large amounts of food to maintain their energy. Shrews can eat twice their own weight in insects each day!

Figure 12-10 *Insect-eating mammals include the hedgehog (left)* and shrew (right). *The hedgehog curls up into a ball when threatened by predators. To keep healthy, shrews must eat twice their weight in insects each day.*

Flying Mammals

Bats look like mice and are the only flying mammals. In fact, the German word for bat is "Fledermaus," which means flying mouse. Bats are able to fly because they have skin stretched over their arms and fingers, which form wings. Other mammals such as the flying squirrels do not really fly. They simply glide to the ground after leaping from high places.

Although a bat's eyesight is poor, its hearing is excellent. While flying, bats give off high-pitched squeaks that people cannot hear. These squeaks bounce off nearby objects and return to the bat as

Figure 12-11 *Bats are the only flying mammals. This fruit-eating bat is carrying a fig in its mouth.*

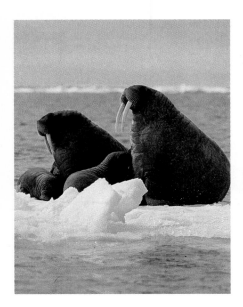

Figure 12-12 *Although most mammals are <u>herbivores, or plant eaters</u>, some are <u>carnivores, or flesh eaters</u>. Flesh eaters have large pointed teeth called canines. Walruses have especially large canines, called tusks.*

Activity

The Fastest Runner

The cheetah is the fastest land animal and can run at speeds of up to 100 kilometers per hour. How far can it run in a second?

echoes. By listening to these echoes, the bat knows where objects are. Bats that hunt insects such as moths also use this method to find their prey.

There are two types of bats: fruit eaters and insect eaters. Fruit-eating bats are found in tropical areas, such as Africa, Australia, India, and the Orient. Insect-eating bats live almost everywhere.

Flesh-Eating Mammals

The ground is frozen solid with ice. Great icebergs move slowly in the sea. The shoreline is almost impossible to see through the ice and snow. The chilling wind makes the air feel colder than it already is. Yet, even in this brutal Arctic environment, there is life. In the distance, a group of walruses pull themselves out of the water onto a sheet of floating ice. As they stretch out on the ice, these large animals resemble sunbathers on a beach.

The frozen sheets of ice and freezing waters of the Arctic are home for the walruses. They are able to live in this freezing environment because they have a layer of fat, called blubber, under their skin that keeps body heat in. In addition to their large size, another very noticeable feature of walruses is their long ivory tusks. These tusks are really special teeth called **canines** (KAY-nighns) that point downward and may grow to 100 centimeters in length.

You also have canines; two in your top set of teeth and two on the bottom. To locate your upper canines, look at your top set of teeth in a mirror. Find your **incisors** (in-SIGH-zers). They are your four front teeth, which are used for <u>biting</u>. On one side of the incisors is a tooth that comes to a point. These teeth are your canines.

Unlike most flesh-eating mammals, walruses do not use their canines for tearing and shredding meat. Instead, the walruses use their tusks to defend themselves from polar bears. The walruses also use their tusks as hooks to help them when climbing onto ice.

All of the mammals in this group, including the walruses, are **carnivores** (KAR-ni-vorz), or flesh eaters. Carnivores are predators. Most carnivores, such as lions, wolves, and bears, have very muscular legs that help them to chase other animals. Carnivores also have sharp claws on their toes to help them hold their prey. Most land-living carnivores include any members of the dog, cat, and bear families. Sea-living carnivores include otters, sea lions, seals, and skunks.

Figure 12-13 *Although most mammals run from a predator, this baboon battles a leopard face to face.*

Career: *Animal Technician*

HELP WANTED: ANIMAL TECHNICIAN Completion of a two-year animal technology program required. Experience handling animals and knowledge of laboratory procedures desirable. Needed to assist veterinarian.

A veterinarian and assistant are called to a farm to treat a horse. The horse had difficulty chewing and swallowing and now is shaking violently. The veterinarian discovers that the horse was injured by a nail sticking out of a board in the horse's stall.

The vet's assistant prepares the medicine that will make the horse well. Then the vet injects the medicine into the horse. The assistant records the visit.

The vet's assistant is an **animal technician,** someone who has had training in assisting vets and working in laboratories and animal research. They work on farms, in kennels and pounds, in hospitals, and in laboratories.

Animal technicians must work under the supervision and instruction of a veterinarian. An animal technician's duties include record keeping, specimen collection, laboratory work, and

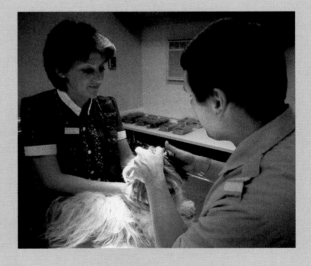

wound dressing. They also help with animals and equipment during surgery.

Patience, compassion, and a willingness to be involved with animal health care are important qualities for one interested in becoming an animal technician. To receive more information about this career, write to the American Veterinary Medical Association, 930 North Meacham Road, Schaumburg, IL 60196.

Figure 12-14 *The armor-plated armadillo* (left) *and two-toed sloth* (right) *are examples of toothless mammals.*

ACTIVITY

Useful Mammals

Visit your library to find out which mammals have benefited people. On a sheet of paper, make a list of these mammals. Beside each mammal, indicate how it benefited people. Discuss with your class whether the uses listed have been harmful, helpful, or had no effect upon the mammal. Was it necessary for people to use these mammals for their own survival?

"Toothless" Mammals

Although "true" anteaters belong to this group of mammals, they are the only members of the group that actually have no teeth. The other members, the armadillos and the sloths, have poorly developed teeth.

Unlike the spiny anteaters mentioned earlier in this chapter, the true anteater does not lay eggs. The young remain inside the female until they are fully developed. However, both types of anteaters have something in common—a long, sticky tongue that is used to catch insects.

The second group of "toothless" mammals are the armadillos. They live in the southern parts of the United States and in Central and South America. These mammals eat plants, insects, and small animals. The most striking feature of the armadillo is its protective, armorlike coat. In fact, the word "armadillo" comes from Spanish, meaning armored.

A type of armadillo called the nine-banded armadillo is the only "toothless" mammal found as far north as the United States. Its special feature is that the female always gives birth to identical quadruplets! This means that the four young are always the same sex and are exactly alike.

Sloths are the third type of "toothless" mammals. There are two kinds of sloths: the two-toed sloth and the three-toed sloth. They eat leaves and fruits and are extremely slow-moving creatures. Sloths spend most of their lives hanging upside down in trees. They can spend up to 19 hours a day resting in this position.

Trunk-Nosed Mammals

Holding its trunk high in the air, the elephant moves clumsily into the deep river. Little by little, the water seems to creep up the elephant's body. Will it drown? The answer comes a few seconds later as the huge animal actually begins to swim!

To an observer on the shore, nothing can be seen of the elephant except its trunk, through which the animal breathes in air. The trunk is the distinguishing feature of all elephants. And it is an amazingly complicated structure whose many kinds of movements are controlled by no fewer than 40,000 muscles!

Elephant trunks are powerful enough to tear large branches from trees. Yet the same trunk is capable of very delicate movements, such as picking up a single peanut thrown by a child at a zoo. These movements are made possible by the work of those 40,000 muscles and the brain that directs them.

Elephants are the largest land animals. There are two kinds of elephants: African and Asiatic. As their names suggest, African elephants live in Africa and Asiatic elephants in Asia, especially in India and

Figure 12-15 *Elephants are the only trunk-nosed mammals. The larger ears of the African elephant* (left) *distinguish it from the Asiatic elephant* (right).

Migration of Mammals

Certain mammals migrate, or move, to places that offer better living conditions. Using posterboard and colored pencils, draw maps that trace the migration of the following mammals: North American bat, African zebra, American elk, and gray whale.

At the bottom of each map, give the reasons why each particular mammal migrates. Display these maps on a bulletin board at school.

Southeast Asia. Although there are a number of differences between the two kinds of elephants, the most obvious one is ear size. The ears of African elephants are much larger than those of their Asiatic cousins.

Hoofed Mammals

What do pigs, camels, horses, and rhinoceroses have in common? No much at first glance. They could not look more different. Yet look again—down where these animals meet the ground—and you see a common characteristic. The feet of these animals end in hoofs—two different kinds of hoofs.

One kind of hoof has an even number of toes and belongs to such mammals as pigs, camels, goats, cows, and the tallest of all mammals, the giraffes. The other kind of hoof has an odd number of toes and belongs to mammals such as horses, rhinoceroses, zebras, and tapirs.

Hoofed animals are among the most important "partners" of human beings and have been so for thousands of years. People eat their meat, drink their milk, wear their skins, ride on them, and use them to pull devices used in farming.

Figure 12-16 *Mammals with hoofs can be even-toed or odd-toed. A giraffe* (left) *has an even number of toes, while the rhinoceros* (top right) *and tapir* (bottom right) *have odd numbers of toes.*

294

Gnawing Mammals

Hardly a day goes by that people in the country or even in cities do not see a gnawing mammal. There are more gnawing mammals than any others on earth. These mammals are commonly known as rodents.

Among the rodents are such animals as squirrels, beavers, chipmunks, rats, mice, and porcupines. As you might guess, what they have in common has something to do with the way they eat—by gnawing. The common characteristics are four special incisors that are used for gnawing. These teeth are chisel-like and constantly grow for as long as the animal lives. Because rodents gnaw or chew on hard objects such as wood, nuts, and grain, their teeth are worn down as the teeth grow. If this were not the case, a rodent's incisors would grow to be so long that the animal could not open its mouth wide enough to eat.

Some rodents, especially rats and mice, compete with human beings for food. They eat the seeds of plants and many other foods used by people. Rodents also spread serious diseases.

Rodentlike Mammals

Rabbits, hares, and pikas (PIGH-kuhz) belong to the group of rodentlike mammals. These mammals have gnawing teeth, similar to rodents. But unlike rodents, they have a small pair of grinding teeth behind their gnawing teeth. Another difference

Figure 12-17 *The most numerous of all mammals are the rodents. The harvest mouse (left) is the smallest rodent, while the capybara (right) is the largest.*

Unlike gnawing mammals, rodentlike mammals have four upper incisors instead of two.

Figure 12-18 *A pika is a close relative of the rabbit and hare, which are rodentlike mammals. Pikas live on the sides of mountains where they eat the sparse vegetation.*

Figure 12-19 *Two groups of mammals live in water. One group includes whales such as the baleen whale (left). The other group includes mammals called manatees (right).*

Activity

Museum Visit

Make plans to visit a natural history museum that has a large collection of mammals.

Prepare an outline in advance of all the types of mammals discussed in this chapter. Take your outline with you to the museum. While at the museum, make notes about these mammals that are in the museum's collection. Be sure to write down the information given about each mammal and note where that mammal fits into your outline.

Using your outline and the information that you gathered, prepare an oral report to present to your class.

between these two groups of mammals is that the rodentlike mammals move their jaws from side to side as they chew their food, while rodents move their jaws from front to back as they chew.

Water-Dwelling Mammals

"Thar she blows!" is the traditional cry of a sailor who spots the fountain of water that a whale sends skyward just before it dives. Sailors of the past recognized this sign of a whale, but they did not have the slightest idea that this sea animal was not a fish but a mammal.

Whales, along with dolphins, porpoises, dugongs, and manatees are intelligent. They have hair and feed their young with milk. They are all mammals—mammals that live in water most or all of the time but breathe air. They are also different from one another. Their differences have allowed scientists to place whales, dolphins, and porpoises in one group and manatees and dugongs in a second group.

Animals in the first group spend their entire lives in the ocean. They cannot survive on land. Animals in the second group live in shallower water, often in rivers and canals. They can move around on land but with great difficulty and only for short periods of time when they become stranded.

Primates

On a visit to your local zoo, you come upon a crowd of people standing and laughing in front of one of the cages. Hurrying over to see what the

Figure 12-20 *The hands and feet of many primates, such as these chimpanzees, are adapted for grasping.*

excitement is about, you hear strange noises. Carefully you make your way to the front of the crowd. What has caused all the excitement and noise? Soon you see a family of chimpanzees entertaining the crowd by running and tumbling around their cage. The baby chimpanzee comes to the front of the cage and extends its hand to you. You are amazed to see how much the chimpanzee's hand looks like yours. It is no wonder they are similar. After all, the chimpanzee along with the gibbon (GIB-uhn), orangutan (oh-RANG-oo-tan), and gorilla are the closest mammals, in structure, to human beings. These mammals, along with baboons, monkeys, and human beings belong to the same group of mammals—the primates.

All primates have eyes that face forward, enabling the animal to see depth. The primates also have five fingers on each hand and five toes on each foot. The fingers are capable of very complicated movements, especially grasping objects.

Primates also have large brains and are the most intelligent of all mammals. There is evidence that chimpanzees can be taught to communicate with people by using a kind of sign language. Some scientists have reported that chimpanzees can *use* tools, such as the use of twigs to remove insects from a log. Human beings, on the other hand, are the only primates that can *make* their own tools.

Figure 12-21 *The gorilla is the largest primate. This gorilla may grow to a height of 1.8 meters and may weigh 200 kilograms.*

SECTION REVIEW

1. What is the placenta?
2. What are canines? Incisors?
3. Define carnivore.

1. Structure through which the developing young receive food and oxygen while in the female
2. Canines are teeth used for tearing and shredding. Incisors are used for biting.
3. Flesh eater

LABORATORY ACTIVITY

For further instructions, see page T-44.

Classifying and Comparing Mammals

Purpose

In this activity, you will classify different mammals and compare their characteristics.

Materials (per group)

Reference materials that provide information on the 14 major orders of mammals

Pictures of mammals of different orders, cut from magazines and old texts

14 sheets of white construction paper

Tape

TABLE 1

Identification Code	Characteristics	Predicted Order

TABLE 2

Identification Code	Name of Organism	Correct Order

Procedure

1. Using reference books, make a list of the fourteen major orders of mammals and their distinguishing characteristics.
2. Fold each of 14 sheets of construction paper in half along its width.
3. Tape the sides of each sheet, forming a pocket envelope. Do not tape the top of the paper.
4. Study the pictures of mammals provided by your teacher. Each picture should have an identification code.
5. Label each pocket envelope with the name of an order.
6. Place each picture in the envelope you think represents that animal's order.
7. Copy Table 1 on a sheet of paper. Place the identification code from each of your pictures in the proper space.
8. In the second column of the table, fill in the characteristics of each of the animals based on your study of the pictures.
9. Fill in the order in which you classified each of the mammals.
10. Copy Table 2 on the same sheet of paper as Table 1. Check with your teacher to find out the correct order and the name of each mammal. Fill in this information in Table 2. Compare the correct order with your predicted order.

Observations and Conclusions

1. How do the monotremes differ from the marsupials?
2. What distinguishes the marsupials from the other mammals?
3. Which orders of mammals appear most similar? Explain your answer.
4. List the characteristics that all mammals have in common.

CHAPTER SUMMARY

12-1 Characteristics of Mammals

▪ Mammals are warmblooded vertebrates that have hair or fur.

▪ Female mammals feed their young milk from the mammary glands. Most mammals give their young more care and protection than do other animals.

▪ Mammals have well-developed brains.

▪ Mammals can be placed into three basic groups depending upon how their young develop. These groups are the egg-laying mammals, the pouched mammals, and the placental mammals.

12-2 Egg-Laying Mammals

▪ Like birds and reptiles, these mammals lay eggs.

▪ The spiny anteater and duckbilled platypus are examples of egg-laying mammals.

12-3 Pouched Mammals

▪ Marsupials are pouched mammals.

▪ The young of the marsupials are born only partially developed. They further develop in the pouch of the mother.

▪ The koala, kangaroo, and opossum are examples of marsupials.

12-4 Placental Mammals

▪ In placental mammals, the placenta provides food for the developing young inside the females.

▪ There are more than 20 groups of placental mammals.

▪ Insect-eating mammals include moles, hedgehogs, and shrews.

▪ Bats are the only flying mammals.

▪ Flesh-eating mammals, or carnivores, include sea-living animals such as walruses. The land-living carnivores include any members of the dog, cat, and bear families.

▪ Armadillos, anteaters, and sloths are "toothless" mammals.

▪ The only members of the trunk-nosed mammal group are the elephants.

▪ Hoofed mammals are divided into those with an even number of toes on each hoof and those with an odd number of toes. Even-toed mammals include pigs, camels, goats, cows, and giraffes. Odd-toed mammals include horses, rhinoceroses, and tapirs.

▪ Gnawing mammals, such as beavers, chipmunks, rats, mice, and porcupines, have chisel-like incisors for chewing.

▪ Rabbits, hares, and pikas are examples of rodentlike mammals.

▪ Mammals, such as whales, dolphins, porpoises, dugongs, and manatees are water-dwelling mammals.

▪ Human beings, monkeys, and apes are known as primates.

VOCABULARY   *Define the following terms.*

canine p.290   **incisor** p.290   **marsupial** p.285

carnivore p.290   **mammary gland** p.283   **placenta** p.287

herbivore p.286

CHAPTER REVIEW

Multiple Choice

Choose the letter of the answer that best completes each statement.

1. All mammals have
   a. pouches.
   b. <u>well-developed brains.</u>
   c. feathers.
   d. fins.
2. The kangaroo is a(n)
   a. <u>pouched mammal.</u>
   b. egg-laying mammal.
   c. placental mammal.
   d. gnawing mammal.
3. The only North American marsupial is the
   a. kangaroo.
   b. koala.
   c. platypus.
   d. <u>opossum.</u>
4. The young mammals that develop totally within the female belong to the group called
   a. egg-laying mammals.
   b. pouched mammals.
   c. <u>placental mammals.</u>
   d. marsupial mammals.
5. Which animal is an insect-eating mammal?
   a. whale
   b. elephant
   c. bear
   d. <u>mole</u>
6. The teeth used for tearing and shredding food are the
   a. carnivores.
   b. <u>canines.</u>
   c. incisors.
   d. all of these.
7. A "toothless" mammal is the
   a. skunk.
   b. mole.
   c. <u>armadillo.</u>
   d. camel.
8. The largest land animal is the
   a. blue whale.
   b. rhinoceros.
   c. <u>elephant.</u>
   d. giraffe.
9. An example of a water-dwelling mammal is the
   a. spiny anteater.
   b. <u>dolphin.</u>
   c. shrew.
   d. elephant.
10. Human beings belong to a group of mammals called the
    a. insect-eating mammals.
    b. rodents.
    c. <u>primates.</u>
    d. carnivores.

Completions

Fill in the word or words that best complete each statement.

1. All mammals are _____warm_____ blooded.
2. Female mammals feed their young with milk from the _____mammary glands_____.
3. An egg-laying mammal that is covered with spines is the _____spiny anteater_____.
4. The internal structure through which the developing young of some mammals receive their food is the _____placenta_____.
5. Another name for flesh-eating mammals is _____carnivore_____.
6. The teeth that are used for biting are the _____incisors_____.
7. Elephants are _____trunk-nosed_____ mammals.

8. Gnawing mammals are also known as _____rodents_____.

9. Rabbits are examples of _____rodentlike_____ mammals.

10. Mammals that have five fingers on each hand and five toes on each foot are called _____primates_____.

True or False

Determine whether each statement is true or false. If it is true, write "true."
If it is false, change the underlined word or words to make the statement true.

1. Mammals are <u>invertebrates</u>. F (vertebrates)

2. In <u>coldblooded</u> animals, the body temperature remains about the same all the time. *

3. The duckbilled platypus is an example of an <u>egg-laying</u> mammal. T

4. Animals that eat only plants are called <u>herbivores</u>. T

5. The <u>flying squirrels</u> are the only examples of flying mammals. F (bats)

6. Fruit-eating bats are found in <u>tropical areas</u>. T

* F (warmblooded)

7. Organisms upon which other organisms feed are called <u>predators</u>. F (prey)

8. A <u>squirrel</u> is an example of a gnawing mammal. T

9. Rhinoceroses are examples of <u>hoofed</u> mammals. T

10. The <u>dolphin</u> has the most well-developed brain of all the mammals. F (human being)

Discussion Topics   Answers appear on page T-44.

Write a brief paragraph discussing each of the following.

1. What are the three groups of mammals? How do they differ from one another?

2. Name two pouched mammals. How are their young born?

3. What features make carnivores good predators?

4. List ten groups of mammals and give an example of each.

EXPAND YOUR KNOWLEDGE

Overbeck, C. *Lions*. Minneapolis, Minn.: Lerner.
   The author traces the life history of lions from birth through adulthood.

Coming Up······SCIENCE GAZETTE·····································

Starting on the next page you will find three special articles. The first tells an exciting story about a scientist. The second tells about a battle of ideas. And the last looks into the future. Each of the articles has been written so you will enjoy reading it. As you read, you may want to jot down thoughts that come to mind. You might then write a report telling what you thought about the articles. Or you might just want to read the articles for the fun of it.

SCIENCE GAZETTE

The articles of this *Science Gazette* have been carefully chosen and designed to inspire and motivate students of all levels in their study of science. Each article is related to one or more topics presented in the unit. See the "Science Reading Skills" section in your Teachers' Resource Book for specific activities and handouts. Also, for further instructions, see page T-45 in this book.

Jane Goodall and the Chimps of Gombe Stream

Deep in the heart of the African jungle, Jane Goodall has been doing research among the wild animals. She is studying one of our closest living relatives, the chimpanzee.

Goodall has always wanted to study the animals in Africa. When she was a young girl, she was inspired by Rudyard Kipling's jungle tales. Ever since reading Kipling's vivid descriptions of the jungle and its inhabitants, Goodall has known where she wanted to spend her time.

For more than 20 years, Goodall has lived at Gombe Stream, Tanzania's Game Preserve on Lake Tanganyika. She is both an ethologist, a person who studies animal behavior, and a primatologist, a person who studies primates. She hopes that her studies will help scientists better understand prehistoric and present-day humans.

In 1960, she stepped off a small boat and came face to face with the majestic mountains of Africa. Over the years, she has learned to live with blistering heat and drenching rain. She has learned how to travel in a country with deep valleys, high mountains, and steep gorges. She has adjusted to living among threatening animals such as cobras and leopards.

But for the first few months after her arrival, Goodall was in despair. Until she discovered wild pig and baboon trails, she had to fight her way through dense underbrush to do her research. Although she could hear the loud calls of the chimps and the rustling of the

302

Chimps often chew leaves, which they then use as "sponges" to soak up drinking water from places such as hollows in logs.

leaves as the chimps moved, she rarely saw them. They would always run when they heard her approaching. After eight months, Goodall had not come within 500 yards of the chimps. She was about to give up!

Suddenly her luck changed. A chimp she had named David Greybeard came shyly to her camp one day. He continued coming to the camp every day. After two weeks of observing her camp, David Greybeard actually took a banana from Goodall's hand. The other chimps, after seeing their leader's bold move, gradually allowed Goodall to get close to them too.

At about the same time, Goodall began to make some amazing discoveries. One of the most important is that chimps use objects as tools. Once again, David Greybeard was the star of the show. Goodall saw David Greybeard and a female chimp she had named Flo strip the leaves from thin branches. They then went over to a termite mound. For protection, termites seal the tops of their tunnels. Chimps look for these protective coverings and peel them off. Goodall watched as David and Flo dipped their branches into the tunnels and pulled them out covered with termites. The chimps then ate the termites off the sticks, just as you might take a piece of meat from a fork. Goodall also noticed that the chimps would go out of their way to select sticks and carry them to termite nests that were far away.

This behavior seems to show that the chimps not only are able to use tools, but can think about their use ahead of time.

In time, Goodall was able to observe other chimp behavior. She saw another male, Evered, strip the leaves off a small branch and stuff them into his mouth. He chewed them for a short time and took them out of his mouth. He then dipped them, like a sponge, into a fallen log to get water. Goodall observed that the other chimps also used leaves to get water. So she collected some leaves and chewed them in order to understand what the chimps were doing. She found that chewing the leaves before dipping them helped to increase their absorbency.

When Goodall is not at Gombe Stream, she and her son live in Palo Alto, California, where she does laboratory research. However, she much prefers studying in the wild. Even in California, she keeps in touch with what is happening at Gombe by corresponding with her assistants there. She has lived among the wild chimps for more than twenty years. If asked why she chooses to live her life this way, Goodall replies that it is her "inborn love of the place and the beasts."

Jane Goodall (left) and companion observe the behavior of an adult and a young chimp.

Bathed in early morning light, a herd of large, dark brown sambar deer grazes on a grassy hillside at the edge of a forest in southern Asia. Suddenly, one of the deer raises its head in alarm and sniffs the air. Soon the entire herd is wary and watchful—ready to flee in an instant.

Conservationists to the Rescue?

The reason for their alarm quickly becomes obvious. Emerging from the woods a mere 225 meters away, a tiger strides up the hillside. The big cat's powerful muscles ripple as it moves. For a moment, the tiger stops and turns its head toward the deer. Then it continues on its way. This morning, at least, the tiger is not hungry. The deer are left to graze in peace.

Tigers are a vanishing species. They have disappeared from many parts of Asia where they were once common. In an effort to save them, conservation groups such as the World Wildlife Fund have raised more than one million dollars. Some of the money has been spent on research into tiger behavior. And the rest of the money has been used to establish preserves in the wild where the cats are protected.

To some extent, the effort has been successful. India now has 11 preserves for tigers. In some of these protected areas, the cat population is increasing once more. Conservationists are hopeful that tigers can continue to live in the wild.

But not everyone wants tigers living in the wild. In areas near some of India's preserves, tigers have killed both animals and people. Some Indians living near preserves oppose the government's attempts to save the tiger. They feel the tiger is not a species that should be saved, but a threat that should be removed.

A Fight to the Finish

Each year, more plants and animals become endangered. As conservationists work to save them, questions often arise about whether all species of living things should be saved. And if not all, which ones should be saved?

The answers are not simple. Some situations involve human needs versus the needs of animals. Other situations require a decision about which species is worth more time, effort, and money. For example, should developers be prevented from building in the Pine Barrens forest of New Jersey if the construction endangers a type of moth that lives there? Or is it worth thousands of dollars to save a kind of sparrow that lives only in a small part of Florida near Cape Canaveral?

Facing the Facts

To do their job, conservationists have to face tough questions like these. Some leading conservationists are very practical about the issues. Norman Meyers, for example, is a well-known environmental scientist. He notes that by the end of the 1980s, one species an hour, counting insects and other invertebrates, will disappear.

"Sad to say," Meyers writes, "the question is not how to save *all* these species; we just do not have the resources to rescue more than a small fraction."

Meyers suggests that first the value of each species be determined. The decision would be based on economics, the environment, and the survival of people. Then, the most valuable species should receive help first.

For example, in the African country of Kenya, lions are a big tourist attraction. Tourism brings lots of money to the country. Therefore, lions may be worth saving.

A tropical plant called the periwinkle is the source of two drugs used to treat cancer. And the venom of the Malayan pit viper, a cousin of the rattlesnake, is used to stop blood clots that cause heart attacks. In Meyers' view, the periwinkle and the pit viper should be among the first to receive help.

Environmental scientists predict that by the end of the 1980s, one species an hour will disappear.

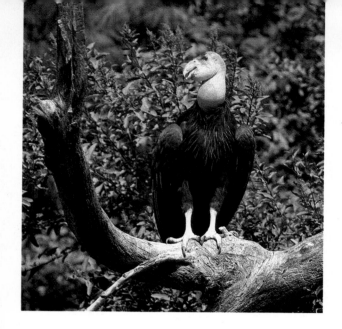

This California condor is one of several species of animals that faces possible extinction.

The Unknown Factor

It is clearly to our advantage to invest time and money in preserving such species of plants and animals. The trouble is, there are probably thousands of species that could be very valuable to people—only no one yet knows it!

Are we wiping out species that hold secrets to curing cancer or solving the energy crisis? Scientists and conservationists Paul and Anne Ehrlich of Stanford University think we might be. And they also see a further complication. When species disappear, the ecosystems, or environments, to which they belong are changed or even destroyed. All life on the earth depends on ecosystems. Ecosystems provide important services such as the maintenance of soils and the control of crop pests and transmitters of human disease. As the Ehrlichs write, "Humanity has no way of replacing these free services should they be lost . . . and civilization cannot persist without them."

The Ehrlichs cite yet another reason for saving as many species as possible—"plain old-fashioned compassion." For many conservationists, stopping the extinction of species is a moral issue.

Concern Around the World

The International Union for the Conservation of Nature and Natural Resources is a worldwide group associated with the United Nations. The union's position is that we are "morally obliged to our descendants and to other creatures" to act wisely when it comes to conserving plants and animals.

Most conservationists would agree that each time a species vanishes, the world is a bit poorer. Consider just the sheer beauty of many of the endangered plants and animals. The main reason for saving tigers and condors, for example, is that they are among the earth's most magnificent creatures.

Perhaps sadly, people tend to feel more concern for species that are pretty or striking than for those that are plain. The black rhinoceros of Africa and the Higgin's eye mussel of midwestern rivers are both in danger. The world knows about the threat to the rhinoceros. But few people know about the Higgin's eye, even though it is closer to extinction than the rhino.

How can conservationists decide which endangered species to help or, at least, to help first? Norman Meyers has an interesting approach. When many people are injured in a big disaster, physicians often first treat victims who are badly hurt but who will recover if treated promptly. Meyers suggests that the same approach be used for species in danger. First help those species that are in the greatest danger and that have a good chance of surviving extinction. Still, says Meyers, it will not be easy to decide which species to aid and which to ignore. Making these decisions, he adds, "will cause us many a sleepless night."

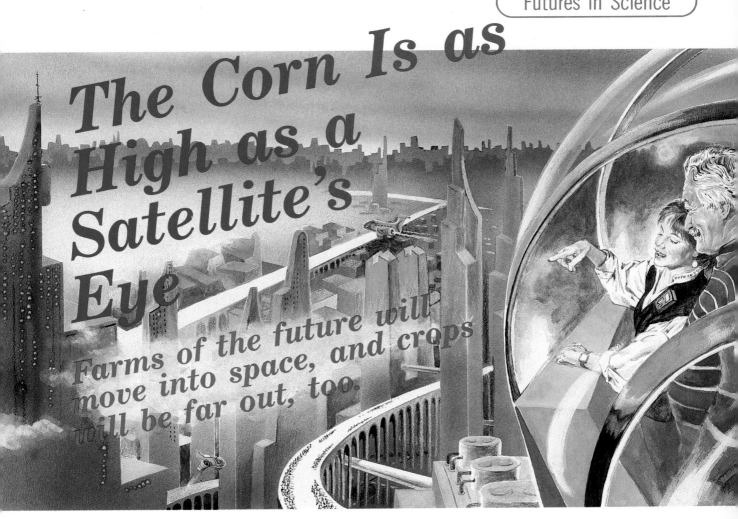

The Corn Is as High as a Satellite's Eye

Farms of the future will move into space, and crops will be far out, too.

The old man held his grandaughter's hand as the high-speed elevator zoomed 180 floors to the top of the Triple Towers. Out on the observation deck, the young girl stared in wonder at the huge city that fanned out to meet the horizon in all directions. Far below, crowds of little dots moved along in neat columns. "Look at all those people!" the girl exclaimed. "There must be millions of them."

The old man nodded. "Twenty-two million, to be exact," he said softly.

"But Grandpa, how do all these people keep from starving? I read that years ago people in cities all over the world couldn't get enough to eat. And there are even more people now than there were back then."

The old man frowned as he remembered his own youth. "Yes, that's true, Lisa," he said with a sigh. "Twenty percent of the world was going hungry when I was a young man in 1985. The farmers could use only a quarter of the earth's land for farming."

"Why couldn't they use more of the land, Grandpa?" Lisa asked.

"Well," he answered, "the rest was either sizzling hot deserts, barren mountains, or frozen tundras. Of the available farmlands, some had to be used for nonfood crops like cotton. Less food was available and more and more people were being born."

"Are people still starving, Grandpa?" Lisa asked in a worried voice.

"Well, dear, some are, but because of techniques that were developed during the late twentieth century, farmers can now produce more food."

"Oh, Grandpa, that sounds interesting. Will you tell me how more food is made?" Lisa asked.

"Of course I will, Lisa. Let's sit down on that bench and I will tell you all about it," the old man said with a smile.

Space Crops

"Look up there. What do you see?" the old man asked.

"Stars, Grandpa. Why?" the girl responded.

"Well, Lisa, much of the world's food is now being grown in space. We have space stations that contain rotating drums filled with plants. The rotation simulates the earth's gravity. The plants are bathed in fluorescent light, which simulates the sun. Crops that do not grow very tall or that grow in the ground, like lettuce, potatoes, radishes, and carrots, are grown in the drums," the old man stated proudly.

"Wow, that's neat, Grandpa. I never knew that salad came from outer space," Lisa said excitedly.

Laughing, the old man said, "Well, most of it does. We also have space stations where plants grow out of the sides of walls or are moved along conveyor belts through humid air."

Genetics Makes the Difference

"Is all our food grown in outer space, Grandpa?" asked Lisa with a curious look on her face.

"Why, of course not. Methods of growing plants on Earth have been improved too. When I was young, Lisa, twenty percent of the crops that were grown on Earth died off. Now, because of changes scientists have made in the genetic material of plants, very few crops die. The genetic changes have resulted in plants with increased resistance to temperature changes, diseases, herbicides, and harsh environments. Plants have been made resistant by several methods. Some plants were altered by a process called protoplast fusion," the old man said.

Short food plants such as lettuce can be grown out of the sides of revolving drums. Such devices could be used in orbiting space stations to grow food crops in the future.

Dwarf trees being grown right now may one day supply enough fruit to fill most of our needs.

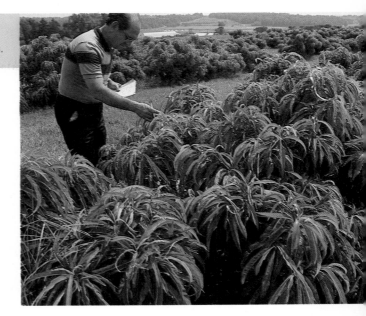

"That sounds complicated," Lisa said.

"It's not really very complicated," he replied. "The plant cell walls are dissolved by enzymes. The part remaining is called a protoplast. This protoplast is then fused to another protoplast from a different strain of the same plant or from an entirely different plant. The cell wall is regrown around the fused protoplasts, and a new plant develops. We now have many varieties of such plants. And you might think it strange, but many are smaller than those that used to be grown."

"Smaller? But that doesn't make sense," Lisa protested.

"Well, the smaller plants can produce as much as or more than the big ones because they have been genetically changed to be highly productive," explained the old man. "Also, more of them can be grown in the same amount of space. Two examples of the smaller plants are dwarf rice plants and dwarf peach trees."

"Wow, that's neat. Tell me more," Lisa said.

"All right. We also have plants that can get the nitrogen they need directly from the air. Plants need nitrogen to build amino acids, proteins, and other cell chemicals. In the old days, most plants got their nitrogen from the soil. But this process was using up all the nitrogen in the soil, and the plants didn't grow well. So fertilizer had to be added to the soil. Soybeans, legumes, alfalfa, and clover have always been able to use nitrogen directly from the air with the help of nitrogen-fixing bacteria. Other plants that can use nitrogen directly from the air were developed by combining genes from these nitrogen-fixing bacteria with genes from plants that normally took their nitrogen from the soil. Now almost all the plants take their nitrogen directly from the endless supply in the air."

"I didn't know that. Are any other plants different from the plants you saw when you were young?" Lisa asked.

"Oh, yes," the old man declared. "Many of the crops are now considered to be high-yield. That means they can be harvested faster than they could before, so that more can be grown. By redesigning the plants genetically, scientists have shortened the plants' growing time."

"It seems that genetic changes have kept people from starving," Lisa said thoughtfully. " That and the growing of food in space or on land."

"That's true," said her grandfather. "But there's still a third place. Some of the crops are grown in the ocean. This leaves more room for crops that can be grown only on land."

"That's a neat story, Grandpa," Lisa exclaimed.

"It's not a story, Lisa. It's the truth. But scientists still have to keep working to improve crop production because the population continues to grow," the old man observed.

Matter

For an overview of this unit, see pages T-46 to T-51. You may want to check the Laboratory Activity following each chapter, as well as the activities and investigations for this unit in your Teacher's Resource Book and Annotated Teacher's Edition, Laboratory Book, so that materials can be ordered, gathered, or prepared in advance.

Whipped by angry waves, a huge white form sweeps across the Antarctic Ocean. Carried eastward by icy currents, this giant raft of ice will circle the Antarctic continent like a ghost ship. Now and again, penguins will hitch a ride and then plunge into the sea in search of fish. To a sailor, the iceberg rising 50 meters into the sky spells great danger. No ship that strikes such an object is likely to survive. But the sailor also knows that a ship must stay far from the iceberg's glistening sides, for there is danger beneath the waves as well. It is there that most of the iceberg hides: more than 400 meters of it deep beneath the smashing waves. Perhaps the sailor does not know why so much of the iceberg sinks below the ocean's surface. The danger is the sailor's only concern. But as you read on, you will learn why there is more to the iceberg than meets the eye!

CHAPTERS

13 General Properties of Matter

14 Physical and Chemical Changes

Adelie Penguins hitch a ride on an iceberg.

13 General Properties of Matter

For a chapter overview, teaching strategies, answers to all activities, a list of A-V materials, and a chapter bibliography, see pages T-46 to T-48.

Consult your Teacher's Resource Book and Annotated Teacher's Edition, Laboratory Book for additional activities and teaching aids.

CHAPTER SECTIONS

CHAPTER OBJECTIVES

After completing this chapter, you will be able to:

13-1 Explain what is meant by the term matter.

13-2 Discuss the relationship between mass and inertia.

13-3 Define gravity and explain its relation to weight.

13-4 Explain what is meant by the term volume.

13-5 Provide a word definition and a mathematical formula for density.

As King Henry VIII of England watched proudly, his fighting ship the *Mary Rose* sailed slowly out of Portsmouth Harbor. The *Mary Rose* was among a fleet of English warships that set out on the morning of July 19, 1545, to battle an invading French fleet. In addition to a crew of 415 sailors, the ship carried 285 soldiers and a number of new, heavy bronze cannons.

But the *Mary Rose* never met the French ships. As the story goes, a sudden gust of wind sprang up, and in seconds the *Mary Rose* tipped over and sank to the bottom of the sea. Did this really happen? Or did the mighty ship actually sink at the hands of the French?

Partly to answer this question, teams of scuba divers began to search for the wreck of the *Mary Rose* in 1965. Some of the divers wore lead belts so that they could hover above the sandy ocean bottom in search of the *Mary Rose*.

In 1970, the divers found it. And with their discovery came the answer to its mysterious disappearance. The weight of the cannons had made the ship top-heavy. And when it tipped, water had flowed into the open spaces inside the ship, replacing the air. Without air inside it, the *Mary Rose* had sunk like a rock to the sea floor. It was as simple as that.

But perhaps there is still a mystery to solve. How can a diver wearing a lead belt hover in the sea, while a ship weighted with cannons and excess water plunges to the bottom? The solution to the mystery can be found as you read on.

Examining ruins of the Mary Rose

13-1 Matter

Stop what you are doing for a moment, and look around you. You are surrounded by a tremendous variety of materials. There are objects such as a desk, a chair, the book you are reading, and a pencil that you may be holding. Through the window you may see the sky and clouds. Observe your surroundings again. Then make a mental list of several of the objects you see. How would you describe them? Would you use such words as "large," "small," "red," "blue," "cold," "hot," "heavy," "light," "rough," "smooth," "sweet," and "sour"?

You see and touch hundreds of things each day. And although most of these things are probably very different from each other, they share one important quality. They are all forms of **matter.** Matter is what the world is made of. All materials consist of matter.

Through your senses of smell, sight, taste, and touch, you are familiar with matter. Some kinds of matter are easily recognized. Wood, water, salt, clay, glass, gold, plants, and animals are examples of matter that are easily observed. Oxygen, carbon dioxide, ammonia, and air are kinds of matter that are not as

Rocks, water, trees, clouds, air, grasses

Figure 13-1 *Many of the various forms of matter can be seen in this photograph. Can you identify at least five examples of matter?*

easily recognized. Are these different kinds of matter similar in some ways? Is salt anything like ammonia? Do water and glass have anything in common?

In order to answer these questions, you must know something about the qualities, or characteristics, that describe an object. Such qualities are called **proper-ties.** Color, odor, shape, and hardness are examples of properties of matter. These properties are very specific, however. They make it easy to tell one kind of matter from another. There are some properties of matter that are more general. Instead of describing the differences among forms of matter, general properties tell you how all matter is the same.

SECTION REVIEW

1. What is matter?
2. What is the difference between a specific and a general property of matter?

1. The material that makes up all things in the world
2. General property: one that all matter has; specific property: one that describes differences among forms of matter

13-2 Mass

The most important general property of matter is that it has **mass.** All of the objects you put on your mental list have mass. But what is mass?

Think of the materials you listed. They are all made up of a certain amount of matter. Mass is the amount of matter in an object. The mass of an object does not change unless some matter is either removed from the object or added to the object. Mass, then, does not change when you move an object from one location to another. You, for example, have the same mass whether you are on top of a mountain, at the bottom of a deep mine, or on the moon! Later in this chapter you will discover why this is a very important concept.

Suppose you were given the choice of pushing either an empty supermarket cart up a hill or a cart full of groceries up the hill. The full cart, of course, has more mass than the empty cart. And you know from experience that it will be easier for you to push the empty cart. Now suppose both carts are at the top of the hill and begin to roll down. Again, you

Figure 13-2 *Because of its large mass, a bowling ball is able to produce the results shown in this photograph. Would a hollow bowling ball or a tennis ball do the same?* No

Figure 13-3 *It's not really magic, just a demonstration of inertia. As the table on which this dinner is set* (left) *is moved quickly, the objects are suspended in midair for an instant* (right).

A good way to help your students remember the meaning of inertia is to tell them that "inertia" comes from the Latin word *iners*, which means lazy or idle.

Activity

Demonstrating Inertia

You can demonstrate that objects at rest tend to remain at rest by using a drinking glass, playing card, and coin.

Put the glass on a table. Lay a flat playing card on top of the glass. In the center of the card, place the coin. Using either a flicking motion or a pulling motion of your fingers, quickly remove the card so it flies out from under the coin. Can you remove the card fast enough so that the coin lands in the glass? You might need to practice a few times.

How does this activity demonstrate inertia? What happens to the coin if you remove the card slowly? How does this demonstrate inertia?

know from experience that the full cart—the cart with more mass—will be harder to stop than the empty cart. In other words, it is harder to get a cart with more mass moving; and it is harder to get it to stop again.

Scientists use this idea to define mass in another way. Objects that have mass resist changes in their motion. For example, if an object is at rest, a force must be used to make it move. If you move it, you notice that it resists your push or pull. In the same way, if an object is moving and you stop it, you see that it resists this effort too. The property of a mass to resist changes in motion is called **inertia** (in-ER-shuh). Thus mass is a measure of the inertia of an object.

The more mass an object has, the greater its inertia. So the force that must be exerted to overcome its inertia is also greater. That is why you must push or pull harder to speed up and slow down a supermarket cart if it is loaded with groceries than if it is empty.

Mass is measured in units called grams, g, and kilograms, kg. One kilogram is equal to 1000 grams. The mass of small objects is usually expressed in grams. A nickel, for example, has a mass of about 5 grams. The mass of this book is about 1600 grams, or 1.6 kilograms.

SECTION REVIEW

1. What is mass? 1. The amount of matter in an object

2. What is inertia? 2. The ability of a mass to resist changes in motion

3. How are mass and inertia related?
3. The more mass, the more inertia

13-3 Weight

In addition to mass giving an object inertia, mass is also the reason an object has **weight.** Weight is another general property of matter. In order to understand what weight is, you must know something about gravity.

You have probably noticed that a ball thrown up in the air soon falls to the ground. And you know that an apple that drops off a tree falls down, not up. The ball and the apple fall to earth because of the earth's force of attraction for these, and all other, objects. The force of attraction between objects is called **gravity.**

Gravitational force is not a property of the earth alone. All objects exert a gravitational attraction on other objects. Indeed, your two hands attract each other, and you are attracted to books, papers, and chairs. Why, then, are you not pulled toward these objects as you are toward the earth? In fact, you are! But the attractions in these cases are just too weak

Figure 13-4 *In his novel* From the Earth to the Moon, *author Jules Verne pictured this condition of weightlessness, or zero gravity, inside a spaceship (left). His prediction came true, as you can see from the orange-juice sphere and book floating in this astronaut's space capsule.*

Weight on Earth

Weight on moon = 1/6 weight on Earth

Weight on Jupiter = 2.7 times weight on Earth

Figure 13-5 *Because of differences in the gravity of the earth, the moon, and Jupiter, this boy's weight changes from one place to another. His mass, however, stays the same.*

for you to notice them. The earth's gravity, however, is great because the earth is so massive. In fact, the greater the mass of an object, the greater its gravitational force. How do you think the gravity of Jupiter compares with that of the earth? It is greater because Jupiter is more massive.

The pull of gravity on an object determines the object's weight. On earth, your weight is a direct measure of the planet's force pulling you toward the surface. The pull of gravity between objects weakens as the distance between the centers of the objects becomes greater. So at a high altitude, on top of a tall mountain for example, you actually weigh less than on the surface of the earth. Again, this is because you are farther from the center of the earth when you are on top of a mountain. And when an object is sent into space far from the earth, the object is said to be weightless. However—and this is a very important point—the object *does not* become massless. Mass, remember, does not change when location changes. So no matter what happens to the force of gravity, mass stays the same. Only weight changes.

ACTIVITY

Weight Changes

Suppose an inhabitant of Jupiter weighs 270 jupes on his home planet. How many jupes will he weigh on Earth? On the moon?

SECTION REVIEW

1. What is gravity?
2. What is weight?
3. What is the basic difference between mass and weight?

1. The force of attraction between objects
2. A measure of the force of gravity on an object
3. When the force of gravity changes, weight changes but mass does not.

13-4 Volume

You may wish to show your students the laboratory equipment used to measure mass and volume: a balance and a graduated cylinder, respectively.

Did you have this book on your mental list of examples of matter? Let's use the book to help discover another general property of matter. Suppose you could wrap a piece of paper around the entire book and then remove the book. How would you describe what is left inside the paper? You probably would use the word "space." For an important property of matter is that it takes up space. And when the book is occupying its space, nothing else can be in that same space. You might go ahead and prove this to yourself.

The amount of space an object takes up is called its **volume.** Volume is expressed in liters, L; milliliters, mL; and cubic centimeters, cm^3. One liter is equal to 1000 milliliters. How many milliliters are there in 2.5 liters? 2500 mL

Activity

Volume of a Solid

The volume of a liquid is easily measured by using a graduated cylinder. Can this method be used for a solid?

Fill a measuring cup with water. Note the volume of the water. Now place a small solid object in the measuring cup. You might choose a rock, a block of wood, or a bar of soap. If the object floats, use a piece of wire to push it under the water's surface. Note the volume again.

Subtract the original volume from the new volume. This difference in volume is the volume of the object.

One milliliter equals one cubic centimeter. For water only, a volume of one mL has a mass of one g.

SECTION REVIEW

1. What is volume?
2. In what units is volume commonly measured?

1. The amount of space an object takes up
2. Liters, L; milliliters, mL; and cubic centimeters, cm^3

Career: *Scuba Diver*

HELP WANTED: SCUBA DIVER To perform tasks under water for limited periods of time. Requires scuba diver certification with advanced scuba training.

On a warm, muggy day in August, a salvage diving crew finally raised a 29-meter-long sailing vessel off the bottom of the Los Angeles harbor. The vessel had been at the bottom of the harbor for a year after mysteriously sinking. The crew consisted of specially trained **scuba divers** who earn their livings by completing underwater tasks with the use of scuba gear.

The tasks of scuba divers differ from job to job. Their work may include inspecting dams, pipelines, and cables. Or it may involve recovering sunken objects, or doing underwater repair and construction. They may work from a boat, off a dock, or from the shore.

Scuba divers must wear wet suits to protect them from the cold temperatures of deep water. They must also wear air tanks. Anyone interested in scuba diving as a career can obtain more information by writing to NASDS Headquarters, P.O. Box 17067, Long Beach, CA 90807.

Collect at least six different kinds of objects as samples of matter. You might include rocks, pieces of wood or metal, and objects made by people. Identify each sample by its general properties and its special properties. Now write a sentence that describes each sample. Be sure to use the following words in your descriptions.

color

density

hardness

mass

matter

property

shape

volume

weight

13-5 Density

Suppose you were asked to determine which is heavier, wood or lead. Could you answer this question right away? How would you go about it? Perhaps you would suggest comparing the masses of both on a balance. You are on the right track, but there is one problem with this solution. What size pieces of lead and wood should you use? After all, a small chip of lead does not have a greater mass than a baseball bat made of wood!

You probably realize now that in order to compare the masses of two objects, you need to use equal volumes of each. In other words, you need to compare the way masses of objects are related to their volumes. When you do, you soon discover that a piece of lead has a greater mass than a piece of wood of the *same* size. A cubic centimeter of lead, for example, is heavier than a cubic centimeter of wood. An object's mass per unit volume is called its **density.**

All matter has density. And the density of a specific kind of matter is a property that helps to identify it and distinguish it from other kinds of matter.

Figure 13-6 *Salt water has a higher density than fresh water, so it's easy to float in the great Salt Lake, Utah.*

Since density is mass per unit volume, the following formula can be used to find the density of an object.

$$\text{density} = \frac{\text{mass}}{\text{volume}}$$

Density is often expressed in grams per milliliter. The density of wood is about 0.8 g/mL. This means that any piece of wood 1 milliliter in volume has a mass of about 0.8 gram. The density of lead is 11.3 g/mL. So a piece of lead has a mass about 14 times that of a piece of wood of the same size.

The density of water is 1 g/mL. Wood floats in water because its density is less than the density of water. What happens to a piece of lead when it is put in water? It sinks.

From the fact that ice floats, you now know that it too is less dense than liquid water. Actually, the density of ice is about 89 percent that of cold water. What this means is that only about 11 percent of a block of ice stays above the surface of the water. The

DENSITIES OF SOME COMMON SUBSTANCES

Substance	Density (g/mL)
Air	0.0013
Aluminum	2.7
Gasoline	0.68
Gold	19.3
Ice	0.9
Steel	7.8
Water (liquid)	1.0

Figure 13-7

Figure 13-8 *Although this iceberg may appear harmless to passing ships, it is really quite dangerous. Only the tip of the iceberg is visible. Nearly 90 percent of it lurks beneath the water's surface!*

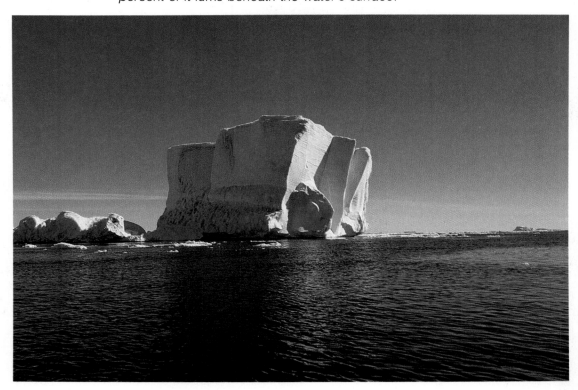

Archimedes and the Crown

The famous Greek mathematician and scientist Archimedes was once faced with a most difficult task. He had to determine whether a crown received by King Hieron was made of gold or a mixture of gold and silver. And he had to accomplish this task without damaging the crown!

Using books and other reference materials in the library, find out how Archimedes solved this problem. Make a report in which you describe Archimedes' discovery and his famous race through town.

rest is below the surface. This fact is what makes icebergs, like the one pictured on page 321, so dangerous. What is visible is only the "tip" of the iceberg. The rest of it lurks silently below the water's surface!

Can you now solve the mystery posed at the beginning of this chapter? An object floats in water if its density is less than 1 g/mL. In order for the scuba diver to sink in the water, the diver's overall density has to be greater than 1 g/mL. So the diver wears a lead belt to increase mass.

Now, the density of water increases as the water gets colder. So below the surface, the density of water is greater than 1 g/mL. At a certain depth, the scuba diver's density becomes equal to the water's density. The diver will not sink further.

With its large volume partly filled with air, the *Mary Rose* was less dense than water, and so it floated. The air was able to balance the added mass of the cannons. However, when its volume was filled with water, the added mass of the cannons made the *Mary Rose*'s overall density greater than that of the surrounding water at any depth. Down, down went the *Mary Rose*!

Figure 13-9 *The objects and liquids in this container have different densities. So some float while others sink.*

Air
0.001 g/cm³

Corn oil
0.93 g/cm³

Water
1.00 g/cm³

Glycerine
1.26 g/cm³

Corn syrup
1.38 g/cm³

Wood
0.85 g/cm³

Plastic
1.17 g/cm³

Rubber
1.34 g/cm³

Steel
7.81 g/cm³

Figure 13-10 *It is the density of an object, not its size, that determines whether it will float or sink in water. This large ocean liner (above) has an overall density less than 1 g/mL, so it floats in water. The density of this coin (left) is greater than 1 g/mL, and so it sinks.*

SECTION REVIEW

1. What is density?
2. What determines whether an object floats or sinks in water?

1. Mass per unit volume
2. Whether its density is less than or greater than that of water (1g/mL)

LABORATORY ACTIVITY

For further instructions, see page T-47.

Inertia

Purpose

In this activity, you will define mass in terms of the behavior of objects, showing that the more resistance to change of position, or inertia, an object has, the more mass it has.

Materials (*per group*)

Several objects of various masses that will fit into shoe boxes
Smooth table surface
Household broom
Several shoe boxes of similar size
Metric ruler

Procedure

1. Place one object in each shoe box and replace the shoe box's lid.
2. Set the box so that it hangs over the edge of the table by 8 cm.
3. Stand the broom directly behind the table. Put your foot on the straw to hold it in place. The handle should be pointing up in the air directly behind the box.
4. Now slowly bring the handle back away from the box.
5. When you release the handle, it should spring forward, striking the middle of the end of the box.
6. Measure how far the box travels across the table owing to the force of the broom.
7. Repeat the procedure with each of the boxes.

Observations and Conclusions

At this point, you will have noticed that when the same force—the impact of the broom handle—is delivered, the distance that the box and its contents move varies from box to box.

1. What part of the definition of inertia applies to your observations about the movements of the boxes?
2. Why do you think some boxes moved farther than others?
3. Open the boxes and examine the contents. What do you notice about the objects that moved the farthest from resting position? What do you notice about the objects that moved the least from resting position?
4. Mass can be determined on a balance, but do you now see another way to compare masses?

CHAPTER SUMMARY

13-1 Matter
- All objects are made up of matter.
- A quality or characteristic that describes an object is called a property.

13-2 Mass
- One property of matter is that it has mass. Mass is the amount of matter an object contains.
- The property of a mass to resist changes in motion is called inertia. Mass is a measure of the inertia of an object.
- Mass is commonly measured in grams and kilograms.

13-3 Weight
- The force of attraction between objects is called gravity.

- The pull of gravity on an object determines the object's weight.
- The weight of an object can vary, but its mass remains unchanged.

13-4 Volume
- The amount of space an object takes up is called its volume.
- Volume is expressed in liters, milliliters, and cubic centimeters.

13-5 Density
- The density of an object is its mass per unit volume.
- Objects with a density less than 1 gram per milliliter, which is the density of water, will float in water. Objects with a density greater than 1 gram per milliliter will sink.

VOCABULARY   *Define the following terms*

density p.320
gravity p.317
inertia p.316
mass p.315

matter p.314
property p.315
volume p.319
weight p.317

CHAPTER REVIEW

Multiple Choice
Choose the letter of the answer that best completes each statement.

1. Air, water, glass, and clay are examples of
   a. energy.
   b. matter.
   c. volume.
   d. properties.

2. Characteristics that tell how all matter is the same are called
   a. specific properties.
   b. universal differences.
   c. density numbers.
   d. general properties.

3. The amount of matter an object possesses is called its
a. <u>mass</u>.
b. volume.
c. density.
d. weight.

4. In describing mass, it is correct to say that
a. mass changes with altitude.
b. mass changes with location.
c. <u>mass remains unchanged</u>.
d. mass changes with weight.

5. An object's resistance to a change in motion is called its
a. density.
b. <u>inertia</u>.
c. mass.
d. volume.

6. The force of attraction between objects is
a. inertia.
b. weight.
c. density.
d. <u>gravity</u>.

7. As an object gets farther away from the earth,
a. its weight increases.
b. <u>its weight decreases</u>.
c. its mass decreases.
d. its weight remains the same.

8. The amount of space an object takes up is called its
a. <u>volume</u>.
b. density.
c. weight.
d. graduated cylinder.

9. The formula for finding density is
a. volume/mass.
b. volume × mass.
c. <u>mass/volume</u>.
d. mass/weight.

10. General properties of matter include
a. mass, shape, and density.
b. <u>mass and volume</u>.
c. weight, volume, and color.
d. volume and density.

Completions

Fill in the word or words that best complete each statement.

1. A quality or characteristic that describes an object is called a(n) ____property____.

2. The amount of matter an object has is called its ____mass____.

3. One kilogram is equal to ____1000____ grams.

4. The force that pulls objects toward the earth is called ____gravity____.

5. The earth's pull on an object determines the object's ____weight____.

6. As an object gets farther from the center of the earth, its weight ____decreases____.

7. In order to compare the masses of two objects, you must use equal ____volumes____.

8. An object's mass per unit volume is called its ____density____.

9. An object with a mass of 10 g and a volume of 5 mL will ____sink____ in water.

10. An ice cube floats because it is ____less____ dense than water.

True or False

Determine whether each statement is true or false. If it is true, write "true." If it is false, change the underlined word or words to make the statement true.

1. All objects are made up of <u>matter</u>. T

2. <u>Volume</u> is a measure of the resistance of an object to any kind of change in its motion. F (Inertia)

3. An object at rest tends to remain at rest because of <u>inertia</u>. T

4. The mass of a small object is usually measured in <u>liters</u>. F (grams)

5. The earth's force of attraction for all objects is called <u>mass</u>. F (gravity)

6. As the pull of gravity decreases, an object's weight <u>decreases</u>. T

7. As an object's weight decreases, its mass <u>increases</u>. F (stays constant)

8. The amount of space an object takes up is called its <u>volume</u> and is measured in liters and milliliters. T

9. One liter is equal to <u>100</u> milliliters. F (1000)

10. An object's mass per unit volume is called its <u>density</u>. T

Discussion Topics Answers appear on page T-48.

Write a brief paragraph discussing each of the following.

1. Air is matter, although it is less easily recognized than other kinds of matter. Using the general properties of matter, suggest two situations in which you could illustrate that air is matter.

2. "I have to lose weight" might be the reaction of a person who discovers that clothes fit too tightly. From a scientific point of view, discuss whether a weight loss will make the clothes fit better. What would be a more accurate way of stating the situation?

3. Aluminum is used to make airplanes. Cast iron is used to make heavy machines. How do the densities of these metals make them useful for these purposes?

4. The common mineral iron pyrite is often called "fool's gold" because it can be mistaken for gold. How would you go about determining whether a particular sample is iron pyrite or gold?

EXPAND YOUR KNOWLEDGE

Asimov, I. *A Short History of Chemistry.* Garden City, N.Y.: Anchor Books.
  This book provides a lively account of the efforts of many scientists to understand the structure and behavior of matter.

Dank, M. *Albert Einstein.* New York: Watts.
  With great feeling for the subject, the author presents a biography of Albert Einstein—his life and contributions. Excellent photographs help capture the personality of Einstein, and a list of books for further reading aids the student's research.

Lapp, R. E., and the editors of Time-Life Books. *Matter.* New York: Time.
  Read all about the forms of matter in this interesting book. You will enjoy looking at the many beautiful photographs.

14 Physical and Chemical Changes

For a chapter overview, teaching strategies, answers to all activities, a list of A-V materials, and a chapter bibliography, see pages T-48 to T-50.

Consult your Teacher's Resource Book and Annotated Teacher's Edition, Laboratory Book for additional activities and teaching aids.

CHAPTER OBJECTIVES

After completing this chapter, you will be able to:

14-1 Distinguish between a physical property and a physical change.

14-2 Describe the four phases of matter.

14-2 State the Gas Laws.

14-3 Identify the various phase changes.

14-3 Relate phase changes to changes in heat energy.

14-4 Distinguish between a chemical property and a chemical change.

All day long, the temperature had been steadily dropping. Only a few people working in the orange grove could remember a day as cold in that area of Florida. The branches of the orange trees were heavy with fruit that was not yet ripe enough for picking. If the temperature fell much lower, the juice in the oranges would freeze. The entire crop of fruit would be ruined.

Something had to be done quickly in order to save the orange crop. So workers lighted small fires in the groves. But they soon realized that this heat would not be enough to save the oranges. Suddenly, some of the workers carried large hoses into the grove. Racing against time and temperature, the workers sprayed the trees with water. As the temperature dropped, this water would freeze and turn into ice. Strange as it may seem, ice was being used to keep the oranges warm!

When the sun rose the next day and temperatures began to climb, the glistening ice that had covered the fruit trees melted away. The fruit was undamaged—cold but not frozen. The orange crop had been saved.

Was this some sort of magic? In a sense, yes. But it was magic that anyone who knows science can do. And as you read further, you will learn how freezing water can sometimes do a better job of keeping things warm than fire can.

Keeping oranges warm with ice!

14-1 Physical Properties and Changes

How would you describe a copper penny? Or a wooden stick? Well, after reading Chapter 13, you would probably say both the penny and the stick are matter. And because they are matter, they have mass, weight, volume, and density. You are using general properties of matter to tell how the penny and the stick are alike.

What else could you say about them? You might say a copper penny is reddish-brown, round, hard to scratch, and dense enough to sink in water. In contrast, a wooden stick is brown, long and narrow, easy to scratch, and floats in water. Now you are using specific properties of matter to distinguish the penny from the wooden stick. Properties such as color, shape, hardness, and density are called **physical properties.**

Now suppose you take the wooden stick and break it into pieces. Are the pieces still wood? To answer that question, you must determine whether the pieces are still the same kind of matter. In this example, they are. You changed the shape of the wood, but it is still wood. In other words, the wood that makes up the stick has not changed into another substance. Changes in which physical properties of a

Figure 14-1 *Various types of matter, each having its characteristic properties, can be seen in this photograph. Can you identify three types and some of their properties? Remember, invisible gases are matter!*

Wooden hockey stick: brown; long and thin with curved bottom; fairly hard but can be broken
Ice: solid; white; hard; turns to water; can be scraped
Cold air: gas; colorless; odorless; tasteless

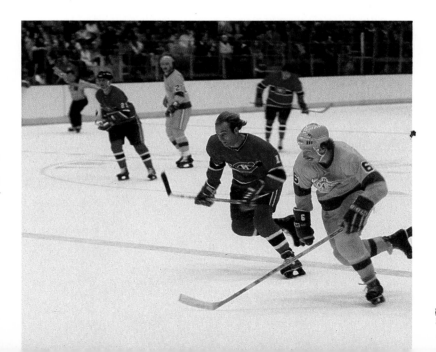

substance are altered, but the substance remains the same kind of matter, are called **physical changes.**

Breaking an object into pieces is one example of a physical change. Another example is dissolving a substance. You can easily dissolve a cube of sugar in a glass of warm water. The sugar disappears from sight, and the liquid remains clear. You might be tempted to think that somehow the sugar has changed its identity—that it is no longer sugar. But the sugar is still there, as you can tell by the sweet taste of the liquid. Taste, then, is another physical property of matter. Although the sugar has lost its white color and its original shape, it is still the same kind of matter. It still has its physical property of sweet taste. This physical property makes it easy to identify. However, scientists rarely use taste to identify substances. Why do you think this is so? Some substances are poisonous.

Figure 14-2 *Even after this karate expert breaks the three boards, the wood remains the same kind of substance. Breaking an object into pieces is a physical change.*

SECTION REVIEW

1. Give three examples of physical properties.
2. Give an example of a physical change.

1. Color, shape, hardness, density
2. Breaking an object into pieces, dissolving a substance

14-2 The Phases of Matter

Ice, liquid water, steam. Perhaps these three materials seem very different to you. Certainly you can use them in very different ways. You can cool a drink with ice, wash a car with liquid water, and cook vegetables in steam. And because they all look and feel different, you usually do not mix them up and, say, use steam to cool a drink!

Ice, liquid water, and steam, however, are all made up of exactly the same substance in different states. These states are called **phases.** Matter can exist in any of four phases. Ice, liquid water, and steam are three familiar phases of the substance water.

Figure 14-3 *Three familiar phases of the substance water are visible in this photograph. Can you identify them?* Ice, liquid water, water vapor

Solids

Cubes of ice, cubes of sugar, metal coins, wooden sticks, rocks, and diamonds are several examples of **solids.** And although they look very different, as sol-

Figure 14-4 *The white cubic crystals in this photograph (left) are sodium chloride, or table salt. They are growing on crystals of calcium sulfate, or gypsum. Crystals have a regular arrangement of particles, as shown in the drawing of the structure of sodium chloride (right).*

ids they share two basic characteristics. All solids have a definite shape and a definite volume.

All the tiny particles in a solid are packed very close together, so it keeps its shape. The particles cannot move far out of their places and, in most solids, the particles cannot flow over or around each other. In many solids, the particles are arranged in a regular, repeating pattern. Such a regular arrangement of particles is called a **crystal** (KRIS-tuhl). Solids made up of crystals are called **crystalline solids.** Common table salt is a good example of a crystalline solid. See Figure 14-4.

Crystals often have beautiful shapes that result from the arrangement of the particles within them. Snowflakes are crystals of water in the solid phase. If you look at them closely, you will see that all the

Figure 14-5 *Snowflakes (left) are six-sided crystals of water in the solid phase. The repeating pattern of the particles in ice can be seen in this computer-generated drawing (right) of a portion of the crystal.*

flakes have six sides. However, what is so amazing is that no two snowflakes in the world are exactly alike!

Have you ever played with sealing wax or silicone rubber? Both of these materials are solids. Yet from your experience, you may know that they do not keep their shapes permanently, as do crystalline solids. Left out on a table top for a long period of time, both of these solids will lose their shape and flatten out into a "puddle." Such solids that do not keep a definite shape are called **amorphous** (uh-MOR-fuhs) **solids.** Unlike crystals, the particles within amorphous solids are not arranged in a rigid way. So these particles can slowly flow around one another.

Some scientists think of amorphous solids as slow-moving liquids. Tar, candle wax, and glass are examples. Are you surprised to learn that glass actually flows? You might be able to see this for yourself if you can look at windowpanes in very old houses. Such windowpanes are thicker at the bottom than at the top because the glass has flowed slowly downward. Given enough centuries, the glass might flow completely out of its frame! Glass is sometimes described as a supercooled liquid. It is formed when a material in the liquid phase is cooled to a rigid condition, but no crystals form.

Figure 14-6 *Amorphous solids like this sealing wax lose their shape under certain conditions.*

Phases of matter differ in how easily their particles can be compressed. A solid is not readily compressed; a gas is most easily compressed.

Liquids

When you put water into a glass, it takes on the same shape as the glass. But when you pour that water onto a table or floor, it takes on a different shape. This behavior is a property of another phase of matter—the **liquid** phase.

Liquids have no definite shape. They take the shape of the container into which they are placed. So liquid water in a square container is square. And liquid water in a round container is round. Liquids can take on different shapes because the particles in them can flow easily around one another, even though they are close together.

Although liquids do not have a definite shape, they do have a definite volume. For example, pouring one liter of water into a two-liter bottle does not fill the bottle. The water does not spread out to fill the entire volume of the bottle. What happens if you try to pour two liters of water into a one-liter bottle?

The water will overflow.

Solid   **Liquid**   **Gas**

Figure 14-7 *The arrangement and movement of particles vary in a solid, a liquid, and a gas.*

Figure 14-8 *A gas has no definite volume and will expand to fill its container. If allowed to, the gas will expand without limit, which is what has happened to the gas in Donald Duck's left hand. A hole in that part of the balloon has enabled the gas to escape into the air.*

Gases

Have you ever pumped air into a bicycle tire or blown up a balloon? If so, you may have observed an important property of another phase of matter—the **gas** phase. Gases have no definite volume. They always fill their container, regardless of the size or shape of the container.

When air is pumped into a bicycle tire or a balloon, a large amount of gas is being squeezed into a small volume. Fortunately, the particles in a gas can be pushed close together.

Just the opposite can also happen. A small amount of gas can spread out to fill a large volume. The smell of an apple pie baking in the oven comes to you because gases from the pie spread out to every part of the room. In fact, if allowed to, gases will expand without limit. If not for the pull of gravity, all the gases making up the earth's atmosphere would do just that!

Like liquids, gases have no definite shape. They take the shape of their container. The particles that make up a gas are not arranged in any set pattern. So it is very easy for gas particles to move around, either spreading apart or moving close together.

The Behavior of Gases

The world inside a container of gas particles is not as quiet as it may seem to you. Although you cannot see the particles of gas, they are in constant motion. Whizzing around at speeds of about 500 meters per second, these bulletlike particles are constantly hitting one another. In fact, each particle undergoes about 10 billion collisions per second! Added to that are the collisions the particles make with the walls of the container. The effect of all these collisions is an outward pressure, or push, by the gas. The pressure is what makes the gas expand to fill its container. What do you think happens to a container when the pressure of the gas becomes too great? The container breaks or explodes.

BOYLE'S LAW Imagine you are holding an inflated balloon. If you press lightly on the outside of the balloon, you can feel the air inside pushing back. Now if you squeeze part of the balloon, what do you feel? You probably feel the air pressing against the walls of the balloon with even greater force.

This increase in pressure is due to a decrease in volume. By squeezing the balloon, you reduce the space the gas particles can occupy. As the particles are pushed a bit closer together, they collide with one another and the walls of the balloon even more. So the pressure from the moving gas particles increases. The relationship between volume and pressure is called **Boyle's Law:** The volume of a fixed amount of a gas varies *inversely* with the pressure of the gas. In other words, as one increases, the other decreases. If the volume increases, the pressure decreases. If the volume decreases, the pressure increases.

opposite

Activity

Boyle's Law

According to Boyle's Law, what will happen to the pressure of a fixed amount of gas if the volume is tripled? If the volume is halved? If the volume is doubled?

BOYLE'S LAW
As the volume of a gas decreases, the pressure it exerts increases. The volume of a fixed amount of gas varies indirectly with the pressure.

CHARLES'S LAW
As the temperature of a gas increases, the volume it occupies increases. The volume of a fixed amount of gas varies directly with the temperature.

Figure 14-9 *The volume of a fixed amount of gas varies inversely with the pressure of the gas and directly with the temperature of the gas.*

Activity

Temperature and Pressure of a Gas

A relationship between the temperature and pressure of a gas can easily be observed. Before going on an automobile or bicycle trip, feel the tires of your car or bike to see how hot or cold they are. Check the pressure in the tires. Then after traveling several miles, stop and again feel the tires and check the air pressure. Determine whether there is a change in the way the tires feel and in the air pressure. Describe the changes, if any, you observe and explain them.

CHARLES'S LAW   Imagine you have that inflated balloon again. This time you heat it very gently. What do you think happens to its volume? As the temperature increases, the gas particles absorb more heat energy. They speed up and move further away from one another. So the increase in temperature results in an increase in volume. If the temperature had decreased, then the volume would have decreased. This relationship between temperature and volume of a gas is called **Charles's Law:** The volume of a fixed amount of gas varies *directly* with the temperature of the gas. What do you think happens as the temperature of a gas drops? Try to support your answer by putting an inflated balloon in your freezer.

Boyle's Law and Charles's Law together are called the Gas Laws. The Gas Laws describe the behavior of gases with changes in pressure, temperature, and volume. *Its volume decreases.

Plasma

The fourth phase of matter is quite rare on the earth. It is called the **plasma** phase. Matter in the plasma phase is very high in energy. In fact, the particles contain so much energy that they are dangerous to living things. Luckily, plasma is not found naturally on the earth. It is, however, common in stars, such as the sun. Plasma can only be made on the earth by using equipment that produces very high energy. But the plasma cannot be contained by the walls of ordinary matter, which it would immediately destroy. Instead, magnetic fields produced by powerful magnets keep the high-energy particles in a plasma from escaping. One day, producing plasmas on the earth may meet most of our energy needs.

SECTION REVIEW

1. What are the four phases of matter? 1. Solid, liquid, gas, plasma
2. How is a crystalline solid different from an amorphous solid?
3. State Boyle's Law and Charles's Law.

2 . Crystalline: regular arrangement of particles, keeps its shape; amorphous: no rigid arrangement of particles, can flow
3. Boyle's: Volume of a fixed amount of gas varies inversely with pressure; Charles's: Volume of a fixed amount of gas varies directly with temperature.

Figure 14-10 *These eruptions on the sun are examples of the high-energy plasma phase of matter.*

14-3   Phase Changes

Ice, liquid water, and steam are all the same substance. What, then, causes the particles of a substance to be in one particular phase rather than another? The answer has to do with energy—energy that can cause the particles to move faster and farther apart.

A solid substance tends to have less energy than that same substance in the liquid phase. A gas usually has more energy than the liquid phase of the same substance. So ice has less energy than liquid water, and steam has more energy than both ice and liquid water. The greater energy content of steam is what makes a burn caused by steam more serious than a burn caused by hot water!

Because energy content is responsible for the different phases of matter, substances can be made to change phase by adding or taking away energy. And the easiest way to do this is to heat or cool the substance, allowing heat energy to flow into or out of it. This idea should sound familiar to you since you frequently increase or decrease heat energy to produce phase changes in water. You put

heating or cooling

You may wish to demonstrate to your students that during a phase change heat energy is absorbed but the temperature of the substance remains the same.

337

liquid water in the freezer to remove heat and make ice. On a hot stove you add heat to make liquid water turn to steam. You can now think of some common kitchen appliances as phase-changing devices!

Changes of phase are examples of physical changes. In a physical change, a substance changes from one form to another, but it remains the same *kind* of substance. No new or different *kinds* of matter are formed, even though physical properties may change.

Solid-Liquid Phase Changes

What happens to your popsicle on a very hot day if you do not eat it fast enough? Right—it begins to melt. **Melting** is the change of a solid to a liquid. Melting occurs when a substance absorbs heat energy. The rigid crystal structure of the particles breaks down, and the particles are free to flow around one another.

The temperature at which a solid changes to a liquid is called the **melting point.** Most substances have a characteristic melting point. It is a physical property that helps to identify the substance. The melting point of ice is 0° C. The melting point of table salt is 801° C, while that of a diamond is 3700° C.

Activity

Comparing Melting Points

How many times greater than the melting point of table salt is the melting point of diamond?

Figure 14-11 *As some solids absorb heat energy, they begin to melt, or change to the liquid phase.*

338

The opposite phase change, that of a liquid to a solid, is called **freezing.** Freezing occurs when a substance loses heat energy. The temperature at which a substance changes from a liquid to a solid is called the **freezing point.** Strangely enough, the freezing point of a substance is equal to its melting point. So water both melts and freezes at 0° C.

Substances called alcohols have freezing points much lower than 0° C. These substances are used in automobile antifreeze because they can be cooled to low winter temperatures without freezing. One such substance, ethylene glycol, when mixed with water can lower the freezing point of the mixture to −49° C.

The fact that freezing involves a loss of heat energy explains the "magic" worked by the orange growers you read about at the beginning of this chapter. The liquid water sprayed onto the trees released heat energy as it froze. Some of this heat energy was released into the oranges, preventing them from freezing and being destroyed.

Liquid-Gas Phase Changes

Have you ever left a glass of water out overnight? If so, perhaps you noticed that the level of the water was lower the next morning. Some of the liquid changed phase and became a gas. The gas then escaped into the air.

The change of a substance from a liquid to a gas is called **vaporization** (vay-puhr-uh-ZAY-shuhn). During

Figure 14-12 *The force of freezing water can cause a violent explosion. A cast-iron container about 0.6 centimeter in width is filled with water and placed in a beaker of dry ice and alcohol (left). As the water freezes and expands, a huge amount of energy is exerted against the walls of the container, causing an explosion (right).*

Figure 14-13 *The mist hanging over this forest is caused by the evaporation of rainwater, which then condenses to form liquid droplets that remain suspended in the air.*

this process, particles in a liquid absorb enough heat energy to escape from the liquid phase. If vaporization takes place at the surface of the liquid, the process is called **evaporation** (ee-vap-uhr-AY-shuhn). So some of the water in the glass left out overnight evaporated.

Evaporation is often thought of as a cooling process. Does this sound strange to you? Think for a moment of perspiration on the surface of your skin. As this water evaporates, it absorbs and carries away heat energy from your body. In this way, your body is cooled. Can you explain why it is important to sweat on a hot day? To cool the body, which otherwise would become overheated

Vaporization does not occur *only* at the surface of a liquid. If enough energy is supplied, particles inside the liquid can change to gas. These particles travel to the surface of the liquid and then into the air. This process is called **boiling.** The temperature at which a liquid boils is called its **boiling point.** The boiling point of water at the earth's surface under normal conditions is 100° C. The boiling point of table salt is 1413° C, and that of a diamond is 4200° C!

The boiling point of a liquid is related to the pressure of the air above it. Since the gas particles must escape from the surface of the liquid, they need to have enough "push" to equal the "push" of the air pressing down. So the lower the air pressure, the more easily the bubbles of gas can form within the liquid and then escape. Lowering the air pressure lowers the boiling point.

At high altitudes, air pressure is much lower and so the boiling point is reduced. If you could go many kilometers above the earth's surface, the pressure of the air would be so low that you could boil water at ordinary room temperature! However, this boiling water would be cool! Certainly you would not be able to cook anything in this water. For it is the heat in boiling water that cooks food, not simply the boiling process.

Gases can change phase too. If a substance in the gas phase loses heat energy, it changes into a liquid. Scientists call this change **condensation** (kahn-den-SAY-shuhn). You have probably noticed that cold objects, such as glasses of iced drinks, tend to become wet on the outside. Water vapor present in the surrounding air loses heat energy when it comes in contact with the cold glass. The water vapor condenses and becomes liquid drops on the glass.

Solid-Gas Phase Changes

If you live in an area where winters are very cold, you may have noticed something unusual about fallen snow. Even when the temperature stays below the melting point of the water that makes up the snow, the fallen snow slowly disappears. What happens to it? The snow undergoes **sublimation** (suhb-luh-MAY-shuhn). When a solid sublimes, its surface

Figure 14-14 _When water vapor in the air cools and condenses, water droplets form. If the droplets become large enough, they fall as rain. Rain can vary from a drizzle to a heavy downpour._

Figure 14-15 *Certain substances such as iodine* (left) *and dry ice* (right) *sublime, or go from the solid phase directly to the gas phase.*

In this photo of iodine subliming, the purple cloud at the top is the iodine vapor. Scattered throughout you can see the crystals of iodine re-forming as small black lines.

Activity

An Almost Ruined Day

Using the following words, write a 250-word story about a day on which your birthday party was almost a disaster.

boiling	melting
freezing	phase
crystal	physical change
evaporation	solid
liquid	sublimation

particles escape *directly* into the gas phase. They do not pass through the liquid phase.

A substance called dry ice is often used to keep other substances, such as ice cream, very cold. Dry ice is solid carbon dioxide. At ordinary pressures, it cannot exist in the liquid phase. So as it absorbs heat energy, it sublimes directly to the gas phase. By absorbing and carrying off heat energy as it sublimes, dry ice keeps materials that are near it cold and dry. Just think what would happen to an ice cream cake if it were packed in regular ice rather than dry ice!

SECTION REVIEW

1. Define melting and freezing.
2. Explain the difference between evaporation and condensation.
3. What is sublimation?

1. Change of solid to liquid; change of liquid to solid
2. Evaporation: liquid-to-gas change at surface of liquid; condensation: gas-to-liquid change
3. Change of solid directly to gas

14-4 Chemical Properties and Changes

At the beginning of this chapter, you learned that you could easily tell a copper penny from a wooden stick by its physical properties. It was easy to see the differences in color, shape, hardness, and density. But now suppose you have to distinguish between two gases—oxygen and hydrogen. Both are colorless, odorless, and tasteless. Since they are gases, they have no definite shape or volume. And although each has a specific density, you cannot drop them into water to see what happens! So in this case, physical properties are not very helpful in identifying the gases.

Fortunately, physical properties are not the only way to identify a substance. Both oxygen and hydrogen can turn into other substances and take on new identities. And the way in which they do this can be useful in determining the gas. The properties that describe how a substance changes into other new substances are called **chemical properties.**

If you collected some hydrogen in a test tube and put a glowing wooden stick in it, you would hear a loud pop. The pop results when hydrogen combines with oxygen in the air. The hydrogen is burning. The ability to burn is called **flammability** (flam-uh-BIL-uh-tee). It is a chemical property. A new kind of

Career: *Firefighter*

HELP WANTED: FIREFIGHTER High school diploma required. Must pass written test and physical examinations. Minimum age 18. Needed for firefighting team.

It was a dry October day when the field caught fire. Responding to the alarm sounded at their fire station, the men and women quickly jumped onto the trucks and raced to the burning field. Their first task was to keep the fire from spreading. The team began by clearing a strip of land a short distance from the approaching flames. They then set another fire between the cleared strip and the raging flames. This would keep the fire contained to a small area. Finally the fire was put out with water.

The brave individuals who often risk their lives in the line of duty are **firefighters.** It is their job to protect people and property from the thousands of fires that occur each year. In doing their job, they are sometimes exposed to explosive, flammable, or poisonous materials.

The duties of firefighters include driving emergency vehicles, hooking up hoses and pumps, setting up ladders, and rescuing victims. Some firefighters are trained to conduct fire safety checks in buildings and homes, while others investigate false alarms and suspicious fires. If you are interested in this career, write to the Department of Fire Protection and Safety Technology, Oklahoma State University, 303 Campus Fire Station, Stillwater, OK 74078.

Figure 14-16 *Burning is a chemical change in which oxygen combines with another substance and produces heat and light.*

Figure 14-17 *Rusting is a chemical change in which iron slowly combines with oxygen to form rust, or iron oxide.*

matter forms as the hydrogen burns. This substance is water—a combination of hydrogen and oxygen.

Oxygen is not a flammable gas. So you can distinguish it from hydrogen through the chemical property of flammability. However, although oxygen does not burn, it does support the burning of other substances. A glowing wooden splint placed in a test tube of oxygen will continue to burn until the oxygen is used up. This ability to support burning is another example of a chemical property.

The changes that substances undergo when they turn into other substances are called **chemical changes.** Chemical changes are closely related to chemical properties, but they are not the same. For example, the *ability* of a substance to burn is a chemi-

Figure 14-18 *This beautiful fireworks display is the result of a chemical change in which substances such as magnesium, phosphorus, and sulfur combine very rapidly with oxygen.*

cal property. However, the *process* of burning is a chemical change. Figures 14-16 to 14-18 show several examples of chemical changes.

Another name for a chemical change is a **chemical reaction.** Chemical reactions often involve chemically combining different substances. For example, during the burning of coal, oxygen combines chemically with carbon—the substance that makes up most of the coal. This combining reaction produces a new substance—carbon dioxide. The carbon and oxygen have changed chemically. They no longer exist in their original forms.

The ability to use and control chemical reactions is an important skill. For chemical reactions produce a range of products from glass to pottery glaze to medicines. Your life is made easier and more enjoyable because of the products of chemical reactions: synthetic fibers such as nylon, plastics, soaps, building materials, even foods you eat. The next time you eat cheese or a slice of bread, remember that you are eating the product of a chemical reaction!

SECTION REVIEW

1. Give two examples of chemical properties.
2. Give an example of a chemical change.

1. Flammability, ability to support combustion
2. Burning

LABORATORY ACTIVITY

For further instructions, see page T-50.

Conservation of Mass

Purpose

In this activity, you will prove that changes in the appearance of substances, whether chemical or physical, do not change the masses of the substances.

Materials (per group)

1 large test tube and stopper
1 small test tube
3 beakers
Balance
Potassium thiocyanate, KSCN
Ferric nitrate, $Fe(NO_3)_3$
Flask with stopper or peanut butter jar with screw cap
Several chunks of rock salt
Water

Stopper

Large tube with $Fe(NO_3)_3$

Small tube with KSCN

Beaker to hold tubes

Balance pan

Procedure

A. *Chemical Change*

1. Fill a large beaker with 100 mL of water. Then add 1.0 gram of KSCN to the beaker.
2. Fill another beaker with 100 mL of water. To this beaker add 2.4 grams of $Fe(NO_3)_3$. **CAUTION:** *KSCN and $Fe(NO_3)_3$ are poisonous if swallowed.*
3. Fill half of the small test tube with the KSCN solution. Carefully put the small test tube into the large test tube.
4. Now put the $Fe(NO_3)_3$ solution in the large test tube so that it comes to a height no higher than the height of the solution in the small test tube. Put the stopper into the large test tube. Then place the test tubes into a beaker.
5. Determine the combined mass of the beaker and the test tubes.
6. Invert the large test tube to observe the reaction. A dark red material, $Fe(SCN)_3$, forms.
7. Redetermine the mass of the total system.

B. *Physical Change*

1. Pour enough water into the glass container to make it half full. Add a few pieces of rock salt to the water and seal the container.
2. Use the balance to determine the mass of the container and its contents.
3. After some of the salt has dissolved, determine the mass of the container and contents again.

Observations and Conclusions

1. Did the mass of the total system in procedure A change after you inverted the test tube?
2. In procedure B, was there a change in the mass of the container, water, and salt after some of the salt had dissolved?

CHAPTER SUMMARY

14-1 Physical Properties and Changes

■ Examples of physical properties of matter include color, shape, hardness, and density.

■ Changes in which physical properties of a substance are altered but the substance remains the same kind of matter are called physical changes.

14-2 The Phases of Matter

■ Matter can exist in any of four phases: solid, liquid, gas, and plasma.

■ A solid has a definite shape and volume.

■ A crystal is the regular, repeating pattern in which particles of a solid are arranged.

■ Amorphous solids do not keep a definite shape because they do not form crystals.

■ A liquid has a definite volume but not a definite shape. It takes the shape of its container.

■ A gas has no definite volume or shape.

■ Boyle's Law states that the volume of a fixed amount of gas varies inversely with the pressure. Charles's Law states that the volume of a fixed amount of gas varies directly with the temperature.

■ Matter in the plasma state is very high in energy.

14-3 Phase Changes

■ Phase changes are accompanied by either a loss or gain of heat energy.

■ Melting is the change of a solid to a liquid at a temperature called the melting point. Freezing is the change of a liquid to a solid at the freezing point.

■ Vaporization is the change of a liquid to a gas. Vaporization at the surface of a liquid is called evaporation. Vaporization throughout the liquid is called boiling.

■ The boiling point of a liquid is related to the air pressure above the liquid.

■ The change of a gas to a liquid is called condensation.

■ Sublimation is the change of a solid directly to a gas.

14-4 Chemical Properties and Changes

■ Chemical properties describe how a substance changes into other new substances.

■ Flammability, the ability to burn, is a chemical property.

■ When a substance undergoes a chemical change, or chemical reaction, it turns into a new and different substance.

VOCABULARY *Define the following terms.*

amorphous solid p.333
boiling p.340
boiling point p.340
Boyle's Law p.335
Charles's Law p.336
chemical change p.344
chemical property p.343
chemical reaction p.345
condensation p.341

crystal p.332
crystalline solid p.332
evaporation p.340
flammability p.343
freezing p.339
freezing point p.339
gas p.334
liquid p.333
melting p.338

melting point p.338
phase p.331
physical change p.331
physical property p.330
plasma p.336
solid p.331
sublimation p.341
vaporization p.339

CHAPTER REVIEW

Multiple Choice

Choose the letter of the answer that best completes each statement.

1. Color, odor, and density are
   a. chemical properties.
   b. general properties.
   c. physical properties.
   d. solid properties.
2. The phase of matter characterized by a definite shape and a definite volume is a
   a. solid.
   b. liquid.
   c. gas.
   d. plasma.
3. A regular pattern of particles is found in
   a. molecules.
   b. crystals.
   c. compressions.
   d. plasmas.
4. It is true that liquids have
   a. definite shape and definite volume.
   b. no definite shape but definite volume.
   c. no definite shape and volume.
   d. definite shape but no definite volume.
5. As the volume of a fixed amount of a gas decreases, the pressure of the gas
   a. decreases.
   b. remains the same.
   c. first increases and then decreases.
   d. increases.
6. As the temperature of a gas increases,
   a. the volume decreases.
   b. the volume remains the same.
   c. the volume increases and decreases.
   d. the volume increases.
7. The state of matter made up of very high-energy particles is
   a. liquid.
   b. plasma.
   c. gas.
   d. solid.
8. A solid changes to a liquid by
   a. evaporation.
   b. freezing.
   c. melting.
   d. sublimation.
9. Vaporization taking place at the surface of a liquid is called
   a. boiling.
   b. evaporation.
   c. sublimation.
   d. condensation.
10. Flammability is an example of a
    a. chemical property.
    b. physical property.
    c. chemical change.
    d. physical change.

Completions

Fill in the word or words that best complete each statement.

1. The phase of matter that has a definite volume but no definite shape is the _____liquid_____ phase.

2. Solids that do not have a definite shape and are sometimes considered slow-moving liquids are called _____amorphous_____ solids.

3. If the volume of a certain amount of gas increases, the pressure _____decreases_____.

4. High-energy particles that make up most of the matter on the sun and other stars are called the _____plasma_____ phase of matter.

5. The temperature at which a solid changes to a liquid is called the _____melting point_____.

6. The boiling point of water at the earth's surface is _____100° C_____.

7. As air pressure decreases, the boiling point of water _____decreases_____.

8. The process by which a gas changes into a liquid is called _____condensation_____.

9. The process by which a solid changes directly to a gas is _____sublimation_____.

10. Another name for a chemical change is a chemical _____reaction_____.

True or False

Determine whether each statement is true or false. If it is true, write "true." If it is false, change the underlined word or words to make the statement true.

1. Hardness, shape, taste, and melting point are <u>chemical</u> properties of matter. F (physical)

2. Particles that make up a <u>solid</u> are packed very close together. T

3. Common table salt, which has a regular, repeating arrangement of particles, is called <u>amorphous</u>. F (crystalline)

4. The particles of matter are spread farthest apart in a <u>liquid</u>. F (gas)

5. The pressure a gas exerts on the walls of its container is due to <u>collisions</u> of the particles of the gas with each other and with the walls of the container. T

6. The relationship between the temperature of a gas and the volume it occupies is described by <u>Boyle's Law</u>. F (Charles's Law)

7. A liquid will freeze when it <u>absorbs</u> heat energy. F (loses)

8. The process by which a liquid changes to a gas is called <u>vaporization</u>. T

9. Drops of water on the outside of a cold glass are water vapor that has <u>sublimed</u> into a liquid. F (condensed)

10. New substances having different properties are formed as a result of <u>physical</u> changes. F (chemical)

Discussion Topics   Answers appear on page T-50.

Write a brief paragraph discussing each of the following.

1. In New York City, it takes three minutes to make a soft-boiled egg. In Denver, Colorado, it takes longer. Explain why.

2. On a hot day, why do you feel cooler when you turn on a fan, even though the air that is being blown around is hot?

EXPAND YOUR KNOWLEDGE

Cobb, V. *Gobs of Goo.* New York: Lippincott.
   Using "goo" learn the how and why of many scientific processes.

Coming Up ·····SCIENCE GAZETTE·····

Starting on the next page you will find three special articles. The first tells an exciting story about a scientist. The second tells about a battle of ideas. And the last looks into the future. Each of the articles has been written so you will enjoy reading it. As you read, you may want to jot down thoughts that come to mind. You might then write a report telling what you thought about the articles. Or you might just want to read the articles for the fun of it.

Adventures in Science

The articles of this *Science Gazette* have been carefully chosen and designed to inspire and motivate students of all levels in their study of science. Each article is related to one or more topics presented in the unit. See the "Science Reading Skills" section in your Teachers' Resource Book for specific activities and handouts. Also, for further instructions, see page T-50 in this book.

W. LINCOLN HAWKINS

He Solved the Puzzle of the Aging Wires

Lincoln Hawkins examines a model of his "miracle" molecule. The molecule is that of a plastic used to protect wires from the weather.

When "Linc" Hawkins was twelve, his father and mother came home to find their son hard at work on a strange project. Linc was drawing plans for building a perpetual-motion machine. Such a machine never stops working. Linc thought that by laying out a series of tilted ramps, he would be able to keep a steel ball bearing rolling forever. What Linc did not realize was that friction and gravity would slow the ball down no matter how he tilted the ramps. But that did not stop Linc from trying to build his machine. After a few years of trying, however, Linc gave up the project. By then he had come to realize that the laws of physics make the invention of a perpetual-motion machine impossible.

Linc's impossible perpetual-motion machine was to be only the first in a series of challenges that awaited him. Although his first efforts had not been successful, they had convinced Linc that his future lay in science and engineering. Several years later, he attended Rensselaer Polytechnic Institute, from which he received a degree in chemical engineering.

Unfortunately for Linc, getting a degree was a lot easier than getting a job! For Linc graduated while the nation was experiencing the Great Depression of the 1930s. There were just no jobs available in engineering. But Linc Hawkins was not ready to call it quits. He went back to school and managed to earn a Master of Science degree from Howard University. A few years later, he received a higher degree, a Ph.D. from McGill University. And still he was not finished with his education. He continued his studies at Columbia University in New York. But was all this education leading anywhere?

Linc Hawkin's first break finally came in 1942. He was hired by the Bell System's Laboratories in New Jersey. There he worked on many chemical problems. But he did not find the problems challenging enough. So Linc convinced his supervisor to let him work with plastics. In this area, Linc believed, his training in chemistry and chemical engineering might be put to better use.

At this time, scientists were beginning to consider the use of plastics as insulators for electrical cables, including telephone cables. Insulators protect the cables. They keep the electricity in the wires. Up until then, lead had been used for this purpose. But lead was expensive, heavy, and in short supply.

Plastics known as polyethylenes, however, were lighter than lead. They were also inexpensive, flexible, strong, and water resistant. Some scientists felt that polyethylenes would make very good insulating coatings for electrical cables. But there was a problem. Tests showed that polyethylenes would wear out quickly when used outdoors. Exposure to light, heat, and moisture sometimes caused them to stiffen and crack. Was there a way to protect polyethylene against the weather?

This is where Linc Hawkins came in. He began to investigate how plastics become "old." And he also performed experiments to find ways of keeping the plastics "young." In other words, Hawkins was looking for a way to protect plastics from light, heat, and exposure to air. Each of these factors speeded up the aging of a plastic.

Hawkins soon realized that the key to keeping plastics young was to mix them with special chemicals. But which chemicals? The answer seemed simple. To keep a plastic safe from light, the plastic should be mixed with a chemical that did not break down when bathed in bright light for a long time. To protect a plastic against heat, the plastic should be mixed with a chemical that stood up to heat. And to keep a plastic from falling apart in air, the plastic should be mixed with a chemical that withstood long-time exposure to air.

Was there a single chemical with all these properties? And, if there were such a chemical, could it be mixed successfully with a plastic? Hawkins knew that such a single, miracle chemical probably did not exist. But

Hawkins and an assistant prepare to test wires coated with protective plastic.

there were different chemicals that were each strong in one way but not in others. So Hawkins began a search for a *combination* of chemicals. If he could find the right combination, he would be on the way to making the almost-perfect insulator.

Days stretched into weeks, weeks into months, and months into years as Hawkins worked on his problem. Little by little he began to solve it. First he found a chemical that could protect plastics against oxygen in the air. Then he found a chemical that could protect plastics against light. And finally he found a chemical that helped plastics stand up to heat.

Today, these chemicals and others like them make up the plastic that covers billions of kilometers of electrical wires. So the next time you pick up the telephone, stop and think how W. Lincoln Hawkin's career has made it easier for your call to reach its destination. And how ability, education, and hard work, even under the most difficult circumstances, can achieve great things.

Issues in Science

This geothermal plant in Iceland helps bring heat and electricity to about 75 percent of homes in the country.

Can the Energy of Volcanoes Be Harnessed?

For many years, people living in different parts of the world have used heat from within the earth as a source of energy. They have done this in many ways. For example, when underground water comes in contact with hot rocks, the water's temperature can rise to above its boiling point.

The water then begins to turn to steam. This causes a tremendous buildup of pressure. The pressure forces steam and hot water to come rushing out through weak spots in the earth's crust. This spouting, steaming water is called a hot spring.

Water from these natural hot springs has been used by people as a source of heat. In cases where the water does not come up naturally, wells have been drilled near hot springs. These wells bring underground steam and boiling water to the surface where they can be put to use.

Heat energy from deep within the earth is called *geothermal* energy. One of the most important uses of geothermal energy is producing electricity. Since 1904, steam from deep underground has been used to run machines that generate electricity. This has been done in Italy, New Zealand, and California. In a year, these power plants can produce the same amount of energy that is in 13 million barrels of oil. That's enough to meet the electricity needs of a city the size of San Francisco! And the energy is there for the taking.

Up until now, most geothermal energy has come only from underground places near natural hot springs. But some engineers say that we could drill into underground hot spots far from hot springs.

If the hot spot turns out to be dry, cold water from the surface could be pumped down into the hot rocks. There the water would turn into steam. The steam would rush to the surface. And it could be used to generate electricity.

But several things could make this hard to do. Rocks hot enough to do the job might be much deeper underground than expected. Drilling very deep could cost a lot of money. Also, the steam rising from deep in the earth might cool on the way up. As a result, it would not provide enough pressure to run

Hot water from deep within the earth can be used to generate electricity.

Electric power plant

Cold water

Hot water

Hot rock

machines that produce electricity. Another problem might be that the deep rocks might have so many cracks and holes that drilling would cause them to break up. Then the ground would collapse, destroying an expensive well and perhaps triggering an earthquake!

Taming a Volcano

Another way to use the earth's underground energy is to get it from an active volcano. This may seem like a crazy idea. After all, volcanoes are among the most powerful and "wild" natural furnaces on Earth. How can they be tamed? For one thing, the molten, or melted, rock of a volcano is often close to the surface of the earth. So there is no need to drill deep wells to get at the heat. Using the heat of volcanic rock is exactly what is done at the Eldfell volcano in Iceland.

Hot lava spurts freely from the ground in Iceland. However, in other parts of the country heat energy from inside the earth is trapped and used to warm homes and produce electricity. But there are risks in "taming" the earth's heat.

There spiral-shaped pipes are put into an area of hardening lava. Lava is molten rock that has reached the earth's surface. Water is then pumped through the pipes. The water is heated and then used to heat homes and do other jobs.

But there is a price to pay for getting heat from volcanoes. The pipes have to be made of a material that can withstand high temperatures. Unfortunately, making such pipes is very expensive. In addition, the water flowing through the pipes might not get hot enough to turn into high-pressure steam.

Of course, pipes don't have to be used. Water could be pumped directly into the cracks of a volcano crater. The steam, gases, and vapors that escape from the cracks could be passed through ordinary pipes to drive machines that produce electricity. But as one scientist said, "fooling around with a volcano involves risks."

Drilling holes and sending water into the cracks of a volcano could touch off a small but dangerous explosion. And a powerful volcanic eruption might be set off!

Does the need for energy make taking risks with volcanoes worthwhile? Many people say yes. They point out that electricity is not the only thing we could get by taming a volcano. For example, water heated up by a volcano could be used to heat homes, buildings, and greenhouses. But that is not all. Both steam and hot water could be used by industry to do a number of jobs. In addition, large amounts of valuable chemicals, particularly sulfur, are present in volcanic steam and hot water. Maybe these chemicals could be obtained from volcanoes. This would be a real bonus, point out many scientists.

Long ago, the people of Iceland learned to harness and use the energy from deep within the earth. Since then, Icelanders have used geothermal energy to improve their quality of living. Miles of greenhouses, warmed by the earth's own heat, provide large crops of fruits and vegetables for Icelanders. About 75 percent of their homes are heated by geothermal energy. Without this source of energy, Iceland would have to import millions of additional gallons of oil each year. Now the people are starting to use the earth's heat for fish farming, industry, and the generation of electricity. In time, Iceland may run entirely on geothermal power.

Is the greatest source of this power locked in volcanoes? Should we try to get at it? What do you think?

WIRED TO THE SUN

THE HOUSE OF THE FUTURE WILL RUN ON ENERGY FROM THE SUN, MAKE ITS OWN ELECTRICITY, AND EVEN SELL SOME OF IT TO THE ELECTRIC COMPANY.

It looks like an ordinary house, nestled among several others just like it. The lights are on in the kitchen. Good—dinner will be ready soon. Let's see . . . what was it you ordered for supper before you left the house this morning? Oh yes, a menu featuring your favorite Italian dishes. Mmm . . .

POWER PANELS

The thought of collapsing into a comfortable chair in a cool room makes you walk even faster. Not such a good idea on a day that saw the temperature reach 35°C—for the sixth time in a row. The only advantage to this heat wave is that it will enable you to sell back lots of electricity to the power company. Yes indeed, those 64 solar panels rising up from the southern side of the roof really do their job. They produce enough electricity to run most of the major appliances in the house. The panels, covering a roof area of 5.5 square meters, are made up of *photovoltaic cells*. These cells change the energy in sunlight directly into electricity.

Now, of course, when there is no strong sunlight—like during the night and on cloudy days—the photovoltaic cells don't work. But you need not worry. At those times, your house is automatically switched to a local electric company's cables. You use its electricity and pay its prices. But so far this summer, the photovoltaic cells have produced more energy than the house needs. Some of the energy has been stored in the hot-water heater. The remainder has been sold back to the electric power company. The electricity is actually sent from the roof through cables to a nearby company station. Just think about it: The electricity you sell back is used to power one of those old-fashioned houses!

COMPUTER COMFORT

As you climb the stairs to the airlock entry, you happily notice that the outside window shutters have been automatically rolled down. These shutters reflect sunlight on hot days and help hold heat in the house on cold days. Shutters inside the windows have also been automatically lowered. Keeping direct sunlight out of the house on a day like today is very important.

Punching your code in the door keypad, you walk into the airlock entry. The airlock keeps hot air from entering the house in summer. In winter, it keeps the cold air out. The burglar-alarm system now shuts itself off. It feels a bit too cool in the house, so you signal the air-conditioning system to quit working so hard by punching a code into the thermostat.

As you pass from room to room, doors open automatically and lights switch on and off. The heat and motion sensors built into the floors, walls, and ceilings keep track of your path. And sure enough, as you enter the family room, your favorite music goes on.

With dinner cooking in the oven, which automatically went on when you walked in,

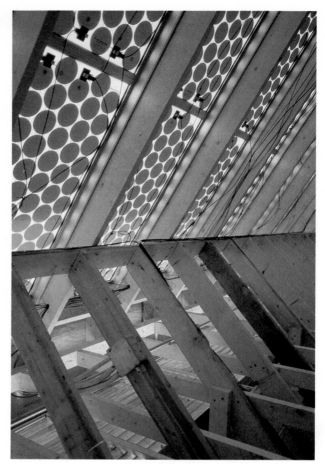

Each one of the 64 solar panels in the roof of this house is made up of photovoltaic cells. These cells capture the energy of the sun and change it directly into electricity.

you can sit down for awhile and relax. The dusting and vacuuming have all been done by the computer-driven robots. The kitchen computer keeps track of what food items you are getting low on. It will "call in" a list of groceries to the supermarket later.

So you're now free to sit and think about just how comfortable your home life is. The main computer of your house-management system takes care of almost everything—from controlling heating and cooling systems to providing news and sports information and educational courses. It opens locks, gives fire-alarm protection, cooks meals, turns lights on and off. It remembers when to turn certain appliances on or turn them off. It even takes readings of the dust level on the solar panels and lets you know when they need washing! Maybe someday soon, the computer will take care of cleaning the photovoltaic cells too!

SOLAR SERVICE

One amazing thing about your house is how well it uses energy. That's because it has several special features. These features are designed to get the most out of the sun's natural heating ability in winter. At the same time, they are designed not to add heat to the house in summer. How can this be done?

Both the trombe wall and the wall containing phasechange salts can be seen in this view of the house. These solar features, designed to get the most out of the sun's natural heating ability, are for winter use only.

The large, rounded shape in the front of the house is the airlock entry, which keeps hot air out of the house in summer and cold air in winter. The automatic shutters that reflect sunlight away in summer can be seen covering the upstairs windows.

That black wall covered with glass along the south side of the house is called a *trombe wall*. Its job is to collect the sun's rays. When these rays pass through the glass, they strike the trombe wall and are absorbed. The wall is painted black to make sure as much of the sun's energy as possible is absorbed. Dark colors absorb sunlight best. The wall heats up as it absorbs energy. Because the wall is very thick, a great deal of heat is stored. At night or on a cloudy day, that heat is slowly released into the house. The glass covering is about 15 centimeters from the wall and creates an air space. This space prevents the heat from escaping to the outside.

The trombe wall is a wintertime-only feature. During the summer months, the wall is shaded.

Phasechange salts are another amazing solar feature. Along the south side of the house, tubes no longer than 76 centimeters are built into the wall. These tubes are painted black on the outside to absorb the greatest amount of solar energy. Inside the tubes are special calcium compounds, which are solids at temperatures below 27.2° C, their melting point. During the day, the sun's radiation is absorbed by the salts. The salts melt if their temperature goes above 27.2° C. But during the time they melt and stay liquid, they store the sun's heat energy. Then at night, when the temperature drops below the melting point, the salts turn back to the solid phase. This phase change releases the stored heat to the house. However, like the trombe wall, the salt-containing tubes must be shaded during the summer months.

Well, these solar features have come a long way since they were first introduced back in the 1970s. Since then, they have been modified and improved. So now in 1997, they help keep your house warm as toast in winter and cool as a cucumber in summer. That thought reminds you your computer is calling— dinner is ready!

Structure of Matter

For an overview of this unit, see pages T-52 to T-57. You may want to check the Laboratory Activity following each chapter, as well as the activities and investigations for this unit in your Teacher's Resource Book and Annotated Teacher's Edition, Laboratory Book, so that materials can be ordered, gathered, or prepared in advance.

Probing ever further into space, scientists have discovered more and more distant objects. Somewhere out there is the most distant object in the universe, a sphere of tightly packed particles shooting out incredible bursts of energy. This object is a quasar. Located perhaps 20 billion light-years from the earth, this quasar has existed for 20 billion years. And its light has been traveling for that long a time. Perhaps by viewing the light from this quasar, scientists can witness the very beginning of the universe. For in that flash of light is evidence of the birth of all the matter in space—galaxies, stars, planets, rocks, molecules, atoms, and even the atoms' tiniest parts. These small particles, set loose billions of years ago, hold many secrets about the world around you.

CHAPTERS

Computer-generated image of Quasar 3C 273

15 Atoms and Molecules

For a chapter overview, teaching strategies, answers to all activities, a list of A-V materials, and a chapter bibliography, see pages T-52 to T-54.

Consult your Teacher's Resource Book and Annotated Teacher's Edition, Laboratory Book for additional activities and teaching aids.

CHAPTER OBJECTIVES

After completing this chapter, you will be able to:

15-1 Discuss an early idea about the nature of matter.

15-1 Describe the models of the atom developed by Thomson and Rutherford.

15-2 Compare the proton, neutron, and electron in terms of charge, mass, and location within the atom.

15-2 Define atomic number and isotopes.

15-2 Describe the structure of the atom according to modern atomic theory.

15-3 Explain what a molecule is.

Beads of mercury gleam on a sheet of cloth. Some beads are small, others are large. But they are all still mercury, a pure substance. If you were to take the smallest bead of mercury and slice it in half once, twice, three times, even a thousand times, you would still be left with mercury—or would you?

Is there some incredibly tiny bead of mercury that if sliced one more time would no longer be mercury? It was just this kind of question that sparked the imagination and curiosity of early scientists. They hypothesized and argued as the years passed—for more than two thousand years, in fact.

Then, slowly, clues were found. Experiments were performed. New ideas were hatched. And finally an answer was developed. In many ways it was a very simple answer. To find it out, let's begin at the beginning.

Silvery beads of liquid mercury

15-1 An Atomic Model of Matter

Can matter be divided into smaller and smaller pieces forever? This was one of the questions that puzzled Greek philosophers more than 2400 years ago. For they were trying to figure out what matter was made of. Some of their ideas were rather strange and were certainly incorrect. Yet others were steps along the trail that would finally lead to the truth.

Early Ideas About the Atom

The search for a description of matter began with the Greek philosopher Democritus (de-MOK-rih-tuhs). He believed that an object could not be cut into smaller and smaller pieces forever. Eventually, the

Figure 15-1 *Alchemists, or early chemists, hoped to find a way to change ordinary metals into gold. Although the alchemists failed, some of their methods led to modern ideas about conducting experiments.*

smallest possible piece would be obtained. And that piece could not be divided any further. It was indivisible. Democritus called this smallest piece of matter an **atom**. The word "atom" comes from the Greek word *atomos* meaning "indivisible."

What were these atoms? Democritus had no way of knowing. But he guessed they were small, hard particles that were all made of the *same* material but came in different shapes and sizes. Although Democritus was on the right trail, his theory of atoms was ignored and forgotten. In fact, it would be another 2100 years before others traveled down that trail.

Modern Ideas About the Atom

In the early 1800s, the English chemist John Dalton did a number of experiments that led to an interesting conclusion. Dalton discovered that gases combined as if they were made of individual particles. These particles were the atoms of Democritus. For the first time, a theory of atomic structure was based on chemical experiments. Dalton had taken an important step along the atomic trail. But like Democritus, Dalton believed that atoms were "uncuttable." Was he right?

In 1897, the English scientist J. J. Thomson was studying the passage of an electric current through a gas. The gas gave off rays that Thomson showed were made of negatively charged particles. But the gas was known to be made of uncharged atoms. So where had the negatively charged particles come from? From within the atom, Thomson reasoned. A particle smaller than the atom had to exist. The atom was divisible! Thomson called the negatively charged particles "corpuscles." Today they are known as **electrons.**

Thomson's discovery of electrons presented him with a new problem to solve. If the atom as a whole was uncharged, yet it contained negatively charged particles, what balanced the negative charge? Thomson reasoned that the atom must also contain a positive charge. But try as he might, he was unable to find this positive charge.

So he proposed a model of the atom that is sometimes called the "plum pudding" model. He pictured the atom as made of a puddinglike, positively

Aristotle believed in the four elements but not in atoms. Because he was so greatly respected, his views in all areas of science were almost totally accepted. His influence tended to retard the progress in the area of atomic theory.

Activity

A Mental Model

Scientists have developed an atomic model based on many experiments. Because scientists cannot see the subatomic particles, they must rely on observing how atoms behave under certain conditions. In this activity, you will develop a mental model of something you cannot see.

Place three to five small items in a shoe box. Seal the box. Exchange boxes with a friend or classmate. Using a variety of tests on the box, describe what you think is inside it. You can shake, turn, weigh, and smell the box. You can also hold a magnet near it. But do not open the box or damage it.

After you have developed a mental model of the contents, open the box and see how close your model is to the actual contents.

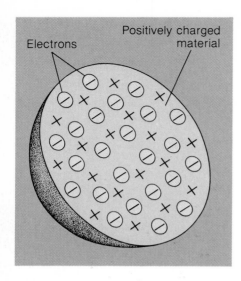

Figure 15-2 *Thomson's model of the atom pictured a "pudding" of positively charged material throughout which were scattered negatively charged electrons.*

Figure 15-3 *In Rutherford's experiment* (left), *most of the positively charged particles passed right through the gold sheet. A few were slightly deflected, while a very few bounced back. From these observations, Rutherford developed his model of the atom* (right) *as an object that was mostly space but had a dense, positively charged nucleus.*

charged material. Scattered throughout this material, like plums in a pudding, were the negatively charged electrons. See Figure 15-2. Thomson's model of the atom was far from correct. But his work was an important step along the trail toward understanding the atom.

In 1908, the British physicist Ernest Rutherford was hard at work on an experiment that seemed to have little to do with the mysteries of the atom. Rutherford was doing experiments in which he fired tiny, positively charged particles at thin sheets of gold. Rutherford discovered that most of these positively charged "bullets" passed right through the gold atoms without changing course at all. This could only mean that the gold atoms in the sheet were mostly empty space! The atoms were not a pudding filled with a positively charged material, as Thomson had thought.

Some of the "bullets," however, did bounce away from the gold sheet as if they had hit something solid. What could this mean? Rutherford knew that positive charges repel other positive charges. So he proposed that an atom had a small, positively charged center that repelled his positively charged "bullets." He called this center of the atom the **nucleus** (NOO-klee-uhs; plural: nuclei, NOO-klee-igh).

In Rutherford's model, the atom looked like a tiny solar system. Electrons circled the nucleus in the same way that the planets circle the sun. Although useful in many ways, this model did not explain the arrangement of the electrons. It would be the job of

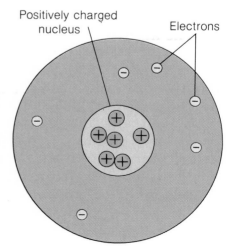

future scientists to improve upon Rutherford's atomic model. And it would not be a simple task! For the atom is only one ten-billionth of a meter in diameter. And examining its structure is much like finding one particular grain of sand among the grains of sand making up all the beaches of the earth!

SECTION REVIEW

1. What atomic particle did J. J. Thomson discover?
2. What is the center of the atom called? Who discovered it?

1. Electron
2. Nucleus; Rutherford

Figure 15-4 *A crystal of tungsten, magnified 3,000,000 times, shows a regular arrangement of atoms.*

15-2 Structure of the Atom

When Thomson performed his experiments, he was hoping to find a single particle smaller than the atom. Certainly Thomson would be surprised to learn that today about 200 different kinds of such particles are known to exist! Because these particles are smaller than an atom, they are called **subatomic particles**.

At this time, you need to know about only three of these subatomic particles. For each particle, you should know its mass, charge, and location within the atom. Let's begin with the nucleus of the atom. For it is the nucleus that makes one kind of atom different from another.

Figure 15-5 *When particles collide, they leave tracks that can be recorded on film, such as this example. Physicists study the tracks to learn about the particles.*

The Nucleus

The nucleus is the "heart" of the atom, the core in which 99.9 percent of the mass of the atom is located. Yet the nucleus is about a hundred thousand times smaller than the entire atom! In fact, the size of the nucleus compared to the entire atom is like the size of a bee compared to a football stadium!

PROTONS Those positively charged "bullets" that Rutherford fired at the gold sheets bounced back because of the **protons** in the nucleus of the gold atoms. Protons are positively charged particles found in the nucleus.

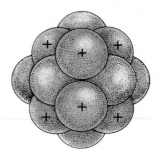

Lithium
nucleus

Carbon
nucleus

Figure 15-6 *A lithium nucleus contains 3 protons and 4 neutrons. A carbon nucleus contains 6 protons and 6 neutrons.*

Because the masses of subatomic particles are so small, scientists use a special unit to measure them. They call this unit an **atomic mass unit**, or amu. The mass of a proton is 1 amu. To get a better idea of how small a proton is, imagine the number 6 followed by 23 zeros. It would take that many protons to equal a mass of 1 gram!

NEUTRONS Sharing the nucleus with the protons are the electrically neutral **neutrons**. Neutrons have no charge. They do have mass, however. Each neutron has a mass of 1 amu.

Atomic Number

You read before that atoms of different substances are different. What is it that accounts for this difference? The answer lies in the nucleus. For it is the number of protons in a nucleus that determines what the substance is. For example, a carbon atom has 6 protons in its nucleus. Carbon is a dark solid. There are 7 protons in the nucleus of a nitrogen atom. That is only 1 more than carbon. Yet nitrogen is a colorless gas.

The number of protons in the nucleus is called the **atomic number**. It identifies the kind of atom. All hydrogen atoms—and *only* hydrogen atoms—have 1 proton and an atomic number of 1. Helium atoms have an atomic number of 2. So there are 2 protons in the nucleus of every helium atom. Oxygen has an atomic number of 8, and 8 protons in the nucleus of each atom. How many protons does uranium, atomic number 92, have?

Isotopes

The atomic number of a substance never changes. This means that there is always the same number of protons in the nucleus of every atom of that substance. But the number of neutrons is not so constant! Atoms of the same substance can have different numbers of neutrons.

Atoms that have the same number of protons but different numbers of neutrons are called **isotopes** (IGH-suh-tohps). Look at Figure 15-8. You will see three different isotopes of hydrogen. Notice that the number of protons does *not* change. Remember that the atomic number, or number of protons, identifies a substance. No matter how many neutrons there are in the nucleus, 1 proton always means the atom is hydrogen.

Figure 15-7 *The number of protons in an atom's nucleus determines what the atom is. Neon atoms, which make up the gas often used in colored lights (left), have 10 protons. Helium atoms, which make up a colorless, odorless gas often used in balloons (right), have 2 protons.*

Figure 15-8 *The three isotopes of hydrogen. Notice that the number of protons remains the same; the number of neutrons changes.*

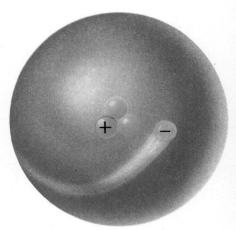

Protium   Deuterium   Tritium

The Electrons

If you think protons and neutrons are small, picture this. Whirling around outside the nucleus are particles that are about 1/2000 the mass of either a proton or a neutron! These particles are electrons. Electrons have a negative charge and a mass of 1/1836 amu. In an atom, the number of negatively charged electrons is usually equal to the number of positively charged protons. So the total charge on the atom is zero. The atom is neutral.

Rutherford pictured electrons moving around the nucleus like planets orbiting the sun. But as scientists learned more about the atom, they had to reject this theory. Their experiments showed that electrons do not move in fixed orbits. In fact, the *exact* location of an electron cannot be known. Only the probability, or likelihood, of finding an electron at a particular place in an atom can be determined.

In fact, the entire space in which electrons are found is what scientists think of as the atom itself. Sometimes this space is called the **electron cloud**. But do not think of the atom as a solid center surrounded by a fuzzy, blurry cloud. For the electron cloud is a *space* in which electrons are likely to be found. It is somewhat like the area around a beehive in which the bees move. Sometimes the electrons are near the nucleus. Sometimes they are farther away from it. In a hydrogen atom, one electron "fills" the cloud. It fills the cloud in the sense that it can be found almost anywhere within the space.

Although the electrons whirl about the nucleus billions of times in one second, they do not do this in a random way. For each electron seems to be locked into a certain area in the electron cloud. The location of an electron in the cloud depends upon how much energy the electron has.

According to modern atomic theory, electrons are arranged in **energy levels**. An energy level represents the *most likely* location in the electron cloud in which an electron can be found. Electrons with the lowest energy are found in the energy level closest to the nucleus. Those electrons with higher energy are found in energy levels farther from the nucleus.

Each energy level within an atom can hold only a certain number of electrons. The energy level closest

Figure 15-9 *An atom is mostly empty space, like this spider web. The electrons are found within that space, although their exact location cannot be determined.*

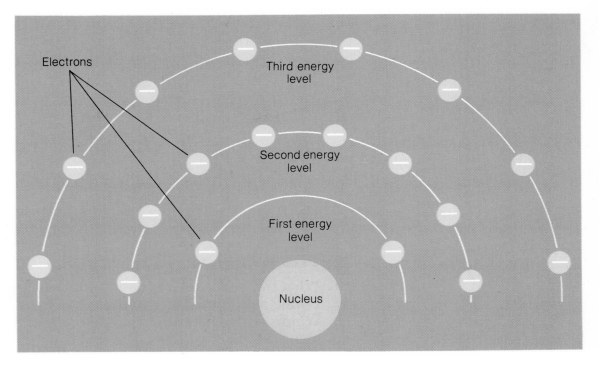

Electrons

Third energy level

Second energy level

First energy level

Nucleus

Figure 15-10 *Each energy level in an atom can hold only a certain number of electrons. How many electrons are there in the first, second, and third energy levels shown here?* 2,8,8

Although the third energy level can actually hold 18 electrons, 10 of the 18 have energies comparable to those of the electrons of the fourth energy level. These electrons are placed more "deeply" in the atom than are the fourth-level electrons. For this reason, the third energy level—and all higher energy levels—can never contain more than 8 *valence* electrons.

to the nucleus—the lowest energy level—can hold at most 2 electrons. The second and third energy levels can each hold 8 electrons. See Figure 15-10. The properties of different kinds of atoms depend on how many electrons are in the various energy levels of the atoms. In fact, the electron arrangement in the electron cloud is what gives the atom its chemical properties.

Do not confuse an energy level with a specific path. For it is not. In fact, some scientists believe that inside the strange world of the atom, electrons do not have a path. Scientists can speak only of the *chances* of finding electrons at various locations, but not of their exact position.

Is the atom "cuttable"? The existence of protons, neutrons, and electrons proves it is. And these particles in turn can be separated into even smaller particles. It is now believed that a new kind of particle makes up all the other known particles in the nucleus. This particle is called the **quark** (kwahrk). There are a number of different kinds of quarks. All nuclear particles are thought to be combinations of three quarks. According to current theory, quarks have properties called "flavor" and "color." There are six different flavors and three different colors.

Activity

Electron Arrangement

Determine the electron arrangement for each of the following elements given their atomic numbers.

sodium 11	lithium 3
nitrogen 7	neon 10
chlorine 17	argon 18

Figure 15-11 *Each subatomic particle in the nucleus is thought to be made up of a different combination of three quarks.*

15-3   The Molecule

Most atoms have a very important property. They can combine chemically with each other to produce new and different structures called **molecules** (MAH-luh-kyoolz). A molecule is made up of two or more atoms chemically bonded.

A molecule is the smallest particle of a substance that has all the properties of that substance. Suppose

Figure 15-12 *This computer-generated image is a hemoglobin molecule. Hemoglobin is the substance that gives red blood cells their color.*

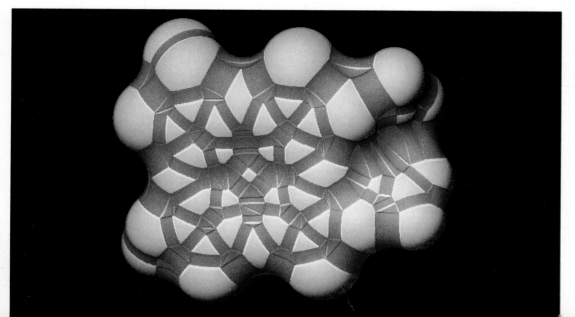

Career: *Science Teacher*

make up tests and quizzes, record pupil attendance and progress, and issue reports to parents. They also attend meetings, conferences, and workshops. If you are interested in this career, you can learn more by writing to the American Federation of Teachers, 1012 Fourteenth Street N.W., Washington, DC 20005.

Saturday afternoon provided ideal weather for some backyard gardening. But the teacher's mind was back in the classroom rather than on the sprouting bean plants. This week the unit on chemistry was to begin. Many students would have trouble understanding what could not be seen with the unaided eye. The teacher thought about the best way to begin the lesson.

Science teachers spend much of their time developing lesson plans for different topics. They create interesting ways to present information to their students. Activities such as lectures, demonstrations, laboratory work, and field trips are often used.

Science teachers have other duties as well. They must correct homework and test papers,

a sample of water was divided up into smaller and smaller samples. Eventually a particle that could not be further divided without losing the properties of water would be reached. This particle is the water molecule. It is made up of two atoms of hydrogen and one atom of oxygen bonded together chemically.

Some atoms form bonds with other atoms very easily. Other atoms hardly ever form bonds. What accounts for the differences in bonding ability? The answer can be found in the arrangement of the electrons in an atom. The bonding ability of an atom is a chemical property. And it is the electron arrangement in the electron cloud that gives an atom its chemical properties.

Single atoms of certain elements, such as helium, can be thought of as molecules because atoms of those elements do not combine with one another to form larger particles.

SECTION REVIEW

1. What is a molecule?
2. Give one example of a molecule.

1. Smallest particle of a substance that has all the properties of that substance
2. Water molecule

LABORATORY ACTIVITY

For further instructions, see page T-53.

Flame Tests

Purpose

In this activity, you will observe the colors produced by excited atoms of different substances. When some substances are heated in a flame, their electrons are raised to higher energy levels by heat energy. When these electrons fall back into the lower energy levels, energy is released. The released energy produces a color characteristic of that substance.

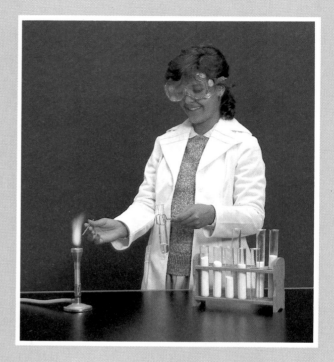

Materials (*per group*)

Bunsen burner
7 test tubes and test tube rack
Test tube clamp
Safety goggles
Wire loop with wooden handle
Hydrochloric acid, 6M HCl
.5M solutions of the nitrates of sodium, barium, calcium, lithium, potassium, strontium
Graduated cylinder
Test tube brush
Distilled water
Lab coat
Rubber gloves

Procedure

1. Put on safety goggles and lab coat. For steps 2 and 3 wear rubber gloves.
2. To clean each test tube thoroughly, hold it with the test tube clamp, place a few milliliters of 6M HCl into it and gently brush. Rinse the test tubes with tap water and then distilled water. **CAUTION:** *HCl burns. Avoid contact with skin, eyes, and clothes. If any should fall on you, immediately wash the area with water and then notify your teacher.*
3. Clean the wire loop by carefully dipping it first into some 6M HCl acid in a test tube and then holding it in the colorless flame of the Bunsen burner. Repeat until the wire adds no color to the flame. **CAUTION:** *Be careful when lighting and using the Bunsen burner.*
4. Pour 4 mL of the sodium nitrate solution into a clean test tube. Dip the tip of the clean wire loop into the solution, and then hold it in the flame just above the wire. Note: Heat only the tip of the wire.
5. Clean the wire loop as in Step 3.
6. Repeat Step 4, using in turn 4 mL of the solutions of the nitrates of barium, calcium, lithium, potassium, strontium. Clean the wire thoroughly after each test. Record the color of the flame for each substance.

Observations and Conclusions

1. How might scientists use a flame test to study unknown substances?

CHAPTER SUMMARY

15-1 An Atomic Model of Matter

■ More than 2000 years ago, Greek philosophers such as Democritus attempted to explain the nature of matter.

■ J. J. Thomson's model of the atom pictured a positively charged material in which negatively charged electrons were scattered.

■ Ernest Rutherford's discovery of the nucleus produced an atomic model in which the negatively charged electrons whirled around the positively charged nucleus.

15-2 Structure of the Atom

■ The positively charged proton and the electrically neutral neutron make up the nucleus of an atom.

■ The number of protons in the nucleus of an atom is the atomic number.

■ Atoms that have the same number of protons but different numbers of neutrons are called isotopes.

■ The area in which electrons are likely to be found is called the electron cloud.

■ Electrons are arranged in energy levels according to how much energy they have.

■ All nuclear particles are thought to be made of smaller particles called quarks.

15-3 The Molecule

■ Two or more atoms chemically bonded together form a molecule.

VOCABULARY   *Define the following terms.*

atom p.363
atomic mass unit p.366
atomic number p.366
electron p.363
electron cloud p.368

energy level p.368
isotope p.367
molecule p.370
neutron p.366
nucleus p.364

proton p.365
quark p.369
subatomic particle p.365

CHAPTER REVIEW

Multiple Choice

Choose the letter of the answer that best completes each statement.

1. The name Democritus gave to the smallest possible piece of matter is
   a. molecule.
   b. atom.
   c. electron.
   d. proton.

2. The scientist J. J. Thomson discovered the
   a. proton.
   b. electron.
   c. neutron.
   d. nucleus.

3. The small, heavy center of an atom is the
   a. neutron.
   b. proton.
   c. electron cloud.
   d. nucleus.
4. Ernest Rutherford's atomic model pictured
   a. a negatively charged center with positively charged particles close to it.
   b. a positively charged material with negatively charged particles in it.
   c. a positively charged center with mostly empty space around it in which negatively charged particles were found.
   d. a positively charged center only.
5. Particles smaller than the atom are
   a. molecules.
   b. elements.
   c. compounds.
   d. subatomic particles.
6. The nucleus of an atom contains
   a. protons and neutrons.
   b. protons and electrons.
   c. neutrons and electrons.
   d. protons, neutrons, and electrons.

7. The number of protons in an atom is called its
   a. mass number.
   b. isotope number.
   c. quark number.
   d. atomic number.
8. An isotope of oxygen, atomic number 8, could have
   a. 8 protons and 10 neutrons.
   b. 10 protons and 10 neutrons.
   c. 10 protons and 8 electrons.
   d. 6 protons and 8 neutrons.
9. All nuclear particles are thought to be made up of a combination of three
   a. electrons.
   b. isotopes.
   c. molecules.
   d. quarks.
10. Two or more atoms chemically bonded together form a(n)
   a. quark.
   b. isotope.
   c. molecule.
   d. nucleus.

Completions

Fill in the word or words that best complete each statement.

1. The smallest particle of matter is a(n) _____atom_____.

2. The negatively charged particles that Thomson called "corpuscles" are today known as _____electrons_____.

3. Rutherford is credited with the discovery of the _____nucleus_____, or the center of the atom.

4. The particles in an atom that have a positive charge and a mass of 1 amu are the _____protons_____.

5. An atom with an atomic number of 18 has _____18_____ protons in its nucleus.

6. Atoms that have the same number of protons but different numbers of neutrons are called _____isotopes_____.

7. The subatomic particle that has a negative charge and a mass almost equal to zero is the _____electron_____.

8. The negative particles in an atom are arranged in _____energy levels_____, which represent the most likely places of finding them based on their energy content.

9. The particle that is now thought to make up all other nuclear particles is called the _____quark_____.

10. When two or more atoms combine chemically, they form a(n) _____molecule_____.

True or False

Determine whether each statement is true or false. If it is true, write "true." If it is false, change the underlined word or words to make the statement true.

1. The idea that matter was made up of indivisible particles called atoms was proposed by <u>Democritus</u>. ^T

2. In the early 1800s, <u>Aristotle</u> developed a theory of atomic structure that was based on chemical experiments. ^{F (Dalton)}

3. In Thomson's experiment, the gas in the tube gave off rays that were made of negatively charged particles called <u>neutrons</u>. *

4. Rutherford's experiments detected the presence of a <u>positively</u> charged center. ^T

5. Most of the mass of the atom is located in the <u>electron cloud</u>. ^{F (nucleus)}

    * F (electrons)

6. Subatomic particles that have a mass of 1 amu and no electric charge are called <u>protons</u>. ^{F (neutrons)}

7. Chlorine has an atomic number of 17. It has <u>17</u> protons in its nucleus. ^T

8. Atoms having the same number of protons but different numbers of neutrons are called <u>isomers</u>. ^{F (isotopes)}

9. Electrons having the least amount of energy are found <u>farthest from</u> the nucleus. *

10. Two atoms of hydrogen and one atom of oxygen chemically bonded together form a water <u>molecule</u>. ^T

    * F (closest to)

Discussion Topics   Answers appear on page T-53.

Write a brief paragraph discussing each of the following:

1. If the letter Z represents the atomic number of a neutral atom and the letter A represents the number of protons plus neutrons, explain how you could use those symbols to find: number of electrons; number of protons; number of neutrons.

2. Explain why an ice cube made of one isotope of oxygen might float, while an ice cube made of another isotope of oxygen might sink. Remember, ice is two atoms of hydrogen bonded to one atom of oxygen.

3. Ordinary water molecules are made up of two hydrogen atoms and one oxygen atom. If there are three hydrogen isotopes and three oxygen isotopes, how many different kinds of water molecules could there be?

EXPAND YOUR KNOWLEDGE

Adler, I., and R. Adler. *Atoms and Molecules.* New York: John Day.
    In this interesting book, you will read about the parts of the atom and learn how atoms combine to form molecules.

Asimov, I. *How Did We Find Out About Atoms?* New York: Walker.
    The story behind what scientists know about the atom is presented here in an informative and entertaining way.

Frisch, O. J. *Working with Atoms.* New York: Basic Books.
    This book provides an explanation of the nature of atoms. The author talks about many of the scientists who have worked with atomic structure, including Ernest Rutherford and J. J. Thomson.

16 Elements and Compounds

For a chapter overview, teaching strategies, answers to all activities, a list of A-V materials, and a chapter bibliography, see pages T-54 to T-55.

Consult your Teacher's Resource Book and Annotated Teacher's Edition, Laboratory Book for additional activities and teaching aids.

CHAPTER OBJECTIVES

After completing this chapter, you will be able to:

16-1 Define an element and give several examples of elements.

16-1 Give the chemical symbols for ten common elements.

16-2 Distinguish between an element and a compound.

16-2 Describe what information a chemical formula provides.

16-2 Explain how a balanced chemical equation describes a chemical reaction.

A reddish stain on a scrap of fabric . . . some bits of dust gathered in the creases of a man's clothing . . . a seemingly unimportant clump of mud upon the floor . . . a few grains of tobacco let fall at the scene of a murder. . . . What could all these details mean? To detective Sherlock Holmes, the creation of British novelist Arthur Conan Doyle, they were clues to some of the most mysterious crimes imaginable. By paying close attention to the evidence, Holmes was able to solve many of the most perplexing crimes. And in so doing, he amazed not only the London police but also his own assistant, Dr. Watson.

Holmes's success had a simple, solid basis: logical thinking combined with a knowledge of chemistry. Using this knowledge, he was able to classify and analyze various substances that were clues to the mysteries. Holmes was a master at using scientific principles to solve crimes.

Criminology, of course, is not the only area in which scientific principles are applied. The whole world is a place of mystery, filled with puzzles and wonders that await the investigation of young detectives like you. But before you set out on your adventure, you will need to know how chemical substances are classified. And soon you will share the feelings of Holmes, who exclaimed at moments of discovery, "By Jove, Watson, I've got it!"

Detective Sherlock Holmes gathering clues

Figure 16-1 *The gold in this rock (left) is an example of a pure substance. Gold has long been used in jewelry and coins. These gold bars (right), called bullion, are part of a nation's money reserves.*

Activity

Getting to Know the Elements

Choose two elements that are commonly found in your surroundings. Mount a sample of each element on poster paper. Then illustrate the element's uses by cutting out and pasting pictures that show the various uses.

16-1 Elements

Suppose you were given a list of 100 different objects—objects common to your world. And you had to sort them out into different groups. How might you do it? Perhaps you would group them according to their color. Or their shape and size. Or their texture. Maybe you would sort them by their uses.

Well, scientists have faced just such a problem with the classification of matter. And by applying the concepts of atoms and molecules, they have been able to sort all forms of matter into logical groups. So a great deal of the work has already been done for you!

But before you discover what scientists have done, you should recall what you have learned about atoms and molecules. An atom is a tiny building block of matter. And a molecule, which is made up of two or more atoms chemically bonded, is the smallest particle of a substance that has all the properties of that substance.

The Simplest Pure Substances

The first thing scientists did was to divide matter into two groups: materials made up of parts that are all alike and materials made up of parts that are not alike. For example, in a sample of water, all the parts making up the water are exactly alike. These parts are water molecules. Scientists call such a material a **pure substance**. A pure substance contains only one *kind* of molecule. The oxygen you breathe is another example of a pure substance. All the molecules in the gas are exactly the same.

Now suppose you are looking at a sample of a rock called granite, like the one in Figure 16-2. You might notice that scattered throughout the granite are different-colored particles. These particles are the minerals quartz, feldspar, and mica. So granite is not made up of only one kind of molecule. It is not a pure substance. You will learn exactly what granite is in Chapter 17.

Let's go back to oxygen for a moment. Every molecule of oxygen is made up of two atoms of oxygen bonded together. So each oxygen molecule contains only one *kind* of atom—the oxygen atom. A pure substance made up of only one kind of atom is called an **element** (EL-uh-ment). Oxygen is an element. So is hydrogen. Carbon, aluminum, iron, mercury, silver, and uranium are also elements.

Elements are the simplest type of pure substance. They cannot be changed into simpler substances by heating or by any chemical process. Suppose you melt a piece of iron by adding heat energy to it. You may think that you have changed the iron into a

Figure 16-2 *Granite, which is not a pure substance, is made up of the minerals quartz, feldspar, and mica.*

Figure 16-3 *The beautiful colors of fireworks* (left) *are produced by the rapid burning of elements such as magnesium, phosphorus, sulfur, barium, and strontium. The element silicon is used to make computer chips* (right).

Iron filings	Zinc	Steel
Gravel	Tin	Clay
Sulfur	Borax	White arsenic
Sea salt	Burned pebbles	Eggshells

Figure 16-4 *These were the symbols used by the alchemists.*

simpler substance. But the liquid you now have still contains only iron atoms. True, the iron has changed phase—from solid to liquid. But it is still iron. No new or simpler substance has been formed.

Chemical Symbols

For many years, scientists had to spell out the full names of elements when writing about them. As you can imagine, this practice was time-consuming. Then in 1813, a system of representing the elements with symbols was introduced. After all, why couldn't chemists do what mathematicians and musicians did?

Chemical symbols are a shorthand way of representing the elements. Each symbol consists of one or two letters, usually taken from the element's name. The symbol for the element oxygen is O. The symbol for hydrogen is H; for carbon, C. The symbol for aluminum is Al; and for chlorine, Cl. You should note that when two letters are used in a symbol, the

Career: *Melter Supervisor*

HELP WANTED: MELTER SUPERVISOR, trainee To train as supervisor of steel company crew. Must complete four- to five-year training program, which includes classroom instruction. High school diploma optional. Minimum age 18.

What do cars, toasters, and business machines have in common? All require steel in their manufacture—steel that must be supplied by one of about 200 companies in the United States. Steel companies use iron ore, iron scrap, carbon, manganese, and other substances to make steel. These materials are placed in furnaces in carefully measured amounts. The molten steel that is produced is poured into molds and then cooled. Finally, it is sent to the manufacturers of steel products.

The steelworker who oversees work crews during the operation of such a furnace is called the **melter supervisor.** As crew supervisor, the melter directs the various activities involved in making steel. These activities include adding materials to the furnace, "charging" the furnace with steel scrap, and adding molten iron from

another furnace to the scrap. Lime is added to the mixture to carry off unwanted compounds.

The melter supervisor determines when the process is complete. If the temperature is over 1000° C, and the quality of the molten steel is acceptable, it is poured into molds.

If you think you might wish to pursue a career in steelwork, for further information write to the American Iron and Steel Institute, Communications and Education Services Department, 1000 Sixteenth Street N.W., Washington, DC 20036.

COMMON ELEMENTS

Name	Symbol	Name	Symbol	Name	Symbol
Aluminum	Al	Hydrogen	H	Oxygen	O
Bromine	Br	Helium	He	Potassium	K
Calcium	Ca	Iodine	I	Silver	Ag
Carbon	C	Iron	Fe	Sodium	Na
Chlorine	Cl	Lead	Pb	Sulfur	S
Copper	Cu	Magnesium	Mg	Tin	Sn
Fluorine	F	Mercury	Hg	Zinc	Zn
Gold	Au	Nitrogen	N		

Figure 16-5

first letter is *always* capitalized, but the second letter is *never* capitalized. Do you know why two letters are sometimes needed for a symbol? Hint: Scientists have already identified more than 108 elements!

What do you think the symbol for gold is? Is it G? Is it Go? The symbol for gold is Au. Does that surprise you? Gold is not spelled with an "a" or a "u." But the reason for the symbol is really not so strange. The Latin name for gold is *aurum*. Scientists often use the Latin name of an element to create its symbol. Here are some other examples. The symbol for silver is Ag, from the Latin word *argentum*. The Latin word for iron is *ferrum*. So the symbol for this element is Fe. Mercury's symbol is Hg, from the Latin name *hydrargyrum*. The table in Figure 16-5 lists some common elements and their symbols.

There are more elements than letters in the alphabet.

SECTION REVIEW

1. What type of pure substance is made up of only one kind of atom? 1. Element
2. What is the shorthand way of representing the elements? 2. Chemical symbols
3. What is the chemical symbol for: bromine; nitrogen; iron; calcium; oxygen; sodium? 3. Br; N; Fe; Ca; O; Na

Figure 16-6 *These symbols were part of Dalton's system for representing the elements.*

Figure 16-7 *Sodium is a highly reactive element that must be stored in oil (top). Chlorine is a yellow-green, poisonous gas (center). The compound formed when these two elements chemically combine is sodium chloride, or common table salt (bottom).*

16-2 Compounds

Let's go back to the sample of water again. Water is a pure substance. It contains only *one kind of molecule.* That molecule is made up of two hydrogen atoms chemically bonded to one oxygen atom. So each molecule of water contains *more than one kind of atom.* Pure substances such as water are known as **compounds.** Compounds are made up of molecules that contain more than one kind of atom. To put it another way, compounds are two or more elements chemically combined. Sugar is a compound. Each sugar molecule is made up of atoms of carbon, hydrogen, and oxygen. Baking soda is a compound you may be familiar with. So are carbon dioxide, ammonia, and TNT.

Unlike elements, compounds can be broken down into simpler substances. Heating is one way of separating some compounds into their elements. For example, the ore known as chalcocite is the compound copper sulfide. When heated to a high temperature, this ore breaks down into the elements copper and sulfur.

Sometimes the elements in a compound are so strongly bonded that heating cannot separate them. So some other form of energy must be used. Often electric energy is used to break down a compound. For example, by passing an electric current through water, this compound can be broken down into the two different elements, hydrogen and oxygen, that make it up.

The properties of the elements that make up a compound are often very different from the properties of the compound itself. Would you want to flavor your French fried potatoes with a poisonous gas and a highly active metal? Probably not! Yet, in a way, this is exactly what you are doing when you sprinkle salt on your potatoes. Chlorine is a yellow-green gas that is poisonous. Sodium is a silvery metal that explodes if placed in water. But when chemically combined, these elements produce a harmless white compound—sodium chloride—that has a tasty flavor! You can reinforce this idea by considering water, a colorless, harmless, relatively unreactive liquid. It is made up of hydrogen, a flammable gas, and oxygen, a highly reactive gas that supports combustion.

Chemical Formulas

When you began to read, you probably started by learning the alphabet. Well, you can think of chemical symbols as the letters of a chemical alphabet. Just as you learned to put letters together to make words, chemical symbols can be put together to make chemical "words." Combinations of chemical symbols are called **chemical formulas.** These formulas are a shorthand for the names of chemical substances.

Most chemical formulas represent compounds. For example, ammonia is a compound made up of the elements nitrogen and hydrogen. A molecule of ammonia has the formula NH_3. Sometimes, however, the formula represents a molecule of an element. For example, the symbol for the element oxygen is O. But oxygen occurs naturally as a molecule containing 2 atoms of oxygen bonded together. So the formula for a molecule of oxygen is O_2. Some other gases that exist only as pairs of atoms are hydrogen, H_2, nitrogen, N_2, fluorine, F_2, and chlorine, Cl_2. Remember, the *symbols* for the elements just listed are the letters only. The *formulas* are the letters with the small number 2 at the lower right.

Carbon dioxide is a compound of the elements carbon and oxygen. Its formula is CO_2. By looking at the formula, you can tell that every molecule is made up of 1 atom of carbon, C, and 2 atoms of oxygen, O. Water has the formula H_2O. How many hydrogen atoms and oxygen atoms are there in a molecule of water? 2 H, 1 O

When writing a chemical formula, you use the symbol of each element in the compound. You also use small numbers called **subscripts.** Subscripts are placed to the lower right of the symbols. A subscript gives the number of atoms of the element in the compound. When there is only 1 atom of an element, the subscript 1 is *not* written. It is understood to be 1.

Can you now see the advantages of using chemical formulas? Not only does a formula save space, but it tells a lot about the compound. It tells you the elements that make up the compound. And it tells you how many atoms of each element combine to form the compound.

Hydrogen molecule

Oxygen molecule

Nitrogen molecule

Chlorine molecule

Figure 16-8 *Hydrogen, oxygen, nitrogen, and chlorine exist as pairs of atoms chemically bonded to form molecules.*
Molecules made up of two of the same kind of atoms are called diatomic molecules. In addition to those mentioned here, iodine, I_2, and bromine, Br_2, are diatomic elements.

Figure 16-9 *A carbon dioxide molecule, CO_2, is made up of two atoms of oxygen bonded to one atom of carbon. A water molecule, H_2O, consists of two hydrogen atoms bonded to one oxygen atom.*

Carbon dioxide molecule

Water molecule

Figure 16-10 *The changing colors of autumn leaves* (left) *are caused by chemical reactions. Several chemical reactions are involved in the manufacture of plastic fibers* (right).

Figure 16-11 *The formation of a carbon dioxide molecule involves the chemical bonding of one carbon atom to one oxygen molecule.*

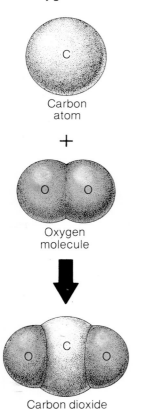

Carbon
atom

+

Oxygen
molecule

↓

Carbon dioxide
molecule

Chemical Equations

If symbols are "letters" and formulas are "words," chemical "sentences" can be written. But what are chemical "sentences"? They are a way of describing a chemical process, or **chemical reaction.** In a chemical reaction, substances are changed into other substances through a rearrangement or new combination of their atoms. New chemical substances with new properties are formed.

Have you ever seen charcoal burning in a barbecue grill? If so, you were watching a chemical reaction. The carbon atoms in the charcoal were combining with the oxygen molecules in the air to form the gas carbon dioxide. This reaction could be written:

carbon atoms plus oxygen molecules
produce carbon dioxide molecules

But using symbols and formulas, this reaction can be written in a simpler way:

$$C + O_2 \rightarrow CO_2$$

The symbol C represents a carbon atom. The formula O_2 represents a molecule of oxygen. And the formula CO_2 represents a molecule of carbon dioxide. The arrow is read "yields," which is another way of saying "produces." This description of a chemical reaction using symbols and formulas is called a **chemical equation.**

Here is the chemical equation for the formation of water from the elements hydrogen and oxygen:

$$H_2 + O_2 \rightarrow H_2O$$

Look closely at this equation. It tells you what elements are combining and what product is formed. But there is something wrong. Do you know what it is?

Look at the number of oxygen atoms on each side of the equation. Are they the same? On the left side of the equation, there are 2 oxygen atoms. On the right side, there is only 1 oxygen atom. Could 1 oxygen atom have disappeared? Scientists know that atoms are *never* created or destroyed in a chemical reaction. Atoms can only be rearranged. So there must be the same number of atoms of each element on each side of an equation. The equation must be balanced.

$$2H_2 + O_2 \rightarrow 2H_2O$$

Now count the atoms of each element on each side of the equation. You will find they are the same: 4 atoms of hydrogen on the left and on the right, and 2 atoms of oxygen on the left and on the right. The equation is correctly balanced.

An equation can be balanced by placing the appropriate number in front of the chemical formula. This number is called a **coefficient** (koh-uh-FI-shuhnt). The equation now tells you that 2 molecules of hydrogen combine with 1 molecule of oxygen to produce 2 molecules of water.

A balanced chemical equation is "evidence" of a chemical reaction. Using your knowledge of elements, compounds, symbols, and formulas, you can now solve the mysteries of chemical reactions. Like Sherlock Holmes, you too can say, "I've got it!"

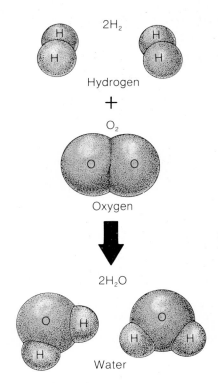

Figure 16-12 *When two molecules of hydrogen chemically combine with one molecule of oxygen, two molecules of water are formed.*

Chemical reactions follow the law of conservation of mass: the number of atoms of each element does not change in a chemical reaction.

Activity

Naming and Counting Atoms

The chemical formula for baking soda is $NaHCO_3$. The chemical formula for table sugar is $C_{12}H_{22}O_{11}$. What elements make up each of these compounds, and how many atoms of each element are there?

SECTION REVIEW

1. What is a compound?
2. What is the shorthand way of representing the names of compounds?
3. Give an example of a balanced chemical equation.

1. A pure substance that contains more than one kind of atom
2. Chemical formulas
3. $C + O_2 \rightarrow CO_2$, $2H_2 + O_2 \rightarrow 2H_2O$

LABORATORY ACTIVITY

For further instructions, see page T-54.

Marshmallow Molecules

Purpose

In this activity, you will make model molecules and use them to learn why coefficients are necessary to balance chemical equations.

Materials *(per group)*

Toothpicks
Food coloring: red, yellow, green, blue,
   purple (red/blue), orange (yellow/red)
25 large marshmallows

Procedure

A. Making Marshmallow Atoms

1. Set 25 marshmallows out overnight so that they dry out.

2. Prepare marshmallow atoms by applying food coloring as follows:
   N (nitrogen)—red (2)
   H (hydrogen)—blue (6)
   Cu (copper)—green (4)
   O (oxygen)—white (8)
   C (carbon)—yellow (1)
   K (potassium)—orange (2)
   Cl (chlorine)—purple (2)

3. Allow the marshmallows to dry for a few hours.

B. Assembling the Marshmallow Molecules

1. Using two red marshmallows and a toothpick, make a molecule of N_2. Then make a molecule of H_2 using blue marshmallows.

2. Ammonia, NH_3, is used in cleaning solutions and fertilizers. A molecule of ammonia contains 1 nitrogen atom and 3 hydrogen atoms. Using the marshmallow molecules that you made in step 1, produce an ammonia molecule of nitrogen and hydrogen. You may use as many nitrogen and hydrogen molecules as you need to make ammonia molecules as long as you do not leave any atoms over. Note: Hydrogen and nitrogen must start out as molecules consisting of two atoms each. Now balance the equation that produces ammonia:

$$\_\_ N_2 + \_\_ H_2 \rightarrow \_\_ NH_3$$

3. Using two green marshmallows for copper and one white one for oxygen, prepare copper oxide, Cu_2O. Using a yellow marshmallow for carbon, manipulate the molecules to represent and balance this equation, which produces metallic copper:

$$\_\_ Cu_2O + \_\_ C \rightarrow \_\_ Cu + \_\_ CO_2$$

4. Using orange for potassium, purple for chlorine, and white for oxygen, assemble $KClO_3$.

5. The decomposition of $KClO_3$ is a way to produce O_2. Take apart your $KClO_3$ to make KCl and O_2. You may need more than one molecule of $KClO_3$ to do this.

Observations and Conclusions

1. How many molecules of N_2 and H_2 are needed to produce two molecules of NH_3?

2. How many molecules of copper are produced from two molecules of Cu_2O?

3. How many molecules of O_2 are produced from two molecules of $KClO_3$?

CHAPTER SUMMARY

16-1 Elements

■ A pure substance is made up of parts that are all alike.

■ Elements are the simplest type of pure substance because they are made up of only one kind of atom. They cannot be broken down into simpler substances by chemical means.

■ Chemical symbols made up of one or two letters are used to represent the elements.

16-2 Compounds

■ Pure substances that contain more than one kind of atom are called compounds.

■ Compounds are two or more elements chemically combined. Compounds can be broken down into simpler substances.

■ The properties of the elements that make up a compound are often very different from the properties of the compound itself.

■ Combinations of chemical symbols, used to represent substances, are called formulas.

■ Subscripts indicate the number of atoms of an element present in a compound.

■ A chemical reaction is described by a chemical equation.

■ In a chemical equation, the same number of atoms of each element must appear on each side of the equation.

■ A balanced chemical equation indicates what substances are combining, what products are formed, and how many atoms and molecules are involved in the reaction.

VOCABULARY   *Define the following terms.*

chemical equation p.385
chemical formula p.383
chemical reaction p.384
chemical symbol p.380
coefficient p.385

compound p.382
element p.379
pure substance p.379
subscript p.383

CHAPTER REVIEW

Multiple Choice

Choose the letter of the answer that best completes each statement.

1. A material made up of parts that are all alike is called a(n)
   a. atom.
   b. pure substance.
   c. mixture.
   d. granite.

2. The simplest form of matter made up of only one kind of atom is a(n)
   a. element.
   b. mixture.
   c. compound.
   d. molecule.

3. Oxygen, iron, and silver are examples of
   a. particles.
   b. formulas.
   c. compounds.
   d. elements.

4. One or two letters used to represent the name of an element are called a chemical
   a. symbol.
   b. formula.
   c. compound.
   d. equation.

5. Two or more elements chemically combined form a(n)
   a. mixture.
   b. atom.
   c. symbol.
   d. compound.

6. Two methods of separating a compound into its elements are
   a. heating and filtering.
   b. heating and electric current.
   c. electric current and magnetizing.
   d. filtering and magnetizing.

7. A shorthand way of representing a chemical substance as a combination of symbols is a(n)
   a. equation.
   b. reaction.
   c. formula.
   d. atom.

8. Numbers that indicate the number of atoms of an element in a certain compound are called
   a. coefficients.
   b. subscripts.
   c. fractions.
   d. superscripts.

9. The process by which substances are changed into other substances as a result of rearranging atoms is called a(n)
   a. chemical equation.
   b. chemical symbol.
   c. chemical reaction.
   d. chemical formula.

10. A chemical equation can be balanced by using numbers called
   a. subscripts.
   b. coefficients.
   c. superscripts.
   d. fractions.

Completions

Fill in the word or words that best complete each statement.

1. A material that contains only one kind of molecule is called a(n) _____pure substance_____.

2. Oxygen, which is made up of only one kind of atom, is called a(n) _____element_____.

3. Chemical _____symbols_____ are used to represent elements.

4. A pure substance made up of more than one kind of atom is called a(n) _____compound_____.

5. Carbon dioxide and water are examples of _____compounds_____.

6. Two forms of energy often used to break down a compound into simpler substances are electricity and _____heat_____.

7. Molecules of gases such as chlorine and oxygen occur naturally as _____two_____ atoms of the element bonded together.

8. Chemical _____formulas_____ are used to represent compounds.

9. A chemical process in which substances are changed into other substances is called a chemical _____reaction_____.

10. In order to balance the equation $MgO \rightarrow Mg + O_2$, the number _____2_____ must be placed in front of MgO and Mg.

True or False

Determine whether each statement is true or false. If it is true, write "true."
If it is false, change the underlined word or words to make the statement true.

1. The tiny building blocks of matter are called underline{atoms}. T
2. Two or more atoms chemically bonded make a underline{mixture}. F (molecule)
3. If a substance is made up of parts that are all alike, the substance is called a underline{complex} substance. F (pure)
4. Silver, gold, and carbon are examples of underline{compounds}. F (elements)
5. Elements underline{cannot} be changed into simpler substances by heating them. T
6. Ca and Fe are examples of underline{formulas} of chemical substances. F (symbols)
7. Two or more elements chemically combined form a underline{compound}. T
8. One molecule of nitrogen, N_2, is made up of underline{one} atom of nitrogen. F (two)
9. Small numbers placed at the lower right of a chemical symbol in a formula are called underline{superscripts}. F (subscripts)
10. The description of a chemical reaction using symbols and formulas is called a underline{chemical equation}. T

Discussion Topics Answers appear on page T-55.

Write a brief paragraph discussing each of the following.

1. The language of chemistry is a universal language. Scientists all over the world use the same representations for chemical substances. Explain why the system of symbols and formulas you learned about is so important to this idea.

2. The equation below is not balanced. Explain why it would be incorrect to balance it by changing H_2O to H_2O_2. Hint: The name for H_2O_2 is hydrogen peroxide.

$$H_2 + O_2 \rightarrow H_2O$$

$$2H_2 + O_2 \rightarrow 2H_2O$$

EXPAND YOUR KNOWLEDGE

Carona, P. B. *Chemistry and Cooking*. Englewood Cliffs, N.J.: Prentice-Hall.
Cooking is a great way to find out about chemical processes and reactions. Through the preparation and cooking of food, you will learn about emulsification, leavening, fermentation, and dehydration.

Drummond, A. H. *Molecules in the Service of Man*. Philadelphia: Lippincott.
What are zeolites and chelates? Find out about these and other molecular structures in this interesting book.

Hyde, Margaret O. *Molecules Today and Tomorrow*. New York: McGraw-Hill.
This interesting book is all about molecules. Read about new discoveries in the field of molecular medicine, the importance of molecules in cryogenics, and how molecules are responsible for plastics.

17 Mixtures and Solutions

For a chapter overview, teaching strategies, answers to all activities, a list of A-V materials, and a chapter bibliography, see pages T-55 to T-57.

Consult your Teacher's Resource Book and Annotated Teacher's Edition, Laboratory Book for additional activities and teaching aids.

CHAPTER OBJECTIVES

After completing this chapter, you will be able to:

17-1 Describe three important properties of a mixture.

17-2 Distinguish between heterogeneous mixtures and homogeneous mixtures.

17-2 Give an example of a suspension and a colloid.

17-3 Define the terms solute, solvent, and solution.

Hold the ketchup! Extra mustard, a dab of mayonnaise, sliced onion, pickle relish, and cheese! Don't forget the lettuce, but no tomato, please!

Is this the way you order your hamburger? Or do you prefer it plain? In either case, you are getting a combination of many ingredients. Substances such as fats, oils, proteins, and minerals are in the hamburger. Flour, salt, water, and other ingredients are mixed together in the bun. If you order a milkshake, you are drinking a blend of milk, sugar, ice cream, various flavorings, and air.

Making a list of all the chemical substances found in your burger and shake might surprise you. For your list would probably contain thousands of entries! After reading this chapter, why not try it?

A dazzling combination of chemical substances

Figure 17-1 *Granite is a mixture that contains crystals of the minerals quartz, feldspar, and mica.*

17-1 Properties of Mixtures

In Chapter 16, you learned that pure substances are made up of a single kind of particle. So it follows that any amount of a pure substance—a gram, a kilogram, or a ton—has the same properties as any other amount. Elements are the simplest type of pure substance. Compounds, which are chemical combinations of two or more elements, are also pure substances.

Do you remember the picture of a piece of granite? See Figure 17-1. Granite contains particles of different minerals. Looking closely at the rock in the photograph, you can see crystals of quartz, feldspar, and mica. Granite, then, is *not* made up of a single kind of particle. Such a material is called a **mixture.**

Figure 17-2 *There are two different mixtures in this photo of a fish tank (top). The air above the water is a gaseous mixture made up mostly of oxygen and nitrogen molecules. The liquid mixture contains water molecules, nitrogen molecules, and oxygen molecules (bottom).*

Oxygen molecules — Water molecules — Nitrogen molecules

Gaseous mixture

Liquid mixture

Makeup of Mixtures

A mixture consists of two or more pure substances that are mixed but not chemically combined. Beach sand is a mixture, as is soil. Salad dressing, concrete, and sea water are other examples of mixtures. The pure substances that make up a mixture can be elements or compounds. For example, in a mixture of sugar and water, there are molecules of the compound sugar, $C_{12}H_{22}O_{11}$, and molecules of the compound water, H_2O. In the mixture known as air, there are molecules of the elements oxygen, O_2, and nitrogen, N_2. There are also other pure substances, such as molecules of the compound carbon dioxide, CO_2.

Because the substances in a mixture are not chemically combined, they keep their separate identities and most of their own properties. Think of the mixture of sugar and water you just read about. The water is still a colorless liquid. And the sugar, although dissolved in the water, still keeps its property of sweetness. Your sense of taste tells you this is so. The same molecules of water and sugar are present after the mixing as before it. No new chemical substances have been formed. Substances in a mixture may change in physical appearance, as when they dissolve. But they do not change in chemical composition.

If you eat cereal for breakfast, you are probably making a mixture. That is what you produce when you pour milk over the cereal. And if you put berries or raisins into your cereal, you make an even more complex mixture. But you do not use exactly the same amount of cereal, milk, and fruit each time. This illustrates another property of mixtures.

The substances that make up a mixture can be present in any amount. The amounts are not fixed. So you can make a mixture of a lot of cereal, a little milk, and loads of fruit. Or, if you prefer, a little cereal with lots of milk and fruit! This property illustrates an important difference between mixtures and compounds. Do you know what this difference is? You might remember that when elements combine chemically to form a compound, they do so in exact amounts. For example, 2 hydrogen atoms always combine with 1 oxygen atom—no more, no less—to form a molecule of water.

Figure 17-3 *A nebula, a cloud of gases and dust in space, is a mixture. Here you see the Dumbbell Nebula, which gets its name from its shape.*

Figure 17-4 *By combining powdered iron (top) with powdered sulfur (center), an iron-sulfur mixture is formed. Because iron has the physical property of magnetism, which sulfur does not, iron can be separated from the mixture (bottom).*

Separation of Mixtures

Look at the photographs in Figure 17-4. A mixture has been made by combining powdered iron with powdered sulfur. Iron is black and sulfur is yellow. The resulting mixture has a grayish color, although particles of iron and sulfur are clearly visible. This mixture illustrates the two properties of mixtures you have just learned: The substances in a mixture retain their original properties. And the substances can be present in varying amounts. Look again at the figure to discover another property.

Iron is attracted by a magnet. Sulfur is not. The powdered iron can be separated from the powdered sulfur by holding a strong magnet near this mixture. If the two elements were chemically combined in a compound, they could not be separated with a magnet. This happens to be the case for a compound called iron sulfide, FeS.

You can use a number of methods to separate substances in a mixture. The method you choose will depend on the type of mixture. See Figure 17-5. You should note that all the methods of separating mixtures are based on physical properties. No chemical reactions are involved.

SECTION REVIEW

1. Is a mixture a physical or a chemical combination of substances?
2. In what amounts are the substances in a mixture present?

1. Physical
2. Varying amounts

Figure 17-5 *Salt water is a mixture of various salts and water. When the water evaporates, which is a physical change, it leaves behind deposits of salt (right). Heavy pieces of gold can be separated from rock, sand, and dirt by shaking the mixture in a pan of water (left). The gold will settle to the bottom of the pan.*

17-2 Types of Mixtures

Does it surprise you to learn that both concrete and stainless steel are mixtures? Concrete is a mixture of pieces of rock, sand, and cement. Stainless steel is a mixture of the elements chromium and iron. But in looking at each of these mixtures, you might describe the stainless steel as "better mixed" than the concrete because you cannot see individual bits of chromium and iron in the steel. Mixtures are classified according to how "well mixed" they are.

Heterogeneous Mixtures

Have you ever looked closely at a piece of broken concrete? If so, you saw the particles of rock mixed in with the sand and cement. And you probably also saw that no two parts of the concrete piece were exactly the same in appearance.

A mixture such as concrete or sand is said to be **heterogeneous** (het-uhr-uh-JEEN-ee-uhs). This means that no two parts of the mixture are identical. A heterogeneous mixture is the least "well mixed" of mixtures. The particles that make up the mixture are large enough to be seen. For this reason, they are easy to recognize and to separate from the mixture. A mixture of different-sized buttons or of different types of coins is an example of a heterogeneous mixture. Can you think of some other examples? Threads of different colors in a fabric, etc.

Not all heterogeneous mixtures contain solid particles. Shake up some pebbles or sand in water to make a solid-liquid mixture. This mixture is easily separated just by letting it stand. Oil and vinegar make up a liquid-liquid heterogeneous mixture. When the mixture is well shaken, large drops of oil spread throughout the vinegar. This mixture, too, will separate when allowed to stand. Both these mixtures contain particles that are mixed together but not dissolved. Such mixtures are called **suspensions.**

Homogeneous Mixtures

When the particles of a mixture are very small, are not easily recognized, and do not settle when the

Figure 17-6 *Pizza is a heterogeneous mixture in which the parts are easy to recognize and to separate from the mixture.*

Figure 17-7 *This suspension of soil and water is a solid-liquid mixture. Notice how the particles separate when the mixture is allowed to stand.*

395

Figure 17-8 *Gelatin is a colloid containing liquid particles mixed in a solid, while whipped cream contains gas particles in a liquid (left). Fog is a type of colloid in which liquid particles are mixed in a gas (right).*

Figure 17-9

TYPES OF COLLOIDS	
Name	**Example**
Fog (liquid in gas)	Clouds
Smoke (solid in gas)	Smoke
Foam (gas in liquid)	Whipped cream
Emulsion (liquid in liquid)	Mayonnaise
Sol (solid in liquid)	Paint
Gel (liquid in solid)	Butter

mixture is allowed to stand, the mixture is "well mixed." As a result, different parts seem to be identical. This type of mixture is said to be **homogeneous** (ho-muh-JEEN-ee-uhs). The stainless steel you read about is a homogeneous mixture.

Although you may not be aware of it, many of the materials you use and eat each day are homogeneous mixtures. Milk, whipped cream, toothpaste, mayonnaise, and suntan lotion are just a few examples. In these homogeneous mixtures, the particles are mixed together but not dissolved. As a group, these mixtures are called **colloids** (KAHL-oyds). The particles in a colloid are larger than ordinary molecules but too small to be easily seen through a microscope. In fact, it is the large size of the particles that often makes a colloid appear cloudy. Have you ever wondered why milk has a white, cloudy appearance? The colloidal particles in milk are just large enough to scatter light in all directions. The result of this scattering is the cloudy white color you see.

Colloidal particles, however, are too small to settle when the mixture is allowed to stand. There are several different types of colloids, as you can see in the table in Figure 17-9.

SECTION REVIEW

1. Based on how "well mixed" they are, what are the two types of mixtures?
2. What is the name given to mixtures such as milk and mayonnaise?

1. Heterogeneous, homogeneous
2. Colloids

17-3 Solutions

When you are thirsty, you might drink a glass of lemonade. But did you know that you were drinking a homogeneous mixture called a **solution?** A solution is the "best mixed" of all mixtures. In fact, the substances making up the solution are not just mixed together. They are dissolved in one another.

Properties of Solutions

By picturing a glass of lemonade, you can discover several important properties of a solution. First of all, how was the lemonade made? Lemon juice and sugar were probably added to water. They dissolved in the water. In a solution, the substance that is dissolved is called the **solute** (SAHL-yoot). The substance that does the dissolving is called the **solvent** (SAHL-vunt). So the lemon juice and the sugar are solutes. The water is the solvent.

Looking at the glass of lemonade, you will notice that the particles are not large enough to be seen.

Career: *Perfumer*

HELP WANTED: PERFUMER To create fragrances for cosmetic company. High school diploma required. On-the-job training provided.

Perhaps you have noticed that the second-hand car your neighbor just bought smells brand new. Or that your friend's new plastic wallet smells like real leather. Companies known as fragrance houses create scents to make products more attractive.

Most of the scents made by fragrance houses are used in soaps, detergents, perfumes, and other grooming items. The people who create the fragrances are **perfumers.** They combine many ingredients, including oils of flowers, to make a desired fragrance.

There are more than 3000 natural and synthetic ingredients used in making fragrances. In a process that can take up to two years, perfumers mix solutions of ingredients, check to make sure the ingredients are properly balanced, and test the fragrances. For more information on this career, write to the Fragrance Foundation, 116 East Nineteenth Street, New York, NY 10003.

TYPES OF SOLUTIONS

Solute	Solvent	Example
Gas	Gas	Air (oxygen in nitrogen)
Gas	Liquid	Soda water (carbon dioxide in water)
Gas	Solid	Charcoal gas mask (poisonous gases on carbon)
Liquid	Gas	Water vapor in air
Liquid	Liquid	Antifreeze (ethylene glycol in water)
Liquid	Solid	Dental filling (mercury in silver)
Solid	Gas	Soot in air (carbon in air)
Solid	Liquid	Seawater (salt in water)
Solid	Solid	Gold jewelry (copper in gold)

Figure 17-10

Activity

Water Dissolves Most Substances

You can find out what substances will dissolve in water by performing the following activity. Fill seven glasses with water. Into each glass of water, add a small amount of one of the substances listed below. Stir and let stand for several minutes. Observe what happens. Make a chart of your observations. Include your conclusions about what substances dissolve in water.

sugar
starch
salt
flour
cooking oil
baking soda
cleaning powder

The particles in a solution are individual atoms or molecules. For this reason, most solutions cannot be easily separated by simple physical means. Unlike many colloids, liquid solutions appear clear and transparent. The particles in a liquid solution are too small to scatter light.

Tasting the lemonade illustrates another property of a solution. Every part of the solution tastes the same. This might lead you to believe that one property of a solution is that its particles are evenly spread out. And you would be right!

There are nine possible types of solutions, as you will see in Figure 17-10. Many liquid solutions contain water as the solvent. Ocean water is basically a water solution containing many salts. Body fluids are also water solutions. Because water can dissolve many substances, it is called the "universal solvent."

Solubility

A substance that dissolves in water is said to be **soluble** (SAHL-yuh-bul). Salt and sugar are soluble substances. Mercury and oil do not dissolve in water. They are **insoluble.**

The amount of solute that will completely dissolve in a given amount of solvent *at a specific temperature* is called **solubility.** What is the relationship between temperature and the solubility of solid solutes? In general, as the temperature of a solvent increases, the solubility of the solute increases. What about gaseous solutes? An increase in the temperature of the solvent usually decreases the solubility of the solute. This explains why soda that warms up goes flat. Remember, the "fizz" of soda is due to bubbles of carbon dioxide dissolved in the solution.

Some substances are not very soluble in water. But they do dissolve easily in other solvents. For example, one of the reasons you use soap to wash dirt and grease from your skin or clothing is that the soap dissolves these substances, while water alone does not. Soap is made up of long molecules, with one end dissolving in water and the other end serving as a solvent for grease. The soap dissolves the grease and then, along with the grease, is washed away by the water.

Not all solutions are liquid, as the table in Figure 17-10 indicates. Metal solutions called **alloys** are examples of solids dissolved in solids. Gold jewelry is actually a solid solution of gold and copper. Brass is an alloy of copper and zinc. Sterling silver contains small amounts of copper in solution with silver. And the stainless steel you read about before is an alloy of chromium and iron. You may find it interesting to learn about the makeup of other alloys such as pewter, bronze, and solder.

SECTION REVIEW

1. What is a solute? A solvent?
2. What condition can increase or decrease the solubility of a substance?

1. The substance that is dissolved; the substance that does the dissolving
2. Temperature

Figure 17-11 *In the process of making steel, a solution of scrap steel and iron is made in a blast furnace (left). Near the end of the process, alloying substances are dissolved in the steel. In a water-purification plant, air dissolves in water as the water flows from sprinklers (right). The air-water solution now contains an increased amount of oxygen.*

Activity

Expressing Solubility

Solubility can be described in several different ways. Using books in the library, find out what each of the following words means. Give an example of each term.

dilute

concentrated

unsaturated

saturated

supersaturated

LABORATORY ACTIVITY

For further instructions, see page T-56.

Examination of Freezing-Point Depression

Purpose

In this activity, you will observe the effects of various dissolved substances on the freezing point of water.

Labels: Thermometer; Stirring rod; Test tube holder; Test tube containing water solution; Flask containing ice-salt mixture

Materials (per group)

Water
Glucose
Sucrose
(table sugar)
Sodium chloride
Test tube holder
Test tube rack
7 large test tubes and stoppers
Thermometer ($-10°$ to $100 °C$)

Glass-marking pencil
Coarse salt
Crushed ice
Glass stirring rod
500-mL beaker
Triple-beam balance
Graduated cylinder

Procedure

1. Label seven large test tubes with the numbers 1 through 7.
2. Place 10 mL of tap water in each of the test tubes.
3. Use the balance to pour out the following amounts of glucose ($C_6H_{12}O_6$), sucrose ($C_{12}H_{22}O_{11}$), and sodium chloride (NaCl).
    1. control
    2. 1.8 g glucose
    3. 3.6 g glucose
    4. 3.4 g sucrose
    5. 6.8 g sucrose
    6. 0.6 g NaCl
    7. 1.2 g NaCl
4. Add the measured substances to the corresponding numbered test tubes. Cover each test tube with a stopper. Shake until the substance is completely dissolved in the water.
5. Set up a low-temperature bath by mixing together 150 mL crushed ice, 100 mL coarse salt, and 100 mL water in a 500-mL beaker. Stir with a glass stirring rod for a

few minutes. If all the ice should melt at any time during the activity, simply add more.
6. Place a thermometer in test tube 1. Using the test tube holder, lower the tube into the ice-salt bath until it is submerged at least up to the level of the liquid it contains. Stirring gently with the thermometer, record the temperature at which the water begins to freeze. Remove the tube and thermometer. Wipe the thermometer clean.
7. Repeat step 6 for tubes 2 through 7.

Observations and Conclusions

1. What effect does the presence of a dissolved substance have on the freezing point of water?
2. What effect does doubling the amount of a given dissolved substance have on the freezing-point?
3. Tubes 2 and 4 contained roughly equal numbers of molecules of dissolved substances. Does the kind of substance have much effect on freezing-point?

CHAPTER SUMMARY

17-1 Properties of Mixtures

▪ Mixtures are made up of different substances mixed together but not chemically combined. They can be separated by ordinary physical means.

▪ Substances in a mixture keep their properties and are present in varying amounts.

17-2 Types of Mixtures

▪ No two parts of a heterogeneous mixture are identical. The particles are large enough to be seen, and they settle when the mixture is allowed to stand.

▪ Homogeneous mixtures, which contain very small particles, have parts that seem to be identical.

▪ Colloids are homogeneous mixtures of very small particles. Colloids often appear cloudy.

17-3 Solutions

▪ A solution consists of a solute dissolved in a solvent. The particles of each are individual atoms or molecules.

▪ Solutions are transparent. They cannot be easily separated by simple physical means.

▪ Soluble substances dissolve in water. Insoluble substances do not.

▪ The amount of solute that completely dissolves in a given amount of solvent is called solubility.

▪ The solubility of a solute depends upon the temperature of the solvent. The solubility of a solid in a liquid usually increases as the temperature of the solvent increases. The solubility of a gas in a liquid decreases as the temperature of the solvent increases.

▪ Alloys are solid solutions.

VOCABULARY   *Define the following terms.*

alloy p.399
colloid p.396
heterogeneous mixture p.395
homogeneous mixture p.396

insoluble p.398
mixture p.392
solubility p.398
soluble p.398

solute p.397
solution p.397
solvent p.397
suspension p.395

CHAPTER REVIEW

Multiple Choice

Choose the letter of the answer that best completes each statement.

1. Which of the following substances is *not* a pure substance?
   a. oxygen
   b. sugar
   c. salt water
   d. carbon dioxide

2. The particles in a mixture
   a. are always too small to be seen.
   b. are identical throughout the mixture.
   c. are chemically combined.
   d. are not identical throughout the mixture.

3. In a mixture, substances are present in
   a. varying amounts.
   b. fixed amounts.
   c. a ratio of 2 to 1.
   d. the liquid phase only.
4. Ways of separating a mixture depend on
   a. chemical properties.
   b. physical properties.
   c. chemical reactions.
   d. nuclear reactions.
5. A mixture in which no two parts are identical is a
   a. homogeneous mixture.
   b. heterogeneous mixture.
   c. solution.
   d. solvent.
6. A mixture that contains large particles that settle when the mixture is allowed to stand is called a
   a. suspension.
   b. solution.
   c. colloid.
   d. solvent.
7. Homogeneous mixtures such as milk, toothpaste, and mayonnaise are examples of
   a. suspensions.
   b. solutions.
   c. colloids.
   d. solvents.
8. In a solution, the substance that is dissolved is called the
   a. solvent.
   b. gel.
   c. solute.
   d. emulsion.
9. In a saltwater solution, the water is the
   a. solute.
   b. solvent.
   c. alloy.
   d. colloid.
10. Metal solutions of solids in solids are
   a. salts.
   b. colloids.
   c. alloys.
   d. suspensions.

Completions

Fill in the word or words that best complete each statement.

1. Two or more pure substances mixed together but not chemically combined form a(n) _____mixture_____.

2. Methods of separating mixtures are based on the _____physical_____ properties of the substances in the mixture.

3. Oil mixed with vinegar is an example of a mixture called a(n) _____suspension_____.

4. Mixtures whose particles are very small and whose different parts seem to be identical are said to be _____homogeneous_____.

5. A mixture that often appears cloudy, does not separate when allowed to stand, and contains very small particles is a(n) _____colloid_____.

6. Mayonnaise, which contains droplets of one liquid spread throughout another liquid, is a colloid known as a(n) _____emulsion_____.

7. In a solution, the substance that does the dissolving is called the _____solvent_____.

8. _____Solubility_____ is the extent to which a substance dissolves in another substance at a given temperature.

9. Substances that do not dissolve in water are said to be _____insoluble_____.

10. Stainless steel, sterling silver, and brass are examples of solid solutions called _____alloys_____.

True or False

Determine whether each statement is true or false. If it is true, write "true." If it is false, change the underlined word or words to make the statement true.

1. The rock granite is a compound. F (mixture)
2. In forming a mixture, substances lose their original properties. F (keep)
3. The substances that make up a mixture are present in varying amounts. T
4. Separating mixtures is based on the chemical properties of the substances. F (physical)
5. A mixture whose parts are identical throughout is said to be heterogeneous. *

  *F (homogeneous)

6. A suspension will separate when allowed to stand. T
7. In a solution of sugar water, the sugar is the solute. T
8. The universal solvent is alcohol. F (water)
9. A gas is usually more soluble in warm water than in cold. F (less)
10. Brass, a solution of copper and zinc, is an example of an alloy. T

Discussion Topics   Answers appear on page T-57.

Write a brief paragraph discussing each of the following.

1. Why can heterogeneous mixtures be separated by filtering but solutions cannot?
2. Explain whether you believe there exists a true "universal solvent," capable of dissolving all other substances. Include a description of the kind of container you would put such a solvent in.
3. Describe what would happen if you were to drop two lumps of sugar into a cup of hot tea; a cup of cold tea.

EXPAND YOUR KNOWLEDGE

Stone, A. H. *The Chemistry of a Lemon.* Englewood Cliffs, N.J.: Prentice-Hall.
This book contains experiments in which you use lemons, which contain acid, to find out about solutions known as bases and salts.

Coming Up······SCIENCE GAZETTE·········

Starting on the next page you will find three special articles. The first tells an exciting story about a scientist. The second tells about a battle of ideas. And the last looks into the future. Each of the articles has been written so you will enjoy reading it. As you read, you may want to jot down thoughts that come to mind. You might then write a report telling what you thought about the articles. Or you might just want to read the articles for the fun of it.

SCIENCE GAZETTE

The articles of this *Science Gazette* have been carefully chosen and designed to inspire and motivate students of all levels in their study of science. Each article is related to one or more topics presented in the unit. See the "Science Reading Skills" section in your Teachers' Resource Book for specific activities and handouts. Also, for further instructions, see page T-57 in this book.

Adventures in Science

Peter Armbruster and the search for an unknown element

How would you like to produce something never before created by a human being? A new piece of music? A beautiful painting? A famous book? Many people would jump at the chance to perform any of these feats. But not many get the opportunity. One who did is the physicist Peter Armbruster.

Armbruster got his chance in 1976 in the city of Darmstadt in Germany. He had joined a team of American and German scientists who were trying to produce a bit of matter never before observed on the earth or in the heavens. What this team of dedicated scientists was after was element 109.

As you know, all of the matter around you is made up of atoms of various elements.

Ninety of these elements occur in nature. Examples are oxygen, iron, gold, copper, and hydrogen. The remaining elements are not found in nature, but are "manufactured" by scientists. By the time Armbruster and his team started the search for element 109, the artificial elements included elements 43, 61, and 93 through 107. The manufacturing of the elements beyond element 107 seemed to be a very difficult, perhaps impossible, job. But it is challenges such as these that spark the imaginations of scientists such as Peter Armbruster.

As you know, the identity of an element is determined by the number of protons in its

Element 109 is born as an iron nucleus hits a bismuth nucleus and they combine.

nucleus. So to produce element 109, an atom with 109 protons in its nucleus would have to be made. But how could Armbruster and his team accomplish this?

After a great deal of analysis of the properties of various atoms, Armbruster and his fellow scientists decided to use bismuth and iron to "build" element 109. A nucleus of a bismuth atom contains 83 protons. A nucleus of an iron atom holds 26 protons. The protons would total 109 when combined. But how do you get two such nuclei to combine? You fire one at the other like a bullet at a target.

The device that "fires" the bullets at tremendous speeds is called a particle accelerator. In such a machine, the team of researchers planned to fire nuclei of iron atoms at nuclei of bismuth atoms. Unfortunately, getting the two nuclei to combine turned out to be a very complex task. For one thing, all atomic nuclei carry a positive charge. Because like charges repel one another, the iron nuclei would be repelled by the bismuth nuclei. So the iron nuclei had to be given enough energy of motion to overcome this repulsion. But the scientists would have to be careful not to give the iron nuclei too much energy. For then, the colliding nuclei would shatter on impact.

The combined efforts of these German-American element-hunters brought element 109 to life on August 29, 1982. Peter Armbruster is seated on the right.

The scientists set about solving all of these problems. Weeks passed, then months, then years. Finally, in the middle of August 1982, the scientists were at last ready to "go for 109."

For ten days, the Darmstadt researchers fired iron "bullets" at bismuth "targets." Billions of collisions took place. A computer analyzed the particles that sprang from the collisions. Nothing new appeared. Then, at 4:10 P.M. on August 29, 1982, the computer detected a single atom that vanished in less than one five-thousandth of a second. Analysis revealed that the fleeting bit of matter had a nucleus that held 109 protons. Element 109 had apparently been born!

Physicists all over the world were astounded. One said that the discovery was "an incredible technological feat." Another declared, "I think it's fantastic." In 1984, the Darmstadt team produced another fantastic feat. They made the missing element 108, which had been even more difficult to make than element 109.

Will elements 108 and 109 be of practical use? No one knows. But the special methods that produced them will certainly be used to make other elements. And some of these elements may be of great benefit to human beings.

Issues in Science

WASTING TIME:
The Nuclear Clock
Ticks Down

Today, nuclear power plants are producing more than energy. They are producing a potentially deadly form of garbage: nuclear wastes!

By the year 2000, there will be enough nuclear garbage to fill a giant box about 40 meters on each side. Such a "box" would not be much larger than a 13-story building on a square city block. If there will be no more waste than this, what's the grave danger? Why all the fuss? The answer, in a single word, is radiation!

Invisible Danger

Radiation is invisible energy. And nuclear radiation is *powerful* invisible energy. It is so powerful, in fact, that even small doses over a period of time can permanently harm, or even kill, living things.

Substances such as uranium and plutonium are common fuels for nuclear power plants. Like other fuels, these substances leave behind waste materials when they are used. But these wastes are not at all like the ashes that are the waste products of burning wood. Ashes are harmless. Nuclear wastes are extremely hazardous. The deadly radiation they give off can penetrate most ordinary substances. And this radiation can last for hundreds of thousands of years. So the disposal of nuclear wastes, even the smallest amount, is a giant problem.

Obviously, nuclear wastes cannot be disposed of like ordinary garbage. And they cannot be kept in giant containers, either. So how and where can they be safely stored? Scientists and engineers are trying to answer this question. But they cannot take forever to find a solution. For the wastes are piling up. Over the next few years, special tanks located near nuclear power plants will serve as temporary storehouses. But what is needed is a permanent home for these hazardous materials.

Space-Bound Garbage

If we cannot find a place on earth to get rid of nuclear garbage, why not send it into space? Rockets loaded with nuclear wastes could be launched into orbit between the earth and Venus. Traveling at the right speeds, the rockets could stay in orbit for a million years or more without bumping into either planet. By that time, the nuclear wastes would have become harmless.

Critics of this idea point to its cost and potential danger. An accident during rocket launch could harm thousands of people. These critics believe that the solution is not in the stars but on earth. Only where can these nuclear burying grounds be found?

Down-to-Earth Alternatives

The Antarctic ice sheet is more than 2500 meters thick in some places. Could nuclear wastes be buried under this huge, frozen blanket? No, according to some critics of this idea. Not enough is known about the behavior of ice sheets. And what is known is not comforting. For example, ice sheets move rapidly about every 10,000 years. Their movement might allow the wastes to get loose. In addition, nuclear wastes produce a tremendous amount of heat—enough heat, in fact, to melt the ice. Where the ice melted, nuclear radiation might leak out into the oceans and air.

If not under the Antarctic ice sheet, then how about a nuclear cemetery under the ocean floor? Thick, smooth rock layers have been building up there for millions of years. Nuclear wastes deposited in these rock layers would probably remain there almost forever.

But as with other proposals, there are problems with this idea. At present, the technology to do the job does not exist. And not enough is known about the various forces to which such rock is exposed. For example, the force of hot currents might pull the stored nuclear wastes out of the rock.

Rock Candidates

With ice sheet cemeteries and underwater graveyards all but impossible, one idea still remains. That idea is to put nuclear wastes in "rooms" dug out of underground rock.

In order to determine the best place to bury nuclear wastes, scientists must know all they can about the rock. Here are the properties scientists have determined are best: The rock must be strong, heat-resistant, and water-proof. The rock must be at least 6100 meters deep. And the ground where the rock exists must be very dry and free of earthquakes.

As you can see from the map, such rock formations exist in the United States. Scientists are now studying many of these formations. They plan to choose the best location and build a nuclear-waste garbage dump there between the years 1998 and 2006. There are four kinds of rocks that scientists believe will be the best.

Basalt is a volcanic rock that is strong and waterproof. It does not lose its strength when heated. However, basalt formations usually contain seams. Some scientists believe that water, which might carry nuclear wastes, could flow along these seams.

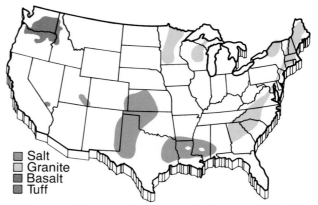

☐ Salt
☐ Granite
☐ Basalt
☐ Tuff

Various underground sites are being considered for the storage of nuclear waste material. There are a number of different kinds of rock in which wastes could be put. The map shows where some of these types of rock are located.

Tuff is another volcanic rock that has some of the properties of basalt. It is being studied in Nevada, where there is little underground water. Scientists point out that there is still much to be learned about tuff.

Granite is a very hard rock that resists heating. But water is found in many granite formations. And in addition, granite is very difficult to drill through. So building a nuclear-waste "room" in granite might be a very tough and costly job.

Salt is found in huge underground deposits. Although salt looks solid, it is really a flowing material. Scientists point out that this property of salt helps to seal cracks in salt formations. Unfortunately, salt is often not dry. And when heated, the salt will dissolve in the water and produce a saltwater solution called brine. The brine could carry nuclear wastes out of the salt formation.

So far, scientists have been unable to find the perfect graveyard for nuclear wastes. But the search goes on. Unfortunately, in the meantime the wastes pile up.

Storage of nuclear wastes requires a complex network of facilities. Here you see an artist's concept of the surface and underground features of a disposal site mined out of rock.

Waste Isolation Facility Concept

THE RIGHT STUFF—

Plastics

Cars, buildings, and appliances of the twenty-first century will be lighter, safer, and stronger than anything we have today.

Standing apart from a group of her classmates, Jennifer bounced her glass ball on the sidewalk. She was not paying attention to the other members of her class or to what her teacher, Ms. Parker, was saying.

As the sparkling ball bounced, Jennifer was barely aware of the sidewalk changing color to reduce the glare of sunlight. She did not notice a young woman hurrying along the street, carrying an auto engine in one hand and groceries in the other. She did not look up as cars sped by towing boats and houses by plastic threads.

Jennifer and her Design for Living class were on a field trip to a brand new "house of the future." The house had just been completed that year—2086. It certainly made the students' homes seem old-fashioned.

For days before the field trip, Ms. Parker had talked about the house of the future. She had described how safety, security, cleaning, maintenance, entertainment, home educa-

tion, and communications systems in the house were completely controlled by a central computer. She had showed the students how the combination of a waste-recycling unit, solar cells, and wind turbines met all of the house's energy needs. Ms. Parker had spent a long time talking about the new materials that made such a house possible. She had drawn pictures of organic and inorganic molecules on the classroom computer screen.

Even with all this preparation, Jennifer did not care about the house. She was interested only in the designs of the past. Jennifer's real love was for twentieth-century antiques. In her opinion, the appliances, furnishings, and materials of 2086 were boring and ugly.

"*Jennifer!*" Ms. Parker's voice cut through the group.

Jennifer scooped up the bouncing ball and thrust it into her shoulder bag.

"Yes, Ms. Parker?"

"Please come forward and give us the benefit of your views on home design."

As Jennifer moved to the front of the group, she knew she was on the spot. The class was already aware of Jennifer's "good-old-days" views, which contrasted with Ms. Parker's enthusiasm for modern materials and designs.

Nervously, Jennifer started to talk. "Plastics, silicones, polymers . . . I don't think the scientists of the late twentieth-century did us a favor by developing all this phony stuff. I wish we could go back to using wood, steel, aluminum, copper, and real glass. Remember those beautiful steel-and-chrome cars and the polished wood furniture in the design museum?"

"Yes," Ms. Parker agreed, "many things produced in the last century were beautiful and well made. It's easy to admire them in museums. But I don't think we'd find them convenient to live with every day."

"I would," Jennifer insisted.

"All right," responded Ms. Parker. "Let's hop into a mental time machine and find out. What age should we go back to?"

"How about the 1980s?" Jeremy suggested.

"Perfect," said Ms. Parker. "The 1980s were just the beginning of the great materials revolution. Great changes in industry, electronics, and materials development began at that time. By the way, Jennifer, you'd better leave your bouncing ball behind. They didn't have elastic glass in the 1980s. Light-sensitive building materials that change color to reduce glare were also unheard of. However, the research to produce these materials was already under way."

A Trip Back in Time

The house of the future was forgotten as Ms. Parker and the class moved to a nearby park to talk about materials of the past.

Ms. Parker began by asking the students, "What would be the first thing you'd notice in the world of the 1980s?"

"Heaviness. The great weight of almost everything," Jeremy volunteered.

"Go on," Ms. Parker said.

"Appliances like refrigerators, stoves, washing machines, and air conditioners were still made of metal at that time. They were so heavy that it was almost impossible for a single person to lift one of them. And a lot of everyday things were much heavier than they are now. Many food items in supermarkets still came in metal cans and glass bottles. A bagful of those containers could weigh a lot. It wasn't until the 1990s that lightweight, tough plastic containers had completely replaced them."

A Safer Future

Turning to another student, Ms. Parker asked: "Carlee, what would you notice most about life in the 1980s?"

"That it wasn't safe," Carlee responded.

"Why?"

Carlee thought for a moment and then said, "I guess what I was thinking of was the danger of riding in a 1984 car. I've seen pictures of how those old metal cars hurt people in accidents. Sometimes the heavy metal engines and batteries in the front end were pushed back to where people were sitting. Sharp pieces of broken metal and glass were all over

This plastic automobile engine weighs much less than an all-metal engine. Plastic engines have already been used to power race cars, and it may not be long before they are used in passenger cars.

Cars of the future may be made entirely of plastics and powered by solar batteries. Such a car would be lightweight, durable, and clean and inexpensive to operate.

the scene of an accident. Cars could blow up or catch fire."

"That can't happen now," Marian said. "Our cars, including the engines, are made of superplastics and silicones inside and out. These materials are very light and strong, and they bounce. Even if a laser brake system fails, no one can get seriously hurt."

"Cars not only are lighter and safer now," Jeremy added, "they require less energy to run. The changeover from metal to plastic engines in the 1990s led to great energy savings. And, the changeover since then to solar battery-powered cars has meant even greater savings. If we'd kept on using heavy metal cars, the world might have run out of oil and other materials by now."

"You're quite right, Jeremy," Ms. Parker agreed. "Let's sum up what's happened since the 1980s. A great materials revolution started at that time. Chemists discovered how to produce polymers, very long chains and loops of carbon, oxygen, hydrogen, and nitrogen atoms.

"Around the same time, other scientists created a new family of polymers. Silicon atoms were used instead of carbon atoms, so the materials were called silicones. The result of all this chemistry was a new range of super strong, light, cheap plastics.

> *The result of all this chemistry was a new range of super strong, light, cheap plastics.*

"The new materials can be made into anything that was once made with metal, wood, glass, or ceramic. In fact, we can do many things with combinations of the new materials that we couldn't do with the old materials, like making a transparent bouncing ball." Ms. Parker smiled at Jennifer.

Jennifer smiled back, still not convinced of the advantages of living in 2086.

Amethyst uncut

Composition of the Earth

For an overview of this unit, see pages T-58 to T-65. You may want to check the Laboratory Activity following each chapter, as well as the activities and investigations for this unit in your Teacher's Resource Book and Annotated Teacher's Edition, Laboratory Book, so that materials can be ordered, gathered, or prepared in advance.

Imagine a place 160 kilometers below the surface of the earth. You are taking a journey deep into the earth in an unbelievably strong bubble—a kind of underground diving capsule. Rivers of orange, glowing rock ooze past your observation window. The temperature gauge on your instrument panel indicates that the outside temperature is a rock-melting 1500° C. You hammer your fist on the pressure gauge. Can it be right? It reads 70,000 kilograms per square centimeter.

Your instruments are accurate. They are giving you a picture of the inside of your planet—the birthplace of rocks and minerals. One day, perhaps millions of years into the future, the molten rocks around you will reach the earth's surface. If conditions are right, unusual and beautiful crystals could form in these rocks as they cool. And what was once formless, glowing ooze may become the rarest rocks on the earth—gemstones!

CHAPTERS

18 Minerals

For a chapter overview, teaching strategies, answers to all activities, a list of A-V materials, and a chapter bibliography, see pages T-58 to T-60.

Consult your Teacher's Resource Book and Annotated Teacher's Edition, Laboratory Book for additional activities and teaching aids.

CHAPTER SECTIONS

CHAPTER OBJECTIVES

After completing this chapter, you will be able to:

18-1 Identify various minerals according to their physical properties.

18-1 Use the Mohs hardness scale to help identify a mineral.

18-2 Describe various uses of minerals.

18-2 Explain what gems are made of and what gives them their colors.

Some of your students may want to read a very exciting detective novel entitled *The Moonstone* by William Wilkie Collins, an English novelist. Collins' story, published in 1868, tells what happens when a valuable diamond is stolen from an idol's eye in India.

Throughout history, diamonds have been prized as a symbol of great wealth and power. Many of the world's largest diamonds decorate the crowns and jewelry of royalty. Take, for example, the Orloff diamond—if you can find it!

The story goes that this diamond was once in the eye of an idol in a Buddhist shrine in India. In the 1700s the diamond was stolen by a French soldier, who sold it to a British sea captain. After many thefts and some violent crimes, including murder, the diamond found its way to Russia. It was bought by Count Gregory Orloff from an Armenian merchant for about four million dollars. The Count gave it to Catherine II, Empress of Russia. Later, the diamond disappeared during the Russian Revolution.

Other diamonds also have disappeared before their owners' eyes—not through magic, but through ignorance. Early diamond hunters in South America thought they had a simple test for diamonds. They knew that diamonds are the hardest natural substance known. When the hunters found a stone that looked like a diamond, they hit it with a hammer. Usually, the stone shattered into bits and pieces. To the hunters, the shattering just proved the object was worthless. Actually, the stone may have been a diamond.

What the hunters did not know was that diamonds are brittle. Tap a diamond with a knife edge at exactly the right angle and it breaks cleanly and beautifully along an absolutely straight line. Tap it at the wrong angle and the diamond shatters.

Why do diamonds and other precious stones behave in this way? The answer is just a part of the fascinating story of minerals.

Rough diamonds

Figure 18-1 *Chalk* (top left), *pearl* (top right), *and aragonite (bottom left) are all made of calcium carbonate, or limestone. But only the aragonite is a mineral.*

Figure 18-2 *This is a chunk of granite rock and the major minerals found in it. From top to bottom, these minerals are hornblende, feldspar, quartz, and mica.*

18-1 What Is a Mineral?

Animal, vegetable, or mineral? In the game of 20 questions, a **mineral** is something that is not alive and was never part of something alive. A mineral, then, is a <u>natural substance that forms in the earth.</u> It is not a product of living things. For instance, a pearl, a piece of chalk, and the needle-shaped crystals shown in Figures 18-1, a, b, c, are all made of the same substance—limestone. The pearl formed in an oyster. A piece of chalk is made up of countless shells of sea creatures that lived long ago. Only the crystals are minerals. The crystals formed underground from water containing dissolved limestone.

There are more than <u>2000 different kinds</u> of <u>minerals. Each kind of mineral is composed of one or more elements.</u> See Figure 18-2. An element is a substance that cannot be separated into simpler sub-

Figure 18-3 *Chalcopyrite* (left) *is a copper-bearing mineral that looks like gold. Gold* (top right) *is arranged in various formations on this quartz rock. These nuggets* (bottom right) *are called "fool's gold." They are actually crystals of pyrite.*

stances by ordinary chemical means. For example, the mineral galena (ga-LEE-na) is made up of the elements lead and sulfur. Quartz is made up of silicon and oxygen. Minerals made up of only one element include copper, sulfur, silver, and gold.

Usually, a rock is made up of several minerals. Each mineral in a rock is a distinct and different substance. So each mineral has different properties that help scientists identify it. Most common minerals are identified by certain physical properties such as hardness, streak, heft, color, luster, crystal form, and cleavage and fracture.

The process of identifying a mineral can be tricky. Suppose, for example, a prospector comes across three rocks. One rock looks as if it is solid gold. A second rock has ribbons and ridges of gold folded around a milky-white stone. The third rock is made up mainly of nuggets of gold. See Figure 18-3. Do all the rocks contain gold? Simply looking at the rocks you might say yes. But only the following tests can give the prospector the correct answer.

MOHS HARDNESS SCALE

Mineral	Hardness
Talc	1
Gypsum	2
Calcite	3
Fluorite	4
Apatite	5
Feldspar	6
Quartz	7
Topaz	8
Corundum	9
Diamond	10

Figure 18-4

Another example is pyrite. This mineral is pale yellow but leaves a greenish to brownish-black streak.

Hardness

The prospector smiles. He has seen rocks studded with golden nuggets like these before. The first Spanish explorers of the Americas sent shiploads of such rocks back to Spain in the belief that they held gold. But the nuggets were not real gold. These nuggets have fooled many people.

Just to make sure he is right, the prospector rubs a corner of a nugget across the flat blade of a steel pocketknife. The nugget scratches the blade, showing that is is harder than the steel blade. However, real gold is very soft, and will not scratch steel. The nugget, then, is not gold. Chemical analysis would reveal that the nugget is made of a combination of iron and sulfur. Geologists call it pyrite. Prospectors call it "fool's gold."

The hardness of a mineral is determined by using the **Mohs** (mohz) **hardness scale.** See Figure 18-4. The softest mineral, talc, is 1 on the scale. The hardest mineral, diamond, is rated 10. A mineral can scratch any other material that is less than or equal in hardness to itself. In other words, the harder mineral always scratches the softer mineral. For example, pyrite has a hardness of 6 to 6.5. Steel is 5.5 on the Mohs scale. Pure gold is 2.5 to 3, while your fingernails are about 2 on the scale. So if you think you have a chunk of gold, try scratching it with your fingernails and then with a steel knife blade. If your nails do not make a scratch but the knife blade does, then you may have found gold!

Streak

Next, the prospector takes the stone that appears to be solid gold and runs the sharp edge of the steel knife blade firmly over it. The knife blade scratches the "gold." But instead of a golden groove, the scratch leaves a trail of greenish–black powder.

The color of a mineral in powder form is called its **streak.** Coloring of the powder may be quite different from the unpowdered mineral, as in this case. Streak color can be an excellent clue to identifying a mineral.

Very soft minerals such as talc leave a streak when rubbed on paper. Talc leaves a white streak.

Graphite, a slightly harder mineral made of carbon, leaves a gray-black, shiny streak. Graphite is the "lead" in a pencil. When you write with a pencil, the line you produce is the streak of the graphite. You can see that the streak is shiny by holding it under a strong light.

The prospector now knows that the solid gold rock is *not* real gold because gold leaves a pale yellow streak. And he knows some other things about this mineral. It is yellow with a greenish-black streak and is easily scratched with a steel knife blade. On the Mohs scale, it is probably no harder than 3.5 or 4. Chemical analysis would reveal that this rock is made up of a combination of copper, iron, and sulfur. From these clues, the prospector knows that the mineral is chalcopyrite (kal-ko-PIE-right).

But what about the third stone, the milky-white stone with ridges of gold? Using the steel blade of the knife, the prospector finds that the blade cuts easily through the gold ridges. The cut leaves a pale yellow streak. From the evidence, it appears that this rock contains gold. Although other tests will have to be performed, the prospector is quite excited about possibly finding real gold.

The prospector has had a good day. In fact, the fool's gold and the chalcopyrite may turn out to be

Activity

Rock-Forming Minerals

Only a small number of minerals make up most of the rocks on the earth's surface. These are called the rock-forming minerals.

Collect between five and ten different rocks from your neighborhood. Use a rock and mineral field guide to identify the minerals that make up each rock you found. Attach an index card to each rock, label the rock, and list the minerals that you were able to identify in that rock.

Figure 18-5 *Talc is a mineral that leaves a white streak (left). Graphite is a mineral that leaves a gray-black, shiny streak (right).*

A Gem of a Gem!

The largest recorded crystal of gem quality was a 520,000-carat aquamarine found in Brazil in 1910. A carat is a unit of mass for gems that is equal to about 200 milligrams. Find the mass of the largest gem.

Hefting is a valid test *only* if the same kind of rock (or rocks with about the same density) contain the gold-colored samples. The prospector is hefting rocks of the same size but not the same density.

valuable finds. Chalcopyrite is an important source of copper. Fool's gold is a source of iron and sulfur, vital to the chemical industry.

Heft

To confirm his hunch about the rock with ridges of gold, the prospector performed another simple test on the three rock specimens. The rocks were all about the same size and contained about the same amount of gold-colored material. So the prospector **hefted** the rocks. He balanced a rock in each hand, comparing their weights. The chalcopyrite and the fool's gold seemed to weigh about the same. The third specimen was noticeably heavier. And the prospector knew that real gold was heavier than either chalcopyrite or fool's gold. So here was another clue that the third specimen probably contained real gold.

Color

A mineral's color can fool you, which is the logic behind the saying "All that glitters is not gold." Put another way, all that has a gold color is not gold. Many minerals come in a variety of colors. The

Figure 18-6 *Quartz is a common mineral found in a variety of colors, such as light purple* (left) *and white* (right).

Figure 18-7 *Color can be a reliable guide to identifying some minerals along with other characteristics. Some of these colors are red-orange* (right), *yellow* (top left), *light green and purple* (bottom left).

milky-white mineral in which the prospector may have found gold is called quartz. It is in most rocks and makes up about 20 percent of the earth's crust. The sand on most beaches is almost all finely powdered quartz. Since quartz comes in almost every color of the rainbow, you would not be able to use color alone to determine whether a mineral is quartz.

On the other hand, color is a reliable guide to some minerals. For example, almost all minerals that contain copper are green or blue-green. The blue-green color of turquoise is due to the copper it contains. The color "turquoise blue" refers to this specific shade of blue-green. And, of course, the color "gold" comes from the mineral that always has that color, which is what probably excited the interest of our prospector in the first place.

Figure 18-8 *The variety of minerals in this photograph have many different metallic and nonmetallic lusters.*

Luster

One reason chalcopyrite and fool's gold are sometimes mistaken for gold is due to the way they reflect light. The way a mineral reflects light is called luster. Chalcopyrite and fool's gold both have a metallic luster. They reflect light the way highly polished metal does. Real gold also has the same kind of luster. What other minerals have a metallic luster? Answers will vary but students might suggest copper, silver, graphite, and other metals.

Other minerals have a nonmetallic luster. These minerals are dull and do not reflect much light. Many are transparent or partly transparent, like glass. Minerals with a glassy luster include quartz and tourmaline, which is used in optical equipment. Another mineral with a glassy luster is calcite, which is made up of calcium carbonate and found in the form of limestone, chalk, or marble. Some mica shows a pearly luster. Mica is a mineral that easily separates into layers. It reflects light with a rainbow display of colors the way a pearl does. Some minerals look as though they are covered with a thin layer of oil. Minerals such as serpentine, which looks like a snake's skin, have this greasy luster. Other minerals have a dazzling, brilliant luster. For example, rays of light reflected from a diamond break up into sparkles and flashes of many colors. Minerals that shine like silk, such as malachite, which is green and used as an ornament, and gypsum, used as a fertilizer, have a silky luster.

Figure 18-9 *Garnet, corundum, sulfur, crocoite, anatase, and kyanite illustrate the six basic crystal systems, which are due to the way the atoms in a crystal bond.*

CRYSTAL SYSTEMS

Cubic	Hexagonal	Orthorhombic	Monoclinic	Tetragonal	Triclinic
Garnet	Corundum	Sulfur	Crocoite	Anatase	Kyanite

Figure 18-10 *Many minerals break into different shapes. Galena cleaves into cubes* (left). *Hematite cleaves into thin sheets* (right).

Crystals

Most minerals from **crystals,** or solids that have a definite geometric shape. The shape of a crystal results from the way the atoms or molecules of a mineral bond, or join together. Each mineral has its own crystalline pattern of atoms or molecules. So each mineral has its own crystal shape.

There are six basic shapes of mineral crystals, or crystal systems. Each shape has a number of faces, or flat surfaces, that meet at specific angles to form sharp edges and corners. The crystal shape of a mineral is one of the most important clues to what the mineral is. Figure 18-9 shows the six crystal systems and examples of each.

Figure 18-11 *Asbestos is a mineral that fractures into fibers.*

Cleavage and Fracture

As you have read, a diamond struck at the correct angle breaks smoothly along a straight line. Many crystalline minerals break in this manner. Halite, the mineral form of common table salt, breaks into cubes. So does galena, a source of lead. Mica is a transparent crystalline mineral that breaks into thin sheets and plates. This breakage occurs along definite lines or smooth, flat surfaces and is called **cleavage.** See Figure 18-10.

Some minerals **fracture.** When these minerals break, they form an irregular surface that may be rough or jagged. Quartz fractures look like curved lines on a sea shell. Asbestos, a mineral used in making fireproof materials, fractures into fibers.

423

Figure 18-12

COMMON MINERALS AND THEIR USES

Minerals	Uses
Alum	Used in cosmetics, dyes, and water purification
Bauxite	Source of aluminum
Calcite	Used in medicine and toothpaste; also found in marble and limestone, which are used as building materials
Corundum	Used to make emery boards and to grind and polish metals
Feldspar	Used to make pottery, china, and glass
Graphite	Used in pencils and as a lubricant in small machines, clocks, and locks
Halite	Table salt
Hematite	Source of iron
Jade	Used to make vases and figurines
Malachite	Used to make table tops and jewelry
Quartz	Used in radios, television, and radar instruments
Sulfur	Used to make matches, medicine, rubber, and gunpowder

SECTION REVIEW

1. What is a mineral?
2. List seven physical properties of minerals.
3. What is the difference between the cleavage and fracture of minerals?

1. A natural substance that forms in the earth
2. Hardness, streak, heft, color, luster, crystal form, cleavage, and fracture
3. Cleavage: breakage that occurs along smooth, flat surfaces. Fracture: breakage that occurs along irregular surfaces.

18-2 Uses of Minerals

Did you ever try to listen to a quartz watch? There is no tick-tock sound that you can hear. But at the heart of any timekeeper is some kind of regular beat. What beats in a quartz timepiece is a quartz crystal. An electric current makes the crystal expand and contract. The crystal beats with a steady rhythm. The rate of the beat depends on the size and shape of the crystal, and nothing else. Because quartz crystals are such accurate timekeepers, they also are used to keep high-quality stereo turntables running at the right speed.

Other minerals also have important uses. See Figure 18-12. Salt, for example, is essential for life. Salt was once more precious than diamonds. Roman soldiers received part of their pay in salt, which is where our word for salary comes from. The word "sal" is Latin for salt.

Ores

Minerals are also the source of metals, without which modern civilization would be impossible. All metals come from minerals. Some metals, especially gold and silver, are found in their pure form in nature. Most metals, however, are combined in rocks with other minerals.

Rocks from which metals and other minerals can be removed in usable amounts are called **ores.** Chalcopyrite, for example, is a copper-containing mineral. It is an ore of copper. Copper and many other metals are removed from their ores by smelting. In this process, the ores are heated to the melting point and then treated chemically to free the metal from the ore.

Career: Gem Cutter

Near the end of their junior year, many students received their high school rings. A few students wondered about the origin of the red gem set firmly in their gold bands. After doing some research, the students learned that their rubies might have been found embedded in rocks in North Carolina, Thailand, or perhaps Burma. The students learned that their rubies had been cut from dull lumps of corundum, which is colorless if pure but appears red with the presence of chromium oxide. Once the red mineral was uncovered, it was cut and polished, into the gems used to decorate the students high school rings and other jewelry.

Gem cutters cut, shape, and polish the rough, dull minerals and stones into brilliant gems including diamonds, emeralds, and rubies. They place the rough stones into machines that cut and slit the stones with the use of diamond dust. The cut stone is then held against a rough, revolving disk that shapes and grinds it to create smooth surfaces called facets. Afterward, the gem cutters examine the stones using a magnifying glass to determine how accurately the cutting was done. Finally, the stone is polished with the use of felt or canvas, a polishing wheel, and polishing compounds.

Gem cutting requires patience and accuracy. Mistakes during cutting could be costly for the cutter. For this reason, beginning gem cutters practice with quartz and other inexpensive minerals until they become skilled enough to cut more expensive stones. If you are interested in gem cutting and would like to learn more, write to the Gemological Institute of America, P.O. Box 2110, 1660 Stewart Street, Santa Monica, CA 90406.

Gems

Some rare, very valuable, and beautiful minerals are called **gems.** But which gems are most desired? Historically, gems made from quartz were often more prized than diamonds. Amethysts, agates, and onyxes were among these gems. Queen Cleopatra of Egypt treasured a ring that contained an amethyst. Diamonds were valuable only because they could be used to cut and polish other gems.

But today, diamonds are highly prized. Diamonds come in different colors and shades. There are many shades of yellow and brown diamonds. Green, red,

Figure 18-13 *Diamonds have many uses such as jewelry* (left) *and as the points of phonograph needles* (right).

Activity

Rubies, Sapphires, and Emeralds

Using reference materials in the library, look up information about rubies, sapphires, and emeralds. In a written report, include answers to the following questions:

1. Why are these gems valuable?

2. How are these gems cut to make jewels?

3. How are these gems different?

4. In what countries are these gems found?

blue, and violet diamonds are much rarer, and therefore more valuable, than colorless diamonds. The yellow Tiffany diamond and the blue Hope diamond are among the most valuable of all gems. The rarest and most valuable gems are called precious stones. Other precious stones include rubies, emeralds, and sapphires.

The different colors of diamonds are due to small traces of various minerals. Such minerals also color rubies red, sapphires blue, and emeralds green. In fact, rubies and sapphires are nothing more than impure crystals of aluminum oxide, which is <u>aluminum rust</u>! Pure aluminum oxide is colorless.

Another name for aluminum oxide is corundum (ko-RUN-dum). It is a very common mineral. Because it is harder than any other mineral except diamonds, corundum is used in emery boards and for grinding and polishing metals. Tons of corundum are mined for such purposes.

But take corundum and add a few impurities and you may have a great sapphire, like the Star of India, which is a crystal of slightly impure aluminum rust. Brilliant emeralds, as precious as diamonds, are nothing more than impure beryl. Beryl is an ore of the metal beryllium, and in its pure form is a common colorless mineral. As for diamonds, the great flawless, colorless ones like the Cullinan are pure carbon. The mineral carbon is the same substance as the graphite in your pencil!

Other gems are not as rare or valuable as <u>precious stones</u>. These gems are called <u>semiprecious</u> stones. Examples of semiprecious stones are zircon, opals, jade, turquoise, amethysts, and malachite.

SOME CHARACTERISTICS OF GEMS

	Uncut	Cut	Color
Amethyst			Purple, blue-violet
Aquamarine			Blue-green, pale blue
Diamond			Yellow, brown, green, blue, violet, black, colorless
Emerald			Green
Ruby			Red, blue-red
Topaz			Yellow, brown, pale blue, pink, red, white
Tourmaline			Black, brown, pink, red, green, blue, colorless

Figure 18-14

SECTION REVIEW

1. What is an ore?
2. What is a gem?
3. List some examples of precious and semiprecious stones.

1. Rocks from which metals and other minerals can be removed in usable amounts
2. Rare, valuable, and beautiful minerals
3. Precious stones: diamonds, rubies, emeralds, sapphires. Semiprecious stones: opal, jade, turquoise, amethysts, malachite, zircon.

LABORATORY ACTIVITY

Answers appear on page T-59.

Forming Mineral Crystals

Purpose

In this activity, you will grow different types of crystals.

Materials *(per group)*

Table salt
Table sugar
Borax
Alum
Copper sulfate
250-mL beaker
Dental floss
Stirring rod
5 petri dishes
Magnifying glass or hand lens
Marking pencil

Procedure

1. Using a beaker and stirring rod, dissolve 25 grams of table salt in 200 mL of hot water.
2. Fill a petri dish with this solution. Use a marking pencil to label the dish.
3. Place a piece of dental floss in the solution and let it hang over the edge of the dish.
4. Repeat steps 1 to 3 four times, using sugar, borax, alum, and copper sulfate instead of salt.
5. Allow the solutions to evaporate slowly for a day or two. Note which crystals form quickly and which form slowly.
6. With a hand lens or magnifying glass, observe the crystals formed in the dish and along the dental floss. Note the difference in the crystal forms. Each substance has its own distinct crystal shape.

Observations and Conclusions

1. Write a brief statement describing the results of this activity.
2. Describe the appearance of each of the different crystals that you grew.
3. Draw a chart showing how long it took each of your crystals to grow.

CHAPTER SUMMARY

18-1 What Is a Mineral?

■ A mineral is a substance that has a definite set of physical properties, a definite chemical composition and is composed of one or more elements.

■ Most minerals can be identified by certain physical properties such as hardness, streak, heft, color, luster, crystal form, cleavage, and fracture.

■ The Mohs hardness scale rates minerals according to their hardness from 1 to 10.

■ Streak is the color of a mineral in powder form.

■ Heft is a way of comparing the weights of rocks.

■ Luster is the way a mineral reflects light.

■ Many minerals form different crystal shapes.

■ Cleavage breaks form definite lines or smooth, flat surfaces; fracture breaks form irregular surfaces that may be rough or jagged in appearance.

18-2 Uses of Minerals

■ Ores are rocks from which metals and other minerals can be removed in usable amounts.

■ Rare and valuable minerals are called gems.

VOCABULARY   *Define the following terms.*

cleavage p.423
crystal p.423
fracture p.423
gem p.425
heft p.420

luster p.422
mineral p.416
Mohs hardness scale p.418
ore p.424
streak p.418

CHAPTER REVIEW

Multiple Choice

Choose the letter of the answer that best completes each statement.

1. A mineral is a substance that forms in the earth and is composed of
   a. only one element.
   b. one or more elements.
   c. the remains of living things.
   d. living plants and animals.

2. An example of a mineral made up of more than one element is
   a. sulfur.
   b. gold.
   c. silver.
   d. quartz.

3. Most common minerals can be identified by certain physical properties such as
   a. hardness.
   b. luster.
   c. streak.
   d. all of the above.
4. The softest mineral on the Mohs hardness scale is
   a. talc.
   b. gold.
   c. pyrite.
   d. diamond.
5. A steel knife will scratch anything softer than
   a. feldspar.
   b. corundum.
   c. gypsum.
   d. calcite.
6. The color of a mineral in powder form is called
   a. luster.
   b. streak.
   c. cleavage.
   d. heft.

7. A mineral with a pearly luster is
   a. calcite.
   b. mica.
   c. chalcopyrite.
   d. copper.
8. An example of a mineral with a dazzling, brilliant luster is
   a. malachite.
   b. gypsum.
   c. diamond.
   d. calcite.
9. An example of a precious stone is a(n)
   a. zircon.
   b. amethyst.
   c. sapphire.
   d. opal.
10. An example of a semiprecious stone is a(n)
   a. emerald.
   b. jade.
   c. ruby.
   d. sapphire.

Completions

Fill in the word or words that best complete each statement.

1. All rocks are made up of _____minerals_____.

2. A mineral will _____scratch_____ any other material that is less than or equal in hardness to itself.

3. The sand on most beaches is almost entirely made of the mineral _____quartz_____.

4. Chalcopyrite and fool's gold both have a _____metallic_____ luster.

5. Malachite and gypsum have a nonmetallic luster called _____silky_____.

6. _____Cleavage_____ is the name of the process by which certain minerals, such as mica, break along definite lines or smooth, flat surfaces.

7. _____Fracture_____ is the name of the process by which certain minerals, such as quartz, break along an irregular surface.

8. Rocks from which metals and other minerals can be removed in usable amounts are called _____ores_____.

9. Aluminum oxide or corundum is a common mineral that is harder than any other mineral except _____diamond_____.

10. Colorless diamonds like the Cullinan are made up entirely of the element _____carbon_____.

True or False

Determine whether each statement is true or false. If it is true, write "true." If it is false, change the underlined word or words to make the statement true.

1. Quartz is a mineral made up of <u>two elements</u>. T
2. Sulfur is a mineral made up of <u>two elements</u>. F (one element)
3. Gold is <u>softer</u> that fool's gold. T
4. Some micas have a <u>pearly</u> luster. T
5. Quartz and tourmaline are minerals that have a <u>greasy</u> luster. F (glassy)
6. <u>Streak</u> is a way of judging the density of a rock. F (Heft)
7. Mica breaks into <u>cubes</u>. F (thin sheets)
8. Metals are extracted from their ores by the process of <u>smelting</u>. T
9. Rubies and sapphires are made up of crystals of <u>aluminum rust</u>. T
10. Colorless diamonds and graphite are made up of the element <u>iron</u>. F (carbon)

Discussion Topics Answers appear on page T-59.

Write a brief paragraph discussing each of the following.

1. Briefly explain how a mineral differs from a nonmineral.
2. Describe six physical properties used to identify minerals.
3. Discuss five different types of nonmetallic lusters and give one or more mineral examples of each type. Explain how metallic and nonmetallic lusters differ.
4. Discuss the uses of ten minerals.
5. Explain what causes gems to have specific colors. Give examples.

EXPAND YOUR KNOWLEDGE

Gilbert, M. *The Science Hobby Book of Rocks and Minerals*. Minneapolis, Minn.: Lerner.
 This interesting book tells you all about the physical properties of minerals. There are excellent discussions of rock-forming minerals, metallic and nonmetallic minerals, and gems.

O'Neil, P., and the editors of Time-Life Books. *Planet Earth: Gemstones*. Alexandria, Va.: Time-Life Books.
 Here is a fascinating discussion of precious and semiprecious gems, their history, and the exciting searches for these rare minerals. There are also excellent photographs of these gems.

Sootin, H., and L. Sootin. *The Young Experimenters' Workbook: Treasures of the Earth*. New York: Norton.
 This book provides over 50 simple experiments that you can do to learn more about the properties of different minerals.

Rocks

For a chapter overview, teaching strategies, answers to all activities, a list of A-V materials, and a chapter bibliography, see pages T-60 to T-62.

Consult your Teacher's Resource Book and Annotated Teacher's Edition, Laboratory Book for additional activities and teaching aids.

CHAPTER OBJECTIVES

After completing this chapter, you will be able to:

19-1 Explain how igneous rocks are formed.

19-2 Explain how sedimentary rocks are formed.

19-3 Explain how metamorphic rocks are formed.

19-4 Describe how the rock cycle works.

On the Giant's Causeway, row after row of black, six-sided rock pillars rise from the shore. The thousands of rocky pillars form huge platforms that look like stepping stones for giants. And according to legend, that is how the Giant's Causeway got its name. As the legend goes, giants built the rocks so they could cross the sea from the northern coast of Ireland to Scotland.

If such giants had existed, they might have discovered another unusual rock formation south of Scotland. On the southeastern coast of England, white cliffs tower 114 meters above the town of Dover. These cliffs form a wall of bright, gleaming stone. But if you were to examine the stone through a microscope, you would discover countless tiny, beautiful shells. From these white cliffs, it is said, comes one of the ancient names for England—Albion, the "White Land."

These are but two examples of different and amazing forms of rock. There are many others. Each has its own history—a history hidden in the earth's past. This history is full of action and change. And although the next rock you see is not likely to move before your eyes, it got to be where it is by great movements on and within the earth—movements that built the Giant's Causeway and the white cliffs of Dover.

The Giant's Causeway

Figure 19-1 *This photograph shows hot, molten lava erupting from a volcano on Hawaii.*

Figure 19-2 *A pattern of roughly six-sided rock columns forms where mud flats dry out. This pattern is similar to the skin of solid rock that shrunk and split to form the Giant's Causeway.*

19-1 Rocks of Liquid and Fire: Igneous Rocks

The strange six-sided rocks of the Giant's Causeway were forged in fire. But not by giants, and not in an ordinary fire.

Deep within the earth it is so hot that some of the minerals that make up rocks melt and flow like liquid. The liquid rock is less dense than solid rock, so the liquid rock tends to rise—just as bubbles rise through water. This hot, molten rock deep inside the earth is called **magma.**

Sometimes the magma reaches the surface. It may erupt from a volcano. Or it may seep through weak spots in the ground. Magma that has reached the earth's surface is called **lava.**

At the site of the Giant's Causeway, melted rock seeped toward the surface, forming large pools of melted rock material. As the rock cooled and solidified, it shrank and cracked. The cracks formed a six-sided pattern. You can see a pattern something like this where mud flats dry out in places like the Painted Desert in Arizona. As the lower levels of the pool of melted rock material cooled and hardened, the pattern of cracks spread downward. Each pool broke up into rows of six-sided rock columns.

The rocks of the Giant's Causeway are basalt. They belong to one group of rocks called **igneous** (IG-nee-us) **rocks.** All rocks formed from molten material are igneous rocks. The word "igneous" may remind you of the word "ignite." Both come from the Latin word "ignis" meaning coming from fire.

Extrusive Rocks

Basalt is only one kind of igneous rock. It is formed from melted rock or lava that cools and hardens at or near the earth's surface. Basalt is a type of igneous rock which is also called **extrusive** (ek-STROO-sive) **rock.** Some extrusive rocks originally were pushed slowly onto the earth's surface, much as toothpaste is pushed out of a tube. Others formed as melted rock material erupted rapidly from places such as volcanoes.

The Devil's Postpile is found in the Sierra National Forest in east-central California. These columns tower about 18 meters above the San Joaquin River. Shiprock is considered by the Indians of New Mexico to be a sacred object.

Figure 19-3 *These photographs show that basaltic rock can have very different shapes. Devil's Postpile National Monument (left) is a spectacular mass of blue-gray basalt columns. Shiprock (right) is the remains of the basaltic inner core of a volcano.*

Figure 19-4 *This obsidian dome is an example of an extrusive rock that cools rapidly on the earth's surface.*

Obsidian is another kind of extrusive rock. Because it is glassy-looking, it is often referred to as volcanic glass. It is usually dark in color and forms from molten material that cools very rapidly on the earth's surface. Rapid cooling is the key to making all kinds of glass.

Sometimes igneous rocks form so quickly that bubbles of volcanic gases are trapped in them. Rocks formed in this way contain many holes and tiny needlelike slivers of volcanic glass. Pumice (PUH-mis) is an example of this kind of rock. Because pumice is filled with bubbles it is a rock that actually floats on water! The particles of volcanic glass in pumice make it a good polishing agent. Have you had your teeth cleaned at a dentist's office? The gritty stuff in the cleaning powder was probably crushed pumice.

Intrusive Rocks

Another kind of igneous rock is granite, one of the earth's most common types of rock. Chemically, granite is similar to obsidian. However, granite is usually white or gray, rather than black. Also granite contains large crystals, while obsidian contains none.

Rocks that form from melted rock or magma that cools and hardens deep below the earth's surface are called **intrusive** (in-TROO-siv) **rocks.** They intrude, or push between surrounding rocks, while in a molten state. Huge masses of granite form within the earth

Figure 19-5 *This batholith is a huge body of igneous rock containing granite that formed underground and was eroded at the earth's surface.*

in this way. In some places, the masses are more than a thousand kilometers long and 200 kilometers wide. Scientists call these gigantic masses of rock batholiths (BA-thuh-liths), or deep stones. Batholiths form the stony base of the earth's great mountains.

Why do obsidian and granite look so different? The reason is because granite forms from molten rock that cools and hardens *within* the earth instead of at the earth's surface. As a result, granite cools and hardens much more slowly than the molten rock that becomes obsidian. Why? Think of a pot of soup on a stove. Exposed to air, it cools quickly. With the lid on the pot, the soup cools much more slowly. Granite forms "with the lid on." Obsidian forms "with the lid off."

The amount of time it takes liquid rock to cool and harden affects the texture of the rock. Texture refers to the size and type of crystals, or grains, that make up that rock. The slower the rate of cooling, the larger the crystals. The faster the rate of cooling, the smaller the crystals.

Most extrusive igneous rocks, such as basalt, have small crystals and are fine-grained because they cool and harden very quickly at the earth's surface.

Most intrusive igneous rocks, such as granite, have large crystals and are coarse-grained because they cool and harden very slowly beneath the earth's surface. Sometimes, magma cools and hardens so quickly that crystals do not form at all. Obsidian, or volcanic glass, is an extrusive rock that did not have time to form crystals.

SECTION REVIEW

1. What is the difference between magma and lava?
2. What is the difference between extrusive and intrusive rocks? Name an example of each.
3. What determines the size and type of crystals in rocks?

1. Magma: found deep inside the earth.
   Lava: found at the earth's surface.
2. Extrusive: cools and hardens at or near the earth's surface; obsidian. Intrusive: cools and hardens deep below the earth's surface; granite
3. Time it takes liquid rock to cool and harden

19-2 Rocks in Layers: Sedimentary Rocks

The rocks in this limestone cliff in Arizona, shown in Figure 19-6, appear to be stacked very neatly. One layer is piled on top of another. The layers are almost as straight as if they had been drawn using a ruler. Layered rocks like these are called **sedimentary** (sed-uh-MEN-tuh-ree) **rocks.**

How did this layering happen? The answers are in the rocks themselves. The rocks of this cliff are made up largely of the same material as the white cliffs of Dover—the shells of small sea creatures.

Figure 19-6 *The sedimentary rocks of this limestone cliff in Arizona (left) are stacked neatly on top of one another. These cliff layers in New Zealand (right), which look like piles of pancakes, are another example of sedimentary rock.*

437

Figure 19-7 *Sedimentary limestone rock contains the shells of once-living marine animals.*

Figure 19-8 *Conglomerates are made up of rock particles of different sizes, as well as sand and mud.*

Some 250 million years ago, this part of Arizona was believed to be at the bottom of a shallow sea. The sea stretched from what is now western Texas north to Canada. The sea was rich in life. Sharks and many kinds of fish swam in the waters. Most abundant of all were sea creatures that had shells. As these animals died, their remains settled to the sea floor. Steadily, more and more shells fell to the bottom. This process continued for millions of years.

Meanwhile, tropical forests of fernlike trees grew. Giant cockroaches scurried on the forest floor. Ancestors of the dinosaurs waddled on the shores of the sea. Rain and wind washed soil into rivers. The rivers flowed down to the sea, carrying muddy soil, pebbles, and rocks. These, too, built up in layers on the sea bottom.

Bones, shells, mud, and pebbles—all this material settled to the sea floor as sediment. The sediment piled up in layers many hundreds of meters thick. Lower layers were pressed together more and more tightly under the weight of the layers above. Larger rock fragments became cemented together by dissolved minerals. Gradually, the sediments hardened into strata, or layers, of rock.

Sedimentary rocks usually are formed in water. Most of the earth was under water at some time in the past. That is true now too—70 percent of the earth is covered by oceans. Consequently, sedimentary rocks are common all over the world. Sedimentary rocks often are rich in fossils—the remains or traces of animals or plants that lived in prehistoric times and were trapped in the layers of sediment.

Fragmental Rocks

Conglomerates, sandstones, and shales are all examples of **fragmental rocks.** They are sedimentary rocks made up of rock fragments mixed with sand, clay, and mud cemented together.

CONGLOMERATES Pebbles and other rocks of different sizes often cement together gradually by sand, mud, and clay to form a single large rock. It is an odd-looking rock. The sand, mud, and clay form the cement surrounding the pebbles. You can see in Figure 19-8 why the scientists who first studied this kind

Figure 19-9 *The unusual sandstone formations in Bryce Canyon, Utah were formed from cliffs made of layers of red sedimentary rocks.*

of rock called it "puddingstone." Later, scientists gave it another name—conglomerate rock. The name means the same thing. Conglomerate rock translates as "rock-made-up-of-many-things-put-together."

SANDSTONE   The layered rocks of sandstone, shown in Figure 19-9, are located in Bryce Canyon National Park, Utah. As their name implies, they form from sand grains cemented together. This sandstone is colored red due to traces of iron. Sandstone is very resistant to wear and decay and is often used as a building stone.

SHALE   Mud and clay that has hardened into layers of rock is called shale. Shales often form in quiet waters such as swamps and bogs. Small particles of clay and mud make up shales. These particles could only settle to the bottom in quiet waters. In fast-moving rivers, these small particles would be swept along by the currents.

Organic Rocks

Not all sedimentary rocks are made from pieces of rock. There are two other kinds of sedimentary rock. Some sedimentary rocks, such as limestone, may be built up from the remains of living things. Such rocks are called **organic rocks.** The name for

Figure 19-10 *This large deposit of shale is made up of small particles of clay and mud.*

Figure 19-11 *As the water in Mono Lake, California dries up, it leaves behind unusual shaped formations of rock salt.*

Why is there such a high concentration of minerals in Mono Lake? The answer is that the lake has no outlet, so the minerals are carried into the lake but not out.

Activity

Coral Conversions

The largest coral reef is the Great Barrier Reef, which parallels the northeastern coast of Australia for a distance of about 2000 kilometers. How many meters long is the Coral Reef? How many centimeters? Compare this distance to the distance across the United States which is 4,517 km from east to west.

these rocks comes from the word "organism," meaning living thing. Shells of animals such as clams and oysters sink to the ocean bottom and eventually form limestone. Limestone may also contain mud and sand. The hard outer coverings of corals are cemented together to become limestone reefs. Chalk is another organic sedimentary rock. It is made up of small pieces of animal shells and crystals of limestone cemented together.

Chemical Rocks

Some sedimentary rocks are formed when a sea or lake dries up leaving large amounts of minerals that were dissolved in the water. These minerals may collect into large formations called **chemical rocks.** Examples of this type of sedimentary rock include rock salt and gypsum (JIP-sum).

SECTION REVIEW

1. What are fragmental rocks made of? What are two examples?
2. What are organic rocks made of? What are two examples?
3. How are chemical rocks made? What are two examples?

1. Rock fragments mixed with sand, clay, and mud cemented together; conglomerates, sandstone, shale
2. Remains of living things; limestone, chalk
3. When a sea or lake dries up leaving large mineral deposits; rock salt, gypsum

19-3 Rocks That Change: Metamorphic Rocks

There is a very simple chemical test to determine if a rock is limestone. Add some strong vinegar to limestone and the rock will fizz and begin to dissolve. If you add strong vinegar to a bit of marble, the marble will also fizz and begin to dissolve. Why? Marble is chemically the same as limestone. However, the resemblance ends there.

Marble does not look like chalk, a kind of limestone. Chalk is soft and powdery, which is one reason you can use it to write on a chalkboard. But you cannot write with a piece of marble. Why? The reason is because marble is much harder and not powdery like chalk. Marble can be smoothed and polished until it gleams. And, unlike chalk, you will find no trace of fossil shells in marble.

Yet all marble was once limestone, including organic limestone made of fossil shells. Any kind of limestone may become buried deep within the earth. Under very high temperatures and tremendous pressures, the limestone changed. For millions of years the limestone was bent, folded, twisted, squeezed, and changed by forces in the earth. A different kind of rock finally formed. In this case, the new rock was marble.

Activity

Rock Quarries

Quarrying is a method of taking solid blocks or smaller pieces of rock from the earth and preparing them for various uses. Using reference materials in the library, write a report about quarrying stone and include the answers to the following questions:

1. What kinds of rocks are usually taken from quarries?

2. Describe three methods used to remove rocks from a quarry.

3. What are some of the uses of rock material taken from quarries?

4. Where are some large rock quarries located in the United States?

Figure 19-12 *Granite, an igneous rock, can be changed by enormous heat and pressure to form the metamorphic rock gneiss.*

Figure 19-13 *Shale, a sedimentary rock, can be changed by enormous heat and pressure to form the metamorphic rock slate.*

Rocks made in this way are called **metamorphic** (met-uh-MAWR-fik) **rocks.** These rocks are usually the hardest and densest rocks. The word "metamorphic" means a rock that has been changed.

Most metamorphic rocks once were either igneous or sedimentary rocks. Slate is a metamorphic rock made from clay or from shale, a sedimentary rock. Shale is porous or leaky. But under high temperatures and pressures, shale turns to slate. Waterproof, slate can be split into sheets and used to make roofs, pathways, and chalkboards.

Figure 19-14 *Sandstone, a sedimentary rock, can be changed by enormous heat and pressure into the metamorphic rock quartzite.*

Another example of metamorphic rock is quartzite (KWORT-zight). This rock is formed from the sedimentary rock sandstone. Under high temperature and pressure, the sand grains change shape and are packed closer together. The result is that quartzite is harder than sandstone.

SECTION REVIEW

1. What are the two physical conditions needed for metamorphic rocks to form?
2. Metamorphic rock was once what kind of rock?
3. Name two metamorphic rocks. Name the rock from which each is formed.

1. High temperatures and high pressures
2. Igneous or sedimentary
3. Marble from limestone; slate from shale; quartzite from sandstone

CAREER: *Geochronologist*

HELP WANTED: GEOCHRONOLOGIST Bachelor's degree in geology or related field required. Graduate study or coursework in geochronology a plus. Training will be provided during fieldwork and laboratory research.

For a very long time scientists could only guess at the age of the earth and the rocks upon it. Scientists tried determining age by estimating the time it took for the ocean to gain its present saltiness. They also made guesses on the time it takes for sediments to deposit, and then they measured the thickness of all the sedimentary rocks. Unfortunately, the scientists came up with age estimates of the earth ranging from 3 million to 1600 million years with no precise answer.

In the early 1900s, scientists began determining the age of rocks by using the half-life of radioactive minerals. Today scientists who specialize in the study of geologic time are called **geochronologists.** They figure out the age of rocks and landforms by the radioactive decay of certain elements such as carbon and uranium. They test igneous, metamorphic, and sedimentary rocks that range in age from being just recently formed to being almost as old as the earth itself, about 4.6 billion years.

Geochronologists work to learn more about how the earth came to be as it is. Through the study of sediments and fossils, they try to provide pictures of the earth throughout its history. These scientists have contributed to knowledge about the development of life from the first single-celled organisms to prehistoric human beings.

Some qualities that lead to a career in geochronology are natural curiosity, problem-solving ability, and enjoyment of the outdoors. Physical stamina is also required to do the fieldwork. More information may be obtained by writing to the American Geological Institute, 5205 Leesburg Pike, Falls Church, VA 22041.

19-4 The Rock Cycle

Rocks go through many changes. Igneous and sedimentary rocks can change to metamorphic rocks. Metamorphic rocks, too, may be remelted and become igneous rocks again. The continuous changing of rocks from one kind to another over long periods of time is called the **rock cycle.**

Figure 19-15 *This diagram of the rock cycle shows the many ways that rocks are changed.*

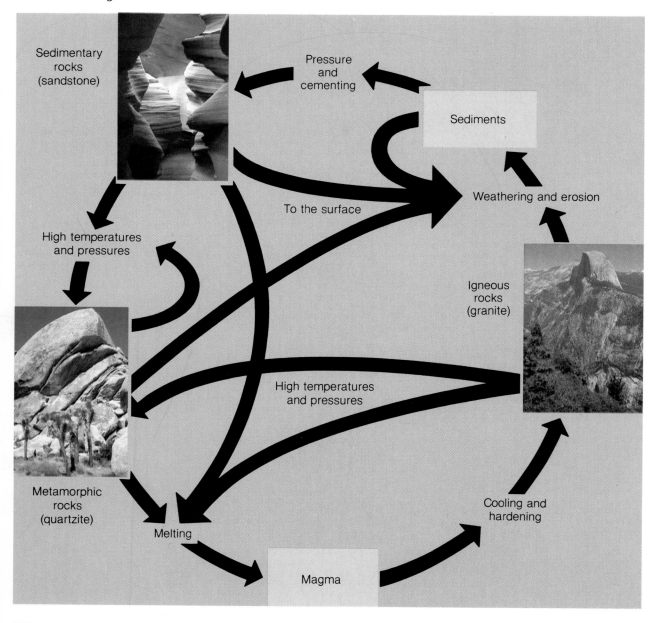

Sedimentary rocks (sandstone)

Pressure and cementing

Sediments

To the surface

Weathering and erosion

High temperatures and pressures

Igneous rocks (granite)

High temperatures and pressures

Metamorphic rocks (quartzite)

Melting

Cooling and hardening

Magma

Let's follow a rock on its ages-long journey through the rock cycle. See Figure 19-15. A huge dome of granite, an igneous rock, lies exposed to the wind and the rain, the cold of winter, and the heat of summer. Millions upon millions of years ago, this mass of granite was seething molten rock within the earth. It pushed upward against the solid rock above it, forming a dome. The dome hardened into solid rock underground. Slowly, the rock and soil that covered the dome were washed and ground away by wind and rain. Now the harder granite stands alone on the earth's surface.

But though the granite is hard, it also eventually will be worn down under the steady force of wind, water, and temperature changes. Bits of granite will flake off. Dragged along in rushing streams, these sediments may be reduced to powder. Much of this powder will be sand grains, which is made up mainly of the mineral quartz. The quartz will mix with water and other minerals, such as aluminum. The small particles that form are called clay. Some of this clay, as you will see in the next chapter, will become part of the soil.

But these sediments may take another path. They may be deposited on the sea floor. Under high pressure, the sediments may be cemented together in layers to form a sedimentary rock such as sandstone. These rocks may become buried deep under the earth's surface.

High pressure and high temperature may then change the sandstone into quartzite, a metamorphic rock. The quartzite may be exposed at the earth's surface and eventually become eroded to sediments again. Or the quartzite may become molten deep inside the earth. The magma that forms may cool and harden back into granite again. So the rock cycle goes on and on.

Activity

Changes in Rocks

Rocks can change with differences in temperature, moisture, soil type, and other environmental conditions. You can see some of these changes in gravestones.

Visit a nearby cemetery and try to find some old gravestones. Compare them to more recent gravestones. You can determine which are the oldest stones by reading the burial dates.

Summarize your findings in a written report. In this report, you should include the answers to the following questions:

1. What kinds of rocks were used for the older and the newer gravestones?

2. Which gravestones show more signs of weathering, the older ones or the newer ones?

3. Which kinds of rock show the most weathering?

4. Why are there more weathering and erosional changes in some gravestones than in others?

SECTION REVIEW

1. What are the three main groups of rocks? Give one example from each group of rocks.

2. How do wind, temperature, and water cause changes in rocks?

3. What is the rock cycle? What two factors in this cycle may change sandstone to quartzite?

1. Igneous, sedimentary, metamorphic; granite, sandstone, quartzite 2. Wear down rocks
3. The continuous changing of rocks from one kind to another. High pressure and high temperature

LABORATORY ACTIVITY

For further instructions, see page T-61.

Making a Sedimentary Rock

Purpose

In this activity, you will make your own sedimentary rock.

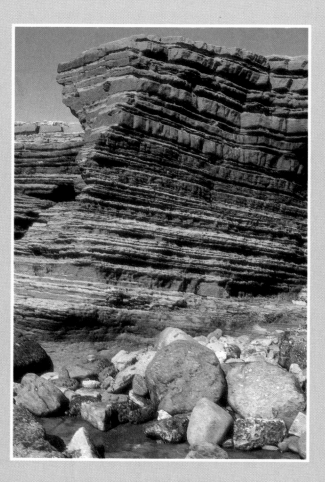

Materials *(per group)*

25 g alum
Sand
Metric ruler
Plastic butter or margarine container
100-mL graduated cylinder
Stirring rod
250-mL beaker
Triple-beam balance

Procedure

1. Use a stirring rod to dissolve 25 g of alum in 100 mL of warm water.
2. Fill the bottom of a plastic container to a depth of 2 cm with sand.
3. Pour the alum solution onto the sand in the container. Stir the mixture so that the alum solution is evenly distributed throughout the sand.
4. Pour off and throw away any excess solution. Gently tap the plastic container to help the sand grains settle together.
5. Place the container in a location where it can cool slowly and evaporate to dryness. This usually takes about a day.
6. Gently twist the sides of the container to free its contents. You have created a sedimentary rock.

Observations and Conclusions

1. Describe your rock in terms of color, heft (density), and overall appearance.
2. How is your rock similar to a piece of real sandstone?
3. How is your rock different from a piece of real sandstone?

CHAPTER SUMMARY

19-1 Rocks of Liquid and Fire: Igneous Rocks

■ Deep within the earth it is so hot that rock-forming minerals exist only in a liquid form known as magma.

■ If magma reaches the surface of the earth, it becomes known as lava.

■ Igneous rocks formed from the cooling of molten rock at or near the earth's surface are called extrusive rocks. Examples include basalt, obsidian, and pumice.

■ Igneous rocks formed from the cooling of molten rock deep beneath the earth's surface are called intrusive rocks. Granite is an example.

19-2 Rocks in Layers: Sedimentary Rocks

■ The hardening of layers of sediment results in the formation of sedimentary rocks. These rocks usually are formed in water.

■ Fragmental sedimentary rocks are formed by the cementing together of rock fragments. Conglomerates, sandstones, and shales are examples of fragmental rocks.

■ Organic sedimentary rocks are formed from the cementing together of the remains of living things. Chalk is an example.

■ Chemical sedimentary rocks are formed as large amounts of minerals—once dissolved in water—harden together.

19-3 Rocks that Change: Metamorphic Rocks

■ Rocks that underwent high temperatures and high pressures without melting lost their original features and are called metamorphic rocks. Marble and slate are examples.

19-4 The Rock Cycle

■ The continuous changing of rocks from one kind to another is called the rock cycle.

VOCABULARY   Define the following terms.

chemical rock p.440   **igneous rock** p.434   **magma** p.434   **rock cycle** p.444
extrusive rock p.434   **intrusive rock** p.435   **metamorphic rock** p.442   **sedimentary rock** p.437
fragmental rock p.438   **lava** p.434   **organic rock** p.439

CHAPTER REVIEW

Multiple Choice

Choose the letter of the answer that best completes each statement.

1. Molten rocks that cool at the earth's surface are
   a. igneous rocks.
   b. extrusive rocks.
   c. volcanic glass.
   d. all of these.

2. A kind of igneous rock that has cooled so quickly that gas bubbles remain trapped inside is called
   a. basalt.
   b. pumice.
   c. obsidian.
   d. granite.

3. Which of these is an example of an intrusive rock?
 a. granite
 b. obsidian
 c. magma
 d. pumice

4. The amount of time it takes molten rock to cool and harden mainly affects the rock's
 a. color.
 b. mass.
 c. texture.
 d. all of these.

5. Which of these igneous rocks cooled most slowly?
 a. obsidian
 b. granite
 c. pumice
 d. volcanic rock

6. Which sedimentary rock is formed from the cementing together of sand grains?
 a. granite
 b. shale
 c. limestone
 d. sandstone

7. Which of these is an example of a fragmental rock?
 a. basalt
 b. shale
 c. chalk
 d. obsidian

8. Organic rocks are formed from
 a. the cooling of magma.
 b. the cementing together of sand and clay.
 c. the remains of living things.
 d. all of these.

9. Which of these is an example of a metamorphic rock?
 a. pumice
 b. shale
 c. chalk
 d. marble

10. In the rock cycle, weathering and erosion can change which rocks into sediments?
 a. igneous
 b. sedimentary
 c. metamorphic
 d. all of these

Completions

Fill in the word or words that best complete each statement.

1. Molten rock that reaches the earth's surface is called _____lava_____.

2. _____Obsidian_____ is often volcanic glass.

3. Gigantic masses of granite called _____batholiths_____ form the bases of the earth's mountain ranges.

4. An example of a rock formed by the cementing together of rock fragments is _____conglomerates_____.

5. _____Shale_____ is a sedimentary rock formed from the hardening of layers of mud and clay.

6. Limestone is _____organic_____ sedimentary rock formed from the shells of ocean animals.

7. Limestone reefs form from the hard outer coverings of _____corals_____ that become cemented together.

8. Sedimentary rocks that form from large amounts of minerals that were once dissolved in water are called _____chemical_____ rocks.

9. _____Slate_____ is a metamorphic rock formed from clay or shale.

10. The continuous changing of rocks from one kind to another over long periods of time is called the _____rock cycle_____.

True or False

Determine whether each statement is true or false. If it is true, write "true." If it is false, change the underlined word or words to make the statement true.

1. Hot, molten rock deep inside the earth is called <u>lava</u>. F (magma)
2. Granite and obsidian are igneous rocks of <u>similar</u> chemical composition. T
3. Molten rocks that cool and harden beneath the earth's surface are called <u>extrusive rocks</u>. F (intrusive rocks)
4. Due to rapid cooling, the crystals of extrusive rocks are <u>smaller</u> than those of intrusive rocks. T
5. <u>Sedimentary rocks</u> may be rich in fossils. T
6. A <u>conglomerate</u> is an example of a(n) <u>chemical rock</u>. F (fragmental rock)
7. <u>Chalk</u> is a sedimentary rock made of small pieces of animal shells and limestone. T
8. Strong vinegar will react chemically with most <u>sandstone</u>. F (limestone)
9. <u>Metamorphic rocks</u> can change into igneous rocks. T
10. Under high temperature and high pressure, sandstone, a sedimentary rock, may change into quartzite, a <u>metamorphic rock</u>. T

Discussion Topics   Answers appear on page T-62.

Write a brief paragraph discussing each of the following.

1. Obsidian and granite are igneous rocks with similar chemical composition, but with different appearances. Describe the differences and explain how they came about.
2. Describe how and where sedimentary rocks form. Explain why scientists study sedimentary rocks to learn about prehistoric life.
3. Fragmental rocks, organic rocks, and chemical rocks are all examples of sedimentary rocks. Describe the differences between these three types and list one example of each.
4. Describe what may happen to a huge dome of granite as it goes through the rock cycle.

EXPAND YOUR KNOWLEDGE

Fenton, C. L., and M. A. Fenton. *The Rock Book.* New York: Doubleday.
    This book describes the properties and the importance of many different rocks. It also contains many useful suggestions for collecting and displaying your rock specimens.
Gallant, R. A., and C. J. Schubeth. *Discovering Rocks and Minerals: A Nature and Science Guide to Their Collection and Identification.* New York: Natural History Press.
    A useful guide for easily identifying many different kinds of rocks and where you can find them. The excellent photographs also help in identifying your rock specimens.
Shepherd, W. *Wealth from the Ground.* New York: John Day.
    What products do you use every day that are made from rocks? Find out about the many uses of sedimentary, igneous, and metamorphic rocks in this beautifully illustrated book.

Soils

For a chapter overview, teaching strategies, answers to all activities, a list of A-V materials, and a chapter bibliography, see pages T-62 to T-65.

Consult your Teacher's Resource Book and Annotated Teacher's Edition, Laboratory Book for additional activities and teaching aids.

CHAPTER OBJECTIVES

After completing this chapter, you will be able to:

20-1 Describe the different soil levels.

20-1 List and describe different environmental factors that produce various kinds of soil.

20-2 Describe how leaching affects soil formation, especially in tropical rain forests.

20-3 Explain why temperate forest soil does not provide enough minerals for widespread plant growth.

20-4 Explain how prairie grassland soil came to be so fertile.

20-5 Explain why little humus forms in desert soil.

20-6 Explain why tundra soil is different from most types of soil.

To the first settlers from Europe, much of North America looked like one vast forest. It stretched westward as far as the settlers could see.

Or so it seemed. The first settlers cleared some forest and built their towns along the Atlantic coast of the new continent. As more settlers arrived and families grew, the settlers slowly pushed westward. By the 1800s, they reached the edge of the forest—the Midwest.

It was like standing between two worlds. Behind the settlers, to the east, lay the forest—shaded, cool and damp. Under a thin layer of leaves, the soil was white and ashlike. To the west, in brilliant sunshine, a sea of grass rippled in the wind. Beneath the grass, though the settlers did not know it yet, lay some of the best farming soil in the world.

Beyond the western edges of the great grasslands, the grass grew scarcer and died away into desert land with cactus plants and shrubs. Here much of the soil was barren powdery rock.

The pioneers that settled on this new continent did not know why soils were different in forests, grasslands, and deserts. They may have guessed that factors in the environment were important. And they would have been right.

The prairie grasslands

20-1 Soil

Some people think of "soil" as being another word for dirt. And when people say something is "dirt cheap," they mean it is practically worthless. But soil is precious and vital to life on the earth. Without soil, most plants could not grow on the land. Without plants, no animals would survive. The earth's surface might look as barren as the moon.

Soil Layers

You can find out a lot about how a house is built by looking at what holds it up and what holds it together—its structure. But usually you cannot see much of the structure without taking the house apart. The framework of a house is hidden in the walls and floors. The foundation is underground.

The structure of soil is much the same. Soil is a covering over most of the earth's land surface. This soil covering can range in thickness from a few millimeters to a few meters. However, all you usually see of the soil covering is the very top. To find out what lies beneath, you must dig.

Like a house with several floors, soil has different levels. The uppermost level is made up of **topsoil.** Topsoil is a mixture of small grains of rock and the decayed matter of plants and animals. How did this mixture come about? You can see its beginnings on the forest floor. Year after year a carpet of wood, pine needles, leaves, and bits of twigs is laid down. A rich variety of animals live on and under this carpet, including worms, snails, insects, and mice.

Year after year, the remains of plant and animal life decay to become a part of the topsoil. The decayed matter combines with rocky soil particles to form a rich, dark soil called **humus.** Humus supplies essential chemicals for growing plants. Because humus is spongy, it stores water. In fact, humus can hold up to 600 times its own weight in water. Humus soil also contains many air spaces, or pores. When mixed well with rock grains, humus forms a soil through which both air and water can reach the roots of plants.

Topsoil
(containing
humus)

Subsoil

Weathered
parent
rock

Unweathered
parent
rock

The thickness of the topsoil may be anywhere from a few centimeters to a meter or more. Beneath it is the **subsoil** level. This level is made up of larger bits of rock and has little or no humus.

As you dig down further into the soil, the rock particles become larger and more numerous. Finally you reach solid rock, which is called the **parent rock.** Most minerals and other rocky particles in the soil first originated from this parent rock. But how could tiny rock particles come from solid parent rock?

Soil and the Environment

If you place a rock on the ground and strike it with a hammer, the rock will break into pieces. Smash these pieces and they become even smaller. Continue smashing the pieces and they may even become part of the soil. Billions of years ago before soil formed, the land surfaces of the earth were solid rock—parent rock. Naturally, there were no giant hammers crushing the parent rock into soil. But in a way environmental factors such as wind, water, heat,

Figure 20-1 *Soil has different layers, as shown in an artist's view* (left) *and in a photograph* (right). *In the photograph, see if you can locate the topsoil, subsoil, and areas of weathered and unweathered parent rock.*

Figure 20-2 *This photograph shows the longest natural bridge in the world. Made of sandstone, it was formed by the process of weathering.*

This natural arch spans about 89 meters and is set about 30.5 meters above the canyon floor. In one place, erosion has narrowed the arch to about 2 meters wide.

Activity

Rain Forest Death Rate

In 1980, the U.S. National Academy of Sciences estimated that 20 million hectares of tropical rain forest are destroyed each year. How many hectares would have to be destroyed each day to make this estimate correct?

and cold acted much like a hammer. The process by which rocks are broken down by the environment is called **weathering.** Weathering helped produce soil when the earth was young, and weathering still is producing soil today.

How can weathering produce soil? There are many ways. Water, for example, may seep into cracks in the rock. In cold weather, the water freezes. As water freezes, it expands to take up more space than liquid water. The ice pushes against both sides of the cracks and splits the rock into smaller pieces. Small plants, such as lichens, may grow on these rocks. These plants produce acids that break down the rocks into even smaller pieces. Eventually, weathering breaks down parent rocks into mineral particles. Remains of plants and animals get mixed in with these mineral particles and soil is formed.

Running water can also break down rocks into smaller soil particles. Whipping winds can do the same. Environmental factors such as these not only help produce soil, they also distribute the soil—often far from the region where it formed. On the steep slope of a mountainside, for example, strong winds and heavy rains can break down rock, which may eventually become a part of the soil. But as fast as the soil forms, floods can sweep it away. The soil may eventually be deposited many kilometers away on a flat plain, forming the rich soil important to farmers.

But to say that soil is created in this way is only part of the story. There are many kinds of soil. Different soils are shaped by different environmental factors, including the weather, the land, and the living things where the soil was formed. At the same time, the kind of soil in a place has an important influence on the kinds of things that can live in that place. For example, plants such as rhododendrons and azaleas grow best in soils containing large amounts of iron. Other plants have special needs for various elements in the soil.

SECTION REVIEW

1. Name the first two layers of soil.
2. Which layer of soil contains the most humus?

1. Topsoil, subsoil
2. Topsoil

20-2 Tropical Rain Forest Soil

There are three major areas in the world where tropical rain forests grow: the Amazon area of South America, parts of Africa, and parts of Southeast Asia. This green belt of tropical rain forests is near the equator, where there is much rain and the temperatures are warm year round.

If you were to walk through a tropical rain forest, you might be amazed by the many different kinds of plants and animals. All around you tall trees, some 60 meters or more in height, soar toward the sky to capture sunlight. And soar they must, for the forest

Figure 20-3 *A tropical rain forest has many kinds of trees that grow very close together.*

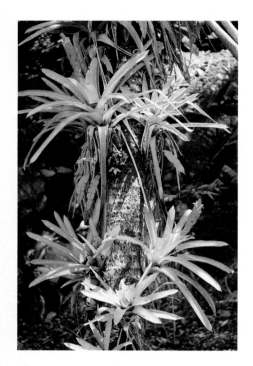

Figure 20-4 *Some plants grow piggyback on the trunks and limbs of trees in a tropical rain forest.*

Some plants that live on tree branches in a tropical rain forest develop tangled masses of aerial roots that act like a net and catch leaves. As these leaves decay, they not only supply nutrients for the plants but also act like a sponge to collect water.

Figure 20-5 *Many interesting animals, such as these colorful macaws (left) and this large orangutan (right), live in a tropical rain forest.*

floor is dim and shadowy. Even at noon only scattered flecks of sunlight shine through the ceiling of trees and reach the forest floor.

You might wander for over a kilometer without seeing the same kind of tree twice! From some trees hang strange vines that weave their way around the tree trunks, forming coils and loops of living matter. Other vines snake through the air, waving in the warm tropical breeze. Colorful plants such as orchids grow on the bark of some trees. Surprisingly, you have little trouble walking on the forest floor. Very few plants would block your way because they cannot grow where the light is so dim.

The tropical rain forest is a biologist's delight. Animals of all kinds, ranging from huge tarantulas that capture small birds for prey to brightly feathered parrots munching on nuts, live in the forest. Some animals, such as hunting leopards, glide through the shadows of the forest floor in search of food. Others, such as lizards and snakes, climb up and down tree trunks. Still others, including over 150 species of bats, fly through the air. In fact, scientists estimate that two-thirds of all plant and animal species make their home in tropical rain forests.

As you continue on your walk, you notice that many plants have leaves with unusually long pointed ends. These ends, called "drip tips," function like rain gutters. They allow water to quickly drip off the leaves of these plants. Drip tips are a big advantage in a tropical rain forest in which rainfall averages more than 200 centimeters per year. If the rain could not quickly flow off the leaves, the plants might become covered with mold and die.

The heavy rainfall in the tropical rain forest plays a role in soil formation. Heavy rains can wash minerals important for plant growth downward into the soil. This process of washing minerals out of the topsoil is called **leaching.** Leaching is important in the formation of soils. Normally, leaching can spread important minerals throughout the subsoil where roots can easily reach them. But in the tropics, there is often too much rain for this to happen. Instead, the minerals are leached so far into the ground that they are lost to the plants.

If leaching removes important minerals from the rain forest soil, why are so many different kinds of plants able to survive? The answer is right above you—all you need do is look up to see the forest's main source of minerals. Leaves, flowers, and other plant parts constantly fall to the forest floor. Added to these remains are the bodies of dead animals. Since the forest is hot and damp all year long, these remains decay very quickly and form a rich supply of food for the plants. Although rain constantly washes away this thin layer of humus, it is constantly replaced by a new layer. Also, the root systems of rain forest plants are so efficient that almost all the decaying matter is absorbed by living plants.

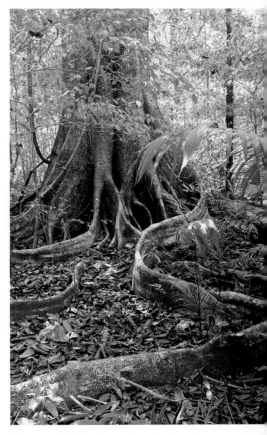

Figure 20-6 *Many tropical rain forest trees have extensive surface root systems that are so efficient they can recycle nearly all the nutrients from decaying plants.*

SECTION REVIEW

1. What is leaching? Why is leaching important in the formation of soils?
2. Tropical soil has a thin layer of humus. Why?

1. Washing of minerals out of topsoil; spreads minerals throughout the subsoil.
2. Rain constantly washes it away.

20-3 Temperate Forest Soils

"The American forests have generally one very interesting quality, that of being entirely free from underwood. This is owing to the extraordinary height and spreading tops of the trees; which thus prevent the sun from penetrating to the ground."

So wrote a traveler in Pennsylvania in 1806. Today only small areas of these temperate forests still exist in the United States. But they still take up a lot of ground. Temperate forests include such trees as beech, maple, oak, hemlock, wild cherry, and dogwood, as well as a variety of evergreens.

The traveler's description of the temperate forest sounds something like that of the tropical rain forest. Of course, there are important differences. The climate of the tropical forest is hot and damp. The climate of the temperate forest ranges from cold and fairly dry in the north to warm and damp further south. There are four different seasons in all temperate forests. In the cold seasons, particularly in the northern forests, most decay of plant and animal remains stops. As you might expect, little humus is produced in the cold weather and few minerals are added to the soil. However, even in warm weather, the temperate forest floor cannot support a wide variety of plant life. Why?

All trees lose leaves in winter. However, evergreens continue to grow new leaves all year, even in winter.

Career: *Soil Conservationist*

HELP WANTED: SOIL CONSERVATIONIST Bachelor's degree in soil conservation or natural resource sciences such as agronomy, forestry, or agriculture necessary.

The rain poured down hard and fast. Most of the valuable topsoil washed into the stream that ran across the farm. Enough soil filled the stream to cause flooding and destruction of the crops beside it. To obtain help, the farmer contacted the area's soil conservation service. A

soil conservationist was immediately sent to inspect the situation.

Soil conservationists advise farmers and ranchers how best to water livestock or to prevent overgrazing. Other concerns include water conservation, sound land use, and environmental improvement. Soil conservationists prepare plans using soil conservation practices such as crop rotation, reforestation, terracing, and permanent vegetation. Usually in planning a soil program, soil conservationists work closely with government workers, farmers, ranchers, foresters, and urban planners.

Anyone who is interested in conserving and protecting our natural resources and who enjoys working with people might consider a career in soil conservation. In rural areas, positions arise in banks, insurance firms, and mortgage companies. Public utility, lumber, and paper companies also employ soil conservationists. Government positions are also available, such as in the Department of the Interior. For more information about this career, write to the United States Department of Agriculture, Soil Conservation Service, Room 5218—South, Fourteenth Street and Independence Avenue S.W., Washington, DC 20250.

Figure 20-7 *Trees in a temperate forest grow many leaves during the summer* (left). *But these leaves do not grow during the winter. In the winter, organic decay and plant growth stop* (right).

In temperate forests, there is no heavy year-round rainfall. However, again, little humus forms. For although the forest floor is matted with leaves and evergreen needles, rainwater often leaches out important minerals. These minerals are carried deep into the subsoil. So, many minerals are lost before the dead plant matter can decay enough to return any minerals to the topsoil.

Because the trees in temperate forests have deep roots, they can reach important minerals that have leached into the subsoil. However, smaller plants with shorter root systems cannot get to these minerals needed for plant growth. The lack of smaller plants is particularly true in northern temperate forests where almost all the plants are evergreen trees. The carpet of evergreen needles is especially poor in many important minerals. In more southern temperate forests, the leafy floor is richer in minerals and the warmer weather allows more decay to proceed at a faster pace. Why is this soil more fertile than soil in the most northern temperate forests?

Leafy material is richer than evergreen needles in important minerals; warmer weather allows more humus to form because there is more decay of plant and animal matter

SECTION REVIEW

1. Where would you expect the rate of decay of dead plant and animal matter to be faster, in a tropical rain forest or in a temperate forest?
2. List three trees, other than evergreens, that grow in temperate forests in the United States.

1. Tropical rain forest
2. Oak, maple, beech

Activity

Leaching

In a 500-word essay describe how leaching affects each of the following soil types: tropical soil, temperate forest soil, prairie grassland soil, desert soil, tundra.

Figure 20-8 *Darrel Coble (far right) was three years old in April 1936 when he and his family fled this dust storm in Oklahoma. During the 1930s, prairie grassland soils became useless for growing crops.*

Activity

The Use of Fertilizers

Fertilizers are natural or artificial chemicals that take the place of humus. In the library, look up information about the many kinds of fertilizers used to improve the soil. What kinds of fertilizers are best suited for different kinds of soil?

Some fertilizers may have harmful as well as beneficial effects. What are some of these harmful effects? What factors should be considered before using certain fertilizers to improve the soil? Prepare a chart of the various fertilizers and their uses. In your chart include the advantages and disadvantages of each kind of fertilizer.

20-4   Prairie Grassland Soil

To the first settlers, the great prairie grasslands of the midwestern United States appeared as a vast sea of grasses. It stretched from the eastern forest region to the Rocky Mountains.

At first, the settlers felt that these prairie grasslands were useless for growing crops. The settlers were used to planting crops in cleared forest land. They had never seen anything like this land and believed that where trees did not grow in large numbers, the ground could not be good for crops.

In time, the settlers discovered that the soil of these regions was some of the richest in the world. Today the Canadian and United States prairie grasslands are considered the "breadbaskets of the world," for here is where great oceans of wheat are grown. Wheat is the grain from which bread is made. There are similar regions in Argentina and the Ukraine region of the Soviet Union. Together, these regions produce nearly all of the grain crops grown in the world. Grain crops include corn, wheat, barley, and rye.

The soils of North America's prairie grassland were not always so fertile. Millions of years ago most of the land west of the Rocky Mountains slowly turned to desert. As the soil dried up and crumbled to dust, winds carried it eastward and deposited the

Figure 20-9 *On the same land in Oklahoma 42 years later, Darrel Coble and his two sons walk through fertile fields of wheat. Changes in climate greatly influence soil and plant changes.*

soil over the prairie. Soon grasses began to grow in the newly laid soil. Year after year, thick mats of grass roots and stems decayed, building a deep layer of humus. Since the prairie, unlike the forests, was exposed to lots of sun and high winds, rainfall quickly evaporated. This prevented important minerals in the humus from leaching out of the topsoil. Today prairie grassland soil is rich in humus, dark brown to black in color, and very fertile.

SECTION REVIEW

1. Why are the Canadian and United States prairies called the "breadbaskets of the world"?
2. Why is there less leaching in prairie soil than in forest soil?

1. Great amounts of wheat are grown in these regions.
2. Rainfall is quickly evaporated by the sun and high winds.

20-5 Desert Soil

You probably imagine deserts as being very hot, dusty places. And, in fact, many deserts are quite hot—at least during the day. However, the main characteristic of all deserts is not heat but a lack of water. This lack of water is a problem for many plants and animals that make their home in the desert. But it also means there is very little leaching of

Figure 20-10 *In the spring, desert flowers bloom in a spectacular display. But the flowers soon vanish so the plants can complete their life cycles before the start of the hot, dry summer.*

Figure 20-11 *These barrellike cacti act like living accordions by swelling up to store water and then contracting slowly as the water supply decreases. Cacti also have a waxy coating that keeps the stored water from evaporating.*

minerals from the desert soil. So you might expect desert soil to be rich in minerals—and it is.

Despite the minerals in the desert soil, there is little or no humus in the soil. Why? Desert plants often have root systems that spread out in a wide area around the plant. In this way, plants can take in as much water as possible whenever an infrequent rain shower occurs. However, because of their widespread root systems, there are often large spaces between desert plants. With so few plants in any one area, there is not a constant "rain" of plant matter onto the desert floor. And what does fall to the floor decays very slowly in the dry desert heat. As a result, very little humus or topsoil can form. How, then, do you think scientists might be able to grow plants and food crops in a desert? By bringing more water to desert regions

SECTION REVIEW

1. What is the main characteristic of all deserts?
2. Why is there little leaching in the desert?

1. Lack of water
2. Lack of water

20-6 Tundra Soil

Beyond the edge of the northern evergreen forests and in much of northern Alaska lies the arctic tundra. Tundra also is found in other arctic regions in the world. In the tundra, the climate is very cold most of the year, and strong winds blow constantly.

There is little or no topsoil in the tundra and much of the soil just below the surface is permanently frozen. This frozen soil is called **permafrost.** As you might expect, few plants can grow in the harsh tundra, particularly during the long winter. Those plants that do grow are small plants, mainly reindeer moss, lichens, and dwarf trees. When these plants die, they decay very slowly due to the cold weather. So little humus forms in the tundra.

Unlike most soils, tundra soil does not have different levels. There is a constant mixing of the soil due to freezing and thawing. In summer, a thin layer at the top of the soil thaws. It stays wet, because the water cannot go through the permanently frozen layers beneath. During this time, small lakes and marshes form on the tundra. Ducks of all kinds flock to the tundra lakes during the short summer months. When winter does return and the ground soil again freezes, the ducks and many other tundra animals will have already migrated to warmer areas farther south.

Figure 20-12 *Another kind of soil is mountain soil. Soil on the slopes of mountains is made up of jagged pieces of weathered parent rock and very small amounts of clay and sand. There usually is no topsoil in these regions.*

Figure 20-13 *Many small plants such as grasses, lichens, and reindeer moss grow on the tundra during summer (left). But during the winter the ground is snow-covered, and animals such as these caribou must keep traveling in search of food (right).*

SECTION REVIEW

1. What is permafrost?
2. Tundra soil has no distinct layers. Why?

1. Permanently frozen soil
2. Constant mixing due to freezing and thawing

LABORATORY ACTIVITY

For further instructions, see page T-64.

Determining Rates of Weathering

Purpose

In this activity, you will find out what effect particle size has on the speed, or rate, at which a rock reacts with its surroundings.

Materials *(per group)*

1 antacid or seltzer tablet	Paper
4 100-mL beakers	Pen or pencil
Graduated cylinder	Water

Procedure

1. Break an antacid tablet in two.
2. Place one of the halves on a piece of paper, and fold the paper so that it covers the tablet.
3. With one end of your pencil or pen, gently tap the half tablet under the paper several times in order to break it into smaller pieces. Be careful not to crush the material to powder.
4. Place the other half of the tablet in one beaker. Place the crushed, smaller pieces in a second beaker.
5. Add 10 mL of water to each of the remaining beakers.

6. At the same time, pour the water from these two beakers into the beakers containing the seltzer tablets.
7. Observe both reactions until they end. Then record your observations. Be sure to describe the reactions you observed in both beakers and the time it took for the reactions to end.

Observations and Conclusions

1. What difference in reaction rates did you observe in the two beakers?
2. When you broke the tablet into very small pieces, you increased the surface area of that part of the tablet. State the relationship between surface area and reaction rate in a chemical change.
3. Your observations in this activity can be used to make a general statement about weathering processes that occur in the natural environment. Draw a graph showing the relationship between the particle size of a substance and the rate at which it weathers.

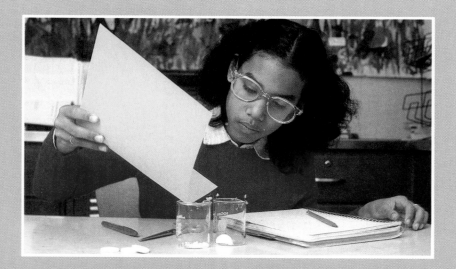

6. The washing of minerals out of the topsoil is called _____leaching_____.

7. Heavy rainfalls cause many minerals to leach from the _____topsoil_____ layer in a tropical rain forest.

8. The topsoil of prairie grassland soils is dark in color because it contains a lot of _____humus_____.

9. The soil of the Arctic is called _____tundra_____ soil.

10. The permanently frozen subsoil of the Arctic is called _____permafrost_____.

True or False

Determine whether each statement is true or false. If it is true, write "true."
If it is false, change the underlined word or words to make the statement true.

1. The uppermost layer of soil is <u>subsoil</u>. F (topsoil)
2. Humus is used by <u>animals</u> as food. F (plants)
3. Humus soil contains <u>few</u> air spaces. F (many)
4. The process in which rock is broken down into soil is called <u>weathering</u>. T
5. If the leaves of plants in tropical rain forests do not dry quickly, <u>molds</u> may grow on them and kill the leaves. T
6. Tropical rain forests are located near the earth's <u>poles</u>. F (equator)
7. Rapid decaying and forming of humus occurs in <u>tropical</u> soils. T
8. A mat of evergreen needles is <u>rich</u> in minerals needed for plant growth. F (poor)
9. Plants and animals of the desert areas can survive because they are able to save and store <u>water</u>. T
10. Constant mixing of the soil due to freezing and thawing prevents <u>tundra</u> soils from having different soil levels. T

Discussion Topics   Answers appear on page T-65.

Write a brief paragraph discussing each of the following.

1. Soil is precious and vital to life on the earth. Compare what the earth is like with soil to what the earth would be like without soil.

2. Many scientists consider the Antarctic among the world's largest deserts. Explain how such a cold place can be a desert.

EXPAND YOUR KNOWLEDGE

Graham, A., and F. Graham. *The Changing Desert*. New York: Scribner's
Each chapter presents an interesting discussion about the desert environment and how people are changing the desert.

Coming Up······SCIENCE GAZETTE·····································

Starting on the next page you will find three special articles. The first tells an exciting story about a scientist. The second tells about a battle of ideas. And the last looks into the future. Each of the articles has been written so you will enjoy reading it. As you read, you may want to jot down thoughts that come to mind. You might then write a report telling what you thought about the articles. Or you might just want to read the articles for the fun of it.

SCIENCE GAZETTE

Adventures in Science

The articles of this *Science Gazette* have been carefully chosen and designed to inspire and motivate students of all levels in their study of science. Each article is related to one or more topics presented in the unit. See the "Science Reading Skills" section in your Teachers' Resource Book for specific activities and handouts. Also, for further instructions, see page T-65 in this book.

Maria Reiche Solving the

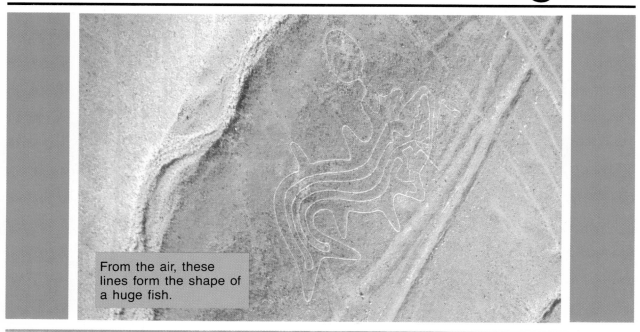

From the air, these lines form the shape of a huge fish.

Mysteries of the Nazca Lines

One of the driest spots on the earth is the Nazca Desert of Peru. Here, huge drawings of animals have been scratched into the earth's surface. These drawings are so large that they can be recognized only from the air.

The figure of a monkey capers across 80 meters of flat, dusty landscape. Nearby, a gigantic bird spreads its wings over more than 270 meters of desert soil. These are just two of about 30 huge mysterious drawings that, from the ground, look simply like furrows in the dirt.

The drawings are called the Nazca Lines, after the desert on which they are drawn. They were made many centuries ago by Peruvian Indians who left behind almost nothing else of their culture. But why did the ancient Peruvians make the drawings? This question remains unanswered.

Many scientists, as well as interested visitors, have tried to unlock the secret of the Nazca Lines. But the efforts of one woman stand out. Her name is Maria Reiche, a woman on a lifelong quest to solve the mystery of the lines. Maria Reiche is an 80-year-old mathematician and geographer. For more than 20 years she has lived in the desert studying the Nazca Lines and making careful measurements.

Speaking of her search for the answer to the mystery of the Nazca Lines, Maria Reiche says, "We have to penetrate into the minds of the Indians who drew these lines and find the way they worked to find the answer."

Reiche came to Peru from Germany in the 1930s. Her fascination with the desert drawings began in 1940, when she met an American archeologist named Paul Kosok. Kosok was in Peru studying ancient systems of watering crop lands. He had charted one of the winding desert markings thinking that it might be part of such a watering system. Instead, he found that the line formed the huge figure of a bird. It was the first drawing to be discovered. Reiche has since devoted herself to the drawings.

From her many years in the desert, Reiche discovered how the ancient Peruvians carved the lines in the soil. They created the 7- to 8-centimeter deep furrows by removing the surface of brown stones to reveal the yellow soil beneath. The yellow soil—a mixture of

Maria Reiche seeks to unlock the secrets of mysterious lines carved into the ground of the Nazca Desert of Peru.

sand, clay, and calcite—contrasts sharply with the stones.

The Indians could not have chosen a better spot for their artwork. The Nazca Desert receives less than one-quarter of a centimeter of rain each year. It is the dryness that has preserved the lines for the one or two thousand years since they were made. A cushion of warm air hovers over the desert surface and helps protect the drawings from being covered by blowing sand.

A Recent Breakthrough

Some scientists, including Reiche, believe that the drawings had something to do with religious ceremonies. But Reiche feels that religious ceremony was not their only function. She has been trying to prove that the lines were a kind of calendar that was used to chart the movement of the sun, moon, and stars. Many ancient civilizations had such calendars and used them to set dates for planting, harvesting, and festivals.

To test her hypothesis, Reiche must find a relationship between the lines and the positions of the sun and moon at special times of the year. Such times are the solstices, which mark the beginning of summer and winter, and the equinoxes, which mark the beginning of spring and fall.

In the early morning, before the desert heat becomes too intense, Maria Reiche can be seen shuffling across the desert. Even before the sun has risen, she is noting the position of the lines in relation to the sunrise. In this way, she has found that some of the straight lines in the figures were solstice lines. They pointed to where the sun rose and set on June 21 and December 21 hundreds of years ago.

Still, many scientists are not convinced that the Nazca Lines were drawn as a calendar. Although Reiche has proven to her own satisfaction that some lines mark ancient solstices and equinoxes, too many lines seemingly point to nothing at all. Also, scientists argue, the animal drawings remain a mystery.

Maria Reiche is not about to give up, however. The lines, she says, "can't be senseless. There is too much work in them."

Issues in Science

DIVING FOR NATURAL TREASURES:

A Risky Business?

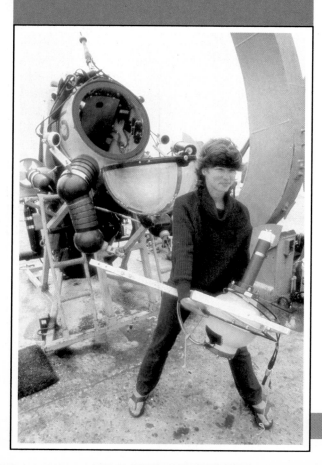

Six hundred meters below the ocean's surface, Edith Widder looks out on a fascinating world. The powerful beam from her lamp illuminates oddly shaped fish. Glowing masses of plankton, or microscopic plants and animals, float within reach of her outstretched arms.

Edith Widder is one of five pioneer scientists who participated in a program of deep-ocean exploration conducted by the University of California at Santa Barbara in the summer of 1984. The program had two purposes. One was to study the strange and beautiful animals that live in the ocean depths. The other was to test a diving suit called the Wasp. As its name suggests, this special new suit makes the wearer look like a wasp, with a big head and a tapered body.

The scientists made a series of dives down to 600 meters in the deep Santa Barbara Channel off the coast of California. Despite the crushing water pressure, each scientist was able to spend long periods of time moving around on the ocean floor. Few divers have ever ventured to such a depth before. Those that have were not able to stay down for long. In fact, most deep-ocean exploration has been done by scientists in submarines and diving bells or by tanklike robots.

The Santa Barbara Channel dives have opened up a whole new way to explore the ocean depths. The Wasp provides deep-ocean protection and life support while giving the wearer remarkable freedom of movement. Some people have dubbed it the "body submarine" because it combines the best features of a submarine and a diving suit. Such a combination is vital for future exploration of the ocean depths and for future use of the ocean's wealth.

Edith Widder, with the Wasp diving suit in the background, prepares for a dive in California's Santa Barbara Channel.

BURIED TREASURE

The treasures that lie beneath the waves are many and varied. People eat some of these treasures, such as fish, sea animals, and sea plants. Scientists have also discovered that many ocean plants and animals are a source of valuable medicines. Vast oil fields lie beneath the ocean floor. Some are being tapped now. Many more lie waiting to be tapped in the future. Large deposits of hard minerals have been discovered on the ocean floor as well. These minerals include manganese, tungsten, vanadium, nickel, cobalt, tin, titanium, silver, platinum, and gold.

Some of the minerals can be found just below the surface of the ocean floor. Others are a bit deeper in the sediment layers and would have to be mined. But perhaps the most interesting minerals are those that are just sitting on the ocean floor waiting to be scooped up. Trillions of tons of these minerals in the form of potato-sized lumps, or nodules, cover the ocean bottom in many places.

A number of American companies have designed equipment to gather these nodules from the ocean floor. One craft, a tractorlike robot, would roam the ocean floor scooping up minerals. The craft would then wash and crush them and pipe them to the surface for further processing.

QUESTIONS RISE TO THE SURFACE

The harvesting of minerals raises some difficult questions. Will ocean mining pollute the water? Will mining in one area hurt

Trillions of tons of valuable metal ores lie on the ocean floor. These potato-sized rocks hold magnesium.

Before the Wasp was invented, deep ocean exploration had to be done in vehicles such as the one shown in this photo.

fishing in nearby areas? Will mining wipe out rare fish and other sea life?

Studies such as the one conducted in the Santa Barbara Channel may help to answer these questions. Divers wearing the Wasp would be able to keep a close watch on mining and drilling operations on the ocean floor. This kind of monitoring might reduce the chances of oil leaks and other such accidents. Deep-ocean divers could also keep track of the effects of mining and drilling operations on marine life.

International political questions also arise. Who has the right to mine the ocean depths? Where should this mining be allowed? Who should set the rules? And who should benefit from ocean mining?

These questions are difficult to answer. Since 1959, representatives from many nations have been meeting to try to create a Law of the Sea. This law would regulate ocean mining, oil drilling, fishing, energy usage, dumping of wastes, exploration, and research. Finally, in 1982, 119 nations signed a Law of the Sea treaty. But the United States was not one of them.

THE LAW OF THE SEA

Under provisions of the treaty, each coastal nation is given an exclusive economic zone 200 nautical miles from its shore. Within that zone, a nation controls all natural resources, dumping, economic use, and scientific research. Where economic zones of different nations overlap, the nations must work out agreements.

Outside of the economic zones, no single nation controls the ocean floor. The International Seabed Authority administers this vast ocean floor region, called the International Seabed Area. The Authority sets the rules for mining in the International Seabed Area. And further, all mining technology must be shared with the Authority.

The United States could not accept these provisions and, therefore, did not sign the Law of the Sea treaty. On March 10, 1983, the United States declared its own economic zone extending 200 nautical miles off the coasts of the United States and all its territories. Since then, a number of American companies have announced that they plan to drill for oil and mine hard minerals in the zone.

Conflict over the zone has already arisen. And it is likely that many disputes will come up when people start mining the sea floor for its mineral wealth.

Offshore oil rigs are already tapping vast oil reserves that lie beneath the ocean floor. Divers wearing the Wasp may be able to repair cracks in the rig and prevent underwater oil leaks.

WANTED! SPACE PIONEERS

KANSAS CITY STAR: JANUARY 12, 2021

WANTED: Moon Miners and Engineers to provide new space colony with building materials. We're looking for people who can turn moon rocks and lunar topsoil into usable metals such as aluminum, magnesium, and titanium. These metals will be used to make tools and to build support structures for the colony. We also want workers who can extract silicon from the moon's silicates. Silicon is needed to make solar cells and computer chips. Glass that will be used for windows in space colony homes also comes from lunar silicates. And iron and carbon mined from the moon need to be turned into steel.

In addition, we're looking for lunar gold miners to search the moon's surface for deposits of gold, as well as nickel and platinum. And oxygen, which will be used for both life-support systems and rocket fuel, needs to be extracted from moon rocks.

Terry had answered the advertisement. Now, in the year 2024, she was hard at work at Moon Mine Alpha.

Terry expertly plunged the heavy shovel of her bulldozer into the soil to pick up another load of valuable material. When she raised the shovel, it was filled with moon rocks and lunar dust. Terry dumped her cargo into her lunar hauler. "My last truckload of the day," she thought, jumping down from the bulldozer. "Now I can go watch the mass driver in action."

Terry swung into the driver's seat of the lunar hauler. Soon she was bumping along the moon highway, a dusty path her hauler and others like it had carved out of the lunar topsoil over the past few months.

A typical lunar colony with all the comforts of home!

Fifteen minutes later, she spotted the huge piece of machinery known as the mass driver. She saw the "flying buckets" of the mass driver suspended magnetically above special tracks. The buckets, filled with packages of lunar rocks, soon would be sent speeding along above these tracks by powerful magnetic forces. When the buckets reached high enough speed, they would fling their contents into space at 2.4 kilometers per second. At this speed, an object can escape the moon's gravity. Hundreds or thousands of kilometers away, a mass catcher would be waiting to grab the lunar cargo. The lunar materials would then be turned into fuel or building materials for a new space colony. Surely the mass driver, developed in the 1970s at the Massachusetts Institute of Technology, had proved to be a valuable tool for space colonization.

What will this space colony be like? Stationed nearly 400,000 kilometers from the earth, a huge sphere more than 1.5 kilometers in diameter will rotate in space. The rotation will create artificial gravity on the inner surface of the sphere. Here 10,000 people or more will live and work inside an earthlike environment powered by the sun. The Space Colony will be constructed of materials mined almost entirely on the moon.

Resources in Space

As many scientists see it, our growing needs for raw materials, energy, and jumping-off places for journeys to the planets and stars make us look into space. Where else is there a free, continuous supply of solar energy, uninterrupted by darkness or weather? Where else does weightlessness, which will aid in the construction of huge structures, exist? Where else is there an untapped source of minerals?

A wealth of energy and materials is available in space. Let's start with the moon, a mere 356,000 kilometers away. This natural satellite could be an important source of aluminum, iron, silicon, and oxygen. A permanent base established on the moon could supply all the resources needed to support space settlement and exploration. Although these resources are abundant on the earth, bringing millions of tons of materials into space is out of the question!

The moon could become a gigantic "supply station" in the sky. Metals and lunar soil could be mined to build huge structures inside of which comfortable, earthlike homes would be

Mining the asteroids yields precious metals, minerals, and water.

constructed. Since the moon's gravitational force is one sixth the strength of the earth's, it would be cheaper and easier to build such space factories and colonies on the moon. These buildings could become part of the permanent moon base.

Almost half of the moon is made up of oxygen. This oxygen could be used to make rocket fuel. Liquid hydrogen mixed with liquid oxygen is a basic rocket fuel. Rockets bound for the outer plants could be launched more easily from the moon than from Earth, where the pull of gravity is six times greater.

A New Frontier

The moon is not the only source of natural materials in near space. Asteroids are also vast treasure houses of minerals. They contain metals such as nickel, iron, cobalt, magnesium, and aluminum. Phosphorus, carbon, and sulfur are also present on asteroids. And they may contain the precious metals gold, silver, and platinum. Asteroids are also important sources of water. One small asteroid can perhaps yield between one and ten billion tons of water.

"Hey, Terry, how's it going?" The voice belonged to Bill, one of the workers who ran the mass driver.

"Oh, I still like being a moon miner," Terry answered, "but a few years from now, I hope to be mining the asteroids instead. It should be a challenge trying to capture a small asteroid or land on a big one."

"I hope you like traveling, Terry," Bill said with a worried look. "The trip could take months or years."

"It would be worth it," said Terry as she waved to Bill and headed to her two-room apartment under the plastic dome of Hadleyville.

Turning on her TV set to watch live coverage from Earth of the 2024 Summer Olympics, Terry first tuned in the *Moon Miner's Daily Herald*, a TV "newspaper." Suddenly, an advertisement caught her eye.

WANTED: *Asteroid Miners and Engineers to capture small asteroids and collect samples from larger asteroids. Workers must be willing to spend long periods of time far from home. Travel to the asteroid belt, which lies between the orbits of Mars and Jupiter about 160 to 300 million kilometers away, is required.*

"Why not?" Terry thought as she began to type out a reply on her computer keyboard.

Structure of the Earth

For an overview of this unit, see pages T-66 to T-72. You may want to check the Laboratory Activity following each chapter, as well as the activities and investigations for this unit in your Teacher's Resource Book and Annotated Teacher's Edition. Laboratory Book, so that materials can be ordered, gathered, or prepared in advance.

Rising from the ocean floor up through the clouds, Hawaii's Mauna Kea from bottom to top is the tallest mountain in the world. Its 10,203-meter height is greater than that of Mount Everest by 1355 meters. Although the skiers who glide down the mountain's gentle slopes may not know it, Mauna Kea is the product of violent forces trapped deep beneath the earth's surface. For Mauna Kea is a volcano, one of many that have molded the Hawaiian Islands. The great eruptions of such volcanoes around the world have done more than change the earth's surface. Clouds of dust and gases shooting into the sky from these thundering mountains have dramatically changed the earth's atmosphere—sometimes for a short while, sometimes permanently.

CHAPTERS

21 Internal Structure of the Earth

22 Surface Features of the Earth

23 Structure of the Atmosphere

Hawaii's Mauna Kea

21 Internal Structure of the Earth

For a chapter overview, teaching strategies, answers to all activities, a list of A-V materials, and a chapter bibliography, see pages T-66 to T-68.

Consult your Teacher's Resource Book and Annotated Teacher's Edition, Laboratory Book for additional activities and teaching aids.

CHAPTER OBJECTIVES

After completing this chapter, you will be able to:

21-1 Describe two kinds of earthquake waves.

21-1 Explain how earthquake waves tell scientists about the structure of the earth's core.

21-2 Describe the structure of the earth's mantle.

21-2 Explain how mantle rocks form new ocean floor.

21-3 Describe the earth's crust and explain how continents can float.

This multiple-exposure photograph shows the progress of a caver descending the Incredible Pit, a 134-meter natural shaft in Ellison's Cave, Georgia.

Would you like to visit the center of the earth? It is not far away—no farther than the distance from New York City to Berlin, Germany. That comes to about 6450 kilometers.

But in some ways, the earth's center is harder to reach than planets that are millions of kilometers away. Scientists are sending probes into outer space that are traveling beyond the solar system. But no mechanical probe into inner space that scientists are able to build today can survive the enormous heat and pressure at the earth's center.

Yet there *are* probes that can reach the center of the earth and return to tell their story. As long ago as 1906, the Irish geologist Richard Dixon Oldham said that such a probe "enables us to see into the earth . . . as if we could drive a tunnel through it."

Oldham was a geologist who studied earthquakes. Great earthquakes topple buildings, shake the ground, and can change the shape of entire mountains. They also send shock waves through the earth. These shock waves penetrate the depths of the earth and return to the surface. Detected by special instruments, the shock waves can be used by scientists to "see" into the inside of the earth.

These shock waves were the probes that Oldham spoke of. Let's take a look at what they let Oldham, and the scientists who followed him, see!

Descending into the earth

21-1 The Earth's Core and Earthquake Waves

In Tokyo, Japan, at a little past two in the morning, a strong earthquake occurs more than a hundred kilometers beneath the ground. The date is April 18, 1889. The earthquake is so deep that few people are aware of it and little damage is done. However, in Tokyo, a special instrument called a **seismograph** (SIGHZ-muh-graf) records a strange message from the earthquake. The message is written as a pattern of squiggly lines.

In Potsdam, Germany, on the other side of the world, it is just past seven on the evening of April 17. There the seismograph is quiet—but not for long. One hour and four minutes after the earthquake in Tokyo, the Potsdam seismograph makes a pattern of squiggles like those in Figure 21-1.

Scientists quickly realized that the message recorded in Potsdam was really due to shock waves from the earthquake in Tokyo. And these waves had traveled through the earth's **core,** or center region, to reach Potsdam! This was the first time one of these messages from an earthquake was recorded by a seismograph on the opposite side of the world.

Figure 21-1 *Earthquake waves* (left) *are recorded on a type of seismograph* (right). *A pen records these waves on a sheet attached to a rotating drum.*

Support vibrates

Heavy object

Drum vibrates

Earthquake waves

Base vibrates

Ground vibrates

Seismograph

Figure 21-2 *A powerful earthquake in Alaska ripped a hole in the ground near this house.*

Here was a chance, scientists believed, to look deep inside the earth. A worldwide network of seismograph stations were set up to record future earthquakes. But how can earthquake waves provide a picture of the earth's interior? To find out, let's take a look at how these waves are produced.

Kinds of Earthquake Waves

Major earthquakes begin with a massive breaking and sliding of rocks underground. Shock waves travel in every direction from the underground point of origin of the breakage. That point is called the **focus,** or center, of the earthquake.

Some of these shock waves pass through the earth's interior and come to the surface at points far away from the earthquake's focus. Seismographs detect and record these emerging waves. The instruments measure the strength of the waves. They also record the time of their arrival.

All earthquakes produce at least two kinds of shock waves at the same time. **Primary waves,** or **P waves,** result from a back-and-forth vibration of

The area on the earth's surface that is directly *above* the earthquake's focus is called the epicenter. The epicenter is where the most violent shaking occurs.

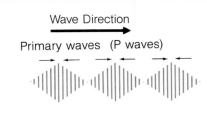

Wave Direction

Primary waves (P waves)

Figure 21-3 *Primary waves, or P waves, vibrate in the same direction as the path of the earthquake wave.*

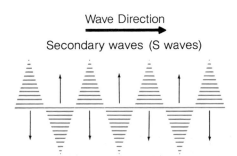

Wave Direction

Secondary waves (S waves)

Figure 21-4 *Secondary waves, or S waves, vibrate at right angles to the path of the earthquake wave.*

rock particles. These particles vibrate in the same direction as the path of the wave. See Figure 21-3. P waves move rapidly and can travel through both solids and liquids. **Secondary waves,** or **S waves,** result from an up-and-down or side-to-side vibration of rock particles. These particles vibrate at right angles to the path of the wave. See Figure 21-4. S waves are slower than P waves and can pass only through solids.

The Mystery of the Shadow Zones

By 1900, a worldwide network of seismographs was in place. And very soon, scientists noticed a regular but mysterious pattern to the P and S waves produced by earthquakes.

Suppose, for example, an earthquake strikes under the North Pole. Seismograph stations around the northern part of the earth record both P and S waves, but from northern Canada to southern Mexico there is a **shadow zone.** See Figure 21-5. In a shadow zone, no earthquake waves are detected by seismographs. Why are there shadow zones? At first scientists could not solve this mystery.

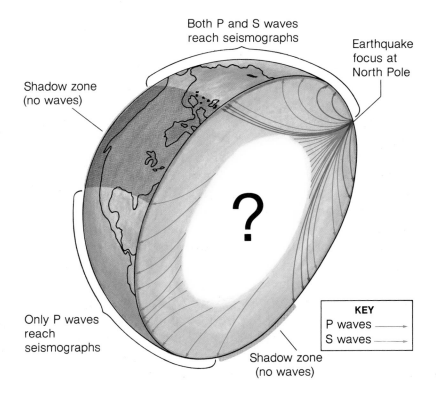

Figure 21-5 *There are no earthquake waves in a shadow zone. Something inside the earth was blocking S waves and concentrating P waves on the other side of the world.*

482

Adding to the mystery is the fact that south of the shadow zone, very strong P waves *are* detected. But *no* S waves are found in this area. The P waves are strongest around the South Pole—the one place on earth directly opposite the North Pole! Scientists needed to find out how this information was related to the mystery of the shadow zones.

Scientists discovered that the pattern is the same for every earthquake. Both P and S waves are detected up to a little more than a quarter of the way around the world from the focus of the earthquake. Beyond that lies a shadow zone. Then a strong concentration of P waves appears on the opposite side of the earth from the focus. S waves do not appear.

Scientists reached two conclusions. The first conclusion was that something inside the earth was blocking S waves and preventing them from getting through to the other side of the earth. The second conclusion was that something inside the earth was concentrating P waves on the other side of the world. The mystery had to be solved.

Seeing the Earth's Core

What did this pattern of shadow zones and concentration of P waves mean? Scientists found out that this pattern is a message from the depths of the earth that actually answers two questions. The answers to these questions are coded into the wiggly lines that record earthquake waves. And by decoding the message of these lines, scientists have been able to look into the earth's core and solve the mystery of this pattern.

THE FIRST QUESTION What happened to the missing S waves? These waves disappear at the edge of the shadow zone and are not found on the opposite side of the world.

Scientists believed that something was deflecting the S waves. And since S waves pass through solids but not liquids, that something must be liquid. The earth's core, scientists concluded, is at least partly liquid. Using data from seismographs, the geologist Richard Dixon Oldham was able to map the boundary of the earth's liquid core at about 2900 kilometers beneath the earth's surface.

Figure 21-6 *This photograph shows a seismologist at the National Earthquake Information Service in Colorado. Each drum records the results from a different seismograph station.*

As you see in Figure 21-5, the earth's core deflects S waves, forming a shadow zone where no S waves appear. This deflection of S waves also explains why there are no S waves on the opposite side of the world from the earthquake's focus. Part of the mystery of the shadow zones had been solved.

THE SECOND QUESTION Why is there a high concentration of P waves on the opposite side of the world from the earthquake's focus? The answer was decoded from earthquake waves by Inge Lehmann, who was chief of the Royal Danish Seismological Department from 1928 to 1953.

To see how she did it, let's look at a straw resting in a glass of water. See Figure 21-7. The straw seems to be broken right at the surface of the water—the boundary between air and water. Actually, the straw only makes visible what happens to light waves as they cross such a boundary—they bend because their speed changes. This bending of light causes the straight straw to appear broken.

Lehmann discovered that what is true of light waves is also true of earthquake waves speeding through the earth. The earthquake's shock waves bend at boundaries between different substances—boundaries that mark changes in the inner structure of the earth. Lehmann suggested that the earth's core is made up of two parts, a liquid outer core and a solid inner core. The answer to the mystery of the S waves had already shown that the liquid outer core boundary begins 2900 kilometers beneath the earth's surface. She suggested that the inner core is like a solid ball within the outer core. Lehmann estimated the radius, or distance from the edge to the center, of the inner core to be about 1200 kilometers.

Now Lehmann could explain why P waves are concentrated on the side of the world opposite the earthquake's focus. The waves would be bent four times—when entering the outer core, when entering the inner core, when leaving the inner core, and when leaving the outer core. The result of all this bending is that the waves are concentrated around the area opposite the earthquake's focus. See Figure 21-8. As you can see, P waves are also bent away from the shadow zones. The mystery of the shadow zones had been solved.

Figure 21-7 *The bending of light makes this straw appear broken. Earthquake waves, like light waves, change speed and bend when they enter a different substance.*

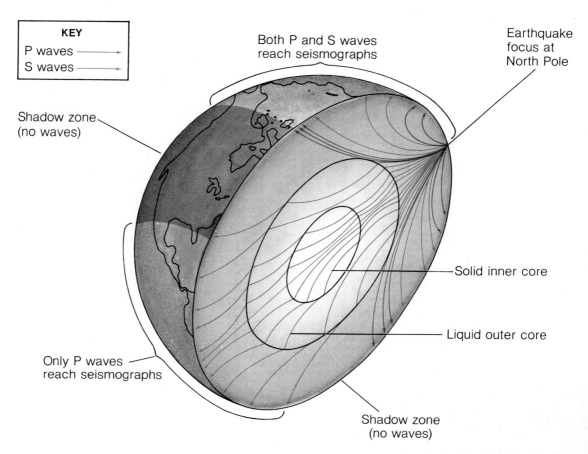

KEY
P waves ———→
S waves ———→

Both P and S waves reach seismographs

Earthquake focus at North Pole

Shadow zone (no waves)

Solid inner core

Liquid outer core

Only P waves reach seismographs

Shadow zone (no waves)

Figure 21-8 *Inge Lehmann solved the mystery of the shadow zones when she explained how P waves bend and change speeds as they move through the earth's outer and inner cores.*

Lehmann wrote about her discovery in 1936. Since then, other scientists using more sensitive instruments have developed an even clearer picture of the earth's core.

Lehmann's estimate of the size of the inner core remains amazingly accurate. Scientists now calculate that the radius of the inner core is about 1300 kilometers. An outer core about 2250 kilometers thick surrounds the inner core. The outside boundary of the outer core begins about 2900 kilometers beneath the earth's surface. Add these three numbers together and you get the approximate distance from the earth's surface to the actual center of the earth—6450 kilometers.

From studies of earthquake waves, scientists have learned much more about the earth's core. For example, they have learned that the hot outer core is probably a region of constantly churning liquid,

Activity

How Many Earths?

The distance from the earth's surface to the center of the earth is about 6450 kilometers. The average distance from the earth to the sun is 150 million kilometers. How many earths lined up in a row are needed to reach the sun?

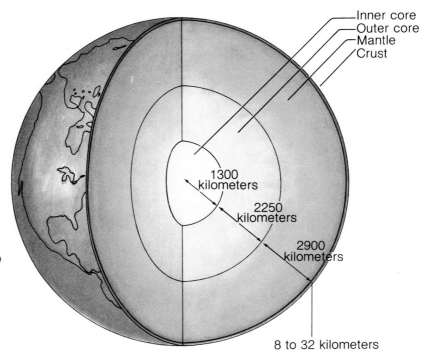

Figure 21-9 *The earth is made up of different layers. This drawing shows the distances you would have to travel through these layers from the surface to the earth's center.*

Inner core
Outer core
Mantle
Crust

1300 kilometers
2250 kilometers
2900 kilometers
8 to 32 kilometers

mostly iron and nickel. The very hot inner core is made up mostly of solid iron and nickel under tremendous pressure. Temperatures probably range from about 2200° C in the upper part of the outer core to about 5000° C in the inner core.

SECTION REVIEW

1. Name two kinds of earthquake waves.
2. What is a shadow zone?
3. What is the outer core made of? What is the inner core made of?

1. Primary or P waves; secondary or S waves
2. Where no earthquake waves are detected
3. Liquid iron and nickel; solid iron and nickel

21-2   Exploring the Earth's Mantle

The distance from the edge of the liquid outer core to the earth's surface is about 2900 kilometers. Most of this distance makes up the earth's **mantle.** Exactly what is the mantle? How is it different from the earth's core? Part of that question was answered in 1909. On October 8, an earthquake shook Croatia, which is now part of the country of Yugoslavia. In

Zagreb, the capital of Croatia, Yugoslavian geologist and seismologist Andrija Mohorovicic (moh-hoh-ROH-vuh-chich) studied seismograph records from many stations.

Mohorovicic noticed something odd about the seismograph recordings. Stations within about 160 kilometers of the earthquake's center showed a pattern of squiggles that indicated a strong earthquake followed by a weak one. But at stations more than 160 kilometers away from the earthquake the pattern of squiggles indicated a weak earthquake followed by a strong one. The second message was the reverse of the first message. But both messages had been sent out by the same earthquake at the same time! Here was a mystery to be solved.

Mohorovicic thought he must be misreading the messages. He knew there was only one earthquake. The stronger signals came from shock waves that had traveled a shorter distance. The weaker signals from the same earthquake came from shock waves that had traveled a longer distance and had lost some strength along the way. That seemed to explain the first set of messages from seismographs within 160 kilometers of the earthquake. The weaker waves traveled a longer distance and came in second. See Figure 21-10.

Figure 21-10 _The stronger earthquake waves arrive before the weaker waves at a seismograph station less than 160 kilometers from the earthquake's focus._

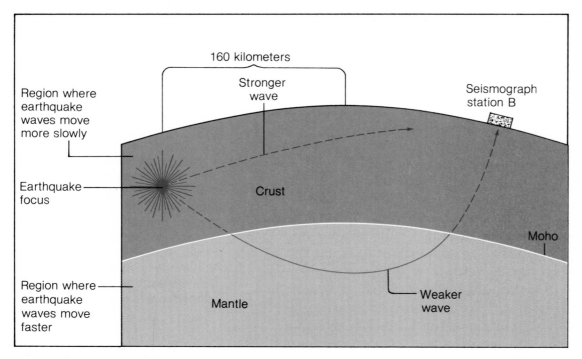

160 kilometers

Stronger wave

Seismograph station B

Region where earthquake waves move more slowly

Earthquake focus

Crust

Moho

Region where earthquake waves move faster

Mantle

Weaker wave

Figure 21-11 *The weaker earthquake waves arrive before the stronger waves at a seismograph station more than 160 kilometers from the earthquake's focus.*

Activity

Drilling into the Earth

During the 1960s, scientists tried to drill through the thin crust of the ocean to look into the mantle. Using reference materials in the library, write a short report on the successes and failures of these drilling projects. What problems did scientists have to solve when building and using such drilling ships as *CUSS 1* and the *Glomar Challenger*? What discoveries have been made by these ships?

But what about those stations farther from the earthquake's center than 160 kilometers? There the weaker waves came in first, although they had traveled farther than the stronger signals. Mohorovicic reasoned that there could be only one answer. Something had speeded up the weaker waves so that they outraced the stronger waves to the station. Mohorovicic calculated that the stronger waves traveled near the surface of the earth. The weaker waves had traveled through a deeper region well beneath the earth's surface. In this region, Mohorovicic thought, the earth's structure must be different than on the surface. The weaker waves speeded up in this lower region and were bent back toward the surface. Although these weaker waves traveled a longer distance, they came in first. See Figure 21-11.

You know that earthquake waves bend. They also change speed. The bending and the change in speed occur as the waves travel through the boundary between different layers of the earth. Mohorovicic calculated that the boundary between the different layers was about 32 kilometers beneath the earth's land surface. He had discovered the boundary between the earth's crust, or outermost layer, and the mantle. This boundary is now called the **Moho.**

Doorway into the Mantle

Over many years, scientists discovered that the Moho extends around the world. Beneath it, the mantle goes down about 2900 kilometers into the earth until it reaches the edge of the outer core.

The distance from the earth's surface to the Moho varies. It is a long distance from the surface of the land to the Moho. In comparison, it is a very short distance from the ocean floor to the Moho. In fact, on the floor of the Atlantic Ocean, scientists have found a doorway into the mantle.

In the 1950s, scientists mapped the floor of the Atlantic Ocean. Ships sailed back and forth, bouncing thousands of sound signals over the entire bottom of the Atlantic Ocean. From these sound signals, Marie Tharp, a draftswoman working for the Lamont-Doherty Geological Observatory in New York, made the first map of the Atlantic Ocean's bottom. Her map showed a great crack, or rift, in the crust that ran down the middle of a massive underwater mountain range in the Atlantic Ocean. This crack and the area on either side of it are called the **Mid-Atlantic Rift Valley.** Later, scientists found that the Mid-Atlantic Rift Valley is part of a much larger system of rift valleys and mountain ranges—a system called the **Mid-Ocean Ridge** that extends for about 74,000 kilometers under all the world's oceans.

Partially molten, or melted, rock from the mantle flows upward through a rift valley. It spreads outward on both sides of the valley. As it spreads, the partially molten rock cools quickly and hardens into solid rock. This rock becomes a new part of the ocean floor. Because it was "frozen" in the act of flowing, the solid rock shows a pattern of twisted ridges like giant fingerprints. See Figure 21-12.

This rock came from the earth's mantle. Now, for the first time, scientists could hold a piece of the mantle in their hands. They could take it to the laboratory and find out what it was made of. The mantle rocks turned out to be mostly silicon, oxygen, iron, and magnesium. So the unknown substance of the mantle is made up of the same ordinary materials found in rocks on the earth's surface.

But the mantle rocks were not acting like ordinary rocks. Are these rocks liquid? Evidence from

Figure 21-12 *Partially molten rock has been "frozen" while flowing from a rift valley. Notice the many ridges that look like giant fingerprints.*

Figure 21-13 *A research vessel travels through a rift valley of the Mid-Atlantic Ridge System. The partially molten rock near the rift's center will eventually become new ocean floor.*

earthquake waves suggests that the temperature in the upper part of the mantle is about 900 to 1000° C—more than hot enough to melt the mantle rocks completely. But these rocks are not completely melted.

Are these rocks solid? Scientists found that S waves can travel through the mantle. And you know that S waves travel through solids but not liquids. But how can solid rock flow? How could a rock act like a solid and like a liquid at the same time? Here was another mystery to be solved.

Flexible Rocks and Conveyor Belts

Scientists found that the answer to this mystery is pressure. Pressure is the amount of force over a certain area. Mantle rocks are under great pressure from the weight of all the rocks above them. Under great pressure, the solid rocks flow very slowly. The mantle rocks do not melt under this great pressure but become a flexible solid that flows slowly like a gooey liquid—like very thick molasses. S waves can travel through this thick liquid.

But why does mantle rock flow steadily upward through the rift valleys? The answer is that the great heat from the earth's core sets up churning motions in the solid-liquid rocks of the mantle. They are much like the churning motions you can see in a pot of boiling soup on a stove. In this case, the soup acts like rocks in the mantle, and the stove provides heat as does the earth's core. The hottest soup, nearest the heat from the stove, rises to the top of the pot. There the soup cools and sinks back to the bottom of the pot. This soup is reheated and again moves upward to the surface.

Scientists reason that material in the mantle must move in the same way. These churning motions keep molten rock pouring out of the rift valleys. This molten rock becomes a new part of the ocean floor. As the flow out of a rift valley goes on, the older parts of the ocean floor are pushed farther away from the rift valley on either side.

Think of a conveyor belt like the ones that move groceries at supermarket counters. Then imagine a

Figure 21-14 *The continents and ocean floor ride on plates that may move by means of "conveyor belts." Plates move away from rift valleys as new ocean floor forms from molten rock. Plates move toward trenches and become molten rock again.*

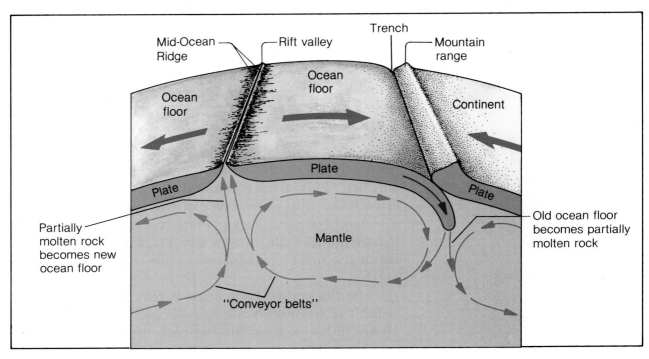

second conveyor belt at the end of the first one. The second belt is moving in the opposite direction. It is as if two such "belts" made of partially molten rock are rolling up out of a rift valley and spreading in opposite directions. See Figure 21-14.

These belts move much more slowly than conveyor belts at the supermarket. They add new floor to the ocean at the rate of only a few centimeters a year. But over millions of years, this adds up to hundreds of kilometers. Over such a length of time, the Atlantic Ocean has become hundreds of kilometers wider.

If you think about it, that is like saying that the continents, or large landmasses, on either side of the Atlantic have moved farther apart. In fact, scientists now have good evidence that all the continents on the earth's surface are slowly moving. And this is part of the story of the earth's crust.

Figure 21-15

ELEMENTS IN THE EARTH'S CRUST	
Element	Percentage in Crust
Oxygen	46.60
Silicon	27.72
Aluminum	8.13
Iron	5.00
Calcium	3.63
Sodium	2.83
Potassium	2.59
Magnesium	2.09
Titanium	0.40
Hydrogen	0.14
Total	99.13

SECTION REVIEW

1. What two changes happen to earthquake waves when they enter a different substance?
2. Where did scientists find a doorway into the mantle?
3. What causes mantle rock to become a flexible solid that flows like thick molasses?

1. Bend and change speeds
2. On the floor of the Atlantic Ocean
3. Pressure

21-3 The Earth's Crust and Floating Continents

You now have traveled 6450 kilometers from the center of the earth's core to the surface on which you live. This surface is called the earth's **crust.** The crust is the thin outer layer of the earth and is made up mainly of solid rocks. These rocks contain mostly two elements—silicon and oxygen. Figure 21-15 is a list of the most abundant elements in the crust of the earth.

The thickness of the crust varies. The crust beneath the continents has an average thickness of about 32 kilometers. But beneath the ocean floor,

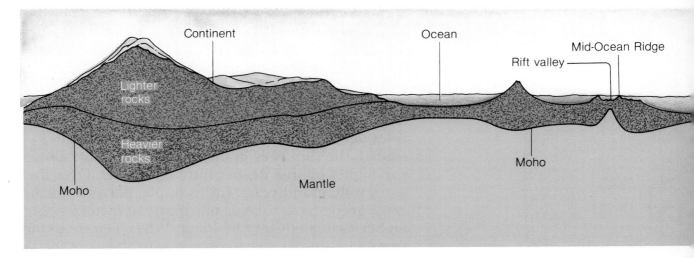

Figure 21-16 *The earth's crust has two layers. The upper layer is made of lighter rocks and is found only under the continents. The lower layer is made of heavier rocks. It is found both under the continents and under the oceans, where it forms the ocean floor.*

the crust has an average thickness of only about 8 kilometers. You learned earlier that new ocean floor is being added on either side of the rift valleys. Then why doesn't the ocean floor pile up higher and higher?

Let's go back to our picture of the supermarket conveyor belts. Although the belts come up to the counter in one place, they also go back under the counter at another. The "belts" that move the continents are like this too.

At a rift valley, the molten rock flows up from inside the earth, forming new crust. At other places, called trenches, older crust moves back down into the mantle to again form part of its solid-liquid rock. See Figure 21-14. After many millions of years the slowly moving mantle rocks once again emerge at a rift valley—just as the supermarket conveyor belt travels part of the time *under* the counter and then comes up again.

The trenches and rift valleys of the earth divide the crust into about 20 floating parts like the pieces of a jigsaw puzzle. Scientists call these parts plates. Plates usually move away from rift valleys and toward trenches. Each plate is like a package riding on the upper, visible part of a supermarket conveyor belt. The motion of these belts moves the continents

In some places, the crust may extend to depths of about 70 kilometers underneath mountain ranges.

Activity

Making a Model of the Earth's Interior

Obtain a Styrofoam ball 15 centimeters or more in diameter. *Carefully* cut out a section that goes halfway through the ball. See Figure 21-9. Draw lines on the inside of the section to represent the four layers of the earth. Use Figure 21-9 to decide how wide each layer should be. Label and color each layer. Which layer is the thickest? Which layer is the thinnest?

and ocean floor, which rest on the upper part of the plates. The plates float on the solid-liquid rocks of the mantle. You can also think of the continents and ocean floor as floating ships slowly riding on the plates.

Balance is the key to the floating continents, as it is to floating ships. When a ship takes on cargo, it rides deeper in the water. When the cargo is unloaded, the ship rises in the water. Continents also rise higher or sink deeper into the mantle. Over the last ten thousand years, for example, parts of northern Europe have risen as much as 250 meters—higher than a 60-story building. Why? Ten thousand years ago, this land was covered with sheets of ice

Career: Cave Guide

HELP WANTED: CAVE GUIDES To conduct and instruct groups of all ages and backgrounds through local natural caves. High school or college students preferred. Courses or interest in geology or public speaking desirable. Summer or part-time work available.

There are more than 50,000 naturally formed caves in the United States. Caves are found at or near the surface of the earth's crust. The deepest cave in the world extends only about 1.5 kilometers into the crust. New caves are discovered, explored, surveyed, and named each year. One cave in Texas, for example, was discovered by highway engineers while building an interstate roadway. Visitors to this cave are shown special formations such as "icicles" made of stone. Fossils of extinct animals have also been discovered in this cave.

Workers who lead groups of visitors safely through a cave are the **cave guides.** Cave guides lecture about a cave's size, history, and how it was formed. They point out features of special interest and answer questions. They are concerned with cave conservation, preservation, and safety.

Each cave is different, so guides must spend time learning about their particular cave before they begin work. Visitors on cave tours walk or ride in vehicles such as jeeps. In caves with underground lakes or rivers, visitors may travel by boat. Besides explaining geologic formations to visitors, guides discuss topics such as underground waterfalls, fossils, Indian artifacts, cave life, and the constant temperature maintained in caves.

If you are interested in experience as a cave guide or would like to know more about the caves in your area, write to the National Caves Association, Route 9, Box 106, McMinnville, TN 37110.

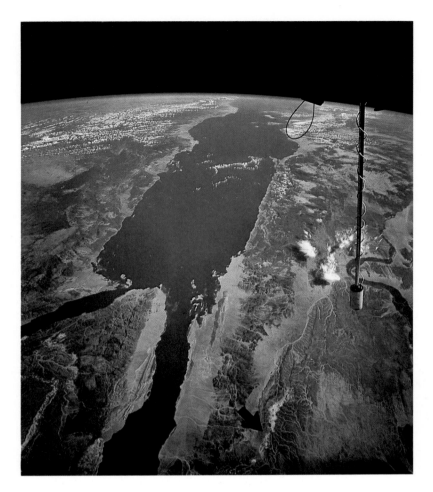

Figure 21-17 *The plate that carries Egypt* (right) *is separating from the plate that carries Saudi Arabia* (left). *The Red Sea has become wider as a result of this separation.*

several kilometers thick. This ice was like a cargo of additional material. As the ice melted, the continent rose like a lightened ship.

You now have come to the end of the journey from the center of the earth to the surface. That familiar land on which you live and walk, with its rocks, and water, and soil is just the top of the earth's crust. And the crust is afloat, sinking and rising on the mantle and powered by heat from the very center of the earth.

SECTION REVIEW

1. What is the average thickness of the crust beneath the continents? Beneath the ocean floor?
2. How is new crust formed?
3. At least how many floating plates make up the crust?

1. 32 kilometers; 8 kilometers
2. Molten rock flows upward from inside the earth and forms new crust
3. 20

Activity

Mohorovicic's Discovery

The boundary between the crust and the mantle is called the Moho after Andrija Mohorovicic. Write a 300 word essay explaining how Mohorovicic discovered this boundary. Your essay should emphasize all of the following vocabulary words: crust, focus, mantle, Moho, P waves, S waves, and seismograph.

LABORATORY ACTIVITY

For further instructions, see page T-67.

Building an Active Geyser

Purpose

In this activity, you will build a model geyser and observe it in action.

> **Materials** *(per group)*
>
> 250-mL beaker
> Bunsen burner
> Glass funnel
> Tripod
> Wire gauze
> Safety goggles
> Water

"Geyser eruption"

Steam

Wire gauze

Water (level with tip of funnel bowl)

Tripod

Bunsen burner

Procedure

1. Place a glass funnel upside-down in a beaker.
2. Add water until the bowl of the funnel is covered.
3. Place the beaker, water, and funnel on a piece of wire gauze resting on a tripod.
4. Put the Bunsen burner beneath the tripod and light it. **CAUTION:** *Be very careful in lighting the burner. Avoid putting your face or hands near the setup when the geyser becomes active. Be sure to wear your safety goggles.*
5. Allow time for the water to boil. Notice the bubbles of steam that push the hot water up the funnel stem. As the steam bubbles expand, you should be able to observe water spurting from the funnel stem, much as water acts in a coffee percolator.

Observations and Conclusions

1. Describe the behavior of your model geyser while it was erupting.
2. A Bunsen burner provided the heat source for your model geyser. What is the source of energy that heats the water in a real geyser?
3. According to your observations of the model geyser, what is the relationship between geyser activity and available heat energy?
4. If a natural geyser stopped erupting, what might have been the cause?
5. "Old Faithful" is a well-known geyser in Yellowstone National Park. It erupts on a very regular basis, just about every 66 minutes! What must be true of the heat source and water supply that keep this geyser operating?

CHAPTER SUMMARY

21-1 The Earth's Core and Earthquake Waves

- Instruments called seismographs detect and record the shock waves from earthquakes.

- Shock waves originate at the focus of an earthquake and travel in every direction.

- Earthquakes produce at least two kinds of waves: primary or P waves and secondary or S waves.

- Primary waves vibrate in the direction of the path of an earthquake wave. They travel through both solids and liquids.

- Secondary waves vibrate at right angles to the path of an earthquake wave. They travel only through solids.

- Shadow zones are areas on the surface of the earth where seismographs cannot detect earthquake waves.

- The earth's solid inner core has a radius of about 1300 kilometers.

21-2 Exploring the Earth's Mantle

- The earth's mantle is about 2900 kilometers thick and surrounds the earth's outer core.

- By knowing that earthquake waves bend and travel at different speeds through different substances, Andrija Mohorovicic was able to calculate how far below the earth's surface the boundary is located that separates the mantle from the crust. This boundary was named the Moho in his honor.

- The Mid-Atlantic Rift Valley is a crack that runs down the middle of an underwater mountain range in the Atlantic Ocean. The Mid-Ocean Ridge is part of a mountain range system that extends under all the world's oceans.

- Mantle rock is a flexible solid that flows like a thick gooey liquid.

- It is believed that heat from the earth's core sets up churning motions that cause mantle rock to move. You can think of this motion as being like very slow conveyor belts in the mantle that bring molten rock up through rift valleys to form new ocean floor.

21-3 The Earth's Crust and Floating Continents

- The crust is the thin, outermost layer of the earth.

- At rift valleys, mantle rocks form new crust. At trenches, old crust becomes mantle rock.

- The crust is divided into about 20 pieces called plates. The continents and ocean floor ride on the upper part of the plates.

- Plates usually move away from rift valleys and toward trenches.

- Floating continents rise higher or sink deeper into the mantle depending on the amount of material the continents have.

VOCABULARY *Define the following terms.*

core p.480
crust p.492
focus p.481
mantle p.486
Mid-Atlantic Rift Valley p.489
Mid-Ocean Ridge p.489

Moho p.488
primary waves (P waves) p.481
secondary waves (S waves) p.482
seismograph p.480
shadow zone p.482

CHAPTER REVIEW

Multiple Choice

Choose the letter of the answer that best completes each statement.

1. Seismographs
   a. detect earthquake waves.
   b. record earthquake waves.
   c. measure the strength of earthquake waves.
   d. do all of these.

2. Primary waves are earthquake waves that can travel through
   a. liquids.
   b. solids.
   c. liquids and solids.
   d. none of these.

3. Areas in which seismographs cannot detect earthquake waves are called
   a. Mohos.
   b. shadow zones.
   c. rifts.
   d. seismozones.

4. The distance in kilometers from the earth's surface to the earth's center is
   a. 1300.
   b. 2900.
   c. 5000.
   d. 6450.

5. Who suggested that the earth's core is a solid center surrounded by liquid?
   a. Inge Lehmann
   b. Andrija Mohorovicic
   c. Richard Dixon Oldham
   d. Marie Tharp

6. The distance from the earth's surface to the Moho
   a. is 2900 kilometers.
   b. is longer than the radius of the earth's core.
   c. is 1300 kilometers.
   d. varies between 8 and 32 kilometers.

7. The crack in the Atlantic Ocean crust through which mantle rock flows to form new ocean floor is called the
   a. Moho.
   b. Mid-Atlantic Rift Valley.
   c. Mid-Ocean Ridge.
   d. Mid-Atlantic Trench.

8. Rocks on the earth's surface are made mostly of
   a. iron and silicon.
   b. oxygen and magnesium.
   c. iron and magnesium.
   d. oxygen and silicon.

9. Which is the thinnest layer of the earth?
   a. mantle
   b. crust
   c. outer core
   d. inner core

10. The earth's crust
   a. is least thick beneath the ocean floor.
   b. is least thick beneath the continents.
   c. is equally thick around the world.
   d. is none of these.

Completions

Fill in the word or words that best complete each statement.

1. An instrument that records shock waves from an earthquake is called a(n) __seismograph__.

2. The center of the earth is inside the __inner core__.

3. The underground point of origin or center of an earthquake is called the __focus__.

4. Earthquake waves that travel through solids and are blocked by liquids are called __secondary or S waves__ waves.

5. The region between the earth's outer core and the earth's crust is called the __mantle__.

6. The boundary between the earth's crust and the mantle is called the __Moho__, in honor of the scientist who discovered it.

7. The mountain range system that runs under all the world's oceans is called the __Mid-Ocean Ridge__.

8. Mantle rocks flow like a thick liquid because of the great __pressure__ from the weight of all the rocks above them.

9. The thin, solid, outer layer of the earth is called the __crust__.

10. About 74 percent of the earth's crust is made of the elements __silicon__ and oxygen.

True or False

Determine whether each statement is true or false. If it is true, write "true." If it is false, change the underlined word or words to make the statement true.

1. Earthquakes produce <u>both</u> primary and secondary shock waves. T

2. There are no <u>P waves</u> in the shadow zones because they are deflected by the earth's core. F (S waves)

3. Each time earthquake waves enter and leave the earth's outer and inner cores, they <u>bend</u>. T

4. The boundary between the earth's mantle and <u>outer core</u> is called the Moho. F (crust)

5. Earthquake waves change <u>speeds</u> as they travel through different substances. T

6. Scientists are able to analyze mantle rock because mantle material flows up through <u>rift valleys</u>. T

7. The temperature of the mantle <u>is not</u> hot enough to melt rocks. F (is)

8. Older crust moves back into the mantle through <u>trenches</u>. T

9. The crust is <u>thicker</u> beneath the ocean floor than beneath the continents. F (thinner)

10. Continents and ocean floors ride on about 20 floating parts called <u>ridges</u>. F (plates)

Discussion Topics   Answers appear on page T-67.

Write a brief paragraph discussing each of the following.

1. Compare the movement of mantle rock to a pot of soup boiling on a stove.

2. Compare the rising and sinking of floating ships to floating continents.

EXPAND YOUR KNOWLEDGE

Adler, I., and R. Adler. *The Earth's Crust.* New York: John Day.
    Discover what the earth's crust is made of, how thick it is, and how it was formed. The authors explain why the inside of the earth is hot and the crust is cool.

22 Surface Features of the Earth

For a chapter overview, teaching strategies, answers to all activities, a list of A-V materials, and a chapter bibliography, see pages T-69 to T-70.

Consult your Teacher's Resource Book and Annotated Teacher's Edition, Laboratory Book for additional activities and teaching aids.

CHAPTER SECTIONS

CHAPTER OBJECTIVES

After completing this chapter, you will be able to:

22-1 Describe the three major kinds of landscapes.

22-1 Explain how mountains are formed.

22-1 Describe several differences between plateaus and plains.

22-2 Identify the major sources of salt water and fresh water.

22-2 Explain how the water cycle works.

A church steeple is all that remains of a village destroyed by the eruption of Paricutín, which is eight kilometers away. The 4000 residents were safely evacuated before the lava destroyed the village in June 1944.

On February 20, 1943, a Mexican farmer, Dionisio Pulido went to work as usual in his cornfield. But his cornfield had changed overnight. He stared in disbelief at a 24-meter-long crack in his land. Hot rocks and ash oozed from the crack. Pulido ran to the nearby village of Paricutín to tell what he had seen.

Pulido had witnessed a dramatic change in the earth's surface—the birth of a volcano! The volcano, called Paricutín after Pulido's village, grew rapidly. It was about 10 meters high by the next morning, and about 168 meters high after the first week. The volcano was about 335 meters high after the first year. By then, great amounts of ash had covered the land around for about 50 square kilometers. On February 25, 1952, Paricutín reached its final height of about 410 meters above the surrounding land.

Nine years and 12 days after its birth, Paricutín became inactive. During its active years it had thrown out about 3.6 billion tons of lava, rocks, and ash. Pulido had lost his cornfield, and about 4500 people in two villages had lost their homes. The surface of the land was completely different.

Volcanoes like Paricutín are among the great forces that shape and reshape the earth's surface. More slowly, folding of the earth's crust forms huge mountain ranges. And even more slowly, the mountains are worn down. The flow of water also changes the shape of the land. This process has been going on for billions of years. It is still going on today.

Paricutín erupting

22-1 The Earth's Surface: Landmasses

Nearly all the visible land on our planet rests on seven great landmasses—the continents. There are many different surface features on these continents. For example, Asia holds the highest place on earth—Mount Everest, the crown of the mighty Himalaya mountain range. Everest's peak is 8848 meters above sea level. Mount Everest is in Nepal, a small country north of India. Thousands of kilometers to the west, but still within Asia, lies the lowest place on earth's land surface—the shore of the Dead Sea in Israel, 392 meters below sea level.

Asia, the largest continent, stretches from the frozen Arctic tundra in the north to the steaming tropical rain forests and rice paddies of places such as Viet Nam and Cambodia in the south. Asia also stretches from the parched Arabian Desert in the west to rich farmlands on the Pacific coasts of China and the Soviet Union.

But even within the smallest continent, Australia, the land takes many shapes. Along the western coast, the land is low and flat. Looking eastward, you can see what appears to be a long line of mountains. As you approach them, you realize that they are not

Figure 22-1 *Mount Everest (left) is the highest place on the earth's surface, and the shore of the Dead Sea (right) is the lowest place.*

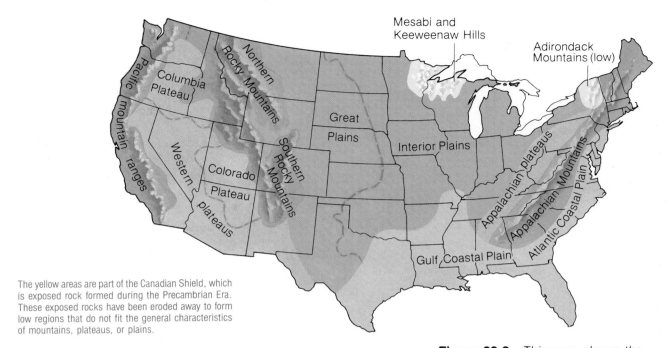

The yellow areas are part of the Canadian Shield, which is exposed rock formed during the Precambrian Era. These exposed rocks have been eroded away to form low regions that do not fit the general characteristics of mountains, plateaus, or plains.

Figure 22-2 *This map shows the major landscape regions of the continental United States.*

mountains but steep cliffs. A climber reaching the tops of these cliffs finds a great area of roughly level land. This highland region covers most of western Australia. It is like an enormous table whose edges are cliffs. In fact, such highlands are often called tablelands.

Mountains, highlands, and lowlands are different kinds of physical features on the earth's land surface. Such areas that have certain physical features are called landscapes. Figure 22-2 shows the major landscape regions of the continental United States. In what landscape region do you live?

There are three main types of landscapes on the earth's surface. Each type has different characteristics. Let's visit them one at a time.

Different physical features of the land surface can influence the weather. For example, Mexico City lies in the tropics. But its weather is cool, dry, and pleasant. The major reason for this weather is that Mexico City is on a level stretch of land about 2380 meters above sea level.

Mountains

You are walking through a region of tall, jagged peaks, long slopes, and high, narrow ridges. You can see deep valleys, forests, and small, rushing streams. Where are you? The region you are visiting is an example of a typical **mountain landscape.**

What is the difference between a mountain and a hill? Most geologists agree that a mountainous area rises at least 610 meters above the surrounding land.

Figure 22-3

SOME OF THE WORLD'S MOST FAMOUS MOUNTAINS

Name	Height Above Sea Level (meters)	Location	Interesting Facts
Aconcagua	6959	Andes in Argentina	Highest mountain in the Western Hemisphere
Cotopaxi	5897	Andes in Ecuador	Highest active volcano in the world
Elbert	4399	Colorado	Highest mountain of Rockies
Everest	8848	Himalayas on Nepal-Tibet border	Highest mountain in the world
K2	8611	Kashmir	Second highest mountain in the world
Kanchenjunga	8598	Himalayas on Nepal-India border	Third highest mountain in the world
Kilimanjaro	5895	Tanzania	Highest mountain in Africa
Logan	5950	Yukon	Highest mountain in Canada
Mauna Kea	4205	On volcanic island in Hawaii	Highest island mountain in the world
Mauna Loa	4169	On volcanic island in Hawaii	Famous volcanic mountain
McKinley	6194	Alaska	Highest mountain in North America
Mitchell	2037	North Carolina	Highest mountain in the Appalachians
Mont Blanc	4807	France	Highest mountain in the Alps
Mount St. Helens	2549	Cascades in Washington	Recent active volcano in the United States
Pikes Peak	4301	Colorado	Most famous of the Rocky Mountains
Rainier	4392	Cascades in Washington	Highest mountain in Washington
Vesuvius	1277	Italy	Only active volcano on the mainland of Europe
Whitney	4418	Sierra Nevadas in California	Highest mountain in California

But the actual height of a mountain is given as its height above sea level. For example, Pikes Peak in Colorado rises about 2700 meters above the surrounding land. But its height in Figure 22-3 is given as 4301 meters. What does this figure mean?*

The height of a mountain on an island is also measured from sea level. For example, Hawaii's Mauna Kea is listed in Figure 22-3 as 4205 meters above sea level. Actually, Mauna Kea is the world's tallest mountain, rising 10,203 meters from the sea floor to its peak.

Most of the world's mountains have been built up by the slow folding and wrinkling of the earth's crust. See Figure 22-4. These mountains include the Appalachians of the eastern United States, the Himalayas of Asia, the Andes of South America, the Rockies of the western United States, the Urals and Caucasus of the Soviet Union, and the Alps of Europe.

You can make a model of this kind of folding with a large piece of cloth. Lay it flat on a table. Put your hands on opposite ends of the cloth and push it slowly together. Wave-shaped wrinkles form in the cloth, making miniature "mountains" and "valleys." You may notice that the wrinkles tend to form parallel rows at right angles to the direction of your push. If you flew over the Alps of Europe, you would see a large-scale version of your cloth model. There are row after parallel row of snow-capped, jagged peaks with steep, narrow valleys in between.

Mountains are built very slowly. It is thought that the Rocky Mountains began to form about 65 million years ago. It took about 10 million years for these mountains to reach their maximum height. It will take much longer for them to wear down. But wear down they will. Someday, many millions of years in the future, the majestic sharp-peaked Rockies will be worn down by the action of wind and moving water. On that day, the Rockies will be little more than low rounded hills.

Some mountains are formed when the earth's crust breaks into huge blocks. See Figure 22-4. The Sierra Nevada Mountains of northern and central California were formed in this way.

Sometimes the crust cracks, and lava and ashes come through the cracks and pile up, layer on layer.

Figure 22-4 *Mountains may form when the earth's crust breaks into great blocks that are then tilted or lifted (top). Folded mountains form when layers of the earth's crust wrinkle into wavelike folds (bottom).*

Figure 22-5 *The Alps are an example of folded mountains. These mountains show parallel rows of snow-capped jagged peaks with steep narrow valleys in between.*

*The surrounding land rises 4301 − 2700 = 1601 meters above sea level.

Such pile-ups may form volcanic mountains, such as the Cascade Mountains of Washington and Oregon. Many individual mountains are volcanoes. For example, Paricutín in Mexico, Vesuvius in Italy, and Kilimanjaro in Africa are all volcanoes.

However, most mountains are part of a group of mountains. A group of mountains is called a **mountain range.** Examples of mountain ranges are the Alps, Andes, Himalayas, Rockies, and Appalachians.

Most mountain ranges are part of a larger group of mountains called a **mountain belt.** The Rocky Mountains, for example, are just one part of a huge chain of mountains that extends along the Pacific Coast of North and South America from Alaska to the southern tip of South America. This chain is one of the two major mountain belts on the earth's surface. Figure 22-6 shows the pattern of these two mountain belts. One is called the circum-Pacific belt. This belt roughly circles the Pacific Ocean. The other belt is the Eurasian-Melanesian belt, which extends across northern Africa, southern Europe, and southern Asia. The two belts meet in Indonesia.

The great mountain belts on the continents are rivaled by the undersea mountains of the worldwide Mid-Ocean Ridge system discussed in Chapter 21. This system extends through the Atlantic, Pacific, Indian, and Antarctic oceans. On either side of the rift valleys of the Mid-Ocean Ridge system are belts of

Figure 22-6 *Most of the mountains on the earth's surface are located in the two major mountain belts shown on this map.*

Figure 22-7 *In this photograph of the Colorado Plateau and Grand Canyon, a barren, dry landscape is revealed.*

high undersea mountains. These mountains were built by volcanic action. Many are still active volcanoes.

Plateaus

Now you are walking through a different landscape. You are in a highland area dotted with enormous flat-topped hills. This region is dry, almost a desert. But the same kind of landscape at another place on earth may be damp and covered with forests. No matter whether it is dry or wet, warm or cold, this type of region is a **plateau landscape,** or simply a plateau.

A plateau begins as flat land that is gradually lifted by movements of the earth's crust. A plateau is usually more than 600 meters above sea level. Some plateaus reach heights of more than 1500 meters.

The plateau upon which you are standing lies west of the Rocky Mountains, among some of the wildest and most beautiful scenery on earth. It is the Colorado Plateau, which includes the Grand Canyon. The Colorado Plateau is roughly centered on the point where the boundaries of Colorado, New Mexico, Arizona, and Utah meet.

Plateaus usually form near mountain ranges. In fact, the Colorado Plateau began rising as the Rocky Mountains were forming some 65 million years ago.

Figure 22-8 *Here you can see the forests and rounded slopes of the Appalachian Plateau.*

Activity

Sizes of Continents

Using tracing paper, trace the outline of the seven continents from a globe. Use scissors to cut out the outlines of the continents. Place the cutouts on graph paper and trace around each of the continents. Lightly shade in the outlined area covered by the continents.

Consider each square on the graph paper as an area unit of 1. Figure the area units for each of the seven continents to the nearest whole unit. For example, if a continent outline covered all of 45 units, approximately half of 20 units, and one-fourth of 16 units, the total number of area units covered would be 45 + 10 + 4 = 59. List the continents from the largest to the smallest, according to your calculations.

But a plateau forms without the sideways folding and buckling of the crust that forms mountains. So its top stays more or less flat. In its youth, the Colorado Plateau was a single broad structure, towering 1500 meters and more above the surrounding land, but lower than the Rockies to the east.

Today, however, the Colorado Plateau is made of many plateaus. As you look around, you see an awesome landscape of huge flat-topped tables of rock. They are separated by steep clifflike canyon walls. Along the cliffsides, layers of brightly colored rock glow in the sun. The canyon walls are often terraced—almost as if a giant hand had carved a series of ledges there to make convenient steps.

Actually, the carving was done by the Colorado River and its branches over millions of years. They sliced deeper and deeper into the rock, cutting it up into separate plateaus. The steps of the terraces are layers of more water-resistant rock. The streams cut around this rock.

The Colorado River has carved the mighty Grand Canyon out of the hard rocks of the Colorado Plateau. It is a huge canyon about 2 kilometers deep, up to 29 kilometers wide, and 349 kilometers long. Today, the Colorado River continues to carve out more of this canyon.

By contrast, the Appalachian Plateau, west of the Blue Ridge Mountains, has more rounded slopes and forests. The Appalachian Plateau gets lots of rain. This plateau is many millions of years older than the

Colorado Plateau. So there has been much more time for rain, streams, and wind to smooth and round its slopes.

Plains

Now you are visiting another of the major landscape types. Here the land is mostly flat and of about equal height, like plateaus. But, unlike plateaus, this landscape is lower than the surrounding land. You are in a lowland area that is not far above sea level. You see broad rivers or streams, and the vegetation is mainly grass. The region you are visiting is a **plains landscape.**

The two major types of plains areas are determined by location and height above sea level. They are either along a coast or farther inland. Let's visit these two types of plains in the United States.

COASTAL PLAINS Low, flat regions called **coastal plains** spread gently upward from the Atlantic and Gulf coasts of the United States. These plains extend along the Atlantic coast from Cape Cod, Massachusetts, to Florida and from the Gulf coast of Florida to Texas. They average about 150 meters above sea level.

Many crops can be grown in coastal plain soil. Why? The reason is that the soil is very rich in substances needed for plant growth. In the United States, citrus crops, cotton, tobacco, and many different kinds of vegetables can be grown on the rich coastal plains.

Where does the rich soil come from? The soil is brought to the coastal plains by rivers. Rivers can break down rocks into sand and mud.

Rivers flow from high mountains and plateaus down to low-lying plains and out to sea. These rivers move fastest at the start of their journey. A fast-moving river is a powerful tool for wearing down rock. Because it is fast-moving, it can carry a large load of sand and mud.

As the river hits the gentler slopes of the lowlands, it slows down. And the more slowly it flows, the more sand and mud drops out of the flow. So, year after year, the rivers help to wear down the highlands and build up the lowland plains.

Figure 22-9 *In this plains landscape, the flat lowlands are not far above sea level. Such landscapes may include broad rivers or streams. The natural vegetation is mainly grass.*

Figure 22-10 *The flat land of the inland plains has very fertile soil that is good for growing crops such as wheat and corn.*

Activity

Surface Features

Suppose you take a trip across the earth's land surface. You will see many different kinds of features. Write a 200 word essay about what you see using the following vocabulary terms: mountain landscape, mountain range, plateau landscape, coastal plains, and inland plains. Your essay should describe the major similarities and differences between these features.

There is another reason that the coastal plains have rich soil. Long ago, shallow oceans covered these areas. As the shallow seas disappeared, they left behind rich deposits of soil that formed the coastal plains.

But not all coastal plains are available for farming. Some of the most fertile soil in coastal plains is not usable because it is found in swamps and marshes. This land is below river level and sometimes below sea level. So the land usually floods with water. Inland plains are also found in the Soviet Union, central and eastern Europe, and parts of Africa and Australia.

INLAND PLAINS The central part of the United States is divided into two very large **inland plains**— the Interior Plains and the Great Plains. See Figure 22-2. Inland plains average about 450 meters above sea level. How were these plains formed? Over millions of years, mountains and hills were worn down by wind, rivers, and glaciers, leaving plains that have become the heartland of the United States farming country.

Why are these plains considered among the world's best for farming? There are three reasons. Many parts of these plains receive very rich soil deposits from such rivers as the Mississippi, Ohio, Missouri, Arkansas, and Red. More than half the material that built up the 65 million-year-old Rocky Mountains has been spread over these plains by rivers. Another reason is that plenty of rain falls on much of the plains during the growing season. A third reason is that these northern and western plains are much higher above sea level than are the coastal plains. So flooding, which could carry away rich soil, tends not to occur there.

Even where there is less water and rainfall, as in the western part of the Interior Plains and in the Great Plains, crops such as corn and wheat cover the land. Only within the "rain shadow" of the Rockies does farmland give way to semidesert and desert. Within a rain shadow, the mountains cut off the rains moving in from the west.

Water is very important to all living things. As you read in this section, too much or too little water can affect the growth of crops and the value of land to farmers. The next section will discuss the other major surface feature of the earth—water.

Career: *Surveyor*

In ancient Egypt, farmers placed boundary stones around their land to mark off property lines. But the annual flooding of the Nile River moved the stones or washed them away. So the Egyptians, who were excellent mathematicians, learned to survey their land. Thus they could replace any lost boundary markers accurately.

Today boundaries and areas of property on the earth's surface are determined by scientists called **surveyors.** They use an instrument called a transit to measure and plot angles and distances. Surveyors can measure the exact location of points and elevations on the earth's surface. The results of their survey are recorded, the data are checked, and sketches, maps, and reports are prepared. This information is used for construction projects, mapmaking, land division, mining, and deciding property ownership.

Surveyors must make very precise measurements. Their maps and land descriptions are recorded in the courthouse for anyone to check. A state licensing exam is taken after several years of work experience.

A person interested in surveying must have good judgment, enjoy problem solving, be able to communicate, and be attentive to detail. For more information, write to the American Congress on Surveying and Mapping, 210 Little Falls Street, Falls Church, VA 22046.

SECTION REVIEW

1. What are the three main types of landscapes on the earth's surface? 1. Mountains; plateaus; plains
2. What are three ways that mountains can form?
3. What are the two major types of plains?

2. Slow folding and wrinkling of earth's crust; earth's crust breaks into huge blocks; volcanic pile-ups
3. Coastal and inland

22-2 The Earth's Surface: Water

The earth is a watery planet. Oceans cover about 70 percent of its surface. And about 97 percent of all the water on our world is in the oceans. This is salt water. Every hundred kilograms of sea water contains about 3.5 kilograms of ordinary salt, as well as a number of other salts dissolved in the water.

Figure 22-11 *Oceans cover most of the earth's surface.*

Where do these salts come from and how do they get into sea water? There are three main sources. Ocean salts are found in undersea volcanoes, in rivers, and along shores. Ocean water dissolves salts in volcanic rocks. Rivers dissolve salts in rocks and soil on land. The rivers then carry these salts to the oceans. As waves constantly pound on shores, the erosion from waves helps to dissolve the salts in rocks.

What about the other 3 percent of the earth's water? Most of it is locked up in the ice packs of the Arctic Ocean, and in the great sheets of ice that cover a large part of the continent of Antarctica. This is fresh water. The rest of the fresh water is in the ground and in lakes, ponds, streams, and rivers. Fresh water does not contain salt, though it does have small amounts of other dissolved minerals. Fresh water is drinking water. It is essential for all plants and animals that live on land.

Where does fresh water come from? Why is it fresh and not salty? That is part of the story of the water cycle.

The Water Cycle

There is an old saying that every drop of water from the ocean rains five times before it returns to the ocean. Although this is not a very scientific statement, it does have a kind of scientific basis. Here is the reason. The oceans hold about 11.4 billion cubic kilometers of water. Water at the surface evaporates constantly, while at the bottom of the ocean water may wait 2000 years before it reenters the water cycle.

Activity

Community Water Supply

Visit a water-treatment plant in your area. Find out what sources your fresh water comes from and how the water is purified before it comes into your community. In a written report, include the answers to these questions:

1. Where does your community's water come from?

2. How is the water treated before it is pumped into the water supply?

3. About how much water is used by your community each year?

4. How could the supply of water be increased?

Every day, the heat of the sun causes water on the earth's surface to change to a gas. This process is called **evaporation** (i-va-puh-RA-shun). Enormous amounts of water are evaporated from the oceans. Water also evaporates from fresh-water sources on land. See Figure 22-12.

When water evaporates, it gets into the air as an invisible gas—water vapor. There is always some water vapor in the air, even over the driest deserts.

Air can hold only a certain amount of water vapor. Warm air can hold more water vapor than can cold air. As warm air, loaded with water vapor, rises, it cools. The cooler air can no longer hold all of its water vapor. Some of the water vapor changes back into a liquid. This process is called **condensation** (kahn-den-SAY-shun). Next, clouds form. They are made up of billions of tiny water droplets so light that they can float in the air. Sooner or later, this water falls to earth as rain, sleet, hail, or snow. It is fresh water. This falling process is called **precipitation** (pree-sip-uh-TAY-shun). When sea water evaporates, the solids dissolved in the water are left behind. Then the cycle begins again.

Figure 22-12 *The water cycle is made up of the processes of evaporation, condensation, and precipitation.*

Figure 22-13 *Air on the western sides of mountains contains much moisture. The wet conditions allow many kinds of vegetation to grow (left). Air on the eastern sides of mountains contains much less moisture, and dry, desert conditions result (right).*

Figure 22-14 *The grooves in these mountains show how running water can cut deeply into mountains over millions of years.*

In some places, high mountain ranges generally prevent moisture from reaching the land, producing a desert climate. For example, moisture-laden air from the Pacific flows eastward over the California coast. Plenty of rain falls on the farms of the Great Central Valley in California. The air reaches the Sierra Nevada Mountains inland and is forced to rise. As it rises it cools. Lots of rain falls on the western slopes of the mountains. But by the time the air crosses the Sierras, it no longer contains enough moisture. So little rain falls on the desert lands east of the Sierras, including Death Valley. For the same reason, the eastern side of the Rockies is mostly desert land.

Running Water

Some of the water that falls to earth evaporates again. But about a third of the water remains on the surface. It begins moving downhill and flows into rivers and streams. The water entering a river or stream is called surface runoff. In the spring, melting snow and ice add to the surface runoff.

From high mountains and steep plateau cliffs, water flows downward. It collects in basins, grooves, and channels worn in the rock by earlier runoffs. Streams like these come together to become the sources of the world's rivers. The rivers return to the oceans. Water evaporates from the oceans, and the cycle repeats endlessly.

Some rain water soaks into the ground. The ground takes on water like a sponge. This water is called **ground water.** About 0.6 percent of the earth's fresh water is in ground water. Even in the driest deserts, there is water underground. There is a place under the desert sands where the ground is soaked with water. Water fills spaces between the grains of soil. Eventually, ground water flows underground to the oceans. This water can then become part of the water cycle again.

The top level to which ground water rises when underground is called the **water table.** In the desert, the water table may be hundreds of meters underground. In places with more rainfall, the water table lies nearer the surface. There, water seeps up from the water table, keeping the roots of plants moist and supplying water for wells. See Figure 22-16. In some places, such as coastal plains, the land lies slightly below the level of the water table. Such land is usually swampy or marshy. When there is a long period without rain—a drought—the water table sinks deeper into the ground. Ponds begin to dry up. Wells go dry, the shallowest wells first.

On the other hand, after unusually heavy rains through much of the year, the water table may rise toward the surface. Normally dry ground becomes muddy. Puddles form everywhere. The ground is waterlogged right up to its top. Plants may be killed because their roots cannot get enough air.

Standing Water

Unlike rivers and streams, the water in lakes and ponds usually stays in one location. Both can be important sources of water. Moosehead Lake, in Maine, for example, is a natural source of fresh water. It is 56 kilometers long and 3 to 16 kilometers wide. The pine-forested shores of the lake can hold huge amounts of water from rains and melting snow. This water is released slowly to the lake, making flooding less likely. During times of drought, the lake holds a huge supply of water in reserve.

Frozen Water

Aside from the oceans, the most enormous store of water on earth lies in the ice sheets around the North and South poles. About 2 percent of the

Figure 22-15 *An oasis can form in a desert when ground water rises to the surface.*

Figure 22-16 *These diagrams show the changes in a water table after a long period of rain and after a long period without rain.*

After a Long Period of Rain

Deep well

Water sinking into ground

Shallow well

Shallow pond

Water table

Ground water

After a Long Period Without Rain

Deep well

Shallow well

Evaporation

Dry pond

Water table

Ground water

earth's fresh water is frozen in ice sheets. If all this ice melted, the oceans would rise about 50 meters above their present level. New York, New Orleans, Houston, and Seattle would be under water. Memphis, Tennessee, now 560 kilometers from the sea, would become a major seaport. In Washington, D.C., the top floors of the Capitol Building and the tip of the Washington Monument would be above water. But the Pentagon would be completely covered.

The very thick ice sheets that cover most of the polar regions are called **continental glaciers.** Glaciers are huge, slow-moving masses of ice. During the Ice Ages, when the earth's climate was much colder, the ice piled up several kilometers thick around both poles. The pressure of the piled-up ice caused it to flow outward away from the poles. At times, these glaciers covered a third of all the land on earth.

Valley glaciers are long, narrow glaciers. They move downhill between the steep sides of mountain valleys. Usually they follow channels worn by running water in the past.

As the glacier slides downward, it tears rock fragments from the mountainside. These fragments become frozen in the glacier. They cut deep grooves in the valley walls. Finer bits of rock sandpaper the walls, smoothing them. Glaciers often turn a steep, V-shaped valley into a U-shaped valley with smooth sides. There are many such valleys in the Alps.

Figure 22-17 *This valley glacier is slowly moving downhill between the steep sides of a mountain valley.*

Figure 22-18 *Glaciers cut valleys into U-shapes* (left), *and rivers cut valleys into V-shapes* (right).

Great chunks of ice break off from the edges of the Arctic and Antarctic ice sheets. These masses of free-floating ice are called **icebergs.** They can be a major hazard to ships. In 1912, the ocean liner *Titanic* sank after smashing into an iceberg in the North Atlantic Ocean. Today, sea lanes are patrolled constantly by ships and planes on the lookout for icebergs.

Around the Great Lakes are masses of boulders, rocks, and sand, heaped up into ridges and hills. They are deposits left by glaciers that covered this area thousands of years ago. As the climate grew warmer, the glaciers melted and dropped their cargo of rocks in piles. These piles mark the farthest advance of the glaciers.

You now have explored what is under your feet—the earth's interior. And you have explored what you are standing on—the earth's surface. What's left to explore? That's right, what's above your head—the earth's atmosphere.

SECTION REVIEW

1. What percentage of the water on earth is fresh water?
2. Name the three processes of the water cycle?
3. Where is most of the earth's fresh water found?

1. 3 percent
2. Evaporation; condensation; precipitation
3. Frozen in glaciers

The U.S. Geological Survey's computer model predicts any glacier's movement by analyzing its position in the water, the rate of ice flow toward the glacier's tip, and the number of icebergs breaking off at the glacier's tip per period of time.

Activity

Reservoirs

The most frequently used sources of fresh water are artificial lakes called reservoirs. Using reference materials in your library, write a short report about reservoirs and include answers to the following questions:

1. How are reservoirs built?
2. How are reservoirs important during periods of heavy rain? During periods of drought?
3. How are some reservoirs used in the generation of electrical power?
4. What are the names and locations of some major reservoirs in the United States? In the rest of the world?

LABORATORY ACTIVITY

For further instructions, see page T-69.

Examining Differences Between Fresh and Salt Water

Purpose

In this activity, you will examine some of the differences in the physical characteristics of salt water and fresh water.

Materials (per group)

1 plastic drinking straw
Small piece of clay
4 to 6 steel BBs or ball bearings
250-mL beaker
Fresh water
Pencil
Metric ruler
3 samples of liquids

Procedure

1. Cut a straw in half and plug one end with a small piece of clay.
2. With a pencil, make a series of marks ½ cm apart along the entire length of the straw.
3. Add water to the beaker or glass container until it is about three-quarters full.
4. Carefully drop two or three BBs into the open end of the straw and let them roll down to the clay at the bottom.
5. With the clay end down, gently place the straw into the water. It should float. Add as many BBs as are necessary to cause your straw hydrometer to float very low in the water. Only two or three pencil lines on the hydrometer should show above the water's surface. Note exactly the level at which it floats. Your hydrometer is now ready to be used to compare densities of liquids. The higher it floats, the more dense (salty) the liquid will be.
6. Examine the three beakers containing sample fluids that have been provided by your teacher. They are labeled A, B, and C.

Each sample has had different amounts of salt added, so each possesses a different density.

7. Gently place your hydrometer into the fluid of the first container. Carefully note and record the level at which it floats. Repeat the procedure for each of the two remaining samples.

Observations and Conclusions

1. List the order of the samples tested, from the one that was least dense to the one that was most dense. Include the sample of fresh water in your list.
2. How would the hydrometer float in a fluid that was less dense than the fresh water?
3. How would the hydrometer float in a fluid that was more dense than any of those tested?
4. How would the level of any floating object in fresh water compare to the floating level of that same object in salt water?
5. What do you think happens to the density of sea water at the surface of the ocean whenever it rains for a long period of time?

CHAPTER SUMMARY

22-1 The Earth's Surface: Landmasses

■ Mountains, plateaus, and plains are the three main types of landscapes on the earth's surface.

■ Most mountains have been formed by the slow folding and wrinkling of the earth's crust.

■ Some mountains are formed when the earth's crust breaks into huge blocks. Volcanic material also can form mountains.

■ Mountains are usually parts of larger groups called ranges and belts.

■ Plateau landscapes are usually areas of flat land of about equal height that have been uplifted to more than 600 meters above sea level and are higher than the surrounding land. Plateaus are sometimes called table-lands or highlands.

■ Plains landscapes are areas of flat land of about equal height that are lower than the sur-rounding land. Plains are lowland areas that are usually not far above sea level.

■ Coastal plains are low, flat regions that ex-tend along coasts and usually average about 150 meters above sea level. Rich soil is brought to the coastal plains by rivers. Flood-ing is a problem in these low-lying plains.

■ Inland plains are low, flat regions that usu-ally average about 450 meters above sea level. Rich soil is brought to such plains by rivers.

22-2 The Earth's Surface: Water

■ About 97 percent of all the water on earth is in the oceans. This ocean water is salt wa-ter. The other 3 percent is fresh water found in glaciers, ground water, lakes, and rivers.

■ The water cycle is a continual process. It involves the processes of evaporation, con-densation, and precipitation.

■ Fresh water from streams, rivers, and ground water eventually returns to the oceans.

■ A water table is the top level to which ground water rises.

■ Fresh water from lakes and ponds usually stays in one location.

■ About 2 percent of all fresh water is frozen in glaciers.

VOCABULARY   *Define the following terms.*

coastal plains p.509
condensation p.513
continental glacier p.516
evaporation p.513
ground water p.515
iceberg p.517
inland plains p.510
mountain belt p.506

mountain landscape p.503
mountain range p.506
plains landscape p.509
plateau landscape p.507
precipitation p.513
valley glacier p.516
water table p.515

CHAPTER REVIEW

Multiple Choice

Choose the letter of the answer that best completes each statement.

1. The highest place on the earth's surface is
   a. Mauna Kea in Hawaii.
   b. Pikes Peak in Colorado.
   c. Mount Everest in Nepal.
   d. Vesuvius in Italy.
2. Most of the world's mountains have been built up by
   a. river deposits.
   b. folding and blocking of the earth's crust.
   c. earthquakes.
   d. all of these.
3. A mountain belt is a
   a. group of volcanic mountains.
   b. group of underwater mountains.
   c. group of mountains such as the Appalachians.
   d. group of mountain ranges.
4. Plateaus
   a. have jagged peaks.
   b. are sometimes called highlands.
   c. are lower than the surrounding land.
   d. are always found in dry, desert areas.
5. On the earth's surface flooding is a major problem for
   a. inland plains.
   b. coastal plains.
   c. plateaus.
   d. mountains.

6. Some of the best farmland is found
   a. in marshes.
   b. on mountain slopes.
   c. on inland plains.
   d. on plateaus.
7. An example of standing water is
   a. rivers.
   b. lakes.
   c. glaciers.
   d. streams.
8. The process by which the sun's heat causes water on the earth's surface to change to a gas is called
   a. precipitation.
   b. evaporation.
   c. condensation.
   d. the water cycle.
9. Fresh water is not found in
   a. lakes.
   b. ground water.
   c. glaciers.
   d. oceans.
10. Long, narrow masses of ice that move downhill along the sides of mountains are called
   a. icebergs.
   b. valley glaciers.
   c. polar ice sheets.
   d. continental glaciers.

Completions

Fill in the word or words that best complete each statement.

1. There are seven large landmasses on Earth called ___continents___.
2. Most mountain ranges are part of a larger group of mountains called a(n) ___mountain belt___.
3. A ___plateau___ is a major landscape feature that forms when a flat land surface is uplifted by movements from within the earth's crust.
4. Lowland areas that are not far above sea level are called ___coastal plains___.
5. The process in the water cycle by which the sun changes surface water to water vapor is called ___evaporation___.

6. The process in the water cycle by which water vapor changes to liquid water is called _____condensation_____.

7. The process in the water cycle by which water falls to earth as rain, sleet, hail, or snow is called _____precipitation_____.

8. The top level at which ground water is found is called the _____water table_____.

9. The thick ice sheets that cover most of the earth's polar regions are called _____continental glaciers_____.

10. Most of the earth's _____fresh_____ water is found frozen in ice sheets.

True or False

Determine whether each statement is true or false. If it is true, write "true." If it is false, change the underlined word or words to make the statement true.

1. Three main types of landscapes on the earth's surface are mountains, <u>hills</u>, and plains. F (plateaus)

2. Most of the world's mountains were built by the slow <u>folding and wrinkling</u> of the earth's crust. T

3. There are two major mountain <u>ranges</u> on the earth's surface. F (belts)

4. <u>Plains</u> are highland areas that look like enormous tabletops. F (Plateaus)

5. Rivers bring rich soil to <u>plateau</u> regions. F (plains)

6. Coastal plains are <u>higher</u> above sea level than inland plains. F (lower)

7. About <u>97 percent</u> of all the water on the earth's surface is salt water. T

8. <u>Evaporation</u> is a process in the water cycle by which water vapor changes back into a liquid. F (Condensation)

9. Rivers and streams are examples of <u>standing</u> water. F (running)

10. Most fresh water is frozen in <u>glaciers</u>. T

Discussion Topics   Answers appear on page T-69.

Write a brief paragraph discussing each of the following.

1. Briefly describe the three major kinds of landscapes.

2. Describe three ways in which mountains are formed.

3. Describe how the Colorado Plateau was formed.

4. Compare the similarities and differences between inland plains and coastal plains.

5. Discuss three reasons why the inland plains of the United States are among the best farming land in the world.

6. Describe the processes of the water cycle and explain how it is a continual process.

EXPAND YOUR KNOWLEDGE

Bauer, E. *Wonders of the Earth.* New York: Watts.
   Volcanoes, geysers, waterfalls, caves, and other geological features on or near the earth's surface are discussed in this easy-to-understand book. The book contains beautiful color photographs and drawings.

23 Structure of the Atmosphere

For a chapter overview, teaching strategies, answers to all activities, a list of A-V materials, and a chapter bibliography, see pages T-70 to T-72.

Consult your Teacher's Resource Book and Annotated Teacher's Edition, Laboratory Book for additional activities and teaching aids.

CHAPTER OBJECTIVES

After completing this chapter, you will be able to:

23-1 Describe how the layers of the atmosphere differ.

23-1 Describe the relationships between temperature and the layers of the atmosphere.

23-1 Explain why the air gets "thinner" and colder at higher altitudes.

23-1 State the importance of ozone and the jet stream.

23-2 Compare the earth to a magnet.

"I caught my breath as I looked out. The scene as we topped 100,000 feet was utterly magnificent. For long moments, we drank in the beauty of earth, sea, and sky. Our horizon lay some 400 miles away. A narrow lower segment of the sky appeared bright and whitish-blue. I recognized it as the troposphere, the layer of the atmosphere closest to the earth. Above came another layer, a much richer, deeper, cleaner blue. Above that and over our heads, the blue darkened to a blue-black towards the void of space." That was the view from the pressurized cabin of a balloon soaring over the Gulf of Mexico.

Today, research balloons commonly explore the lower parts of the atmosphere. Rockets go up even farther, crossing that vague boundary where the last bit of earth's air fades into outer space. And down below, people travel through the lowest parts of the atmosphere—by foot, in elevators and cable cars, and in airplanes. These trips are not often scientific or mysterious. Yet there are mysteries in the air and scientists to solve them.

For example, a flight up through the clouds is often bumpy. But, above the clouds, the flight is smooth. There seems to be an invisible wall above which clouds and bumpy weather cannot rise. What is this wall?

Clouds in the lower atmosphere

Figure 23-1 *In the last century, scientists studied the atmosphere from wicker baskets attached to balloons* (left). *Today, scientists use high-altitude balloons carrying instruments to study the atmosphere* (right).

23-1 The Layers of the Atmosphere

In the nineteenth century, some weather scientists began exploring the atmosphere. Their ships of exploration were wicker baskets! Baskets? Yes, that's right. The scientists soared into the sky in huge baskets hanging from hydrogen-filled balloons.

James Glaisher, an English scientist, was one of these early explorers. On a warm day in September 1862, he and another scientist, Henry Coxwell, began a balloon trip. They soon found themselves in serious danger.

Twenty-five minutes after leaving the ground, they reached an altitude of 4800 meters. They were nearly as high as the tallest mountain in Europe, Mont Blanc. The temperature had dropped to −11° C. Ice coated the basket and the rigging of the balloon. The explorers could have returned to the ground by slowly releasing hydrogen gas and deflating the balloon. They decided to go on instead.

The temperature continued to drop as they rose. At 5000 meters it was −12.5° C. At 10,000 meters it was −45° C. Finally they reached 11,000 meters, well over 2000 meters higher than the top of Mount Everest. Though warmly dressed and in bright sunshine, the two men were numbed with cold. It was −52° C.

And something else was wrong. The scientists could move only very slowly. It was almost as if they were paralyzed. The bright sun turned dim as their eyesight failed. Glaisher lost consciousness. Coxwell tried to open the gas valves to get them down. But the valve cord was tangled up with the ropes that held the basket under the balloon. Although frostbitten, Coxwell somehow climbed up the ropes. He was surrounded by long icicles hanging from the balloon.

At last he was able to untangle the valve cord. His hands were completely numb. He climbed back down into the basket by clinging to the ropes with his elbows. Coxwell knew they would both soon die if he could not bring the balloon down. He grabbed the valve cord with his teeth and tugged the valve open. They were on their way to safety.

The two explorers lived to tell their story—and to make other balloon flights. Some other daring scientists were not so lucky. But around the world, scientists continued to explore the atmosphere in balloons. Everywhere, the picture of the atmosphere was the same. The temperature, scientists discovered, drops at an average rate of 6.5° C per kilometer of altitude.

The air also gets "thinner," or less dense, with increasing altitude. It becomes more spread out. So there is less of it in a given space at a higher altitude. This is why Glaisher and Coxwell moved so slowly and why Glaisher became unconscious. They did not have enough oxygen to breathe. In fact, at 11,000 meters, they had to take about four breaths to get the same amount of oxygen that is in one breath at the surface of the earth.

What causes air to be less dense at higher altitudes? Suppose you take a couple of handfuls of cotton and squeeze them into a small ball. Obviously, the ball has the same amount of cotton in it that once filled up both your hands. But it is squeezed into a much smaller space.

In much the same way, the air around you is pressed together by the weight of all the air above it.

Figure 23-2 *The air contains less oxygen at higher altitudes, so pilots must wear oxygen masks.*

AIR PRESSURE AND ALTITUDE

Altitude (meters)	Air Pressure (g/cm²)
Sea level	1034
3000	717
6000	450
9000	302
12,000	190
15,000	112

Figure 23-3 *Air pressure decreases as you go higher into the atmosphere.*

*It is not really air inside your body that changes, but changes in the liquid pressure inside your cells that balances outside pressure.

Activity

Air Pressure

Air exerts a pressure of about 1000 grams per square centimeter at sea level. Use the following steps to demonstrate the effects of air pressure. Obtain a glass juice or milk bottle, a hard-boiled egg with the shell removed, scrap paper, a match, and a pencil.

Stuff most of the paper into the bottle. Have your teacher light the rest of the paper and push it into the bottle with a pencil. Immediately place the egg on the top of the open bottle. What happens to the egg? Why?

This pressing force due to the weight of the air above you is called **air pressure.** Air pressure at sea level is about 1000 grams on each square centimeter. The air pressure on your body is around 12 tons. That would be enough to flatten you into a very thin pancake—except that there is also air inside your body under the same pressure, balancing the outside pressure.

As you go upward into the atmosphere, whether by climbing a mountain or flying in an airplane, or even riding in an elevator, the air pressure decreases. See Figure 23-3. That's because there is less air above you, so there is less weight and less air pressure. The air pressure inside your body decreases too, but a little more slowly. That is why you sometimes sense the change in pressure in your ears.*

Air is like a spring. Under pressure, it is squeezed into a smaller space. When the pressure is lower, the air expands, taking up more space. This not only explains why the air is thinner at higher altitudes. It also explains why the air gets colder there.

Have you ever felt the stream of air coming out of a tire when you open the valve? The tire may be warm, and the day may be warm—but the air stream is cold. The air in the tire is under higher pressure than the air around it. When you open the valve, the air rushes out and expands. And when air expands, it cools.

As air rises from the earth's surface, it expands because the air pressure becomes less and less. The higher it rises, the more it expands. And the more it expands, the colder it gets up to a certain height.

Air is always rising from the earth's surface. As you know, the earth's surface is heated by the sun. So air near the surface is warmed by that heat. Warm air is less dense than cold air. So the warm air heated at the surface floats up through the colder air above it. Cold air sinks to take its place.

So in the lower atmosphere, the air is constantly in motion. These churning motions or currents caused by heat are like the currents in the earth's mantle that you read about in Chapter 21.

Scientists who study the earth's atmosphere have divided it into four layers. *The division of these layers is based on changes in temperature.* Let's travel upward through these four layers and see what is there.

The Troposphere

The lowest layer of the atmosphere is called the **troposphere** (TRAH-puh-sfeer). This name means "turning over." Turning gives you the idea of constant change, and that is what the troposphere is all about. It is the place where storms are born, grow in power, weaken, and die. All of the earth's weather takes place in the troposphere. So are 99 percent of the clouds, water vapor, dust, and pollution. The great currents and the swirling storm winds are what make plane flights in the troposphere bumpy. The

Figure 23-4 *Here fog covers the Golden Gate Bridge in San Francisco. Fog is simply low-lying clouds. It results when the water vapor in cool, moist air condenses near the earth's surface.*

Figure 23-5 *Winds and thunderstorms occur in the troposphere.*

currents and winds also keep the air in the troposphere well mixed.

The most important single fact about the troposphere is that it gets steadily colder from bottom to top. This is what makes the churning of its air possible. Suppose the troposphere were nearly the same temperature throughout. Then there would be no rising of warm air, no settling of cold air—no currents at all.

For a long time, scientists thought that the atmosphere just kept getting colder all the way up to the edge of space. By 1902, a French scientist, Léon Philippe Teisserenc de Bort, had showed this was not so. He had checked the temperatures instruments recorded from 236 balloon flights. The balloons rose from altitudes between about 9.5 kilometers and 14.5 kilometers. The instruments showed that at an altitude of about 12 kilometers, the temperature stopped falling. There seemed to be a "roof" over the troposphere!

The troposphere actually is like a sloping roof. On the average, the troposphere's roof is lowest at the poles and slopes upward toward the equator.

Figure 23-6 *Rainbows* (left) *and clouds* (right) *are caused by weather conditions in the troposphere.*

Over the United States, which is about halfway between the poles and the equator, the roof of the troposphere is 11 kilometers up. The temperature of the roof of the troposphere over the United States is about −55° C. About 76 percent of the earth's air is found in the troposphere. Warmer temperatures at the equator, which cause the warmer air to rise higher, and the greater mixing of air due to equatorial wind patterns, are responsible for the higher altitude of the troposphere above the earth's equator.

The Stratosphere

The layer of the earth's atmosphere above the troposphere is called the **stratosphere** (STRAT-uh-sfeer). The stratosphere extends from about 16 kilometers to about 48 kilometers above the earth's surface. About 24 percent of the air lies in the stratosphere.

From about 12 kilometers high in the troposphere layer up to about 24 kilometers in the stratosphere layer, the temperature usually stays the same. The temperature remains about −55° C. Above that height, the air in the stratosphere actually warms up slowly with increasing height. At the top of the stratosphere, the temperature normally reaches between −2° C and 0° C.

Why doesn't the stratosphere get colder with the increasing height? Because **ozone** is present. Ozone is a high-energy form of oxygen. It has a sharp smell, something like the smell given off by sparking electric wires. Oxygen in the stratosphere reacts with sunlight to form ozone. The ozone forms a layer in the stratosphere. This ozone layer absorbs powerful ultraviolet rays from the sun. These rays warm the stratosphere. The ozone layer also acts as a screen, shielding the earth's surface from these harmful ultraviolet rays. Without this shield, most living things on earth would be killed. The ozone layer ends at the top of the stratosphere.

In the troposphere, air rises when there are layers of colder air above it. This does not happen in the stratosphere. The temperature is constant or rises with increasing height. So there are no currents. There are no storms. This is why airliners fly in the stratosphere when they can.

Another reason for flying in the stratosphere is the **jet stream.** The jet stream is a narrow, fast-moving current of air that forms along the troposphere-stratosphere boundary.

Figure 23-7 *Jets fly in the stratosphere to avoid the storms and strong winds of the troposphere.*

Ozone is a reactive form of oxygen containing three oxygen atoms per molecule, with the formula O_3. Normal oxygen has the formula O_2.

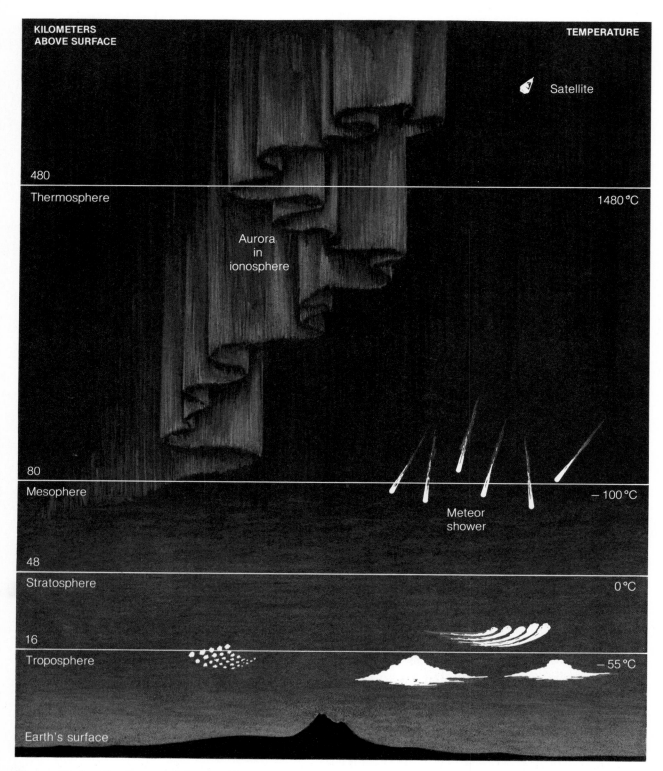

KILOMETERS ABOVE SURFACE

TEMPERATURE

Satellite

480

Thermosphere   1480 °C

Aurora
in
ionosphere

80

Mesosphere   − 100 °C

Meteor
shower

48

Stratosphere   0 °C

16

Troposphere   − 55 °C

Earth's surface

Figure 23-8 *The layers of the earth's atmosphere, from lowest to
highest altitude, are the troposphere, the stratosphere, the
mesosphere, and the thermosphere. Scientists determine the height of
each layer by measuring the temperature changes at various altitudes.*

In 1922, a weather balloon was sent aloft at Hampshire, England. It crossed the boundary between the troposphere and the stratosphere. Suddenly, it started sailing eastward at great speed. It came down four hours later in Leipzig, Germany, 900 kilometers east of its starting point. The balloon had been carried by a jet stream blowing at more than 200 kilometers an hour.

A jet stream usually forms where cold air from the poles meets warmer air from the equator. So there are two major jet streams that circle the earth. One jet stream is roughly halfway between the North Pole and the equator. The other is roughly halfway between the South Pole and the equator. Each usually blows in an easterly direction at more than 105

The jet stream, a high-altitude river of wind that marks the dividing line between cool and warm air, usually is flowing across Canada when the United States is in mid-summer. To the south of this jet stream there is warm air. To the north of this jet stream there is cool air. By midwinter the jet stream usually is flowing across the middle of the United States.

Career: *Physical Meteorologist*

HELP WANTED: PHYSICAL METEOROLOGIST Bachelor's degree in meteorology required. Master's degree preferred. Courses in air pollution and hydrology helpful. Apply to National Weather Service.

As you read these words, it is possible that somewhere in the world a volcano is "blowing its top." Almost countless tons of rock, dust, and gases are exploding into the earth's atmosphere. Wind will carry this volcanic "junk" around the world—perhaps to the sky above

your head. At the same time, factories near your home and cars on your street will puff more dust and gases into the atmosphere. Not so strangely, all of this material can affect the weather where you live. How? That is a question that **physical meteorologists** try to answer.

These scientists study the effects of gases and other particles in the air on weather and on other important things that affect the lives of people. The work of physical meteorologists can aid in the fight against air and water pollution.

Physical meteorologists study both the electrical and the chemical properties of the atmosphere. They observe the processes that produce winds and those that produce clouds, rain, snow, and hail. They do research to learn how the atmosphere affects light, sound, and radio waves. Meteorologists work for the government, universities, airlines, aerospace companies, and the radio and television industry.

If you are a curious person who enjoys detailed work in a laboratory and outdoors, physical meteorology may be a career for you. High school courses in physics, chemistry, and mathematics are very helpful. To learn more, write to the American Meteorological Society, 45 Beacon Street, Boston, MA 02108.

kilometers per hour. However, speeds may exceed 320 kilometers per hour. Airplanes flying eastward use the jet stream to make a faster trip and to save fuel. Airplanes traveling westward climb above the jet stream to avoid a head wind that would slow them down. There, of course, they do not get a push from the jet stream. That's why an airline flight schedule will show a shorter time for a flight from San Francisco to New York than a return flight, for example.

Jet streams also can steer large storms. You may have seen a television weather forecaster showing a jet stream on a map of the United States. Usually the jet stream is shown as a sort of twisted, moving belt snaking its way east across the country. As the jet stream changes its path, usually from day to day, the track of big storms changes with it.

The Mesosphere

The layer of the earth's atmosphere above the stratosphere is called the **mesosphere** (MES-uh-sfeer). This layer extends from about 48 kilometers above the earth to about 80 kilometers high. The air in the mesosphere is many thousands of times less dense than the air at sea level. Here again, the temperature begins to drop. At the top of the mesosphere, the temperature has dropped to about − 100° C. This is the coldest part of the atmosphere.

Why does the temperature drop? Because there is no more ozone. Above the stratosphere, there is not enough oxygen left to form an ozone layer.

With very little air in the mesosphere, you might think that nothing ever happens there. But something does happen. You may have seen that something when you look up into the sky at night. For it is in the mesosphere where most **meteoroids** (MEE-ti-uh-roids) burn up. A meteoroid is a chunk of rocklike matter from outer space.

At speeds of 160,000 kilometers an hour or more, a meteoroid may strike the atmosphere. As it rubs against the air, the meteoroid is quickly heated and glows white hot.

This is what happens to the heat shield of a spacecraft as it reenters the atmosphere. But meteoroids do not have heat shields to protect them. If

The streak of light or meteor is sometimes called a shooting star.

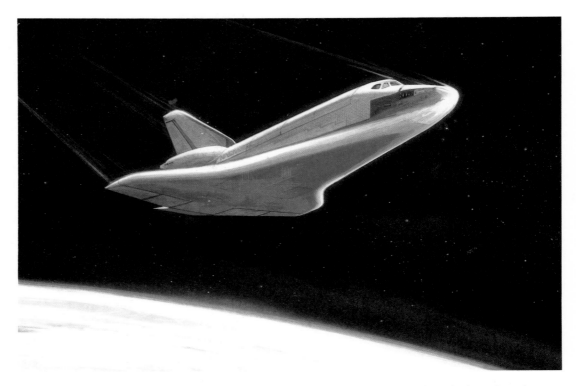

Figure 23-9 *A heat shield protects the Space Shuttle from burning up in the earth's atmosphere.*

you are looking at the sky at night, you may see a streak of light, or **meteor** (MEE-tee-er). That streak of light is a meteoroid burning up in the mesosphere.

The Thermosphere

The upper layer of the atmosphere is called the **thermosphere** (THER-muh-sfeer). This layer extends upward from about 80 kilometers to between 480 kilometers and 600 kilometers. At the top of the thermosphere is the beginning of space. But there is no sharp line where one ends and the other begins. As you travel near the top of the thermosphere, you are in the neighborhood of that invisible boundary.

"Thermosphere" means "heat sphere" or "warm layer." And in the thermosphere the temperature rises to more than 1480° C. But don't be fooled about the high temperatures in the thermosphere. This is a very different kind of heat. On the earth's surface, such temperatures would melt many metals. However, a thermometer placed in the thermosphere would register far below zero!

Figure 23-10 *Most artificial satellites orbit above the thermosphere layer of the atmosphere.*

533

Heat is a measure of *total* energy. There is little heat energy in the thermosphere because there are very few particles despite the high temperature of these particles.

Figure 23-11 *Radio waves can be bounced off the ionosphere to transmit radio messages long distances around the world.*

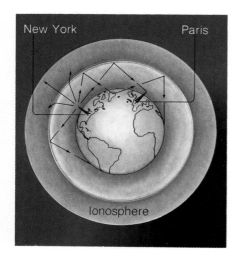

Why? Temperature is a measure of how fast particles in air move. The faster the air particles travel, the higher the temperature. On the earth, particles in the air are packed so tightly together that a particle travels a very short distance before hitting another particle—about 0.06 microns. A micron is a millionth of a meter. In the thermosphere, however, the particles are few and far between. About 99.999 percent of the earth's atmosphere lies below the thermosphere. So the particles travel a long distance before they hit other particles.

A thermometer on the earth's surface is bombarded by countless billions of air particles. But in the thermosphere, few particles ever strike the thermometer. These particles are moving very fast and are far apart. They are very hot, but there would not be enough of them to warm a thermometer. However, special instruments can measure the temperature of particles in the thermosphere.

The particles are moving very fast because they are absorbing energy from the sun and outer space. This energy causes many of the particles to become charged with electricity. These charged particles are called **ions.**

Ions are found mainly in the lower part of the thermosphere and extend up for several hundred kilometers. This part of the thermosphere is a kind of sphere within a sphere—the **ionosphere** (ī-AH-nuh-sfeer).

There are a number of layers of ions in the ionosphere. They act like a mirror, reflecting radio waves back to earth. Radio waves, like light waves, travel in straight lines. But when reflected by the ionosphere, they can travel long distances around the earth. These radio waves can be received thousands of kilometers from their source.

Sometimes streams of fast-moving ions from the sun streak through the ionosphere. They collide with other particles in the air, which causes them to glow. This is much the same thing that happens in a neon sign. A stream of electrically charged particles is passed through a small amount of neon gas in the sign. The neon glows brightly.

These sky glows are called the northern and southern lights or **auroras** (aw-RAW-ruhz). They are most brilliant in the polar regions. Why? As you will

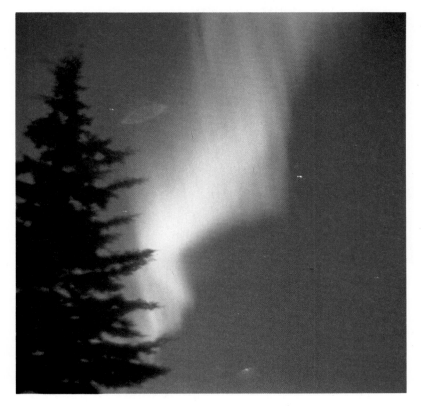

Figure 23-12 *Auroras are bright bands of light in the upper atmosphere caused by electrically charged particles.*

Activity

Listening to the Radio

To find out from how far away radio waves can be received during the day and night, try the following: Listen to an AM radio during the day and late at night. Record the number of stations you can receive during the day and at night. Record what city these stations are broadcasting from. Plot the location of these stations on a map.

Answer the following questions:

1. Which of the radio stations you were able to receive during the day was the farthest away? At night?

2. How many kilometers away is the farthest station you heard during the day? During the night?

3. On the average, the ionosphere at night is higher above the earth's surface. What happens to radio signals when the ionosphere is higher?

see in the next section, the earth is like a giant magnet. The ends of this magnet are in the polar regions. Electrically charged particles are attracted toward the ends of this magnet.

SECTION REVIEW

1. In what layer are weather and most clouds found?
2. List two reasons that airplanes fly in the stratosphere.
3. What is the coldest layer of the atmosphere?
4. In what layer are ions and auroras found?

1. Troposphere
2. No air currents and storms; jet stream
3. Mesosphere
4. Thermosphere

23-2 The Magnetosphere

Place a pane of thin glass over a bar magnet. Sprinkle some iron filings over the top of the glass. Tap it gently. The tapping moves the filings and

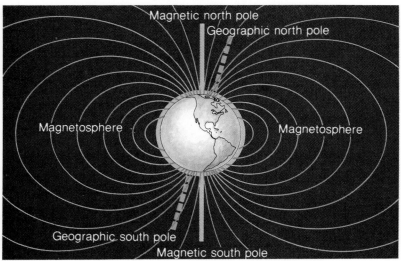

Figure 23-13 *The earth acts like a giant bar magnet* (right) *whose lines of force produce the same pattern as a small bar magnet* (left).

they form a pattern around the magnet, as shown in Figure 23-13.

The pattern of the iron filings shows you the invisible lines of force that are between the north and south poles of a bar magnet. The earth acts like a giant bar magnet whose lines of force produce the same pattern.

You can see in Figure 23-13 that the magnetic poles of the earth are in a different location from the geographic poles. The magnetic north pole is near Bathurst Island in northern Canada, about 1600 kilometers from the geographic north pole. The magnetic south pole is in Wilkes Land, a part of Antarctica, about 2570 kilometers from the geographic south pole.

The magnetic field around the earth extends beyond the earth's atmosphere. This field is called the **magnetosphere** (mag-NEE-toh-sfeer). The magnetosphere begins at an altitude of about 1000 kilometers and extends out into space about 64,000 kilometers on the side of the earth facing the sun. This magnetic field extends even farther out into space on the other side of the earth. Why? The difference is caused by streams of electrically charged ions from the sun. These ions form a kind of solar wind. This wind pushes the magnetosphere farther into space on the side of the earth away from the sun.

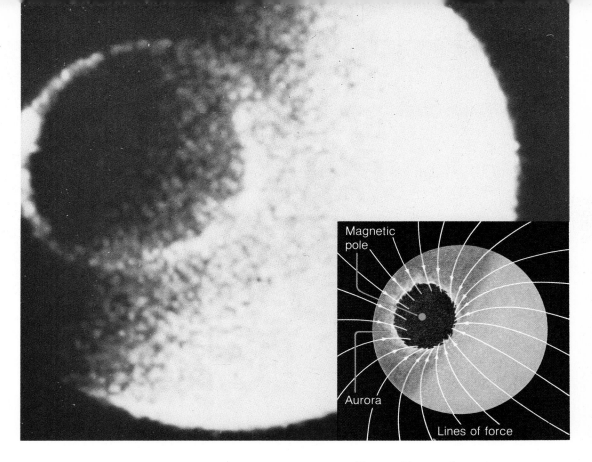

Magnetic
pole

Aurora

Lines of force

What causes the earth's magnetic field? Most scientists believe that the magnetic field probably is caused by a combination of the earth's rotation and electric currents in the earth's core. As the earth spins, these currents produce earth's magnetic field.

By studying the magnetic direction of iron particles found in Earth's rocks, scientists such as Allan Cox and Richard Doell of the U.S. Geological survey have discovered that Earth's magnetic poles have reversed many times. When poles reverse, magnetic north becomes magnetic south, and magnetic south becomes magnetic north. It is estimated that the magnetic poles have reversed 171 times in the last 76 million years. How? Scientists do not know the answer.

Figure 23-14 *An entire aurora was photographed for the first time by a satellite approximately 22,000 kilometers above the earth's magnetic north pole on September 15, 1981. An artist's drawing shows the magnetic lines of force that give the aurora its shape (lower right).*

SECTION REVIEW

1. What is the magnetic field around the earth called?
2. What may cause the earth's magnetic field?
3. When poles reverse, what does magnetic north become?

1. Magnetosphere
2. Combination of earth's rotation and electric currents in the core
3. Magnetic south

LABORATORY ACTIVITY

For further instructions, see page T-71.

Using Atmospheric Pressure to Crush a Can

Purpose

In this activity, you will demonstrate the presence of atmospheric pressure by using the force caused by the weight of the air to crush a metal can.

Materials *(per group)*

Safety goggles
A metal can that can be securely sealed
Graduated cylinder
Tripod
Bunsen burner
Oven mitten
Wire gauze

Procedure

1. Put on your safety glasses and wear them during the entire activity.
2. Add 200 mL of water to a metal can. Place the unsealed can on a tripod. Position a Bunsen burner under the can and light it. **CAUTION:** *Be careful when lighting the Bunsen burner.*
3. Heat the water to boiling and allow it to boil for a few minutes after you have seen condensed water droplets leaving the opening of the can. Heating the liquid water will cause it to change to water vapor, which will force the air out of the can.
4. Turn off the Bunsen burner. Using the oven mitten, hold the heated can and carefully place the top on the can. Be sure it is on securely. **CAUTION:** *Be very careful; the can will be extremely hot.*
5. At the sink, carefully pour cold water over the hot can to cool it.

Observations and Conclusions

1. What happened when the heated can was sealed and allowed to cool? Why?
2. Describe a procedure to restore the can to its original state.

CHAPTER SUMMARY

23-1 The Layers of the Atmosphere

▪ Air pressure decreases as altitude increases.

▪ Warm air is less dense than cold air, and so it rises.

▪ The atmosphere is divided into four layers based on temperature changes.

▪ The troposphere contains most of the earth's air. It is the weather layer. The temperature in the troposphere decreases with increasing altitude but then levels off.

▪ The stratosphere contains ozone, which absorbs ultraviolet rays from the sun. This accounts for the gradual warming within the stratosphere.

▪ The jet stream is the narrow, fast-moving current of air found between the troposphere and the stratosphere.

▪ The mesosphere is the coldest part of the atmosphere.

▪ Meteoroids, chunks of rocklike matter from outer space, are found in the mesosphere. A meteoroid burning up in the mesosphere is called a meteor.

▪ The thermosphere, the outer limit of the atmosphere, is heated by the sun's energy. It contains electrically charged particles called ions in an area called the ionosphere. A stream of these ions causes auroras.

23-2 The Magnetosphere

▪ The earth acts like a giant bar magnet surrounded by a magnetic field called the magnetosphere. This magnetic field is probably the result of the combination of the earth's rotation and electric currents in its core.

VOCABULARY   *Define the following terms.*

air pressure p.526   **jet stream** p.529   **meteoroid** p.532   **troposphere** p.527
aurora p.534   **magnetosphere** p.536   **ozone** p.529
ion p.534   **mesosphere** p.532   **stratosphere** p.529
ionosphere p.534   **meteor** p.533   **thermosphere** p.533

CHAPTER REVIEW

Multiple Choice

Choose the letter of the answer that best completes each statement.

1. The force pressing down on the earth's surface due to the weight of the air is called air
   a. density.
   b. mass.
   c. temperature.
   d. pressure.

2. Generally, as air rises it expands, and its temperature as recorded by an ordinary thermometer
   a. decreases.
   b. increases.
   c. remains the same.
   d. first increases, then decreases.

3. The division of the earth's atmosphere into four layers is based on
 a. surface pressure.
 b. wind currents.
 c. temperature.
 d. density.

4. The weather layer of the atmosphere is the
 a. troposphere.
 b. stratosphere.
 c. mesosphere.
 d. thermosphere.

5. As the altitude increases within the troposphere, the temperature
 a. increases continuously.
 b. increases and then decreases.
 c. decreases and then increases.
 d. decreases and then levels off.

6. The layer of the atmosphere that extends from about 16 kilometers to about 48 kilometers above the earth's surface is called the
 a. mesosphere.
 b. stratosphere.
 c. troposphere.
 d. thermosphere.

7. A high-energy form of oxygen produced when oxygen reacts with sunlight is
 a. hydrogen.
 b. helium.
 c. water vapor.
 d. ozone.

8. The coldest layer of the atmosphere is the
 a. mesosphere.
 b. stratosphere.
 c. ionosphere.
 d. troposphere.

9. The upper layer of the atmosphere is the
 a. mesosphere.
 b. thermosphere.
 c. stratosphere.
 d. troposphere.

10. Scientists believe that the earth's magnetic field is caused by
 a. a combination of the earth's revolution and rotation.
 b. a combination of the earth's revolution and electric currents in its core.
 c. a combination of the earth's rotation and electric currents in its core.
 d. a combination of the magnetic poles and geographic poles.

Completions

Fill in the word or words that best complete each statement.

1. Within the atmosphere, as the altitude decreases, the air pressure _____increases_____.

2. Clouds, dust, and pollution are characteristics of the layer of the atmosphere called the _____troposphere_____.

3. Pilots prefer to fly in the layer of the atmosphere called the _____stratosphere_____ because there are no air currents or storms.

4. The _____ozone_____ layer in the stratosphere shields the earth from harmful ultraviolet rays.

5. The narrow, fast-moving current of air that forms at the boundary of the troposphere and the stratosphere is the _____jet stream_____.

6. The layer of the atmosphere characterized by the lowest ordinary temperatures and very little oxygen is the _____mesosphere_____.

7. Chunks of rocklike matter from outer space are called _____meteoroids_____.

8. Electrically charged particles found in the thermosphere are called _____ions_____.

9. The glowing of the sky due to a stream of electrically charged particles is call a(n) _____aurora_____.

10. The area beyond the earth's atmosphere that is a magnetic field is called the _____magnetosphere_____.

True or False

Determine whether each statement is true or false. If it is true, write "true." If it is false, change the underlined word or words to make the statement true.

1. Warm air is <u>less</u> dense than cold air. T
2. Most of the air is in the <u>stratosphere</u>. *
3. When sunlight and oxygen react in the stratosphere, a gas called <u>peroxide</u> is formed. F (ozone)
4. The coldest part of the atmosphere is the <u>mesosphere</u>. T
5. A <u>meteoroid</u> burning up in the mesosphere is called a <u>northern light</u>. F (meteor)
6. The part of the thermosphere in which charged particles can be used to transmit radio waves is the <u>mesosphere</u>. F (ionosphere)

   * F (troposphere)

7. Magnetic lines of force are the strongest at the <u>poles</u> of a magnet. T
8. The magnetic field around the earth extends farthest into space on the side of the earth facing <u>toward</u> the sun. F (away from)
9. Most scientists believe it is the earth's <u>revolution</u> that is partly responsible for its magnetic field. F (rotation)
10. When the poles of the earth reverse, magnetic north becomes magnetic <u>south</u>. T

Discussion Topics Answers appear on page T-72.

Write a brief paragraph discussing each of the following.

1. In the 1968 Summer Olympic Games held in Mexico City, Mexico, long jumper Bob Beamon set a world's record. Since that time, no other long jumper has exceeded his jump of 8.90 meters. The altitude of Mexico City is 2309 meters. Relate this distance above sea level to the density of air and the resistance the air offers a jumper. Then explain how Beamon was helped to achieve his extraordinary jump.

2. Official airline guides give flying time from Seattle, Washington, to New York City, New York, as 5 hours, 5 minutes. The reverse trip, from New York City to Seattle, takes 5 hours, 35 minutes. Explain this difference.

EXPAND YOUR KNOWLEDGE

Weiss, M. *Storms: From the Inside Out.* New York: Julian Messner.
A storm is one of the most exciting shows that nature puts on. If you have ever wondered what was really happening during a thunderstorm, a hurricane, or a tornado, you can find out by reading this book.

Coming Up······SCIENCE GAZETTE···

Starting on the next page you will find three special articles. The first tells an exciting story about a scientist. The second tells about a battle of ideas. And the last looks into the future. Each of the articles has been written so you will enjoy reading it. As you read, you may want to jot down thoughts that come to mind. You might then write a report telling what you thought about the articles. Or you might just want to read the articles for the fun of it.

SCIENCE GAZETTE

Adventures in Science

The articles of this *Science Gazette* have been carefully chosen and designed to inspire and motivate students of all levels in their study of science. Each article is related to one or more topics presented in the unit. See the "Science Reading Skills" section in your Teachers' Resource Book for specific activities and handouts. Also, for further instructions, see page T-72 in this book.

William Haxby Maps the Invisible Ocean Floor

William Haxby's undersea maps provided a view of the ocean floor never before seen by people. In this photo, parts of Africa and South America are shown in gray. Red dots show locations of underwater earthquakes. Dark blue indicates areas of the ocean that have a greater depth than light-colored areas.

Vast canyons and craggy mountains make the ocean floor as mysterious as the surface of a far-off planet. It may be centuries before the bottom of the world's seas are fully explored. Yet using information from a space satellite, a 33-year-old scientist has created a startling map of the undersea landscape. This map is almost as detailed as if the water had been drained out of the seas and a man had walked over the land, making a map as he went.

That man is William Haxby of the Lamont Geological Observatory in Palisades, New York. Haxby fed readings from the satellite *Seasat* into a computer. Using computer graphics, he produced a three-dimensional map in vivid colors. This map provided a view of the ocean floor never before seen by people. Cracks in the sea bottom, underwater volcanoes, and other features of the ocean floor popped up on Haxby's map. These features provided new evidence about some of the most important earth science theories.

One of these theories, continental drift, suggests that all continents were once part of a single, large landmass. This landmass gradually broke up into the fragments now called continents. And the continents drifted to their present positions. Another theory, called plate tectonics, states that the earth's crust is made up of a number of very large plates. Heat and motion deep within the earth cause the plates to move. The movement of plates triggers earthquakes, thrusts up mountain ranges, and cuts deep ridges.

Haxby's map shows many signs of plate movement along the sea floor. One deep crack under the Indian Ocean may have been made when India drifted away from Antarctica and headed for Asia millions of years ago. Geologists believe a twisting ridge on the ocean floor off the southern tip of Africa was also formed millions of years ago, when Africa, South America, and Antarctica separated. The ridge, concealed under layers of sediment, was detected by Haxby's computer.

Mapping the Ocean Floor

Haxby started his mapping project, which took 18 months, in 1981. His work was based on *Seasat's* measurements of height differences on the sea's surface. Even if there were no waves or wind, Haxby points out that the surface of the ocean would not be perfectly flat. The height of the sea's surface varies by dozens of meters from one place to another. The reason for the variations in the sea's surface is the gravitational pull of structures on the bottom. Structures with large mass, such as undersea mountains, pull on the water with more force than those with less mass, such as canyons. The stronger the pull, the more water is attracted to a place above the structure. "As a result," says Haxby, "water piles up and there is a bump in the sea over a big object." So the sea surface imitates the sea bottom.

Measurements of differences in the sea's surface were recorded on *Seasat* by an instrument called an altimeter. It measured distances between the satellite and the surface of the sea to within a few centimeters. The satellite sent out 1000 electronic pulses a second. The altimeter measured the time it took for the pulses to hit the sea's surface and bounce back. Launched in 1978 for a five-year orbit, *Seasat* became silent after three months due to a short circuit in its electrical system. But the eight billion readings it had radioed back to tracking stations on the earth were enough for Haxby to start his computer work.

Tall and slender, Haxby has been interested in geology since his boyhood, when he was a "rockhound." At the University of Minnesota, he became interested in continental drift and plate tectonics. He eventually did graduate work in geophysics, leading to a doctoral degree from Cornell University. When he first began computer analysis of the satellite information, however, he did not intend to map the

William Haxby is an expert on continental drift and plate tectonics. His maps of the sea floor have helped scientists all over the world solve riddles about the earth.

entire ocean bottom. All he wanted to do was chart some small areas by matching sea surface heights with the gravitational forces that created them. This would enable him to figure out the mass of objects on the sea floor. His first maps were so detailed, however, that Haxby decided to go further.

Colorful Results

Sitting at his computer, often working late into the night, Haxby gradually expanded his map to include all of the ocean floor. He assigned different colors—ranging from blue to pink—to various sea levels. More than 250 different color intensities helped him create his three-dimensional map. Ridges, mountains, trenches, and canyons stand out by color. The detail—Haxby can pinpoint objects as small as 30 kilometers across—and colors reveal structures that are not on other large maps of the sea bottom. In fact, the images produced by Haxby's computer look so real that people looking at the images feel as if they are standing on the bottom of the sea. And around the globe, scientists now use Haxby's maps to help solve riddles about the earth.

Issues in Science

Lakes affect the land around them. Runoff from a lake feeds surrounding trees and plants. More plant life attracts birds and animals to the area. But artificial lakes, if not well planned, can harm the environment.

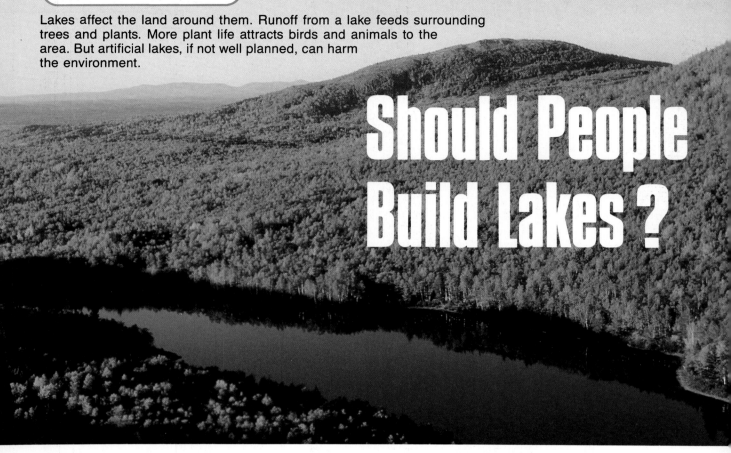

Should People Build Lakes ?

The Benefits May Be Obvious, But What Are the Drawbacks?

Although it was a tiring trip, I looked forward to seeing my friend Jeff again. But I didn't look forward to leaving the air-conditioned comfort of the bus.

All around me, the landscape was dry, dusty, and sun-baked. There were few trees. I knew the temperature outside must be about 38° C.

Moments later, as we pulled into town, I spotted Jeff's car. And there was Jeff, looking tanned and happy.

I was neither tanned nor happy by the time we reached Jeff's house about four miles out of town. In fact, I was hot, dusty, and sweaty. So, Jeff's suggestion that we go for a swim at a nearby lake was very welcome. The suggestion was also surprising.

"I don't remember any lakes in this area," I remarked.

Jeff replied, "It's brand new. It was built since the last time you were here."

I had always thought that lakes were created only by nature way back when the earth was young. Then I realized that Jeff's artificial lake was probably no more than a muddy pond.

Did I get a pleasant surprise when we arrived at the lake! A great expanse of beautiful, clean water sparkled before us. It was surrounded by green grass, bushes, and young trees. There were sandy beaches at several spots along the winding shore. People were swimming and fishing in the clear water. A few boats bobbed on the lake's surface.

Lakes Influence Climate

"This is great," I said. "Even the air here feels fresher and cooler."

"Lakes influence local climate and vegetation," Jeff responded. "Water vapor rising from the lake surface makes the air moist and cool. Wait until you come back in a few years. The trees will be taller and the greenery will have spread. It will be a brand new ecosystem."

"But where does the water for this new lake come from?" I asked.

"The water for this lake comes from an underground spring," Jeff replied. "It's part of the groundwater system. There's lots of water down there."

"Do all artificial lakes get their water from underground springs?"

"Oh, no! Most of these lakes are created by damming rivers or streams. A few have their water piped in. If necessary, we could pipe water all the way down from Canada."

Over the following two weeks, I became very fond of Jeff's lake. In a dry, hot, dusty world, it was a delightful change. I was convinced that it would be a good idea to build lakes in all the dry regions of the country.

Life and Death of Lakes

By the time I got home, I was fascinated by the subject of lakes. But as I learned more and more about lakes, I realized that artificial lakes could have serious drawbacks as well as benefits. The drawbacks are caused by the very nature of lakes.

For example, all lakes eventually die. But artificial lakes tend to have much shorter life spans than natural lakes.

Lakes die in various ways. For one thing, water evaporates from the surface. If the loss of water through evaporation is greater than the incoming flow of water, the level of the lake will go down rapidly.

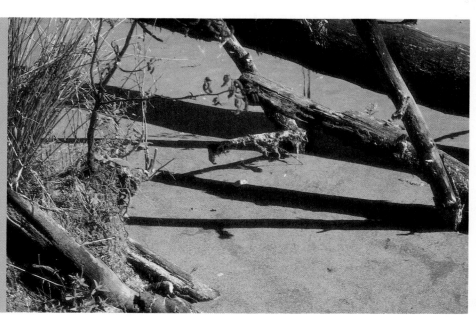

Artificial lakes tend to have shorter lives than do natural lakes. In each case, old age often turns a lake into a swamp.

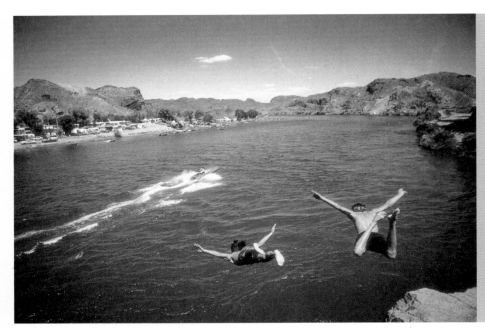

Lake Meade in Nevada is an artificial lake that is a recreation spot for many people.

This is a problem especially in hot, dry areas. So unless the flow of water from the underground spring into Jeff's lake is greater than the evaporation from its surface, that lake might disappear in just a few years.

Evaporation is not the only thing that kills a lake. Water flowing into a lake is likely to carry with it large quantities of soil, sand, salts, and minerals. This material settles on the bottom of a lake to form a layer of sediment. It may be joined by leaves, branches, and other decaying vegetation.

Layer by layer, the sediment builds up. And if this process is combined with evaporation, a once clear lake might quickly turn into a muddy swamp.

This is more likely to happen to an artificial lake than to a natural lake. The reason is that artificial lakes are usually shallow and built in areas where water is scarce to begin with. Also, soil and sand are usually more easily washed into a lake in those areas.

A number of lakes that were built for resort communities over the past 30 years have turned into swamps. Others have become bitter or salty as a result of the seepage of fertilizers from surrounding farms and from the fall of acid rain—rain polluted by smoke and gases from industry.

A big drawback of creating lakes that might soon die is that water that could be used for other purposes is wasted. Also, taking great amounts of water from the ground may injure the earth. In Arizona, for example, so much water has been pumped out of the ground that great cracks have opened in the earth's surface. As ground water is removed, empty spaces form deep under ground. These spaces can collapse, creating depressions called sinkholes that can swallow homes and people.

In order for a lake to survive over a long period, it should be deep. Its water output should not exceed its input. And the water in the lake should be able to circulate. Care should be taken to prevent the buildup of soil, sand, salts, acids, fertilizers, and other pollutants. If these things are not considered, it might be better not to build any lakes at all. What do you think?

the longest winter

The team of Survivors shivered as the bouncing raft made its way across the river. An icy July wind whipped up the water all around the raft. The shore to which the Survivors were heading was covered with a thick coat of new snow. Although it was noon, the day was strangely dark.

Jonah, the Team Leader, peered into the strange darkness ahead. Members of the team lowered long poles into the water and pushed the raft toward the shore.

"There," Jonah said, pointing to a good landing spot. "Head for that flat beach."

Within seconds, the team members were ashore. Soon after, they had built a fire and cooked a meal of canned foods. And then they had settled down for Jonah's afternoon "story" about the past.

"Well, my friends," Jonah began, "this day makes me think of a frightening story that began long, long ago. If I remember correctly, the time was winter, 1983. The football season was in full swing. The holidays were approaching. Everything was kind of normal and happy. Of course, people were worried about such things as taxes and war. But that wasn't too unusual for those days. Then something happened that scared a lot of people. A group of some of the finest scientists in the United States made a report.

The scientists—there were 20 of them—had been trying to figure out what might happen if there were a nuclear war. And the report described what they had discovered."

Jonah paused and looked up at the dark sky as if searching for the July sun. But all he could see was an unbroken gray cloud that seemed to stretch forever. Jonah sighed and went on.

"To get an idea of what the scientists concluded, you must first know some basic facts about this planet of ours. Our atmosphere is very special. For one thing, as one of the scientists said, our atmosphere normally 'acts as a window for sunlight, but as a blanket for heat'."

"What does that cause," one of the Survivors asked as she tugged a blanket tightly around her shoulders.

"Normally, it causes the earth to stay warm. You see, the light from the sun is a form of energy. When this energy hits the earth, a new kind of energy is produced. It is called heat. Our atmosphere normally traps a lot of this heat. The heat keeps us warm. It keeps our oceans and lakes from freezing. And it makes plant and animal life possible on the earth. Now what do you think would happen if the 'window for sunlight' had a shade pulled down over it?"

A young Survivor, busily rubbing his hands together to keep them warm, answered. "The light from the sun would not reach the earth. So heat energy would not be produced. And the earth would cool down."

"Right," said Jonah. "And that's exactly what the scientists said could happen if there were a nuclear war. The scientists figured out that such a war would set millions of fires. Tons of black, sooty smoke would rise into the atmosphere. This smoke, they said, would have a mass of more than 100 million tons!

"The particles of soot would rise very high into the atmosphere, the scientists calculated. As high, maybe, as 20 kilometers. There the winds of the atmosphere would spread the soot over the entire earth.

"Now there's something very special about these two things—the soot and the height to which it would rise. Experiments showed that small particles of black soot absorb sunlight better than other kinds of particles. But that's not all. Researchers also found that the higher in the air particles are found, the longer they are going to stay there."

"That means that the soot closes the

'windows for sunlight.' And if the soot is high in the air, the 'window' stays closed for a long time," said one of the Survivors.

"Sadly, that's true," Jonah replied in a whisper. "Using the very best computers of the time, the scientists figured out that about 95 percent of the sun's light would not reach the ground. In their report, the scientists said that in some places the brightness at noon 'could be as low as that of a moonlit night'."

"Just like it is now," another Survivor said softly.

Jonah sighed. Telling this story wasn't easy, he thought to himself.

"So what would happen then?" asked another Survivor.

"Again, the computer came up with some answers. And they were chilling. Temperatures over land areas like North America, Europe, and Asia would suddenly drop about 40°C! That means that the average temperature in these places would be about −25°C."

"Why that's way below the freezing point of water!" exclaimed a Survivor.

"I'm afraid so," said Jonah. "And these freezing temperatures would last for months, said the scientists. The scientists called it a 'nuclear winter.' And the winter would cover the whole world."

"But that would kill off all sorts of plants, and animals that live on plants," the Survivor continued. "Why there would be no trees, no grass, no cows and sheep that feed on grass, no corn or wheat, no food for us."

"How about fish in lakes and streams?" another Survivor asked.

"Frozen solid," said Jonah about these waters. "Life in the water would die out."

"But wouldn't living things survive in the oceans and on the coasts of oceans? After all, ocean water holds a lot of heat for a long time. It might keep the land nearby warm enough to grow crops," suggested a Survivor.

"The scientists thought of that too," replied Jonah. "But the very cold air over the land meeting the warm air over the sea would cause terrible storms. Farming in areas struck by constant hurricanes would be impossible."

Jonah stopped speaking. Again he looked up at the sky, searching for a ray of sunshine. But there was none to be seen. The Survivors sat very quietly. Finally, one of them spoke.

"If that had happened, Jonah, the whole world would have looked and felt like this day. Everywhere it would be winter in July—not just here in Argentina and other southern countries. And we would be real survivors instead of members of an outdoor club."

"That's right," said Jonah, who now smiled. "But leaders of our country and of the other countries of the world saw to it that there was no nuclear war. So we still have our trees, and our grass, our forests, our animals . . . and our wilderness to explore. So let's pack up our gear and be on our way. We've got a long hike ahead of us."

Appendix A THE METRIC SYSTEM

The metric system of measurement is used by scientists throughout the world. It is based on units of ten. That is, each unit is ten times larger or ten times smaller than the next unit. The most commonly used units of the metric system are given below. After you have finished reading about the metric system, try to put it to use. How tall are you in metrics? What is your mass? What is your body temperature in degrees Celsius?

COMMONLY USED METRIC UNITS

Length The distance from one point to another

meter (m)

(a meter is slightly longer than a yard)

1 meter = 1000 millimeters (mm)

1 meter = 100 centimeters (cm)

1000 meters = 1 kilometer (km)

METRIC RULER

GRADUATED CYLINDER

(26 mL)

Volume The amount of space an object takes up

liter (L)   1 liter = 1000 milliliters (mL)

(a liter is slightly larger than a quart)

Mass The amount of matter in an object

gram (g)   1000 grams = 1 kilogram (kg)

(a gram has a mass equal to about one paper clip)

Riders   Beams

TRIPLE BEAM BALANCE

THERMOMETER

Boiling point of water

Human body temperature

Freezing point of water

Temperature The measure of hotness or coldness

degrees Celsius (°C)   0° C = freezing point of water

100° C = boiling point of water

METRIC-ENGLISH EQUIVALENTS

2.54 centimeters (cm) = 1 inch (in.)

1 meter (m) = 39.37 inches (in.)

1 kilometer (km) = 0.62 miles (mi.)

1 liter (L) = 1.06 quarts (qt.)

250 milliliters (mL) = 1 cup (c.)

1 kilogram (kg) = 2.2 pounds (lb.)

28.3 grams (g) = 1 ounce (oz.)

$^{\circ}C = 5/9 \times (^{\circ}F - 32)$

METRIC COMPARISONS

Ruler = 12 inches or 30.48 centimeters

Blue Whale = 110 feet or 33.5 meters

Statue of Liberty = 151 feet or 45.7 meters

Football Field = 100 yards or 91.44 meters

Golden Gate Bridge = 1400 yards or 1280 meters

Mount Everest = 29,000 feet or 8840 meters

Nile River = 4132 miles or 6649 kilometers

Distance to the Sun = 93,000,000 miles or 150,000,000 kilometers

Light Year = 6 trillion miles or 9.65 trillion kilometers

Ping Pong Ball = .09 ounces or 2.53 grams

Mouse = .79 ounces or 22.39 grams

Football = 15 ounces or 425 grams

Wright Brothers Plane = 750 pounds or 340 kilograms

African Elephant = 14,000 pounds or 6350 kilograms

Jumbo Jet Plane = 775,000 pounds or 351,540 kilograms

Saturn Rocket = 6,526,000 pounds or 2,960,194 kilograms

Butter Melts = 87° F or 30.6° C

Body Temperature = 98.6° F or 37° C

Hottest Temperature ever recorded on Earth = 136.4° F or 58° C

Coldest Temperature ever recorded on Earth = -130° F or -90° C

Appendix B   THE LABORATORY BALANCE

The laboratory balance is an important tool in scientific investigations. You can use the balance to determine the mass of materials that you study or experiment with in the laboratory.

Different kinds of balances are used in the laboratory. One kind of balance is the double-pan balance. Another kind of balance is the triple-beam balance. The balance that you may use in your science class is probably similar to one of the balances illustrated in this appendix. To use the balance properly, you should learn the name, function, and location of each part of the balance you are using.

THE DOUBLE-PAN BALANCE

The double-pan balance shown in this appendix has two beams. Some double-pan balances have only one beam. The beams are calibrated, or marked, in grams. The upper beam is divided into 10 major units of one gram each. Each of these units is further divided into units of 1/10 of a gram. The lower beam is divided into 20 units, and each unit is equal to 10 grams. The lower beam can be used to find the masses of objects up to 200 grams. Each beam has a rider that is moved to the right along the beam. The rider indicates the grams used to balance the object in the left pan.

Before you begin using the balance, you should be sure that both riders are pointing to zero grams on their beams and that the pans are empty. The balance should be on a flat, level surface. The pointer should be at the zero point. If your pointer does not read zero, slowly turn the adjustment knob until it does.

The following procedure can be used to find the mass of an object with a double-pan balance:

1. Place the object whose mass is to be determined on the left pan.

2. Move the rider on the lower beam to the 10-gram notch.

3. If the pointer moves to the right of the zero point on the scale, the object has a mass less than 10 grams. Return the rider on the lower beam to zero. Slowly move the rider on the upper beam until the pointer is at zero. The reading on the beam is the mass of the object.

4. If the pointer did not move to the right of the zero, move the rider on the lower beam notch by notch until it does. Move the rider back one notch. Then move the rider on the upper beam until the pointer is at zero. The sum of the readings on both beams is the mass of the object.

5. If the two riders are moved completely to the right side of the beams and the pointer remains to the left of the zero point, the object has a mass greater than the total mass that the balance can measure.

The total mass that most double-pan balances can measure is 210 grams. If an object has a mass greater than 210 grams, return the riders to zero.

PARTS OF A BALANCE AND THEIR FUNCTIONS

DOUBLE-PAN BALANCE

Scale   Graduated instrument along which the pointer moves to show if the balance is balanced

Pointer   Marker that indicates on the scale if the balance is balanced

Zero point   Center line of the scale to which the pointer moves when the balance is balanced

Adjustment knob   Knob used to balance the empty balance

Left pan   Platform on which an object whose mass is to be determined is placed

Right pan   Platform on which standard masses are placed

Beams   Scales calibrated in grams

Riders   Moveable markers that indicate the number of grams needed to balance an object

Stand   Support for the balance

The following procedure can be used to find the mass of an object greater than 210 grams:

1. Place the standard masses on the right pan one at a time, starting with the largest, until the pointer remains to the right of the zero point.

2. Remove one of the large standard masses and replace it with a smaller one. Continue replacing the standard masses with smaller ones until the pointer remains to the left of the zero point. When the pointer remains to the left of the zero point, the mass of the object on the left pan is greater than the total mass of the standard masses on the right pan.

3. Move the rider on the lower beam and then the rider on the upper beam until the pointer stops at the zero point on the scale. The mass of the object is equal to the sum of the readings on the beams plus the mass of the standard masses.

THE TRIPLE-BEAM BALANCE

The triple-beam balance is a single-pan balance with three beams calibrated in grams. The back, or 100-gram, beam is divided into 10 units of 10 grams each. The middle, or 500-gram, beam is divided into 5 units of 100 grams

Beams

Riders

Pointer
(at zero)

each. The front, or 10-gram, beam is divided into 10 major units of 1 gram each. Each of these units is further divided into units of 1/10 of a gram.

The following procedure can be used to find the mass of an object with a triple-beam balance:

1. Place the object whose mass is to be determined on the pan.

2. Move the rider on the middle beam notch by notch until the horizontal pointer drops below zero. Move the rider back one notch.

3. Move the rider on the front beam notch by notch until the pointer again drops below zero. Move the rider back one notch.

4. Slowly slide the rider along the back beam until the pointer stops at the zero point.

5. The mass of the object is equal to the sum of the readings on the three beams.

Appendix C THE MICROSCOPE

The microscope is an essential tool in the study of life science. It enables you to see things that are too small to be seen with the unaided eye. It also allows you to look more closely at the fine details of larger things.

The microscope you will use in your science class is probably similar to the one illustrated on the following page. This is a compound microscope. It is called compound because it has more than one lens. A simple microscope would only contain one lens. The lenses of the compound microscope are the parts that magnify the object being viewed.

Typically, a compound microscope has one lens in the eyepiece, the part you look through. The eyepiece lens usually has a magnification power of 10×. That is, if you were to look through the eyepiece alone, the object you were viewing would appear 10 times larger than it is.

The compound microscope may contain one or two other lenses. These two lenses are called the low- and high-power objective lenses. The low-power objective lens usually has a magnification of 10×. The high-power objective lens usually has a magnification of 40×. To figure out what the total magnification of your microscope is when using the eyepiece and an objective lens, multiply the powers of the lenses you are using. For example, eyepiece magnification (10×) multiplied by low-power objective lens magnification (10×) = 100× total magnification. What is the total magnification of your microscope using the eyepeice and the high-power objective lens?

To use the microscope properly, it is important to learn the name of each part, its function, and its location on your microscope. Keep the following procedures in mind when using the microscope:

1. Always carry the microscope with both hands. One hand should grasp the arm, and the other should support the base.

2. Place the microscope on the table with the arm toward you. The stage should be facing a light source.

3. Raise the body tube by turning the coarse adjustment knob.

4. Revolve the nosepiece so that the low-power objective lens (10×) is directly in line with the body tube. Click it into place. The low-power lens should be directly over the opening in the stage.

5. While looking through the eyepiece, adjust the diaphragm and the mirror so that the greatest amount of light is coming through the opening in the stage.

6. Place the slide to be viewed on the stage. Center the specimen to be viewed over the hole in the stage. Use the stage clips to hold the slide in position.

7. Look at the microscope from the side rather than through the eyepiece. In this way, you can watch as you use the coarse adjustment

MICROSCOPE PARTS AND THEIR FUNCTION

1. **Arm** Supports the body tube

2. **Eyepiece** Contains the magnifying lens you look through

3. **Body tube** Maintains the proper distance between the eyepiece and objective lenses

4. **Nosepiece** Holds high- and low-power objective lenses and can be rotated to change magnification

5. **Objective lenses** A low-power lens which usually provides 10X magnification, and a high-power lens which usually provides 40X magnification

6. **Stage clips** Hold the slide in place

7. **Stage** Supports the slide being viewed

8. **Diaphragm** Regulates the amount of light let into the body tube

9. **Mirror** Reflects the light upward through the diaphragm, the specimen, and the lenses

10. **Base** Supports the microscope

11. **Coarse adjustment knob** Moves the body tube up and down for focusing

12. **Fine adjustment knob** Moves the body tube slightly to sharpen the image

knob to lower the body tube until the low-power objective *almost* touches the slide. Do this slowly so you do not break the slide or damage the lens.

8. Now, looking through the eyepiece, observe the specimen. Use the coarse adjustment knob to *raise* the body tube, thus raising the low-power objective away from the slide. Continue to raise the body tube until the specimen comes into focus.

9. When viewing a specimen, be sure to keep both eyes open. Though this may seem strange at first, it is really much easier on your eyes. Keeping one eye closed may create a strain, and you might get a headache. Also, if you keep both eyes open, it is easier to draw diagrams of what you are observing. In this way, you do not have to turn your head away from the microscope as you draw.

10. To switch to the high-power objective lens (40×), look at the microscope from the side. Now, revolve the nosepiece so that the high-power objective lens clicks into place. Make sure the lens does not hit the slide.

11. Looking through the eyepiece, use only the fine adjustment knob to bring the specimen into focus. Why should you not use the coarse adjustment knob with the high-power objective? The objective is very close to the slide in high power, and by turning the coarse adjustment knob you could cause the objective to hit the slide.

12. Clean the microscope stage and lens when you are finished. To clean the lenses, use lens paper only. Other types of paper may scratch the lenses.

PREPARING A WET-MOUNT SLIDE

Most specimens to be observed with the compound microscope are placed on a slide in a liquid solution. This preparation is know as a wet-mount slide. To make a wet-mount slide, follow these directions along with the accompanying diagrams.

Eyedropper —

Drop of — water

Slide

1. Place the specimen to be observed in the middle of a clean slide. For you to observe any specimen with a compound microscope, the specimen must be thin enough for light to pass through it.

2. Using an eye dropper, place a drop of water on the specimen.

3. Place one side of a clean cover slip at the edge of the drop of water. Using a needle or probe, slowly lower the cover slip over the specimen and water. Try not to trap any air bubbles under the cover slip since these will interfere with your view of the specimen.

Cover slip

Needle or probe

4. Your wet-mount slide is now ready to be viewed with your microscope. Be sure you do not tilt the microscope when viewing a wet-mount slide. What do you think might happen if you did?

The water from the slide will drip onto the microscope.

Glossary

air bladder: tiny grape-shaped structure that acts like an inflatable life-preserver in brown algae

air pressure: pressing force due to the weight of air

alga (AL-guh; plural: algae, AL-gee): member of the largest group of nonvascular plants

alloy: solid metal dissolved in another solid metal

amino acid: building block of protein

amorphous (uh-MOR-fuhs) **solid:** solid that does not keep a definite shape

anal pore: tiny opening through which a paramecium eliminates waste

angiosperm (AN-jee-oh-sperm): type of seed plant whose seeds are covered by a protective wall

annual ring: one year's growth of xylem cells

antibiotic: substance produced by helpful bacteria that destroys or weakens disease-causing bacteria

asexual reproduction: formation of an organism from a single parent

astronomy: study of planets, stars, and other objects beyond the earth

atom: tiny particle of matter consisting of a nucleus that contains protons and neutrons and an electron cloud that contains electrons

atomic mass unit (amu): unit used to measure the masses of subatomic particles; a proton has a mass of one amu

atomic number: number of protons in the nucleus of an atom; number that identifies the kind of atom

aurora (aw-RAW-ruh): bands of light in the upper atmosphere caused by electrically charged particles

autotroph (AWT-uh-trohf): organism that makes its own food from simple substances

bacillus (buh-SIL-uhs; plural: bacilli): rod-shaped bacterium

bacteriophage (bak-TEE-ree-uh-fayj): virus that infects bacterial cells

bacterium (plural: bacteria): unicellular microorganism

binary fission: reproductive process in which a cell divides into two cells

binomial nomenclature (bigh-NOH-mee-uhl NOH-muhn-klay-cher): naming system in which organisms are given two names: a genus and a species

bioluminescence (bigh-oh-loo-muh-NE-suhns): firefly-like glow produced by a kind of fire algae

boiling: process in which particles of a liquid change to gas, travel to the surface of the liquid, and then into the air

boiling point: temperature at which a liquid boils

botany: study of plants

Boyle's Law: law stating that the volume of a fixed amount of gas varies indirectly with the presure of the gas

budding: reproductive process in yeast, in which a new yeast cell is formed from a tiny bud

cambium (KAM-bee-uhm): growth tissue of the stem where xylem and phloem cells are produced

canine (KAY-nighn): pointed tooth next to the incisor

cap: fruiting body of a mushroom

carbohydrate: organic compound made up of the elements carbon, hydrogen, and oxygen, and a main source of energy for living things

carnivore: (KAR-ni-vor): flesh-eating animal

cartilage: flexible tissue that gives support and shape to body parts

catalyst: substance that speeds up or slows down chemical reactions, but is not itself changed by the reaction

cell: basic unit of structure and function in a living thing; building block of life

cell membrane: thin, flexible envelope of protoplasm that forms the outer covering of an animal cell and that is inside the cell wall of a plant cell; controls movement of materials into and out of the cell

cell wall: outermost boundary of plant and bacterial cells that is made of cellulose

Celsius: temperature scale used in the metric system at which water freezes at 0° and boils at 100°

Charles's Law: law stating that the volume of a fixed amount of gas varies directly with the temperature of the gas

chemical change: change a substance undergoes when it turns into another substance

chemical equation: description of a chemical reaction using symbols and formulas

chemical formula: combination of chemical symbols used as a shorthand for the names of chemical substances

chemical property: property that describes how a substance changes into another new substance

chemical reaction: process by which a substance is changed into another substance through a rearrangement or new combination of its atoms

chemical rock: sedimentary rock formed from large amounts of minerals when a body of water dries up

chemical symbol: shorthand way of representing the elements; usually consists of one or two letters, the first of which is always capitalized, but the second is never capitalized

chemistry: study of what substances are made of and how they change and combine

chlorophyll: green substance, needed for photosynthesis, found in green plant cells

chloroplast: large, irregularly shaped structure that contains the green pigment chlorophyll; food-making site in green plants

chromosome: thick, rodlike object found in the nucleus that directs the activities of the cell and passes on the traits of the cell to new cells

cilium (SIHL-ee-uhm; plural: cilia): small, hairlike projection on the outside of a cell

class: classification group between phylum and order

cleavage: breakage of a mineral along definite lines or smooth, flat surfaces

coastal plains: low, flat areas that average about 150 meters above sea level

coccus (KAHK-suhs; plural, cocci): sphere-shaped bacterium

coefficient (koh-uh-FI-shuhnt): number placed in front of a chemical formula in a chemical equation so that the equation is balanced

coldblooded: having a body temperature that can change somewhat with changes in the temperature of the environment

colloid (KAHL-oyd): homogeneous mixture in which the particles are mixed together but not dissolved

commensalism: symbiotic relationship in which one organism benefits and the other is neither helped nor harmed

community: the living part of an ecosystem; all the different organisms that live together in an area

competition: struggle among living things to get the proper amount of food, water, and energy from the environment

compound: substance made up of molecules that contain more than one kind of atom; two or more elements chemically combined

compound light microscope: microscope containing more than one lens that uses light to make an object look larger

condensation (kahn-den-SAY-shun): process in which a gas loses heat energy and changes into a liquid

conjugation (kahn-joo-GAY-shun): type of sexual reproduction in which hereditary material is exchanged

consumer: organism that feeds directly or indirectly on producers; heterotroph

continental glacier: very thick ice sheet that covers most of both polar regions

contour feather: largest bird feather needed for flight

control: experiment run exactly the same way as the experiment with the variable, but the variable is left out

core: center region of the earth

cotyledon (kaht-uh-LEE-duhn): leaflike structure of an embryo plant that stores food

crop: saclike organ that stores food in an earthworm

crust: thin outer layer on the earth's surface made up mainly of solid rocks

crystal (KRIS-tuhl): regular, repeating pattern of particles in a solid

crystalline solid: solid made up of crystals

cytoplasm: jellylike substance outside the nucleus

data: recorded observations and measurements

decomposer: organism that breaks down dead plants and animals into simpler substances

density: mass per unit volume, or how much mass is contained in a given volume of an object

diffusion: process by which food, oxygen, water, and other materials enter and leave a cell through openings in the cell membrane

digestion: process by which food is broken down into simpler substances

division of labor: division of the work that keeps an organism alive among the different parts of its body

DNA: (deoxyribonucleic acid) nucleic acid that stores the information needed to build proteins and carries genetic information about an organism

down feather: short, fuzzy bird feather that acts as insulation

ecology: study of the relationships and interactions of living things with one another and with their environment

ecosystem: group of organisms in an area that interact with one another and with their nonliving environment

electron: negatively charged particle that moves around the nucleus of an atom in a region called the electron cloud

electron cloud: space in which electrons are most likely to be found

electron microscope: microscope that uses a beam of electrons to magnify the image of an object

element (EL-uh-ment): pure substance made up of only one kind of atom that cannot be broken down into simpler substances by ordinary means

endoplasmic reticulum (en-doh-PLAZ-mik ri-TIK-yuh-luhm): maze of clear tubular passageways that leads out from the nuclear membrane; involved in the manufacture and transport of proteins

endospore: oval-shaped structure that protects a bacterium

energy level: most likely location in the electron cloud in which an electron can be found

environment: all the living and nonliving things with which an organism may interact

enzyme: special type of protein that regulates chemical activities within the body

epidermis (e-puh-DER-mis): outer protective layer of the leaf

evaporation (ee-va-puh-RA-shun): process in which a liquid changes into a gas by absorbing heat energy

excretion: process of getting rid of waste materials

exoskeleton: rigid, outer covering of an organism

extrusive (ek-STROO-sive) **rock:** igneous rock formed

from melted rock or lava that cools and hardens at or near the earth's surface

eyespot: light-sensitive organ in lower organisms

family: classification group between order and genus

fat: energy-rich organic compound made up of carbon, hydrogen, and oxygen, that is solid at room temperature

fermentation: energy-releasing process in which sugars and starches are changed into alcohol and carbon dioxide

fertilization: joining of egg and sperm

flagellum (fla-JEL-um; plural, flagella): whiplike structure that propels some one-celled organisms

flammability (flam-uh-BIL-uh-tee): ability to burn

flower: structure containing the reproductive organs of the angiosperm

focus: underground center of an earthquake

food chain: illustration of how groups of organisms within an ecosystem get their food and energy

food web: all the food chains in an ecosystem

fracture: mineral breakage that forms an irregular surface that may be rough or jagged

fragmental rock: sedimentary rock made up of rock fragments mixed with sand, clay, and mud cemented together

freezing: change of a liquid to a solid

freezing point: temperature at which a liquid changes to a solid

frond: leaf of a fern plant

fruit: ripened ovary of an angiosperm

fruiting body: in a fungus, the spore-containing structure

fungus (FUHNG-guhs; plural: fungi): group of simple organisms that have no chlorophyll and must get food from other organisms

gas: phase in which matter has no definite shape or volume

gem: rare, very valuable, and beautiful mineral

genus (plural: genera): group of organisms that are closely related; classification group between family and species

germination (jer-muh-NA-shuhn): early growth stage of an embryo plant; also called sprouting

gill: structure through which fish and other aquatic animals breathe; in a mushroom, the spore-producing structure

gizzard: in an earthworm, the organ that grinds up food

glucose: simple sugar into which all carbohydrates are broken down in the body to produce energy

gravity: force of attraction between objects

ground water: water that has soaked into the ground

guard cell: sausage-shaped cell that regulates the opening and closing of stomata

gullet: funnel-shaped structure in the paramecium extending from the oral groove to the food vacuole

gymnosperm (JIM-nuh-sperm): type of seed plant whose seeds are not covered by a protective wall

habitat: place in which an organism lives

heft: comparing the weights of two rocks of similar size by balancing one in each hand

herbaceous (her-BAY-shuhs) **stem:** green, soft stem

herbivore (HER-bi-vor): animal that eats only plants

heterogeneous (het-uhr-uh-JEEN-ee-uhs) **mixture:** mixture in which no two parts are identical

heterotroph (HET-uhr-u-trohf): organism that is not able to make its own food and thus feeds on other organisms

hibernation: winter sleep during which all body activities slow down

homeostasis (ho-mee-o-STAY-sis): ability of an organism to keep conditions inside its body the same even though conditions in its external environment change

homogeneous (ho-muh-JEEN-ee-uhs) mixture: mixture in which different parts seem to be identical

host: organism in which a parasite lives

humus: dark, rich soil made of decayed plant and animal matter combined with rocky soil particles

hypha (HIGH-fuh; plural: hyphae, HIGH-fee): threadlike structure in a fungus that produces digestive enzymes

hypothesis (high-PAH-thuh-sis): suggested solution to a scientific problem

iceberg: mass of free-floating ice that has broken off from the edges of the Arctic or Antarctic ice sheets

igneous (IG-nee-us) **rock:** rock formed from cooled and hardened magma or lava

incisor (in-SIGH-zer): one of the four front teeth used for biting

inertia (in-ER-shuh): property of a mass to resist changes in motion

ingestion: eating

inland plains: low, flat areas that average about 450 meters above sea level and are confined to the interior or central part of a country or region

inorganic compound: compound that does not usually contain the element carbon

insoluble: cannot be dissolved in water

intrusive (in-TROO-siv) **rock:** rock that forms from melted rock or magma that cools and hardens deep below the earth's surface

invertebrate: animal without a backbone

ion: electrically charged particles

ionosphere (i-AH-nuh-sfeer): lower part of the thermosphere that contains ions

isotope (IGH-suh-tohp): atom of a substance that has the same number of protons but a different number of neutrons as another atom of the same substance

jet stream: narrow, fast-moving current of air that forms along the troposphere-stratosphere boundary

kilogram: basic unit of mass in the metric system

kingdom: largest classification grouping

larva: stage of insect that emerges from the egg

lava: magma that has reached the earth's surface

leaching: process in which rain washes minerals out of the top soil

lens: curved pieces of glass that bends light rays as they pass through it

lichen (LIGH-kuhn): organism made up of a fungus and an alga that live together

life span: maximum length of time a particular organism can be expected to live

liquid: phase in which matter has no definite shape but does have a definite volume

liter: basic unit of volume in the metric system

liverwort: nonvascular, green leaflike plant; similar to moss but smaller

luster: way a mineral reflects light

lysosome: small, round structure involved with the digestive activities of a cell

magma: hot, molten rock deep inside the earth

magnetosphere (mag-NEE-toh-sfeer): magnetic field of the earth

mammary gland: milk-producing gland in mammals

mantle: part of mollusk that produces material that makes up the hard shell; layer that extends from the edge of the liquid outer core to where the earth's crust begins

marsupial (mahr-SOO-ip-uhl): mammal that has a pouch

mass: amount of matter in an object

matter: what all materials are made of

meiosis (migh-OH-sis): form of cell division that halves the number of chromosomes in a male and female sex cell as they form

melting: change of a solid to a liquid

melting point: temperature at which a solid changes to a liquid

mesosphere (MES-uh-sfeer): coldest layer of the atmosphere

metabolism (muh-TA-buh-li-zuhm): all chemical activities in an organims essential to life

metamorphic (met-uh-MAWR-fik) **rock:** rock changed by heat, pressure, or chemical action

metamorphosis (met-uh-MAWR-fuh-sis): change in appearance due to development

meteor (MEE-tee-er): bright trail or streak of light that results when a meteoroid burns up in the mesosphere

meteoroid (MEE-tu-uh-roid): chunk of rocklike matter from outer space

meter: basic unit of length in the metric system

metric system: universal system of measurement

microbiology: science of microorganisms

microscope: instrument that produces an enlarged image of an object

Mid-Atlantic Rift Valley: great crack, or rift, and the area on either side of it in the earth's crust that runs down the middle of a massive underwater mountain range in the Atlantic Ocean

Mid-Ocean Ridge: system of rift valleys and mountain ranges that extends for 74,000 kilometers under all the world's oceans

migrate: to move to a new environment during the course of a year

mineral: natural substance that forms in the earth

mitochondrion (plural: mitochondria): rod-shaped structure that is referred to as one of the powerhouses of a cell

mitosis (migh-TOH-sis): duplication and division of the nucleus and of the chromosomes during cell reproduction

mixture: two or more pure substances that are mixed but not chemically combined

Moho: boundary between earth's crust and mantle

Mohs (mohz) **hardness scale:** scale used to determine the hardness of a mineral

molecule (MAH-luh-kyool): smallest particle of a substance that has all the properties of that substance; made up to two or more atoms that are chemically bonded

moss: nonvascular plant that contains chlorophyll

mountain belt: group of mountain ranges

mountain landscape: area of tall, jagged peaks, long slopes, and high, narrow ridges

mountain range: group of mountains

multicellular: having many cells

mutualism: symbiotic relationship in which both organisms benefit

nematocyst (NEM-uh-toh-sist): stinging cell around the mouth of a coelenterate

neutron: electrically neutral particle found in the nucleus of an atom

niche: everything an organism does and everything an organism needs within it habitat

nonvascular plant: plant that does not have transportation tubes to carry water and food

nuclear membrane: thin membrane that separates the nucleus from the protoplasm of the cell

nucleic acid: large organic compound that stores information that helps the body make the proteins it needs

nucleolus (noo-KLEE-uh-luhs): cell structure located in the nucleus and made up of RNA and protein; may play important role in making proteins for the cell

nucleus (NOO-klee-uhs; plural: nuclei, NOO-klee-igh): spherical cellular structure that directs all activities of the cell; positively charged center of an atom

oil: energy-rich organic compound made up of carbon, hydrogen, and oxygen that is liquid at room temperature

oral groove: mouthlike indentation in the paramecium

order: classification group between class and family

ore: rock from which metals and other minerals can be removed in usable amounts

organ: group of different tissues working together

organic compound: compound that contains the element carbon

organic rock: sedimentary rock built up from the remains of living things

organism: entire living thing that carries out all the basic life functions

osmosis: special type of diffusion by which water passes through the cell membrane

ovule (OH-vyool): structure that contains the female sex cells of a plant

ozone: high-energy form of oxygen that forms a layer mainly in the stratosphere

parasite (PA-ruh-sight): organism that feeds on other living organisms

parasitism: symbiotic relationship in which one organism benefits and the other is harmed

parent rock: solid rock found where soil is formed

permafrost: permanently frozen soil just below the surface

petal: colorful leaflike structure that surrounds the male and female reproductive organs in a flower

phase: state in which matter can exist; solid, liquid, gas, plasma are the phases of matter

pheromone (FER-uh-mohn): chemical substance given off by insects and other animals to attract a mate

phloem (FLOH-uhm): tubelike plant tissue that carries food down the plant

photosynthesis (foh-tuh-SIN-thuh-sis): process by which green plants make glucose for food by combining carbon dioxide and water by using the sun's energy

phylum (FY-luhm; plural: phyla): second largest classification group; between kingdom and class

physical change: change in which physical properties of a substance are altered, but the substance remains the same kind of matter

physical property: characteristic that distinguishes one type of matter from another and can be observed without changing the identity of the substance

physics: study of different forms of energy

pistil: female reproductive organ of the flower

placenta (pluh-SEN-tuh): structure through which developing young receive food and oxygen while in the mother

plains landscape: broad, flat lowland area divided into coastal or inland plains that are not far above sea level

plasma: phase in which matter is very high in energy and cannot be contained by the walls of ordinary matter; very rare on Earth

plateau landscape: broad, flat highland area usually more than 600 meters above sea level

pollen: particle containing the male sex cells of a plant

pollination: transfer of pollen to the stigma of a flower

population: group of the same type of organism living together in the same area

pore: opening on the outer surface of an animal through which materials enter and leave

precipitation (pree-sip-uh-TA-shun): water falling to the earth as rain, sleet, hail, or snow

primary waves (P waves): shock waves produced by a back-and-forth vibration of rock particles during an earthquake

producer: green plant that makes its own food; autotroph

property: quality or characteristic that describes an object

protein: organic compound made up of carbon, hydrogen, oxygen, nitrogen, and sometimes sulfur and phosphorus, necessary for the growth and repair of body structures

proton: positively charged particle found in the nucleus of an atom

protoplasm: all the living material found in both plant and animal cells

protozoan: unicellular animal-like organism

pseudopod: "false foot" in amoeba

pupa (PYOO-puh): stage in an insect's life cycle when it is wrapped in a cocoon

pure substance: substance that contains only one kind of molecule

quark (kwark): particle that makes up all subatomic nuclear particles

radula: filelike structure in the mouth of a univalve used to scrape food from an object

reproduction: process by which living things give rise to the same type of living thing

respiration: process by which living things take in oxygen and use it to produce energy

response: some action or movement of the organism brought on by a stimulus

rhizoid (RIGH-zoid): rootlike structure through which mosses absorb water

rhizome (RIGH-zohm): stem growing along or under the ground

ribosome: grainlike body made up of RNA and attached to the inner surface of an endoplasmic passageway; a protein-making site of the cell

RNA (ribonucleic acid): nucleic acid that "reads" the genetic information carried by DNA and guides the protein-making process

rock cycle: continuous changing of rocks from one kind to another

saprophyte (SA-pruh-fight): organism that feeds on dead things

scavenger: animal consumer that feeds on the bodies of dead animals

scientific method: basic steps that scientists follow in uncovering facts and solving scientific problems

secondary waves (S waves): shock waves produced by an up-and-down or side-to-side vibration of rock particles during an earthquake

sedimentary (sed-uh-MEN-tuh-ree) **rock:** rock formed in layers

seed: structure from which a plant grows; contains a young plant, stored food, and a seed coat

seismograph (SIHGZ-muh-graf): instrument that records shock waves due to earthquakes

sepal (SEE-puhl): leaflike structure enclosing a flower when it is still a bud

sexual reproduction: formation of an organism from the uniting of two different sex cells

shadow zone: area in which no earthquake waves are detected by seismographs

slime mold: bloblike organism found on decaying material

solid: phase in which matter has a definite shape and volume

solubility: amount of solute that will completely dissolve in a given amount of solvent at a specific temperature

soluble (SAHL-yuh-bul): can be dissolved in water

solute (SAHL-yoot): in a solution, substance that is dissolved

solution: homogeneous mixture in which particles are dissolved in one another

solvent (SAHL-vunt): in a solution, substance that does the dissolving

species (SPEE-sheez): group of organisms that are able to interbreed, or produce young

spirillum (spigh-RIL-uhm); plural: spirilla): spiral-shaped bacterium

spontaneous generation: theory that states that life can spring from nonliving matter

stalk: in a mushroom, a stemlike structure with a ring near its top

stamen (STAH-muhn): male reproductive organ of the flower

stimulus: signal to which an organism reacts

stoma (STOH-muh; plural: stomata): opening in the

surface of a leaf through which carbon dioxide enters and oxygen and water vapor pass out

stratosphere (STRAT-uh-sfeer): layer of the atmosphere where the ozone layer and jet streams are found

streak: color of a mineral in powder form

subatomic particle: particle that is smaller than an atom

sublimation (suhb-luh-MAY-shuhn): process in which the surface particles of a solid change directly into gas

subscript: number placed to the lower right of a chemical symbol to indicate the number of atoms of the element in the compound

subsoil: level beneath topsoil that is made up of larger bits of rock with little or no humus

suspension: heterogenious mixture containing particles that are mixed together but not dissolved

swim bladder: sac in a bony fish that enables the fish to rise or sink in water

symbiosis: (sim-bigh-OH-sis): relationship in which one organism lives on, near, or even inside another organism

system: group of organs that work together to perform certain functions

talon: sharp claw on the toe of birds of prey

taxonomy: (tak-SAH-nuh-mee): science of classification

thermosphere (THER-muh-sfeer): upper layer of the atmosphere where the ionosphere and auroras are found

tissue: group of cells similar in structure and joined together to perform a special function

topsoil: uppermost level of soil that is made of a mixture of small grains of rock and decayed matter of plants and animals

toxin: poison produced by bacteria

transpiration: process for regulating water loss through the leaves of a plant

troposphere: (TRAH-puh-sfeer): lowest layer of the atmosphere where all the earth's weather occurs

unicellular: having one cell

vacuole (VA-kyoo-ohl): large, round sac floating in the cytoplasm of a cell in which water, food, enzymes, and other materials are stored

valley glacier: long, narrow glacier that moves down hill between the steep sides of mountain valleys

vaporization (vay-puhr-uh-ZAY-shuhn): change of a liquid to a gas

variable: factor being tested in an experiment

vascular plant: plant that contains transporting tubes that carry material throughout the plant

venom: poison produced in special glands by snakes

vertebra (plural: vertebrae): one of the bones that make up a vertebrate's backbone

vertebrate (VER-tuh-brit): animal with a backbone

virus: tiny particle that contains hereditary material

volume: amount of space an object takes up

warmblooded: able to maintain a constant body temperature

water table: top level to which ground water rises when underground

weathering: process by which rocks are broken down by such factors as wind, water, heat, and cold

weight: measure of the force of attraction between objects due to gravity

woody stem: rigid stem containing woody xylem tissue

xylem (ZIGH-luhm): tubelike plant tissue that carries water and minerals through the plant

zoology: study of animals

Index

phase changes with solids, 341–42
Gas Laws, 335–36
Gems, 425–26
Genus, in biological classification, 134, 137
Germination, 210
Giant squid, 229–30
Gibbon, 297
Gila monster, 267
Gills
of crustaceans, 237
of fish, 255
of tadpoles, 262
Gills, of mushrooms, 182
Gingkoes, 204, 205
Gizzard, 228
Glaciers, 516–17
Glucose, 49, 101, 203
Gnawing mammals, 295
Gold, 417, 418, 420
Gorilla, 297
Gram, 22, 316
Granite, 435–36, 445
Grasshopper, 242–43
Grasslands, 460–61
Gravity, 22–23, 317–18
Great Barrier Reef, 222, 234
Great Plains, 510
Great white shark, 258
Green plants, 101, 104, 105, 140, 172
Green turtle, 269–70
Grierson, James, 28–29
Ground water, 515
Growth
of arthropods, 236–37
of mollusks, 231
of trees, 199–200
Growth and development, 40–41, 71–73
of birds, 274–75
of insects, 243–45
of mammals, 283
Growth rings
of coral, 221
of trees, 200
Guard cells, 204
Gullet, 161
Gymnosperms, 197, 204–206

H

Habitats, 99–100
Hardness test for minerals, 418
Hares, 295
Head, of insect, 242
Head-footed mollusks, 233
Hedgehogs, 288
Heft of minerals, 420
Herbaceous stems, 201, 202
Herbivores, 286

Heterogeneous mixtures, 395
Heterotrophs, 102, 141, 179
Hibernation, 261–62
Hives, insect, 245–46
Homeostasis, 47–48, 60
Homogeneous mixtures, 395–96
Honey guide bird, 111
Hoofed mammals, 294
Hookworm, 227
Hormones, 62, 84
Host, 226
Human beings, 283, 297
Human diseases, 157, 162, 295
Humus, 452
Hydra, 221
Hyphae, 180, 181, 183
Hypocotyl, 210
Hypothesis, forming of, 16–17

I

Icebergs, 517
Ice sheets, 515–17
Igneous rocks, 434–47
Iguanas, 264
Incisors, 290, 295
Incubation, 275
Inertia, 316
Information, gathering, 16
Ingestion, 39
Inland plains, 510
Inorganic compounds, 49
Insect-eating mammals, 288–89
Insects, 241–47
anatomy of, 242–43
behavior of, 245–46
defense mechanisms of, 246–47
growth and development of, 243–45
role in pollination of, 207, 208–209
Insoluble, 398
Insulin, produced by bacteria, 156–57
Interior Plains, 510
Internal fertilization, 265
Intestine, 228
Intrusive rocks, 435–37
Invertebrates, 218–47
characteristics of, 219
Ionosphere, 534
Ions, in atmosphere, 534, 536
Isotopes, 367
Iwanowski, Dimitri, 148–49

J

Jawless fish, 256–57
Jellyfish, 221, 222
Jet stream, 529–32

K

Kangaroos, 285, 286
Kelp, 172, 177
Kilogram, 22, 316
King cobra, 266
Kingdom, in biological classification, 136
Koalas, 286
Komodo dragon, 267
Krakatoa, 172

L

Lampreys, 112, 256–57
Landmasses, 492–95, 502, 506
Landscapes, 503–510
Larva, 245
Lasers, 27
Latin
used in biological classification, 134, 137
used for chemical symbols, 381
Lava, 434
Leaching, 457
Leaves, 195, 196, 202–204, 207, 210
functions of, 202, 204
structure of, 202
types of, 202
Leeches, 227
Legionnaires' Disease, 147
Lehmann, Inge, 484–85
Length, 21–22
Lens, microscope, 26
Levels of organization, in living things, 81–87
Lichens, 184–85
Life science, 19
Life span, 41–42
Limestone, 222, 416, 437–38, 439–40, 441
Linnaeus, Carolus, 134
Liquids, 333
phase changes with gases, 339–41
phase changes with solids, 338–39
Liter, 22, 319
Liverworts, 187
Living space, needed by living things, 46–47
Living things
arising only from other living things, 37
characteristics of, 36–43
chemistry of, 48–51
needs of, 44–48
and their environment, 94–100
Lizards, 264, 265, 267–68
Lobsters, 237
Lungfish, 260
Lungs, 262

Luster of minerals, 422
Lysosomes, 65–66

M

Magma, 434
Magnetosphere, 535–37
Malaria, 163
Mammals, 282–97
  characteristics of, 282–83
  egg-laying, 284–85
  flesh-eating, 290–91
  flying, 289–90
  gnawing, 295
  hoofed, 294
  insect-eating, 288–89
  placental, 287–97
  pouched, 285–87
  primates, 296–97
  rodentlike, 295–96
  "toothless," 292–93
  trunk-nosed, 293–94
  water-dwelling, 296
Mammary glands, 283, 284, 287
Manatees, 296
Mantle, of earth, 486, 489–92
Mantle, of mollusks, 230–31
Marble, 441
Marsupials, 285–87
Mary Rose, 313, 322
Mass, 22, 315–16
  units of, 316
  and weight, 22–23
Matter, 314–15
  atomic model of, 362–65
  general properties of, 314–22
  phases of, 331–37
  specific (physical) properties of, 330
Mauna Kea, 477, 505
Megalosaurus, 13
Meiosis, 73
Melting, 338–39
Melting point, 338
Mesosphere, 532–33
Metabolism, 39–40
  in cell, 68–69
Metals, 424
Metamorphic rocks, 441–43
Metamorphosis, 243
Meteoroids, 532
Meteors, 533
Meter, 21
Metric system, 20–24
  length, 21–22
  mass and weight, 22–24
  temperature, 24
  units, *20*
  volume, 22
Mica, 422, 424
Microbiology, 149
Microscopes, 24–27

Mid-Atlantic Rift Valley, 489
Mid-Ocean Ridge, 489, 506
Migration, 275
Milk, 283, 284, 286, 287
Milliliter, 319
Millipedes, 238
Minerals, 416–26
  identifying, 417–23
  physical properties of, 417
  uses of, 424–26
Mites, 238, 239, 241
Mitochondria, 64–65, 66
Mitosis, 71–73
Mixtures, 392–96
  heterogeneous, 395
  homogeneous, 395–96
  properties of, 392–94
  separation of, 395
  types of, 395–96
Moho, 488, 489
Mohorovicic, Andrija, 487–88
Mohs hardness scale, 418
Molds, 182–83
Molecules, 370–71
Moles, 288
Mollusks, 229–33
  anatomy of, 230
  classification of, 231
Monerans, 173
  classification of, 141, 152
Monkeys, 297
Monocots, 210
Mono Lake, Calif., 114–15
Mosses, 186–87
Mountains, 503, 505–507
  famous, *504*
  formation of, 505
  volcanic, 506, 507
Mountain belts, 506
Mountain landscapes, 503
Mountain ranges, 506, 507–508, 514
Mouth
  coelenterate, 221–22
  insect, 242
Movement, 38
  in amoebas, 159
  in amphibians, 262–63
  in bacteria, 154
  in ciliates, 160
  in fish, 255, 260
  in mollusks, 230, 231, 232–33
  in reptiles, 267, 268
  in slime molds, 186
  in snakes, 267
  in spiny-skinned animals, 234–35
Mudskipper, 260
Multicellular organisms, 81–87, 171–72, 219
  classification of, 140–41
Mushrooms, 181–82
Mussels, 232
Mutualism, 110–12

N

Nautiluses, 233
Navigation
  in birds, 275
  in turtles, 269
Nematocysts, 221–22
Nervous system, 84, 86–87
  of earthworm, 229
Neutrons, 366
Newts, 263
Niches, 99–100
Nitrogen-fixing algae, 173
Nitrogen-fixing bacteria, 157
NMR (Nuclear Magnetic Resonance), 28
Nonvascular plants, 170–87
Nuclear membrane, 61, 63, 72
Nucleic acids, 51, 61–62
Nucleolus, 62–63
Nucleus, of atom, 364, 365–66
Nucleus, of cell, 60–63, 71–72, 153
  in paramecia, 161
  in protozoans, 159

O

Obsidian, 435, 436, 437
Ocean floor, 489, 491–94
Oceans, 511–12
Octopus, 230, 233
Oils, fats and, 49–50
Oldham, Richard Dixon, 479, 483
One-celled organisms. *See* Unicellular organisms
One-shelled mollusks, 231–32
Open circulatory system, 243
Opossums, 286–87
Oral groove, 161
Orangutan, 297
Order, in biological classification, 137
Ores, 424
Organic compounds, 49–51
Organic rocks, 439–40
Organisms, 86–87
  classifying, 137–38, 140–41
  interactions among, 101–104
Organization of living things, 81–87
Organs, 83–84, 219
Organ systems, 84–85, 219, 255
Osmosis, 70
Ovary, of flower, 207
Ovules, 205
Oxygen
  in photosynthesis, 203
  used by living things, 39–40, 46, 101, 172, 237
Oysters, 225, 230
Ozone, 529

Associates; **511,** © Pam Taylor/*Bruce Coleman;* **512,** *dpi;* **514,** top left, Stuart L. Craig/*Bruce Coleman;* top right, Keith Gunnar/*Bruce Coleman;* bottom, William E. Ferguson; **515,** Hackenberg/*Leo de Wys;* **516,** G. R. Roberts/*OPC;* **517,** left, F.G. Love; right, G.R. Roberts; **522,** Margot Conte/© *Earth Scenes;* **524,** left, The Bettman Archive, Inc.; right, National Center for Atmospheric Research; **525,** Novak/*Leo de Wys;* **527,** top, J. Alex Langley/*dpi;* bottom, Monty Monsees/*dpi;* **528,** left, Breck P. Kent; right, Keith Gunnar/*Bruce Coleman;* **529,**

Jerome Wyckoff; **531,** © Pat Lanza Field/*Bruce Coleman;* **533,** top, NASA; bottom, NASA; **536,** William E. Ferguson; **537,** NASA; **555,** Don Benson/*Tom Stack & Associates.*

Gazette Photographs

120, Anne Meylan; **121,** left, Archie Carr/Univ. of Florida; right, Archie Carr; **122,** David Scharf/Peter Arnold; **123,** Eric Kroll/Taurus; **124,** Michael Habicht/Animals Animals; **126,** left, Smithsonian Institution; middle, Ken Karp/OPC; right, Joel Greenstein/OPC; **303,** bottom, Wrangham/Anthro Photo; top, Wrangham/Anthro Photo; **306,** Jeff Foott/Bruce Coleman; **308,** Merle H. Jensen; **309,** Runk/Schoenberger/Grant Heilman; **350,** Ken Karp, **351,** Ken Karp; **352,** K.D. Franke/Peter Arnold; **354,** Robert Rose/Picture Group Charles Belinsky/Photo Researchers; **356,** Georgia Power Co.; **357,** bottom, Georgia Power Co.; top, Georgia Power Co.; **405,** John McGrail, Discover Magazine © 1982. Time, Inc.; **406,** © 1980 Roy H. Blanchard/DPI; **408,** top, DOE; bottom, DOE; **410,** Amoco Chemical Co.; **468,** Peru National Tourist Office; **469,** Dr. Georg Gerster/Photo Researchers; **470,** Univ. of California; **471,** left, Dr. Bruce Heezen/Lamont-Doherty; right, Dave Woodward/Taurus; **472,** © C. B. Jones 1982/Taurus; **542,** William Haxby; **543,** Anita Brosius; **544,** © Dan Budnik 1982/Woodfin Camp; **545,** Alfred Owczarzak/Taurus; **546,** Chuck O'Rear/West Light

Text illustrations by Lee Ames & Zak Ltd. with special acknowledgement to David Christensen. Gazette art by Phil Carver & Friends, Inc.